The Decline of Latin American Economies
Growth, Institutions, and Crises

Edited by **Sebastian Edwards, Gerardo Esquivel, and Graciela Márquez**

The University of Chicago Press

Chicago and London

SEBASTIAN EWARDS is the Henry Ford II Professor of International Economics at UCLA's Anderson Graduate School of Management and a research associate at the National Bureau of Economic Research. GERARDO ESQUIVEL is a professor of economics at El Colegio de Mexico, and GRACIELA MÁRQUEZ is a professor of history at El Colegio de Mexico.

The University of Chicago Press, Chicago 60637
The University of Chicago Press, Ltd., London
© 2007 by National Bureau of Economic Research
All rights reserved. Published 2007
Printed in the United States of America

16 15 14 13 12 11 10 09 08 07   1 2 3 4 5
ISBN-13: 978-0-226-18500-2 (cloth)
ISBN-10: 0-226-18500-1 (cloth)

Library of Congress Cataloging-in-Publication Data

The decline of Latin American economies : growth, institutions, and
  crises / edited by Sebastian Edwards, Gerardo Esquivel, and Graciela
  Márquez.
    p. cm.
  Includes bibliographical references and index.
  ISBN-13: 978-0-226-18500-2 (cloth : alk. paper)
  ISBN-10: 0-226-18500-1 (cloth : alk. paper)
  1. Latin America—Economic conditions. 2. Latin America—
Economic policy. 3. Latin America—Politics and government.
4. Latin America—History. I. Edwards, Sebastian, 1953–
II. Esquivel, Gerardo. III. Márquez, Graciela.
HC125 .D384 2007
330.98—dc22
                                                        2006101997

∞ The paper used in this publication meets the minimum requirements of the American National Standard for Information Sciences—Permanence of Paper for Printed Library Materials, ANSI Z39.48-1992.

National Bureau of Economic Research

Officers

Elizabeth E. Bailey, *chairman*
John S. Clarkeson, *vice-chairman*
Martin Feldstein, *president and chief executive officer*
Susan Colligan, *vice president for administration and budget and corporate secretary*
Robert Mednick, *treasurer*
Kelly Horak, *controller and assistant corporate secretary*
Gerardine Johnson, *assistant corporate secretary*

Directors at Large

Peter C. Aldrich
Elizabeth E. Bailey
John H. Biggs
Andrew Brimmer
John S. Clarkeson
Don R. Conlan
Kathleen B. Cooper
George C. Eads
Jessica P. Einhorn
Martin Feldstein
Jacob A. Frenkel
Judith M. Gueron
Robert S. Hamada
Karen N. Horn
Judy C. Lewent
John Lipsky
Laurence H. Meyer
Michael H. Moskow
Alicia H. Munnell
Rudolph A. Oswald
Robert T. Parry
Marina v. N. Whitman
Martin B. Zimmerman

Directors by University Appointment

George Akerlof, *California, Berkeley*
Jagdish Bhagwati, *Columbia*
Ray C. Fair, *Yale*
Michael J. Brennan, *California, Los Angeles*
Glen G. Cain, *Wisconsin*
Franklin Fisher, *Massachusetts Institute of Technology*
Saul H. Hymans, *Michigan*
Marjorie B. McElroy, *Duke*
Joel Mokyr, *Northwestern*
Andrew Postlewaite, *Pennsylvania*
Uwe E. Reinhardt, *Princeton*
Nathan Rosenberg, *Stanford*
Craig Swan, *Minnesota*
David B. Yoffie, *Harvard*
Arnold Zellner (director emeritus), *Chicago*

Directors by Appointment of Other Organizations

Richard B. Berner, *National Association for Business Economics*
Gail D. Fosler, *The Conference Board*
Martin Gruber, *American Finance Association*
Arthur B. Kennickell, *American Statistical Association*
Thea Lee, *American Federation of Labor and Congress of Industrial Organizations*
William W. Lewis, *Committee for Economic Development*
Robert Mednick, *American Institute of Certified Public Accountants*
Angelo Melino, *Canadian Economics Association*
Jeffrey M. Perloff, *American Agricultural Economics Association*
John J. Siegfried, *American Economic Association*
Gavin Wright, *Economic History Association*

Directors Emeriti

Carl F. Christ
George Hatsopoulos
Lawrence R. Klein
Franklin A. Lindsay
Paul W. McCracken
Peter G. Peterson
Richard N. Rosett
Eli Shapiro
Arnold Zellner

Relation of the Directors to the Work and Publications of the National Bureau of Economic Research

1. The object of the NBER is to ascertain and present to the economics profession, and to the public more generally, important economic facts and their interpretation in a scientific manner without policy recommendations. The Board of Directors is charged with the responsibility of ensuring that the work of the NBER is carried on in strict conformity with this object.

2. The President shall establish an internal review process to ensure that book manuscripts proposed for publication DO NOT contain policy recommendations. This shall apply both to the proceedings of conferences and to manuscripts by a single author or by one or more coauthors but shall not apply to authors of comments at NBER conferences who are not NBER affiliates.

3. No book manuscript reporting research shall be published by the NBER until the President has sent to each member of the Board a notice that a manuscript is recommended for publication and that in the President's opinion it is suitable for publication in accordance with the above principles of the NBER. Such notification will include a table of contents and an abstract or summary of the manuscript's content, a list of contributors if applicable, and a response form for use by Directors who desire a copy of the manuscript for review. Each manuscript shall contain a summary drawing attention to the nature and treatment of the problem studied and the main conclusions reached.

4. No volume shall be published until forty-five days have elapsed from the above notification of intention to publish it. During this period a copy shall be sent to any Director requesting it, and if any Director objects to publication on the grounds that the manuscript contains policy recommendations, the objection will be presented to the author(s) or editor(s). In case of dispute, all members of the Board shall be notified, and the President shall appoint an ad hoc committee of the Board to decide the matter; thirty days additional shall be granted for this purpose.

5. The President shall present annually to the Board a report describing the internal manuscript review process, any objections made by Directors before publication or by anyone after publication, any disputes about such matters, and how they were handled.

6. Publications of the NBER issued for informational purposes concerning the work of the Bureau, or issued to inform the public of the activities at the Bureau, including but not limited to the NBER Digest and Reporter, shall be consistent with the object stated in paragraph 1. They shall contain a specific disclaimer noting that they have not passed through the review procedures required in this resolution. The Executive Committee of the Board is charged with the review of all such publications from time to time.

7. NBER working papers and manuscripts distributed on the Bureau's web site are not deemed to be publications for the purpose of this resolution, but they shall be consistent with the object stated in paragraph 1. Working papers shall contain a specific disclaimer noting that they have not passed through the review procedures required in this resolution. The NBER's web site shall contain a similar disclaimer. The President shall establish an internal review process to ensure that the working papers and the web site do not contain policy recommendations, and shall report annually to the Board on this process and any concerns raised in connection with it.

8. Unless otherwise determined by the Board or exempted by the terms of paragraphs 6 and 7, a copy of this resolution shall be printed in each NBER publication as described in paragraph 2 above.

Contents

Introduction Sebastian Edwards, Gerardo Esquivel, and Graciela Márquez	1

I. ECONOMIC GROWTH, TAXATION, AND INSTITUTIONS

1. When Did Latin America Fall Behind? Leandro Prados de la Escosura	15
2. Before the Golden Age: Economic Growth in Mexico and Portugal, 1910–1950 Pedro Lains	59
3. Inequality and the Evolution of Institutions of Taxation: Evidence from the Economic History of the Americas Kenneth L. Sokoloff and Eric M. Zolt	83

II. FINANCIAL CRISES, LENDING, AND INFLATION

4. Financial Crises, 1880–1913: The Role of Foreign Currency Debt Michael D. Bordo and Christopher M. Meissner	139
5. The True Measure of Country Risk: A Primer on the Interrelations between Solvency and the Polity Structure of Emerging Markets, Argentina 1886–1892 Gerardo della Paolera and Martín Grandes	195

6. Related Lending: Manifest Looting or Good Governance? Lessons from the Economic History of Mexico   213
Noel Maurer and Stephen Haber

7. Sudden Stops and Currency Drops: A Historical Look   243
Luis A. V. Catão

8. Establishing Credibility: The Role of Foreign Advisors in Chile's 1955–1958 Stabilization Program   291
Sebastian Edwards

III. PROTECTIONISM AND ECONOMIC PERFORMANCE

9. Some Economic Effects of Closing the Economy: The Mexican Experience in the Mid-Twentieth Century   333
Gerardo Esquivel and Graciela Márquez

10. The Political Economy of Protectionism: The Mexican Textile Industry, 1900–1950   363
Aurora Gómez-Galvarriato

Contributors   407
Author Index   409
Subject Index   415

Introduction

Sebastian Edwards, Gerardo Esquivel, and
Graciela Márquez

For a long time Latin America's economic performance has puzzled economists and historians. How can we explain that a region so rich in natural resources has had such a mediocre economic performance? Why has Latin America lagged behind, while its neighbors to the north—the United States and Canada—have developed and flourished? Why is it that after being one of the wealthiest nations in the world in the late nineteenth century, Argentina has joined the ranks of the crisis-prone countries? The papers collected in this volume deal with these issues from a historical perspective. In December 2004 the authors met at El Colegio de Mexico in Mexico City and spent two days discussing why Latin America's history has been characterized by mediocre growth, rampant protectionism, very high inflation, low productivity growth, and successive crises. Two themes run through these papers: (a) institutions have played an important role in shaping the Latin American economies; and (b) political considerations—including, in particular, distributional struggles—have been crucial in determining economic outcomes in the region.

Inequality and backwardness have been two central features of Latin American economies during the last two centuries. The region's skewed income distribution was already apparent to European travelers journeying in the Spanish colonies at the beginning of the nineteenth century. Many of

---

The papers collected in this volume were presented at the National Bureau of Economic Research's (NBER) Inter-American Seminar on Economics (IASE), held on December 6–8, 2004, at El Colegio de Mexico, Mexico City.

Sebastian Edwards is the Henry Ford II Professor of International Economics at UCLA's Anderson Graduate School of Management and a research associate at the National Bureau of Economic Research. Gerardo Esquivel is a professor of economics at El Colegio de Mexico, and Graciela Márquez is a professor of history at El Colegio de Mexico.

them pointed out the enormous gap that existed between the rich and the poor in the region.[1] Inequality has remained a salient feature of Latin America despite the profound economic transformations that have taken place in the region in the last two centuries. At the same time, Latin America's growth record has been insufficient to close its income gap with north Atlantic economies. Initial studies on international comparisons of long-run growth reveal that, relative to the United States, Latin America fell behind between 1700 and 1900.[2]

The study of colonial institutions and economic performance in the half century after Independence remains crucial for understanding how Latin America fell behind. Inequality inherited from the colonial past (and reproduced in the nineteenth century) shaped Latin American structures of taxation in ways that not only differed radically from the United States and Canada, but also from other developing economies. Differences prevailed well into the twentieth century. Lessons learned from the study of fragmented markets, political instability, and weak institutional structures—salient characteristics of nineteenth-century Latin America—illuminate not only our knowledge of the past, but also provide important elements to understanding present-day problems of this and other developing regions of the world.

At the end of the nineteenth century, and after decades of virtual stagnation, Latin American economies began to experience a slow but sustained recovery. This resumption of growth coincided with a process of globalization in the world economy that was characterized by an increased worldwide integration of commodity and factor markets. The expansionary cycle of the world economy increased the demand for raw materials and foodstuffs, benefiting export sectors throughout the region. However, only in Argentina did the export sector truly become the engine of growth for the three decades before the First World War.[3] The resumption of sustained per capita gross domestic product (GDP) growth elsewhere faltered due to a number of factors, including weak institutions, poor infrastructure, and misguided economic policies.

Throughout 1870–1913 the vast majority of Latin American countries became recipients of international capital inflows in the form of foreign direct investment and foreign loans. Virtually every government borrowed in international capital markets, mostly in gold-denominated debt.[4] While in many instances external debt financed the construction of railroad net-

---

1. "Mexico is the country of inequality. Nowhere does there exists such a fearful difference in the distribution of fortune, civilization, cultivation of the soil, and population" (von Humboldt, 1811, p. 134).
2. This conclusion is best presented by John Coatsworth's "Economic and Institutional Trajectories in Nineteenth-Century Latin America" (1998).
3. For an examination of the export-led growth see Victor Bulmer-Thomas (1994).
4. The pioneering study of the history of foreign debt in Latin America from a long-run perspective is Carlos Marichal (1989).

works, port facilities, and public works, it also exposed Latin American economies to banking and currency crises. Indeed, the accumulation of external debt denominated in foreign currency precipitated financial crises in countries like Brazil and Argentina, where foreign debt and fiscal mismanagement led to economic catastrophes.[5] Interestingly, in other then-emerging and peripheral economies, including British offshoots (Australia, Canada, New Zealand, and the United States) and small European countries (Norway and Finland), stronger fiscal and financial systems helped reduce the frequency and virulence of financial crises.

The disruption of trade and capital flows brought about by World War I and its aftermath resulted in the expansion of the manufacturing sector in more diversified economies; at the same time, export sectors suffered from cyclical movements in commodities markets. Latin America was still highly vulnerable to external shocks, and the Great Depression reduced income per capita throughout the region. Individual outcomes, however, varied, depending on the degree of openness, the behavior of export prices, and the degree of diversification of the nonexport sector. The recovery from the slump of the early 1930s was in part helped by unorthodox policy measures, including very large real devaluations and increases in government spending, which facilitated import substitution and appeased social protests.[6] The outbreak of World War II resulted in renewed external restrictions in commodity and capital markets, further reducing export earnings and foreign borrowing for the region as a whole. In the late 1940s, economic policy deliberately promoted domestic manufacturing in countries such as Brazil, Mexico, Colombia, Argentina, Chile, and Peru. In these countries a diversified industrial base and a sizeable domestic market gave credence to theories supporting industrialization through import substitution. Thus, the larger economies in the region followed an inward-looking strategy based on the rise of protection levels, capital controls, exchange controls, multiple exchange rate schemes, and public intervention in labor markets.[7]

In the period 1950–1960, average GDP growth rate for the twenty largest Latin American economies was 5.3 percent. Yet, the variance across the region was significant, and the acceleration of population growth lowered GDP per capita rates. For instance, the larger economies (Argentina, Brazil, Chile, Colombia, Mexico, Peru, and Venezuela) averaged only 2.4 percent in GDP per capita growth in the period 1950–1973. Growth rates masked problems associated with trade and capital controls and protec-

5. See, for example, the paper by Bordo and Meissner in this volume, as well as the references cited therein.
6. Latin American responses to the 1930s Depression were systematically analyzed in Rosemary Thorp (1984).
7. For an evaluation of price distortions of inward-looking development see Sebastian Edwards (1992). For a recent treatment see Alan Taylor (1998).

tionism: inefficient allocation of resources, inflationary pressures, monopolistic industrial structures, and growing current account and public deficits. Concerns about macroeconomic behavior appeared at different junctures in different countries, and stabilization programs attempted solutions that had varying degrees of success. By the 1960s, under the auspices of the United Nations Economic Commission for Latin America, the model of inward-looking development was present in virtually every country in the region. In the period 1950–1973, the economies of Argentina, Brazil, Chile, Colombia, Mexico, Peru, and Venezuela grew, on average, at a rate of 2.4 percent, whereas smaller and less diversified economies had a much lower growth rate.[8] Even if we consider the first group of countries as representative of Latin America, GDP per capita growth rate was only higher than that of African countries, and was similar to that of the western offshoots (Australia, Canada, New Zealand, and the United States). During this period, other regions in the world expanded at a more rapid pace: Asia (2.6 percent), Eastern Europe (4.0 percent), Southern Europe (4.8 percent), and western Europe (3.8 percent).[9]

In the 1960s, most Latin American governments considered regional integration to be the means to remedy some of the pitfalls of the inward-looking strategy, in particular growing external imbalances. Yet, the lack of harmonization between exchange rate, fiscal and monetary policies produced poor results. More importantly, the dominant autarkic orientation remained unchanged, as did the price distortions associated with it. Not implementing a policy shift at that time (the 1960s) was a lost opportunity for Latin America; price distortions became more severe in the 1970s and 1980s, and distortive policies had long-run effects on accumulation and growth.

In other latitudes, developing economies also industrialized, following similar inward-looking strategies. In particular, the economies of East Asia promoted import substitution industrialization in the early post–World War II period, with policies and instruments similar to those implemented in Latin America. In the 1960s and 1970s, however, the policy menu in East Asia shifted away from inward-looking development and increasingly moved toward outward orientation. Integrating with global markets allowed East Asia to maintain a fast-growing development until the 1990s, a trajectory that contrasts sharply with the dismal economic growth record of Latin America in the last quarter of the twentieth century.

A key conclusion from the study of the Latin American economic past is that history matters. Despite its simplicity, this observation points out the complexities involved in understanding the fundamental connections

---

8. For figures on average and individual GDP growth rates see Bulmer-Thomas, op. cit., table 9.4, 309.

9. Growth estimates correspond to estimates by Angus Madison (1995).

between growth trajectories and institutional paths. The essays in this volume show important dimensions of the historical interaction of economic performance and institutions in Latin America. This book also offers analytical insights into today's debates on the implications that political and institutional changes may have on economic development.

The volume is divided into three parts: part one deals with economic growth, taxation, and institutions, and has three papers. Part two includes five papers and focuses on financial crises, lending, and inflation. The third part has two papers on protectionism and economic performance. In the rest of this introduction I provide a reader's guide to the volume.

Economic Growth, Taxation, and Institutions

The volume opens with a paper by Leandro Prados de la Escosura titled "When Did Latin America Fall Behind?" In this piece Prados de la Escosura asks one of the fundamental questions in Latin America's economic history: has the income gap between Latin American countries and the core of advanced nations widened over time? And if so, when did this widening begin? Was there an era when Latin America grew at a rate comparable to that of the core nations? And, perhaps more important, why did Latin America fall behind? In an effort to address these issues Prados de la Escosura uses some tools of the inequality literature. He addresses long-run intercountry inequality in terms of real GDP per head (purchasing power adjusted). He also uses an improved human development index as an indicator of welfare for present-day Organization for Economic Cooperation and Development (OECD) countries and for Latin American nations. Prados de la Escosura's analysis shows that there has been a long-term rise in income inequality for this sample of countries. The main determinant of this increased cross-country inequality is the widening gap between the OECD and Latin America. The author argues that contrary to popular belief, Latin America fell behind, in terms of income, in the late twentieth century—not in the nineteenth century. Furthermore, the author argues that "the decline that probably took place in the decades after independence seems hardly comparable to the dramatic fall that took place in Latin America's relative position to the OECD in the late twentieth century." Prados de la Escosura also shows that, although cross-country inequality in terms of human development declined over time, the gap between OECD and Latin American countries remained largely unchanged.

In "Before the Golden Age: Economic Growth in Mexico and Portugal, 1910–1950," Pedro Lains provides a comparison of Mexico's and Portugal's economic growth during the first half of the twentieth century. He argues that what makes these countries particularly interesting is that they experienced solid growth in the interwar years, a period when most of the world was either stagnant or experiencing economic retrogression. Economic expansion in these two countries was the result of structural changes at the aggregate level as well as at the industrial sector level. These reforms favored those sectors with above-average total factor productivity and, thus, contributed to faster growth. Perhaps more importantly, during the interwar period the exchange rate was used as the most important tool for protecting local industries. This contrasts sharply with both countries' later experiences—Portugal after 1973 and Mexico after 1982—when import tariffs and quantitative restrictions were used as the main sources of protection. Lains also argues that his results call into question the traditional interpretation of Mexico's and Portugal's industrialization. According to traditional views, this process took off after World War II; the data discussed by the author suggest that strong industrialization forces were already gathering momentum during the interwar years. The author also discusses some of the most important differences between Mexico and Portugal, including political differences, differences in external policy, and demographic differences.

The next chapter, "Inequality and the Evolution of Institutions of Taxation: Evidence from the Economic History of the Americas," is by Kenneth L. Sokoloff and Eric M. Zolt. The authors analyze the role played by institutions in shaping Latin American countries' ability to raise revenues through taxation. Sokoloff and Zolt argue that the way in which nations organize their tax systems has widespread economic and social effects. It affects economic performance, productivity, inequality, and the degree of decentralization. The main interest of Sokoloff and Zolt is to analyze the relationship between inequality and taxes. They ask how and why tax institutions have differed and evolved throughout the countries of the Americas. They argue that there are striking contrasts in the tax systems of developed and developing countries; while advanced nations rely heavily on income and broad-based consumption taxes, emerging countries rely on taxes on international trade, value-added taxes, and turnover taxes. Sokoloff and Zolt also argue that developing countries are more likely to raise taxes at the national level rather than at the state and local level. Departing from traditional works that have asked how taxation affects inequality, Sokoloff and Zolt analyze the ways in which inequality may influence the design and implementation of tax systems. They argue that one of the most important reasons why tax structures in Latin America look so different from tax structures in North America is *not* that one region is rich and the other poor. Even when incomes across the North and the South were relatively equal, the tax structures were very different. Sokoloff and Zolt ask whether these differences in taxes (and spending) might play a role in explaining the divergent paths of long-run development. Their thesis, that inequality plays an important independent role in influencing the structure of taxation, is supported by comparisons between Latin America and

North America, as well as by comparisons between the respective countries within each of these regions.

Financial Crises, Lending, and Inflation

The first chapter in part two of the volume is "Financial Crises, 1880–1913: The Role of Foreign Currency Debt," by Michael D. Bordo and Christopher D. Meissner. In this paper, Bordo and Meissner inquire what has been the role of foreign currency debt in precipitating financial crises in Latin America. This question, which has recently been discussed in the context of modern crises, has received the name *liabilities dollarization,* as the cause of financial crises. According to this literature, countries that have a high proportion of their debt in foreign currency are more prone to having a financial crisis. Moreover, in countries with a high degree of liabilities dollarization, crises will tend to be profound and costly. In their paper, Bordo and Meissner put together a data set for nearly thirty countries between 1880 and 1913, and examine debt crises, currency crises, banking crises, and twin crises. Bordo and Meissner pay special attention to the role of foreign currency and gold clause debt, currency mismatches, and debt intolerance. They argue that there is strong evidence that suggests that a larger proportion of foreign currency debt leads to a higher chance of having a debt crisis or a banking crisis. An important finding, however, is that countries with strong institutions, with very different historical backgrounds, such as Australia, Canada, New Zealand, Norway, and the United States, were able to manage their exposure to hard currency debt, and were able to avoid having recurrent crises. Furthermore, these countries never had severe financial meltdowns. Bordo and Meissner also find that a strong international reserve position seems to be correlated with a lower likelihood of a debt crisis, currency crisis, or banking crisis. According to them, "this strengthens the evidence for the hypothesis that foreign currency debt is dangerous when mismanaged." An important finding is that a history of defaults matters: countries with previous default histories seem prone to debt crises, even when they have low debt ratios.

In "The True Measure of Country Risk: A Primer on the Interrelations between Solvency and the Polity Structure of Emerging Markets: Argentina 1886–1892," Gerardo della Paolera and Martin Grandes use Argentine data from the late nineteenth century to analyze the behavior of a true measure of country risk. What makes this period particularly interesting is that in 1890 the world suffered the first widespread emerging market capital and debt crisis—the so-called *Barings* crisis. Della Paolera and Grandes' most important contribution is constructing a measure of country risk that takes into account the evolution of both national, provincial, and local debt. This measure acknowledges the importance of the political structure of an emerging nation, such as Argentina, in determining its degree of participation and its strategies in international debt markets. The authors argue that the rationale for constructing this index of the true degree of risk premium is that the polity structure of a country matters for the conduct and outcome of the public debt phenomenon. This is particularly the case if the country has—as in Argentina—a federal structure with a significant struggle between the provinces and the federal government. The authors argue that this index informs policymakers and investors about the true country risk in federal countries where subsovereign entities are fiscally interdependent and potential time inconsistencies and sovereign moral hazards are present. Della Paolera and Grandes show that their true measure of country risk departs from the traditional typical sovereign risk spread by 200 to 350 basis points as Argentina approached its 1890 financial crisis.

In "Related Lending: Manifest Looting or Good Governance? Lessons from the Economic History of Mexico," Noel Maurer and Stephen Haber use Mexican historical data to analyze the extent to which banks lent to related firms during the 1884–1910 period. This has become an important question in modern economics, as scholars have tried to determine whether managers channel bank resources to related firms. Maurer and Haber argue that the dominant view among academics and policymakers is that related lending, a widespread practice in most emerging nations, should be discouraged, because it provides a mechanism through which bankers can loot their own banks at the expense of minority shareholders and depositors. The authors, however, take a different view, and argue that neither looting nor credit misallocation are necessary outcomes of related lending. According to them, related lending is the natural outcome of economic, financial, and institutional structures that result in very high information costs and contract enforcement costs. Maurer and Haber argue that whether related lending encourages looting depends on the other institutions that support the banking system. According to them, a particularly important factor is whether existing institutions give depositors and minority shareholders incentives and mechanisms to monitor directors, as well as incentives for directors to monitor other directors. On the basis of their empirical analysis using Mexican data from the Porfiriato period, the authors conclude that related lending does not need to be economically inefficient. They identify four conditions that would prevent related lending from becoming a form of organized looting. First, banks must be well capitalized. Second, bank directors must have a substantial equity position in their own banks. This gives them incentives to monitor one another. Third, minority and outside shareholders must have their own money at risk. And fourth, there should not be deposit insurance that covers one hundred percent of deposits.

In "Sudden Stops and Currency Drops: A Historical Look," Luis A. V.

Catão uses a data set for 1870 through 1913 to analyze the salient characteristics of sudden stops of capital inflows to both core and periphery countries. Catão argues that the behavior of capital markets during the period preceding World War I was remarkably similar to what we have observed during the last two decades. The analysis focuses on four issues: first, Catão shows that during the period under study all main capital-importing countries sporadically faced capital flow reversals. During these reversal episodes the volume of capital flowing out amounted to approximately 4.5 percent of GDP, on average. Second, the analysis shows that these sudden stop episodes affected both fixed and floating exchange rate countries. Moreover, according to Catão's results, there were no significant differences in sudden stops under the two regimes. Third, the results discussed in this paper show that most sudden stop episodes displayed significant cross-country synchronization. Moreover, they were all immediately preceded by an increase in international interest rates. This important result provides some evidence for the existence of contagion during the late nineteenth and early twentieth centuries. Fourth, Catão shows that not all sudden stop episodes resulted in currency collapses: while some countries did experience dramatic currency depreciations, others managed to preserve exchange rate stability. According to the author, "these distinct responses are related to domestic factors that heightened the pro-cyclicality of capital inflows and domestic absorption in some countries—notably in Latin America and Southern Europe—relative to others."

In "Establishing Credibility: The Role of Foreign Advisors in Chile's 1955–1958 Stabilization Program," Sebastian Edwards analyzes Chile's experience with anti-inflationary policies in the mid-1950s. In 1955–1958 Chile implemented a stabilization package with the advice of the U.S. consulting firm of Klein-Saks. At the time the program was put in place inflation had reached the extremely high annual level (for that time) of 85 percent. The policies adopted contradicted the newly dominant orthodoxy in Latin America that associated inflation with *structural* problems. The Klein-Saks program took place in a period of acute political confrontation. After what was considered to be an initial success—inflation declined to 38 percent in 1956, and was further reduced to 17 percent in 1957—the program failed to achieve durable price stability. Edwards argues that the foreign advisors of the Klein-Saks Mission gave *initial* credibility to the stabilization program launched in 1955. According to him, these foreign advisors played the role of independent, nonpartisan, technocratic arbiters. It was precisely because they were foreigners that they could rise above the political fray and suggest a specific program, whose main components were rapidly approved by a highly divided Congress. The fact that the program was very similar to one proposed earlier by the government—and that was rejected by Congress—underscores the view that, while locals are suspect of being excessively partisan, foreigners are often (but not always) seen as independent policy brokers. But providing *initial credibility* was not enough to ensure success. In spite of supporting trade reform, foreign exchange rate reform, and the de-indexation of wages, Congress failed to act decisively on the fiscal front. Consequently, the fiscal imbalances that had plagued Chile for a long time were reduced but not eliminated. In 1957, a sharp drop in the international price of copper—the country's main export—resulted in a major decline in fiscal revenue and an increase in the fiscal deficit. The Mission recommended a series of belt-tightening measures, but politicians had had enough of orthodoxy. No adjustment was made, and inflationary expectations once again shifted for the worse. Edwards presents empirical results on the evolution of inflation, exchange rates, and interest rates that support his analysis.

Protectionism and Economic Performance

The last two chapters in the volume deal with protectionism and economic performance, an issue that has been of great interest to Latin American scholars for a long time. Indeed, a number of analysts have argued that Latin America's mediocre growth and its historically unequal income distribution have been, at least in part, the result of pervasive protectionist policies. In "Some Economic Effects of Closing the Economy: The Mexican Experience in the Mid-Twentieth Century," Gerardo Esquivel and Graciela Márquez investigate the closing of the Mexican economy in the mid-twentieth century and how it affected the Mexican economy. They are particularly interested in understanding how protectionism affected the economic structure, as well as conventionally defined economic performance. In the first part of the chapter the authors describe the type of commercial policies implemented in Mexico during the first part of the twentieth century. The authors then use data from the Industrial Census for 1945–1965 to investigate the way in which these policies affected employment, wages, and the regional location of economic activity. Their results provide support for the wage and employment implications of standard international trade theory. An important finding, however, is that commercial policy in Mexico during the mid-twentieth century does not appear to have affected the geographical pattern of production. Esquivel and Márquez reach this conclusion after having analyzed the evolution of a "location index" and a "regionalization index."

The final paper in the volume is "The Political Economy of Protectionism: The Mexican Textile Industry, 1900–1950," by Aurora Gómez-Galvarriato. In this paper Gómez-Galvarriato uses microdata from a textile mill in Mexico to analyze the evolution of prices, costs, and productivity during a period of increasing protectionism. In order to have a benchmark for comparison, Gómez-Galvarriato also analyzes the behavior of key data in textile mills in the United States, Great Britain, and

Japan. What makes this analysis particularly interesting is that the data come from the archives of one of the oldest textile firms in Mexico: the Compañia Industrial Veracruzana S.A. (CIVSA). According to Gómez-Galvarriato's analysis, in 1911 CIVSA was quite efficient, and its levels of productivity compared favorably with those in the United States and in the United Kingdom. CIVSA's productivity levels, however, did not increase during the rest of the twentieth century. According to the author, this dismal performance was not the result of a single factor; it was the consequence of a complex confluence of policies and circumstances. At the time of the Great Depression the different actors in this saga—unions, stock owners, management, and the government—decided that maintaining the status quo was the best way of dealing with the crisis. Subsequently, however, every effort to improve technology was opposed by unions and, to some extent, by industrialists, who could do well as long as import tariffs were sufficiently high. According to Gómez-Galvarriato the government also benefited from this arrangement, as it could maintain a relatively peaceful labor-relations regime in a sector that was considered to be politically very important.

References

Bulmer-Thomas, V. 1994. *The economic history of Latin America since independence.* New York: Cambridge University Press.

Coatsworth, J. H., and A. M. Taylor, eds. 1998. *Latin America and the world economy since 1800.* Cambridge, MA: Harvard University Press.

Edwards, S. 1992. Trade orientation, distortions and growth in developing countries. *Journal of Developing Economics* 39:31–57.

Madison, A. 1995. Monitoring the world economy. Paris: OECD.

Marichal, C. 1989. *A century of debt crisis in Latin America: From independence to the Great Depression, 1820–1930.* Princeton, NJ: Princeton University Press.

Taylor, A. M. 1998. On the costs of inward-looking development: Price distortions, growth and divergence in Latin America. *Journal of Economic History* 58:1–28.

Thorp, R., ed. 1984. *Latin America in the 1930s: The role of the periphery in the world crisis.* New York: St. Martin's.

Von Humboldt, A. 1811. Political essay on the kingdom of New Spain. Trans. John Black. London: Brown.

I

Economic Growth, Taxation, and Institutions

1
When Did Latin America Fall Behind?

Leandro Prados de la Escosura

1.1 Introduction

When did Latin America fall behind, and has the gap between the developed countries and Latin America widened over time are recurrent questions among economic historians. The idea of long-run relative decline since independence has been favored in the literature (Bulmer-Thomas 1994, 410), while it is widely accepted that the origins of modern Latin American economic retardation are located in the nineteenth century (Coatsworth 1993; Haber 1997). Coatsworth (1998) emphasizes that Latin America fell behind between 1700 and 1900, while the gap with the United States remained unchanged during the twentieth century. The evidence on comparative real product per head, assembled by Pablo Astorga and Valpy Fitzgerald (1998, 353), lends support to this view.[1]

Explanatory hypotheses for the early failure of Latin America emphasize the initial colonial conditions. The radically different evolution of Anglo and Latin Americas reflects the imposition of distinct metropolitan institutions on each colony (North 1990). Initial inequality of wealth, human capital, and political power conditioned institutional design and, thus,

---

Leandro Prados de la Escosura is professor of economic history at Universidad Carlos III de Madrid.

This essay was presented at the 2004 Inter-American Seminar on Economics sponsored by the National Bureau of Economic Research and El Colegio de Mexico in México, DF. I am grateful to the organizers, Sebastian Edwards, Gerardo Esquivel, and Graciela Márquez, to its participants, and especially to my discussant, Luis Felipe López Calva, for their remarks and suggestions. Useful comments by Pablo Astorga, Luis Bértola, Joan Rosés, and two anonymous referees are acknowledged. The usual disclaimer applies.

1. In a recent paper, however, Astorga, Bergés, and Fitzgerald (2005) stress that the per capita income trend for a sample of thirteen countries diverged from that of the United States in the second half of the twentieth century.

poor performance in Latin America relative to the United States (Engerman and Sokoloff 1997). Latin America's fate could thus be explained with Acemoglu, Johnson, and Robinson's (2002) "reversal of fortune" theory: in areas of relative affluence, with abundant population, such as Meso-America and the Andes, Europeans established "extractive institutions," with political power concentrated in the hands of an elite, as the most efficient choice—in spite of its long-term negative effects on growth. While in poor, less densely populated areas, Europeans settled in large numbers and developed their own institutions that encouraged investment and growth.[2]

Another view stresses the role of colonial independence in modern Latin America's destiny. The break with colonial rule destroyed institutions that provided credible commitments to rights and property within the Spanish empire and, as a result, widespread turmoil, violence, and political instability took place after independence, with the consequence of sluggish economic growth (North, Summerhill, and Weingast 2000). Views from the *Dependencia* school concur. The failure to achieve sustained and balanced growth in the new republics over the nineteenth century resulted from the persistence of colonial heritage (Frank 1967; Stanley and Barbara Stein 1970). *Dependentists* saw the opening to the international economy as a cause of increasing inequality across and within countries, stressing the role of the terms of trade in Latin American retardation by shifting resources to primary production (Singer 1950) and by provoking *immiserizing* growth (Prebisch 1950).

Interpretations of Latin America's early backwardness rest on a long-run comparison with the United States. It must be pointed out, however, that most countries, including those of Western Europe, fell behind over the nineteenth century when measured by American standards (Maddison 2003; Prados de la Escosura 2000). Moreover, the claim that Latin America's relative position to the United States remained mostly unaltered during the twentieth century, as proof that her economic retardation occurred in the nineteenth century (Astorga and Fitzgerald 1998; Coatsworth 1998) is at odds with the post-1950 catching-up experience in large areas of the periphery (southern Europe, southeast Asia), in which the gap with the United States in income per head was significantly reduced. The United States appears, therefore, a questionable yardstick to assess Latin America's economic performance.[3]

Whether Latin America fell behind in the late twentieth century or in the

---

2. A forerunner of this view is Stanley and Barbara Stein's (1970, 128) counterfactual argument: "had the Englishmen found a dense and highly organized Amerindian population, the history of what is called the United States would record the development of a stratified, bi-racial, very different society."

3. The U.S. exceptionalism was emphasized by Stanley and Barbara Stein (1970, 128): "the existence of a huge, under-populated virgin land of extraordinary resource endowment directly facing Europe and enjoying a climate comparable to that of Europe represented a potentiality for development which existed nowhere else in the New World."

early nineteenth century has important consequences for the ongoing debate on its causes. If her backwardness originated in the decades after independence, institutional and factor endowments differences with the United States and western Europe are relevant to provide an explanation. If, however, her retardation occurred in the late twentieth century, discrepancies between Latin and British Americas during the colonial and the post-independence periods become secondary to exploring what went wrong in Latin America during the phase of widespread catching up to the developed countries in regions of the periphery (southern Europe, East Asia). Explanations that emphasize the cost of inward-looking policies, macroeconomic instability, and poor contract enforcement would then come to the fore.[4]

My purpose in this paper is to reexamine the timing of Latin America's economic retardation—first, by using a more representative comparator, such as a group of countries included under the OECD acronym, and second, by resorting to the tools employed in the inequality literature.[5] Interestingly, in their pioneering contribution, Bourguignon and Morrisson (2002, 738) did not discuss the case of Latin America, "because its economic growth over the last two centuries has roughly coincided with the world average."[6]

Among the main findings of the paper that can be highlighted are that, contrary to widespread belief, it was during the late twentieth century when Latin America fell behind more dramatically. A long-term rise in real average per capita income inequality is found for a large sample of countries encompassing most of Europe, the Americas, and Oceania. The rise in intercountry inequality resulted from the widening gap between the OECD countries and Latin America, as opposed to the reduction in income differences within each of these country groups. As a result, polarization emerged.

This chapter is organized as follows: section 1.2 compares per capita income levels and growth rates. Section 1.3 presents new measures of long-run intercountry economic inequality that can be decomposed into the underlying changes within and across regions' inequality. When did Latin America fall behind is re-assessed in the concluding section.

1.2 Real Income Trends

In international comparisons, dissatisfaction with *nominal* income (that is, GDP per head in national currency converted into a common currency,

---

4. Such as those proposed, among others, by Cardoso and Fishlow (1992), Edwards (1995), de Gregorio (1992), and Taylor (1998).
5. I describe OECD, for short, as a sample of today's advanced nations from Europe, the so-called "areas of new settlement" or Maddison's (2003) "European offshoots" (Australia, Canada, and New Zealand), the United States, and Japan.
6. No systematic assessments of international inequality over the long run exist other than Bourguignon and Morrisson's (2002) and Lindert and Williamson's (2003) contributions.

using the trading exchange rate) has led to an almost generalized use of *real income* (the conversion of per capita income into a common currency is carried out with a purchasing power parity [PPP] exchange rate).[7] Unfortunately, the construction of PPP converters involves high costs in terms of time and resources. Only PPPs for a restricted country sample that does not include any of Latin America have been constructed for earlier periods, and most of them for output components.[8]

An indirect method to derive historical estimates of real income levels for a large sample of countries is the backward projection of PPP-adjusted GDP per capita for a recent benchmark with volume indices (or growth rates) of product per head derived from national accounts data.[9] It is worth noting that fixed-base *real* (PPP-adjusted) product data represent a most convenient alternative to carrying out painstaking direct comparisons across space and time, and have the presentation advantage that their growth rates are identical to those calculated from national accounts.[10] Alas, a distant PPP benchmark introduces distortions in intertemporal comparisons, since its validity depends on how stable the basket of goods and services used to construct the original PPP converters remains over time. As growth occurs over time the composition of output, consumption, and relative prices all vary, and the economic meaning of comparing real product per head based upon remote PPPs becomes entirely questionable. Hence, using a single PPP benchmark for long-run comparisons implies the hardly realistic assumption that no changes in relative prices (and hence, no technological change) takes place over time.

---

7. Empirical evidence gathered in recent years strongly rejects the conventional results obtained through the trading exchange rate converter (Summers and Heston 1991, van Ark 1993). Trading exchange rates only reflect the purchasing power of goods traded internationally, and are influenced by capital movements, exchange controls, and speculation (Maddison 1995, 162). In other words, foreign exchange rates do not measure relative price levels and do not move with them over time (Ahmad 1998).

8. In addition to O'Brien and Keyder's (1978) and Fremdling's (1991) PPP computations for commodity output, there are sectoral PPP estimates: for agriculture, Luiten van Zanden (1991) and O'Brien and Prados de la Escosura (1992), and for manufacturing, Broadberry and Fremdling (1990), Broadberry (1994, 1997), Burger (1997), and Dormois and Bardini (1995). Exceptionally, Williamson (1995) used an income approach. Recently, Ward and Devereux (2003a, 2003b) have accepted the challenge to build direct PPP estimates from the expenditure side for twelve western economies at five benchmarks (1872, 1884, 1905, 1930, and 1950).

9. Maddison's (2003) 1990 Geary-Khamis dollar estimates provide the best example.

10. A significant strand of the literature defends the view that the best estimates of growth rates are those obtained from national accounts (Bhagwati and Hansen 1973; Isenman 1980; Kravis and Lipsey 1991; Maddison 1991, 1995) on the grounds that "using domestic prices to measure growth rates is more reliable, because those prices characterize the trade offs faced by the decision making agents" (Nuxoll 1994, 1423). Kravis and Lipsey (1991, 458) argued that growth rates derived from domestic prices were preferable because the basket of goods used "reflected the preferences of purchasers of final product in one of the years being compared."

Since PPP exchange rates were not computed directly for Latin American countries in 1990 (Maddison 1995, 2001), I have resorted to a set of own-country weights (Paasche) PPP direct computations by the Economic Commission for Latin America (ECLA) for 1960, never used before in historical studies, which provides a wider spatial coverage. The commodity basket included 261 consumption goods and 113 investment goods for capital cities in nineteen Latin American countries and the United States (Houston and Los Angeles). Prices were collected in 1960–62. Quantity expenditure weights for a Latin American average and the United States in 1960 were used (ECLA 1968; Stanley Braithwaite 1968).[11] Alternatively, Geary-Khamis PPPs, derived by the UN's International Comparisons Project (ICP), could have been used for most Latin American countries in 1980[12] (and for all in 1996).[13] There are two reasons for the choice of the 1960 benchmark: (a) in absence of current price PPP-adjusted GDP levels, real income at 1960 U.S. prices provides an intermediate year for the time span considered that it is preferable to the use of a benchmark year for the end of the twentieth century,[14] and (b) GDP volume series expressed in U.S. relative prices (derived with Paasche PPPs) facilitate the comparison with available OECD countries' real (PPP-adjusted) income per head, expressed in U.S. relative prices (Prados de la Escosura 2000). A set of real product per head estimates, which includes Europe, the Americas, Oceania, and Japan, has been constructed at 1960 U.S. relative prices by projecting backward with volume indices the benchmarks for Latin America (ECLA 1968) and my own one for OECD countries (Prados de la Escosura 2000).[15]

Figure 1.1 and table 1.1 present trends in population-weighted measures of real GDP per head in Latin America and OECD over one and a half centuries for different country samples in which time and spatial coverage are inversely related, so the lengthier the time span covered the lower the number of countries comprised in the sample. Hence, the figures for wider cov-

---

11. PPPs in ECLA (1960) appear, thus, to be superior in country coverage but not in commodity coverage to Program of Joint Studies on Latin American Economic Integration and Development (ECIEL) benchmark estimates for 1970 and 1975 (Salazar-Carrillo 1983; Salazar-Carrillo and Tirado de Alonso 1988; Salazar-Carrillo and Prasada Rao 1988).

12. I have replicated the whole exercise presented here at 1980 international prices with no major discrepancies in the results, except for the fact that relative levels of Latin America's per capita GDP in terms of OECD average are significantly higher when expressed in 1980 international dollars.

13. It is worth noting that the 1970 benchmark, originally published by CEPAL (the Spanish acronym of ECLA; 1978) and used in Astorga, Bergés, and Fitzgerald (2005), is just a projection of the 1960 benchmark levels with each Latin American country's inflation differential to the United States.

14. I am currently preparing new shortcut *current* price estimates of *real* income (at U.S. relative prices) for Latin America.

15. The sources for the volume indices of GDP per head are provided in appendix A.

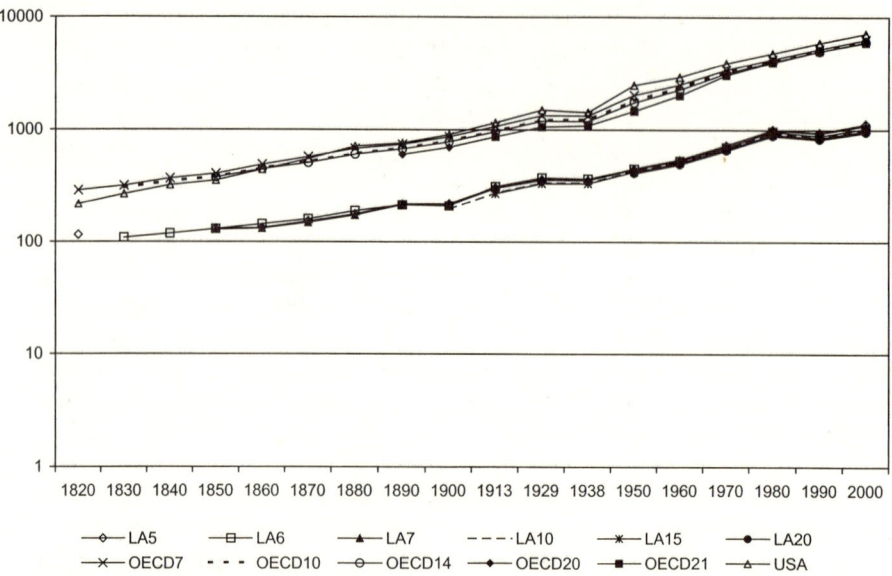

Fig. 1.1 Real per capita GDP in Latin America, the OECD, and the United States (1960 U.S. relative prices)

erage in table 1.1 (columns in bold) should be preferred.[16] Some main features of historical performance in Latin America can be pointed out. In the first place, the origins of modern economic growth, as defined by a sustained increase in output per person, can be traced back at least to the midnineteenth century. Latin America appears to have experienced a sustained and gradual growth over one and a half century, a trend only broken during the 1890s, the Great Depression, and, especially, the 1980s crisis, in which per capita GDP multiplied by 8.5 times.

Alas, only scant quantitative evidence exists for the early nineteenth century. Growth rates varied substantially across Latin America. Mexico seems to have experienced a decline in per capita income during the period of independence and a very mild recovery between the 1820s and midnineteenth century (Coatsworth 1989, 2003; Salvucci 1997), and the fate of Peru was probably similar (Quiroz 1993), while Brazil appears to have experienced stagnation (Leff 1982) and, perhaps, also Colombia (Kalmanovitz 2005; Jaramillo Uribe, Meisel, and Urrutia 2001). A long-run improvement in income per head occurred in Cuba until 1860 (Fraile, Salvucci, and Salvucci 1993; Santamaría 2005), Venezuela (Baptista 1997), Chile (Díaz, Lüders, and Wagner 1998), and it can be guessed, also in the

---

16. The data in figure 1.1 correspond to roughly decadal benchmarks in order to facilitate its reading. Table 1.1 presents all the available benchmarks.

Table 1.1   Per capita GDP in Latin America, the OECD, and the United States (1960 U.S. relative prices; population weighted averages)

	LA5	LA6	LA7	LA10	LA15	LA20	OECD7	OECD10	OECD14	OECD20	OECD21	U.S.
1820	*115*						*289*					217
1830		*109*					318	*305*				268
1840		*119*					370	*349*				322
1850	131	130	*129*				407	382	*378*			354
1860	133	144	*132*				490	453	*447*			443
1870	153	160	*149*				573	519	*508*			550
1880	177	189	*173*				680	612	*605*			712
1890	217	214	*214*				739	685	675	*602*		760
1900	219	210	213	*196*			866	796	779	*698*		905
1913	305	313	302	275	*271*		1,068	976	961	865	*865*	1,154
1925	338	336	333	311	*305*		1,215	1,100	1,074	963	*961*	1,354
1929	361	376	359	339	*333*		1,337	1,220	1,194	1,062	**1,060**	1,498
1933	303	309	298	286	*282*		1,070	976	962	889	**888**	1,065
1938	356	367	355	339	*334*		1,331	1,237	1,187	1,089	**1,087**	1,427
1950	445	450	455	432	*424*	*410*	2,028	1,831	1,740	1,464	**1,462**	2,484
1955	488	489	498	476	466	**451**	2,329	2,164	2,056	1,766	**1,764**	2,808
1960	535	531	546	520	509	**492**	2,512	2,384	2,268	2,016	**2,013**	2,941
1965	609	594	622	591	579	**559**	2,989	2,846	2,736	2,497	**2,493**	3,459
1970	727	698	733	691	675	**654**	3,426	3,281	3,178	3,059	**3,054**	3,907
1975	867	848	869	817	796	**772**	3,747	3,610	3,546	3,436	**3,431**	4,197
1980	1,004	966	994	933	906	**879**	4,256	4,128	4,045	3,969	**3,963**	4,800
1985	937	880	925	870	841	**815**	4,667	4,516	4,413	4,368	**4,360**	5,302
1990	945	884	933	877	848	**820**	5,243	5,088	5,000	5,014	**5,007**	5,918
1995	1,031	989	1,007	952	919	**887**	5,538	5,359	5,274	5,283	**5,278**	6,246
2000	1,127	1,031	1,093	1,017	980	**947**	6,357	6,112	6,042	5,959	**5,961**	7,175

Sources: See appendix A.

Notes: Numbers in *italics* are based on estimates for most countries. See text for explanation. LA5 = Argentina, Brazil, Chile, Mexico, and Uruguay; LA6 = Argentina, Brazil, Chile, Cuba, Uruguay, and Venezuela; LA7 = Argentina, Brazil, Chile, Cuba, Mexico, Uruguay, and Venezuela; LA10 = LA7 plus Colombia, Ecuador, and Peru; LA15 = LA10 plus Costa Rica, El Salvador, Guatemala, Honduras, and Nicaragua; LA20 = all Latin America; OECD7 = Australia, Denmark, France, the Netherlands, Sweden, the United Kingdom, and the United States; OECD10 = Austria, Belgium, Denmark, France, Germany, the Netherlands, Norway, Sweden, the United Kingdom, and the United States; OECD14 = Australia, Austria, Belgium, Canada, Denmark, France, Germany, the Netherlands, Norway, Portugal, Spain, Sweden, the United Kingdom, and the United States; OECD20 = OECD14 plus Finland, Greece, Italy, Japan, New Zealand, and Switzerland; and OECD21 = OECD20 plus Ireland.

River Plate (Newland 1998; Newland and Poulson 1998).[17] On the whole, and if the fragmented evidence and conjectures for each country are weighted by its population, it can be hypothesized that, once independence was completed, moderate per capita income growth (below 0.5 percent per year) took place between the 1820s and mid-nineteenth century. If we accept these conjectures, it could be hypothesized that real per capita income multiplied by 10 between 1820 and 2000.

In table 1.2 growth rates are presented for different aggregates of Latin American countries; fortunately, the picture they offer of Latin America's long-run performance appears quite robust. After a slow start, Latin America grew significantly during the three decades following 1860 and, after the 1890s slowdown, growth accelerated in the early years of the twentieth century up to World War I. A comparison with the advanced countries shows that Latin America experienced faster growth than the OECD group in the 1880s and from 1900 to 1913. Latin America's output per head slowed down during World War I and reached a halt in the years of the Great Depression, but its comparative performance was not dissimilar from that of OECD countries during the interwar years. After the Depression, Latin America enjoyed its fastest phase of growth, which lasted more than four decades (1938–80). Its rate of growth remained, however, below that of OECD countries, and only exhibited a better performance in the 1970s. As for the "Golden Age" (1950–73), Latin America only managed to match the U.S. growth rate, but was way behind that of the OECD group. The 1980s represented a major break in the long-run performance of Latin America that the sluggish growth of the 1990s failed to offset. On the whole, the last two decades of the twentieth century offer the poorest relative economic record in the last one hundred and fifty years of Latin American history.

To sum up, during the decades after independence Latin America experienced moderate economic growth that fell short of that achieved by a small group of rich countries. Latin America then kept pace with the growth of the advanced countries' club throughout the period 1860–1938. The second half of the twentieth century represents, in turn, a phase of relative decline that was exacerbated in its last twenty years. In an

17. For Venezuela, Baptista (1997) estimates indicate an annual compound rate of 2.2 percent for real income per head between 1831–35 and 1851–55. As for Cuba, figures suggested by Fraile, Linda and Richard Salvucci (1993), and Santamaría (2005) allow us to suggest that per capita GDP grew at 0.6 percent per year between 1830 and 1850. In the case of Chile, Díaz, Lüders, and Wagner (1998) figures suggest that real output per head grew at 1.4 percent between 1820 and 1850. In turn, Argentina's littoral agricultural output per head grew at 2 percent per year over 1825–1865 (Newland and Poulson 1998; Newland 1998). Assuming that this sector was representative of the littoral economy as a whole, and that no per capita growth occurred in Argentina's interior provinces, an overall rate of growth of 0.8 percent would result for per capita GDP. It could reasonably be assumed that Uruguay evolved as did Argentina. As regards Mexico, a mild rise in GDP per capita at 0.2 percent per year over the period 1820–45 is suggested by Coatsworth (2003).

Table 1.2   Per capita GDP growth in Latin America, the OECD, and the United States

	LA5	LA6	LA7	LA10	LA15	LA20	OECD7	OECD10	OECD14	OECD20	OECD21	U.S.
1820–1850	*0.4*											1.6
1830–1850		*0.9*										1.4
1850–1860	0.1	1.0	0.2				1.1	1.1				2.2
1860–1870	1.4	1.0	1.2				1.2	1.7	1.7			2.2
1870–1880	1.5	1.7	1.5				1.9	1.4	1.3			2.6
1880–1890	2.1	1.2	2.1				1.6	1.6	1.7			0.7
1890–1900	0.1	−0.2	0.0				1.7	1.1	1.1			1.7
1900–1913	2.6	3.1	2.7	2.6			0.8	1.5	1.4	1.5	1.3	1.9
1913–1929	1.1	1.1	1.1	1.3	1.3		1.6	1.6	1.6	1.7	0.3	1.6
1929–1938	−0.2	−0.2	−0.1	0.0	0.0		1.4	1.3	1.3	1.2	2.5	−0.5
1938–1950	1.9	1.7	2.1	2.0	2.0	1.8	−0.1	0.2	−0.1	0.3	3.2	4.6
1950–1960	1.8	1.7	1.8	1.9	1.8	2.8	3.5	3.3	3.2	2.5	4.2	1.7
1960–1970	3.1	2.7	2.9	2.8	2.8	3.0	2.1	2.6	2.7	3.2	2.6	2.8
1970–1980	3.2	3.2	3.0	3.0	2.9	−0.7	3.1	3.2	3.4	4.2	2.3	2.1
1980–1990	−0.6	−0.9	−0.6	−0.6	−0.7	1.4	2.2	2.3	2.4	2.6	1.7	2.1
1990–2000	1.8	1.5	1.6	1.5	1.5		2.1	2.1	2.1	2.3		1.9
1860–1890	1.6	1.3	1.6				1.9	1.8	1.9	1.7		
1890–1913	1.5	1.7	1.5				1.4	1.4	1.4		0.9	1.8
1913–1938	0.6	0.6	0.7	0.8	0.8		1.6	1.5	1.5	0.9	1.4	1.8
1938–1950	1.0	1.0	1.1	1.2	1.2		0.9	0.9	0.8	1.4	3.3	0.8
1950–1980	2.7	2.5	2.6	2.6	2.5	2.5	1.7	1.7	1.6	3.3	2.0	2.1
1980–2000	0.6	0.3	0.5	0.4	0.4	0.4	2.5	2.7	2.8	2.0		2.2
1860–1929	1.4	1.4	1.5				2.0	2.0	2.0			2.0
1860–1938	1.3	1.2	1.3				1.5	1.4	1.4			1.8
1938–1950	2.5	2.3	2.4	2.4			1.3	1.3	1.3			1.5
1850–2000	1.4	1.4	1.4				2.8	2.9	2.9	3.1	3.1	2.9
1850–1980	1.6	1.5	1.6				1.8	1.8	1.8			2.0
1900–2000	1.6	1.6	1.6	1.6			1.8	1.8	1.8	2.1		2.0
1913–2000	1.5	1.4	1.5	1.5	1.5		2.0	2.0	2.0	2.2	2.2	2.1
1820–2000	*1.3*						2.1	2.1	2.1			2.1
1830–2000		*1.3*					1.7	1.8				1.9
							1.8					1.9

Sources: See appendix A.

Notes: Numbers in *italics* are based on estimates for most countries. See text for explanation. See table 1.1 notes for explanations of abbreviations.

increasingly globalized world, in which access to the latest technological vintage depends upon a country's social capability, Latin American performance appears especially disappointing. The cases of southern Europe and, more recently, of southeast Asian nations provide a most interesting counterpoint. Starting from lower levels of GDP per head and, subsequently, with a poorer endowment of human and physical capital, a faster growth rate could, ceteris paribus, have been expected. However, only in the 1880s, 1900–13, and in the 1970s, did Latin America grow above the OECD average (and the United States).

Decomposing per capita GDP growth using identity (I) provides a more accurate description of Latin American slowdown in the late twentieth century. If low case represents annual rates of variation, per capita income growth can be broke down into the addition of the rates of variation of output per economically active population (EAP), of the activity rate (the EAP ratio to population ages 15 to 64, or potentially active population [PAP]), and of the share of PAP in total population.

$$(1) \qquad y_{pc} = \frac{y}{\text{eap}} + \frac{\text{eap}}{\text{pap}} + \frac{\text{pap}}{\text{population}}$$

In the 1950s and 1960s, labor productivity overcame per capita GDP growth, making for a declining activity rate and a higher dependency rate (the ratio of population below 15 and above 65 to PAP; table 1.3). Since the 1970s, however, labor productivity lagged behind GDP per head growth but was offset by the rise in the activity rate and by the demographic gift of an increasing share of potentially active population, that, from 1980 onward, constituted the only basis for rising per capita income. The increase in the activity rate was related to the reduction of unemployment and, especially during the nineties, to the incorporation of women into the labor force (Astorga, Bergés, and Fitzgerald 2003, 35).

A further decomposition of labor productivity into physical and human capital per worker and total factor productivity (TFP) is necessary to un-

Table 1.3 Per capita GDP growth and its components in Latin America (%; annual logarithmic growth rates)

	Per capita GDP	GDP per EAP	EAP/PAP	PAP/Population
1950–1960	1.9	2.5	–0.2	–0.3
1960–1970	2.8	3.5	–0.3	–0.1
1970–1980	3.0	1.9	0.5	0.4
1980–1990	–0.7	–1.0	0.0	0.6
1990–2000	1.4	–0.3	0.6	0.6

Sources: See appendix A.

Notes: EAP = economically active population; PAP = potentially active population, that is, population ages 15 to 64.

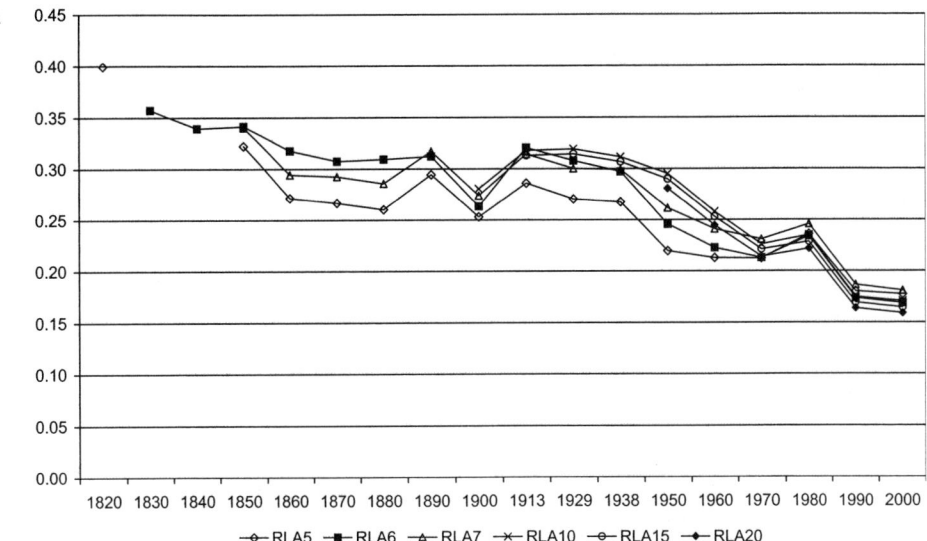

Fig. 1.2 Relative real per capita GDP in Latin America: *A*, OECD = 1; 1960 U.S. relative prices; *B*, U.S. = 1; 1960 U.S. relative prices)

derstand the slowing down in workers' efficiency. For the 1980–2000 period, Astorga, Bergés, and Fitzgerald (2003, 34) suggest an average decline in TFP growth together with a deepening fall in capital. A more benign view of TFP growth is offered by André Hofman (2001), who points out that the decline in labor productivity reflects a "strong increase" in labor inputs.[18]

So far, the focus of attention has been on Latin America as a whole (figure 1.2), but the region comprises a heterogeneous group of countries that exhibit substantial discrepancies in their factor endowments and long-run performance. The fact that most economic historians only focus their research on a country or just one of its regions supports the case. Latin America as a whole is, however, what scholars see from the outside and, therefore, remains a valid concept once allowance is made for the wide dispersion in terms of performance and policies.

Growth rates in per capita GDP for major Latin American countries at roughly decadal benchmarks are presented since 1850 in table 1.4. The high variance of growth rates across countries and across different periods is worth highlighting. Argentina, Chile, and Mexico's income per head grew above Latin America's average between 1870 and 1913, while Brazil, Colombia, Peru, and Venezuela achieved it during 1913–38. On the whole,

---

18. Also, Fajnzylber and Lederman (2000) and Hofman (2000) found a negative TFP growth in the 1980s.

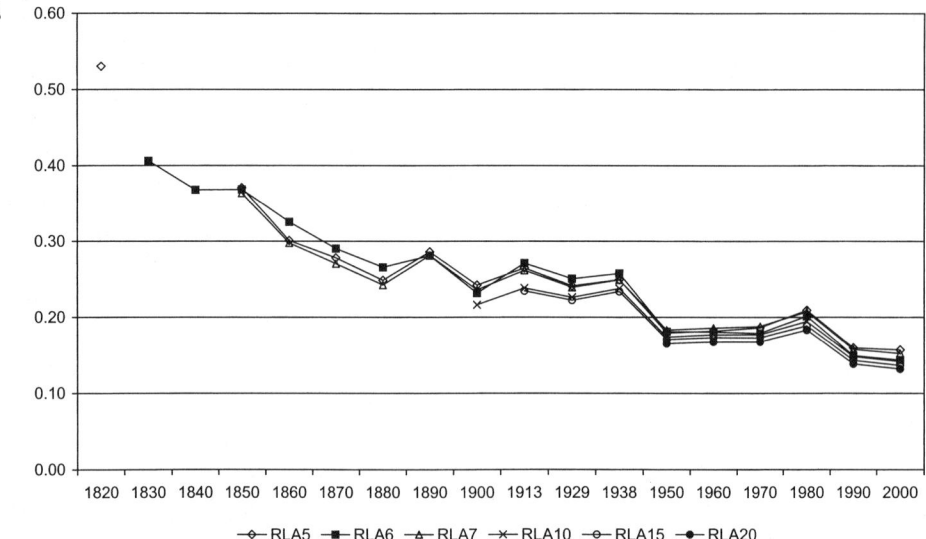

Fig. 1.2 (cont.) Relative real per capita GDP in Latin America: *A*, OECD = 1; 1960 U.S. relative prices; *B*, U.S. = 1; 1960 U.S. relative prices)

during the early phase of modern economic growth Colombia, Peru, Venezuela, and, to a lesser extent, Argentina grew above the region's average. In the second phase of sustained expansion (1938–80), Mexico and especially Brazil emerge above the average, while Chile stands alone as the best performer in the last two decades of the twentieth century. As countries starting from lower income levels (Colombia, Peru, Venezuela) have grown faster than average, while richer countries (Uruguay, Argentina) have grown at a slower pace over the long run, a pattern of convergence among Latin American nations has been building up over time (see figure 1.3). It is worth noticing that the southern cone countries, and Argentina, in particular, conditioned divergence and convergence trends within the region. In the pre-World War I era Argentina's economic success determined per capita income divergence across countries. Conversely, Argentina's slowing down from 1914 onward is behind the process of convergence observed during the twentieth century.

The comparison with other regions or countries allows us to place Latin America's achievements into an international perspective. But, which is the adequate yardstick to assess Latin America's success or failure? Usually Latin America is examined in the U.S. mirror, and widespread interpretations of early failure and moderate success in the twentieth century are derived that way. However, even western European economies fell behind relative to the United States over the nineteenth century (Prados de la Escosura 2000). Moreover, the fact that Latin America's relative position

Table 1.4 Per capita GDP growth in Latin American countries (%)

	Argentina	Brazil	Chile	Colombia	Costa Rica	Cuba	Ecuador	El Salvador	Guatemala	Honduras	Mexico	Nicaragua	Peru	Uruguay	Venezuela
1820–1850	*0.8*	*0.0*	*1.4*								*0.1*			*0.8*	
1830–1850	*0.8*	*0.0*	*2.0*											*0.8*	*2.2*
1850–1860	0.8	−0.1	1.7			0.6					−1.3			2.0	−1.3
1860–1870	0.8	0.5	1.8			1.8					1.3			2.0	−1.1
1870–1880	0.8	0.4	3.0			0.0					1.1			0.0	2.4
1880–1890	1.9	0.0	1.1			1.7					4.3			0.8	2.8
1890–1900	−0.8	−0.9	1.2			3.2					0.4			0.8	−1.5
1900–1913	2.5	2.2	2.3	1.8		−2.8					1.6		1.4	3.1	2.6
1913–1929	0.9	1.4	0.9	3.9	0.1	5.1	1.6	0.6	0.7	1.4	0.6	3.3	3.6	0.9	6.8
1929–1938	−0.8	1.0	−0.8	1.4	1.9	−2.0	2.2	−0.7	2.6	−3.4	0.4	−5.4	0.1	0.1	0.5
1938–1950	1.7	1.6	1.3	1.5	0.4	0.8	0.8	3.8	−0.1	1.4	3.5	3.7	1.2	1.5	4.3
1950–1960	1.1	3.7	1.5	1.6	2.4	3.1	3.4	1.8	0.6	1.1	2.3	2.2	2.9	0.6	3.4
1960–1970	3.9	3.1	1.9	2.2	3.3	−1.0	1.7	2.1	2.2	1.0	3.4	4.1	2.3	0.8	2.4
1970–1980	2.1	5.8	0.9	2.9	3.0	−0.7	2.0	0.4	2.8	1.3	2.5	−3.5	1.7	2.1	0.1
1980–1990	−2.4	−0.2	1.2	1.1	−0.1	3.2	3.8	−1.3	−1.6	−0.1	−0.1	−5.1	−3.3	−0.1	−1.9
1990–2000	2.8	0.8	5.0	0.7	0.9	1.1	−0.3	2.4	1.5	0.2	1.7	0.5	2.3	2.1	−0.1
1860–1890	1.2	0.3	1.9			−2.0	−0.4				2.2			0.9	1.3
1890–1913	1.0	0.9	1.8			1.6					1.0			2.1	0.8
1913–1938	0.3	1.2	0.3	3.0	0.7	1.7	1.7	0.2	1.4	−0.3	0.5	0.2	2.3	0.6	4.5
1913–1950	0.7	1.3	0.6	2.5	0.6	−1.0	2.2	1.4	0.9	0.3	1.5	1.3	2.0	0.9	4.5
1950–1980	2.4	4.2	1.4	2.2	2.9	0.3	2.5	1.4	1.9	1.1	2.7	1.0	2.3	1.2	2.0
1980–2000	0.2	0.3	3.1	0.9	0.4	0.5	−0.5	−0.3	0.6	0.0	0.8	−2.3	−0.5	0.9	−1.0
1860–1929	1.1	0.7	1.6			0.8					1.5			1.3	2.4
1860–1938	0.8	0.8	1.4			0.8					1.3			1.2	2.2
1938–1980	2.2	3.4	1.4	2.0	2.2	1.3	2.7	2.1	1.3	1.2	2.9	1.7	2.0	1.3	2.6
1850–2000	1.1	1.4	1.6			0.8					1.5			1.2	1.7
1850–1980	1.3	1.6	1.4			1.0					1.6			1.3	2.1
1900–2000	1.3	2.1	1.6	2.0		0.9	1.7				1.7		1.5	1.3	2.4
1913–2000	1.2	2.1	1.5	2.1	1.4	0.2	1.7	1.2	1.0	0.5	1.8	0.4	1.5	1.0	2.3
1820–2000	1.1	1.2	1.6								1.3			1.2	
1830–2000	1.1	1.2	1.7			0.8								1.2	1.7

Sources: See appendix A.
Notes: Numbers in *italics* are based on estimates. See text for explanation.

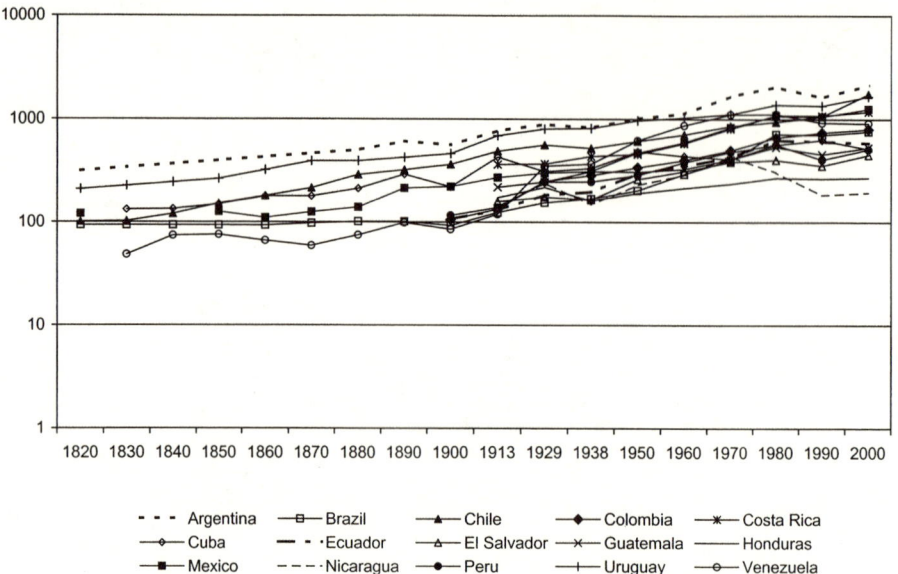

Fig. 1.3 Real per capita GDP in Latin American countries (1960 U.S. relative prices)

to the United States remained mostly unaltered during the twentieth century seems at odds with the catching-up experience in large areas of the periphery. Southern Europe and southeast Asia reduced their gap with the United States significantly after 1950 (Maddison 2003), whereas Latin America only grew faster than the United States in the 1970s. The United States represents, therefore, a questionable yardstick. Thus, alongside the U.S. yardstick, I propose to use a more comprehensive one, the group of advanced countries from the Old and New World that are today part of the OECD.[19]

Figure 1.3 and table 1.5 compare the evolution of population-weighted averages of per capita incomes in Latin America and the OECD for different country samples, and the results tend to be robust. Two phases can be depicted. The first one, between mid-nineteenth and mid-twentieth century, shows for Latin America a rather stable relative position, around 30 percent of OECD income per head. A second phase covers the late twentieth century, in which in spite of sustained growth a decline in Latin America's relative position occurred, with the exception of the slight recovery of the 1970s. The fall in the 1980s appears particularly intense, from which

---

19. This sample includes countries that belonged to the European periphery but that today are part of the core, such as Italy, Ireland, or Spain.

Table 1.5   Relative per capita GDP in Latin America and the OECD (OECD = 1)

	RLA5	RLA6	RLA7	RLA10	RLA15	RLA20
1820	*0.40*					
1830		*0.36*				
1840		*0.34*				
1850	0.32	0.34	0.34			
1860	0.27	0.32	0.29			
1870	0.27	0.31	0.29			
1880	0.26	0.31	0.29			
1890	0.29	0.31	0.32			
1900	0.25	0.26	0.27	0.28		
1913	0.29	0.32	0.31	0.32	0.31	
1925	0.28	0.31	0.31	0.32	0.32	
1929	0.27	0.31	0.30	0.32	0.31	
1933	0.28	0.32	0.31	0.32	0.32	
1938	0.27	0.30	0.30	0.31	0.31	
1950	0.22	0.25	0.26	0.30	0.29	0.28
1955	0.21	0.23	0.24	0.27	0.26	0.26
1960	0.21	0.22	0.24	0.26	0.25	0.24
1965	0.20	0.21	0.23	0.24	0.23	0.22
1970	0.21	0.21	0.23	0.23	0.22	0.21
1975	0.23	0.23	0.25	0.24	0.23	0.23
1980	0.24	0.23	0.25	0.24	0.23	0.22
1985	0.20	0.19	0.21	0.20	0.19	0.19
1990	0.18	0.17	0.19	0.17	0.17	0.16
1995	0.19	0.18	0.19	0.18	0.17	0.17
2000	0.18	0.17	0.18	0.17	0.16	0.16

Sources: See appendix A.

Notes: Numbers in *italics* are based on estimates for most countries. See text for explanation. RLA5 = LA5: OECD7; RLA6 = LA6: OECD10; RLA7 = LA7: OECD14; RLA10 = LA10: OECD20; RLA15 = LA15: OECD21; and RLA20 = LA20: OECD21. See table 1.1 notes for explanations of abbreviations not listed here.

Latin America had not recovered by 2000, when her average income per head relative to OECD was practically half the share it represented in 1950.

When, instead, the comparison is carried out with the United States (figure 1.3 and table 1.6), a decline is observed between 1850 and 1870 (from 36 to 27 percent of the U.S. GDP per head), followed up to 1938 by stability—around one-fourth of the U.S. per capita income. A two-step decline, in 1938–50 and the 1980s, reduced Latin American GDP per head relative to the United States by the end of the twentieth century to just half its share in 1938. These results do not warrant, therefore, the widely held view of Latin America's relative stability in terms of U.S. income throughout the twentieth century.

And what can be conjectured about Latin America's relative position in the early nineteenth century? The outcome is highly sensitive to the inclusion of Coatsworth's (1989, 2003) guesstimates about Mexican perfor-

Table 1.6 Relative per capita GDP in Latin America and the United States (U.S. = 1)

	RLA5	RLA6	RLA7	RLA10	RLA15	RLA20
1820	*0.53*					
1830		*0.41*				
1840		*0.37*				
1850	0.37	0.37	0.36			
1860	0.30	0.33	0.30			
1870	0.28	0.29	0.27			
1880	0.25	0.27	0.24			
1890	0.29	0.28	0.28			
1900	0.24	0.23	0.24	0.22		
1913	0.26	0.27	0.26	0.24	0.23	
1925	0.25	0.25	0.25	0.23	0.23	
1929	0.24	0.25	0.24	0.23	0.22	
1933	0.28	0.29	0.28	0.27	0.26	
1938	0.25	0.26	0.25	0.24	0.23	
1950	0.18	0.18	0.18	0.17	0.17	0.17
1955	0.17	0.17	0.18	0.17	0.17	0.16
1960	0.18	0.18	0.19	0.18	0.17	0.17
1965	0.18	0.17	0.18	0.17	0.17	0.16
1970	0.19	0.18	0.19	0.18	0.17	0.17
1975	0.21	0.20	0.21	0.19	0.19	0.18
1980	0.21	0.20	0.21	0.19	0.19	0.18
1985	0.18	0.17	0.17	0.16	0.16	0.15
1990	0.16	0.15	0.16	0.15	0.14	0.14
1995	0.17	0.16	0.16	0.15	0.15	0.14
2000	0.16	0.14	0.15	0.14	0.14	0.13

Sources: See appendix A.
Notes: Numbers in *italics* are based on estimates for most countries. See text for explanation. See tables 1.5 and 1.1 for explanations of abbreviations.

mance. Thus, population-weighted average income per head in Latin America might have fallen from around half (53 percent) the U.S. income in 1820 to above one third (37 percent) between 1820 and 1850 when a large country as Mexico is taken on board. If, alternatively, Mexico is not considered, a milder contraction appears between 1830 and 1850: from 41 to 37 percent of OECD income. Hence, a significant decline in the relative position of Latin America can be posited only if we accept Coatsworth's conjectures on Mexico's per capita income. The question, then, remains open until further research is carried out for Brazil and Mexico, the largest countries that decisively condition the aggregate results for Latin America.

Latin America's position relative to the OECD group per capita income is decomposed in table 1.7. It can be noticed that labor productivity systematically reaches higher relative levels than GDP per head as a consequence of a lower share of population in working age, which results from

Table 1.7 Decomposing of Latin America's relative per capita GDP, 1900–1990

	Per capita GDP			GDP/EAP				EAP/PAP				PAP/Population			
	RLA4	RLA5	RLA9	RLA20	RLA4	RLA5	RLA9	RLA20	RLA4	RLA5	RLA9	RLA20	RLA4	RLA5	RLA9	RLA20
1900	0.41				0.47				0.94				0.92			
1913	0.46	0.43			0.57				0.87				0.92	0.92		
1925	0.48	0.46			0.60	0.59			0.88	0.87			0.90	0.90		
1929	0.46	0.45			0.61	0.60			0.84	0.83			0.91	0.90		
1933	0.47	0.46			0.61	0.60			0.85	0.85			0.90	0.89		
1938	0.44	0.44	0.31		0.59	0.58	0.40		0.85	0.85	0.90		0.88	0.88	0.86	
1950	0.42	0.42	0.29	0.28	0.52	0.52	0.36	0.34	0.91	0.91	0.93	0.95	0.89	0.89	0.87	0.87
1955	0.37	0.38	0.27	0.26	0.47	0.48	0.34	0.32	0.90	0.90	0.91	0.93	0.88	0.88	0.87	0.86
1960	0.35	0.36	0.26	0.24	0.45	0.46	0.33	0.31	0.89	0.88	0.90	0.92	0.87	0.87	0.87	0.86
1965	0.33	0.34	0.24	0.22	0.43	0.44	0.30	0.28	0.90	0.90	0.91	0.93	0.85	0.85	0.85	0.85
1970	0.31	0.32	0.23	0.21	0.45	0.46	0.30	0.28	0.83	0.83	0.89	0.91	0.84	0.84	0.85	0.84
1975	0.30	0.31	0.24	0.23	0.42	0.42	0.30	0.29	0.86	0.86	0.92	0.92	0.85	0.85	0.86	0.85
1980	0.30	0.30	0.24	0.22	0.41	0.40	0.30	0.28	0.86	0.87	0.92	0.93	0.85	0.85	0.85	0.85
1985	0.25	0.25	0.20	0.19	0.36	0.36	0.25	0.24	0.80	0.80	0.90	0.90	0.86	0.86	0.87	0.86
1990	0.22	0.22	0.17	0.16	0.32	0.31	0.22	0.21	0.79	0.80	0.89	0.90	0.88	0.87	0.89	0.88

Sources: See appendix A.
Notes: EAP = economically active population; PAP = potentially active population, that is, population ages 15 to 64. See tables 1.5 and 1.1 for explanations of abbreviations.

Table 1.8 Dependency rates in Latin America: A comparison with OECD countries

	Dependency rates				Relative dependency rates			
	LA4	LA5	LA9	LA20	RLA4	RLA5	RLA9	RLA20
1850								
1860								
1870								
1880								
1890								
1900	0.634				1.02			
1913	0.745	0.746			1.22	1.22		
1925	0.702	0.706			1.31	1.32		
1929	0.699	0.702			1.29	1.30		
1933	0.700	0.704			1.33	1.34		
1938	0.708	0.711	0.750		1.40	1.41	1.48	
1950	0.734	0.739	0.777	0.780	1.35	1.36	1.43	1.44
1955	0.774	0.782	0.777	0.785	1.38	1.40	1.39	1.40
1960	0.822	0.830	0.836	0.842	1.40	1.42	1.43	1.44
1965	0.857	0.863	0.823	0.834	1.49	1.50	1.43	1.45
1970	0.879	0.883	0.857	0.864	1.55	1.56	1.51	1.52
1975	0.834	0.837	0.790	0.804	1.52	1.53	1.44	1.46
1980	0.783	0.784	0.782	0.792	1.51	1.51	1.51	1.53
1985	0.732	0.733	0.698	0.719	1.50	1.50	1.43	1.47
1990	0.699	0.701	0.674	0.694	1.44	1.44	1.38	1.43

Sources: See appendix A.
Note: See tables 1.5 and 1.1 for explanations of abbreviations.

higher dependency rates, and from a lower activity rate (a feature related to a lower female participation in the labor force). The persistence of high dependency rates in Latin America (table 1.8) hints at the lack of incentives to reduce fertility and to the weak demand of human capital that helped to bring about the demographic transition in OECD countries (Galor 2004).

In sum, modern Latin America experienced sustained growth since the second quarter of the nineteenth century—only brought to a halt during the 1890s, the Great Depression, and, overall, the 1980s. Growth was accompanied by relative backwardness, in particular during the second half of the twentieth century, and especially since 1980. It is true that Latin America fell behind in the early years of independence if she is compared to the core's richest countries, but in order to understand Latin America's long-run economic retardation, the late twentieth century appears a more suitable period to be explored than early independence years.

1.3 Long-Run Intercountry Inequality

A more rigorous assessment of intercountry average income inequality for the large country sample considered, which encompasses most of Europe, the Americas, and Oceania, can be obtained with the comprehensive measures provided by entropy decomposable indices. Was inequality significantly larger in 2000 than in 1850? Can different phases be distinguished in inequality over time, or, as suggested by Bourguignon and Morrison (2002), for the world, was there a sustained rise in inequality up to 1950 that tended to stabilize thereafter? Did the widening gap between OECD countries (the core) and Latin America (the periphery) discussed in the previous section contribute to the rise in long-term inequality? All are pressing questions that deserve a response.

All measures of inequality between OECD and Latin American countries are simultaneously provided for alternative sets of countries that allows us to test the sensitivity of the results to changes in their national composition.[20] Only countries for which data on GDP actually exists are in the sample. Needless to say, the quality and coverage of the estimates show a large variance, and usually fall as one goes back in time.[21]

Population-weighted, MLD (mean logarithmic deviation), and income-weighted, Theil measures of inequality[22] are obtained as

(4) $$\text{MLD}_y = \sum p_i \ln\left(\frac{p_i}{y_i}\right)$$

(5) $$\text{Theil}_y = \sum y_i \ln\left(\frac{y_i}{p_i}\right),$$

with p_i and y_i representing the shares of country i in total (OECD and Latin America) population and GDP.

The detailed results for the alternative country samples of OECD and Latin American countries are presented in the appendix (tables 1A.1–1A.4). In addition to inequality levels, yearly rates of inequality reduction—in other words, the speed at which inequality falls (positive sign) or rises (negative sign)—are shown at the bottom of each table.

A rise in per capita income inequality over the long run is observed for all the alternative Latin America and OECD countries sets (at an annual rate of around 1 percent over 1850–2000). It can be noticed that when measured with the MLD index, which gives more weight to changes at the bottom of the distribution, a larger inequality increase and level is obtained.

---

20. The more comprehensive country the sample, the shorter its time span. The countries included in each group for real income inequality estimates are listed at the bottom of tables 1A.1–1A.4.
21. But neither heroic assumptions are introduced in an attempt to widen the geographical coverage of the sample, nor imaginative solutions for missing countries, such as assuming identical levels of income or growth rates as their neighbors, are employed.
22. Mean Logarithmic Deviation (MLD) is also known as Bourguignon's L, Theil's population-weighted index, and GE(0). Theil is short for Theil's income weighted index of inequality, also known as GE(1).

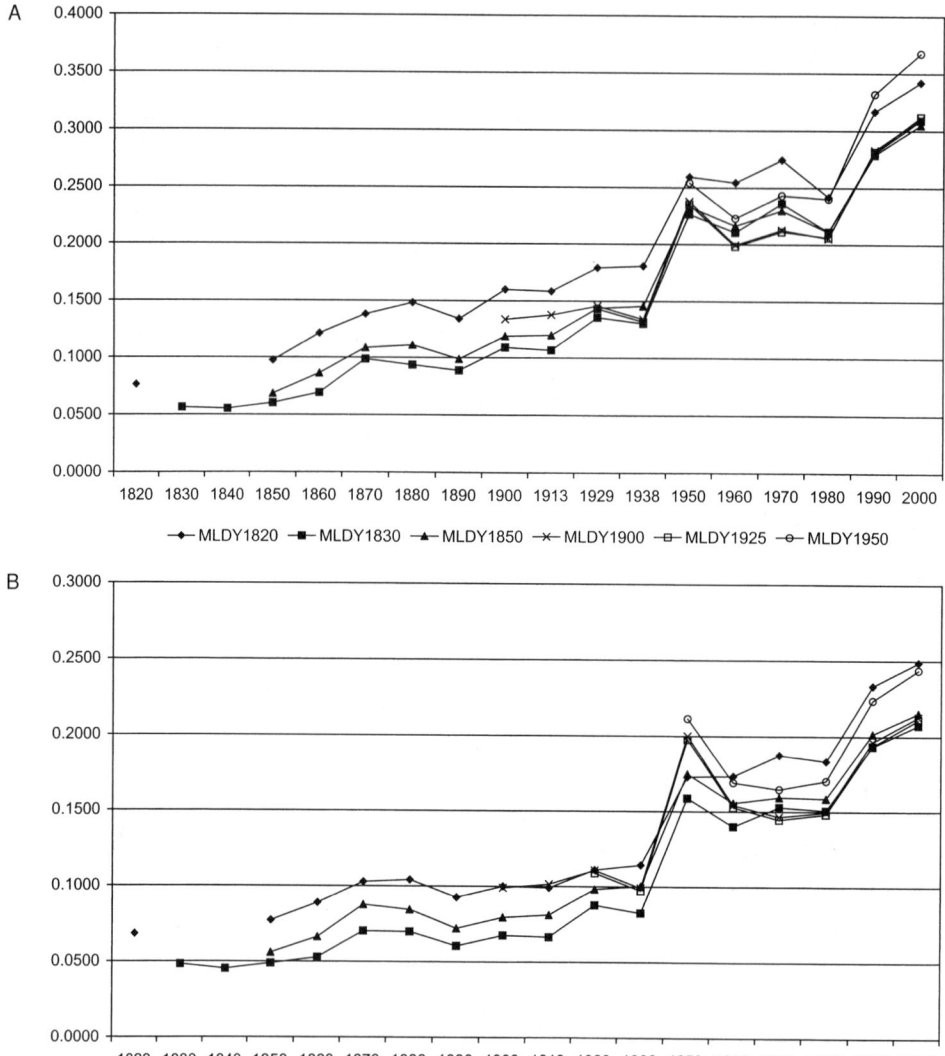

Fig. 1.4 Inter-country inequality of real per capita GDP in Latin America and the OECD: *A,* MLD indices; *B,* Theil indices

Moreover, the more comprehensive the country coverage, the deeper the inequality (figure 1.4).[23]

Two breaks in 1938 and 1980 allow us to identify three distinctive phases in the evolution of intercountry inequality. After a rapid increase in in-

23. Alternative MLD and Theil indices are computed for country samples starting at different dates; thus, MLD1870 means that the computed MLD index covers the period from 1870 to 2000.

equality during 1850–70, it rose at a steady pace up to 1938, in which episodes of shrinking inequality took place in the 1880s and the 1930s. The disruption brought about by World War II provoked a dramatic upsurge in inequality, and although it fell during the following three decades, its level remained high. A major rise occurred again with the 1980s debt crisis in Latin America, which reached up to the end of the twentieth century. Inequality shifted upward during 1938–50 and in the 1980s at yearly rates of 4.8 and 3.2 percent, reaching levels of 0.24 and 0.36 for MLD in 1950 and 1990, respectively. It is worth recalling that it is in these two periods when the gap in per capita income widened between Latin America and the OECD group.

The nineteenth and twentieth centuries witnessed population and GDP growth that proceeded with different intensity across different countries. To what extent did the variance in their rates of growth have an impact on income inequality? I have simulated the yearly rates at which, other things being equal, inequality would have fallen if all countries in the sample had enjoyed identical population (or per capita income) growth. The actual way of carrying out the simulation was to compute weighted inequality measures in which, ceteris paribus, population (or per capita income) remained unchanged over each epoch. This amounts to allocating identical growth rates to population (or per capita income) for all countries in the sample. The simulation exercise has been carried out for each of the three epochs established in the evolution of inequality: 1870–1938, 1938–80, and 1980–2000.

Table 1.9 offers the results of simulating what would have happened in our country sample had the variance of population (or income) growth been zero. Without a significant variance in population and per capita income growth, the rise in inequality would have been larger over 1870–1938. During 1938–80, the variance in per capita GDP growth prevented a larger rise in inequality, while the population growth variance contributed to increasing it. Both population and per capita income growth differentials had a part in inequality shifting upward during the last two decades of the twentieth century.

A glance at the simulations for OECD countries (table 1.10) shows that per capita income catching up was a main instrument in the decline in intercountry inequality, especially during the Golden Age. Prior to World War I, discrepancies in population growth mattered for the decline in inequality, suggesting that higher fertility and dependency rates in the New World might have contributed to checking inequality during the first phase of globalization.

When we focus on simulations for Latin America (table 1.11) it emerges that, over 1870–1913, differences in the pace of per capita GDP growth across the region contributed to rising inequality, associated to the economic progress in the areas of new settlement (Argentina and Uruguay), while discrepancies in population growth (in which immigration mattered)

Table 1.9 Assessing the impact of population and per capita GDP growth differences on inter-country inequality: Yearly rates of inequality reduction in OECD and Latin American countries

	Actual value	Counterfactual zero variance in:		Actual value	Counterfactual zero variance in:		Actual value	Counterfactual zero variance in:	
		Per capita GDP growth	Population growth		Per capita GDP growth	Population growth		Per capita GDP growth	Population growth

MLD indices

1870–1929	−0.48	−1.60	−1.65							
1870–1938	−0.42	−1.54	−1.40							
1938–1980	−0.85	−1.99	−0.51	−0.96	−2.01	−0.49				
1980–2000	−1.94	−0.91	−0.64	−2.01	−0.93	−0.66	−2.13	−1.05	−1.20
1870–1913	−0.30	−1.00	−1.05							
1900–1950	−1.28	−2.15	−2.41	−1.20	−1.94	−1.78				
1913–1938	−0.41	−1.26	−0.69	0.25	−1.36	0.13				
1913–1950	−1.64	−1.59	−1.93	−1.45	−1.76	−1.56				
1950–1980	0.50	−1.87	1.09	0.65	−1.78	1.35	0.19	−1.60	2.33
1950–2000	−0.48	−1.48	0.40	−0.42	−1.44	0.54	−0.74	−1.38	0.92

Theil indices

1870–1929	−0.19	−1.76	−1.87							
1870–1938	−0.17	−1.67	−1.52							
1938–1980	−1.01	−1.51	−0.75	−0.93	−1.67	−0.72				
1980–2000	−1.64	−0.82	−0.69	−1.73	−0.69	−0.76	−1.79	−0.75	−1.17
1870–1913	0.11	−0.89	−1.37							
1900–1950	−1.47	−2.26	−2.63	−1.45	−1.98	−2.22				
1913–1938	−0.45	−1.11	−0.76	0.27	−1.20	0.10				
1913–1950	−1.94	−1.24	−2.21	−1.79	−1.53	−2.02				
1950–1980	0.61	−1.51	1.05	1.13	−1.44	1.57	0.72	−1.11	2.45
1950–2000	−0.29	−1.23	0.35	−0.01	−1.14	0.64	−0.28	−0.97	1.00

Sources: See text.

Table 1.10 Assessing the impact of population and per capita GDP growth differences on inter-country inequality: Yearly rates of inequality reduction in OECD countries

		Counterfactual zero variance in:			Counterfactual zero variance in:			Counterfactual zero variance in:	
	Actual value	Per capita GDP growth	Population growth	Actual value	Per capita GDP growth	Population growth	Actual value	Per capita GDP growth	Population growth
				MLD indices					
1870–1929	0.41	−1.77	−2.84						
1870–1938	0.40	−1.65	−2.48						
1938–1980	1.17	−1.07	−0.85	1.92	−1.04	−1.19			
1980–2000	0.01	−0.71	−0.69	−0.33	0.12	−0.66	−0.22	0.83	−1.93
1870–1913	0.83	−0.70	−2.13						
1900–1950	−2.07	−2.47	−3.41	−1.97	−1.94	−3.55			
1913–1938	−0.24	−0.90	−1.11	1.53	−1.04	−0.48			
1913–1950	−3.05	−1.00	−2.48	−2.40	−1.44	−2.57			
1950–1980	5.20	−1.01	0.94	6.92	−0.55	1.11	6.85	0.51	4.05
1950–2000	3.12	−0.89	0.29	4.02	−0.28	0.40	4.02	0.64	1.66
				Theil indices					
1870–1929	0.59	−2.02	−2.64						
1870–1938	0.65	−1.88	−2.21						
1938–1980	0.96	−0.91	−1.14	1.81	−1.07	−1.39			
1980–2000	0.00	−0.69	−0.73	−0.29	−0.10	−0.73	−0.19	0.83	−1.90
1870–1913	1.06	−0.69	−2.11						
1900–1950	−2.00	−2.65	−3.28	−1.94	−2.16	−3.48			
1913–1938	−0.01	−0.96	−1.01	1.40	−1.06	−0.22			
1913–1950	−2.97	−0.87	−2.65	−2.46	−1.33	−2.81			
1950–1980	5.00	−1.00	0.84	6.74	−0.74	1.34	6.67	0.66	3.85
1950–2000	3.00	−0.88	0.21	3.93	−0.48	0.51	3.93	0.73	1.55

Sources: See text.

Table 1.11 Assessing the impact of population and per capita GDP growth differences on inter-country inequality: Yearly rates of inequality reduction in Latin American countries

		Counterfactual zero variance in:			Counterfactual zero variance in:			Counterfactual zero variance in:	
	Actual value	Per capita GDP growth	Population growth	Actual value	Per capita GDP growth	Population growth	Actual value	Per capita GDP growth	Population growth
MLD indices									
1870–1929	−0.84	0.47	−1.52						
1870–1938	−0.46	0.27	−1.12						
1938–1980	2.73	−0.92	2.86	2.31	−0.58	3.18			
1980–2000	−0.36	−0.46	2.02	−0.25	−0.45	1.24	−1.27	−0.47	−0.87
1870–1913	−1.29	0.95	−1.99						
1900–1950	0.22	−0.25	−0.05	0.38	−0.27	0.26			
1913–1938	0.97	−0.89	0.37	1.37	−0.68	0.99			
1913–1950	0.67	−0.80	0.82	0.92	−0.58	1.14			
1950–1980	3.80	−1.05	3.30	3.25	−0.66	3.88	1.94	−0.69	1.63
1950–2000	2.14	−0.81	2.79	1.85	−0.58	2.82	0.66	−0.60	0.63
Theil indices									
1870–1929	−0.55	0.87	−1.73						
1870–1938	−0.23	0.62	−1.32						
1938–1980	2.55	−1.17	3.01	2.17	−0.82	3.31			
1980–2000	−0.14	−0.54	1.95	−0.05	−0.53	1.71	−0.71	−0.65	−0.31
1870–1913	−0.89	1.41	−2.13						
1900–1950	0.28	−0.06	−0.38	0.45	−0.08	−0.03			
1913–1938	0.91	−0.76	0.08	1.27	−0.55	0.62			
1913–1950	0.77	−0.74	0.65	1.00	−0.52	0.99			
1950–1980	3.38	−1.36	3.48	2.86	−0.95	3.92	2.00	−1.14	2.24
1950–2000	1.97	−1.03	2.87	1.70	−0.78	3.04	0.92	−0.94	1.22

Sources: See text.

prevented a larger increase. During most of the twentieth century (1913–80) differences in economic growth contributed to reducing inequality, as a local process of convergence among Latin American countries was taking place (as the southern cone and, especially, Argentina, was experiencing a relative decline). After 1980, discrepancies in growth contributed to an increase in inequality, as not all countries reacted similarly after the debt crisis.

In sum, differentials in population growth, mostly stemming from Latin America's late demographic transition, represented an obstacle to reducing inequality in the OECD and Latin America country sample over 1938–2000. Such a finding is in conflict with Bourguignon and Morrison's (2002) contention that population growth rates are not associated with significant changes in world income distribution. In turn, differences in economic growth rates within Latin America help explain local convergence over 1913–80.

Another way to look at inequality trends is to decompose OECD and Latin American weighted inequality into the share attributable to distribution changes within each region and the share that stems from differences among regions. I have followed Theil (1979, 1989) in decomposing aggregate inequality into within-regions and between-regions inequality. Within-regions inequality is obtained by adding up the results of weighting each region's inequality measure by its population share, in the case of MLD, and by its income share in the case of Theil. Between-regions inequality is, then, obtained as the difference between total (OECD and Latin America) inequality and the computed within-regions inequality.

In figure 1.5 one can observe that in within-regions inequality a moderate rise occurred in MLD up to 1929, while a slight decline happened in the case of Theil, followed in both cases by the dramatic rise up to 1950 and a decline during the Golden Age that led to stability for the rest of the century (although a rise since 1990 is noticeable for MLD). Figure 1.6 shows, in turn, that between-regions inequality—that is, between OECD countries and Latin America—is a smoothed replica of total inequality for both MLD and Theil. It appears, then, that the main element underlying the observed increase in overall inequality was the deepening gap between OECD countries and Latin America.

When inequality within each region is examined, OECD countries exhibit (figure 1.7) a sustained decline in inequality since 1870, only interrupted by the upsurge resulting from World War II and its aftermath, and shadows closely the trend in within-regions inequality. Actually, when viewed in the long run, the inequality decline during the Golden Age is to a large extent the recovery of the level achieved prior to World War II.

Two clear trends emerged in inequality within Latin America (figure 1.8): a steep rise prior to 1914, followed by a sustained decline thereafter that seems to reverse since 1990, with the final result of similar levels of in-

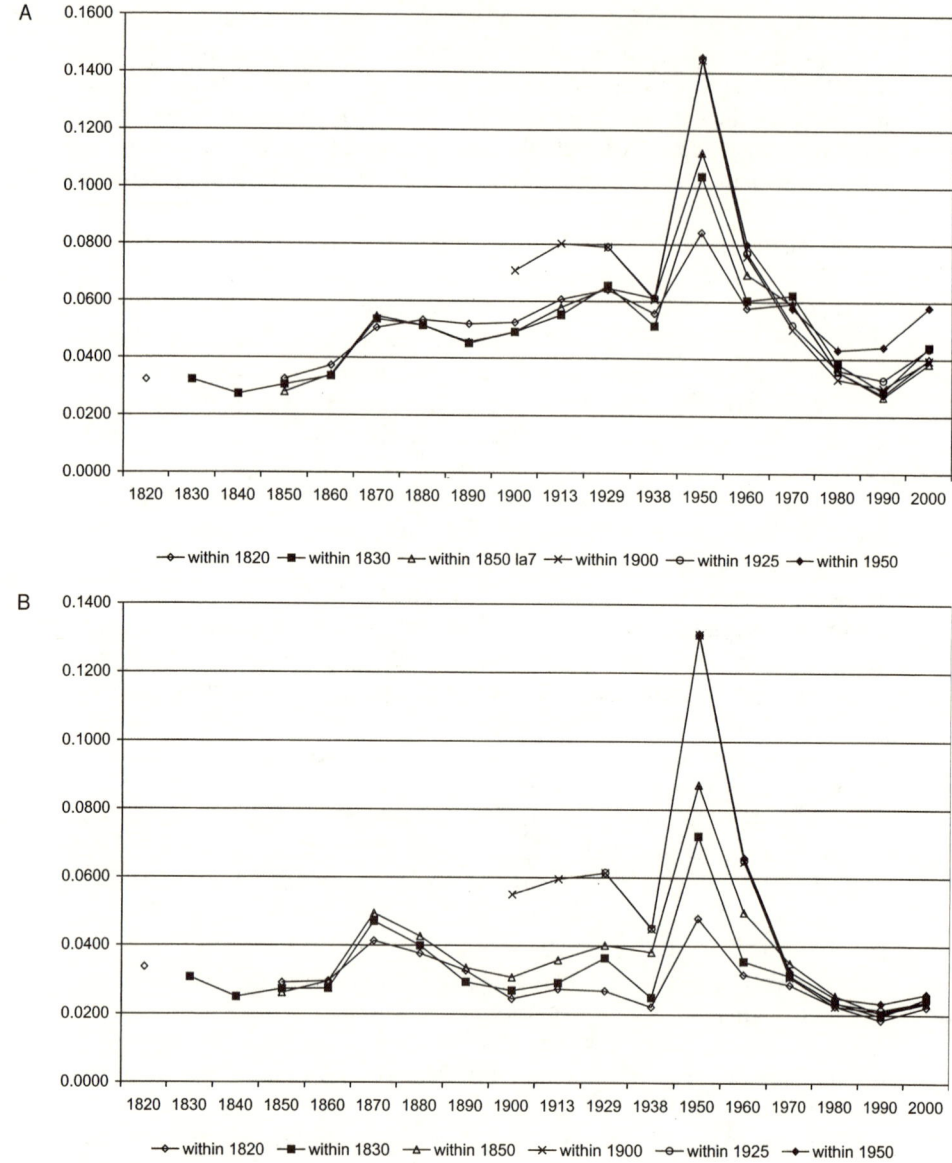

Fig. 1.5 Within-regions inequality of real per capita GDP in Latin America and the OECD: *A*, MLD indices; *B*, Theil indices

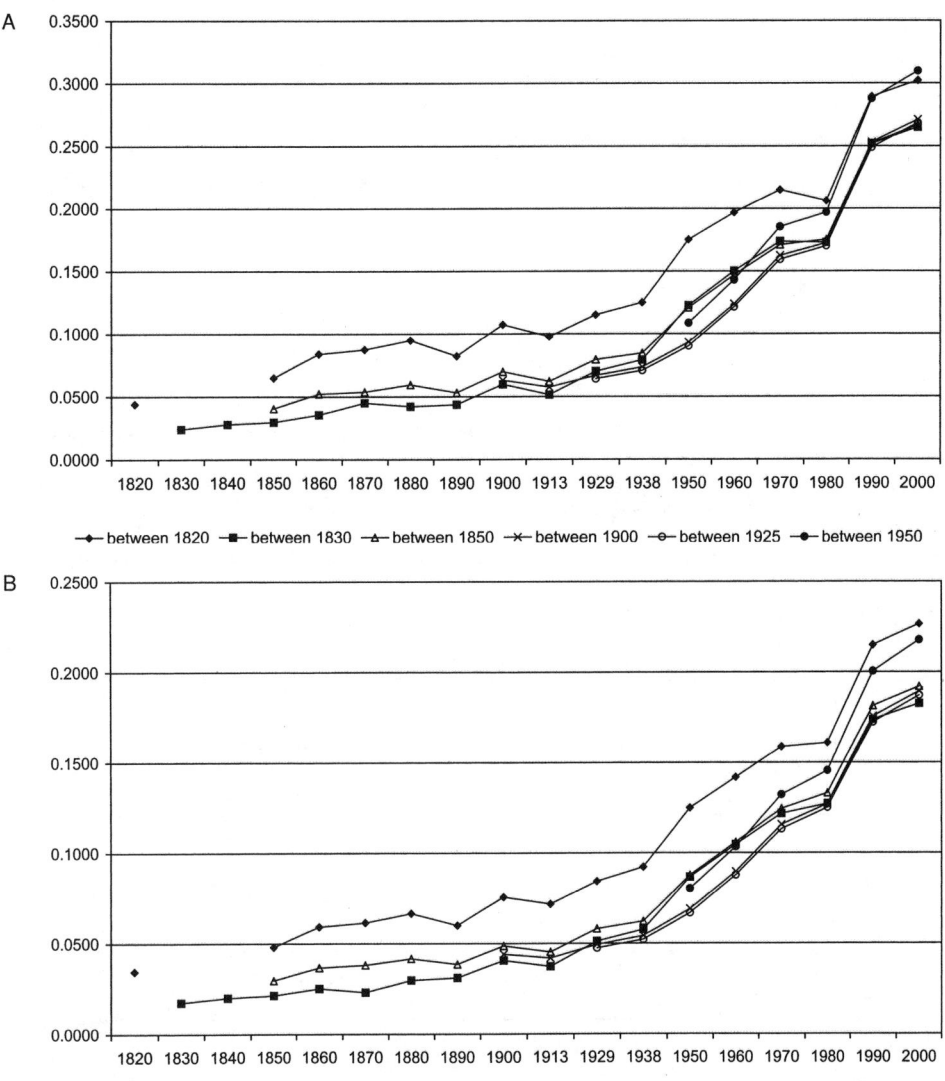

Fig. 1.6 Between-regions inequality of real per capita GDP in Latin America and the OECD: *A*, MLD indices; *B*, Theil indices

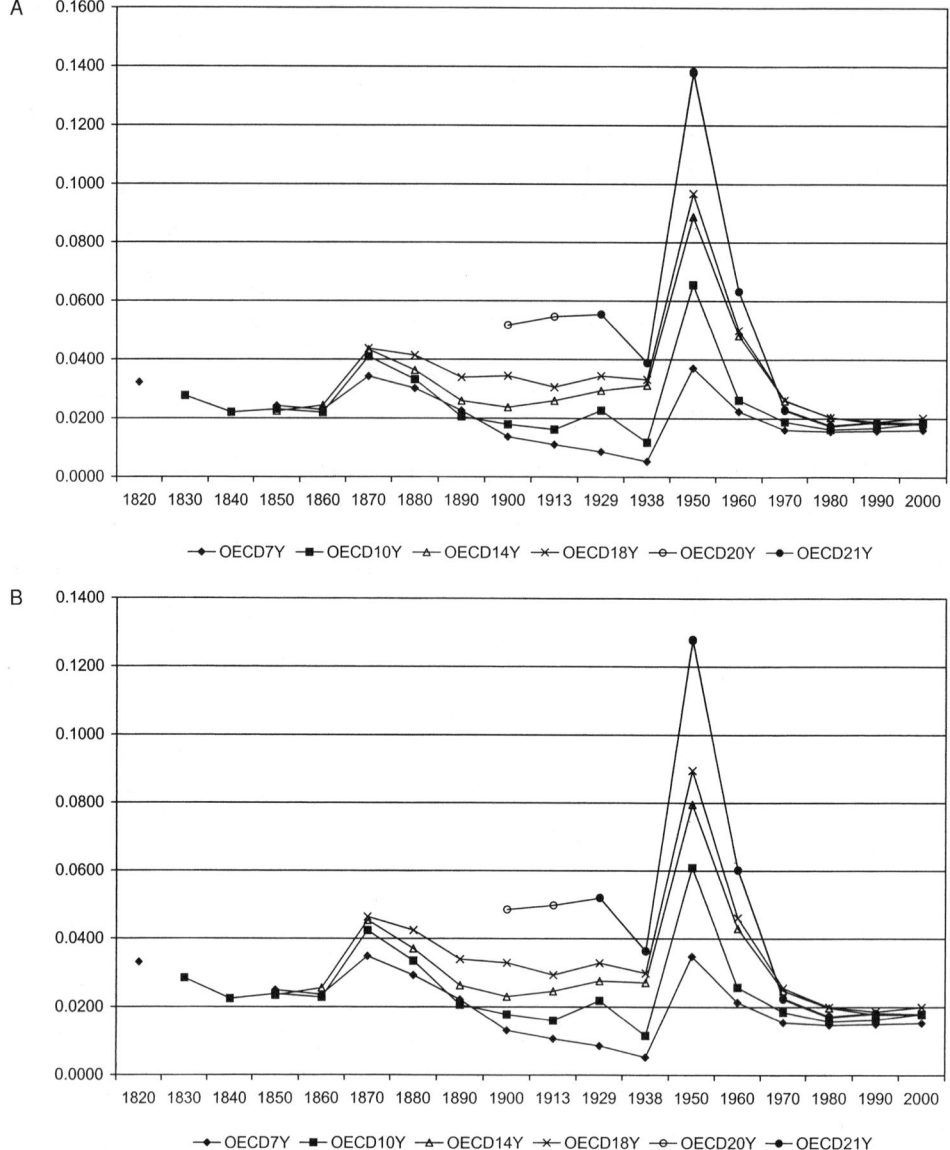

Fig. 1.7 Inter-country inequality of real per capita GDP in the OECD: *A*, MLD indices; *B*, Theil indices

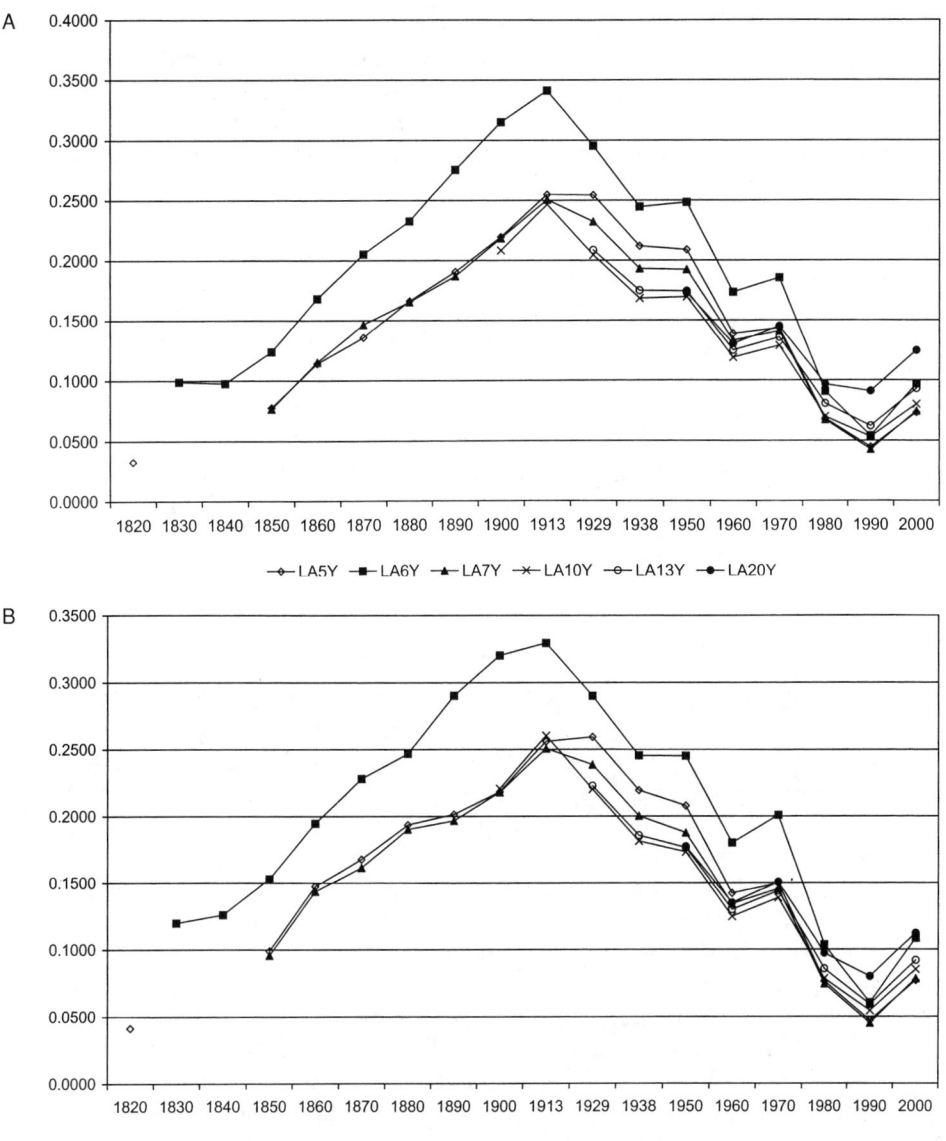

Fig. 1.8 Inter-country inequality of real per capita GDP in Latin America: *A*, MLD indices; *B*, Theil indices

equality levels to those prevailing by mid-nineteenth century. Inequality across Latin American countries increased during the first phase of globalization, as countries reacted very differently, depending on their exposure to international commodity and factor movements. Argentina's economic success determined per capita income divergence across countries. Deglobalization in the interwar years spawned a reduction in across-country inequality. The long-run fall in twentieth century inequality, in spite of a new phase of globalization after 1950, is associated with a process of convergence within Latin America, as lower-income countries achieved faster growth than richer ones—among which Argentine's collapse had a major part. Argentina's slowing down from World War I onward contributed to the process of local convergence.

To sum up, the long-run increase in inequality is mainly due to the widening gap between average incomes between OECD countries and Latin America that peaked in the late twentieth century. It is then when Latin America appears to have fallen behind. A process of convergence within Latin America paralleled its divergence with respect to the advanced countries.

1.4 Concluding Remarks and Research Agenda

A long-term rise in real per capita income inequality for a partial sample of the world that includes Latin America and OECD countries is confirmed. The deepening gap and subsequent polarization between the OECD group and Latin America was the major factor behind the observed increase. National differences in population growth, largely a consequence of the late demographic transition in Latin America, held up a fall in inequality during the twentieth century. This finding contradicts the benign view of a rise in inequality up to the mid-twentieth century that stabilized thereafter, as proposed by Bourguignon and Morrison (2002) and Sala i Martín (2002).

These results provide an answer to the question of when did Latin America fall behind. It is true that when compared to the select club of the core's richest countries that experienced sustained per capita income growth prior to 1850, Latin America fell behind in the early years of independence—as did most countries at the time. However, the empirical findings presented here seriously challenge conventional assessments that locate Latin American economic retardation in the early nineteenth century and link it to geography, initial inequality of wealth and power, colonial heritage, and post-independence political instability and turmoil. They all certainly hindered long-run growth and a counterfactual scenario with law and order, lower inequality, and British-like institutions would have cast a higher growth rate in Latin America. However, blaming Latin America's long-term backwardness on the post-colonial epoch seems far-fetched. Contrary to a widely held view, Latin America's retardation appears to be a late-twentieth century phenomenon that should be explored if we want to understand why Latin America remains a backward region in a global world.

Ascertaining why Latin America's retardation occurred in the late twentieth century provides a research agenda. Why, during the period of fastest growth in Latin America—1938–80—did Latin America fall behind OECD countries, unlike southwestern Europe and East Asia? Is it misleading, as claimed by Astorga, Bergés, and Fitzgerald (2003), to associate import-industrialization strategies to faltering performance, as, when such policies were implemented, growth intensified and welfare improved? Were neoliberal policies the causes of post-1980 economic stagnation and relative decline? Or was it because of poor institutional quality and lack of government credibility? These are among the pressing questions that will require further research.

Appendix A

Sources for GDP per Capita Volume Indices for the OECD and Latin America

GDP volume or quantity indices and population, potentially active population (PAP), and economically active population (EAP) data for OECD countries come from the national sources stated in Prados de la Escosura (2000), Maddison (2003), Mitchell (1992, 1993, 1994), and the League of Nations and UN yearbooks. Data for twentieth-century Latin American GDP volumes and total and potentially active population and economically active population comes from Astorga and Fitzgerald (1998), Astorga, Bergés, and Fitzgerald (2004), The Oxford Latin American Economic History Database (OxLAD), The Latin American Centre, Oxford University, http://oxlad.thedesignfly.net/, and Mitchell (1993). Otherwise, the sources are:

Argentina: Della Paolera, Taylor, and Bózolli (2003), GDP, 1884–1990, spliced with Cortés Conde and Harriague (1994) for 1875–84. I assumed the level for 1870 was identical to that of 1875. Newland and Poulson (1998) estimated Argentina's littoral agricultural output per head grew at 2 percent per year over 1825–65. I have assumed that this sector was representative of the littoral's economy as a whole, and that no per capita growth occurred in Argentina's interior provinces, reaching a per capita GDP rate of growth of 0.8 percent. Population data comes from Newland (1998).

Brazil: Goldsmith (1986), 1850–1980.

Chile: Díaz, Lüders, and Wagner (1998), and Braun, Braun, Briones, and Díaz (1998).

Colombia: GRECO (2002), since 1906. I assumed the level for 1900 was identical to that of 1906.

Cuba: Fraile, Salvucci, and Salvucci (1993) and Santamaría (2005).

México: Instituto Nacional de Estadística Geografica e Informática (INEGI; 1995), 1850–1990. GDP figures from 1845 to 1896, interpolated from the original benchmark estimates. Following Coatsworth (2003), I accepted a mild rise in GDP per capita at 0.2 percent per year over 1820–45.

Uruguay: Bértola and Associates (1998), since 1870. I have assumed that Uruguay evolved as did Argentina's littoral between 1850 and 1870, as Argentina as a whole over 1820–50.

Venezuela: Baptista (1997).

Central America (Costa Rica, El Salvador, Guatemala, Honduras, and Nicaragua): I obtained the level for 1913 by assuming a growth for 1913–20 identical to that of 1920–25, the latter taken from OxLAD.

Table 1A.1   Inter-country inequality in per capita GDP, 1850–2000

	MLD indices			Population shares		Inequality	
	OECD and Latin America	OECD	Latin America	OECD	Latin America	Within regions	Between regions
1850	0.0685	0.0224	0.0766	0.8974	0.1026	0.0280	0.0405
1860	0.0863	0.0244	0.1152	0.8933	0.1067	0.0341	0.0522
1870	0.1086	0.0433	0.1465	0.8898	0.1102	0.0547	0.0539
1880	0.1110	0.0363	0.1654	0.8826	0.1174	0.0515	0.0595
1890	0.0987	0.0259	0.1869	0.8780	0.1220	0.0456	0.0532
1900	0.1190	0.0237	0.2184	0.8689	0.1311	0.0493	0.0698
1913	0.1199	0.0260	0.2505	0.8578	0.1422	0.0579	0.0620
1913	0.1272	0.0259	0.2505	0.8482	0.1518	0.0600	0.0672
1925	0.1337	0.0304	0.2149	0.8340	0.1660	0.0610	0.0727
1929	0.1439	0.0294	0.2322	0.8266	0.1734	0.0646	0.0793
1933	0.1284	0.0192	0.1939	0.8207	0.1793	0.0506	0.0778
1938	0.1456	0.0312	0.1931	0.8149	0.1851	0.0612	0.0844
1950	0.2329	0.0888	0.1923	0.7735	0.2265	0.1122	0.1207
1955	0.2281	0.0653	0.1623	0.7599	0.2401	0.0886	0.1395
1960	0.2164	0.0481	0.1331	0.7471	0.2529	0.0696	0.1468
1965	0.2326	0.0350	0.1565	0.7316	0.2684	0.0676	0.1650
1970	0.2299	0.0260	0.1411	0.7139	0.2861	0.0590	0.1710
1975	0.2059	0.0196	0.0846	0.6962	0.3038	0.0393	0.1666
1980	0.2110	0.0205	0.0673	0.6741	0.3259	0.0357	0.1752
1985	0.2491	0.0231	0.0475	0.6610	0.3390	0.0314	0.2177
1990	0.2790	0.0182	0.0428	0.6509	0.3491	0.0268	0.2522
1995	0.2812	0.0170	0.0666	0.6496	0.3504	0.0344	0.2469
2000	0.3051	0.0181	0.0743	0.6389	0.3611	0.0384	0.2667
	Annual rates of inequality reduction (%)						
1850–1913	−0.89	−0.23	−1.88			−1.15	−0.67
1870–1913	−0.23	1.19	−1.25			−0.13	−0.33
1900–1950	−1.34	−2.64	0.25			−1.65	−1.10
1913–1938	−0.54	−0.74	1.04			−0.08	−0.91
1913–1950	−1.63	−3.32	0.71			−1.69	−1.58
1950–1980	0.33	4.89	3.50			3.82	−1.24
1938–1980	−0.88	1.01	2.51			1.28	−1.74
1980–2000	−1.84	0.61	−0.50			−0.36	−2.10
1950–2000	−0.54	3.18	1.90			2.14	−1.58

	Theil indices			GDP shares		Inequality	
	OECD and Latin America	OECD	Latin America	OECD	Latin America	Within regions	Between regions
1850	0.0559	0.0234	0.0958	0.9625	0.0375	0.0262	0.0297
1860	0.0663	0.0256	0.1435	0.9660	0.0340	0.0296	0.0367
1870	0.0876	0.0454	0.1614	0.9650	0.0350	0.0494	0.0382
1880	0.0844	0.0371	0.1903	0.9634	0.0366	0.0427	0.0417
1890	0.0721	0.0263	0.1967	0.9578	0.0422	0.0335	0.0385
1900	0.0794	0.0230	0.2180	0.9603	0.0397	0.0308	0.0486

(*continued*)

Table 1A.1   (continued)

	Theil indices			GDP shares		Inequality	
	OECD and Latin America	OECD	Latin America	OECD	Latin America	Within regions	Between regions
1913	0.0811	0.0246	0.2506	0.9505	0.0495	0.0358	0.0453
1913	0.0853	0.0243	0.2506	0.9475	0.0525	0.0362	0.0491
1925	0.0930	0.0286	0.2162	0.9418	0.0582	0.0395	0.0535
1929	0.0982	0.0276	0.2386	0.9407	0.0593	0.0401	0.0581
1933	0.0876	0.0178	0.2078	0.9366	0.0634	0.0298	0.0577
1938	0.1003	0.0271	0.2002	0.9363	0.0637	0.0382	0.0622
1950	0.1749	0.0796	0.1876	0.9289	0.0711	0.0872	0.0876
1955	0.1666	0.0594	0.1617	0.9288	0.0712	0.0667	0.1000
1960	0.1557	0.0430	0.1342	0.9246	0.0754	0.0498	0.1059
1965	0.1607	0.0328	0.1569	0.9230	0.0770	0.0424	0.1183
1970	0.1595	0.0248	0.1455	0.9153	0.0847	0.0350	0.1244
1975	0.1507	0.0189	0.0934	0.9033	0.0967	0.0261	0.1246
1980	0.1587	0.0198	0.0745	0.8938	0.1062	0.0256	0.1331
1985	0.1853	0.0223	0.0517	0.9029	0.0971	0.0252	0.1602
1990	0.2016	0.0178	0.0452	0.9091	0.0909	0.0203	0.1814
1995	0.2005	0.0167	0.0711	0.9066	0.0934	0.0218	0.1788
2000	0.2154	0.0178	0.0783	0.9072	0.0928	0.0234	0.1920
	Annual rates of inequality reduction (%)						
1850–1913	−0.59	−0.08	−1.53			−0.50	−0.67
1870–1913	0.18	1.42	−1.02			0.75	−0.40
1900–1950	−1.58	−2.48	0.30			−2.09	−1.18
1913–1938	−0.65	−0.45	0.90			−0.22	−0.94
1913–1950	−1.94	−3.21	0.78			−2.38	−1.56
1950–1980	0.32	4.64	3.08			4.09	−1.39
1938–1980	−1.09	0.75	2.35			0.95	−1.81
1980–2000	−1.53	0.53	−0.25			0.45	−1.83
1950–2000	−0.42	3.00	1.75			2.63	−1.57

Sources: See text.

Notes: **Boldface** indicates interwar borders. Latin America (LA7) is comprised of Argentina, Brazil, Chile, Cuba, Mexico, Uruguay, and Venezuela. OECD (14) is comprised of Australia, Austria, Belgium, Canada, Denmark, France, Germany, the Netherlands, Norway, Portugal, Spain, Sweden, the United Kingdom, and the United States.

Table 1A.2   **Inter-country inequality in per capita GDP, 1900–2000**

	MLD indices			Population shares		Inequality	
	OECD and Latin America	OECD	Latin America	OECD	Latin America	Within regions	Between regions
1900	0.1338	0.0517	0.2084	0.8783	0.1217	0.0707	0.0630
1913	0.1377	0.0546	0.2465	0.8666	0.1334	0.0802	0.0575
1913	0.1440	0.0569	0.2465	0.8602	0.1398	0.0834	0.0605
1925	0.1366	0.0512	0.1959	0.8478	0.1522	0.0732	0.0634
1929	0.1457	0.0554	0.2045	0.8417	0.1583	0.0790	0.0667
1933	0.1184	0.0280	0.1679	0.8368	0.1632	0.0508	0.0676
1938	0.1341	0.0388	0.1683	0.8311	0.1689	0.0607	0.0734
1950	0.2377	0.1383	0.1695	0.7975	0.2025	0.1446	0.0931
1955	0.2198	0.0995	0.1427	0.7850	0.2150	0.1088	0.1111
1960	0.1996	0.0632	0.1188	0.7717	0.2283	0.0759	0.1237
1965	0.2105	0.0412	0.1389	0.7561	0.2439	0.0650	0.1455
1970	0.2128	0.0228	0.1288	0.7393	0.2607	0.0504	0.1624
1975	0.1966	0.0176	0.0825	0.7225	0.2775	0.0356	0.1610
1980	0.2054	0.0173	0.0699	0.7026	0.2974	0.0330	0.1725
1985	0.2461	0.0205	0.0528	0.6887	0.3113	0.0306	0.2156
1990	0.2830	0.0187	0.0532	0.6773	0.3227	0.0298	0.2532
1995	0.2838	0.0183	0.0691	0.6722	0.3278	0.0349	0.2488
2000	0.3106	0.0185	0.0800	0.6581	0.3419	0.0395	0.2711
		Annual rates of inequality reduction (%)					
1900–1950	−1.15	−1.97	0.41			−1.43	−0.78
1913–1938	0.28	1.53	1.53			1.27	−0.77
1913–1950	−1.36	−2.40	1.01			−1.49	−1.16
1950–1980	0.49	6.92	2.96			4.93	−2.06
1938–1980	−1.02	1.92	2.09			1.45	−2.03
1980–2000	−2.07	−0.33	−0.68			−0.91	−2.26
1950–2000	−0.54	4.02	1.50			2.59	−2.14
	Theil indices			GDP shares		Inequality	
	OECD and Latin America	OECD	Latin America	OECD	Latin America	Within regions	Between regions
1900	0.0990	0.0485	0.2206	0.9626	0.0374	0.0549	0.0441
1913	0.1015	0.0497	0.2605	0.9534	0.0466	0.0596	0.0420
1913	0.1060	0.0515	0.2605	0.9511	0.0489	0.0617	0.0442
1925	0.1042	0.0486	0.2080	0.9453	0.0547	0.0573	0.0469
1929	0.1107	0.0519	0.2202	0.9433	0.0567	0.0614	0.0494
1933	0.0865	0.0268	0.1861	0.9409	0.0591	0.0362	0.0503
1938	0.0991	0.0363	0.1813	0.9405	0.0595	0.0449	0.0542
1950	0.2001	0.1280	0.1731	0.9303	0.0697	0.1312	0.0689
1955	0.1783	0.0939	0.1480	0.9313	0.0687	0.0976	0.0807
1960	0.1543	0.0602	0.1247	0.9291	0.0709	0.0647	0.0895
1965	0.1518	0.0406	0.1454	0.9291	0.0709	0.0480	0.1038
1970	0.1465	0.0223	0.1387	0.9262	0.0738	0.0309	0.1156
1975	0.1412	0.0174	0.0936	0.9163	0.0837	0.0238	0.1175

(*continued*)

Table 1A.2 (continued)

	Theil indices			GDP shares		Inequality	
	OECD and Latin America	OECD	Latin America	OECD	Latin America	Within regions	Between regions
1980	0.1496	0.0170	0.0784	0.9095	0.0905	0.0225	0.1271
1985	0.1765	0.0199	0.0574	0.9174	0.0826	0.0230	0.1535
1990	0.1964	0.0181	0.0544	0.9231	0.0769	0.0208	0.1755
1995	0.1968	0.0177	0.0740	0.9192	0.0808	0.0222	0.1746
2000	0.2129	0.0180	0.0851	0.9186	0.0814	0.0234	0.1895
	Annual rates of inequality reduction (%)						
1900–1950	−1.41	−1.94	0.48			−1.74	−0.89
1913–1938	**0.27**	**1.40**	**1.45**			**1.27**	**−0.81**
1913–1950	−1.72	−2.46	1.10			−2.04	−1.20
1950–1980	0.97	6.74	2.64			5.87	−2.04
1938–1980	−0.98	1.81	2.00			1.64	−2.03
1980–2000	−1.76	−0.29	−0.41			−0.20	−2.00
1950–2000	−0.12	3.93	1.42			3.44	−2.02

Sources: See text.

Notes: **Boldface** indicates interwar borders. Latin America (LA10) is comprised of Argentina, Brazil, Chile, Colombia, Cuba, Ecuador, Mexico, Peru, Uruguay, and Venezuela. OECD (20) is comprised of Australia, Austria, Belgium, Canada, Denmark, France, Finland, Germany, Greece, Italy, Japan, the Netherlands, New Zealand, Portugal, Spain, Sweden, Switzerland, the United Kingdom, and the United States.

Table 1A.3   Inter-country inequality in per capita GDP, 1925–2000

	MLD indices			Population shares		Inequality	
	OECD and Latin America	OECD	Latin America	OECD	Latin America	Within regions	Between regions
1925	0.1332	0.0513	0.1981	0.8521	0.1479	0.0730	0.0602
1929	0.1431	0.0554	0.2086	0.8459	0.1541	0.0790	0.0641
1933	0.1160	0.0279	0.1727	0.8410	0.1590	0.0509	0.0651
1938	0.1319	0.0389	0.1749	0.8354	0.1646	0.0613	0.0706
1950	0.2352	0.1377	0.1744	0.8022	0.1978	0.1450	0.0902
1955	0.2187	0.0993	0.1496	0.7893	0.2107	0.1099	0.1088
1960	0.1984	0.0632	0.1249	0.7760	0.2240	0.0770	0.1214
1965	0.2092	0.0414	0.1454	0.7606	0.2394	0.0663	0.1429
1970	0.2112	0.0231	0.1357	0.7438	0.2562	0.0519	0.1593
1975	0.1965	0.0179	0.0915	0.7271	0.2729	0.0380	0.1585
1980	0.2062	0.0176	0.0806	0.7072	0.2928	0.0361	0.1701
1985	0.2482	0.0209	0.0658	0.6931	0.3069	0.0347	0.2135
1990	0.2816	0.0189	0.0622	0.6819	0.3181	0.0326	0.2489
1995	0.2855	0.0183	0.0837	0.6764	0.3236	0.0395	0.2461
2000	0.3120	0.0184	0.0930	0.6617	0.3383	0.0436	0.2684

Table 1A.3 (continued)

	MLD indices			Population shares		Inequality	
	OECD and Latin America	OECD	Latin America	OECD	Latin America	Within regions	Between regions
	Annual rates of inequality reduction (%)						
1925–1938	0.08	2.14	0.96			1.35	–1.23
1925–1950	–2.27	–3.95	0.51			–2.74	–1.62
1950–1980	0.44	6.85	2.57			4.64	–2.12
1938–1980	–1.06	1.88	1.84			1.26	–2.09
1980–2000	–2.07	–0.22	–0.71			–0.95	–2.28
1950–2000	–0.57	4.02	1.26			2.40	–2.18

	Theil indices			GDP shares		Inequality	
	OECD and Latin America	OECD	Latin America	OECD	Latin America	Within regions	Between regions
1925	0.1020	0.0488	0.2079	0.9461	0.0539	0.0573	0.0446
1929	0.1089	0.0520	0.2228	0.9445	0.0555	0.0615	0.0474
1933	0.0846	0.0268	0.1896	0.9421	0.0579	0.0362	0.0484
1938	0.0973	0.0364	0.1857	0.9416	0.0584	0.0451	0.0522
1950	0.1977	0.1277	0.1764	0.9317	0.0683	0.1310	0.0667
1955	0.1768	0.0938	0.1538	0.9328	0.0672	0.0978	0.0790
1960	0.1528	0.0603	0.1298	0.9306	0.0694	0.0651	0.0877
1965	0.1502	0.0408	0.1509	0.9305	0.0695	0.0484	0.1017
1970	0.1446	0.0226	0.1439	0.9275	0.0725	0.0314	0.1132
1975	0.1398	0.0177	0.1002	0.9179	0.0821	0.0244	0.1153
1980	0.1483	0.0172	0.0857	0.9112	0.0888	0.0233	0.1250
1985	0.1754	0.0202	0.0660	0.9191	0.0809	0.0239	0.1515
1990	0.1936	0.0182	0.0591	0.9242	0.0758	0.0213	0.1723
1995	0.1950	0.0177	0.0822	0.9206	0.0794	0.0228	0.1722
2000	0.2110	0.0179	0.0919	0.9196	0.0804	0.0238	0.1871
	Annual rates of inequality reduction (%)						
1925–1938	0.36	2.25	0.87			1.85	–1.20
1925–1950	–2.65	–3.85	0.66			–3.30	–1.61
1950–1980	0.96	6.67	2.41			5.75	–2.09
1938–1980	–1.00	1.78	1.84			1.57	–2.08
1980–2000	–1.76	–0.19	–0.35			–0.11	–2.02
1950–2000	–0.13	3.93	1.30			3.41	–2.06

Sources: See text

Notes: Latin America (LA13) is comprised of Argentina, Brazil, Chile, Colombia, Costa Rica, Cuba, El Salvador, Guatemala, Honduras, Mexico, Nicaragua, Uruguay, and Venezuela. OECD (21) is comprised of Australia, Austria, Belgium, Canada, Denmark, France, Finland, Germany, Greece, Ireland, Italy, Japan, the Netherlands, New Zealand, Norway, Portugal, Spain, Sweden, Switzerland, the United Kingdom, and the United States.

Table 1A.4   Inter-country inequality in per capita GDP, 1950–2000

	MLD indices			Population shares		Inequality	
	OECD and Latin America	OECD	Latin America	OECD	Latin America	Within regions	Between regions
1950	0.2541	0.1377	0.1729	0.7768	0.2232	0.1456	0.1086
1955	0.2408	0.0993	0.1522	0.7635	0.2365	0.1118	0.1290
1960	0.2229	0.0632	0.1304	0.7497	0.2503	0.0800	0.1429
1965	0.2376	0.0414	0.1514	0.7333	0.2667	0.0708	0.1668
1970	0.2432	0.0231	0.1450	0.7155	0.2845	0.0577	0.1854
1975	0.2281	0.0179	0.1051	0.6978	0.3022	0.0443	0.1838
1980	0.2402	0.0176	0.0966	0.6768	0.3232	0.0432	0.1970
1985	0.2895	0.0209	0.0878	0.6613	0.3387	0.0435	0.2460
1990	0.3320	0.0189	0.0909	0.6487	0.3513	0.0442	0.2878
1995	0.3367	0.0183	0.1129	0.6423	0.3577	0.0521	0.2846
2000	0.3677	0.0184	0.1246	0.6268	0.3732	0.0581	0.3097
	Annual rates of inequality reduction (%)						
1950–1980	0.19	6.85	1.94			4.05	−1.99
1980–2000	−2.13	−0.22	−1.27			−1.48	−2.26
1950–2000	−0.74	4.02	0.66			1.84	−2.10

	Theil indices			GDP shares		Inequality	
	OECD and Latin America	OECD	Latin America	OECD	Latin America	Within regions	Between regions
1950	0.2116	0.1277	0.1772	0.9254	0.0746	0.1314	0.0802
1955	0.1920	0.0938	0.1563	0.9266	0.0734	0.0984	0.0936
1960	0.1692	0.0603	0.1349	0.9245	0.0755	0.0659	0.1033
1965	0.1684	0.0408	0.1556	0.9245	0.0755	0.0494	0.1190
1970	0.1648	0.0226	0.1506	0.9215	0.0785	0.0327	0.1322
1975	0.1601	0.0177	0.1091	0.9112	0.0888	0.0258	0.1344
1980	0.1704	0.0172	0.0973	0.9042	0.0958	0.0249	0.1455
1985	0.2012	0.0202	0.0814	0.9126	0.0874	0.0256	0.1756
1990	0.2237	0.0182	0.0799	0.9185	0.0815	0.0233	0.2004
1995	0.2254	0.1077	0.1012	0.9144	0.0856	0.0249	0.2005
2000	0.2437	0.0179	0.1121	0.9136	0.0864	0.0260	0.2177
	Annual rates of inequality reduction (%)						
1950–1980	0.72	6.67	2.00			5.54	−1.99
1980–2000	−1.79	−0.19	−0.71			−0.22	−2.02
1950–2000	−0.28	3.93	0.92			3.24	−2.00

Sources: See text.

Notes: Latin America (LA20) is comprised of all Latin America. OECD (21) is comprised of Australia, Austria, Belgium, Canada, Denmark, France, Finland, Germany, Greece, Ireland, Italy, Japan, the Netherlands, New Zealand, Norway, Portugal, Spain, Sweden, Switzerland, the United Kingdom, and the United States.

References

Acemoglu, D., S. Johnson, and J. A. Robinson. 2002. Reversal of fortune: Geography and institutions in the making of the modern world income distribution. *Quarterly Journal of Economics* 117 (4): 1231–94.
Ahmad, S. 1998. International comparisons of incomes: Why should one bother using PPP Conversion? Poverty Reduction and Economic Management (PREM) seminar, Price and Purchasing Power Parities. Washington, DC: World Bank.
Astorga, P., A. R. Bergés, and V. Fitzgerald. 2003. Productivity growth in Latin America during the twentieth century, University of Oxford Discussion Papers in Economic and Social History no 52.
———. 2004. The Oxford Latin American Economic History Database (OxLAD). Oxford, UK: The Latin American Centre at Oxford University. Retrieved from http://oxlad.qeh.ox.ac.uk.
———. 2005. The standard of living in Latin America during the Twentieth Century. *Economic History Review* 58:765–96.
Astorga, P., and V. Fitzgerald. 1998. Statistical Appendix. In *Progress, poverty and exclusion. An economic history of Latin America in the 20th century,* ed. R. Thorp, 307–65. Washington: Inter-American Development Bank.
Baptista, A. 1997. *Bases cuantitativas de la economía venezolana 1830–1995.* Caracas: Fundación Polar.
Beckerman, W. 1966. *International comparisons of real incomes.* Paris: OECD Development Centre.
Bértola, L. y asociados. 1998. *El PBI de Uruguay 1870–1936 y otras estimaciones.* Montevideo, Uruguay: Universidad de la República.
Bhagwati, J. N. 1984. Why are services cheaper in the poor countries? *Economic Journal* 94:279–86.
Bhagwati, J. N., and B. Hansen. 1973. Should growth rates be evaluated at international prices? In *Development and planning essays in honor of Paul Rosenstein-Rodan,* ed. J. N. Bhagwati and R. S. Eckaus, 53–68. Cambridge, MA: MIT Press.
Bourguignon, F., and C. Morrisson. 2002. Inequality among world citizens. *American Economic Review* 92 (4): 727–44.
Braithwaite, S. N. 1968. Real income levels in Latin America. *Review of Income and Wealth* 14:113–82.
Braun, J., M. Braun, I. Briones, and J. Díaz. 1998. Economía chilena, 1810–1995. Estadísticas histórica. Documento de Trabajo 187, Pontificia Universidad Católica de Chile.
Broadberry, S. N. 1994. Comparative productivity in British and American manufacturing during the nineteenth century. *Explorations in Economic History* 31: 521–48.
———. 1997. Forging ahead, falling behind and catching-up: A sectoral analysis of Anglo-American productivity differences. *Research in Economic History* 17: 1–37.
Broadberry, S. N., and R. R. Fremdling. 1990. Comparative productivity in Britain and German industry, 1907–1937. *Oxford Bulletin of Economics and Statistics* 52:403–21.
Bulmer-Thomas, V. 1994. *The economic history of Latin America since independence.* Cambridge: Cambridge University Press.
Burger, A. 1997. Dutch industry in international perspective 1850–1913. Paper presented at conference, Historical National Accounts for the Netherlands: Eco-

nomic Growth and Structural Change 1800–1913. Utrecht: N. W. Posthumus Institut.
Cardoso, E., and A. Fishlow. 1992. Latin American development. *Journal of Latin American Studies* 24:197–218.
CEPAL. 1978. Series históricas del crecimiento de América Latina. *Cuadernos Estadísticos de la CEPAL.* Santiago de Chile: CEPAL.
Coatsworth, J. H. 1989. The decline of the Mexican economy, 1800–1860. In *América Latina en la época de Simón Bolívar: Latin America formación de las economías nacionales y los intereses económicos europeos 1800–1850,* ed. R. Liehr, 27–53. Berlin: Colloquium Verlag.
———. 1993. Notes on the comparative economic history of Latin America and the United States. In *Development and underdevelopment in America: Contrasts in economic growth in North America and Latin America in historical perspective,* ed. W. L. Bernecker and H. W. Tobler, 10–30. Berlin: Walter de Gruyter.
———. 1998. Economic and institutional trajectories in nineteenth-century Latin America. In *Latin America and the world economy since 1800,* ed. J. H. Coatsworth and A. M. Taylor, 23–54. Cambridge, MA: Harvard University Press.
———. 2003. Mexico. In *The Oxford Encyclopedia of economic history,* ed. J. Mokyr, 501–7. New York: Oxford University Press.
Cortés Conde, R., and M. Harriague. 1994. El PBI argentino, 1875–1935. Unpublished paper. Buenos Aires: Universidad de San Andrés.
De Gregorio, J. 1992. Economic growth in Latin America. *Journal of Development Economics* 39:59–84.
Della Paolera, G., A. M. Taylor, and C. G. Bozolli. 2003. Historical statistics. In *A new economic history of Argentina* (with CD-ROM), ed. G. Della Paolera and A. M. Taylor, 376–85. New York: Cambridge University Press.
Díaz, J., R. Lüders, and G. Wagner. 1998. *Economía chilena 1810–1995: Evolución cuantitativa del producto total y sectorial.* Santiago: Pontificia Universidad Católica de Chile.
Dormois, J. P., and C. Bardini. 1995. La productivité du travail dans l'industrie de divers pays d'Europe avant 1914. *Economies et Sociétés. Histoire Quantitative de l'Economie Française.* Série A F 21, 12, 77–103.
Economic Commission for Latin America (ECLA). 1968. The measurement of Latin American real income in U.S. dollars. *Economic Bulletin for Latin America* 12 (2): 107–41.
Edwards, S. 1995. *Crisis and reform in Latin America: From despair to hope.* New York: Oxford University Press.
Engerman, S. L., and K. L. Sokoloff. 1997. Factor endowments, institutions, and differential paths of growth among new world economies. In *How Latin America fell behind: Essays on the economic histories of Brazil and Mexico, 1800–1914,* ed. S. Haber, 260–304. Stanford, CA: Stanford University Press.
Fajnzylber, P., and D. Lederman. 2000. Economic reforms and total factor productivity growth in Latin America and the Caribbean, 1950–95: An empirical note. World Bank working paper no. 2114. Washington, DC: World Bank.
Fraile, P., R. J. Salvucci, and L. K. Salvucci. 1993. El caso cubano: Exportaciones e independencia. In *La independencia americana: Consecuencias económicas,* ed. L. Prados de la Escosura and S. Amaral, 80–101. Madrid: Alianza.
Frank, A. G. 1967. *Capitalism and underdevelopment in Latin America.* New York: Monthly Review Press.
Fremdling, R. R. 1991. Productivity comparisons between Great Britain and Germany, 1855–1913. *Scandinavian Economic History Review* 29:28–42.

Galor, O. 2004. The demographic transition and the emergence of sustained economic growth. Centre for Economic Policy Research discussion paper no. 4714.
Goldsmith, R. W. 1986. *Desenvolvimento fianceiro sob um século de inflaçao.* Rio de Janeiro: Harper & Row do Brasil.
GRECO (Grupo de Estudios de Crecimiento Económico). 2002. *El crecimiento económico columbiano en el siglo XX.* Bogotá, Colombia: Fondo de cultura Económico.
Haber, S., ed. 1997. *How Latin America fell behind: Essays on the economic histories of Brazil and Mexico, 1800–1914.* Stanford, CA: Stanford University Press.
Hofman, A. A. 2000. *The economic development of Latin America in the twentieth century.* Cheltenham, UK: Elgar.
———. 2001. Long run economic development in Latin America in a comparative perspective: Proximate and ultimate causes. ECLAC *Macroeconomía del Desarrollo* series 8.
Horlings, E. 1997. The contribution of the service sector to gross domestic product in Belgium, 1835–1990. Unpublished paper, International Institute of Social History [IISH], Universiteit Utrecht.
INEGI. 1995. *Estadísticas históricas de México.* México DF: INEGI.
Isenman, P. 1980. Inter-country comparison of "real" (PPP) incomes: Revised estimates and unresolved questions. *World Development* 8:61–72.
Jaramillo Uribe, J., A. Meisel, and M. Urrutia. 2001. Continuities and discontinuities in the fiscal and monetary institutions of New Granada, 1783–1850. In *Transferring wealth and power from the Old to the New World: Monetary and fiscal institutions in the 17th through the 19th Centuries,* ed. M. D. Bordo and R. Cortés-Conde, 414–50. Cambridge: Cambridge University Press.
Kalmanovitz, S. 2005. La economía de la Nueva Granada (unpublished paper, David Rockefeller Center of Latin American Studies, Harvard University).
Kravis, I. B., and R. E. Lipsey. 1991. The international comparison program: Current status and problems. In *International economic transactions: Issues in measurement and empirical research,* ed. P. E. Hooper and J. D. Richardson, 437–64. Studies in Income and Wealth, vol. 55. Chicago: University of Chicago Press.
Leff, N. H. 1982. *Underdevelopment and development in Brazil.* 2 vols. London: Macmillan.
Lindert, P. H., and J. G. Williamson. 2003. Does globalization make the world more unequal? In *Globalization in historical perspective,* ed. M. D. Bordo, A. M. Taylor, and J. G. Williamson, 227–70. Chicago: University of Chicago Press.
Maddison, A. 1991. *Dynamic forces in capitalist development: A long-run comparative view.* Oxford: Oxford University Press.
———. 1995. *Monitoring the world economy, 1820–1992.* Paris: OECD Development Centre.
———. 2001. *The world economy: A millennial perspective.* Paris: OECD Development Centre.
———. 2003. *The world economy: Historical statistics.* Paris: OECD Development Centre.
Mitchell, B. R. 1992. International historical statistics: Europe 1750–1988. New York: Stockton.
Mitchell, B. R. 1993. International historical statistics: The Americas 1750–1988. New York: Stockton.
Mitchell, B. R. 1994. International historical statistics: Africa, Asia and Oceania 1750–1988. New York: Stockton.
Newland, C. 1998. Economic development and population change: Argentina, 1810–

1870. In *Latin America and the world economy since 1800*, ed. J. H. Coatsworth and A. M. Taylor, 207–22. Cambridge, MA: Harvard University Press.

Newland, C., and B. Poulson. 1998. Purely animal: Pastoral production and early Argentine economic growth 1825–1865. *Explorations in Economic History* 35 (3): 325–45.

North, Douglass C. 1990. *Institutions, institutional change and economic performance.* Cambridge: Cambridge University Press.

North, D. C., W. R. Summerhill, and B. R. Weingast. 2000. Order, disorder, and economic change: Latin America versus North America. In *Governing for prosperity*, ed. B. Bueno de Mesquita and H. L. Root, 17–58. New Haven, CT: Yale University Press.

Nuxoll, D. A. 1994. Differences in relative prices and international differences in growth rates. *American Economic Review* 84:1423–36.

O'Brien, P. K., and C. Keyder. 1978. *Economic growth in Britain and France 1780–1914: Two paths to the twentieth century.* London: George Allen & Unwin.

O'Brien, P. K., and L. Prados de la Escosura. 1992. Agricultural productivity and European industrialization, 1890–1980. *Economic History Review* 45:514–36.

Prados de la Escosura, L. 2000. International comparisons of real product, 1820–1990: An alternative data set. *Explorations in Economic History* 37 (1): 1–41.

Prebisch, R. 1950. *The economic development of Latin America and its principal problems,* New York: United Nations, Economic Commission for Latin America.

Quiroz, A. W. 1993. Consecuencias económicas y financieras del proceso de la independencia en el Perú, 1800–1850. In *La independencia americana: consecuencias económicas,* ed. L. Prados de la Escosura and S. Amaral, 124–46. Madrid: Alianza.

Sala i Martín, X. 2002. The disturbing "rise" of global inequality, NBER Working Paper no. 8904. Cambridge, MA: National Bureau of Economic Research.

Salazar-Carrillo, J. 1983. Real product and price comparisons for Latin America and other world countries. *Economic Development and Cultural Change* 31 (4): 757–73.

Salazar-Carrillo, J., and D. S. Prasada Rao. 1988. Real product and price comparisons among Latin American countries. In *World comparison of incomes, prices and product,* ed. J. Salazar-Carrillo and D. S. Prasada Rao, 195–205. Amsterdam: North Holland.

Salazar-Carrillo, J., and I. Tirado de Alonso. 1988. Real product and price comparisons between Latin America and the rest of the world. *Review of Income and Wealth* 34 (1): 27–43.

Salvucci, R. J. 1997. Mexican national income in the era of independence, 1800–1840. In *How Latin America fell behind: Essays on the economic histories of Brazil and Mexico, 1800–1914,* ed. S. Haber, 216–42. Stanford, CA: Stanford University Press.

Santamaría, A. 2005. Las cuentas nacionales de Cuba, 1690–2005 (unpublished paper, Centro de Estudios Históricos, Centro Superior de Investigaciones Científicas, Madrid).

Singer, H. W. 1950. The distribution of gains between investing and borrowing countries. *American Economic Review Papers and Proceedings* 11 (2): 473–85.

Stein, S. J., and B. H. Stein. 1970. *The colonial heritage of Latin America: Essays on economic dependence in perspective.* New York: Oxford University Press.

Summers, R., and A. Heston. 1991. The Penn World Table (Mark 5): An expanded set of international comparisons, 1950–1988. *Quarterly Journal of Economics* 106:327–68.

Taylor, A. M. 1998. On the cost of inward-looking development: Price distortions, growth and divergence in Latin America. *Journal of Economic History* 58 (1): 1–19.
Theil, H. 1979. World income inequality and its components. *Economics Letters* 2:99–102.
———. 1989. The development of international inequality: 1960–1985. *Journal of Econometrics* 42 (1): 145–55.
Ward, M., and J. Devereux. 2003a. Measuring British decline: Direct versus long span measures. *Journal of Economic History* 63:826–51.
———. 2003b. New evidence on catch-up and convergence after 1870 (unpublished paper, Loyola College, Baltimore, and Queens College, CUNY).
Williamson, J. G. 1995. The evolution of global labor markets since 1830: Background evidence and hypotheses. *Explorations in Economic History* 32:141–96.
Zanden, J. L. van. 1991. The first green revolution: The growth of production and productivity in European agriculture, 1870–1914. *Economic History Review* 44:215–39.

2   Before the Golden Age
Economic Growth in Mexico and Portugal, 1910–1950

Pedro Lains

2.1 Introduction

During the interwar period some countries of the world periphery, in particular in southern Europe and Latin America, experienced relatively high rates of economic growth, which helped pave the way to the golden age of growth in the three decades following the end of World War II. Economic growth in the periphery during the interwar period has still not received the attention it deserves, but its analysis is of utmost importance to understand what drives economic growth and structural change in less developed economies. The fact that growth occurred during a period of receding international transactions is not compatible with many growth theories that focus on the benefits of international trade and specialization according to a country's patterns of comparative advantage.[1] Inward-looking growth during the interwar period was a direct consequence of the slowing down of the development of the international economy, as well as of international trade, capital flows, and emigration.

The countries studied in this chapter—Mexico and Portugal—stand out as two examples of positive economic performance during the interwar period.[2] The growth of these two economies was driven by structural change at the aggregate national economic level as well as at the level of the agrar-

---

Pedro Lains is a research fellow in economic history at the Institute of Social Sciences, University of Lisbon.

I would like to thank Graciela Marquéz Colín and a referee for their comments. The usual disclaimer applies.

1. For the most recent revisions of openness and growth theories, see for all Clemens and Williamson (2004).
2. See Cárdenas (1997, 2004), Haber (1990) and Bortz and Haber (2002) for Mexico, and Batista et al. (1997) and Lains (2003a, 2003c) for Portugal.

ian or the industrial sector. In other words, the share of the industrial sector in total output increased, and within agriculture and manufacturing there was also an increase in industries with high levels of factor productivity.[3] Such a pattern of structural change was a consequence of a series of favorable factors. First, thanks to the industrialization in the previous period, the two economies had already achieved, by around 1910, a minimum level of infrastructural as well as industrial development, upon which further advancements were based. Second, another crucial factor that enabled those changes was excess capacity, revealed in both the industrial and the agrarian sectors. Third, after the turn of the century, investment in physical capital continued to rise, thanks to the growth of domestic savings and capital imports. Fourth, domestic demand expanded and monetary and exchange rate policies eased the conditions of financing the current account deficit. The main difference between the interwar period and other periods of globalization backlash or receding international economic conditions—namely in the decades after 1973, in Portugal, and after 1982, in Mexico—was the fact that protection was obtained by exchange rate devaluation, and thus tariffs and economic policies were not biased against the export sector.[4]

The political histories of Mexico and Portugal differ in many important ways, and that is reflected in their economic history as well. Mexico gained its independence in 1821 and started the liberal era with a strong surplus in her government and external accounts (for most of the nineteenth century, Mexico had a surplus in her balance of trade). Portugal lost her Brazilian colony in 1822, and throughout the rest of the century had trouble in financing the government and external accounts, and was largely dependent on capital imports and emigrant remittances for that purpose. The two countries also differed markedly in terms of demographic patterns, as Mexico had rates of population growth that were double those of Portugal. Mexico was—and is—a larger country, with a larger economy and a large natural resource base. The list of differences is, of course, unlimited (as for any set of countries). Yet the two countries had some relevant similarities, too. The two most important in terms of the present comparison is, first, that by 1910 they had similar income per capita levels and, second, that their economies were much influenced by what happened in their larger and more industrialized neighbors, respectively, the United States and the

---

3. Brazil stands out as a case with some similarities with the two countries studied in this chapter, as it also followed a pattern of inward-looking economic growth and structural change during the interwar period. Brazil was Portugal's most important colony for a long time, but the linkages between the two economies were historically weak, except for the role of emigrant remittances in Portugal's balance of payments from the 1870s to the 1920s. On Brazil see Cortés Conde (1992) and Coatsworth and Taylor (1998). See also Haber (1997) and Hofman (2000).

4. On the effects of exchange rate devaluation, see Campa (1990) and Eichengreen and Sachs (1985).

European powers. The study in this chapter questions some views about long-run economic development that have dominated the economic historiography of both Mexico and Portugal. In fact, many would argue that economic growth and industrialization gained momentum in the two countries only after World War II and as a consequence of the opening up of their economies to positive influences of growth from their more developed neighbors.

This work is a contribution to the exploration of the causes of economic growth in the periphery of the industrialized world during the interwar period. Economic growth in the two countries here studied was marked by a path of intensive structural change at the national and industrial levels. The comparative study of the organization and structure of industry is crucial to understand such processes.[5] The available data is not sufficient to endeavor in detailed analyses of total factor productivity, but the observed changes in the structure of output and labor input enlighten the most important factors behind interwar growth. The chapter is structured as follows. The next section briefly presents the historiography of economic growth in Mexico and Portugal. Section three presents the data on output growth, structural change, and labor productivity growth. Section four shows how structural change was driven by domestic demand and how labor productivity gains were achieved in the process. Section five concludes.

2.2 The Historiography of Backwardness and Growth

The distinction of center and periphery is a useful tool for many typologies of growth and retardation, from Gerschenkron (1962) to Abramovitz (1986) and the studies on convergence that followed. That distinction implies that we ask why backward countries in the periphery did not follow more closely the pattern of growth of the forerunners in the center. Such typologies have been used to study the development of both the European and the American economies in the last two centuries, and we have gained many insights in understanding why the Latin American countries failed to follow more closely the speed of economic growth in the United States, or why countries in southern Europe lagged behind the pace of the economic development of their northern neighbors. The understanding of economic backwardness in the peripheries of the two fastest-growing regions of the world can be enhanced by comparing their respective experiences.

Historical explanations for economic retardation in Mexico and Portugal have some common features. First, economic backwardness is associated by many historians of both countries with the consequences of eighteenth-century institutions that constrained growth. For Mexico, Coatsworth (1978, 90–91) summarizes those interpretations quite clearly:

---

5. See Haber (1989, 9).

"three main obstacles to economic growth have been postulated to explain Mexico's relative backwardness at the end of the colonial period: Spanish colonial rule, the system of land tenure, and the Roman Catholic Church." Historians have for a long time held that Portugal's economic backwardness was a consequence of the Church and the imperfect property rights that prevailed in the Ancien Régime. Colonial rule ended in Mexico about the same time that Portugal lost Brazil, in 1821 and 1822, respectively. The two countries were part of the same historical process, which was a consequence of the Napoleonic wars and the liberal revolutions in Portugal and Spain.[6] According to Coatsworth (1978), Mexico's colonial heritage was almost completely eliminated after independence, except for two remaining negative factors—inadequate transport and inefficient economic organization, or geography and feudalism.[7] Engerman and Sokoloff (1997), however, argue that the extremely unequal social structure of the colonial period did not disappear after independence, and that it had a negative impact in the development of the Mexican economy in the nineteenth century. Portugal's Ancien Régime was also slow to die out, and one could argue that the lack of transport infrastructures and the institutional framework, particularly concerning property rights, were among the most important heritages from the eighteenth century that influenced economic performance in the nineteenth century. Thus, in both Mexico and Portugal, liberation from colonial power and from the Ancien Régime, respectively, did not have an immediate impact, and the obstacles to economic growth that those systems imposed were only slowly removed.

How were those obstacles overcome? Three interconnected factors emerge in the historiography of both countries: political stability, railways, and capital imports. In Mexico, those factors gained increasing relevance during the Porfiriato era, from 1876–1911, when political stability was gradually attained. In Portugal there also was an increase in the level of political stability in the second half of the nineteenth century, which allowed a consolidation of the power of the State. Thus, governments in both countries gained strength to intervene in the economy and to invest in social overhead capital that was partially financed by capital imports.[8] The fact that two countries in such different parts of the world had such common patterns in their political history is no coincidence. Both were affected by the turmoil provoked by the revolutionary period following the French wars and the independence of the Latin American colonies. Liberalism ensued in the Iberian Peninsula and Latin America, but it took a long time for the new constitutional order to consolidate. That consolidation was to a large extent stimulated by the benefits of an increasing participation in

---

6. See for Portugal Lains and Silva (2005, vol. 1).
7. See also Cárdenas (1997) and Maurer (1999).
8. See Lains and Silva (2005, vol. 2).

the international economy, which expanded faster after midcentury, particularly since around 1870.

Thus, the increasing pace of growth and development in Mexico and Portugal derived directly from their participation in the international economy through exports, capital imports, and, in the case of Portugal, through emigration. Yet, in the last quarter of the nineteenth century, Mexico outperformed Portugal. Part of Mexico's better performance after 1870 was probably due to the fact that the depression of the first half of the nineteenth century was more severe than in Portugal. Coatsworth (1988) has estimated a decline of about thirty percent in per capita income between 1800 and 1860. Portugal also had a bad period before 1870, but not as bad as Mexico. In any case, the fact was that Mexico caught up to Portugal's level of income per capita in 1913 (see section three, following). Mexico's faster per capita income growth since 1870 was also related to the fact that it had a higher availability of natural resources. Mexico was rich in terms of land, silver, and copper, which allowed the growth of a wider range of sectors with high levels of factor productivity.[9]

Liberalism in its different forms ended in both countries in 1910, and the following decade was one of relative economic stagnation. The 1910 Mexican Revolution was considerably more severe than the one that occurred in Portugal in the same year, and it evolved into a civil war with an immense death toll. In 1917, a new Constitution was an important turning point for political stabilization in Mexico, but complete peace came only by the end of the 1920s. In the case of Portugal, the consequences of the 1910 Revolution, which ended the monarchy and installed a Republican regime, were eventually overshadowed by the outbreak of World War I and by the participation of Portugal in that war, starting in 1916.

The extent of the impact of the civil war in the Mexican economy is, however, under revision. Haber and Razo (1998, 481–82), for example, do not agree with the contention that "the Porfirian boom was followed by a period of relative economic stagnation during the Revolution and postrevolutionary years [and that] it was not until the mid-1930s that growth again reignited, led by import substituting industrialization and government intervention designed to overcome market failures."[10] Their analysis of productivity growth in the Mexican textile industry shows an altogether different pattern. In fact, they conclude that productivity in the textile sector expanded rapidly during the Porfiriato era, in particular after 1890, and

9. See Hofman (2000, 8–11).
10. Razo and Haber (1998). The authors add that such a definition of the pattern of Mexican economic growth is based on slim evidence, namely estimates of national income by Banco de México, which they do not fully trust. We should add, though, that the description they provide is also based on an incorrect interpretation of the same estimates. In fact, the peak-to-peak analysis presented in table 2.1 show that the 1910 Revolution was followed by recovery, with a peak in 1926, and that the downturn happened well before the 1929 crash and the Great Depression. See also Haber and Razo (1998).

that it was only temporarily affected by the revolution. Moreover, productivity growth trends recovered in the following decades and were not affected by the Great Depression. The impact of the revolution was only temporary because the revolutionary wars did not affect to a considerable extent the existent stock of capital. Moreover, the change in the labor regime imposed by the revolution (the eight-hour day and collective contracts) led to the substitution of capital for labor and thus to an increase in capital-output ratios, which impacted positively on labor productivity growth. The authors argue that proximity to large urban markets had a positive impact on factor productivity of the textile industry, as it allowed the specialization on "high value, fine weave textiles" (Haber and Razo 1998, 506). It is important to note that external factors are not considered important in this analysis: changes in tariff protection, devaluations, export prices, and capital imports do not seem to be relevant in explaining the development of factor productivity in the most important sector of the Mexican economy throughout almost a century. Instead, economies of scale and proximity of large urban markets appear as the relevant factors. Part of the conclusions regarding Mexican textiles can be extended to the rest of the industrial sector.

The impact of the 1910 Revolution on Mexican agriculture may have been quite different. Sandos and Cross (1983) estimated a decline of fixed assets value in agriculture in northern Mexico of between 50 and 75 percent. There were also important changes in the structure of land ownership in favor of laborers which affected investment levels in agriculture. In the North, the response to the decline in investment and output was emigration to the irrigated fields of California as well as to Mexico City and other urban centers. Emigration across the border was, however, stopped in 1929, and many Mexican laborers were repatriated from the United States. The increase in the rural population compelled the government to implement a system of land distribution, which, according to Sandos and Cross (1983), had a negative impact on agrarian productivity.[11] That negative trend was reversed in the 1940s with the resurgence of emigration to the United States and the increase in American investment in Mexico.[12] This became known as the "Green Revolution," which complemented the high growth rates in the industrial sector to accomplish the Mexican economic miracle from 1945 to 1965. During the years 1949 to 1955 investment expanded rapidly and at even higher rates in agriculture than in industry,

---

11. Navarrette (1959) has a different perspective on the impact of the agrarian reform. According to him, the redistribution of land was accompanied by an increase of investment pushed by loans by Banco de México, the central bank founded in 1925, and public works of irrigation, starting in 1926. In the same year an agrarian mortgage bank was founded.

12. The relations between Mexico and the United States were stressed by the nationalization of the oil fields and railways in 1937–1938, but after World War II the United States conformed to the new policies, due to its need to improve its relationship with its southern neighbor.

although the growth of industrial output was higher (Navarrete 1959). Recovery in the 1930s was in part due to President Lázaro Cárdenas' macroeconomic management that paved the way to stable macroeconomic policies that lasted until the 1970s—the "desarollo estabilizador" period (see Sandos and Cross [1983] and Cárdenas [1997]).

Mexican industrial growth that occurred during the 1930s was led by import substitution. Cárdenas (1997) asks, though, how did that happen in the context of the negative impact of the Great Depression, which was translated into the contraction of external demand and a fall in terms of trade. He concludes that rapid industrial growth was made possible by the convergence of three factors. First, economic policy was flexible as it adjusted to changing conditions in the product and monetary markets. Money supply was increased, the exchange rate was left to float, and the government ran budget deficits. In short, economic policy was countercyclical. Second, due to devaluation, the relative prices of imports increased, which promoted import-substitution. Third, the industrial sector responded to changes in relative prices because it had excess capacity that had developed in the previous decades as a consequence of favorable trends in investment and the supply of labor.[13]

The alternative of specialization toward exports would have brought positive effects in the case of Mexico, given that it would allow the full utilization of underused capacity in the industrial sector. This was a major problem, according to Haber (1989, 39–43), because of the large share of large-scale manufacturing units in the Mexican industrial sector. But, according to the same author, "Mexican industrialists tried to pursue that strategy" (1989, 39) but did not succeed, and the reasons for the failure are most relevant here. Haber (1989) points out the fact that Mexico was relatively isolated from the outside world because of high transport costs, which derived from its geographical location. Most industrial production occurred inland around Mexico City, and the country had few maritime ports and no merchant marine. Moreover, moving produce to the sea was expensive, even after the railway network was accomplished. A further problem mentioned by Haber (1989) was the fact that Mexican industrialists had to compete with output from neighboring countries who produced similar products. Due to high transport costs across the major industrial nations of Latin America, regional or country specialization was low, which implied a small basis for exchange of industrial products. And this was not substituted by increasing trade with the United States and Europe, because competition for industrial products was very hard in those markets.

In Portugal, the interwar period was marked by large government and foreign deficits, high inflation, and exchange rate devaluation.[14] The 1910

---

13. See also Cárdenas (2004).
14. For what follows see Lains (2003c) and Lains and Silva (2005, vol. 3).

Revolution was the ultimate consequence of the instability that dominated political life there in the last years of the liberal monarchy. The revolution, however, did not put an end to that instability, because instability was not due to the constitutional form of political regime or of government, but to the fact that a substantial proportion of the population was disenfranchised and did not have access to power—a problem which Portugal had in common with Mexico. Whatever the reasons, political instability was aggravated by the advent of World War I; its impact on the Portuguese economic and financial situation derived from the adverse conditions in the international economy. The direct participation of Portugal in the war increased the burden on the economy. The participation in the war was financed by printing money and raising loans from the British government, and an aggravated government deficit was added to the deficit in the external accounts. Financial distress translated into inflation, one of the highest in Europe at the time, and exchange rate depreciation. Financial instability was not fully controlled because of the lack of political power of successive governments; the first Republic ultimately fell with another military coup, in 1926, that paved the way for Salazar's dictatorship. Monetary and exchange rate stability was recovered in 1924, briefly interrupted, and finally consolidated from 1928 onward.

The high levels of instability in Portugal during the 1920s have been closely identified with economic depression by many historians. Increasing public debt and large government deficits, together with high levels of price inflation and steep devaluation of the escudo, were the consequence of both the financial effort to participate in the war and of the contraction of export revenues and taxes. However, such imbalances were ultimately followed by economic recovery in response to increasing levels of protection and state intervention. The developments described earlier are fully recognized in Portuguese political historiography, most of all because they go together with the development of the institutional framework associated with the dictatorship and its quasi-fascist nature. However, historians—economic and otherwise—have paid more attention to the financial world and its distresses, as well as to the overall backwardness of the country, failing to recognize the important elements of growth and structural change that were occurring simultaneously. For a long time, too much attention has been paid to political factors in the explanations of economic performance in Portugal.[15]

Economic policy helped in shaping the international specialization and the structure of the two economies, but it was certainly not the only factor and probably not the most important. As a matter of fact, the 1920s were years of economic growth for Portugal, as shown by data on the evolution of national income. Growth in this period was marked by the growth of in-

---

15. For Mexico, see Cárdenas (1997, 7).

vestment in physical and human capital and by import substitution, in both the agrarian and the industrial sectors. Part of this investment was financed by the repatriation of capital, which had flown the country during the war, and contributed to the financing of the current account. In fact, the 1920s saw many positive developments in the agrarian and industrial sectors. In agriculture, there was an increase in the area under acreage, particularly in the wheat fields of the south. Moreover, there was an increase in the sectors of transformation of primary products, namely flour, as well as of the industries that catered to the primary sector, namely chemical fertilizers. There was also an expansion of other industries, including large-scale industries. This process proceeded during the 1930s and also during World War II. Portuguese exporters benefited from the country's officially neutral position and exports of canned fish and minerals boomed, for a considerable gain for the industrial sector.

Mexico and Portugal thus seem to fall under the general conclusion put forward by Thorp (1998, 114) in relation to Latin America. According to her, "The 1930s in Latin America may not have represented a sharp break with the past, but the decade did not represent a lost opportunity either. In the face of a generally hostile external environment, most republics did well to rebuild their export sectors; where it was feasible republics with only a few exceptions expanded the production of importables and increased the supply of non-traded goods and services. These changes provided the basis for a significant growth in intra-regional trade in the early 1940s when access to imports from the rest of the world was cut off." The author adds that "changes in economic policy in the 1930s were also generally rational; a wholesale retreat from the export sector and the construction of a semi-closed economy would have involved a massive increase in inefficiency; a slavish commitment to the export-led model of growth would have locked the region into an allocation of resources no longer consistent with long-run comparative advantage. Economic historians searching for the period of the twentieth century when Latin America economic policy and performance go seriously wrong need to look beyond the 1930s" (Bulmer-Thomas, 114). Mexico performed better than Portugal because its domestic market was larger, as well as its economic development before 1929. As Hofman and Mulder (1998, 88) put it: "A minimum size in the domestic market plus a minimum degree of autonomy regarding the exchange rate and fiscal and monetary policies were necessary conditions for industrialization in Latin America in the 1930s." The good performance of the 1930s was not replicated later on, after the first oil shock in 1973 or the debt crisis in 1982, because the economic policies then adopted strongly discriminated against exports. Those policies led to foreign exchange constraint and affected the financing of the current account deficit (Ffrench-Davis, Muñoz, and Palma 1998, 115).

Table 2.1 GDP per capita: Real annual growth rates (peak-to-peak; %)

Mexico		Portugal	
1870–1898	1.86	1870–1882	0.15
1898–1905	1.44	1882–1902	1.03
1905–1926	1.16	1902–1922	0.60
1926–1936	–1.07	1922–1934	1.54
1936–1944	2.30	1934–1947	1.11
1944–1958	2.65	1947–1958	2.16
1958–1973	3.15	1958–1973	7.15

Sources: Mexico: Maddison (1995), for 1870, and Cárdenas (1997); Portugal: Lains (2006).

2.3 Growth Trends

At the eve of its industrialization age, in 1870, Mexico's per capita income was low by European and North American standards. In fact, at 710 1990 United States dollars, in 1870, Mexico was poorer than any European country for which there is data for that year. Part of that lag was recovered in the decades leading up to 1910, as the Mexican income per capita expanded at an annual rate of 1.7 percent. None of the poorer European countries, including Portugal, attained such a rapid level of income growth during the same period.[16] Mexico's better performance can be explained in the same manner used to explain the United States' advantage over industrialized Europe in the nineteenth century. That would lead us to take into account the role of natural resource endowments, in terms of mineral wealth per capita and land-labor ratios. Mexico's rapid growth up to 1910 was due to rapid industrialization and to the growth of capital-intensive industrial sectors. This was helped by large amounts of capital imports and foreign direct investment. Interestingly, however, the Mexican agrarian sector remained stagnant in the same period, which contrasts with what happened in the United States. Portugal's income growth was driven by the industrial sector, which was largely dominated by the growth of industries that were not competitive in the international markets—in particular, cotton textiles—and under tariff protection. The agrarian sector also lagged behind, although there were some periods of positive performance in terms of labor (but not land) productivity.[17]

Table 2.1 presents the rates of growth of GDP per capita in Mexico and Portugal during the main growth trends, defined as periods between peak years (see also figure 2.1). The table shows that the Mexican economy expanded at rates of over 1 percent per year before 1926, and that after the recession, starting in that year and ending in 1936, the economy expanded

---

16. See Maddison (1995, 2001).
17. See Lains (2003b).

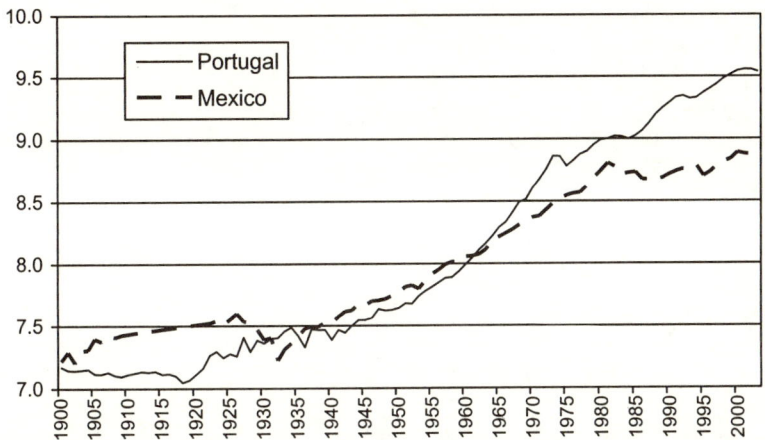

Fig. 2.1 GDP per capita in Mexico and Portugal, 1900–2003 (semi-log scale; 1990 US$)
Sources: See table 2.1.

at rates above 2 percent. In contrast, the Portuguese economy expanded at rates below 1 percent before 1922; thereafter the pace of growth increased, but still remained below that of Mexico until 1958. Between 1958 and 1973, the Portuguese economy took off, whereas Mexico increased its rate of economic growth only slightly. One important fact revealed by the data in table 2.1 is that these two countries had a good performance in terms of rates of economic growth during the interwar years and, in particular, during the late 1920s and 1930s. The upsurge in economic growth is more relevant in the case of Portugal, where the contrast between the periods before and after the 1922 peak is higher. Mexico had a deep depression during 1926–36, which weighed heavily in the performance of the economy during the interwar period. Despite the sharp decline in income per capita that occurred then, the fact is that Mexican income growth reached 1.4 percent per year in the whole period from 1926 to 1958, which was similar to growth in the years 1898 to 1905 and faster than growth in the years from 1905 to 1926.

Table 2.2 gives a comparison of income per capita levels of the two peripheral countries and their industrialized neighbors. The table shows that Mexico followed the United States closely between 1870 and 1913, as relative income levels remained rather similar in those two years, namely, 28.9 and 27.6 percent. Between 1913 and 1929, the relative position in comparison to the United States declined to 21.6 percent, and from then on it remained at that level until 1950, to increase only slightly during 1950–73. Portugal's experience in comparison to western Europe is remarkably different from the Mexico–United States comparison, as there was a sharp

Table 2.2   Levels of income per capita

	Absolute levels (1990 US$)				Relative levels (%)		
	Mexico	Portugal	United States	Western Europe	Mexico/ United States	Portugal/ Western Europe	Mexico/ Portugal
1870	710	1,085	2,457	1,986	28.9	54.6	65.4
1913	1,467	1,354	5,307	3,482	27.6	38.9	108.3
1929	1,489	1,536	6,907	4,538	21.6	33.8	96.9
1938	1,380	1,787	6,134	4,685	22.5	38.4	76.8
1950	2,085	2,132	9,573	5,513	21.8	38.7	97.8
1973	4,189	7,568	16,607	11,694	25.2	64.7	55.4

Source: Maddison (1995), pp. 23–24, 194–198 and 202.

decline in relative income levels, from 54.6 percent in 1870 to 38.9 percent in 1913. From 1913 to 1929 the decline in Portugal's relative position continued, albeit at a slower pace, and after 1929 there was a recovery. The last column on table 2.2 shows the comparison between the two peripheral countries. Mexico caught up with Portugal after 1870, and in 1913 the two countries reached a similar level of income per capita, which was maintained until 1929. In the following decades Portugal outperformed Mexico first, and then the opposite happened, in such a way that in 1950 the two countries were again parallel. The periods chosen for comparison on table 2.2 do not take into account the cycles of growth in each country, and thus they are only indicative. The table shows, however, that the 1910s and the 1920s were less positive in Mexico than they were in Portugal. Moreover, the same table shows that Mexico closely followed the United States' pattern of economic growth. The most important conclusion from these comparisons is that Mexico and Portugal had levels of income per capita within a close range, and that the distances of development in comparison to their respective more industrialized neighbors were also rather similar.

The higher degree of synchrony of Mexico's economic cycles in relation to its northern neighbor was not due to a higher degree of openness, but to the fact that the United States had a larger share in Mexican foreign trade and capital flows (as well as northbound emigration) than any single European economy had in regard to the Portuguese economy. Table 2.3 shows average trade ratios for the two countries. Mexico's export ratio was larger than Portugal's until the period from 1929–37 and then it declined substantially, whereas Portugal's export ratio increased, particularly after 1950. Mexico's import ratio fell below that of Portugal during the whole period, and Mexico also had trade surpluses throughout. In contrast, Portugal had large trade deficits. All in all, the Mexican economy remained more closed than the Portuguese. In fact, the two economies ranked among the most closed economies in the world. At its lowest levels, in 1932–37, the United States accounted for 57.7 percent of Mexican exports and 60.8 per-

Table 2.3 Trade ratios (current values)

	Mexico				Portugal		
	Export/ GDP	Import/ GDP	(Export + Import)/ GDP		Export/ GDP	Import/ GDP	(Export + Import)/ GDP
1900–1910	11.3	9.3	20.7	1910–1913	9.0	19.4	28.4
1921–1928	13.6	7.7	21.3	1918–1928	8.4	24.9	33.3
1929–1937	13.2	8.1	21.4	1929–1937	6.6	14.7	21.3
1938–1950	8.9	9.8	18.7	1938–1950	11.5	16.3	27.8

Sources: Mexico: computed from Mitchell (1993, table E1) and Cárdenas (1997), pp. 190–1; Portugal: Lains (2006).

Table 2.4 Growth of monetary and fiscal indicators (annual growth rates; %)

	Mexico				
	GDP deflator	Money supply (M1)	Ex rate (Pesos/US$)	Total public debt	Budget deficit (–)/ surplus (+) (% of GDP)[b]
1890–1913	2.66	15.46[a]	2.42	6.71	–0.03
1913–1929	2.23	2.29	–0.01	4.41	+0.44
1929–1939	2.05	4.14	9.58	2.48	+0.03
1939–1950	10.39	19.18	4.77	12.97	+0.02
	Portugal				
	GDP deflator	Money supply (M1)	Ex rate (PTE/£)[c]	Total public debt	Budget deficit (% of GDP)
1891–1914	0.92	0.68	0.69	0.46	–0.3
1914–1929	26.91	22.50	25.04	20.85	–6.4
1929–1939	–0.10	6.21	1.85	–2.84	+0.9
1939–1945	15.22	27.77	–1.58	5.54	–0.9

Sources: Mexico: Estadísticas Historicas de Mexico (data in current pesos); Portugal: Lains (2006).
[a] 1910–1913.
[b] 1895–1910, 1921–28, 1929–38, 1939–49.
[c] Before 1910, 1 PTE = 1$000 reis.

cent of imports. In 1938–50 the same shares were, respectively, 80.6 and 94.2 percent (Mitchell 1993). Clearly, though, Portugal had to finance large trade deficits throughout most of the period, and as such it was more dependent than Mexico on capital imports as well as on emigrant remittances.

Table 2.4 shows the evolution of main monetary and fiscal indicators in the two countries. As is shown there, the evolution of price inflation in Mexico was less erratic, growing at rates above or close to 2 percent per year until 1939, and increasing to 10.4 percent in 1939–50. In contrast,

Portugal had a period of very high inflation, with prices increasing on average by 27 percent per year between 1914 and 1929, a period that was followed by stable or slightly declining inflation up to 1939. The major changes in the levels of inflation in Portugal mirror changes in the growth of money supply, the exchange rate, public debt, and the budget deficit. Mexico's financial indicators depict higher levels of stability, and although total public debt increased at high rates throughout, that increase had a more stable pattern than in Portugal. Stability was achieved through successive exchange rate adjustments down to the mid-1950s. Moreover, Mexico's government accounts were kept balanced, even showing small surpluses.[18]

The interwar period stands out in the experience of growth of the Mexican and Portuguese economies. Both countries attained rates of growth of GDP per capita that compare favorably with growth elsewhere in the peripheries at the same time, as well as with growth in the two countries before 1914. Growth in the two countries was inward looking, mainly because there was a globalization backlash resulting from World War I, the decline in world trade, emigration, and international prices for primary products. The 1929–32 Great Depression also had a negative impact on the growth of the two countries, particularly in Mexico. Taking the whole interwar period into account, Mexico outperformed Portugal and in the next section we explore the reasons for that. The better performance is reflected on a more stable monetary and financial situation, which probably was also favorable, in a two-way effect, for the high growth levels achieved in Mexico. Portugal's financial distress during the interwar period were certainly not helpful for growth.

2.4 Structural Change

To explain the performance of the economies of Mexico and Portugal during the interwar period and, in particular, after 1930, we need to look at changes in their structures and reveal which sectors expanded faster. Table 2.5 shows data on structural change for the two countries in three periods, taking into account six economic sectors.[19] The pattern of structural change in the two countries is what one might expect, namely, a contraction of the share of the agrarian sector and an increase in the shares of industry and services. There are, though, two main differences. First, Mexico had a higher share of output originating in the mining sector, and that is, of course, related to her specific resource endowments, namely silver, copper, and oil. Thus, whereas mining in Portugal was marginal, in Mexico it peaked at 14 percent of output value in 1930 to decline to 6.4 percent

---

18. See Cárdenas (1997, 2004) and Bazant (1995).
19. The availability of the data is restricted for different reasons. See Keesing (1969) and Cárdenas (1997, 2004).

Table 2.5   Structural change (%)

	Mexico			Portugal		
	1895	1930	1950	1890	1930	1950
Labor						
Agriculture	66.5	68.7	58.3	66.9ª	60.9ª	53.8ª
Mining	1.8	1.0	1.2	n.a.	n.a.	n.a.
Manufacturing[b]	13.8	12.2	15.6	18.3	20.7	24.6
Transports[c]	1.6	2.0	2.5	14.8	18.4	21.6
Trade[d]	5.6	5.8	9.1	n.a.	n.a.	n.a.
Other services[e]	10.7	10.4	13.2	n.a.	n.a.	n.a.
Total	100	100	100	100	100	100
Output						
Agriculture	49.2	25.4	25.1	40.9ª	31.5	32.1
Mining	6.4	14.0	6.4	n.a.	0.4	0.6
Manufacturing[b]	15.6	20.6	28.4	21.5	27.6	29.7
Transports	3.3	5.5	5.2	37.6[c]	3.8	4.3
Trade	12.3	18.6	16.1	n.a.	16.3	17.0
Other services[e]	13.3	15.8	18.7	n.a.	20.4	16.3
Total	100	100	100	100	100	100

Sources: Mexico: Keesing (1969); Portugal: Lains (2006). The source for Mexico provides data on labor and output per unit of labor, from which output data was derived.

Note: n.a. = not available.

[a]Includes "Mining."
[b]Includes "Energy and construction."
[c]Data for Portugal includes "Trade" and "Other services" and, for both countries, "Communications."
[d]Data for Portugal includes "Finance and rents."
[e]Data for Mexico includes "Other services" and "Insufficiently specified sectors."

at the end of the period. Second, in 1895, Mexico had a higher share of output originating in the agrarian sector and a lower share originating in the industrial sector. From then on structural change was faster in Mexico than in Portugal, in such a way that the percentage of agricultural productivity in Mexico fell below that of Portugal in 1950 and the percentage of the industrial sector reached 28.4 percent, which compares to the percentage of 30.1 percent in Portugal. Portugal kept a larger proportion of resources in the agrarian sector for a longer period of time than did Mexico, due to a large extent to the fact that the labor productivity gap between agriculture and the rest of the economy was considerably smaller. In fact, in 1895, Mexican total labor productivity was 1.36 times that of the agrarian sector alone, and in 1950 the same ratio had increased to 2.32.

Table 2.6 shows that labor productivity in Mexican agriculture increased at an annual rate of 3.3 percent between 1930 and 1950, whereas in the industrial sector growth was 2.9 percent annually. These high rates of growth were achieved in spite of the fact that labor expanded in both sectors at very

Table 2.6   Growth of output and labor (annual; %)

| | Mexico | | | | Portugal | | | |
| | Output | | Labor | | Output | | Labor | |
	1895–1930	1930–1950	1895–1930	1930–1950	1890–1930	1930–1950	1890–1930	1930–1950
Agriculture[a]	0.21	4.75	0.62	1.37	1.01	2.32	0.58	0.70
Mining	4.45	0.83	−1.27	3.25	n.a.	n.a.	n.a.	n.a.
Manufacturing[b]	2.96	6.50	0.17	3.48	2.37	3.09	1.07	2.21
Transports[c]	3.63	4.54	1.19	3.44	1.69	2.20	1.32	2.15
Trade[d]	3.36	4.04	0.64	4.56	n.a.	n.a.	n.a.	n.a.
Other services[e]	2.65	5.69	0.45	3.42	n.a.	n.a.	n.a.	n.a.
Total	2.13	4.81	0.53	2.20	1.62	2.50	0.79	1.33

Sources: Mexico: Keesing (1969); Portugal: Lains (2006). The source for Mexico provides data on labor and output per unit of labor, from which output data was derived.

Note: n.a. = not available.

[a] Includes "Mining."
[b] Includes "Energy and construction."
[c] Data for Portugal includes "Trade" and "Other services" and, for both countries, "Communications."
[d] Data for Portugal includes "Finance and rents."
[e] Data for Mexico includes "Other services" and "Insufficiently specified sectors."

Table 2.7   Growth of labor productivity

	Mexico			Portugal		
	1895–1930	1930–1950	1895–1950	1890–1930	1930–1950	1890–1950
Agriculture[a]	−0.41	3.34	0.94	0.43	1.62	0.83
Mining	5.80	−2.34	2.76	n.a.	n.a.	n.a.
Manufacturing[b]	2.78	2.92	2.83	1.30	0.88	1.16
Transports[c]	2.41	1.06	1.92	0.37	0.05	0.26
Trade[d]	2.70	−0.50	1.52	n.a.	n.a.	n.a.
Other services[e]	2.18	2.20	2.19	n.a.	n.a.	n.a.
Total	1.57	2.58	1.93	0.82	1.17	0.94

Sources: Mexico: Keesing (1969); Portugal: Lains (2006). The source for Mexico provides data on labor and output per unit of labor, from which output data was derived.

Note: n.a. = not available.

[a]Includes "Mining."
[b]Includes "Energy and construction."
[c]Data for Portugal includes "Trade" and "Other services" and, for both countries, "Communications."
[d]Data for Portugal includes "Finance and rents."
[e]Data for Mexico includes "Other services" and "Insufficiently specified sectors."

high rates (see table 2.7). In Portugal, the period from 1930 to 1950 was comparatively positive, as the economy expanded faster than in any previous period since industrialization began. Yet, in this case, growth was mainly due to the performance of the agrarian sector, where labor productivity increased at 1.6 percent per year. The industrial sector expanded at just 0.9 percent per year in the same period of time. The larger contribution of the agrarian sector was due to a great extent to the fact that the primary sector was protected from foreign competition, either through tariffs or special price arrangements, or as a consequence of the contraction in international trade. Protection, in one form or the other, had positive consequences, because it enhanced the growth of agrarian output with above-average factor (i.e., land and labor) productivity levels, and for which domestic demand was also growing at rates above the national average. Evidence on land and labor productivity levels, albeit partial in some cases, indicate that the primary sector in some regions of the country and in some sectors, such as animal products or fruits and legumes, had higher levels of productivity than, for example, the textile sector. Portugal was a very backward country in those years, which meant that there was still the possibility of obtaining productivity gains by shifting resources to certain products within the traditional sectors. Moreover, those were products with higher levels of domestic demand price and income elasticities. This was the mechanism through which a higher level of isolation from the international markets could have had, and did have, a positive impact on average productivity levels.

A similar process happened in Mexico but with higher productivity gains, due to the fact that Mexico had an advantage in terms of certain industrial branches. Again, it is possible to reach such conclusions with the analysis of structural changes, particularly of changes within the industrial sector. The detailed analysis provided in Keesing (1969) is crucial to understand such processes. According to this author, the Mexican economy went through important structural changes within the industrial sector in the 1930s and 1940s—which ultimately "served as a transition to the rapid industrialization and structural change that have subsequently distinguished the economy" (1969, 720). He provides several examples of structural change. The number of workers in the food and beverages industries doubled in the period from 1895 to 1950, but there was a decline in the more traditional activities, such as tortilla makers (which accounted for a third of the total), bakers, and butchers, whereas the number of workers in sugar, alcohol, and beverage industries increased, with overall productivity gains. Also, in the chemical industries, workers were mainly traditional artisans in 1895, namely candle or soap makers, with their numbers declining to give way to more modern industries such as basic chemicals. Keesing concludes that it is at this level that we need to take into account the impact of structural changes in productivity. He argues that "between 1930 and 1950 skill-intensive subsectors typically grew by a factor of three to five times or more, though they remained very small relative to the rest of the economy, by standards of industrial economies" (Keesing 1969, 737). Keesing also points out to structural changes that occurred in the service sector. All changes suggest "that economic development involves at least a two-stage transformation. First there occurs a modernization of techniques that tends to shrink the labor force in each nonagricultural sector. Only later comes a structural transformation of the labor force" (Keesing 1969, 737).

We may conclude, then, that the economies of Mexico and Portugal were going through important shifts in their structure that were ultimately fundamental to future stages of growth. Historically, such changes occurred in periods of diminishing importance of international economic relations, and thus there is a link between such changes and protection of the domestic market. But that evidence tells us nothing about the mechanisms that allowed such changes and thus allowed such productivity gains in the labor force. One key element in illustrating that mechanism is by analyzing the extent to which greater isolation from world commerce allowed the exploration of excess capacity in the economy. That hypothesis is plausible for Portugal's agrarian sector. In fact, land was abundant and still far from totally used by the 1930s, and there was also a large underemployed agrarian population. In the case of Mexican industry the point has also been made that the period since the 1910 revolution until well into the 1920s was one of underutilization of capacity. That would have been a consequence of the high rates of growth of industrial investment prior to 1910, pushed by capital imports.

This conclusion is derived from Bruton (1967) in his study of economic growth in the Latin American economies during the period of high growth from 1940 to 1964. This author devises a simple method to analyze whether "the ability to exploit capacity is an important factor in potential output, and that changing utilization is a key variable explaining productivity growth in the Latin American countries" (1967, 1101). His device is to estimate regressions of productivity growth on the growth of inputs and on the growth of output. The outcomes of those estimates differ for Latin America (LAC), compared to a group of advanced economies (AG).[20] For Latin America in 1940–1964 the author gets (where r_A, r_N and r_P stand respectively for growth of total factor productivity, inputs and output):

(1a) $$\text{AG } r_A = 2.47 + 0.17 \, r_N \quad r^2 = 0.02$$
$$(0.21)$$

(1b) $$\text{LAC } r_A = 1.26 + 0.06 \, r_N \quad r^2 = 0.00$$
$$(0.40)$$

(2a) $$\text{AG } r_A = 0.64 + 0.44 \, r_P \quad r^2 = 0.51$$
$$(0.10)$$

(2b) $$\text{LAC } r_A = -1.71 + 0.74 \, r_P \quad r^2 = 0.75$$
$$(0.10)$$

According to this model, the growth of inputs does not explain the growth of total factor productivity in both the advanced group of countries and Latin America (equations [1a] and [1b] have zero r^2). In contrast, factor productivity can be explained by the growth of output, as shown in equations (2a) and (2b). In fact, in Latin America the growth of output explains 75 percent of the variance in factor productivity. Moreover, the fact that the intercept is negative implies that productivity growth can be negative unless output growth is substantially positive, that is, over 2.3 percent per year (i.e., 1.71/0.74).

Does the data on factor productivity and output growth in Portugal confirm this general finding, for both Latin America and in particular for Mexico? Table 2.8 shows the available estimates for output and factor productivity growth for Portugal, for which we have data concerning the agrarian sector for 1865–1951, and for the whole economy for 1910–47 (the years in the table are peak years). We may see that there is a positive correlation between changes in the rate of growth of output and TFP for agriculture. In fact, both declined in 1902–27 as compared to the previous period,

---

20. The countries in each group are the following. Latin America: Argentina, Brazil, Chile, Colombia, and Mexico; Advanced: Belgium, Canada, Netherlands, Sweden, United Kingdom, France, Italy, West Germany, Israel, Japan, and United States.

Table 2.8 Growth of output and productivity in Portugal

	Output	Labor productivity	Capital productivity	Total factor productivity
Agriculture				
1865–1902	1.41	0.74	0.63	0.72
1902–1927	0.35	0.13	0.86	0.20
1927–1951	2.36	0.97	1.44	1.59–1.63
All sectors				
1910–1934	2.17	1.00	1.25	0.72
1934–1947	2.09	1.31	3.89	−0.02

Source: Lains (2003a, 2003b).

whereas both increased again in the subsequent 1927–51 period. For the whole economy there is evidence for only two periods, and the correlation is again positive. Although the evidence is far from conclusive, as it is based on a small number of observations, we may conclude that also in Portugal total factor productivity growth was positively correlated to the growth of output, implying the existence of unused excess capacity in both the agrarian and the industrial sector. This seems to have been a major source of growth in Mexico and Portugal during the interwar period, which eventually counterbalanced the negative effects of receding international economic relations.

2.5 Conclusion

The conditions analyzed here for economic growth in the two peripheral countries during the interwar period are unique and will not be easily replicated. Mexico and Portugal had comparatively good economic performance under protection in that period because they could benefit from particularly favorable conditions. Those conditions stemmed from the fact that the financing of their external imbalances was facilitated by continuing exports and capital imports. The two economies also reacted positively to higher levels of protection from international competition because they had excess capacity that was put into use. That was particularly evident in the Mexican economy as a whole, as well as in the Portuguese agrarian sector. In addition to these positive factors, we also have to consider the fact that nineteenth century industrialization in the two countries had provided a sufficient economic background for higher growth. The accumulation of investment in manufacturing and agriculture, investments in social overhead capital, urbanization, and the (albeit limited) spread of education paved the way for the response to higher levels of protection after 1910.

One further element that makes the interwar period distinct from any other period when import substitution was implemented was the fact that protection was mainly the outcome of devaluation, and thus it was provided to all of the sectors in the economy. Instead, post-World War II protectionism in Mexico was differentiated and thus imposed changes in the structure of its economy (Portugal entered a period of higher free trade in the late 1950s, although levels of state intervention did not decline during that golden age). The question of why backward countries follow the path of inward-looking industrialization can thus be understood under the light of the Mexican and Portuguese experiences in the interwar period. Political factors and the intervention of interest groups certainly helped to build barriers to international transactions. Yet there were also gains to obtain from protection, which depend on specific favorable circumstances.

What lessons can we derive from the interwar period to the present times? Conditions for growth since the early 1980s are of course drastically different from those of the period analyzed in this paper, but there are nevertheless some lessons to be drawn. In periods of receding international transactions, import substitution can bring higher growth if it leads to structural change that benefits sectors with above-average factor productivity levels. For that to occur, labor and capital have to be available, which means that either there is some degree of excess capacity or that labor force and investment can expand at the prevailing wage and interest rate levels. For investment to expand it may also be crucial that capital imports continue. In periods of expanding international trade and capital flows, countries should be allowed to exploit export opportunities as well, which means that tariff protection is to be abandoned as a major framework for economic policy (if some relation is assumed to exist between domestic and foreign commercial policies). It may be the case, though, that the country's comparative advantages lay in industries with below-average productivity levels, and thus that economic policy has to step in to help in changing the pattern of comparative advantages. It is harder for governments to help promoting the development of new sources of comparative advantages. Two main options are at hand: either to intervene directly by selecting industries where comparative advantages are assumed to be possible, or to intervene indirectly by providing social overhead capital, such as transport infrastructures, education, or financial services. In any case, help from the outside may be crucial, and there the political and financial framework provided by the European Union to Portugal is probably more favorable than the one provided by NAFTA to Mexico.

References

Abramovitz, Moses. 1986. Catching-up, forging ahead and falling behind. *Journal of Economic History* 46 (2): 385–406.

Batista, D., C. Martins, M. Pinheiro, and J. Reis. 1997. New estimates for Portugal's GDP, 1910–1958. *Historia Económica* 7:1–128.
Bazant, Jan. 1995. *Historia de la deuda exterior de México, 1823–1946*. Mexico (D.F.): El Colegio de México.
Bortz, Jeffrey L., and Stephen Haber, eds. 2002. *The Mexican economy, 1870–1930: Essays on the economic history of institutions, revolution and growth*. Stanford, CA: Stanford University Press.
Bruton, Henry J. 1967. Productivity growth in Latin America. *American Economic Review* 57 (Dec.): 1099–1116.
Bulmer-Thomas, Victor. 1998. The Latin American economies, 1929–1939. In *Latin America: Economy and society since 1930*, ed. Leslie Bethell, 65–114. Cambridge: Cambridge University Press.
Campa, José M. 1990. Exchange rates and economic recovery in the 1930s: An extension to Latin America. *Journal of Economic History* 50 (3): 677–82.
Cárdenas, Enrique. 1997. *La industrialización Mexicana durante la Gran Depresión*. Mexico (D.F.): El Colegio de México.
———. 2004. *La hacienda pública y la política económica, 1929–1958*. Mexico (D.F.): El Colegio de México.
Clemens, M. A., and J. G. Williamson. 2004. Why did the tariff-growth correlation change after 1950? *Journal of Economic Growth* 9:5–46.
Coatsworth, John H. 1978. Obstacles to economic growth in nineteenth-century Mexico. *The American Historical Review* 83 (1): 80–100.
———. 1988. La historiografía económica de México. *Revista de Historia Económica* 6 (2): 277–91.
Coatsworth, John H., and Alan M. Taylor, eds. 1998. *Latin America and the world economy since 1800*. Cambridge, MA: David Rockefeller Center Series on Latin America Studies.
Córtes Conde, Roberto. 1992. Export-led growth in Latin America: 1870–1930. *Journal of Latin America Studies* 24 (Suppl.): 163–79.
Eichengreen, Barry, and Jeffrey Sachs. 1985. Exchange rates and economic recovery in the 1930s. *Journal of Economic History* 45 (4): 925–46.
Engermann, Stanley, and Kenneth Sokoloff. 1997. Factor endowments, institutions, and differential paths of growth among New World economies: A view from economic historians of the United States. In *How Latin America fell behind*, ed. Stephen Haber, 206–304. Stanford, CA: Stanford University Press.
Estadísticas Históricas de México. 2000. Instituto Nacional de Estadística, Geografia e Informática. Aguascalientes (Ags), on CD-ROM.
Ffrench-Davis, R., O. Muñoz, and J. G. Palma. 1998. The Latin American economies, 1950–1990. In *Latin America: Economy and society since 1930*, ed. L. Bethell, 149–237. Cambridge: Cambridge University Press.
Gerschenkron, Alexander. 1962. *Economic backwardness in historical perspective*. Cambridge, MA: Harvard University Press.
Haber, Stephen H. 1989. *Industry and underdevelopment: The industrialization of Mexico, 1890–1940*. Stanford, CA: Stanford University Press.
———. 1990. La economía mexicana, 1830–1940: Obstáculos a la industrialización (I) and (II). *Revista de Historia Económica* 8 (1 and 2): 81–93 and 335–62.
———, ed. 1997. *How Latin America fell behind: Essays on the economic history of Brazil and Mexico, 1800–1914*. Stanford, CA: Stanford University Press.
Haber, Stephen H., and Armando Razo. 1998. Political instability and economic performance: Evidence from revolutionary Mexico. *World Politics* 51 (1): 99–143.

Hofman, André. 2000. *The economic development of Latin America in the twentieth century.* Northampton: Edward Elgar.
Hofman, André, and Nanno Mulder. 1998. The comparative productivity performance of Brazil and Mexico, 1950–94. In *Latin America and the world economy since 1800,* ed. John H. Coatsworth and Alan M. Taylor, 85–109. Cambridge, MA: David Rockefeller Center Series on Latin America Studies.
Keesing, Donald B. 1969. Structural change early in development: Mexico's changing industrial and occupational structure from 1895 to 1950. *The Journal of Economic History* 29 (4): 716–38.
Lains, Pedro. 2003a. Catching-up to the European core: Portuguese economic growth, 1910–1990. *Explorations in Economic History* 40:369–86.
———. 2003b. New wine in old bottles: Output and productivity trends in Portuguese agriculture, 1850–1950. *European Review of Economic History* 7 (1): 43–72.
———. 2003c. *Os progressos do atraso: Uma nova história económica de Portugal, 1842–1992.* Lisbon, Portugal: Imprensa de Ciências Sociais.
———. 2006. Growth in a protected environment: Portugal, 1850–1950. *Research in Economic History* 24: 121–63.
Lains, Pedro, and Alvaro Ferreira da Silva, eds. 2005. *História económica de Portugal, 1700–2000.* Lisbon, Portugal: Imprensa de Ciências Sociais.
Maddison, Angus. 1995. *Monitoring the world economy, 1820–1992.* Paris: OECD.
———. 2001. *The world economy: A millennial perspective.* Paris: OECD.
Maurer, Noel. 1999. Progress without order: Mexican economic history in the 1990s. *Revista de Historia Económica* 17 (special issue): 13–36.
Mitchell, B. R. 1993. *Internacional historical statistics: The Americas, 1750–1988.* London: Macmillan.
Navarrete, Alfredo, Jr. 1959. El crecimiento económico de México: Perspectivas y problemas. *Journal of Inter-American Studies* 1 (4): 389–404.
Razo, Armando, and Stephen H. Haber. 1998. The rate of growth of productivity in Mexico, 1850–1933: Evidence from the cotton textile industry. *Journal of Latin America Studies* 30 (3): 481–517.
Sandos, James A., and Harry E. Cross. 1983. National development and international labour migration: Mexico, 1940–1965. *Journal of Contemporary History* 18 (1): 43–60.

3
Inequality and the Evolution of Institutions of Taxation
Evidence from the Economic History of the Americas

Kenneth L. Sokoloff and Eric M. Zolt

3.1 Introduction

The importance of institutions in the processes of economic growth and development is now well recognized.[1] Despite the consensus about their significance, our understanding of where institutions come from and how institutions that do not work well persist over time remains limited. How institutions matter depends, in part, on whether they are exogenous or endogenous and on the factors and processes that shape or determine them. Unfortunately, the study of how institutions evolve is not straightforward. Not only does institutional change take place gradually over long periods of time, but the likelihood of different causal mechanisms being involved further complicates analysis. Despite these formidable challenges, in recent years researchers have made significant contributions to our knowledge of how institutions as fundamental as universal adult suffrage, prop-

---

Kenneth L. Sokoloff is a professor of economics at the University of California, Los Angeles, and a research associate of the National Bureau of Economic Research. Eric M. Zolt is a professor of law at the University of California, Los Angeles.

We would like to express our appreciation to Luis Zegarra, Jason Breen, and Ana Maria Loboguerrero for outstanding research assistance. We have also benefited from discussions with Alberto Alesina, Richard Bird, Roberto Cortes-Conde, William Easterly, Sebastian Edwards, Stanley Engerman, Jeff Frieden, Claudia Goldin, Stephen Haber, Karla Hoff, Daniel Kaufmann, Zorina Khan, Naomi Lamoreaux, Peter Lindert, Jean-Laurent Rosenthal, Kirk Stark, William Summerhill, John Wallis, as well as from participants in seminars or other presentations we gave at Harvard, Toronto, Oxford, the National Bureau of Economic Research, Royal Holloway, University of London, the University of Texas, at the All-UC Group in Economic History, and of course at the conference the editors of this volume organized in Mexico City. We gratefully acknowledge the financial support we have received for this research from All Souls College at the University of Oxford, the Russell Sage Foundation, and the Academic Senate at the University of California, Los Angeles.

1. For a classic statement of this view, see North (1981).

erty rights in intellectual capital, and public schools evolved over time and place.[2]

Tax systems are among the oldest and most fundamental of institutions. Taxes are necessary to raise revenue for governments to fund their operations and to finance investments in public goods and other sorts of public services conducive to general welfare and economic growth. How governments raise revenue can have profound effects on society. First, the technical efficiency of the tax system is important. Taxes alter the decisions of private agents, as taxpayers strive to reduce their tax liabilities.[3] Taxes also impose enforcement costs on governments and compliance costs on taxpayers. The structure of taxes, as well as of other forms of government regulation, may also influence the organization of economic activities, such as whether firms operate in the formal or informal sector or whether firms enter into formal employment arrangements with workers.

Second, the tax system helps determine how much of the costs of publicly provided goods and services are borne by different segments of the population. The incidence of taxes affects both the distribution of disposable income across the population as well as the constellation of political support for various public projects. Individuals are more willing to support government programs if they expect that the benefits they, or their peer groups, would realize from the higher level of expenditures will roughly match or exceed the corresponding increase in their tax liabilities.[4]

Third, although the lines of causation are not always clear, how societies choose to raise tax revenue is related to the relative degrees of authority of local, state, and national governments. Control over public expenditures generally follows the power to tax. As the political and administrative feasibility of levying certain taxes may be sensitive to economy-specific circumstances, those circumstances may also influence the structure of government as well as the extent and direction of government activities. For example, to the extent that local governments are more dependent on taxes on property than other levels of government are, societies that lack the public authority or administrative capacity to effectively implement such

---

2. See, e.g., Engerman and Sokoloff (1997, 2002, 2005). Also see Acemoglu and Robinson (2000), and Khan and Sokoloff (2001).

3. Such adjustments can often lead economies to operate below their productive capacity, as taxpayers allocate their resources to those activities that yield the highest net returns after taxes, as opposed to those that would make the most productive use of resources.

4. Recent studies of quite distinct settings have yielded remarkably consistent findings regarding less government provision of public services in ethnically or otherwise heterogeneous polities. The mechanisms that account for this pattern remain unclear, but may have to do with more diverse populations being hampered by higher costs of reaching a consensus (resolving the collective action problem) or with there being greater economic and political inequality across social groups in such contexts. For examples of this literature, see Alesina, Baqir, and Easterly (1999); and Chaudhary (2006). For discussion of the mechanisms by which the option of the rich to substitute private goods for public goods can inhibit reform or provision of government services, see Hirschman (1970).

taxes might be expected to have relatively small local governments and low levels of public investments and expenditure programs (e.g., schools or local roads) whose benefits accrue primarily to local residents.

Striking contrasts exist today between the tax systems of developed and developing countries.[5] Tax systems in developed countries derive most of their revenue from individual income taxes, corporate income taxes, and broad-based consumption taxes. Such tax systems are commonly regarded as more progressive in incidence than those of developing countries—whose tax revenues come largely from taxes on consumption, in the form of value-added or turnover taxes, excise taxes, and taxes on foreign trade. As a percentage of gross domestic product, aggregate tax revenues in developing countries are only about half the tax revenues of developed countries. Developing countries are also more likely to impose and collect taxes at the national level rather than extend substantial taxing authority to state and local governments.

Why tax systems vary is a difficult question. Scholars have noted that both the level of taxation and the relative use of different tax instruments tend to be systematically related across economies to factors such as per capita income, the share of wages as a percentage of national income, the share of national income generated by large establishments, the share of agriculture in total production, and the level of imports and exports.[6] Many observers have suggested that these patterns arise primarily from technical or resource issues in the design of tax structures. Proponents of this view highlight how, for example, it is less feasible to administer an individual income tax in countries with a large informal sector than it would be in countries where most individuals have stable full-time employment relationships with large firms.[7] They contend that the major reason for the striking differences between the tax systems of the developed and less-developed nations is that rich countries have more choices in deciding the level of taxation and the tax mix (the relative use of different tax instruments).[8] Although not inconsistent with this common wisdom, other scholars have emphasized how political factors can influence the design and administration of tax systems.[9] Groups with great influence are not infrequently able to tilt or shape the structures of taxation, if not of public finance more generally, in their favor.

We turn to history to gain a better perspective on how and why tax systems vary. Our focus is on the societies of the Americas over the nineteenth and twentieth centuries. Our interest in the experiences in North and Latin

5. See Tanzi (1987); and Burgess and Stern (1993).
6. See, e.g., Tait, Gratz, and Eichengreen (1979).
7. See Goode (1984); and Musgrave and Musgrave (1984, 790–96).
8. See Tanzi and Zee (2000).
9. For a pioneering discussion of the influence of politics on the design of tax systems in Central America, see Best (1976). More generally, see Reese (1980).

America has two principal sources. First, despite the region having the most extreme inequality in the world, the tax structures of Latin America are generally recognized as among the most regressive, even by developing country standards.[10] Moreover, Latin American countries typically (though there are exceptions) have low levels of taxation and collect relatively modest tax revenues at the provincial or local level. Improving our knowledge of when and how these rather distinctive patterns in taxation and public finance emerged may help us to better understand both the long-term development of the region as well as the processes of institutional formation and change more generally.

Second, as has come to be appreciated by social scientists, the colonization and development of the Americas constitute a natural experiment of sorts that students of economic and social development can exploit. Beginning more than 500 years ago, a small number of European countries established colonies in diverse environments across the hemisphere. The different circumstances meant that largely exogenous differences existed across these societies, not only in national heritage, but also in the extent of inequality. Relatively high per capita incomes (by the standards of the time) prevailed throughout the Americas, at least through the late eighteenth century, and many of these colonies had gained their independence from their European overlords by the early nineteenth century. The record of what sorts of institutions these new, prosperous, and nominally democratic nations established, and how they evolved over time, provides scholars with a useful laboratory to study the sources of systematic patterns in the evolution of tax systems.

When tax scholars explore the relationship between inequality and taxation, they tend to focus on how tax systems may alter the after-tax distribution of income or wealth, either directly through government takings or transfers, or indirectly through their influence on the decisions of individuals (or households) about labor supply, savings, or investments.[11] Here we take a different approach, by examining whether exogenous differences in the extent of inequality might have influenced the design and implementation of tax systems. We highlight how even when the income levels across the societies of the Americas were relatively similar, the tax structures in the United States and Canada looked very different from those in Latin America. Moreover, we raise the question of whether these differences in taxes, and in related spending patterns, might have played a role in accounting for quite divergent paths of long-run development. Our thesis that inequality plays an important independent role in influencing the

---

10. For estimates of income inequality in Latin America and extensive treatment of these issues, see De Ferranti et al. (2004). Also see the discussion of the regressivity of tax systems in Latin America, Bird (2003).

11. For example, see Slemrod and Bakija (2001).

structure of taxation is also supported by comparisons across regions of the United States.

Previous studies have shown how initial and rather extreme differences in the extent of inequality seem to have contributed to systematic differences in the ways that strategic economic institutions evolved across the Americas. The earlier work explored how a number of mediating mechanisms (paths of institutional development) through which high initial inequality may have led to poor economic outcomes through its impact on the evolution of fundamental policies influencing access to suffrage, schooling, and land, but did not look at tax policy (or at the level and type of government expenditures). The purpose of this paper is to examine whether the extreme differences in inequality that were present across the economies of the Americas soon after colonization also affected the ways tax institutions evolved. We argue that they did, and proceed as follows. Part two sets forth a brief history of the emergence of extreme differences in inequality across the Americas not long after the Europeans began to colonize the hemisphere. Part three then examines the tax systems in Latin America and North America in the nineteenth century. Part four discusses how these tax structures evolved over the twentieth century. In part five we offer some tentative conclusions about what the legacy of extreme inequality in Latin America meant for the long-run pattern of tax design and expenditure policy in that region.

Several salient patterns emerge. The United States and Canada (like Britain, France, Germany, and even Spain) were much more inclined to tax wealth and income during their early stages of growth, and into the twentieth century, than were their neighbors to the south.[12] Although the United States and Canadian federal governments were similar to those of their counterparts in Latin America in relying primarily on the taxation of foreign trade (overwhelmingly tariffs) and excise taxes, the greater success or inclination of state (provincial) and local governments in North America to tax wealth (primarily in the form of property or estate taxes) and income (primarily in the form of business taxes), as well as the much larger relative sizes of these subnational governments in North America, accounted for a radical divergence in the overall structure of taxation. Tapping these progressive (at least as conventionally understood) sources of government revenue, state and local governments in the United States and Canada, even before independence, began directing substantial resources toward public schools, improvements in infrastructure involving transportation and health, and other social programs. In contrast, the societies of Latin America, which had come to be characterized soon after initial

---

12. For example, land and other assessed taxes generally accounted for between 15 and 40 percent of revenue to the British government over the period 1690 to 1790. See Brewer (1990, 98).

settlement by rather extreme inequality in wealth, human capital, and political influence, tended to adopt tax structures that were significantly less progressive in incidence and manifested greater reluctance or inability to impose local taxes to fund local public investments and services. These patterns have persisted well into the twentieth century—indeed, up to the present day.

3.2 Differences in Inequality across the Americas

Our study builds on recent scholarship that has highlighted how radical differences in the extent of inequality across New World societies were present early on in the histories of the colonies established by the Europeans.[13] These differences, it is argued, were due primarily to factor endowments (or initial conditions more generally). Common to nearly all of the colonies was a high marginal product of labor, as evidenced by the historically unprecedented numbers of migrants who traversed the Atlantic from Europe and Africa despite high costs of transportation, as well as by the roughly similar levels of per capita income that prevailed until well into the eighteenth century (or more than two centuries after the colonies began to be established).

Scholars seem increasingly to accept that whereas the great majority of colonies in the Americas came to be characterized early on by substantial inequality, the colonies that came to make up the United States and Canada were quite unusual in that their factor endowments predisposed them toward paths of development with relative equality and population homogeneity. In explaining the logic and empirical basis for this theory, it is convenient to distinguish between three types of New World colonies. A first category encompasses those colonies with climates and soils that were well suited for the production of sugar and other highly valued crops characterized by extensive scale economies associated with the use of slaves. Most of these sugar colonies, including Barbados, Cuba, and Saint Domingue (known now as Haiti), were in the West Indies, but some (mainly Brazil) were located in South America. They soon specialized in the production of such crops, and their economies came to be dominated by large slave plantations and their populations by slaves of African descent. The overwhelming fraction of the populations that came to be black and slave in such colonies, as well as the greater efficiency of the very large plantations, made their distributions of wealth and human capital extremely unequal.[14]

The second category of New World colonies comprises the Spanish

---

13. See Engerman and Sokoloff (1997, 2002).

14. Even among the free population, such economies exhibited greater inequality than those on the North American mainland. For a detailed examination of the distribution of wealth among free household heads on a sugar island, see Dunn (1972).

colonies, such as Mexico and Peru, that were characterized both by a substantial native population that survived contact with the European colonizers and by the distribution among a privileged few of claims to often enormous blocs of land, mineral resources, and native labor. The resulting large-scale estates and mines, established early in the histories of these colonies, were to some degree based on preconquest social organizations in which Indian elites extracted tribute from the general population, and the arrangements endured even when the principal production activities were lacking in economies of scale. Although small-scale production was typical of grain agriculture during this era, the essentially nontradable property rights to tribute (in the form of labor and other resources) from rather sedentary groups of natives gave large landholders the means and the motive to operate at a large scale. For different reasons, therefore, this category of colonies was rather like the first in generating very unequal distributions of wealth. The elites relied on the labor of Native Americans instead of slaves, but like the slave owners, they were racially distinct from the bulk of the population and they enjoyed higher levels of human capital and legal standing.[15]

To almost the same degree as in the colonial sugar economies, the economic structures that evolved in this second group of colonies were greatly influenced by the factor endowments, viewed in broad terms. The fabulously valuable mineral resources and the abundance of low human-capital labor certainly contributed to the extremely unequal distributions of wealth and income that generally came to prevail in these economies. Moreover, without the abundant supply of native labor, the generous awards of property and tribute to the earliest settlers would not have been worth so much (if even possible), and it is highly unlikely that Spain would have introduced the tight restrictions on European migration to its colonies that it did. The early settlers in Spanish America had endorsed, and won, formidable requirements for obtaining permission to go to the New World—a policy that surely helped to preserve the political and economic advantages they enjoyed and kept the share of the population that was of European descent low.

The final category of New World colonies is typified by those on the northern part of the North American mainland, chiefly those that became the northern United States, but also Canada. These economies were not endowed either with substantial native populations able to provide labor or with a climate and soils that gave them a comparative advantage in the pro-

---

15. It is not clear whether the existence of scale economies, such as slavery, supported the competitive success or persistence of the largest units of production in this second class of colonial economies. Rather, large-scale enterprises may have been sustained by the natives' inability or disinclination to evade their obligations to the estate-owning families. For an excellent and comprehensive overview of the *encomienda* and the evolution of large-scale estates, see Lockhart and Schwartz (1983).

duction of crops characterized by major economies in using slave labor. Their growth and development were therefore based on populations of European descent who had similar levels of human capital. Owing to the abundant land and low capital requirements, the great majority of adult men were able to operate as independent proprietors. Efforts to implant a European-style organization of agriculture based on concentrated ownership of land, with labor provided by tenant farmers or indentured servants, invariably failed in such environments. Conditions were somewhat different in the southern colonies, where crops such as tobacco and rice exhibited limited scale economies. Even so, the size of the slave plantations and the share of the population composed of slaves were both quite modest by the standards of Brazil or the sugar islands.[16]

Overall, there seems to be strong evidence that various features of the factor endowments of the three categories of New World economies, including soils, climates, and the size or density of the native population, predisposed them toward paths of development associated with different degrees of inequality in wealth, human capital, and political power. Although these conditions might reasonably be treated as exogenous at the beginning of European colonization, it is clear that such an assumption becomes increasingly tenuous as one moves later in time after settlement. Particularly given that both Latin America and many of the economies of the first category, such as Haiti, Brazil, and Jamaica, are still among the most unequal in the world, however, the initial conditions seem to have had long-lingering effects. Not only were certain fundamental characteristics of New World economies difficult to change, but government policies and other institutions tended generally to reproduce them. Specifically, in those societies that began with extreme inequality, the elites may have been better able to shape the evolution of rules, laws, and other institutions to advantage themselves—contributing to persistence over time in the extent of inequality.

The history of the evolution of suffrage institutions provides a powerful demonstration of how there were indeed systematic patterns across societies in the degree to which elites established a legal framework that ensured them a disproportionate share of political power.[17] Summary information about differences in how the right to vote was restricted across New World societies in the late nineteenth and early twentieth centuries is reported in table 3.1. The estimates reveal that while it was common in all countries to reserve the right to vote to adult males until the twentieth century, the United States and Canada were the clear leaders in doing away with

16. See Galenson (1995); and Greene (1988).
17. Our discussion of the evolution of suffrage institutions draws from Engerman and Sokoloff (2005). It is perhaps worth emphasizing that most of the countries featured here were independent of their colonial masters and were nominal democracies by the middle of the nineteenth century.

Table 3.1   Laws concerning the franchise and voting participation in selected countries, 1840 to 1940

Period and country	Year	Lack of secrecy in balloting	Wealth requirement	Literacy requirement	Percent of the population voting
1840–1980					
Chile	1869	No	Yes	Yes	1.6
Costa Rica	1890	Yes	Yes	Yes	
Ecuador	1856	Yes	Yes	Yes	0.1
Mexico	1840	Yes	Yes	Yes	
Peru	1875	Yes	Yes	Yes	
Uruguay	1880	Yes	Yes	Yes	
Venezuela	1880	Yes	Yes	Yes	
Canada	1878	No	Yes	No	12.9
United States	1850	No	No	No	12.9
1881–1920					
Argentina	1916	No	No	No	9.0
Brazil	1914	Yes	Yes	Yes	2.4
Chile	1920	No	No	Yes	4.4
Colombia	1918	No	No	No	6.9
Costa Rica	1919	Yes	No	No	10.6
Ecuador	1894	No	No	Yes	3.3
Mexico	1920	No	No	No	8.6
Peru	1920	Yes	Yes	Yes	
Uruguay	1920	No	No	No	13.8
Venezuela	1920	Yes	Yes	Yes	
Canada	1917	No	No	No	20.5
United States	1920	No	No	Yes	25.1
1921–1940					
Argentina	1937	No	No	No	15.0
Brazil	1930	Yes	Yes	Yes	5.7
Colombia	1936	No	No	No	5.9
Chile	1938	No	No	Yes	9.4
Costa Rica	1940	No	No	No	17.6
Ecuador	1940	No	No	Yes	3.3
Mexico	1940	No	No	No	11.8
Peru	1940	No	No	Yes	
Uruguay	1940	No	No	No	19.7
Venezuela	1940	No	Yes	Yes	
Canada	1940	No	No	No	41.1
United States	1940	No	No	Yes	37.8

Sources: Engerman and Sokoloff (2002, 2005).

Notes: The information on restrictions refers to national laws. In Colombia, the 1863 Constitution empowered provincial state governments to regulate electoral affairs. Afterward, elections became restricted (in terms of the franchise for adult males) and indirect in some states. It was not until 1948 that a national law established universal adult male suffrage throughout the country. This pattern was followed in other Latin American countries, as it was in the United States and Canada to a lesser extent. Two states, Connecticut and Massachusetts, introduced literacy requirements during the 1850s. Sixteen states—seven southern and nine northern—introduced literacy requirements between 1889 and 1926.

restrictions based on wealth and literacy, and much higher percentages of the populations voted in these countries than anywhere else in the Americas. Although there was important variation in these requirements within Latin America, it is clear that there was much greater political equality in the United States and Canada during the nineteenth century than there was elsewhere in the hemisphere. Indeed, as there were other channels through which elites could influence political outcomes, the rules specifying who could vote likely understates the extent to which elites were able to wield disproportionate power in the formulation and implementation of government policies. Not only did the United States and Canada attain the secret ballot and extend the franchise to even the poor and illiterate much earlier (restrictions that were reintroduced in the United States at the expense of blacks in the 1890s), but the evolution of the proportion of the population that voted was at least a half-century ahead of even the most progressive countries of South America (namely, Uruguay, Argentina, and Costa Rica, whose initial factor endowments and extent of inequality were most like those of the United States and Canada). It is remarkable that as late as 1900, none of the countries in Latin America had the secret ballot or more than a miniscule fraction of the population casting votes.

Although many factors may have contributed to the comparatively very low levels of voting participation in Latin America, the wealth and literacy (which were increasingly introduced over the course of the nineteenth century and maintained in much of South America well into the twentieth century) requirements were obviously (given the literacy rates reported subsequently) serious constraints. The contrast between the United States and Canada, on the one hand, and the Latin American countries, on the other, was not so evident at the outset, and not due to differences in ideology related to national heritage. Despite the sentiments popularly attributed to the Founding Fathers, voting in the United States was largely a privilege reserved for white men with significant amounts of property until early in the nineteenth century. Even as late as 1815, only four states had adopted universal white male suffrage. The first-movers in the movement to broadening access to suffrage were the states on the frontier, those entering the Union after the original thirteen, who virtually all chose in their very first state constitutions to extend voting rights to white men (with explicit racial restrictions generally introduced in the same constitutions that did away with economic requirements). Older states were then spurred, through intense political debates and struggles, to revise their laws.

The leadership of the relatively more egalitarian frontier states in extending the franchise not coincidentally paralleled liberal policies toward public schools, access to land, and other issues of interest to potential migrants.[18] Labor scarcity exerted a direct influence on the initial level of in-

---

18. See the more detailed discussion in Engerman and Sokoloff (2005).

equality across New World colonies, because of its impact on the returns to labor, but it also had indirect effects. It is to us significant that the leaders in extending suffrage (and establishing other institutions providing broad access to opportunity), such as the new states to the United States, Argentina, and Uruguay, did so during periods in which they were striving to attract migrants and when such policies were thought to be attractive to those contemplating relocation. When elites—such as landowners or other asset holders—desire common men to locate in the polity, they thus may freely choose, finding it in their own private interests, to extend access to privileges and opportunities; indeed, a polity (or one set of elites) may find itself competing with another to attract the labor or whatever else is desired.

Differences in the distribution of political power seem to have fed back on the distribution of access to economic opportunities and in investment in public goods in ways that had fundamental implications for the persistence of inequality and long-run paths of institutional and economic development more generally. Schooling institutions are an excellent example. Although most New World societies were so prosperous by the early nineteenth century that they clearly had the material resources to support the establishment of a widespread network of primary schools, only a few made such investments on a scale sufficient to serve the general population before the twentieth century. The exceptional societies, in terms of leadership in investing in institutions of primary education, were the United States and Canada. Virtually from the time of settlement, these North Americans began to develop institutions that would provide local children with a basic education, including the ability to read and write. It was common for schools to be organized and funded at the village or town level, especially in New England. The United States is generally credited with having the most literate population in the world by the early nineteenth century, but the common school movement, which got under way in the 1820s (following closely after the movement to extend the franchise), put the country on an accelerated path of investment in educational institutions that served a broad range of the population. Between 1825 and 1850, nearly every northern state that had not already done so enacted a law strongly encouraging or requiring localities to establish free schools open to all children and supported by general taxes.[19] Although the movement made slower progress in the South, schooling had spread sufficiently by the mid-nineteenth century that over 40 percent of the school-age population was enrolled, and nearly 90 percent of white adults were literate (see table 3.2). Canada soon followed the United States in establishing tax-supported schools with universal ac-

---

19. See the discussion in Cubberley (1920), as well as in Engerman, Mariscal, and Sokoloff (2002).

Table 3.2   Literacy rates in selected countries of the Americas, 1860–1920

Country	Year	Age	Rate (%)
Argentina	1869	6 and above	23.8
	1900	10 and above	52.0
Bolivia	1900	10 and above	17.0
Brazil	1872	7 and above	15.8
	1900	7 and above	25.6
	1920	10 and above	30
Chile	1865	7 and above	18
	1900	10 and above	43
Colombia	1918	15 and above	32
Costa Rica	1892	7 and above	23.6
	1925	10 and above	64
Guatemala	1893	7 and above	11.3
	1925	10 and above	1.5
Mexico	1900	10 and above	22.2
Paraguay	1886	10 and above	19.3
	1900	10 and above	30
Peru	1925	7 and above	38
Uruguay	1900	10 and above	54
	1925	10 and above	70
Venezuela	1925	All	34
Canada	1861	All	82.5
United States	1870	10 and above	80 (88.5, 21.1)
	1910	10 and above	92.3 (95.0, 69.5)

Source: Engerman and Sokoloff (2002).

Note: In the United States, the figures for whites and nonwhites, respectively, are reported within parentheses.

cess, and its literacy rates were nearly as high by the second half of the nineteenth century.[20]

The rest of the hemisphere trailed far behind the United States and Canada in primary schooling and in (the closely related) attainment of literacy. Despite great wealth, the British colonies elsewhere in the hemisphere (such as Guyana and Jamaica) lagged badly in providing basic schooling to broad segments of the population.[21] Similarly, even the most progressive Latin American countries, such as Argentina and Uruguay, were more than seventy-five years behind. Although Argentina had one of the highest per capita incomes in the world, the literacy rate of native-

---

20. See the discussion in Phillips (1957).
21. Indeed, no significant steps at all were taken in this direction until the 1870s, when the British Colonial Office, perhaps spurred by several important expansions of public provision of elementary education in Great Britain itself (such as the 1870 Education Act) began promoting schooling in the colonies.

born Argentines was less than that of nonwhites in the United States at 1900. These societies began to boost their investments in public schooling at roughly the same time that they intensified their efforts to attract migrants from Europe. While this association might be interpreted as providing for the socialization of foreign immigrants, it is also consistent with the idea that elites were inclined to extend access to opportunities as part of an effort to attract increasingly scarce labor from Europe, for which they were directly or indirectly competing. The latter perspective is supported by the observation that major investments in public schooling did not generally occur in any Latin American country until the national governments provided the funds. In stark contrast to the pattern in North America, local and state governments in Latin America proved reluctant to take on this responsibility on their own. Nowhere in this latter region were high levels of literacy achieved until well into the twentieth century.

What accounts for these patterns? Although differences in resources, or per capita income, must certainly play a role in their explanation, it seems likely that the greater inequality that prevailed in Latin America and in the British colonies in the West Indies likely exacerbated the collective-action problems associated with the establishment and funding of universal public schools, because the distribution of the benefits to establishing a broad system of public schools would have been quite different from the incidence of taxes that would have been necessary to finance them. Where the wealthy enjoyed disproportionate political power, they were able to procure schooling services for their own children and to resist being taxed to underwrite or subsidize services to others. Although the children of the elite may have been well schooled in such polities, few other children were so fortunate.

Land policy is yet another important example of how differences in the extent of political and economic inequality across societies may have influenced the evolution of strategic institutions. Virtually all the societies in the Americas had ample supplies of public lands well into the nineteenth century and beyond. Since the respective governments were regarded as the owners or custodians of this resource, they could directly affect the distribution of wealth, as well as the pace of settlement for effective production, by implementing policies to control the availability of land, set prices, establish minimum or maximum acreages, provide credit for such purposes, and design tax systems. The decisions about how to best employ these public resources were everywhere widely recognized as having an important bearing on how a society would develop, and the subject of protracted political debates and struggles.

As we would expect of a country with relative equality and labor scarcity, land policies in the United States never posed major obstacles to acquiring land.[22] The Homestead Act of 1862, which essentially made land

---

22. For a comprehensive overview of U.S. land policy, see Gates (1968). For discussions of Canadian land policy, see Solberg (1987), and Adelman (1994).

free in plots suitable for family farms to all those who settled and worked the land for a specified period, was perhaps the culmination of this institutional orientation. Canada pursued similar policies: the Dominion Lands Act of 1872 closely resembled the Homestead Act in both spirit and substance. Argentina, however, opted for a very different approach. Despite the support of some leaders (such as President Sarmiento) for land policies modeled on the United States and Canadian practices, Argentina chose instead to dispose of public lands by making grants of large blocs of land, at first to individuals and later to private development companies. Given that private agents with control of vast land holdings, especially in this setting, would be expected to set higher prices for land than public authorities focused on broad access, it is perhaps not surprising that the Argentine programs were much less successful at getting land to smallholders than those in the United States and Canada.[23]

Argentina, Canada, and the United States all had an extraordinary abundance of public lands to transfer to private hands, but the issues and circumstances facing policymakers in societies such as Mexico, with large indigenous populations, were very different. Good land was relatively scarce. Here the lands in question had long been worked by communities of Native Americans, but without individual private property rights. Mexico was not unique in pursuing policies, especially in the final decades of the nineteenth and the first decade of the twentieth century, that had the effect of conferring ownership of much of this land in large tracts on non-Native American landholders.[24] The 1856 Ley Lerdo and the 1857 Constitution had set down methods of privatizing these public lands in a manner that could originally have been intended to help Native American farmers enter a national land market and commercial economy. Under the regime of Porfirio Díaz, however, these laws became the basis for a series of new statutes and policies that effected a massive transfer of such lands (over 10.7 percent of the national

---

23. For detailed discussions of the evolution of policies in Argentina, and comparisons with what happened in Canada, see Solberg (1987) and Adelman (1994). The latter makes a number of interesting arguments for why the outcome in Argentina was rather different from that of Canada (as well as in the United States). First, the elites of Buenos Aires, whose interests favored keeping scarce labor in the province, if not the capital city, were much more effective at weakening or blocking programs than were their urban counterparts in North America. Even those policies nominally intended to broaden access tended to involve large grants to land developers (with the logic that allocative efficiency could best be achieved through exchanges between private agents) or transfers to occupants who were already using the land (including those who were grazing livestock). They thus generally conveyed public lands to private owners in much larger and concentrated holdings than did the policies of the United States and Canada. Second, the processes by which large landholdings might have broken up in the absence of scale economies may have operated very slowly in Argentina: once the land was in private hands, the potential value of land in grazing may have set too high a floor on land prices for immigrants and other ordinary, would-be farmers to manage, especially given the underdevelopment of mortgage and financial institutions more generally. Moreover, livestock production increased dramatically during the late nineteenth century, and scale economies in the raising of livestock may have helped maintain the large estates.

24. For further discussion of Mexico, see McBride (1923), Tannenbaum (1929), and Holden (1994).

territory) between 1878 and 1908 to large holders such as survey and land development companies, either in the form of outright grants for services rendered by the companies or for prices set by decree.

In table 3.3, we present estimates for these four countries of the fractions of household heads, or a near equivalent, that owned land in agricultural areas in the late nineteenth and early twentieth centuries. The figures indi-

Table 3.3   Landholding in rural regions of Mexico, the United States, Canada, and Argentina, c. 1900

Country, year, and region	Proportion of household heads who own land[a]
Mexico, 1910	
North Pacific	5.6
North	3.4
Central	2.0
Gulf	2.1
South Pacific	1.5
Total rural Mexico	2.4
United States, 1900	
North Atlantic	79.2
South Atlantic	55.8
North Central	72.1
South Central	51.4
Western	83.4
Total United States	74.5
Canada, 1901	
British Columbia	87.1
Alberta	95.8
Saskatchewan	96.2
Manitoba	88.9
Ontario	80.2
Quebec	90.1
Maritime[b]	95.0
Total Canada	87.1
Argentina, 1895	
Chaco	27.8
Formosa	18.5
Missiones	26.7
La Pampa	9.7
Neuquén	12.3
Río Negro	15.4
Chubut	35.2
Santa Cruz	20.2

Source: Engerman and Sokoloff (2002).

[a] Landownership is defined as follows: in Mexico, household heads who own land; in the United States, farms that are owner operated; in Canada, total occupiers of farmlands who are owners; and in Argentina, the ratio of landowners to the number of males between the ages of 18 and 50.

[b] The Maritime region includes Nova Scotia, New Brunswick, and Prince Edward Island.

cate enormous differences across the countries in the prevalence of land ownership among adult males in rural areas. On the eve of the Mexican Revolution, the figures from the 1910 census suggest that only 2.4 percent of household heads in rural Mexico owned land. The number is astoundingly low. The dramatic land policy measures in Mexico at the end of the nineteenth century may have succeeded in privatizing most of the public lands, but they left the vast majority of the rural population without any land ownership at all. The evidence obviously conforms well with the idea that in societies that began with extreme inequality, such as Mexico, institutions evolved so as to greatly advantage the elites.

In contrast, the proportion of adult males that owned land in rural areas was quite high in the United States, at just below 75 percent in 1900. Although the prevalence of land ownership was markedly lower in the South, where blacks were disproportionately concentrated, the overall picture is one of rather broad access to this fundamental type of economic resource. Canada had an even better record, with nearly 90 percent of household heads owning the agricultural lands they occupied in 1901. The estimates of landholding in these two countries support the notion that land policies made a difference, especially when compared to those for frontier areas in Argentina.[25] Nevertheless, all of these countries were far more effective than Mexico in making land ownership available to the general population. This evidence on how land policies evolved provides yet another support to our view that the initial extent of inequality influenced the way in which strategic institutions evolved across the societies of the Americas.

3.3 Tax Systems in Latin America and North America in the Nineteenth Century

The colonial tax structures established by the Europeans in the Americas were generally alike in obtaining much of their revenue from trade or closely related activities. Great Britain levied relatively light tax burdens on the residents of its colonies. Revenues came from regulation of trade and from the taxes it imposed on the importation into Britain of New World-produced commodities such as sugar and tobacco. Given that the demand for these goods was likely highly inelastic, British consumers likely bore most of the burden of these duties. When Britain attempted to increase tax revenues to offset more of the costs of defending its colonies on the North American mainland through excise taxes, import duties, and higher fees, the change in policy was fiercely and famously resisted.[26]

---

25. We are not able at this time to provide estimates of land ownership rates in all provinces of Argentina, but would expect higher rates in the frontier regions we report than in the country at large.

26. See Brewer (1990). For excellent discussions of how Britain and Spain collected revenue from its colonies, and of how local authorities in their colonies raised revenue, see Gipson (1936), Perkins (1980, 1994), and Elliott (2006).

Spain and Portugal, in contrast, were much more intent on, and effective at, raising revenue directly from the colonies. This was at least partly attributable to the enormous wealth their colonies possessed. The Spanish Crown levied a vast range of taxes, with revenue derived from impositions on a variety of activities, commodities, commercial and administrative transactions, and from tribute exacted from Native Americans varying across colonies and districts with the composition of the economy and of the population. In general, however, most of the revenues seem to have come from taxes on the sales of various commodities (the *alcabala*), custom duties, mining (especially silver and gold production), and from various state monopolies in tobacco, salt, and other commodities.[27]

In Brazil, the sugar industry was the primary source of revenue to Portugal during the colony's early history, but direct taxes on sugar production hampered the competitiveness of Brazilian producers as sugar cultivation spread across the West Indies.[28] By the end of the sixteenth century Portugal introduced new taxes on imports into Brazil, as well as sales taxes on goods exported by Brazil to Portugal. The diversification of taxes, and the eventual boom in gold production (another activity ripe for taxation), contributed to a relative, if gradual, decline in the burden on the sugar industry. Taxation of trade, or of production of commodities intended for export, however, was to remain a central feature of the tax system.

Although the various taxes levied by the British Crown on the residents of their colonies were relatively light, the local and provincial governments set up by the colonists themselves seem to have raised more revenues from their populations (at least those segments that were not Native Americans) than did their counterparts in Latin America. This pattern both reflected and contributed to a more decentralized structure of British America. These taxes allowed local or colonial governments greater autonomy in how they operated. The New England colonies exhibited a preference for property or faculty taxes (based on estimated earnings potential) at both the colonial and local government levels rather early in their histories, and indeed in 1634 the General Court of Massachusetts held that "in all rates and publique charges," every man should be taxed "according to his estate." The expenses of the provincial governments were quite modest, generally consisting of the bare necessities of civil government, but local authorities used their revenues to support investments in quasi-public or public goods and services such as public schools and roads. In contrast, the southern colonies, perhaps influenced by the interests of large landowners (as well as the inelastic demand for some of their prominent

---

27. For example, in Mexico during the late 1780s about a quarter of the colonial government's revenue came from the *alcabala*, nearly 45 percent from state monopolies, and roughly 20 percent from taxes on gold, silver, and other mining activities. See Tenenbaum (1986). The relative importance of taxes on mining seems to have declined, and the relative importance of the tobacco and other monopolies increased over time. See Burkholder and Johnson (1998).

28. Even municipal or local governments at times assessed taxes on sugar production.

exports, such as tobacco), tended to rely more on taxing imports and exports. The Middle Atlantic colonies' tax institutions fell somewhere in between, but already by the time of the Revolution both the Middle Atlantic colonies and the New England colonies made extensive use of property taxes.[29]

The reliance on taxes on trade as the principal source of tax revenue continued (at least at the national government level) throughout the hemisphere after the wave of independence movements of the late eighteenth and early nineteenth centuries. In the United States, a 1789 law establishing the tariff was one of the first laws enacted by the federal government. Although the federal government had other sources of revenues, such as excise taxes, proceeds from sales of public lands, a duty on receipts for legacies, and even taxes (generally of brief duration and during wartime) on dwelling houses, land, and slaves, tariffs provided by far the dominant share (typically well above 80 percent) of national government revenue up through the Civil War. These revenues amounted to roughly 1 to 2 percent of GNP (except for spurts during wartime), and were almost exclusively consumed in covering the costs of defense, paying off the debt, and of general government expenses. Only a small fraction, about 5 percent of federal government expenditures, went to support capital investments such as public buildings, roads and canals, and improvements to rivers and harbors. As was recognized, and has often been noted, the U.S. government was extremely conscientious about maintaining its reputation in financial markets, and was loath to finance much of its expenditures through borrowing or issuance of paper money. In Canada, tariffs were the major source of revenue for the national government after the confederation in 1867, generally accounting for between 60 and 70 percent of dominion revenue (and over 80 percent of dominion tax revenue) into the twentieth century.[30]

The overall patterns of national government taxation, if not of the extent of reliance on debt, in Latin America were remarkably similar to that in the United States and Canada over the nineteenth century. Although wars and other shocks occasionally generated transitory impositions of, or increases in, *direct contributions* (direct levies, applied to land or a proxy for income),

---

29. See Perkins (1980) and for an exceptionally fine treatment of how the tax structures of the colony, commonwealth, and state of Massachusetts evolved from colonial times through the early twentieth century (and the quotation from the order of the General Court; see Bullock 1907, 2).

30. Together with excise taxes (levied primarily on liquors and tobacco), the revenue from tariffs generally accounted for between 75 and 85 percent of dominion revenue. In 1870, the tariffs on sugar and molasses, spirits and wine, tea, cottons, and woolens were the largest contributors, jointly accounting for 65.8 percent of all tariff revenue. See Perry (1955; table III). Customs revenue had been the major source of provincial revenue before the Confederation, but the terms of the unification agreement stripped the provinces of the right to levy such taxes.

customs duties and excise taxes (on commodities such as liquors) normally accounted for the bulk of revenues. Indeed, there were only two notable differences in how Latin American central governments financed themselves. First, unlike in the United States and Canada, state monopolies (a holdover from the colonial period) and levies on the production of certain staples and minerals intended for export (such as coffee, sugar, guano, gold, silver, nitrates, and copper) were at times significant generators of revenue.[31] The other salient divergence was the greater inclination of Latin American countries to incur debt or issue paper money to finance operating deficits.[32] Notwithstanding these differences, Latin American central governments were like the North American central governments in raising most of their revenue from tariffs and from taxes levied on commodities generally thought to be income inelastic. In Mexico, for example, port taxes, income from the tobacco monopoly, and excise taxes yielded 75 to 85 percent of national government revenue over the latter half of the nineteenth century. Taxes on property and on businesses existed, but these typically accounted for less than 10 percent of revenue. In Brazil, between 1823 and 1888, more than 50 percent of total national revenue consistently came from tariffs on imports, with excise taxes and assessments on exports contributing roughly 14 and 25 percent of total revenue, respectively. In Chile, taxes assessed at ports and revenue raised by state monopolies consistently accounted for just under 80 percent of national government revenue throughout the second half of the nineteenth century and well into the twentieth century. Colombia provides yet another example. Already by the 1830s, soon after independence, customs duties and income from state monopolies on commodities such as tobacco and salt brought in 60 percent of national revenues. By the 1840s, their cumulative share rose to nearly 80 percent.

Wars and other threats to the social order (such as the War of 1812, the U.S. Civil War, the war between Mexico and the United States, and various internal uprisings) did sometimes stimulate the imposition of direct taxes that extended the reach of national governments in progressive directions (i.e., the income tax in the United States during the Civil War, and the property tax in Mexico during its war with the United States), but the general

---

31. Most countries did collect some government revenue from duties on exports, but their ability to rely on such taxes was constrained by international competition and the power of exporters. It was generally only in cases where exporters had market power and could pass on some significant portion of taxes to the consumers (such as coffee in Brazil, guano in Peru, or nitrates in Chile) that duties on exports accounted for substantial shares of national government revenue.

32. Not only were Latin American countries more willing to borrow, but they also seem to have been less committed to maintaining confidence in their service of the debt. Their poor record at debt service constrained their ability to tap external credit, and thus Latin American countries were typically quite reliant on internal sources. This may have had unfortunate effects on the development of banks and other financial institutions.

pattern throughout the hemisphere was reliance by national governments on taxes that targeted commodities or trade rather than income or wealth.[33] As is evident in table 3.4, and discussed in more detail in section four, it was only in the twentieth century that national governments in the United States, Canada, and Latin American countries introduced permanent peacetime taxes on income and wealth (including estates and gifts).[34]

Stark contrasts existed across the societies of the Americas, however, in the size and revenue sources of state/provincial and local governments. Local governments were far more prominent in the United States and Canada than in Latin America (see table 3.5), and this feature is of fundamental importance because of the radically different tax instruments used by state and local governments as compared to those of the national governments. A predisposition of the North American populations to organize and support local governments was evident as early as the seventeenth century, despite the absence during that era of distinctively high per capita incomes (as compared to other societies in the Americas). Likewise distinctive was the tendency of these governments to raise the vast majority of revenue through property taxes.

Local governments certainly grew very rapidly in the United States during the early decades of the nineteenth century as the *common school movement* progressed, and there were substantial investments in building roads and other infrastructure demanded by an early industrializing economy. Indeed, they were the largest component of the overall government sector throughout the nineteenth century (with a share of total government revenue of 57.1 percent in 1855, for example), with only a few brief exceptions intervals during and after major wars. Their heavy reliance on the property tax (see table 3.6) suggests that a rather progressive tax structure prevailed among local governments, and given the relative prominence of this level of government, in the overall government sector as well.

For example, between 1861 and 1905, property taxes accounted for between 76 and 87 percent of all the tax revenue collected by the state and

---

33. A close examination of the variation over time in the amounts of tax revenue raised, and the manner by which national governments in Latin America financed their operations, suggests that there was often a reluctance to increase taxes during periods of war. Rather, the approach seemed to be either inflating the money supply or borrowing from foreign lenders or domestic banks. This pattern stands in stark contrast to the behavior of the U.S. government during wartime, but it is interesting to note the resemblance to how the Confederacy financed its operations during the U.S. Civil War. In her intriguing article, which explores the voting patterns among members of the Confederate Congress, Rose Razaghian finds that it was those that came from the states and districts with large slave plantations (and likely the greatest inequality) that were (until the very late stages of the war) most opposed to taxing income—and thus most inclined toward financing the Confederacy through inflationary monetary policy, loans, and excise taxes. See Razaghian (2005).

34. These new assessments, together with payroll taxes, came to be the dominant source of revenue—especially in the United States and Canada—during the 1930s and 1940s, and coincided with a sharp increase in the size of the central governments.

Table 3.4 The shares of national government revenue accounted for by tariffs and excise taxes, and by taxes on income and wealth (%)

Country/Year	Customs	Income and wealth taxes	Country/Year	Customs	Income and wealth taxes
Argentina			Mexico[b]		
1872	94.0		1870	92.3	3.6
1895	71.2	3.2	1890	79.7	4.7
1920	58.4	2.9	1910	86.0	11.1
1940	24.7	17.9	1929	29.8	10.6
Brazil[a]			1940	29.5	17.0
1870	71.4		Peru[d]		
1888	69.1		1871	95.6	
1900	65.5		1899	59.1	3.6
1920	56.8		1920	51.9	6.0
1940	50.3	10.2	1920	26.5	18.4
Chile			Uruguay		
1895	73.8	0.6	1895	66.7	
1920	70.2	6.0	1910	60.0	
1940	41.1	23.7	1929	32.2	18.6
Colombia			1940	40.0	14.0
1872	69.5		Canada		
1928	56.0	5.3	1870	63.2	
1940	36.7	30.4	1905	57.5	
Costa Rica[c]			1920	37.3	10.5
1871	91.4		1940	15.0	28.4
1885	81.3		United States		
1910	86.8		1820	83.3	
1918	64.4	18.3	1860	94.6	
1930	78.1	7.2	1870	47.5	9.3
El Salvador[a]			1900	41.1	
1897	84.0		1927	17.0	64.8
1910	75.0		1940	5.8	43.0
Guatemala[a]					
1872	76.0				

Sources: The general source for the estimates is Mitchell (1993), but the estimates reported by Mitchell were interpreted with, and complemented by, the greater detail obtained for a number of individual countries in other sources. For Argentina, Oficina de Estadistica Nacional (1875). For Brazil, Carreira (1889), and Fundação Instituto Brasileiro (1999). For Chile, Molina (1898). For Colombia, Melo-Gonzalez (1989); Park (1985); and López Garavito (1992). For Costa Rica, Guell (1975); Ministerio de Economia y Hacienda (1953); and Román (1995). For Mexico, Marichal, Miño Grijalva, and Riguzzi (1994). For Peru, Ministerio de Hacienda y Comercio (1928 and 1940); and Tantalean Arbulu (1983).

[a]The revenue included under customs includes sales and excise taxes as well as customs.

[b]The estimates of customs revenue for 1870 through 1910 include the amounts collected from indirect taxes (almost exclusively levies on imports and exports), as well as revenue from stamps (the major component), ports, the post office, lotteries, railroads, and coinage. The income and wealth figures for those years encompass indirect taxes, most of which are taxes on property held in districts under the federal government authority. The share in total revenue accounted for by indirect taxes trends from 72.7 percent in 1870 to 50.8 in 1890 to 44.4 percent in 1910.

[c]The revenues reported under customs revenue include tariffs on imports, a tax on coffee exports, sales or excise taxes (mostly composed of a levy on tobacco consumption until 1908), and revenue obtained from the state monopoly on liquors.

[d]The customs revenue for Peru includes the revenue from the export of guano.

Table 3.5 Distribution of tax revenues across levels of government during the nineteenth century: Brazil, Chile, Colombia, Mexico, Canada, and the United States (%)

Country/Year	National government	Provincial governments	Municipalities or other local
Brazil			
1826	30.8	69.2	0.0
1856	79.5	17.1	3.3
1860	78.2	18.2	3.5
1885/86	76.3	18.5	5.2
Chile			
1913	92.5		7.5
1915	90.8		9.2
1920	87.9		12.1
Colombia			
1839	88.4	2.9	8.7
1842	91.8	1.6	6.7
1850	85.4	8.7	5.8
1870	46.6	30.8	22.6
1894	60.0	32.0	8.0
1898	66.7	28.6	4.8
Mexico			
1882	69.1	19.5	11.5
1890	74.7	16.3	9.0
1900	67.3	19.8	12.9
1908	70.6	17.1	12.3
Canada			
1933	42.5	17.9	39.6
United States			
1855	25.5	17.4	57.1
1875	39.6	16.4	44.0
1895	36.0	14.0	50.0
1913	29.1	13.2	57.6
1927	35.5	18.0	46.5

Notes: For Brazil, see Carreira (1889). The substantial change in the distribution of tax revenues between 1826 and 1856 reflects the growth in the relative power of the national government, relative to the provinces, after independence. There were explicit divisions of authority across the levels of government as regards what could be taxed, but those divisions changed somewhat over time. In 1834, the national government was given the authority to raise revenue through collecting taxes on imports, exports, slaves, and the production of gold, sugar, cotton, and various other products, as well as through port fees, stamp requirements, and the sale of official posts and titles. The division of authority changed over time, with perhaps the principal impact being the shift of taxes on slaves to provinces, with the right to tax immobile property going to the national government.

For Colombia, see Melo-Gonzalez (1989). As seen in the table, in the 1830s and 1840s, the national government collected a major part of the fiscal revenues. The situation changed drastically after the reform of 1850, which intended to decentralize fiscal revenues and spending. The states would be in charge of the elaboration of their own budgets. In the case of revenues, the national government would keep mainly the revenues from customs, salt monopoly, stamped paper, income from the mint, and the postal and telegraph service, while the states would collect the revenues from taxes on the gross value of the production of gold and certain agricultural commodities. These taxes were phased out during mid-century, however, and the

Table 3.5 (continued)

states created new taxes then, such as a direct tax, in order to raise more revenues. Not only taxation was decentralized: spending was also reallocated. The states were put in charge of the spending on public instruction, police, prisons, justice administration, roads, and public works. Between 1863 and 1886 the decentralization process became more significant. The Constitution of 1863 established the federal system in the Estados Unidos de Colombia (United States of Colombia), which was confirmed by nine sovereign states: Antioquia, Bolívar, Boyacá, Cauca, Cundinamarca, Magdalena, Panamá, Santander, and Tolima. The decentralization of revenues had a significant impact: while in 1850 the revenues collected by states represented 8.7 percent of total revenues, in 1870 they represented 30 percent. In the case of the municipalities, their revenues also increased in importance from 6 percent to 23 percent between 1850 and 1870. It is important to notice that Antioquia and Cundinamarca, the two states that realized the most growth over the period in both income and state tax revenue, had been characterized by relative labor scarcity and likely had greater equality.

For Canada, see J. Harvey Perry (1955): appendix C, table 1.

For the United States, the figures for 1855, 1875, and 1895, were computed as a weighted average of regional estimates of per capita revenue raised for different levels of government. The federal figures include revenue raised through land sales. See Lance E. Davis and John Legler (1966). The estimates for 1913, 1927, and 1950, see U.S. Bureau of the Census (2001).

Table 3.6 Sources of tax revenue for U.S. local governments, 1890–1950

Taxes	1890	1902	1913	1927	1940	1950
Income					0.4	0.9
Sales and excise			0.2	0.6	2.8	5.9
Property	92.5	88.6	91.0	96.8	91.3	86.2
Payroll			0.2	0.6	1.5	2.3
Other	7.5	11.4	8.6	2.1	3.9	4.7
Total	100.0	100.0	100.0	100.0	100.0	100.0

Notes: For the 1890 estimates, see Morris A. Copeland (1961). Copeland also provides extensive discussion, as well as estimates that conform with those presented in Sidney Ratner (1980), table 1. We employ Ratner for the estimates after 1890, as this source covers the years up to 1950. The estimates represent the share of local government tax revenues accounted for by the respective taxes. Transfers of resources to local governments accounted for less than 10 percent of total resources available for local government expenditures through 1913 (and most of those transfers were grants for schools or roads), rose to a bit less than 15 percent by 1932, but jumped to more than 25 percent by the early 1940s.

local governments in Massachusetts.[35] The contours of public finance, as regards both the prominence of local governments and the importance of

35. These figures (computed from data reported in Bullock (1907; 135) are all the more striking, because the state of Massachusetts depended much more on taxing corporations than did most other states. Moreover, the implication of the figures in Bullock (1907; 127, 135), is that property taxes accounted for more than 90 percent of the tax revenue raised by local governments in that state between 1880 and 1900, if not before as well. We do not yet have evidence from many states on the shares of revenue coming to local governments from different taxes earlier in the nineteenth century, but scattered information is consistent with the implication of the estimate for 1902 in table 3.6, that local governments obtained well over 90 percent of revenue from property taxes. See Wallis (2001) for further discussion of how the relative importance of the property tax as a source of state revenue varied over the nineteenth century.

Table 3.7   Sources of revenue for Canada's municipal governments, 1913–1950 (%)

Revenue	1913	1933	1950
Income taxes		1.4	
Sales and excise taxes			4.3
Property/Wealth taxes	82.2	78.6	69.6
Other taxes	6.0	6.1	9.2
Nontax revenues	11.8	13.9	14.3
Subsidies from other governments			2.6
Total	100.0	100.0	100.0

Source: Statistics Canada (1983, Series H 52–74).

property taxes to them appear to have been much the same in Canada. Our earliest estimate is that property taxes accounted for over 82 percent of local government revenue in 1913 (see table 3.7), but less comprehensive information suggests that the share of tax revenue accounted for by levies on property may have been even greater during the nineteenth century, especially in Ontario.[36]

State governments in the United States and provincial governments in Canada generally represented relatively small parts of their respective aggregate government sectors during the late nineteenth and early twentieth centuries—at least as measured by share of tax revenues. In neither country did state/provincial governments account for more than 20 percent of aggregate government tax revenues before the 1920s. They differed, however, in how they obtained revenues to finance their expenditures. Even after the confederation of Canadian provinces in 1867, provincial governments in Canada raised most of their revenues from either subsidies or transfers from the Dominion (whose revenues came primarily from tariffs or excise duties) or from assessments levied on mining, cutting timber, and other exploitation of natural resources. It was only after the scale of provincial programs increased, inspired by rapid population and economic growth on the eve of the twentieth century, that provincial governments enacted new levies, such as taxes on corporations, property, and succession duties, to increase their revenues. These measures did not raise substantial amounts, however, and as late as the first decade of the twentieth century, they generally yielded less than a quarter of provincial revenue.

36. See Perry (1955), especially chapters 2, 5, and 12. Perry finds that property taxes played an important role in the development of municipal or local governments. These taxes were extensively used in upper Canada during the early nineteenth century. Indeed, Perry suggests that virtually wherever in Canada significant municipal government developed, the property tax was the dominant source of revenue. Property taxes were less important in Quebec than Ontario, because French Canada was able to obtain substantial revenue from customs fees and statutory road levies. Property taxes were also low in the Maritime Provinces (especially Nova Scotia) because of the limited development of local government in that region. Perry attributes the limited development of local government there to the heterogeneity of the population.

Table 3.8   Sources of tax revenue for U.S. state governments, 1890–1950 (%)

Tax revenue	1890	1902	1913	1927	1940	1950
Individual income				4.0	4.7	7.4
Corporate income				5.3	3.5	6.0
Sales and excise	a	17.9	19.9	42.8	51.0	55.6
Property	70.0	52.6	46.5	21.2	5.9	3.1
Payroll				7.9	24.5	18.8
Death and gift		29.5	33.6	18.9	10.3	9.1
Other		30.0				
Total	100.0	100.0	100.0	100.0	100.0	100.0

Notes: See the note to table 3.6. The estimates represent the share of state government tax revenues accounted for by the respective taxes. Nontax revenues appear to have been substantial, however, accounting perhaps for as much as 40 percent of revenue in 1913.
^aThe sales and gross receipts taxes for 1890 are included in the Other category.

The state governments in the United States made much more use of direct taxes than their counterparts in Canada, and indeed overall relied heavily on property taxes both early and late in the nineteenth century.[37] The property tax was likely the largest single source of state government revenue in the United States at the beginning of the nineteenth century, but the onset of industrialization opened up or improved alternative means of states raising funds. By the 1820s and 1830s, state governments began to reduce or even eliminate property taxes, as more and more revenues rolled in from other sources, including fees assessed for issuing corporate charters, taxes on corporate capital (especially banks and insurance companies), and returns on investments they had made to stoke development in various banks, transportation companies, and other infrastructure. When the economic contractions of the late 1830s and early 1840s sharply curtailed these sources of revenue, however, many state governments found themselves on (or over) the brink of bankruptcy. These fiscal challenges compelled them to revive their property taxes and/or design other relatively stable revenue sources, which were particularly crucial if they hoped to issue debt for the financing of additional investments in infrastructure. Although states were creative in devising a wide variety of alternative methods of raising revenue, property taxes were restored to being the most important tax revenue source for state governments by the end of the nineteenth century (roughly 70 percent of tax revenue in 1890; see table 3.8).

Given the very large size of the local governments in the United States and Canada, and their heavy reliance on property and wealth taxes into the twentieth century, it should perhaps not be surprising that these same

---

37. Another direct tax sometimes levied by state governments in the United States was the poll tax, but the significance of poll taxes as a revenue source diminished greatly over the nineteenth century.

Table 3.9 Sources of tax revenue in the United States, for all levels together, 1902–1950 (%)

Tax revenue	1902	1913	1927	1940	1950
Individual income			9.8	8.1	29.3
Corporate income		1.5	13.9	8.7	19.6
Sales and excise	19.8	16.1	13.2	28.5	23.6
Customs duties	17.7	13.6	6.0	2.3	0.7
Property	51.4	58.6	48.8	30.3	13.0
Payroll		0.1	2.4	13.3	9.7
Death and gift	11.1	10.1	5.8	8.9	4.2
Other					
Total	100.0	100.0	100.0	100.0	100.0

Source: Ratner (1980), table 1.
Note: The estimates represent the share of total government tax revenue (national, state, and local considered together) accounted for by the respective taxes.

Table 3.10 Sources of revenue in Canada, for all levels together, 1933–1950 (%)

Revenue	1933	1950
Income taxes	12.4	44.5
Sales and excise taxes	26.2	32.0
Customs duties	13.5	7.9
Property/Wealth taxes	39.2	10.8
Other taxes	8.7	4.8
Total	100.0	100.0

Source: Statistics Canada (1983, Series H 52–74).

taxes loom large when one considers the total tax revenue collected by governments at all levels. For the United States, in both 1902 and 1913 (see table 3.9), property, gift, and estate taxes account for between 60 and 70 percent of the revenue to the overall government sector. Although our estimates for Canada do not extend that far back (see table 3.10), it is clear that there, too—largely due to the prominence of local or municipal governments—taxes on property and wealth were very important sources of revenue for the government sector overall (nearly 40 percent as late as 1933). Even if the respective levels of government in Latin America relied on the same tax instruments as did their counterparts to the north, the fact that local governments were so much smaller implies that property and wealth holders would contribute a relatively modest proportion of government revenue overall. Local/municipal authorities accounted for only about 10 percent of total government tax revenue in Brazil, Colombia, and Mexico throughout the nineteenth century (and in Chile, between 10 and 20 percent during the second decade of the twentieth century, despite the

Table 3.11   Sources of revenue to Chile's municipal governments (%)

Year	Taxes on income	Taxes/Fees on professions and industries	Taxes on alcoholic beverages	Taxes on slaughtering	Taxes on mines	Taxes on carriages	Other
1913	39.0	7.1	6.0	4.0	2.1	3.0	38.8
1915	50.0	6.7	4.1	3.3	2.5	2.5	30.9
1920	38.7	15.7	2.7	2.1	2.3	2.4	36.1

Source: Oficina Central de Estadistica Sinopsis Estadistica de la Republica de Chile (1921).

absence of state/provincial governments). The contrast with the United States and Canada is dramatic. In the United States, local governments generated 57.1 percent of total government tax revenue in 1855, and the figure remained near 50 percent for the rest of the century. Even as late as the 1930s, the share of local government revenue was near 40 percent in both the United States and Canada.

From the exceedingly modest investments in public schooling characteristic of Latin America into the twentieth century (and reflected in the low literacy rates that prevailed throughout the region until national governments became more aggressive in promoting public schooling) the qualitative pattern evident in the figures for Brazil, Colombia, and Mexico seems to be representative.[38] Local/municipal governments in Latin American countries never grew very large, especially in rural areas and where Native Americans composed larger proportions of the population. The basis for our claim that during the nineteenth century the overall tax structures in the United States and Canada were much more progressive (in the sense of placing more of the burden on wealthy elites) than in Latin America, however, does not rest solely on the relative sizes of the different levels of government. The evidence on the relative use of tax instruments suggests that local governments in Latin America relied much less on the property tax than did their counterparts in the United States and Canada. Early in the twentieth century, local governments in Chile and Colombia (see tables 3.11 and 3.12) raised less than half of their revenue from property and income taxes (less than 25 percent in Cundinamarca, Colombia), while these taxes were dominant in the accounts of Canada (78 percent) and the United States (over 90 percent). When one considers these local governments in Latin America, as compared to even U.S. state governments (which, as reported in table 3.7, were raising more than 80 percent of their revenue from property, death, and gift taxes as late as 1913), the disinclination of Latin American governments to tax property holders and the will to do stands out in especially stark terms.

---

38. See Engerman, Mariscal, and Sokoloff (2002) for more discussion of the evolution of schooling institutions in the Americas.

Table 3.12 Sources of revenue to Colombia's municipal governments in the Department of Cundinamarca, 1918 (%)

Revenue	Total for all municipalities in Cundinamarca	City of Bogota alone
Property tax	22.5	14.2
Almotacen and plaza (tax on market)	11.7	15.0
Taxes on slaughtering	5.7	4.0
Bullfighting and other legal games	1.7	1.0
Rental income	1.2	0.1
Fines	2.7	1.6
Other sources	54.5	64.1
Total	100.0	100.0

Source: Republica de Colombia (1919).

The underdevelopment of local government in Latin America, where both economic and political inequality was extreme and elites might have been expected to resist the levying of property and wealth taxes to fund broad provision of public services, raises the issue of whether the two conditions are causally related to each other. A theoretical argument can certainly be made that elites might have had an interest in resisting the growth of public services, especially those provided to segments of the population that were perceived as quite unlike their own. This notion receives some support from the observation that during the nineteenth century local governments in the United States were relatively larger (as judged both by the local government share of regional income as well as relative to the income share of state income) in regions with less inequality such as the Midwest, or even the Northeast (see table 3.13).

Not only were local governments much smaller in Latin American countries generally, but the state or provincial governments in that region made less use of property taxes, and relied more on taxes that placed a lighter tax burden on the elite. As reflected in tables 3.14 and 3.15, which present the sources of revenue (in percentage terms) for all of the state or provincial governments in Argentina and Colombia, and a sampling of them for Brazil and Mexico at various points during the second half of the nineteenth century, taxes on land or property (the so-called *direct contributions*) accounted for markedly lower proportions of state government revenue in Latin America than such taxes did in the United States. In these four countries (the first three of which are among the most decentralized in Latin America), taxes on different types of property or on business rarely accounted for more than 10 to 15 percent (and generally less) of state/provincial revenue, as compared to 70 percent in the United States in 1890. Instead, state/provincial governments in Latin America relied on excise taxes (such as on liquors, tobacco, flour, slaughtered livestock, and foreign

Table 3.13   Local and state taxes, as shares of income, by region in the United States, 1860 and 1880

Year/Region	Percent state taxes	Percent local taxes	Per capita income (1860$)
1860			
Northeast	0.91	3.65	181
North central	1.25	6.22	89
South Atlantic	2.21	3.07	81
East south central	1.12	1.79	89
West south central	0.68	2.20	184
National average	1.22	2.58	128
1880			
Northeast	0.93	4.08	244
North central	0.84	4.40	170
South Atlantic	2.04	3.33	84
East south central	1.23	1.97	95
West south central	0.97	4.31	112
National average	0.90	3.97	173

Source: Both the regional and national average shares of state and local revenues in regional were calculated from the estimates of government receipts in Davis and Legler (1966), and the per capita income estimates in Robert W. Fogel (1988).

Notes: We do not include estimates for the national government as a share of income, because the receipt is based on point of collection, and thus implies higher taxes in regions with ports or substantial land sales. However, our estimates of the national figures for the total tax revenue relative to income are 6.67 and 8.96 percent in 1860 and 1880, respectively. Some of the later-settled regions are excluded here because of incomplete information.

merchandise), tolls on roads and other modes of transportation, fines and various fees for government services, levies on products intended largely for export (such as coffee in Brazil), and a variety of other sources. Although patterns of incidence are not always transparent, the methods of raising revenue to fund the operations of state and provincial governments in Latin America would generally be expected to impose a proportionally rather light burden on the wealthy classes.

In Brazil, for example, the allocation of taxing authority between the provinces and the national government changed several times over the nineteenth century. Under the 1840 constitution, the main provincial taxes were taxes on sugar and coffee production, but revenues were also obtained from taxes/fees on legacies and inheritance, on transference of properties, the sale of *novhos e velhos direitos* (official posts and titles), taxes on the slave trade, and especially fees for traveling along provincial roads and rivers. Taxes on property generated only a tiny share of total revenue. Until relatively late in the nineteenth century, the fees charged for traveling on provincial roads (*estradas provinciais*) and internal/small rivers (*rios internos*)—fees that were called by different names such as itinerary fees, fees on departure or fees on traveling—were among the most important sources of

Table 3.14 Sources of revenue to state/provincial governments in Argentina and Colombia, c. 1870 (%)

	1872
Argentina	
Revenue of the provincial governments	
Direct contribution (taxes)	13.2
Constitution-mandated share of tariff revenue	15.2
Other subvention from national treasury	9.7
Sales of land	30.5
Alcabala (sales tax)	0.2
Rent of land	0.2
Inheritances	0.1
Stamped paper, tolls, tax on fruit, and other miscellaneous	30.9

	1870
Colombia	
Revenue of the state governments	
Direct taxes on industry and capital	11.7
Tax on real estate	7.1
Tax on slaughtered livestock	18.3
Tax on liquors	15.1
Tax on foreign merchandise	12.9
Excise taxes on cacao, tobacco, and anise	7.0
Stamps	5.7
Miscellaneous/Other	22.1

Source: For Argentina, Oficina de Estadística Nacional (1875). For Colombia, López Garavito (1992).

provincial revenues. For example, in the province of São Paulo in the period 1871–72, the rights to departure raised 56 percent of the total revenues of the province, while the taxation on slavery trade and the tax on legacies accounted for 6 percent and 8 percent, respectively. In the province of Minas Geraes, in 1876 the main sources of provincial revenue were taxes on coffee (20 percent of the total revenues of the province), itinerary fees (16 percent), and taxes on transfer, registration, and trade of slaves (15 percent).

Direct taxes did not become important until late in the nineteenth century, but even then the reliance in Brazil on property and other taxes progressive in character was quite modest compared to the United States. The Constitution of 1891 established a republic, and the provinces then became designated states with expanded rights to collect taxes on exports (rights previously reserved for the national government), as well as taxes on property, on transference of property, and on industries and profits. This change transformed the tributary structure of the most prosperous states, such as Minas Geraes, whose economies were largely directed at foreign trade. In Minas Geraes, levies on exports had raised only 5 percent of the

Table 3.15 Sources of revenue to selected state/provincial governments in Brazil and Mexico, c. 1870 to 1910 (%)

	1871–1872	1910
Brazil		
Sao Paulo		
Taxes on exports		40.7
Transit fees/taxes	79.1	3.6
Tax/Fees on inheritances and property transfers	7.9	15.9
Taxes on property	1.2	2.0
Taxes on capital of producers		5.7
Taxes on slaves and slave trade	5.8	
Taxes on water and sewers		8.4
Judiciary, state stamps, lotteries, fines, fees, and other miscellaneous	6.0	24.7

	1876	1892	1905
Minas Geraes			
Taxes on exports	5.7	64.4	59.0
Taxes on coffee, gold, salt, and diamonds	22.3	0.8	1.5
Transit fees/taxes	16.4	0.9	1.0
Tax/Fees on inheritances and property transfers	7.9	14.1	8.7
Transfer and registration of slaves	17.4		
Taxes on property	2.8		6.1
Taxes on private consumption		7.6	2.3
Taxes on industries and profits			8.0
Judiciary, state stamps, and other fees	1.0	8.2	4.9
Official posts and titles	7.4		2.8
Lotteries, water, sewers, and other miscellaneous	19.1	4.0	5.7

	1870
Mexico	
Yucatan	
Income from public lands and sea salt fields	27.5
Taxes on liquors	14.6
Sales taxes on livestock and flour	20.6
Taxes on imports	3.5
Transfer fees and fines	19.1
Other miscellaneous fees and taxes	14.6

Sources: For Brazil, in 1876 and 1892, Torres (1961), and for 1905, Barbosa (1966). For Mexico, Levy (2005).

Notes: The relatively high figure for the miscellaneous/other category in Minas Geraes in 1876 is due to 9.9 percent of the revenue coming from "direitos de 6% sobre outros generos." The high transit tax revenue in Sao Paolo in 1871 is due primarily to the Taxas das Barreiras, which was a state road tax, whereby stations on state roads collected tolls for carts, wagons, coaches, and animals on the hoof.

total revenues of the province in 1889, but with the expanded power to tax, this share jumped to 64 percent in 1892. Similarly, in 1910 the tax on exports raised 40 percent of the total revenues of São Paulo, whereas in 1871 it had yielded no revenue for the province.

The states also increased the shares of revenue they derived from taxes on property, legacies and others transferences of property, and on industrial profits. In Minas Geraes, the tax on property (*imposto predial* or territorial tax) accounted for 2.8 percent of the total revenues of the province in 1876, but its take rose to 6.1 percent in 1905. There were no taxes on industries and profits prior to the establishment of the republic, but they accounted for 8 percent of revenue in 1905. Taxes and fees on inheritance and transfers of property generated 8.7 percent of total revenues. Such taxes were of similar importance in São Paulo. In 1910, the state of São Paulo raised 2 percent of state revenue from property taxes, 5.7 percent of revenue from a tax on the capital of producers, and 15.9 percent of revenues from taxes/fees on inheritances, legacies, and transfers of property. Thus, in Minas Geraes and São Paulo, perhaps the two major states of Brazil, these progressive taxes accounted for 22.8 and 23.6 percent of state revenue, respectively. As is evident in table 3.8, the corresponding figure for state governments in the United States in 1902 was 82.1 percent. The contrast is dramatic and telling.

If it is indeed true that less reliance on taxation of property or wealth is indicative of elites bearing a lighter tax burden, then the evidence does sustain the idea that the tax institutions that characterized Latin America during the nineteenth century were especially favorable to their interests. Not only were the local authorities (which everywhere were more likely to tax wealth than those at other levels of government) extremely stunted as regards the scale of their activities (and demands for revenue), but both local and state/provincial governments in Latin America made much less use of property, wealth, or other taxes than did their counterparts in the North. Of course, the burdens of taxation should not be assessed solely by the mix of tax instruments applied to raise revenue, but also by the amount of revenue raised. It might be argued, for example, that the United States and Canada were generally more disposed toward government involvement, and thus had a greater need to levy taxes.

One response to this sort of explanation of the comparatively small size of local governments in Latin America is to point out that any bias against governments in Latin America was obviously not neutral across levels of government. The evidence is clear that the local governments in Latin America were stunted relative to national governments, a pattern we find particularly interesting because local governments in virtually all contexts seem to rely more on taxing wealth and property than other levels of government. We explore the issue further in table 3.16, where estimates of the amount of national government taxes collected per capita in 1870, as well

Table 3.16   National government tax revenue per capita, c. 1870

	Taxes per capita (1870 US$)	Index of tax revenue relative to national income (100 = US)
Americas		
Argentina	9.4	155
Bolivia	1.2	
Brazil	6.7	195
Chile	6.7	
Colombia	1.1	
Costa Rica	9.0	
Ecuador	1.3	
El Salvador	2.2	
Guatemala	1.7	
Honduras	0.9	
Mexico	3.1	94
Nicaragua	2.9	
Peru	14.0	
Venezuela	5.1	
United States	11.4	100
Europe		
Belgium	7.1	58
Denmark	9.3	104
England	13.0	86
France	12.3	143
Germany	5.6	63
Greece	4.8	
Holland	14.0	114
Portugal	4.5	
Sweden and Norway	3.7	51
Switzerland	2.0	20

Notes: The information on taxes per capita is from Lopez Garavito (1992, 202–203). The values of the index of tax revenue relative to national income were computed as the respective ratios of the estimates of taxes per capita to the estimates of per capita income for 1870 contained in Angus Maddison (1995). The index values are expressed relative to the U.S. value, which was normalized to a standard of 100.

as the shares of these taxes to national income are presented for a range of countries around the world. Perhaps not surprisingly, given its higher per capita income, the U.S. national government collected substantial taxes on a per capita basis. The only country in the Americas that collected more was Peru, which realized extensive revenue over a period of several decades from exports of guano—a natural resource that was all too soon depleted.[39] Judged as a share of national income, however, the amount of revenue going to the national government was not at all high in the United States. On

39. For a brief account of the rise and fall of this remarkably lucrative industry, see Mathew (1976).

the contrary, Argentina and Brazil (and undoubtedly Peru) raised far more revenue for their respective central government, relative to national income, than did the United States, and Mexico collected nearly as much.

Admittedly, if one considers the much larger share of total government revenue that goes to local and state governments in the United States than in Latin America, it is evident that the revenue going to the government sector in the aggregate is far higher as a share of national income in the United States than in any other country in the hemisphere with the exception of Brazil (and Peru, during the bonanza from guano), where the ratio of total taxes to income (in the 7 to 8 percent range) seems roughly similar. Nevertheless, the substantive point remains. It is not the case that the Latin American countries were in general lightly taxed, but rather that that property and wealth taxes, and the levels of government that were more reliant on these sources of revenue, during the nineteenth and early twentieth centuries especially, were of minor significance, by the standards of their neighbors in North America, in the structure and financing of government.

The striking contrast we have highlighted is consistent with our conjecture that the legacy of extreme inequality in Latin America encouraged a distinctly different path of evolution of tax institutions and/or government structures among the societies of the Americas over the nineteenth century. One alternative hypothesis of this pattern, however, is that the reluctance or inability to tax property and wealth in Latin America was due to conditions characteristic of less developed economies that made it difficult to administer such levies. There may indeed be some merit to this type of explanation, but we would emphasize how the colonies in the northern part of North America, such as those in New England and the Middle Atlantic, made effective use of these sorts of instruments for raising tax revenue in support of local and state governments as early as the seventeenth century. It seems unlikely that these latter polities could be considered more developed than many of the nineteenth century Latin America nations. Other possible rationales are that the Latin American societies may have had less demand for the sorts of public goods and services that were provided by local governments, or that they simply chose to satisfy that demand through national government programs. These interesting theories deserve further study, but it is worth noting that Latin American societies were characterized by low rates of investment in public schools (and the low literacy rates that accompanied them) well into the twentieth century (if not the present day), even after accounting for their levels of per capita income.[40] Moreover, even if a radically different demand for public services, such as schools, does explain the patterns in the size of local governments and in government revenue sources, might this be considered yet another mechanism by which extreme inequality impacts on the institutions of taxation?

---

40. See Engerman, Mariscal, and Sokoloff (2002), as well as De Ferranti et al. (2004).

3.4 Tax Systems in the Twentieth Century

Throughout the Americas, the size of the government sector grew substantially over the twentieth century, and major changes in the tax structures were introduced to fund the increase in government expenditures. But in some respects, much has remained the same. As compared to the United States and Canada, Latin American governments continue to be highly centralized, and to generally rely on consumption taxes instead of taxes on wealth, income (especially those of individuals), or other levies that place a serious burden on elites. Indeed, most observers judge the progressivity of Latin American tax (and expenditure) programs to be remarkably modest, especially in light of the extreme inequality prevailing in that region of the world.[41]

3.4.1 Developments in the United States and Canada

At the beginning of the twentieth century, the U.S. federal, state, and local governments together accounted for only about 7 percent of GDP. Even by 1930, they had grown to no more than 10 percent. During the Depression and World War II, however, the size of the government sector exploded, to roughly 25–30 percent of the economy, with the federal government coming to assume the dominant role it plays today.[42] In Canada, similar developments took place.[43] Most of the major tax changes at the U.S. and Canadian federal levels were related to the need to finance the higher level of expenditures associated with the conduct of World Wars I and II, but in both countries the expanded revenues were tapped in the aftermath of those conflicts to support the peacetime growth of the national governments (Brownlee 1996). Facilitated by the passage of the constitutional amendment in 1913 that cleared away legal obstacles to a federal individual income tax (which followed the passage of a corporate income tax in 1909), the relative tax and spending shares between the federal and state and local governments began to shift. The fiscal landscape changed further with the adoption of social security taxes in 1937.

Over the course of the twentieth century, the individual income tax in the United States replaced the property tax as the primary tax on individuals.[44]

---

41. This discussion relies on several excellent cross-country studies of tax systems in Latin America as well as Government Finance Statistics from the International Monetary Fund. See Bird (1992, 2003), Shome (1999), Tanzi (2000), Stotsky and WoldeMariam (2002), and International Monetary Fund (2001, 2004).

42. See Steuerle (2004); and Slemrod and Bakija (1996). See also Weisman (2002).

43. See Treff and Perry (2004), at http://www.ctf.ca/FN2003/finances2003.asp

44. It is interesting that when Congress required additional revenue during the War of 1812, the solution was a supplemental property tax collected through a direct assessment of the states. By the time of the Civil War, funding the revenue needs of war financing through property taxation had less political appeal. See Brownlee (1996) and Weisman (2002) for more discussion.

The federal government first adopted an income tax during the 1860s, following the British approach for raising funds to finance the Crimean War. After the Civil War, the income tax was subject to political attacks and was eliminated, restored, and then struck down on constitutional grounds. Following the passage of the Sixteenth Amendment in 1913, however, the Underwood-Simmons Tariff Act reestablished the income tax in a less progressive and less ambitious form than the Civil War version or the 1894 legislation.[45] The scope of the individual income tax was changed greatly by the revenue demands associated with the world wars. For example, in the United States, the number of individual income taxpayers grew from 3.9 million in 1939 to 42.6 million in 1945, and tax revenues increased from $2.2 billion in 1939 to $35.1 billion in 1945. This increase in federal tax revenue from the income tax changed the balance in the relative size of the federal government. Only during World War II did federal tax revenues begin to exceed state and local tax revenues.

As discussed previously, national or central governments were, except for periods of wartime, quite small throughout the Americas during the nineteenth century. This was certainly true of the U.S. federal government, whose peacetime activities were largely confined to defense, foreign affairs and oversight of foreign trade, and general administration, with only extremely modest contributions going to infrastructure. State and local government assumed nearly all of the responsibility for the provision of schooling and publicly-provided transportation such as roads. Much of this division of activities evolved naturally, as local governments took on the tasks that communities wanted to get done and were willing to pay for. State governments succeeded the provincial governments of colonial times, and were keen to undertake programs that would stimulate economic activity or otherwise improve welfare within their polities, whether supporting transportation projects beyond the scope of towns, such as railroads, or contributing supplemental funds to encourage the expansion of public education. It might well be argued that the state and local governments were dominant in the provision of these sorts of public services, because these levels of government were more responsive to microlevel concerns, or that the population was more willing to pay taxes for projects that were clearly visible and likely to benefit those bearing the cost. Part of the relatively small size of the federal government during this era, however, may have been attributable to constitutional restrictions imposed on the federal government's taxing authority. The framers severely limited the power of the federal government to impose and collect direct taxes and they required any duties, imposts, or excises to be uniform throughout the

---

45. For more discussion of the history of the income tax, see Brownlee (1996) and Weisman (2002).

Table 3.17 Shares of tax revenue for the aggregate government sector in the United States, 1902 through 2000 (%)

Year	Federal tax revenues (excluding Social Security)	State tax revenues	Local tax revenues	Social Security revenues
1902	37.4	11.4	51.3	
1912	29.2	13.3	57.6	
1922	45.6	12.8	41.5	
1932	22.7	23.7	53.6	
1940	33.9	23.0	31.2	11.9
1950	63.4	14.3	14.4	7.9
1960	60.3	14.1	14.1	11.5
1970	52.5	17.2	14.0	16.3
1980	47.9	18.7	11.8	21.6
1990	41.8	19.8	13.3	25.1
2000	45.6	19.2	11.9	23.3

Sources: U.S. Bureau of the Census (1975); U.S. Census Bureau (1983, 1992, 2003); and C. Eugene Steurle (2004, 260).

United States.[46] Both measures were adopted to prevent regional interests from using the federal government to shift a disproportionate tax burden to other groups. While the constitutional limitation on direct taxes became better known as a barrier to adopting a federal income tax,[47] the limitation was primarily adopted by the founding fathers to prevent federal government property taxes.[48]

As is evident from table 3.17, as the federal government has grown since the 1940s, the relative shares of tax revenue for the federal, state, and local governments have changed dramatically. Even though their tax revenues increased from roughly 6.1 percent of GDP early in the twentieth century to a post-WWII high of 9.7 percent of GDP in 1972, the relative size of local governments plunged over the first half of the century (from over 50 to

46. Article 1, Section 8 provided Congress with the general authority to lay and collect taxes, duties, imposts, and excises, subject to the limitation that such taxes be uniform throughout the United States. Article 1, Section 9 limited the ability of the federal government to impose direct taxes by requiring "No capitation or other direct tax shall be laid, unless in proportion to the census." See generally, Brownlee (1996; 11–20).

47. In *Pollock v. Farmers' Loan & Trust Co.*, 157 US 429, aff'd on rehearing 158 US 601 (1895), the Supreme Court held the income tax of the Wilson-Gorman Tariff unconstitutional because it violated the prohibition on unapportioned direct taxes in Article 1, Section 9. The Sixteenth Amendment, adopted in 1913, allowed Congress the power to impose income taxes without apportionment among the States and without regard to any census or enumeration.

48. Representatives from slave states were concerned that a federal property tax would treat slaves as property, farm states' representatives were concerned that the tax might be based on the size rather than the value of landholdings, and representatives of urban commercial areas were concerned that the property tax would be based on assessed value. Brownlee (1996, 14–15).

below 15 percent), and has drifted down a bit more since (particularly as constitutional and statutory limitations on the use of property taxes began to bite).[49]

The composition of tax revenues for state and local governments in the United States has changed as well. Although property taxes continue to be the major source of tax revenues for local governments, state governments rely far less on them than before. Some of the impetus for this latter shift was the growing dissatisfaction with the property tax that began to surface during the late nineteenth century.[50] Spurred both by these concerns and perhaps by the reintroduction of the federal income tax as well, most states abolished general state-level property taxes during the first half of the twentieth century and replaced them with state-level income taxes, excise taxes (including levies on automobiles and gasoline to help pay for roads), and sales taxes.[51] Taxes on real property were left to local governments. Property taxes contributed over half the revenues of state governments at the beginning of the century, but by the 1940s they accounted for less than 6 percent. Today, property taxes account for 28.6 percent of total state and local revenue, general sales taxes for 24.7 percent, selective sales taxes for 10.8 percent, individual income taxes for 24.3 percent, and corporate income taxes account for 4.1 percent (other taxes account for 7.6 percent; U.S. Bureau of the Census [2001]).

The regional variation noted in the relative size of local governments and the use of tax instruments noted earlier for the nineteenth century per-

---

49. See Steuerle (2004, 37), for changes in the size of local governments relative to the economy. A series of changes in state constitutions and statutes during the late 1970s and 1980s restricted the use of property taxes. In 1978, California voters passed Proposition 13, which imposed a maximum property tax rate of 1 percent. As of 2002, forty-four states had some type of restriction on the ability of local government to impose property taxes. These limitations take different forms: thirty-three states impose property tax rate limitations, twenty-seven states impose limitations on property tax revenue limits, and six states impose limits on increases in assessed property values (Brunori 2003, 61–62).

50. The property tax worked well (or was politically palatable) when the bulk of personal wealth consisted of real property, there was confidence in the ability of the electorate to monitor the expenditures of local (or state) governments, and there was a sense that tax revenue funded public goods and services that enhanced property values. As the variety of assets available to individuals increased, however, criticisms that property taxes were both inequitable and inefficient because either design or enforcement issues led to different forms of wealth being taxed at different rates. State governments responded by nominally increasing the legal scope of their property taxes to cover all types of property, such as cash, bonds, stocks, and mortgages, but in reality the burden fell primarily on owners of real estate. Among the prominent critics of the property tax were Richard T. Ely and Edwin R. Seligman. See Ely (1888) and Seligman (1969 [1895]). Seligman contended that the property tax was defective in five ways: (a) lack of uniformity or inequality in assessment; (b) lack of universality in its failure to effectively tax personal property; (c) incentives to dishonesty in reporting and classifying property; (d) potential for regressivity; and (e) potential for double taxation (see also Seligman, 19–32). He suggested that in the early 1900s the property tax in New York fell 95 percent on real property and only 5 percent on personal property, despite the relative increase in the proportion of wealth held in intangible personal property.

51. See the discussion in Einhorn (2006).

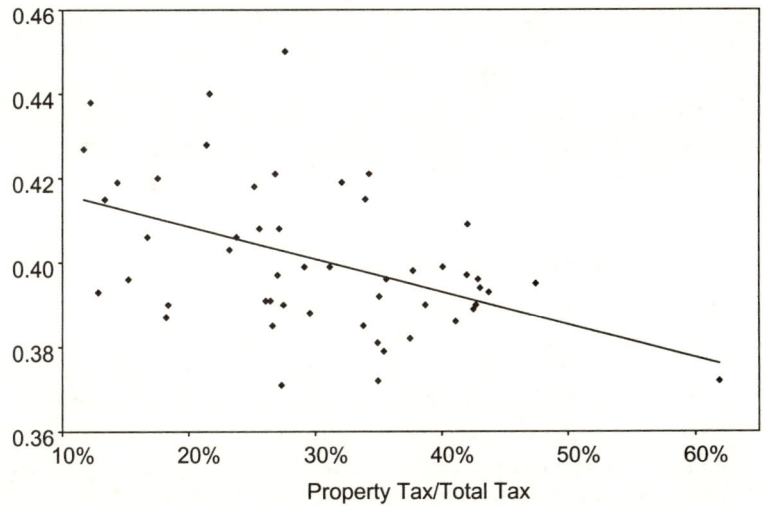

Fig. 3.1 Income inequality and the importance of property tax revenue: A plot of the Gini coefficients by the share of property taxes in total state and local government revenue across all states, 1980

Source: For the state and local government revenue information, see U.S. Bureau of the Census (1983, table 477, p. 284); and for the state-level Gini coefficients for income inequality, see table 702, p. 426.

sisted through the late twentieth century. Not only did the Midwest and the Northeast continue to have relatively larger local governments, and rely more on property taxes as a share of total state and local government revenue than did the South and the West, but a marked association across states between the extent of income inequality and the importance of property taxes for financing government goods and services was evident until late in the twentieth century (for example, see figure 3.1 for the pattern in 1980).

In Canada, the government sector began to grow rapidly following independence in 1867. Not only did the British North America Act provide for a centralized federal government with general taxing authority, but provincial governments came under more pressure to raise revenues to support the increasing demand for public services that accompanied the population and economic booms of the late nineteenth and early twentieth centuries. Tariffs and revenues obtained from public lands and resources taxes were at first the major sources of funds for the national and provincial governments, but this began to change after Canada introduced its first federal income tax, in 1917, to fund the costs of Canada's participation in World War I. Overall, the record of the evolution of tax institutions in Canada over the twentieth century resembled that in the United States, perhaps most notably in the prominence of the income tax (both to the federal and provincial governments; Brownlee 1996). The Canadian pattern was also much like that of the United States in the relative importance of the local governments declining markedly over time (from nearly 40 percent of the government sector as late as the 1920s to less than 10 percent today) and the property tax remaining the dominant source of revenue for local governments (with property tax receipts accounting for roughly 70 percent of revenue at 1950).[52]

3.4.2 Developments in Latin America

Latin American countries experienced major economic and political changes over the late-nineteenth and twentieth centuries. Of greatest significance was a sharp and broad (extending across much of Latin America) acceleration in economic growth that began during the 1870s and 1880s, spurred in large part from exogenous factors such as the expansion of international trade around the world and higher prices for commodities in which the region had a comparative advantage. Although this boom was fueled by improvements in the technology and organization of international transport and trade, as well as increases in demand for raw materials and foodstuffs from rapidly-industrializing Europe, another major stimulus to expanded production of tradable goods came from the real depreciation of the silver-backed currencies (common throughout Latin America) that occurred during the late-nineteenth and early twentieth centuries, as the price of silver declined relative to gold. Where this latter development occurred, the surge in commodity output extended beyond agricultural produce (coffee, sugar, animal products, etc.) and natural resources (such as oil, copper, and other minerals) to manufacturing production (which helped to nurture the development of a powerful constituency for higher tariffs) as well. Although there were interruptions in the ascent of their economies, and the records and rates of progress varied somewhat across countries, Latin America as a whole has grown at nearly the same rate as the United States since 1870, after a period of relative stagnation for roughly the previous century.[53]

The initial phase of relatively sustained economic growth in Latin America was powered largely by the production of goods for foreign markets. The growth in trade that this pursuit of international comparative advantage led to increased revenues from tariffs (some of which had been raised

---

52. Substantial variation exists among the provinces as to the percentage of total local government revenue from property and related taxes. In New Brunswick, Ontario, and Saskatchewan, property tax revenues are about half of total revenues while in Newfoundland and Labrador, Prince Edward Island, and the Northwest Territories property taxes are only about 20 percent of total local government revenues. See Treff and Perry (2004).
53. For an overview of industrial development in Latin America over the late nineteenth and twentieth centuries, see Haber (2006). For general histories of economic, political, and social changes in Latin America during the era, see Halperin Donghi (1993), Thorpe (1998), and Bulmer-Thomas (2003).

Table 3.18 National government tax revenue as a share of GDP (%)

Country	1900	1910	1920	1930	1940	1950	1960	1970	1980	1990	2000
Argentina	10	7	5	7	8	10	10	8	13	10	14
Bolivia	n.a.	n.a.	n.a.	n.a.	n.a.	n.a.	5	10	5	14	18
Brazil	10	11	9	8	10	7	7	10	10	24	23
Chile	n.a.	n.a.	n.a.	n.a.	9	11	17	16	32	21	24
Colombia	n.a.	n.a.	n.a.	n.a.	4	7	8	10	12	13	14
Costa Rica	n.a.	n.a.	n.a.	n.a.	n.a.	10	12	14	18	23	21
Mexico	5	4	n.a.	6	7	9	8	9	16	16	15
Peru	n.a.	n.a.	n.a.	n.a.	n.a.	11	16	16	17	13	16
Uruguay	n.a.	n.a.	n.a.	n.a.	n.a.	n.a.	n.a.	n.a.	22	24	28
Venezuela	n.a.	n.a.	8	9	12	18	27	19	26	24	20

Sources: University of Oxford Latin American Centre (2006); United Nations Online Network in Public Administration and Finance (UNPAN, 2006).
Note: n.a. = not available.

to protect local industry) and export taxes (or other means of procuring revenues from the exploitation of natural resources) that supported an expansion of central governments.[54] In the more progressive and prosperous countries, such as Argentina, Chile, Costa Rica, and Uruguay, this era of trade-based growth yielded a sharp increase in national government support for public services such as schools (which local governments had conspicuously failed to do a good job at providing). In other generally less democratic regimes such as Mexico and Peru, where military officers were not infrequently prominent in political affairs, the increases in revenue were often diverted to enhancing domestic security or the armed forces.[55] Central governments in Latin America did grow during the economic expansion of the late-nineteenth and early twentieth centuries, but in general—with exceptions, such as Argentina and Brazil—their sizes remained quite modest by the standards of the United States or Canada (especially considering the relatively large local and state/provincial governments in those countries), as gauged relative to GDP, until the second half of the twentieth century. Unlike the experience of their neighbors to the north, it was not until the 1950s that most central governments in Latin America began to realize substantial growth relative to their respective economies (see table 3.18). At first, the additional tax revenues were obtained by the introduction and raising of income taxes on individuals and corporations.

54. For example, Brazil, Chile, Ecuador, Mexico, Panama, and Venezuela generally had substantial nontax revenues to support government operations, mostly obtained from mining, oil production, or (in the case of Panama), income from the Canal.
55. Such contrasts call attention to the slow pace of democratization in Latin America and its implications for tax structures and government policies overall. As highlighted in table 3.1, even the more progressive countries did not achieve rates of participation in elections comparable to those in the United States and Canada until the second half of the twentieth century.

The major increases in tax revenues that came during the 1960s, 1970s, and 1980s, however, were generated largely by greater collections from turnover taxes and the value-added tax (VAT). In a few countries (most notably Venezuela), expansions of the public sector were financed by taxes on the production of petroleum or other natural resources.[56]

Given the widespread recognition that the relative size of the government sector typically increases with per capita income, it is perhaps not surprising that tax burdens in Latin American countries were lower throughout the twentieth century than in the United States and Canada. What is more striking is that tax burdens are typically lighter in Latin American countries than in other comparable developing countries.[57] For example, using estimates from the 1997 IMF Government Finance Statistics, we can compare the aggregate tax burdens for Latin American countries to those of other economies with similar levels of per capita income. Low-income developing countries (GDP per capita less than $1,000) are reported as having a tax revenue/GDP ratio of 12.1 percent, medium-income developing countries (GDP per capita between $1,000 and $5,000) a ratio of 17.1 percent, and high-income developing countries (GDP per capita greater than $5,000 and less than $20,000) a tax revenue/GDP ratio of 25.6 percent.[58] With the exceptions of Uruguay, Nicaragua, and Panama (which derives revenue from the Canal), the aggregate tax burdens in Latin American countries are lower than the average for their respective income classes of developing countries.

Looking at aggregate tax burdens tells only part of the story. In order to better appreciate how the structure of taxes evolved in Latin America over the twentieth century and the factors that contributed to those changes, it is necessary to examine the relative use of different tax instruments. What

---

56. For example, in Venezuela during the late 1950s, taxes on petroleum accounted for two-thirds of total tax revenue (see Sommerfield 1966, 57).

57. Economic theory provides relatively little guidance as to optimal levels of taxation, but at least until some level of taxation there is a positive correlation between per capita GDP and tax levels (Burgess and Stern 1993). For the poorer developing countries, Burgess and Stern find a stronger correlation between increasing GDP and levels of taxation than in either richer developing countries or in developed countries. They note that the richer developing countries often have substantial nontax revenue sources, either from revenue from state-owned resources or from natural resources. For example, in Latin America, Brazil, Chile, Ecuador, Mexico, Panama, and Venezuela have substantial nontax revenues to support government operations (see Inter-American Development Bank 1997, table C-10).

58. These statistics are roughly comparable to estimates available from other studies. For example, Tanzi and Zee (2000) estimated that the tax-revenue-to-GDP ratio for all developing countries was 18.2 percent, and for OECD countries the ratio was 37.9 percent for the period 1995–97 (see Tanzi and Zee 2000). Using a larger sample of countries, Fox and Gurley (2005) found that low-income countries (per capita GDP of less than $1,000) raised tax revenue amounting to 15.8 percent of GDP, medium-income countries (per capita GDP of between US $1,000–17,000) raised about 20.0 percent, and high-income countries (per capita GDP greater than US $17,000) raised 27.2 percent. These estimates do not include social insurance payments.

stands out from this record is that despite the substantial increase in the tax revenues raised over the twentieth century, the pattern of Latin American tax institutions generally avoiding taxes that are commonly understood as progressive has persisted. As we have discussed previously, during the first decades of the twentieth century, Latin American countries continued to rely heavily on customs revenue, with tariffs set both to raise central government revenue as well as to protect influential economic interests (including local industry and workers generally) from foreign competition.[59] In 1930, for example, taxes on international trade (primarily tariffs but some taxes on exports) accounted for: 44 percent of central government revenue in Brazil; 48 percent in Argentina; 54 percent in Chile; 55 percent in Colombia; 41 percent in Mexico; and 51 percent in Venezuela. The importance of these taxes on international trade decreased dramatically over the second half of the century, however, and nowhere today do they account for more than 15 percent. For a short interval, during the 1950s, 1960s, and 1970s, income taxes (which fell much more heavily on corporations than on individuals) replaced tariffs as the major source of revenue, but in recent decades there has been a return to the longstanding practice of relying on commodity taxes. Perhaps encouraged by international movements toward greater openness, taxes on domestic goods and services (particularly the VAT) have assumed the dominant role in raising revenue.[60]

Table 3.19 provides a representative snapshot of the current sources of tax revenue to the central governments in Latin America and in the United States and Canada. Most salient is the much greater importance of indirect taxation in Latin America (and the corresponding much greater importance of income taxation in the two northern countries). Even aside from the obvious centrality of the VAT,[61] it is striking that nearly everywhere in

---

59. Haber (2006) and Bulmer-Thomas (2003).

60. Our characterizations of the change over time in the relative use of tax instruments are based on the data and estimates presented in Bulmer-Thomas (2003, table 6.6); International Monetary Fund (various years); Richard Musgrave and Malcolm Gillis (1971, 271–73, tables 3–5), Sommerfield (1966, 56, table 5); Thirsk (1997, 289, table 7.1), and Thorp (1998, 346, tables VII.1–2).

61. As is well known, the introduction and diffusion of the VAT over the second half of the twentieth century changed the tax landscape throughout the world (with the notable exception of the United States). See Liam P. Ebrill et al. (2001) for a review of this development. Latin American countries were among the leaders in replacing an inefficient collection of turnover taxes with VATs. From a political economy perspective the relative success of the VATs came along at a very good time. It allowed many Latin American countries to increase tax revenues (and reduce tariffs) without substantial reliance on income taxes. See Keen and Ligthart (1999). Brazil was the first Latin American country to adopt the VAT (1967), followed by Ecuador (1970), Uruguay (1970), Bolivia (1973), Argentina (1975), Colombia (1975), Honduras (1976), Peru (1976), Panama (1977), Guatemala (1983), Mexico (1980), and the Dominican Republic (1983).

Table 3.19 Sources of tax revenue for current national governments in the Americas (%)

Country	Income tax			Property	Domestic tax on goods and services		Taxes on international trade and transportation	Social security	Other taxes
	Total	Corporate	Individual		Total	Excises			
United States	59	10	50	1	3	3	1	35	0
Canada	58	12	43	0	18	4	1	23	0
Argentina	19	13	6	4	45	15	6	27	0
Bolivia	9	9	0	10	58	22	7	13	3
Brazil	24			0	26	9	3	41	5
Chile	23			0	57	12	7	8	5
Colombia	41	39	2	3	46	4	10		0
Costa Rica	15	13	1	1	45	11	6	33	0
Dominican Republic	21	9	12	1	35	31	38	4	1
Mexico	38			0	30	3	4	24	3
Nicaragua	14			0	59	24	9	18	0
Panama	27			2	16	8	15	35	4
Paraguay	19	19	0	0	59	16	18	0	4
Peru	23	13	10	0	56	13	10	8	4
Uruguay	16	9	7	6	42	12	4	30	3
Venezuela	30	29	2	8	44	8	12	6	1

Sources: International Monetary Fund 2006.

Notes: The figures represent averages for tax years 1998–2003. Certain country data for 1998–2003 were incomplete and only the years in the parentheses are included for Brazil (1998), Colombia (1998–2000), Mexico (1998–2000) and Panama (2001). Paraguay makes use of budgeted data only. Social security and other taxes were removed for Colombia to better reflect consistent categories over time. Additionally, breakdowns of income taxes between individual and corporate taxes were frequently not available for Latin American countries. In some cases, rounding causes the sum of component shares to appear to exceed or fall below aggregate shares.

Table 3.20   Relative use of different tax instruments by national governments, by per capita income level: World averages (1990–1995 GDP estimates; %)

	150–500	500–5,000	5,000–20,000	>20,000	All
Tax revenue as percent of total government revenue	84	87	87	87	87
Total tax revenue					
Individual and corporate tax	23	21	35	33	26
Corporate tax	11	11	13	8	10
Individual income tax	12	10	22	25	16
Taxes on property	3	1	2	3	2
Domestic taxes on goods and services	43	45	34	32	39
Excises	17	13	12	9	12
Taxes on international trade and transportation	21	10	9	1	9
Import duties	20	9	9	1	9
Social security	11	23	20	30	24

Source: International Monetary Fund (2004), for years 1998–2002.

Latin America more revenue (and often far more) is raised from both trade taxes as well as excise taxes than from individual income taxes.[62]

It is to be expected that low-income countries employ different types of taxes than do high-income countries, but Latin American societies stand out relative to other economies at similar levels of development. Table 3.20 presents a summary of the relative use of different tax instruments by countries at different per capita income levels. First, consider general taxes on domestic goods and services as well as excise taxes. As discussed previously, Latin American countries rely on these taxes for about 57 percent of their total tax revenue.[63] Moreover, they generally rely more on these revenue sources than do their counterparts in the respective ranges of per capita income. For example, while most Latin American countries would be considered richer developing countries (per capita income of between

---

62. Stotsky and WoldeMariam (2002, table 7). Today, revenues from excise taxes account for over 20 percent of total tax revenues in Bolivia, the Dominican Republic, and Nicaragua, but less than 5 percent in Colombia and Mexico. For most other countries in Latin America, revenues from excise taxes account for about ten to fifteen percent of total tax revenues. In contrast, revenues from excise taxes represent only three to four percent of the total tax revenues in the United States and Canada. In the early 1980s, only in Chile, Colombia, and Mexico did individual income tax revenues exceed excise tax revenues.

63. The statistics in table 3.19 are in line with the estimates of Tanzi and Zee (2000). They confirm that most countries rely on general consumption taxes, such as the VAT, excise taxes, and trade taxes to fund a substantial portion of government operations. In OECD countries, general consumption tax revenues for 1995–97 account for 11.4 percent of GDP. By comparison, in developing countries, general consumption tax revenues for the same time period account for 10.5 percent of GDP.

$5,000–20,000), the average for that class is 46 percent.[64] Perhaps the most distinguishing feature of this perspective on Latin American tax systems, however, is again in their neglect of income taxes, especially individual income taxes. On average, Latin American countries raise about 25 percent of total tax revenues from income taxes, with about 19 percent from corporate tax revenues and about 6 percent from individual income tax revenues. In contrast, the richer developing countries on average raise about 36 percent of tax revenues from income taxes (13 percent from corporate and 22 percent from individual income tax revenues).[65] Given that the individual income tax is often viewed today as the most progressive major tax instrument, its minor role in Latin America might seem a continuation of a long tradition of gentle treatment of the elite by the tax institutions of that region.

As we emphasized earlier, perhaps the most distinctive and fundamentally important feature of Latin American governmental and tax structures during the nineteenth century was the high degree of centralization. Local governments in Latin America were quite small by the standards of North American countries. In recent decades there has been an increased awareness in Latin America of the possible implications of stunted local governments, especially for the provision of public services. This has led to a wave of policies across the region that are aimed at transferring more resources from the central government to local (if not provincial as well) governments. Table 3.21 presents estimates for five Latin American countries of the distribution of tax revenues and expenditures across levels of government, before and after the first generation of decentralization that began in the early 1980s.[66] Substantial variation in the size of local and

64. A few Latin American countries, such as Bolivia and Paraguay, belong in the middle-income group (with per capita income between $500 and $5000), but their reliance on domestic taxes on goods and services as well as excises (58 and 59 percent, respectively), is roughly equal to the average for this category (58 percent).

65. It may also be useful to compare the relative use of tax instruments by Latin American countries to choices made by governments in developing countries in other parts of the world. Perhaps the most interesting comparisons are between developing countries in Africa and in Latin America. As compared to Latin America, African countries rely more on income taxes (28—14 percent from corporate and 14 percent from individual income tax revenues) and taxes on international tax (31 percent), and less on domestic taxes on goods and services (22 percent), excise taxes (11 percent), and social security taxes (5 percent). Again, what is striking is the relative use of individual income taxes. Whereas African countries raise 14 percent of total tax revenues from individual income taxes, Latin American countries raise only about 6 percent. For the period between 1996 and 2002, developing countries in Asia raised, on average, about 37 percent of total tax revenue from income taxes (16 percent from individual income taxes and 21 percent from corporate income taxes), 45 percent from general consumption and excise taxes, and 14 percent from trade taxes (IMF 2004, online version).

66. See Wiesner (2003, 10), describing the first generation of decentralization as characterized by: (a) implementation of constitutional reforms that provided for automatic and largely unconditional transfers from central government to subnational governments; (b) introduction of targeted fiscal transfers through formulas to specific sectors and to low-income groups; (c) an alleged process of devolving resources together with devolving responsibilities; (d) delegation of some limited taxing and spending authority; and (e) a general lack of any in-

Table 3.21 Shares of total government tax revenues and of expenditures by level of government in selected Latin American countries: Before and after programs to decentralize (%)

	Share of total government tax revenue collected by level of government		Share of total government expenditure by level of government	
	Before decentralization	With decentralization	Before decentralization	With decentralization
Argentina[a]				
Central	79.3	80.0	63.5	51.9
Provincial	13.7	15.4	31.0	39.5
Local	7.0	4.6	5.4	8.6
Brazil[b]				
Central	59.8	47.1	50.2	36.5
State	36.9	49.4	36.2	40.7
Local	3.8	3.6	13.6	22.8
Colombia[c]				
Central	82.2	81.6	72.8	67.0
Departmental	12.2	11.1	16.7	15.7
Local	5.6	7.3	10.5	17.3
Mexico[d]				
Central	90.7	82.7	90.2	87.8
State	8.3	13.4	8.8	9.5
Local	1.0	3.9	1.0	2.8
Venezuela[e]				
Central	95.8	96.9	76.0	77.7
State	0.1	0.1	14.9	15.7
Local	4.0	3.1	9.1	6.5

Sources: For Argentina and Colombia, López Murphy (1995, 22, 25, 33). For Brazil, Anwar Shah (1990, 15). For Venezuela, World Bank (1992, 5). For Mexico, Victoria E. Rodríguez (1987, 271); and INEGI (1994).
[a]Figures before decentralization as of 1983, under decentralization as of 1992.
[b]Figures before decentralization as of 1974, under decentralization as of 1988.
[c]Figures before decentralization as of 1980, under decentralization as of 1991.
[d]Figures before decentralization as of 1982, under decentralization as of 1992.
[e]Figures before decentralization as of 1980, under decentralization as of 1989.

provincial governments is evident, with Argentina, Brazil, and Colombia having the largest subnational governments (especially Brazil, which has relatively large provincial governments), Venezuela, Mexico, and Bolivia somewhere in the middle, and all other countries having even smaller sub-

---

dependent evaluation of results. The second generation of decentralization policies began in the late 1990s and provided for tighter macroeconomic budget constraints, stronger intergovernmental regulatory frameworks, and more intensive use of incentives at the sectoral level (Wiesner 2003, 12).

national governments.[67] Largely because of the enormous increase in the size of the federal governments in the United States and Canada, as well as the large transfers from the central to the provincial governments in Brazil and Argentina, the contrast between the rich countries in the North and their neighbors in Latin America is not nearly so stark in this dimension as it was in the past. Nevertheless, subnational governments remain quite modest throughout Latin America, and the nineteenth century pattern endures, especially when gauged by tax revenues.

3.5 Conclusion

In this paper we have begun to explore how the extreme inequality that came to characterize nearly all Latin American countries during their colonial periods may have influenced how their tax institutions evolved. We seek to understand why the tax structures of Latin American countries are so distinctive today, even relative to other developing countries with roughly similar per capita incomes, and why their national governments have historically been so dominant and their local governments stunted. One traditional explanation for the types of tax regimes adopted by Latin American countries highlights technical or resource constraints. Developing countries have a much more limited administrative capacity to collect income and other complex taxes involving the monitoring of individuals than developed countries. The existence of large informal service and agricultural sectors further complicates the task of tax design and enforcement. Thus, it is not surprising that Latin American and other developing countries focus more on revenue sources such as taxes on trade, taxes imposed on foreign corporations, and general consumption and excise taxes.

That being said, our examination suggests that the government and tax structures of the Latin American societies had already diverged from those in the United States and Canada by, if not before, the middle of the nineteenth century—not long after attaining independence and before there were substantial differences in per capita income. Although the causal mechanisms remain to be explored, we emphasize the striking parallels between how the institutions of taxation evolved across the hemisphere and how other fundamental social and economic institutions evolved (such as those involving suffrage, education, and ownership of land). In Latin America, where a substantial gap existed and persisted in the economic cir-

---

67. Wills, Garman, and Haggard (1995) review the movements toward decentralization in Argentina, Brazil, Colombia, Mexico, and Venezuela, examining the influence that central government has over local finances. They examine the relative discretion the federal government has in determining the amount of transferred funds, the ability of central governments to impose conditions on the use of funds, and the ability of local governments to borrow funds. They find that the degree of decentralization reflects the relative political power of presidents, legislators, and subnational governments, and that the structure of political parties in the respective countries influences the level of autonomy of lower levels of government.

cumstances and political influence between elites and the bulk of the population, these institutions tended to develop along paths that greatly advantaged those elites. Control over voting rules assured elites of greatly disproportionate political representation. Very modest commitments to public investments, such as schooling, kept taxes low and competition in the labor markets for individuals from good backgrounds limited. Land policies kept land ownership in the hands of a relative few. Where government services were provided, funds were raised primarily through means other than direct taxation of income, wealth, or property.

This path of institutional development was radically different from those followed by the relatively homogenous Canada and the United States. Although there may be other explanations for these patterns, the evidence seems consistent with our hypothesis that differences in the extent of inequality across these societies contributed to the different political decisions they made regarding the nature and size of different levels of government and the relative use of different tax instruments (if not the types and scale of government expenditure programs as well). As we have shown, there were no major differences during the nineteenth century in how national governments chose to raise their revenue. The United States, Canada, and Latin American countries all relied overwhelmingly on customs duties, other levies on foreign trade, and excise taxes. However, the United States and Canada were quite unlike their Latin American counterparts in financing local governments whose programs (generally public schools, roads, water and sanitation projects, other public health measures, etc.) were so extensive that they rivaled or exceeded their respective central government in resources consumed and services rendered. The funding for these substantial local governments came overwhelmingly from taxes on property, wealth, and income. State and local governments were successful in raising revenue through such instruments primarily because the large share of nineteenth century wealth was held in land, but it is telling that Latin American societies did not experience the same growth of local governments. Given that the record in Canada and the United States, where local governments funded primarily by property taxes trace back to the seventeenth and eighteenth centuries, it appears very difficult to argue that the Latin American policies were dictated by technical or resource constraints on their ability to administer such taxes.

Latin American countries continue to have the highest rates of income inequality in the world. They still have relatively low aggregate tax burdens and generally rely on taxes on consumption, rather than on taxes on individual income, wealth, or property. Likewise, the central governments are still more dominant, relative to state and local authorities, than they are in the United States, Canada, and other regions of the world. It is not clear whether the persistence in the character of tax institutions and government structures can be attributed to the same factors and processes that operated during the nineteenth century. Much has changed in Latin America over the twentieth century. The progress in broadening the distribution of political influence (democratization), for example, would lead one to expect that the relative influence of elites on the design of institutions should be diminished and the demand for certain types of government programs should be increased. Even with political changes, however, it is difficult to design progressive tax structures in societies marked by great inequality. In addition, in recent years, the range of options available to government tax authorities has narrowed as economies have become more open and capital more mobile. While changes in Latin America over the last 10 to 15 years have increased expenditures on social programs and, often, increased the resources available to local governments to fund those programs, the changes on the tax side have been less dramatic. Perhaps future political and economic developments will change the patterns of taxation in Latin America. In looking at the current structures, however, the evidence suggests that the long history of extreme inequality in Latin America is central to understanding the distinctive set of tax institutions that have evolved in Latin America.

References

Acemoglu, Daron, and James A. Robinson. 2000. Why did western Europe extend the franchise? *Quarterly Journal of Economics* 115 (Nov.): 1167–99.
Adelman, Jeremy. 1994. *Frontier development: Land, labor, and capital on wheatlands of Argentina and Canada, 1890–1914.* Oxford: Oxford University Press.
Alesina, Alberto, Reza Baqir, and William Easterly. 1999. Public goods and ethnic divisions. *Quarterly Journal of Economics* 114 (November): 1243–84.
Barbosa, Francisco de Assis. 1966. *João Pinheiro, Documentário sôbre sua Vida Pública.* Belo Horizonte, Brazil: Arquivo Pública Mineiro.
Best, Michael H. 1976. Political power and tax revenues in Central America. *Journal of Development Economics* 3:49–82.
Bird, Richard M. 1992. Tax reform in Latin America: A review of some recent experiences. *Latin American Research Review* 27 (1): 7–36.
———. 2003. Taxation in Latin America: Reflections on sustainability and the balance between equity and efficiency. University of Toronto, Institute for International Business, Unpublished Working Paper.
Brewer, John. 1990. *The sinews of power: War, money, and the English state, 1688–1783.* Cambridge, MA: Harvard University Press.
Brownlee, W. Elliot. 1996. *Federal taxation in America: A short history.* Washington, DC: Woodrow Wilson Center Press.
Brunori, David. 2003. *Local tax policy: A federalist perspective.* Washington, DC: Urban Institute Press.
Bullock, Charles J. 1907. Historical sketch of the finances and financial policy of Massachusetts. *Publications of the American Economic Association* 3rd series 8 (May 1907): 1–144.

Bulmer-Thomas, Victor. 2003. *The economic history of Latin America since independence.* New York: Cambridge University Press.
Burgess, Robin, and Nicholas Stern. 1993. Taxation and development. *Journal of Economic Literature* 31 (June): 762–830.
Burkholder, Mark A., and Lyman L. Johnson. 1998. *Colonial Latin America.* New York: Oxford University Press.
Carreira, Liberato de Castro. 1889. *Historia Financiera e Ornamentaria do Imperio do Brazil desde a sua fundação.* Rio de Janeiro, Brazil: Imprenta Nacional.
Chaudhary, Latika. 2006. Social divisions and public goods provision: Evidence from colonial India. Stanford University, Department of Economics, Unpublished Working Paper.
Cubberley, Ellwood P. 1920. *The history of education.* Boston: Houghton Mifflin.
De Ferranti, David, Guillermo Perry, Francisco Ferreira, and Michael Walton. 2004. *Inequality in Latin America and the Caribbean: Breaking with history.* New York: World Bank and Oxford University Press.
Dunn, Richard S. 1972. *Sugar and slaves: The rise of the planter class in the English West Indies, 1624–1713.* Chapel Hill: University of North Carolina Press.
Ebrill, Liam P., Michael Keen, Jean-Paul Bodin, and Victoria Summers. 2001. *The modern VAT.* Washington, DC: International Monetary Fund.
Einhorn, Robin. 2006. *American taxation, American slavery.* Chicago: University of Chicago Press.
Elliott, J. H. 2006. *Empires of the Atlantic world: Britain and Spain in America: 1492–1830.* New Haven, CT: Yale University Press.
Ely, Richard T. 1888. *Taxation of American states and cities.* New York: Thomas Y. Crowell.
Engerman, Stanley L., Elisa V. Mariscal, and Kenneth L. Sokoloff. 2002. The evolution of schooling institutions in the Americas, 1800–1945. UCLA, Department of Economics, Unpublished Working Paper.
Engerman, Stanley L., and Kenneth L. Sokoloff. 1997. Factor endowments, institutions, and differential paths of growth among new world economies: A view from economic historians of the United States. In *How Latin America fell behind,* ed. Stephen Haber, 260–304. Stanford, CA: Stanford University Press.
———. 2002. Factor endowments, inequality, and paths of development among new world economies. *Economia* 3 (Fall): 41–102.
———. 2005. The evolution of suffrage institutions in the Americas. *Journal of Economic History* 65 (December): 891–921.
Fox, William F., and Tami Gurley. 2005. An exploration of tax patterns around the world. *Tax Notes International* 37:794–95.
Galenson, David W. 1995. The settlement and growth of the colonies: Population, labor, and economic development. In *The Cambridge economic history of the United States.* Vol. 1, *The colonial period,* ed. Stanley L. Engerman and Robert E. Gallman, 135–237. Cambridge: Cambridge University Press.
Gates, Paul W. 1968. *History of public land law development.* Washington, DC: Government Printing Office.
Gipson, Lawrence. 1936. *The British empire before the American revolution.* Caldwell, ID: The Caxton Printers.
Goode, Richard. 1984. *Government finance in developing countries.* Washington, DC: Brookings Institution.
Greene, Jack P. 1988. *Pursuits of happiness.* Chapel Hill: University of North Carolina Press.
Guell, Tomas. 1975. *Compendio de Historia Económica y Hacendaria de Costa Rica.* San José: Editorial Costa Rica.

Haber, Stephen H. 2006. Development strategy or endogenous process: The industrialization of Latin America. Stanford University Department of Economics and Hoover Institution, Unpublished Working Paper.
Halperin Donghi, Tulio. 1993. *The contemporary history of Latin America.* Ed. and trans. John Charles Chasteen. Durham, NC: Duke University Press.
Hirschman, Albert O. 1970. *Exit, voice, and loyalty.* Cambridge, MA: Harvard University Press.
Holden, Robert. 1994. *Mexico and the survey of public lands: The management of modernization, 1876–1911.* Dekalb: Northern Illinois University Press.
Inter-American Development Bank. 1997. *Latin America after a decade of reforms: Economic and social progress.* Baltimore: Johns Hopkins University Press.
International Monetary Fund. Various years. *Government finance statistics yearbook.* Washington, DC: International Monetary Fund.
Keen, Michael, and Jenny E. Ligthart. 1999. Coordinating tariff reduction and domestic tax reform. IMF Working Paper no. 99-93. Washington, DC: International Monetary Fund, July.
Khan, B. Zorina, and Kenneth L. Sokoloff. 2001. Intellectual property institutions in the United States: Early development. *Journal of Economic Perspectives* 15 (Summer): 233–46.
Lockhart, James, and Stuart B. Schwartz. 1983. *Early Latin America: A history of colonial Spanish America and Brazil.* Cambridge: Cambridge University Press.
López Garavito, Luis Fernando. 1992. *Historia de la Hacienda y el Tesoro y en Colombia, 1821–1900.* Bogota, Colombia: Banco de Republica.
Marichal, Carlos, Manuel Miño Grijalva, and Paolo Riguzzi. 1994. *El primer siglo de la Hacienda Pública del Estado de México, 1824–1923.* Mexico: Secretaría de Finanzas y Planeación del Estado de México y El Colegio Mexiquense A.C.
Mathew, W. M. 1976. A primitive export sector: Guano production in mid-nineteenth-century Peru. *Journal of Latin American Studies* 8 (May): 35–57.
McBride, George McCutchen. 1923. *The land systems of Mexico.* New York: American Geographical Society.
Melo-Gonzalez, Jorge Orlando. 1989. La evolucion economica de Colombia, 1830–1900. In *Nueva Historia de Colombia,* vol. 2, ed. Êlvaro Tirado.
Ministerio de Economía y Hacienda. 1963. *Anuario de la Dirección General de Estadística.* San José, Costa Rica: Imprenta Nacional.
Ministerio de Hacienda y Comercio. 1928. *Extracto Estadistico del Peru 1927.* Lima, Peru: Imprenta Americana.
Mitchell, Brian. 1993. *International historical statistics: The Americas.* New York: Stockton.
Molina, Evaristo. 1889. Bosquejo de la Hacienda Publica de Chile desde la Independencia hasta la fecha. Santiago, Chile: Imprenta Nacional.
Musgrave, Richard A., and Malcolm Gillis. 1971. *Fiscal reform for Colombia: Final report and staff papers of the Colombian Commission on Tax Reform.* Cambridge, MA: Harvard University International Tax Program.
Musgrave, Richard A., and Peggy B. Musgrave. 1984. *Public finance in theory and practice,* 4th ed. New York: McGraw-Hill.
North, Douglass C. 1981. *Structure and change in economic history.* New York: Norton.
Oficina de Estadistica Nacional. 1875. *Registro Estadistico de la Republica Argentina. Tomo Setimo Ano de 1872 y 1873.* Buenos Aires: Sociedad Anonima.
Park, James William. 1985. *Rafael Núñez and the politics of Colombian regionalism 1863–1886.* Baton Rouge: Louisiana State University Press.

Perkins, Edwin J. 1980. *The economy of Colonial America.* New York: Columbia University Press.
———. 1994. *American public finance and financial services, 1700–1815.* Columbus: Ohio State University.
Perry, J. Harvey. 1955. *Taxes, tariffs, & subsidies: A history of Canadian fiscal development.* Toronto: University of Toronto Press.
Phillips, Charles E. 1957. *The development of education in Canada.* Toronto: W. J. Gage.
Razaghian, Rose. 2005. Financing the Civil War: The Confederacy's financial strategy. Yale ICF Working Paper no. 04-45. New Haven, CT: Yale University Press.
Reese, Thomas J. 1980. *The politics of taxation.* Westport, CT: Greenwood.
Rodríguez, Victoria E. 1987. The politics of decentralization: Divergent outcomes of policy implementation. PhD diss., University of California, Berkeley.
Román, Ana. 1995. *Las Finanzas Públicas de Costa Rica: Metodología y Fuentes (1870–1948).* San José: Universidad de Costa Rica.
Seligman, Edwin R. 1969 [1895]. *Essays in taxation.* New York: A. M. Kelley.
Shah, Anwar. 1991. The new fiscal federalism in Brazil. World Bank Working Paper no. 124, Washington, DC: World Bank.
Shome, Parthasarthi. 1999. Taxation in Latin America: Structural trends and impact of administration. IMF Working Paper no. 99-19. Washington, DC: International Monetary Fund, February.
Slemrod, Joel, and Jon M. Bakija. 2001. Growing inequality and decreased tax progressivity. In *Inequality and tax policy,* ed. Kevin A. Hassett and R. Glenn Hubbard, 192–226. Washington, DC: American Enterprise Institute Press.
———. 1996. *Taxing ourselves.* Cambridge, MA: MIT Press.
Solberg, Carl E. 1987. *The prairies and the pampas: Agrarian policy in Canada and Argentina 1880–1913.* Stanford, CA: Stanford University Press.
Sommerfield, Raynard M. 1966. *Tax reform and the Alliance for Progress.* Austin & London: University of Texas Press.
Steuerle, C. Eugene. 2004. *Contemporary US tax policy.* Washington, DC: Urban Institute Press.
Stotsky, Janet, and Asegedech WoldeMariam. 2002. Central American tax reform: Trends and possibilities. IMF Working Paper no. 02-227. Washington, DC: International Monetary Fund, December.
Tait, Alan A., Wilfrid L. M. Gratz, and Barry J. Eichengreen. 1979. International comparisons of taxation for selected developing countries, 1972–1976. *IMF Staff Papers* 26 (March).
Tannebaum, Frank. 1929. *The Mexican agrarian revolution.* New York: Macmillan.
Tantalean Arbulu, Javier. 1983. *Politica Economico-Financiera y la Formacion del Estado Siglo XIX.* Lima, Peru: CEDEP.
Tanzi, Vito. 1987. Quantitative characteristics of the tax systems in developing countries. In *The theory of taxation for developing countries,* ed. David Newbery and Nicholas Stern. New York: Oxford University Press.
———. 2000. Taxation in Latin America in the last decade. Stanford University, Center for Research on Economic Development and Policy Reform, Working Paper no. 00-76.
Tanzi, Vito, and Howell Zee. 2000. Tax policy for emerging markets: Developing countries. IMF Working Paper no. 00-35. Washington, DC: International Monetary Fund, March.
Tenenbaum, Barbara. 1986. *The politics of penury: Debt and taxes in Mexico, 1821–1856.* Albuquerque: University of New Mexico Press.

Thirsk, Wayne, ed. 1997. *Tax reform in developing countries.* Washington, DC: World Bank.

Thorpe, Rosemary. 1998. *Progress, poverty and exclusion: An economic history of Latin America in the 20th century.* Baltimore: Johns Hopkins University Press.

Tôrres, João Camillo de Oliveira. 1961. *A Formação do Federalismo no Brasil.* São Paolo, Brazil: Companhia Editora Nacional.

Treff, Karin, and David B. Perry. 2004. *Finances of the nation 2003.* Toronto: Canadian Tax Foundation.

United States Bureau of the Census. 2001. *State and local revenue.* Washington, DC: Government Printing Office.

Wallis, John Joseph. 2001. A history of the property tax in America. In *Property taxation and local government finance: Essays in honor of C. Lowell Harriss,* ed. Wallace E. Oates, 123–147. Cambridge, MA: Lincoln Institute of Land Policy.

Weisman, Steven R. 2002. *The great tax wars.* New York: Simon & Schuster.

Wiesner, Eduardo. 2003. *Fiscal federalism in Latin America: From entitlements to markets.* Washington, DC: Inter-American Development Bank.

Wills, Eliza, Christopher da C. B. Garman, and Stephan Haggard. 1995. The politics of decentralization in Latin America. *Latin American Research Review* 34 (1): 7–56.

II

Financial Crises, Lending, and Inflation

4
Financial Crises, 1880–1913
The Role of Foreign Currency Debt

Michael D. Bordo and Christopher M. Meissner

4.1 Introduction

The period from 1870 to 1913 was a period of globalization in both goods and financial markets that is comparable to the present era of globalization. Also, it was a period rife with emerging market financial crises, which has great resonance for the experiences that we have observed in the past decade. In both eras many emerging countries faced frequent currency crises, banking crises, and twin crises. They also faced a number of debt crises. In the terminology of Eichengreen and Hausmann (1999), many of these countries suffered from *original sin*. The external debt that they accumulated to finance their development was almost totally denominated in foreign currency or in terms of gold (or had gold clauses) before 1914, just as emerging market debt today is almost entirely denominated in dollars, euros, or yen. When the exchange rate depreciates, debt service in gold or foreign currency becomes very difficult—leading to default, the consequent drying up of external funding, and economic collapse.

The emerging country experience was in contrast to that of the advanced core countries, which were financially mature, had credibility, and could issue bonds denominated in terms of their own currency. There were few

---

Michael D. Bordo is a professor of economics at Rutgers University and a research associate at the National Bureau of Economic Research. Christopher M. Meissner is a University Lecturer at the University of Cambridge, a fellow at King's College, and a faculty research fellow at the National Bureau of Economic Research.

We thank Antonio David and Wagner Dada for excellent research assistance. Comments from Luis Catão, Barry Eichengreen, Marc Flandreau, Daniel Lederman, Kim Oosterlinck, Anna Schwartz, and participants at a conference at Humboldt University, Berlin, are also appreciated. Errors remain our responsibility. The financial assistance from ESRC grant RES 000-22-0001 is gratefully acknowledged.

crises in these countries. This leads us to ask whether these very different debt structures might play a role in explaining the difference in crisis incidence. We also wonder if debt management policies that created or alleviated balance sheet mismatches mattered, as discussed in Goldstein and Turner (2004). Finally, we examine whether poor reputation and accumulated default experience was a problem, as hypothesized by Carmen Reinhart, Kenneth Rogoff, and Miguel Savastano (2003) in their work on *debt intolerance*.

We have developed a database to allow us to identify and distinguish original sin and balance sheet crises from more traditional currency and banking crises for roughly thirty countries (both advanced and emerging) from 1880–1913. We have data both on the type of crisis incidence and on the fundamentals that economists believe are determinants of crises.

Our results do not find unambiguous support for the idea that hard currency debt for emerging markets is always associated with more financial turbulence. In fact, we find evidence that the emerging markets of the day that had significant amounts of original sin can be divided into two subgroups. One group includes countries such as Argentina, Brazil, Chile, Italy, and Portugal, each of which suffered a financial catastrophe between 1880 and 1913. The other group, including Australia, Canada, New Zealand, Norway, and the United States, had relatively little trouble with financial crises in terms of frequency or virulence. We ascribe this to special country characteristics that other independent peripheral countries did not possess.

We also find that many countries matched their hard currency liabilities with hard currency reserves or took out such debt in proportion to their export earning potential. This helped reduce exposure to currency and banking crises and kept banking and currency crises that did occur from becoming too severe. Nevertheless, even after controlling for the mismatch position, original sin still appears to be associated with crises for many vulnerable countries. Finally, there is a possibility that countries with better international repayment records were able to avoid debt crises despite high levels of debt.

4.2 History, Financial Crises, Balance Sheets, and Hard Currency Debt

In this paper we view banking trouble, currency crises, and debt crises that occur in the same or consecutive years as interrelated phenomena. This is perhaps different from first-generation models that viewed currency crises as events arising from unsustainable fiscal policy under a pegged exchange rate. It is also different from a strand of the literature that views banking crises as arising uniquely from poor supervision, weak structure, or stochastic liquidity runs. Our view is that while some countries had crises that unfolded in ways the older generation of models would predict, other countries faced financial meltdown by having twin (banking and currency crises) or even triple crises, where in addition to a large depreciation and disruption in the banking sector the sovereign debt went into default. One important factor determining the ultimate outcome may be an interaction between the nature of the debt contracts in place and the robustness of the financial system. Our framework for thinking about financial crises is very much parallel to that enunciated in Mishkin (2003), which in turn is inspired by an open-economy approach to the credit channel transmission mechanism of monetary policy. Balance sheets, net worth, and informational asymmetries are key ingredients in this type of model.

In our view, initial trouble might begin in the banking sector for a number of reasons. One possibility is that international interest rates rise. This worsens the balance sheets of nonfinancial firms and banks alike. As the number of nonperforming loans rises and net worth falls, a decline in lending can occur, contributing further to output losses. At this point, internationally mobile capital may take a decidedly pessimistic view of returns in the debtor country and either stop coming in (a sudden stop) or reverse itself, leaving significant short-term financing gaps. This reversal leads to more trouble in the financial sector and obviously increases stress for nonfinancial firms that are forced to cut investment because of the lack of financing. Governments may have trouble making interest payments on debt coming due as capital markets become unwilling to continue rolling debt over. The capital flow reversal, if large enough, could also force the abandonment of an exchange rate peg and a large change in the nominal exchange rate. Floating regimes could also see large depreciation occur under such a scenario.

A contemporary view of the impact of such exchange rate changes is that they may be contractionary.[1] This is where original sin enters the picture. Since the majority of obligations for nearly all countries are in foreign currency or, in the late nineteenth century, denominated in terms of a fixed amount of gold, depreciation vis-à-vis creditor countries or breaking the link between gold and the domestic currency could lead to increases in the real value of debt. This is a redistribution of wealth from domestic borrowers to their creditors, who are expecting a certain amount of gold or foreign currency.[2] When net worth matters for lending decisions, this decline in the net worth of creditors can lead to another round of "disintermediation," causing widespread bankruptcies due to liquidity problems. All else equal,

---

1. Theoretical work by Céspedes, Chang, and Velasco (2004) demonstrates how under certain very plausible circumstances original sin can lead to contractionary depreciations.

2. Eichengreen, Hausmann, and Panizza (2003) argue that what matters is the aggregate external mismatch, and that if all debt is domestic, that one sector's losses are the others' gains. Our view, however, is that net worth matters. When a debtor's net worth deteriorates, borrowing capacity falls, and the capital markets seize up. This is one reason why we focus on domestic and external hard-currency debt rather than just foreign holdings (or issues) of hard-currency debt.

the deterioration to debtors' balance sheets would be more severe the greater the amount of fixed interest rate hard-currency debt outstanding.

There is some contention in the literature as to whether all is in fact equal. Goldstein and Turner (2004) have argued that often countries insure themselves against exchange rate movements. Hard currency debt can be, and often is, backed up by hard currency assets. Alternatively, countries could have enough export capacity to offset changes in liabilities due to exchange rate swings. To gauge the actual effect of original sin one must take account of the mismatch position or the entire balance sheet position of an economy. We describe how we do this in the following. Moreover, Reinhart, Rogoff, and Savastano (2003) have argued that original sin is a proxy for a weak financial system and poor fiscal control. As we describe later, we control for some of these fundamentals, too, allowing for a test of this hypothesis.

4.2.1 The Role of Original Sin

It has been the case since at least the eighteenth century that debt issued on international capital markets has been denominated in the currency of the market of issue and not the currency of the issuing country. It has also long been noted that such debt can become more onerous to repay in the face of depreciations, and that since emerging markets often face rapid exchange rate depreciations associated with sudden stops and reversals of capital inflows or very loose monetary policy, these countries are more often the victims of such a volatile combination.

Over the last ten years, these phenomena have started to be addressed in the economics literature. Eichengreen and Hausmann (1999) argued that the danger of exchange rate fluctuations in the face of foreign currency borrowing might oblige many countries to adopt hard currency pegs. They coined the term "original sin" because they argued that foreign currency-denominated debt was imposed by international capital markets. Nations with poor reputations, and *even nations with good reputations or solid fundamentals* are obliged to issue debt in key international currencies. In other words, domestic policies or problems were not the only reason countries could not borrow in their own currencies. Because of original sin and the problems that could be generated in the face of a devaluation, Eichengreen and Hausmann (1999) argued that exchange rate policy was of the utmost importance, even for those countries where fundamentals and fiscal policies were sound but which might fall victim to a liquidity run.

While we have a bit more to say about the origins of original sin in section 4.4.4, one key controversy remains. Exactly how harmful is original sin? Early work by Eichengreen and Hausmann used mainly anecdotal evidence both on the incidence of original sin and its effects. Very recent work by the same authors along with Ugo Panizza (Eichengreen, Hausmann, and Panizza 2005) has shown that countries with higher original sin have higher exchange rate volatility and higher macroeconomic volatility. Flandreau (2003) argues that in the nineteenth century depreciation increased the debt burden because of original sin, which led to sovereign debt crises. He illustrates this with reference to several cases. But we are unaware of any work which has attempted to find a systematic empirical association between original sin and financial crises.[3]

We collected data from various national sources on hard currency debt and augmented and compared this with data made available by Flandreau and Zúmer (2004). What we refer to as hard currency debt is debt that carried a gold clause or was made payable at a fixed rate in a foreign currency.[4] Our measure of original sin is the ratio of this quantity to total public debt outstanding.

This measure is different from, but related to, the measures of original sin defined in Eichengreen, Hausmann, and Panizza (2005). One of their measures of international original sin for country i based on securities issued by residents and nonresidents internationally is

$$OS_i = \max\left(1 - \frac{\text{Securities issued in currency } i}{\text{Securities issued by country } i}, 0\right).$$

One key difference between markets today and in our period under study is that recently debt has been issued in quite a few small-country currencies by agents from lending countries, allowing opportunities for debt swaps. That is, for some countries, the numerator and the denominator in the difference term differ substantially because many other countries issue debt in their currency. To the best of our knowledge it does not appear that foreigners pre-1914 were issuing debt in other exotic currencies. In the pre-1914 case, original sin was not reduced through swaps (Flandreau 2003, 20), hence we can restrict attention in the numerator of this expression to securities issued in local currency (without gold clauses) only by residents.

The other key difference between our measure and the workhorse mea-

---

3. Our conclusions differ from Flandreau's, as we take on a wider set of hypotheses and cases. Empirical work by Flandreau and Zúmer (2004), which regresses sovereign bond yields on a ratio of interest service to government revenues and a number of other variables, also argues that hard currency or gold debt was dangerous. Their tests are quite different from ours since our dependent variables are debt crises, banking crises, currency crises, or twin crises. Frankel and Rose (1996) examined "currency crashes," external debt, and exchange rate fluctuations, but their approach to measuring original sin, its impact, and the type of crises considered is different than ours.

4. Our data appendix has more to say about the structure of this debt. Flandreau and Zúmer (2004) highlight just some of the difficulties in defining this type of debt. Italian bonds, for example, had de facto gold clauses for foreigners but not for residents, but de jure gold clauses for both classes of creditors for a certain proportion of the debt. Likewise, Spain arbitrarily implemented a residency distinction for manner of repayment around 1900. U.S. debt was sometimes vague ex ante about the terms of repayment and often repayment was promised "in specie." Mostly this was meant to be gold but could have meant silver, which secularly depreciated against gold after 1873. Still, our measure is at least a good proxy for the variable of interest.

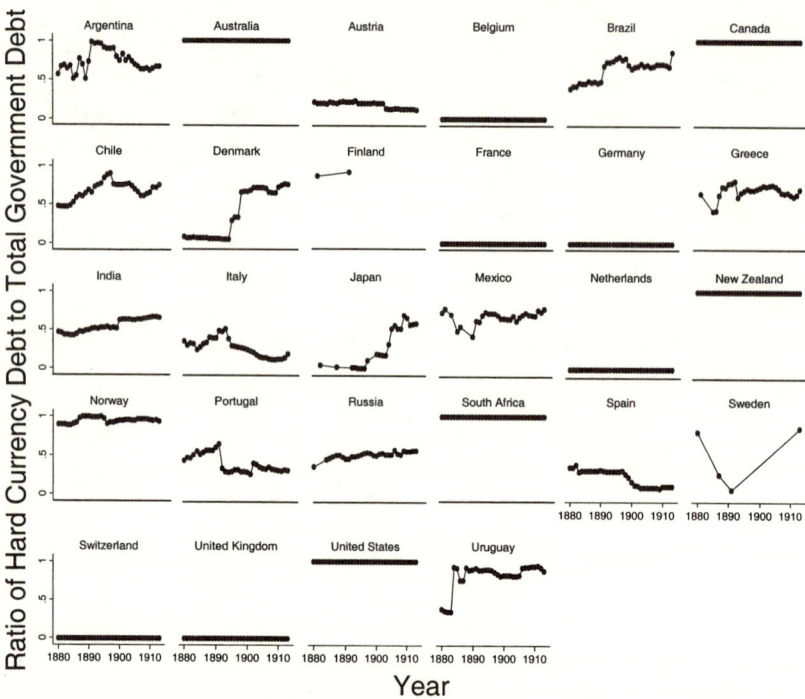

Fig. 4.1   Hard currency debt as a percentage of total public debt, 1880–1913

sure in Eichengreen, Hausmann, and Panizza (2005) is that we look at debt issued in domestic and international markets instead of looking only at international issues. One reason we view this as important is because many domestic issues of the day carried gold clauses. As described previously, in the case where monetary authorities devalued the local currency in terms of gold this would have a similar effect to a depreciation when a country had foreign currency debt. In either event, real debt repayments for local currency gold clause debt and for foreign currency debt would both increase.[5] Hence, we do not classify debt as "debt issued in currency i" if it contained a gold clause stipulating a fixed quantity of gold per unit of local currency payable. Only debt payable in local paper currency without mention of the gold-local currency exchange rate upon payment of coupons and principal is included in the ratio above.

Figure 4.1 shows the ratio of hard-currency government debt to total

---

5. We are finessing the question of what happens to the real exchange rate and prices in general. We assume here that nominal depreciations are perhaps equivalent to real depreciations in the short-run because of sticky prices. On the domestic side we assume going off gold or a depreciation implies a depreciation of the local currency versus gold and that domestic prices are constant over the short run.

government debt by country between 1880 and 1913. Our time series plots reveal most countries' measure of original sin to be constant over time. Some countries' situations worsened. Japan became more exposed to foreign currency debt as it entered global capital markets from the late 1890s. Argentina and Brazil converted local currency paper debt into gold clause debt in the 1890s. Only Spain and Italy appear to have decidedly decreased their reliance on hard currency debt relative to internal currency debt. These nations often had floating currencies throughout the period. As noted by Flandreau and Sussman (2005), their situations appear similar to those of Russia and Austria-Hungary, countries which had relatively low degrees of original sin and which also had floating currencies over most of the period we cover. These are the counterexamples to those who believe that poor fiscal history, a shaky exchange rate policy, and economic backwardness are causes of original sin. Nearly all of these countries had previous episodes of debt default and chronically poor fiscal situations. We subsequently return to this story.

The long-run averages of our original sin measure in figure 4.2 also reveal a counterintuitive ranking, but are consistent with previous findings by Flandreau and Sussman (2005) and Eichengreen, Hausmann, and Panizza (2005). Financial centers have less original sin. Small peripheral countries have a lot of original sin. Countries with ostensibly rotten fiscal institutions and poor international track records have intermediate levels of original sin. Notice that Spain, Russia, Austria-Hungary, Italy, and Argentina are all toward the lower middle of the spectrum. However, some countries with sound fiscal, financial, and monetary records, like Denmark and Sweden, also fall into this range. These countries, like others in west-

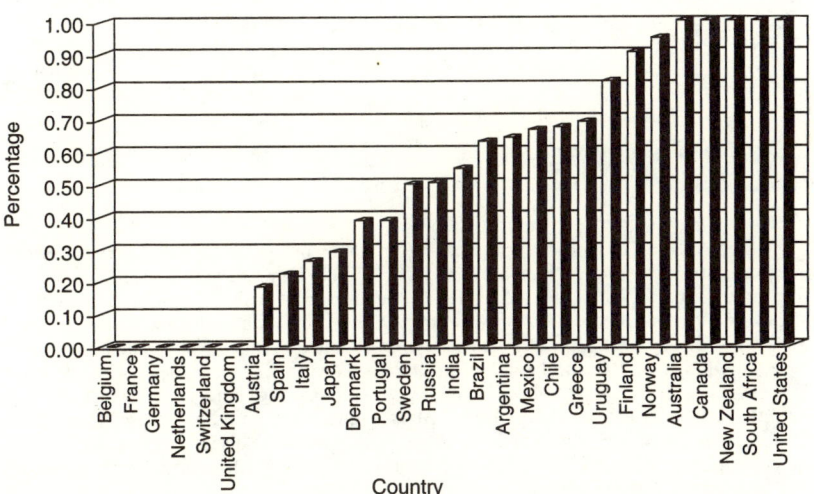

Fig. 4.2   Average ratio of hard currency public debt to total public debt, 1880–1913

ern Europe, had financial institutions that were evolving in the same direction as the core. The question then becomes: are these fundamentals, along with the historical and current fiscal positions, more important for explaining crisis incidence than the actual level of hard-currency debt?

4.2.2 Currency Mismatches

Goldstein and Turner (2004) have argued that currency mismatches are the main problem with foreign currency debt. Countries that have foreign currency liabilities that are not offset by foreign currency assets may be more likely than countries with more foreign assets to find it difficult to repay their foreign currency debts in the event of a depreciation. On the margin, changes in the exchange rate can become a problem the greater the mismatch, as local currency assets lose value in terms of foreign liabilities. Goldstein and Turner have three key ingredients in their overall measure of a nation's mismatch. They first use the difference between all reported foreign assets and foreign currency liabilities outstanding. They then divide this measure by exports (or imports if the difference is positive) to account for openness to trade.[6] For example, the mismatch decreases when exports are higher because a depreciation would likely attract a larger amount of extra revenue and thus such a country would be more naturally hedged. Finally, they premultiply this ratio by the ratio of all reported foreign currency liabilities to all reported liabilities outstanding.

Data on bank and nonbank foreign assets is difficult to assemble today and probably impossible for the pre–World War I era. We focus on the government's mismatch and believe this is a relatively good proxy for the economy-wide mismatch. The functional form we choose is different from Goldstein and Turner and slightly closer to that found in Eichengreen, Hausmann, and Panizza (2003).[7] For country i we have

$$\text{Mismatch}_i = \frac{\text{international reserves} - \text{total hard currency debt outstanding}}{\text{exports}}$$

Our measure of reserves usually only includes gold reserves held at the central bank, in the banking system, or held by the government treasury.

---

6. Goldstein and Turner (2004) choose a functional form so that the boost to exports from a depreciation improves a nation's balance sheet. Though the Goldstein and Turner measure (and our version of theirs) is one measure of the balance sheet position, it is not the ideal measure of a nation's balance sheet. There are omitted ingredients that could make a difference to the balance sheet. For example, for this period, one could theoretically refine this measure by including foreign currency and gold revenues collected through tariffs, exports to gold standard countries, and imports from such countries as a measure of hard currency earnings and liabilities, and foreign assets held in banks. Most of these data would be impossible to collect for a reasonable number of observations. Also, in section 4.4 we discuss how the omission in our mismatch measure of certain types of assets could explain the fact that some countries with high original sin seem less crisis prone.

7. Eichengreen, Hausmann, and Panizza (2003) report that the correlation between their measure of mismatch and the Goldstein and Turner measure is 0.82.

The sources are listed in the appendix. Total hard currency debt (domestic and international issues) is calculated directly if the data is available or by multiplying the total debt outstanding by the percentage of total debt that is payable in gold or foreign currencies. A higher mismatch measure should be correlated with fewer financial crises. As such it compares with the Goldstein and Turner measure. Nevertheless, it does take a different functional form and potentially does leave out a significant fraction of total assets and liabilities in the economy. One should also note that as the mismatch measure increases, damage to the net worth of a country inflicted by a depreciation should be smaller.[8]

The mismatch measure above risks combining flow measures (exports) with stock measures. As an alternative measure of mismatch, we substitute the amount of total hard-currency debt outstanding by the total amount of interest payments due in gold or foreign currency. This is estimated as the product of the ratio of hard currency debt outstanding to the total interest payments on all types of debt.[9] Interest payments come from Flandreau and Zúmer (2004) and are only available for a smaller set of countries.

4.2.3 Debt Intolerance

A new literature on sovereign financial difficulties emphasizes the role of past defaults in creating current difficulties. Reinhart, Rogoff, and Savastano (2003; RRS) have coined the term *debt intolerance*. This line of research tries to explain why some countries are able to sustain very high debt-to-GDP ratios while other emerging-market countries run into debt problems with comparatively low debt-to-GDP ratios. Their evidence suggests that past defaults generate poor sovereign ratings. Countries with worse track records in international capital markets suffer greater financial fragility due to increased borrowing costs at a given level of debt to GDP. An alternative view might be that default history or sovereign ratings are proxies for other underlying structural or institutional problems. Hence we would also like to control for such fundamentals, as far as possible, to allow for the possibility of graduation from debt intolerance.

Given these hypotheses, we would like our tests to include a measure of default history. Accordingly, we take two routes to control for this. First we interact a public debt to government revenue ratio with an indicator

---

8. Goldstein and Turner (2004) note that net worth increases with depreciation for net creditors. To get around the fact that an increase in the denominator of mismatch would decrease the mismatch measure for net creditors they divide by imports when assets exceed liabilities. For all of the results we present we divide by exports. We also tried dividing by imports when appropriate. The two measures have a correlation of 0.999. Our results do not change significantly when we divide by imports for those observations with positive numerators.

9. Of course, different face value interest rates for paper and gold debts will affect how accurate this measure is for the countries that have original sin measures between 0 and 1. The actual difference between the face value interest rate for a gold and paper debt was one percentage point for Brazil in the 1890s.

variable that equals one if a country had at least one default episode between 1800 and 1880. Alternatively, we interact the debt-to-revenue ratio with an indicator equal to one if the country is in the periphery.[10] If the increase in the probability of a financial crisis for a marginal increase in the debt-to-revenue ratio is larger for a peripheral country or a past defaulter, we would argue there is evidence in support of the debt intolerance hypothesis.

4.2.4 Other Data and Hypotheses

The literature on predicting financial crises with econometric techniques is abundant. Our approach is inspired by the pared down methodology of Frankel and Rose (1996), who looked at currency crashes at the annual level. Many subsequent papers have made modifications to this early attempt and have largely been equally unsuccessful at accurately predicting any type of financial crisis.[11] However, some approaches and explanatory variables have done reasonably well in predicting crises, or at least being strongly and statistically significantly correlated with crises in a way consonant with priors based on economic theory.

We attempt to control for the union of the most important variables from the extant literature that is applicable to the time period at hand. The list includes total outstanding government debt divided by government revenue, growth in the terms of trade, the deviation of the real exchange rate from the period average, the current account balance divided by nominal GDP, the yield spread between British consols and long-term government bonds, an indicator for whether the country maintained a gold standard, growth of the money supply, the ratio of gold reserves in the banking system to notes in circulation, and the GDP-weighted average spread on British consols for long-term bonds. The variables used depend on which type of crisis we are examining and are well indicated in the respective tables. Our sources and definitions of these variables are located in the data appendix.

Our sample includes the twenty-one countries examined in Bordo et al. (2001). We have also added information on crises and macrodata for nine other countries. These new additions include Austria-Hungary, Egypt, India, Mexico, New Zealand, Russia, South Africa, Turkey, and Uruguay. To the best of our knowledge, this is the most comprehensive macrohistorical data set ever constructed to analyze the determinants of various types of financial crises.

---

10. The periphery indicator comes from Obstfeld and Taylor (2003). The periphery countries are Argentina, Austria-Hungary, Brazil, Chile, Egypt, Finland, Greece, India, Italy, Japan, Mexico, Portugal, Russia, Spain, Turkey, and Uruguay.
11. See Berg and Patillo (1999) for a broad comparison of some important papers in this literature.

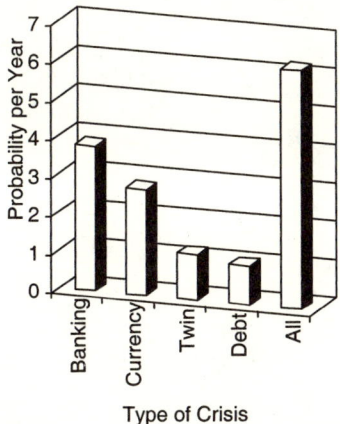

Fig. 4.3   Crisis frequency in percent probability per year, 1880–1913

4.2.5   Crises, 1880–1913

In figure 4.3 we present the frequency of various types of crises (banking, currency, twin, debt, and any type of crisis).[12] This is the number of years a country was in crisis divided by total possible years of observation. We use the country-year as the unit of observation, and eliminate all country-years that witness ongoing crises from the denominator, to come up with a total number for years of observation. We note the pattern found in Bordo et al. (2001) in terms of the relative frequency of types of crises (i.e., that the predominant form of crises before 1914 was banking crises, followed by currency crises, twin, and debt crises).[13] Nevertheless, the absolute magnitude of the probability for each type of crisis increases slightly compared to their figure with our addition of another ten countries.

Figures 4.4 and 4.5 present scatter plots of the percentage of time a country was in a crisis episode versus our measure of original sin and our mismatch variables.[14] There appears to be a quadratic relationship between debt crises and original sin. Countries with intermediate ranges of original sin seem to take longer to resolve their debt crises than those at either end of the spectrum.

It seems intuitive that the financial centers which were more economically developed had fewer crises than nations like Russia, Argentina, and

---

12. Our crisis dates and the methodology we use to classify years of crisis are listed in the appendix.
13. Debt crises were not demarcated by Bordo et al. (2001).
14. Our measure of the percentage of time spent in a crisis is the ratio of the number of years in which a crisis first occurred or was ongoing divided by the number of years in the sample, which is 34. For debt crises, the numerator is the number of years in which there was no resolution or international agreement on debt repayment.

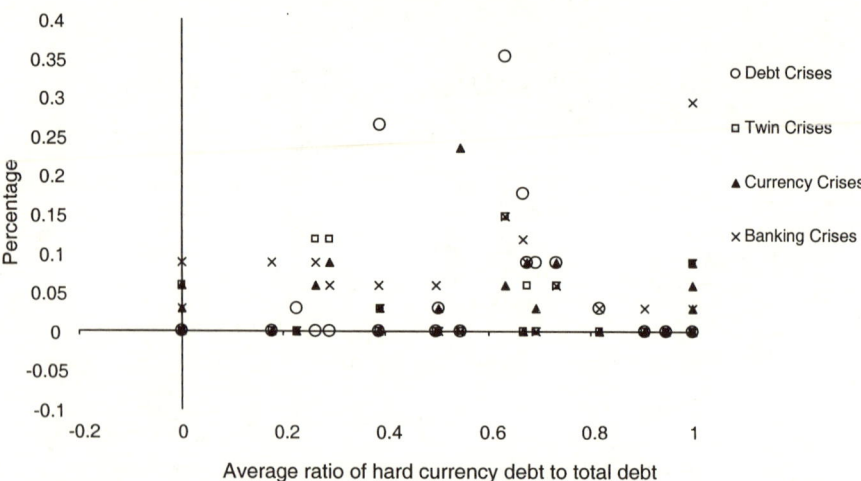

Fig. 4.4 Crisis frequencies by country versus the average level of hard currency public debt to total public debt, 1880–1913

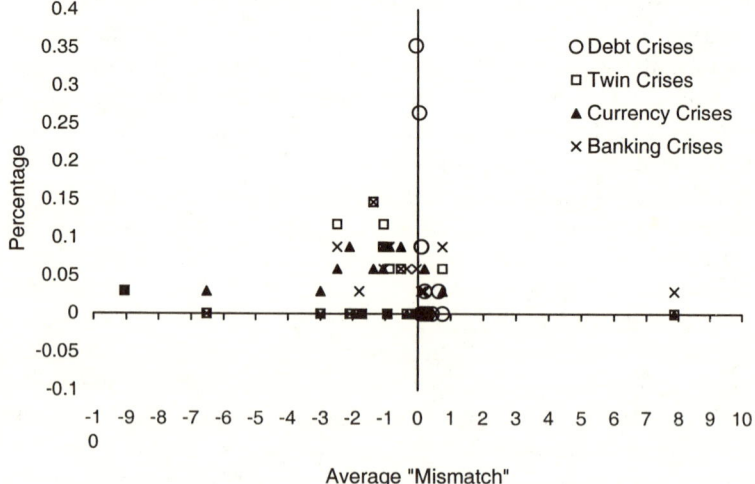

Fig. 4.5 Crisis frequencies by country versus the average level of the "mismatch" measure, 1880–1913

Notes: The mismatch variable for debt crises uses interest payments. The mismatch for other types of crises uses debt outstanding. See text for explanations.

Italy. But what about the countries with high measures of original sin but fewer crises? These data points include primarily the British offshoots like Australia, Canada, New Zealand, and the United States, but also small European countries like Norway and Finland. Perhaps this hump-shaped relationship is evidence that original sin is not always related to more financial fragility. It could be that these countries avoided crises because of their strong financial systems and fiscal institutions, especially when compared to the southern European periphery and the Latin American countries, which make up most of the observations in the middle ground. The next section looks at some case studies that illuminate this finding. The following section uses econometrics to control for a host of other plausible factors that might be omitted from this sample scatter plot. We conclude that for debt crises and banking crises this quadratic relationship is still visible and quite meaningful in telling us what matters for managing original sin.

4.3 Historical Evidence

How well does the overarching framework of financial crises discussed previously match up to the historical record? What role did contemporaries assign to hard currency debt and fiscal mismanagement as causes of the numerous financial crises that occurred between 1880 and 1913? We discuss the cases of Argentina, Brazil, Australia, and the United States to address these questions. These places shared the distinction of being peripheral capital-importing countries, and so these, in many respects, make for good comparisons in a case study.[15] Figures 4.6 through 4.9 plot the levels of our original sin measure, the mismatch variable (measured using total debt outstanding), and the gold reserve ratio for them. The original sin and mismatch variables look fairly similar in levels. They also take the same paths in the run-up to their crises. The notable exception to this pattern is the evolution of the ratios of gold to bank notes in circulation. These are rather high and fairly level for Australia and the United States, but they are low and decreasing for Brazil and Argentina. This highlights the division of the periphery into the two subgroups we mentioned earlier. All four of these countries had a financial crisis in the 1890s. Brazil and Argentina had near total financial meltdowns and sovereign debt defaults. Australia and the United States experienced relatively serious banking crises in 1893 but by no means faced financial disintegration. They both avoided debt default and massive currency depreciations. The robustness of the financial systems and the governments' fiscal position, along with a few other idiosyncratic factors, make the difference between the outcomes.

Perhaps the most notorious of the late nineteenth-century crises is the Baring crisis that hit London and Argentina in late 1890.[16] In Argentina,

---

15. It is debatable whether the United States qualifies as a peripheral country in this period; indeed, our periphery indicator does not classify it as such. Its real income in both total and per capita terms was as high as the advanced countries of western Europe that comprised the core countries. It was also similar in overall economic development. However, before 1900 it was, like the other emergers, a major capital importer. See Bordo and Schwartz (1996) and Flandreau and Jobst (2004).

16. See Eichengreen (1997) for an in-depth discussion of this event and a comparison between it and the Mexican crisis of 1994.

this crisis was a triple crisis involving a banking meltdown, a currency crisis, and a suspension of payments on national debt. The 1880s witnessed a "fiesta financiera." Fiscal excess and a dubious banking situation reigned. Government spending also took off in the 1880s. Much of the spending was financed by local and foreign borrowing, and it was unaccompanied by short-term revenue increases. Bank lending to the national and state governments increased at a harried pace. Foreign purchases of the large amount of (paper peso) bonds issued by local mortgage banks rose throughout the 1880s. Note issues by banks in excess of statutory levels also made the Argentine position even more precarious. There was also a lack of political will to increase tax revenues from import duties in the late 1880s.

Borrowing became harder and harder for Argentina in the late 1880s. As foreign lending started to dry up, the government propped up the mortgage banks through the mortgage bond (*cedulas*) market by guaranteeing that these bonds, which were originally issued in paper, would be paid in gold. This policy increased Argentina's hard-currency liabilities as a percentage of the total at a time when reserves were being used (unsuccessfully) to prop up the paper peso. Figure 4.6 shows how this simultaneously raised the original sin measure and made the mismatch worse.

When the Bank of England raised its discount rate from 2.5 to 6 percent in 1889, the disaster exploded. Baring, overextended because of Argentina's insolvency, was bailed out by a consortium of British banks in a lifeboat operation arranged by the Bank of England (Bordo 2003). The government of Argentina suspended payments on its debts. The two major banks

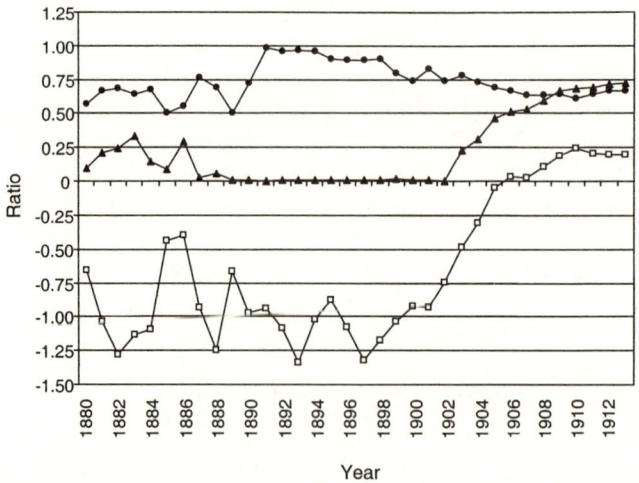

Fig. 4.6 Original sin, mismatch, and gold cover ratio for Argentina, 1880–1913

of Buenos Aires were liquidated in 1890. The most notable facets of this crisis are its near textbook sequence of events and the striking move by Argentine authorities to "dollarize" its debts when in such a precarious position. The ease with which this occurred suggests that decreasing currency risk made the debt seem more attractive for foreign investors. But of course this would only be true as long as these investors neglected the possibility that depreciation itself would cause the debt burden to become unsustainable.

It is also extremely interesting that Brazil (also under a floating exchange rate regime) undertook a local currency to hard-currency debt conversion in 1890 similar in effect to Argentina's. The government converted 5 percent paper bonds to 4 percent gold bonds and instituted collection of tariffs in gold in order to help pay these obligations. Levy (1995) argues that authorities viewed gold bonds as a less expensive way to fund deficits. The conversion itself helped raise Brazil's original sin measure from less than 0.5 to nearly 0.7 (see figure 4.7). According to our data, the Brazilian mismatch using total debt service worsened from –1.26 to –1.38 while the mismatch measure using interest service improved from –0.058 to –0.049. Neither move seems extremely large in comparison with the increase in the original sin measure we have seen. But this conversion surely contributed to Brazil's fragility, culminating in the banking crisis of 1897 and the currency and debt crisis of 1898.

Like in Argentina, the run-up to the Brazilian crisis witnessed fairly

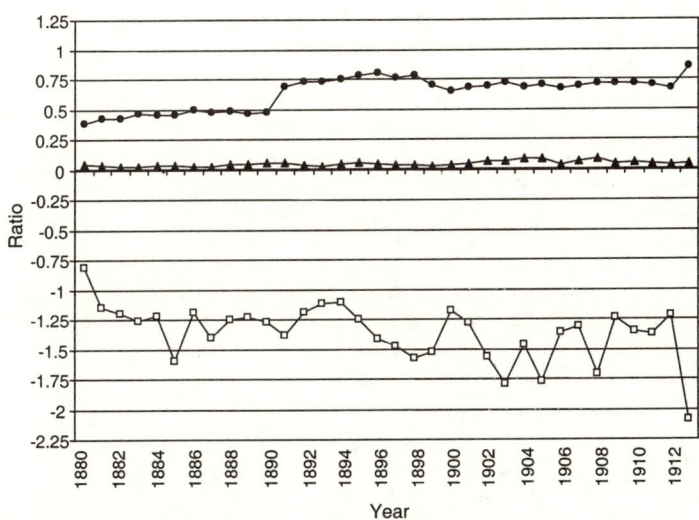

Fig. 4.7   Original sin, mismatch, and gold cover ratio for Brazil, 1880–1913

heavy depreciation of the real as well as civil unrest. The price of coffee, an important export, also tumbled. The depreciation of the real was caused by excessive note issues, weak bank regulation, and continual government pressure for advances. Moreover, the gold tariff was eliminated in 1891, further damaging the government's balance sheet. The government reassumed the monopoly over note issues from the domestic banks of issue in 1895.

All was not bleak in the 1890s. London markets accepted new issues from Brazil, and these funds were used to continue servicing the external debt. Moreover, coffee prices recovered somewhat and rubber exports began to take off. If the government had not embarked upon a number of new military operations and continued with the construction of military installations up to 1898, the fiscal position might not have looked so grim. As it happened, the banking crisis of 1897 and heavy depreciation in 1897 conspired to create a currency crash and finally a suspension on debt payments in 1898.

For the United States and Australia the 1890s were also a turbulent decade. Australia had a banking crisis in 1893. The U.S. Treasury suffered heavy gold losses in 1891 (see figure 4.8). In 1893 the United States was hit by a short-lived banking panic coupled with more gold reserve losses. Despite the turbulence, neither country ended up with a debt crisis, the exchange rates were not allowed to depreciate, and the banking systems withstood the pressure. Moreover, it is worthwhile to note that, by our

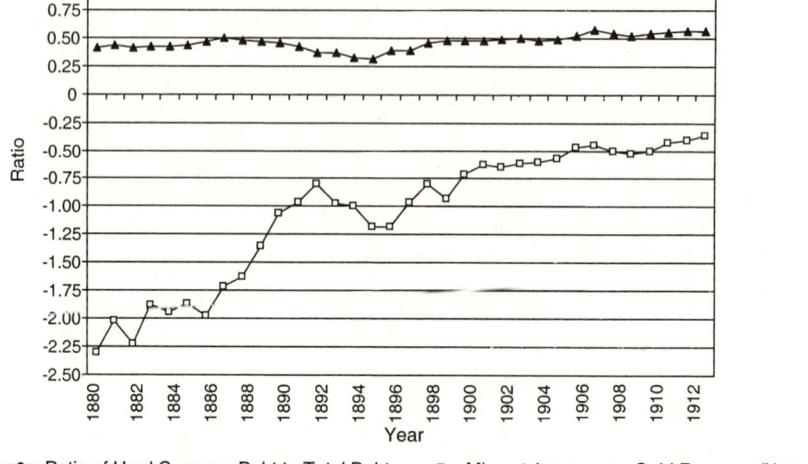

Fig. 4.8 Original sin, mismatch, and gold cover ratio for the United States, 1880–1913

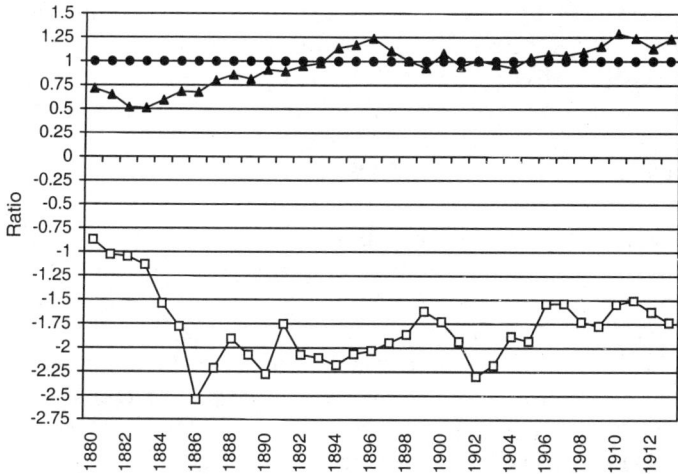

─●─ Ratio of Hard Currency Debt to Total Debt ─□─ Mismatch ─▲─ Gold Reserves/Notes in Circulation

Fig. 4.9 Original sin, mismatch, and gold cover ratio for Australia, 1880–1913

measures, Australia at this time had a debt-to-revenue ratio of roughly nine, which is in the 90th percentile of our sample, and a slightly worse mismatch position than Brazil had in the 1890s.

The story of the crisis in Australia (see figure 4.9) is that land speculation had reached a frenzied pace by the early 1890s. Banks were lending for long-term projects. Historians have called attention to the maturity mismatch that characterized such lending. A tariff rise in 1892 contributed to falling government revenues, probably weakening market confidence at the same time. London markets also tightened up in response to global financial turmoil in the early 1890s. Banks formed an association to protect themselves in 1892, but public depositor confidence was shattered in 1893 when an important bank was allowed to fail. Finally, export prices fell, making debt servicing all the more difficult.

Some observers have claimed that the crisis was not all that severe and that recovery had begun by 1893 (Dowd 1992). Adalet and Eichengreen (2005) emphasize that the crisis and current account reversal that accompanied it depended on deflation and a reduction in expenditures. They note that debt default never occurred as it did in Argentina and later in Brazil, perhaps because membership in the British Empire ruled it out.

Policy measures that surely helped alleviate the financial severity of the crisis include: a five day bank holiday, the government policy, which allowed for a slight increase in the legal maximum note issue, and paper money being declared legal tender in New South Wales. Dowd also suggests that no balance sheet problems or disintermediation occurred, since there is no evidence that advances declined during the period. Moreover, he observes that the biggest banks had prudently prepared for the worst by 1890 by divesting themselves of speculative assets.

In the United States, a combination of luck and a strong financial system averted a total meltdown in the 1890s. The main characteristic of the currency turbulence in 1891 and in 1893 was the heavy loss of the Treasury's reserves. Open market purchases of securities by the Treasury, a tax of 40 cents per $1,000 on gold exports, the McKinley tariff, and a bumper crop in the United States, which was swiftly exported to Europe, where there was a major crop failure, all combined to avert massive disaster and bring calm to markets by late 1891.

In 1893 international markets once again doubted the U.S. commitment to the gold standard. A move to a de facto silver standard was factored into expectations.[17] The closure of the mint to silver in June 1893 in India created expectations of continued depreciation of silver in terms of gold. This would have meant continuing depreciation against gold currencies for a silver-based dollar, and so provided a possible speculative opportunity. In fact, a self-fulfilling attack on the dollar was nearly successful. The Treasury's gold reserves dropped quickly and obligations to repay debt in gold stood at a high level. Markets speculated that gold reserves would continue to diminish. This contributed to further gold outflows. In June of 1893 the clearing house syndicate of New York met, but many banks were still pushed to the limit of their legal reserve requirements. Nevertheless, prominent political defeats for prosilver activists, including the repeal of the Sherman Silver Purchase Act (a sop to prosilver forces passed in 1890) helped assuage market fears. A rescue package engineered by Belmont and Morgan, who purchased $62 million in bonds yielding nearly $35 million in gold for the treasury, also helped suppress the attack.

The strength of the U.S. and the Australian financial systems in comparison to the South American cases mentioned earlier is evident here.[18] We think that the outbreak of crisis in these examples follows a fairly systematic pattern, very similar in nature to the framework laid out previously. This is so especially as it relates to credit expansion, overindebtedness, and vulnerability induced by rises in foreign interest rates. But there is a major divergence at the point when we try to understand how hard-currency debt matters. For the two southern cone countries, hard-currency debt proved dangerous and default ensued. For Australia and the United States, two places where debt was payable strictly in a fixed amount of gold or foreign currency, balance sheet effects did not overwhelm the

---

17. Calomiris (1992) argues that markets were expecting a good chance of a temporary suspension of gold convertibility and a small devaluation of the dollar.

18. Caballero, Cowan, and Kearns (2004) look at the success of dealing with capital market shocks over the last 100 years and make an interesting comparison between Australia and Chile.

economies. Exchange rate commitments did not fail. Most importantly, the financial systems were robust. And finally, in Australia, Empire made the difference. In the United States, Belmont and Morgan and the material interests and strength of the New York banking industry mattered. These are key differences from Argentina and Brazil. The U.S. and Australian case illustrate why original sin is not always dangerous. The statistical work we turn to now provides more support for these assertions.

4.4 Statistical Findings

Our statistical approach is fairly basic. We seek mainly to find a multivariate way to summarize the data by correlating crisis probabilities with a set of explanatory variables.[19] We use probit specifications, and the dependent variable is the first year of a debt crisis, currency crisis, banking crisis, or twin crisis. Our data set is an unbalanced panel, and the observational unit is the country year. We omit country years that include ongoing crises. Throughout, we control for the lack of statistical independence between country observations by using heteroscedasticity robust, country-clustered standard errors.[20] We first present specifications with as many variables as is feasible and then as a robustness check we drop the most statistically insignificant variables so as to avoid possible collinearity problems and to include more observations.[21]

One thing we find consistently, even when conditioning on other variables and in other sensitivity analysis, is a quadratic relationship between the ratio of hard currency debt to total debt and the frequency of debt and banking crises. This suggests that original sin may contribute to more financial crises but that sometimes the damage can be limited by other means.

Holding our measure of the currency mismatch constant however, no relationship between original sin and currency crises is apparent. We view most currency crises as a symptom of capital flight from a crumbling financial sector and liquidity problems, and think that original sin is *indirectly* associated with currency crises. As the framework provided previously would predict, we see that initial problems in the banking sector

---

19. Endogeneity of the regressors as well as usual specification problems may be present in our specifications. We attempted to mitigate endogeneity biases in unreported specifications by using lagged values of the explanatory variables. Results in these cases did not change drastically in qualitative terms. Of course, this solution is only valid if variables are not too persistent. Also, using lags creates measurement error issues that are likely to be problematic for estimation.
20. We estimated random effects probit models as well but found them to perform weakly. The estimated correlation between within-country observations was poorly estimated.
21. The appendix lists the key variables and their availability for each country so the reader can see what the various samples look like. The issue of model specification is, of course, not trivial. We are taking a decidedly reduced form approach, and we use the econometrics as supplements to the qualitative theoretical conclusions and historical record.

(proxied by one-year ahead indicators of debt crises and banking crises) are strongly associated with currency crises. Hence one possibility is that original sin affects debt sustainability or the soundness of the banking sector, and then these problems with debt and the banking system can create a currency run, which further contributes to balance sheet trouble and possibly financial implosion.

Moreover, we document a link between currency crises and mismatches or weak reserve positions. This is evidence supportive of the idea that the outbreak of currency crises is the symptom of liquidity problems or perhaps deeper solvency troubles in the economy that contribute to speculative capital outflows and sudden stops. Some weak evidence shows that mismatches are associated with debt crises, too. Finally, some inconclusive evidence points also to debt intolerance as a factor in debt crises, without ruling out a role for original sin or mismatches.

4.4.1 Debt Crises

Table 4.1 presents results from various specifications where the initial year of a debt crisis is the dependent variable. Column (1) presents a comprehensive specification that includes a variable set as large as possible and that also allows for controls for original sin and currency mismatches. We see that there is a quadratic in original sin, in mismatches (as measured using interest payments rather than total debt outstanding), and there is evidence of debt intolerance. These variables are statistically significant (at better than the 90 percent level of confidence) at the means for each for each of these controls.[22] The size of the estimated coefficients is symptomatic of the low predicted incidence of debt crises. Since the incidence in the sample is barely two percent, this is understandable.

We interpret the quadratic in original sin as stating that more original sin is associated with a higher likelihood of a debt crisis, but those observations with very high levels of original sin face a lower likelihood. Again, these are the countries in the areas of recent settlement like Canada, Australia, New Zealand, and the United States, which had strong financial systems, good fiscal institutions, and which borrowed largely for productive investments.

In terms of mismatch, there is evidence that past a certain level a better

---

22. As usual in a probit model, the actual marginal effect, the standard error, and statistical significance depend on the levels of the covariates in a nonlinear way. We calculated these effects for each observation for particular specifications and found that magnitudes and statistical significance varied considerably (e.g., see figures 4.10 and 4.11). On the whole, we often find that the coefficients of interest are statistically significant and have the most impact at the extremes of the empirical distributions. Moreover, the statistical significance of the interaction effect must be approached with caution. We are interested in the statistical significance of the partial derivative of the probability with respect to, say, hard-currency debt at various values (e.g., the average) but do not always report the *p*-values here. For simplicity we focus mainly on this first partial derivative.

Table 4.1   Determinants of debt crises

Regressors	(1)	(2)	(3)	(4)
Hard-currency debt as a percentage of total debt	6.44 (1.89)***	2.32 (0.92)**		3.44 (1.07)***
Square of hard-currency debt ratio	−4.71 (2.05)***	−3.46 (0.61)***		−4.33 (0.82)***
Debt/Revenue	−0.40 (0.11)***	0.16 (0.07)**	0.23 (0.08)***	−0.05 (0.12)
Debt/Revenue · pre-1880 default	1.04 (0.26)***			0.28 (0.15)
Pre-1880 default	−8.81 (2.83)***			−2.74 (1.18)**
Mismatch	7.41 (4.17)		4.16 (1.67)**	
Square of mismatch	−25.7 (13.13)**		−11.40 (6.61)	
Growth of terms of trade	−31.93 (19.66)	−13.98 (11.42)	−13.22 (9.86)	−16.56 (14.24)
ln (deviation of real exchange rate from period average)	−6.02 (4.33)	−2.39 (1.72)	−2.46 (1.77)	−3.22 (2.06)
Trade balance/GDP	−4.94 (5.22)			
Spread on U.K. consol	−0.18 (0.17)			
Gold standard dummy	1.65 (0.73)***			
Growth of the money supply	−1.59 (3.14)			
Gold reserves/notes in circulation	−12.01 (3.43)***	−3.76 (2.11)	−5.69 (1.41)***	−4.32 (1.19)***
Market portfolio spread	3.44 (1.72)***	1.92 (0.77)**	2.40 (1.15)**	1.77 (0.86)**
Constant	−3.88 (3.67)	−5.72 (1.31)***	−6.30 (2.24)***	−3.80 (1.31)***
No. of observations	371	533	427	533
Percentage of correct positives	83	66.67	66.67	66.67
Percentage of correct negatives	97	98	97	98
Pseudo R^2	0.60	0.45	0.45	0.48
Log-likelihood value	−12.11	−17.9	−17.21	−17.04

Notes: Dependent variable is a binary indicator for a debt crisis. "Robust" clustered standard errors are in parentheses. See the text for precise definitions of variables. Positive signifies crisis year.
***Significant at the 1 percent level.
**Significant at the 5 percent level.

mismatch position leads to a lower likelihood of a debt crisis.[23] But the quadratic pattern suggests that in the neighborhood of an intermediate level of mismatch a marginally better mismatch is associated with a higher chance of a default. The reason is likely to be because those countries that have in fact recently defaulted on their debt but still have the fundamentals that strongly suggest a default have cut their interest payments and thereby have drastically improved their mismatch position (e.g., Argentina and Brazil in the mid-1890s). This makes it appear as if intermediate mismatch positions are associated with fewer crises, when in fact the opposite is the case. We think that the data show that better mismatches are intuitively associated with a lower chance of a debt debacle.

Most other variables have signs that fit our priors. Improvements in the terms of trade, real depreciations, more gold reserves relative to notes outstanding, slower growth of monetary aggregates, and a calmer international environment in capital markets are all associated with lower probabilities of debt crises. The statistical significance of the coefficients on these variables varies, however. Meanwhile, lower local bond spreads (statistically insignificant) and adherence to the gold standard (statistically significant) imply a higher propensity to have a crisis. The positive coefficient on the gold standard does not disappear if we include it in the other specifications, but the coefficient is not statistically indistinguishable from zero.[24]

In figure 4.10 we also present a scatter plot of the marginal effects of the hard-currency debt ratios (calculated at the actual values of the covariates) versus the actual levels of hard-currency debt. We see that for intermediate ranges of original sin that the coefficient varies a lot but is likely to be positive, whereas, toward the extremes, the marginal effects are likely to be near zero or even negative. Figure 4.11 presents the z-statistics for the test that the marginal effect is different from zero. When evaluated at the actual values, only a minority of these have z-statistics high enough to be considered statistically significant. Only the highest in absolute value are significant. This roughly backs up the visual impression received from the previous figure.

We also provide a measure of the fit of the model. This is gauged by the percentage of actual crises that were predicted to be crisis episodes, and the percentage of noncrisis years that are predicted to be noncrisis years. We use a predicted probability of greater than 0.1 to classify a country as having a debt crisis. This is a low threshold, but debt crises are relatively rare in the raw sample. (The sample frequency is 0.01.) For the debt crises, the

---

23. Recall that our mismatch variable increases as the mismatch decreases.

24. Unreported, likelihood ratio tests between the shorter and longer models cannot reject their equivalence. Perhaps the positive coefficient on the gold standard variable is compatible with theories that argue that rigid exchange rates amplify negative external shocks more than flexible rates. But since the statistical significance varies a lot by specification we do not see overwhelming evidence for any hypothesis suggesting a positive or negative coefficient here. See Edwards (2003) for a thorough discussion of exchange rate regimes and crises.

Fig. 4.10   Marginal effect of the ratio of hard currency debt to total debt
Note: Figures are calculated based on the model in column (1) of table 4.1.

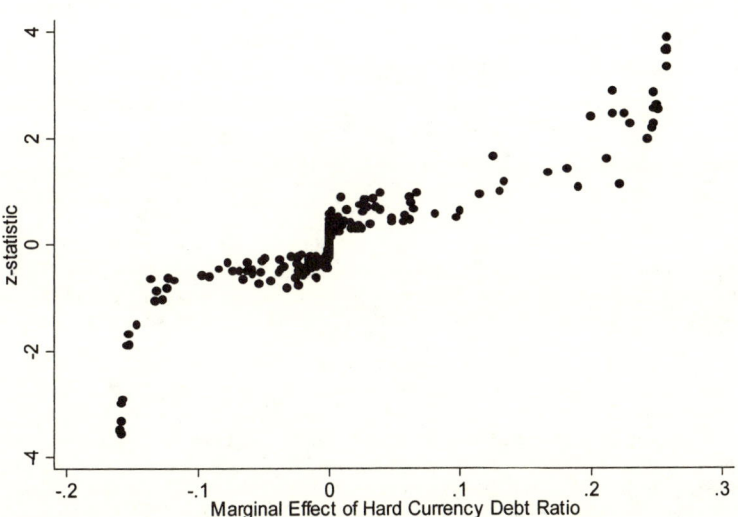

Fig. 4.11   Z-statistics by observation from a test of the hypothesis that the marginal effect is zero

fit is relatively good and the type II errors are mainly concentrated in the country years immediately preceding or coming after actual crises.[25]

Column (2) of table 4.1 pares down the number of variables in the specification and looks more closely at the relationship between original sin and debt crises. The quadratic is still evident. The point where the partial derivative of the predicted probability with respect to a change in the hard currency debt ratio became negative is located around 0.35—the point where over a third of all debt becomes payable in hard currency. At the average ratio of hard-currency debt to total debt of 0.45, the marginal effect of an increase in the hard currency to total debt ratio is not statistically distinguishable from zero. It is also interesting to note that observations where the gold cover ratio is high and the level of hard-currency debt is very low or very high provide excellent predictors for the outcome "no debt crisis." For column (1) the statistical software (Stata) reports that over 140 of such outcomes are completely determined. We believe this is the reason why the statistical significance of these factors is so high, and we are reassured that these findings are consistent with priors based on the theoretical framework outlined earlier.[26]

Column (3) shows that mismatches between *interest payments* in hard currency and available reserves can also contribute to crises.[27] Mismatch ratios extend from –0.45 to 1.7, while the marginal effects, evaluated at each observation's covariates and defined as a function of the actual mismatch, extend from about –1 to 2.7. For mismatch ratios from –0.45 to about 0.2, the marginal effects are zero or positive. For mismatch ratios between 0.2 and 0.5, a marginally better mismatch position decreases the predicted likelihood of a debt crisis (i.e., there is a negative coefficient). After a mismatch ratio of around 0.5 is attained, the marginal effect returns to zero. This is to say that there appears to be a point where additions to the reserve base relative to foreign currency interest payments or increases in export capacity have a limited effect on crisis probability. Our previous discussion is one reason why improvements in the mismatch ratio are associated with more crises at low/intermediate levels of the variable.

---

25. For other types of crises we fail to correctly classify many crisis episodes even at low thresholds. We use the 0.1 barrier for currency and banking crises and 0.03 for the even rarer twin crises. Obviously, our tabulations are sensitive to these thresholds. Our maximum predicted probabilities rarely exceed 0.2 for any type of crisis. Further modifications to the methodology to allow for the rare events nature of the data should be pursued in further work on the topic.

26. The hard-currency debt ratio is not a perfect predictor of debt crises.

27. We found no evidence that mismatches, measured using total debt outstanding (instead of interest payments due), were statistically significant. If we use the mismatch variable with debt outstanding in column 1 instead of current interest payments, we find a statistically insignificant quadratic with nearly the same shape as the reported regressions. If we enter the mismatch variable by itself without the square term then there is a statistically significant and positive relationship between (better) mismatches and debt crises. Our discussion of why there is a quadratic in mismatches probably explains the counterintuitive positive relationship, and the insignificance of the quadratic of the mismatch could be due to errors in trying to capture the actual mismatch position.

Column (4) addresses the relationship between debt intolerance and debt crises in a slightly larger sample than in column (1). Like in column (1), an increase in the debt-to-revenue ratio is negatively associated with crisis incidence when a country has no previous default history. However, when a country had a default prior to 1880, a higher debt-to-revenue ratio increases the chance of having a debt crisis (p-value 0.06). This would appear to be evidence in favor of the debt intolerance hypothesis, but it does not come at the expense of a role for original sin or other debt management policies. Moreover, there still appears to be a quadratic in original sin in this specification.

4.4.2 Currency Crises

Column (1) of table 4.2 presents an inclusive specification where the dependent variable is the probability of having a currency crisis. There are seventeen events to be predicted in this sample. Few variables are statistically significant except for the market portfolio spread and two indicator variables that indicate if a debt crisis or a banking crisis occurred in the next year.

The practical reason we include these *leads* for debt crises and banking crises is because they are good proxies for initial troubles in the banking sector or for unsustainable debt levels.[28] The theoretical reason is that we view a financial crisis unfolding in three stages: first, problems in the banking sector and deterioration in bank, firm, and government balance sheets arise; this generates a currency crisis; finally, a more widespread crisis may ensue, resulting in a full-blown banking crisis and/or debt default. The results in table 4.2 are consistent with this story.

In terms of signs on the coefficients, we still see a quadratic in original sin (though of opposite shape to that found in table 4.1)—a negative relationship between our mismatch variable and no sign of debt intolerance. Some parameters on the other variables have the expected signs while others do not. However, nothing in column (1) besides the crisis leads and the market spread is statistically significant.[29]

---

28. Better indicators for early trouble in the banking sector might include growth rates of nonperforming assets or bank insolvencies in the year of the currency crisis. None of these are available in a systematic way. In terms of debt, various ratios could be used to judge sustainability. Another reason we use this variable is to show how currency crises precede debt crises and hence indirectly feed through to balance sheet problems associated with original sin.

29. As Flandreau and Zúmer (2004) have emphasized, the debt revenue ratio and the original sin variables can increase when the nominal exchange rate changes and when there is hard-currency debt. To the extent that this supports the argument that a banking crisis or a debt crisis is more likely with a depreciation, then there is no problem here. One problem could arise if we predict currency crises with variables that are functions of the nominal exchange rate. To avoid this issue we tried lagging such variables in the currency crisis specifications. Our results regarding such variables in the currency crisis regressions are similar in qualitative terms when we use one or two lags of mismatch, external to total debt and the debt to revenue ratio.

Table 4.2 **Determinants of currency crises**

Regressors	(1)	(2)	(3)	(4)
Hard-currency debt as a percentage of total debt	−0.53 (0.72)	−0.34 (0.71)		
Square of hard-currency debt ratio	0.40 (0.75)	0.18 (0.76)		
Debt/Revenue	−0.03 (0.04)	−0.03 (0.04)	−0.06 (0.04)	−0.04 (0.04)
Debt/Revenue · periphery indicator	−0.09 (0.10)	−0.11 (0.10)		−0.09 (0.09)
Periphery indicator	0.72 (0.44)	0.59 (0.50)		0.47 (0.46)
Mismatch	−0.08 (0.11)	−0.12 (0.10)	−0.07 (0.04)	−0.12 (0.08)
Growth of terms of trade	8.72 (6.35)	7.56 (6.82)		
ln (deviation of real exchange rate from period average)	0.19 (0.66)	−0.1 (0.78)	0.02 (0.78)	0.06 (0.75)
Trade balance/GDP	0.79 (1.73)	1.31 (1.81)	3.25 (1.45)**	2.65 (1.26)**
Spread on U.K. consol	−0.02 (0.07)	−0.04 (0.08)		
Gold standard dummy	0.43 (0.52)			
Growth of the money supply	−0.89 (1.01)			
Gold reserves/notes in circulation	−0.34 (0.45)	−0.18 (0.44)	−0.19 (0.27)	−0.13 (0.40)
Market portfolio spread	0.73 (0.18)***	0.75 (0.20)***	0.47 (0.16)***	0.48 (0.16)***
Debt crisis in $t+1$	0.83 (0.34)**	0.68 (0.34)**	0.42 (0.33)	0.50 (0.38)
Banking crisis in $t+1$	0.74 (0.31)**	0.68 (0.27)**	0.71 (0.30)**	0.70 (0.30)**
Constant	−3.00 (0.79)***	−2.69 (0.57)***	−2.24 (0.29)***	−2.48 (0.47)***
No. of observations	499	505	613	613
Percentage of correct positives	23.5	17.6	23.5	23.5
Percentage of correct negatives	95.4	95.8	96.4	96.1
Pseudo R^2	0.12	0.10	0.10	0.11
Log-likelihood value	−63.8	−65.3	−69.6	−68.57

Notes: Dependent variable is a binary indicator for a currency crisis. "Robust" clustered standard errors are in parentheses. See the text for precise definitions of variables. Positive signifies crisis year.
***Significant at the 1 percent level.
**Significant at the 5 percent level.

We pare down the specification in column (2) and find an intuitive negative relationship between the mismatch variable (measured using total debt outstanding rather than interest payments), which is significant only at the 81 percent level of confidence. This is some very weak evidence that liquidity problems are at play in a currency crisis. The trade balance has a positive sign, as it did in the Frankel and Rose (1996) study of the late twentieth century. Lagging this variable causes the magnitude of the coefficient and its statistical significance to fall, suggesting some endogeneity problems.

We give mismatches a second chance in column (3). Mismatches are associated with a higher probability of a currency crash (p-value of 0.09). This finding does not suggest that original sin is innocuous, but rather suggests that countries that have original sin may be able to avoid currency crises if they manage to collect adequate reserves or are sufficiently open. Moreover, it may back up the argument in Eichengreen, Hausmann, and Panizza (2003) that original sin is a second-best outcome. If countries cannot issue own-currency debt and then are forced by market discipline to hold costly reserves to insure themselves against currency speculation, this may not be socially optimal. Finally, we note that a higher gold cover ratio is associated with a lower probability of a crisis, although it is not statistically significant, and a greater trade surplus relative to GDP is associated with a higher chance of a currency crisis.[30]

In column (4) we drop some of the least significant variables and focus on debt intolerance. This makes for a slightly larger sample. There is no sign that a spotty record on debt combines with the debt burden to generate an increased chance of currency crises. The interaction of the debt ratio with the periphery dummy is negative and larger in absolute terms than the uninteracted coefficient. But all coefficients are far from statistically significant. Though we do not report it, using the pre-1880 default indicator only makes this negative result stronger. It also makes the coefficient on mismatch become highly statistically significant and negative. This implies that improvement in the mismatch is associated with less of a chance of a crisis.

4.4.3 Banking Crises

Banking crises also seem to be associated with original sin and currency mismatches, but not with debt intolerance. The latter might be expected as international perceptions of sovereign debt management and fiscal constraints might not necessarily have an effect on the liquidity or solvency of the banking system. On the other hand, banking trouble associated with

---

30. The seemingly counterintuitive result that net exporters have a higher chance of a crisis seems to arise from the fact that the small peripheral countries in our sample tend to be net exporters while Great Britain, France, and Switzerland, for example, have highly negative ratios for this variable and have had, of course, very few crises.

currency mismatches and hard-currency liabilities might be expected. We have already seen that currency crises are likely to be followed by banking crises.

When the exchange rate changes precipitously, bank balance sheets could be at risk, for various reasons. In countries with bond-based banking systems, if governments neglected to redeem their bonds in gold terms or had to default because of the increased burden placed on them by gold debt, bank balance sheets could suffer. For similar reasons, if loans are made by international banks or through domestic banks that have international liabilities, currency depreciation could easily impair the net worth of the banking sector. International lending through correspondent banks was prevalent in South America—for example, through the Rothschilds (Brazil) and the House of Baring (in Argentina). Moreover, our results suggest that when countries have a stronger gold reserve position the danger of hard currency debt is lower.

Column (1) of table 4.3 shows again the quadratic relationship between hard currency debt and banking crises. It also shows a significant and negative relationship between our mismatch variable and the probability of a crisis. The existence of a central bank, adherence to the gold standard, lower growth of the money supply (or of the note circulation), appreciation of the real exchange rate, lower gold cover ratios, higher trade deficits, and improvement in the terms of trade are associated with lower chances of a crisis. The square of original sin, mismatch, the trade balance, and the gold standard variable are significant at better than the 10 percent level.[31] Little else is statistically significant here, and the signs on the gold cover ratio and the trade balance are opposite of what one might expect.

Column (2) of table 4.3 shows how the coefficients on the two controls for original sin provide a quadratic fit, but both are statistically insignificant. Nevertheless, the mismatch control has a negative sign and is significant at the 86 percent level of confidence. Column (3) drops the mismatch variable and provides more support for a link between original sin and banking crises as the standard errors on the original sin variables shrink in relation to their point estimates, making them both significant at about the 90 percent level of confidence. Finally, column (4) provides no evidence of debt intolerance. However, mismatches are again significant, as is the negative relationship between the gold standard and banking crises.

Table 4.4 shows that finding determinants of twin crises is more difficult. In the comprehensive specification of column (1), only the trade balance is significant at conventional levels. Nevertheless, the quadratic relationship between original sin and such crises is evident, and each coefficient is

---

31. The negative gold standard coefficient may be contradictory to the positive coefficient we found in table 4.1. Again, the results are fragile to the particular specification so there is little we can say definitively.

Table 4.3   **Determinants of banking crises**

Regressors	(1)	(2)	(3)	(4)
Hard-currency debt as a percentage of total debt	1.32 (0.71)	0.62 (0.92)	1.10 (0.67)	
Square of hard-currency debt ratio	−2.36 (0.70)***	−0.90 (0.84)	−1.20 (0.71)	
Debt/Revenue	−0.05 (0.05)	−0.05 (0.04)	−0.01 (0.02)	−0.05 (0.05)
Debt/Revenue · periphery indicator	−0.04 (0.08)			
Periphery indicator	−1.15 (0.92)			
Debt/Revenue · pre-1880 default				−0.10 (0.07)
Pre-1880 default				0.02 (0.52)
Mismatch	−0.17 (0.07)**	−0.07 (0.05)		−0.16 (0.08)**
Growth of terms of trade	−7.01 (5.47)			−6.67 (5.52)
ln (deviation of real exchange rate from period average)	−0.81 (0.85)	−0.24 (0.72)	−0.21 (0.70)	−0.33 (0.29)
Trade balance/GDP	6.50 (2.11)***	4.93 (1.98)**	4.17 (1.83)**	4.60 (2.41)
Central bank indicator	−0.54 (0.43)	−0.12 (0.28)	−0.02 (0.23)	0.07 (0.32)
Gold standard dummy	−0.87 (0.42)**	−0.33 (0.33)	−0.23 (0.28)	−0.65 (0.35)
Growth of the money supply	1.03 (1.11)	0.67 (0.87)	0.65 (0.88)	
Gold reserves/notes in circulation	0.82 (0.47)	0.99 (0.40)***	0.65 (0.25)***	0.78 (0.48)
Market portfolio spread	0.38 (0.30)	0.41 (0.27)	0.39 (0.25)	0.42 (0.25)
Constant	−0.82 (0.84)	−2.26 (0.39)***	−2.43 (0.34)***	−1.95 (0.53)***
No. of observations	485	549	549	491
Percentage of correct positives	27.7	10.5	5.2	21
Percentage of correct negatives	96	97.1	98.1	96.6
Pseudo R^2	0.11	0.07	0.06	0.08
Log-likelihood	−68.46	−76.9	−77.8	−74.1

Notes: Dependent variable is a binary indicator for a banking crisis. "Robust" clustered standard errors are in parentheses. See the text for precise definitions of variables. Positive signifies crisis year.
***Significant at the 1 percent level.
**Significant at the 5 percent level.

Table 4.4   Determinants of twin crises

Regressors	(1)	(2)	(3)
Hard-currency debt as a percentage of total debt	1.33 (0.77)	0.39 (0.47)	1.51 (0.61)**
Square of hard-currency debt ratio	−1.83 (0.98)		−1.46 (0.72)**
Hard-currency ratio · (reserves/imports)		−1.21 (0.89)	
Reserves/Imports		1.42 (0.66)**	
Debt/Revenue	0.008 (0.08)	0.04 (0.03)	0.03 (0.02)
Debt/Revenue · periphery indicator	−0.05 (0.13)		
Periphery indicator	−0.42 (0.65)		
Mismatch	−0.09 (0.09)		
Growth of terms of trade	−11.39 (8.38)		
ln (deviation of real exchange rate from period average)	0.18 (0.47)	−0.13 (0.37)	0.09 (0.33)
Trade balance/GDP	5.14 (2.6)**		3.11 (1.80)
Spread on U.K. consol	0.08 (0.06)		
Gold reserves/notes in circulation	−0.52 (0.61)	−1.57 (0.53)***	−0.56 (0.41)
Market portfolio spread	0.12 (0.22)	0.25 (0.13)	0.16 (0.15)
Constant	−2.04 (0.51)***	−2.68 (0.45)***	−2.58 (0.25)***
No. of observations	497	625	605
Percentage of correct positives	50	50	50
Percentage of correct negatives	89.9	87	88.7
Pseudo R^2	0.13	0.10	0.11
Log-likelihood value	−35.6	−38.3	−37.9

Notes: Dependent variable is a binary indicator for a twin crisis. "Robust" clustered standard errors are in parentheses. Positive signifies crisis year. See the text for precise definitions of variables.
***Significant at the 1 percent level.
**Significant at the 5 percent level.

significant at a bit better than the 90 percent confidence level (*p*-values are 0.083 and 0.060 respectively). In column (2) we control for mismatches with an interaction between original sin and the reserve-to-import ratio. We find that the debt revenue ratio is positively associated with twin crises (*p*-value 0.118) and that higher gold cover ratios and a more tranquil international environment (*p*-value 0.053) are associated with fewer twin crises.[32] The interaction terms suggest that more reserves decrease the chances of having a twin crisis, but this effect is not statistically significant. The specification in column (2) also suggests that a higher ratio of reserves to imports is associated with a greater chance of a twin crisis. Perhaps this is because crisis-prone countries stock up on reserves prior to a crisis. Column (3) eliminates some of the variables and still finds a hump-shaped relationship (positive below a ratio of about 0.5 and negative above) between original sin and twin crises, with each coefficient significant when evaluated at the means. Further specifications revealed no particular relationships between our other measure of mismatches, default history, and twin crises.

4.4.4 Robustness and Reflections

Earlier, we found some evidence that after a certain point more hard currency debt relative to the total seemed to be associated with fewer debt crises and banking crises. One possibility is that the level of original sin is correlated with factors or characteristics of countries we have left out of the analysis. That is to say, perhaps those most at risk take care to protect their financial systems from crises or have effective ways of dealing with crises despite their high levels of original sin. If these factors were constant over time, an econometric solution to such a problem is to include country-level indicator variables.

Since this is infeasible to do in a limited dependent variable model with our particular data configuration, we move to a "fixed effects" linear probability model estimated by ordinary least squares (OLS). Table 4.5 respecifies the models of column (1) from tables 4.1 through 4.4 in this way. Like the previous results, the models fit fairly poorly since there are so few crises compared to noncrisis years. Many of the coefficients on the basic macro-controls are statistically insignificant. Nevertheless, the results regarding the coefficients on the original sin and mismatch variables are qualitatively very similar to the findings in the previous tables.

For debt crises, we find evidence of the very same quadratic pattern from table 4.1. We cannot reject the hypothesis that the coefficients on hard-currency debt and its square are different from zero at the 95 percent confidence level. For currency crises, the link between a crisis and original sin is indirect and seems to be coming through the outbreak of banking problems or eventual debt crises. Also, columns (3) and (4) show that better mismatches are associated with lower chances of having a banking crisis or a

---

32. Throughout the paper we have used the GDP-weighted spread on consols as a time-specific measure of international capital market turbulence. It is also a fact that this measure declines strongly over time and could be picking up other factors, such as increased liquidity in international capital markets, a more tranquil political environment, the shift from deflation after 1896 (as Flandreau, Le Cacheux, and Zúmer [1998] argue), and other environmental factors that change over time in step.

Table 4.5 "Fixed effects" linear probability specifications

Regressors	Debt crises (1)	Currency crises (2)	Banking crises (3)	Twin crises (4)
Hard-currency debt as a percentage of total debt	0.14 (0.10)	−0.11 (0.14)	0.14 (0.16)	0.08 (0.10)
Square of hard-currency debt ratio	−0.29 (0.11)***	−0.06 (0.14)	−0.19 (0.16)	−0.19 (0.11)
Debt/Revenue	0.01 (0.01)	0.004 (0.01)	−0.01 (0.01)	0.002 (0.01)
Debt/Revenue · periphery indicator		−0.01 (0.02)	0.0003 (0.01)	0.003 (0.01)
Debt/Revenue · pre-1880 default	0.01 (0.01)			
Mismatch	0.11 (0.09)	−0.01 (0.01)	−0.03 (0.01)***	−0.02 (0.01)***
Square of mismatch	−0.11 (0.08)			
Growth of terms of trade	−0.39 (0.43)	0.66 (0.58)	−0.72 (0.62)	−0.51 (0.41)
ln (deviation of real exchange rate from period average)	−0.22 (0.06)***	0.02 (0.08)	−0.11 (0.08)	−0.03 (0.05)
Trade balance/GDP	−0.18 (0.20)	−0.01 (0.29)	0.29 (0.30)	0.1 (0.20)
Spread on U.K. consol	0.04 (0.01)***			
Central bank indicator			0.02 (0.08)	
Gold standard dummy	−0.02 (0.03)	−0.08 (0.04)	−0.08 (0.04)	
Growth of the money supply	0.02 (0.06)	−0.12 (0.09)	0.23 (0.10)**	
Gold reserves/notes in circulation	0 (0.07)	0.03 (0.06)	0.03 (0.07)	0.01 (0.04)
Market portfolio spread	−0.01 (0.02)	0.04 (0.03)	0.02 (0.03)	−0.002 (0.02)
Debt crisis in $t + 1$		0.08 (0.05)		
Banking crisis in $t + 1$		0.1 (0.04)**		
Constant	−0.14 (0.06)**	0.05 (0.09)	0.04 (0.11)	0.01 (0.06)
No. of observations	371	499	485	497
R^2	0.06	0.004	0.008	0.01
F-stat	6.81	1.34	1.93	2.02

Notes: Dependent variable is a binary indicator for a banking crisis. Estimation is by OLS. "Robust" clustered standard errors are in parentheses. See the text for precise definitions of variables.
***Significant at the 1 percent level.
**Significant at the 5 percent level.

twin crisis. The coefficients are highly statistically significant as well. For these latter types of crisis it could be said that better reserve positions or being more open to exports for a given level of original sin helped avoid trouble.

We are also apparently left with the result that time-invariant underlying fundamentals like empire status or resource endowments cannot explain how places like the United States, Canada, Australia, and Scandinavia managed to carry high original sin and also avoid severe financial crises. This suggests the possibility that these places had a more active approach to managing crises or that their financial systems were structured in a way that helped stave off financial meltdown following a major shock.[33] Opposite these is little evidence that places like Argentina, Brazil, Greece, Italy, and Portugal faced financial meltdowns because of time-invariant characteristics such as bad government or institutions or simply because they were in the geographic or economic periphery.

In part, such omitted factors may be playing a role in giving rise to the hump-shaped relationship between crisis probability and hard-currency debt.[34] They probably explain why the positive marginal effect of original sin becomes negative at high levels of original sin. Predicted values of having a debt crisis from the regression in column (2) of table 4.1 and the actual values of original sin are shown in figure 4.12. The countries at the far right end of the figure (the United States, Canada, and Australia) with total foreign currency and gold clause debt were special cases.[35] They may have had other means of protecting themselves from reversals and long, drawn-out crises.

33. The endogeneity of the level of original sin should be explored and other experiences across time should be compared. The endogeneity bias would appear to be small. Eichengreen, Hausmann, and Panizza (2003, 2005), and Flandreau and Sussman (2005) take the view that original sin is inversely related to country size. Having a financial center also decreases original sin. Being large and/or having a financial center makes for liquid markets in the domestic currency and increases the demand for such assets in the portfolio of international investors. Because of this, endogeneity may be less of an issue than one might conjecture at the outset. Evidence from Australia, New Zealand, and the United States in Bordo, Meissner, and Redish (2005) suggests that wars and large shocks that closed international markets and forced governments into the domestic markets catalyzed the process. Still other factors are obviously necessary for these factors to be viable explanations.

34. In other un-reported specifications, we tried using proxies for good institutions and financial development in our probit models. We included the ratio of the money stock to GDP, a British Empire indicator, a central bank indicator, and a branch bank indicator. None of these variables eliminated the quadratic pattern or gave rise to a conditionally positive relationship between original sin and debt crises, currency crises, or banking crises. In the debt crisis specifications, it is not feasible to estimate the equations with an empire dummy simply because no included dominion, colony, or other member of the British Commonwealth ever had a debt default in this period. This indicator would be a perfect predictor of not having a debt crisis. So we are left clinging to the notion that the small countries with lots of original sin, like Canada, Australia, and New Zealand, and perhaps the Scandinavian countries, were different along other dimensions than those captured by these proxy variables. Caballero, Cowan, and Kearns (2004) talk about currency-trust and country-trust, which could be factors at play here but are not easily captured by any one explanatory variable.

35. Two data points, Argentina in 1893 and 1894, just after the Baring crisis, are notable exceptions to the rest of the scatter. The fact that the crisis had not yet been fully resolved explains why the predicted values are so high, and because of this we do not believe that this negates the quadratic relationship we have identified.

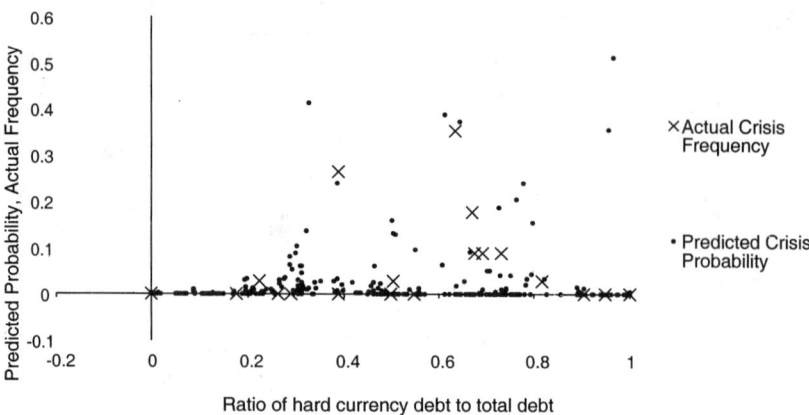

Fig. 4.12   Actual and predicted debt crisis frequencies versus the ratio of hard currency public debt to total public debt, 1880–1913

Notes: Predicted values come from the probit "regression" in column (2) of table 4.1. They are the predicted probabilities arising from the probit likelihood function using the estimated coefficients and evaluating the function at the actual covariates for each country year observation. Actual frequencies of debt crises are calculated as in figure 4.4. The actual frequencies are plotted against the period average values of the hard currency debt ratio. The predicted probabilities are plotted against the ratio in the given year. See text for other definitions.

The United States was lucky to have had a deep and relatively well-functioning financial system, allowing it to resolve crises rapidly. Public debt levels were fairly low, were well-managed since Alexander Hamilton's funding plan in 1790, and from a long-term perspective had sound economic fundamentals. Canada, Australia, and New Zealand had branch banking. The short maturities at which intermediaries lent their funds allowed for more prudent risk-taking by borrowers. The dominions and the United States, then, shared the fundamentals, the fiscal institutions, and the creditor protections necessary to maintain good borrowing practices.

The commitment and ability to maintain gold pegs in the British Commonwealth were stronger and more durable than in the independent countries with sovereign governments and national monetary systems. New Zealand banks held large sterling asset positions in London and also had an incentive to maintain the peg against sterling. Creditors to the dominions often felt that repayment was a certainty because many issues carried the guarantee of the British government. Debt was also given trustee status later in this period. This channelled Trustee Saving Bank funds into colonial securities, raising bond prices and making investors feel that such securities were less risky than they probably were. In such a case, this debt was less likely to give rise to self-fulfilling crises.

All of this suggests that without the special relationships and other idiosyncrasies that allowed for a robust reaction in turbulent times unique to these British offshoots and the United States (and perhaps others, such as the Scandinavian countries), original sin is positively associated with the frequency of crises. The countries in the southern cone of Latin America and southern and eastern Europe (e.g., Argentina, Brazil, Portugal, Spain, Italy, Greece, and Russia) that embraced global financial flows but did not adequately fortify their financial systems each faced at least one severe financial crisis enveloping the banking system, the currency, and usually the national debt between 1880 and 1913.[36]

The other group of countries toward the left hand side of figure 4.12 deserves some mention too. First, many financial centers, like Great Britain, France, and the Netherlands are here. Their low levels of original sin, liquid markets, and sound fundamentals made crisis management easier. One notable exception that looks more like a periphery country, however, seems to have been Austria-Hungary, which had established a significant domestic debt market in our period. This likely reflected much-improved fiscal fundamentals (see Flandreau and Komlos 2002 and Komlos 1987).[37]

A number of other European countries in the middle group that had lower levels of original sin than the settler countries and Scandinavia but were financially crisis prone (e.g., Spain, Portugal, and Italy) had sizeable domestic currency debt markets, and some even had sovereign bond issues denominated in their own currencies listed on the exchanges in London and Paris. These countries were quite open to international trade and had developed financial centers much earlier, reflecting their entrepôt position within European trade (Flandreau and Sussman 2005).

While the precedent of domestic debt issue had been established in these countries, fiscal and financial soundness did not prevail. In reaction to their vulnerability, some of these countries developed methods of crisis prevention not used in the dominions or in the United States. The affidavit system required domestic creditors be paid in paper money while foreigners were paid in gold (see Tattara 2003). But these experiences also further demonstrate that hard currency debt made it more difficult to manage a crisis event, and the repercussions of a bad shock were all the greater when not dealt with in a just and efficient way.

Overall, our results suggest that the contemporary theoretical framework that views balance sheets as important determinants of financial crises are just as valid during the late nineteenth century. Like the late twentieth century, this period was one of freely flowing cross-border cap-

---

36. Eichengreen, Hausmann, and Panizza (2003, 15) might agree: "In particular, countries with strong institutions, capable of running strong policies, are in the best position to cope with the potential mismatch problem." To solve the problem of original sin, policymakers must decide whether it is easier to take steps to eliminate original sin or to fortify the financial system and live with original sin in the medium run.

37. There was also an effort to increase the transparency of the budgetary process and an increase in creditors' protection in this period. See Becker (1913).

ital flows that met with various levels of financial sophistication and fiscal rigor in its global reach for yield. As financial weaknesses became apparent, the markets reacted in ways reminiscent of the financial crises of the 1990s.

4.5   Conclusions

We believe we have found some interesting features in the data that have not previously been systematically addressed in either contemporary or historical literatures. Most importantly, we find that hard-currency debt may not always generate financial crises. Some countries with very high levels of original sin have apparently been less prone to debt crises than those with intermediate levels. Aside from these extreme cases where original sin seems less dangerous, there appears to be a positive relationship between original sin and the incidence of debt crises.

It is interesting that we find that holding our currency mismatch measure constant, more original sin makes countries more crisis prone up to a certain point, and then less vulnerable to debt crises that are often the culmination of a full-blown financial catastrophe. One plausible explanation is that countries with high levels of original sin also had natural hedges, better balance sheets, or better ways of dealing with financial stress that are hard to quantify. This is compelling, because we know anecdotally that the dominions had large sterling balances and that they had good fiscal institutions. A question for further research is whether it was the structure of their financial systems or the actual level of sterling bank assets which we cannot determine. We tend to think it is the former rather than the latter.

Holding original sin levels constant, we also find that mismatches matter. When countries have hard-currency obligations, they seem less prone to debt, banking, or currency crises when they offset these liabilities with gold reserves or are more open. This obviously does not negate the idea that original sin could be responsible for currency and banking trouble. Those countries that do not hold sufficient reserves in their banking sectors, which may be a reflection of either weak banking structure, and/or a lack of political will to take adequate insurance, face a higher chance of a crisis situation. The absence of original sin could be an improvement for such countries if the goal is to reduce crisis incidence.[38] At the same time, it also highlights our key finding—that countries can and have found ways to avoid financial fragility when they have dollarized liabilities.

These results also tend to confirm that it is difficult to find robust determinants of financial crises. This suggests that standard econometric ap-

---

38. This, of course, leaves open the question of social optimality. Perhaps hard-currency debt is a disciplining device, or asset holders would be worse off without hard-currency debt. The question deserves more research.

proaches may not be resoundingly successful or that the theory is too abstract to deal with the messy reality of historical crisis episodes. These complications are in addition to the other data problems we mentioned. Still, as a means of summarizing the data, multivariate analysis can be useful.

The ostensible quadratic relationship between hard-currency debt relative to total debt and debt crises is the most novel. Why is it there? We believe that this quadratic is obscuring a positive relationship between hard-currency debt and debt crises that exists for the average small, independent, emerging market type of country.

So the lesson for today's and tomorrow's emerging market economies is to become more like today's advanced countries. Many of the leading economies today had original sin even as they received massive capital inflows from abroad. They also faced limited exposure to crises. What was involved was following careful debt management policies and the development of sound fiscal and financial institutions. In the interim, large foreign exchange reserves and a strong export position can also help governments and firms to navigate the choppy waters of global finance.

Data Appendix

General Notes

Debt: In general we have defined external debt or hard currency debt as the amount outstanding of long-term debt issued abroad plus the amount outstanding of domestic gold (or silver) debt. Internal debt refers to the outstanding stock of debt payable exclusively in domestic currency. However, in a few cases listed below we have not been able to discern from the sources how much of the domestic or internal debt was payable in gold. More work will have to be put into these cases. However, one will note that for these cases the total amount of domestic debt is rather small.

Real exchange rates: The real exchange rate is defined as the product of the exchange rate (price of local currency per pound) and the U.K. price level divided by the local price level. Price levels come from Obstfeld and Taylor (2003). We use the percentage deviation from the within country average to obviate problems with levels. The average is taken over the entire period 1880–1913.

Market portfolio spread: We use a GDP-weighted average spread of long-term bonds against the British consol constructed by Obstfeld and Taylor (2003) to control for time-specific international changes in capital markets.

Exchange rate regimes: Data on gold standard adherence comes from Meissner (2005), augmented with data from Obstfeld and Taylor (2003).

Default indicator: Our default indicator was created if there were one or more defaults prior to 1880. This data is taken from a spreadsheet underlying Reinhart, Rogoff, and Savastano (2003).

Crisis dating: As in Bordo et al. (2001) we date currency and banking crises using both qualitative and quantitative evidence. For all countries besides Austria-Hungary, Russia, New Zealand, South Africa, Mexico, Turkey, Egypt, Uruguay, and India we have relied on the dates of Bordo et al. We have tried to date currency crises, when possible, by using an approach based on the exchange market pressure (EMP) methodology, which looks at changes in reserves, the exchange rate, and the interest rate.

Debt crisis dates were based on Beim and Calomiris (2001). Only private lending to sovereign nations is considered when building those default dates. Not every instance of technical default is included in the chronology. The authors identified periods (six months or more) where all or part of the interest/principal payments were suspended, reduced, or rescheduled. Some of those episodes are outright debt repudiations, while others were reschedulings agreed upon mutually by lenders and borrowers. Also, data is taken from a spreadsheet underlying Reinhart, Rogoff, and Savastano (2003). We have relied extensively on data underlying Bordo et al. and Obstfeld and Taylor (2003). We cite these papers below though data is available by personal communication.

Argentina

Total outstanding government debt, external hard-currency debt, and domestic paper debt: Total funded debt from 1880 to 1913 from Vázquez-Presedo (1988). The external debt data from 1880 to 1891 comes from Conde (1995). The percentage of debt serviced in gold was taken from Flandreau and Zúmer (2004).
Government revenue: Flandreau and Zúmer (2004).
Terms of trade: Obstfeld and Taylor (2003).
Interest service on debt: Flandreau and Zúmer (2004).
Real exchange rate: Obstfeld and Taylor (2003).
Exports: Flandreau and Zúmer (2004).
Imports: Barbieri (2000).
Nominal GDP: Obstfeld and Taylor (2003).
Yield spread between British consols: Obstfeld and Taylor (2003).
Growth of the money supply: Data underlying Bordo et al. (2001).
Gold reserves: Flandreau and Zúmer (2004).
Notes in circulation: Flandreau and Zúmer (2004).

Australia

Total outstanding government debt, external hard-currency debt, and domestic paper debt: Total debt: Ferguson and Schularick (2006); percentage

of debt payable in gold or foreign currency, Bordo, Meissner, and Redish (2005).
Government revenue: Mitchell (1993a).
Terms of trade: Obstfeld and Taylor (2003).
Real exchange rate: Obstfeld and Taylor (2003).
Exports: Mitchell (1993a).
Imports: Mitchell (1993a).
Nominal GDP: Bordo et al. (2001).
Yield spread between British consols: Obstfeld and Taylor (2003).
Growth of the money supply: Data underlying Bordo et al. (2001).
Gold reserves: Mitchell (1993a).
Notes in circulation: Mitchell (1993a).
GDP-weighted average spread on British consol: Obstfeld and Taylor (2003).

Austria-Hungary

Total outstanding government debt, external hard-currency debt, and domestic paper debt: The source is the statistical yearbooks for both countries. External debt consists of domestic gold debt and foreign currency debt. Internal debt is domestic paper debt. Data for 1880 is from Flandreau and Zúmer (2004).
Interest service on debt: Flandreau and Zúmer (2004).
Government revenue: Flandreau and Zúmer (2004).
Terms of trade: Obstfeld and Taylor (2003).
Real exchange rate: Obstfeld and Taylor (2003).
Exports: Flandreau and Zúmer (2004).
Imports: Mitchell (1992).
Nominal GDP: Obstfeld and Taylor (2003).
Yield spread between British consols: Obstfeld and Taylor (2003).
Growth of the money supply: Bordo et al. (2001).
Gold reserves: Flandreau and Zúmer (2004).
Notes in circulation: Flandreau and Zúmer (2004).

Belgium

Total outstanding government debt, external hard-currency debt, and domestic paper debt: Total public debt from *Annuaire Statistique and Fenn's Compendium*. Level of debt payable in gold is from Flandreau and Zúmer (2004).
Interest service on debt: Flandreau and Zúmer (2004).
Government revenue: Flandreau and Zúmer (2004).
Terms of trade: Obstfeld and Taylor (2003).
Real exchange rate: Obstfeld and Taylor (2003).
Exports: Flandreau and Zúmer (2004).
Imports: Barbieri (2000).

Nominal GDP: Obstfeld and Taylor (2003).
Yield spread between British consols: Obstfeld and Taylor (2003).
Growth of the money supply: Bordo et al. (2001).
Gold reserves: Flandreau and Zúmer (2004).
Notes in circulation: Flandreau and Zúmer (2004).

Brazil

Total outstanding government debt, external hard-currency debt, and domestic paper debt: Debt in foreign currency (1880–1914), domestic paper, and gold debt (1880–1912) from *Statistical Yearbook* and Levy (1995). For 1913 and 1914 the data given in the sources for external debt only included foreign currency debt and was denominated in sterling.
Interest service on debt: Flandreau and Zúmer (2004).
Government revenue: Flandreau and Zúmer (2004).
Terms of trade: Clemens and Williamson (2004).
Real exchange rate: Obstfeld and Taylor (2003).
Exports: Flandreau and Zúmer (2004).
Imports: Barbieri (2000).
Nominal GDP: Obstfeld and Taylor (2003) and Bordo et al. (2001).
Yield spread between British consols: Obstfeld and Taylor (2003).
Growth of the money supply: Bordo et al. (2001).
Gold reserves: Flandreau and Zúmer (2004).
Notes in circulation: Flandreau and Zúmer (2004).

Canada

Total outstanding government debt, external hard-currency debt, and domestic paper debt: Bordo, Meissner, and Redish (2005).
Government revenue: Mitchell (1993b).
Terms of trade: Obstfeld and Taylor (2003).
Real exchange rate: Obstfeld and Taylor (2003).
Exports: Mitchell (1993b).
Imports: Mitchell (1993b).
Nominal GDP: Bordo et al. (2001).
Yield spread between British consols: Obstfeld and Taylor (2003).
Growth of the money supply: Data underlying Bordo et al. (2001).
Gold reserves: Mitchell (1993b).
Notes in circulation: Mitchell (1993b).

Chile

Total outstanding government debt, external hard-currency debt, and domestic paper debt: External and domestic debt from 1880 to 1897 from Molino (1898; no information about domestic gold debt). From 1898 onward the source is the statistical yearbook for Chile for internal gold,

external and domestic paper debt. 1911–12, total and foreign debt come from Ferguson and Schularick (2006).
Government revenue: Mitchell (1993b).
Terms of trade: Obstfeld and Taylor (2003).
Real exchange rate: Obstfeld and Taylor (2003).
Exports: Barbieri (2000).
Imports: Barbieri (2000).
Nominal GDP: Obstfeld and Taylor (2003).
Growth of the money supply: Data underlying Bordo et al. (2001).
Gold reserves: 1887–95, Molino (1898).
Notes in circulation: Mitchell (1993b).

Denmark

Total outstanding government debt, external hard-currency debt, and domestic paper debt: For 1880, 1886 and 1890 the source is *Fenn's Compendium*. No information about domestic gold debt was available but our numbers are highly consistent with Flandreau and Zúmer's (2004) for the total debt payable in gold. Total debt: 1881, 1882, 1884, 1885, 1887–89, 1891–93, Ferguson and Schularick (2006). 1894–1913, Statistical Yearbook. Debt payable in gold 1881–85, 1887–89, 1891–93, Flandreau and Zúmer (2004); 1894–1913 Statistical Yearbook.
Interest service on debt: Flandreau and Zúmer (2004).
Government revenue: Flandreau and Zúmer (2004).
Terms of trade: Obstfeld and Taylor (2003).
Real exchange rate: Obstfeld and Taylor (2003).
Exports: Flandreau and Zúmer (2004).
Imports: Barbieri (2000).
Nominal GDP: Bordo et al. (2001).
Yield spread between British consols: Clemens and Williamson (2004).
Growth of the money supply: Bordo et al. (2001).
Gold reserves: Flandreau and Zúmer (2004).
Notes in circulation: Flandreau and Zúmer (2004).

Egypt

Total outstanding government debt, external hard-currency debt, and domestic paper debt: 1880–1915 total public debt, Government revenues and government expenditures from Crouchley (1938). Consumer Price Indexes 1913 to 1915, Money supply 1901–15 (includes Currency and Bank notes in circulation and deposits in savings banks), are from Mitchell (1993b) and Crouchley. For foreign trade aggregates and crisis dates the source is Crouchley.
Government revenue: Mitchell (1993a).
Terms of trade: Obstfeld and Taylor (2003).

Real exchange rate: Obstfeld and Taylor (2003).
Exports: Barbieri (2000).
Imports: Barbieri (2000).
Nominal GDP: Obstfeld and Taylor (2003).
Yield spread between British consols: Obstfeld and Taylor (2003).
Growth of the money supply: Bordo et al. (2001).
Gold reserves: Not available.
Notes in circulation: Not available.

Finland

Total outstanding government debt, external hard-currency debt, and domestic paper debt: 1880–1915 public debt in marks from statistical yearbook. 1881, 1891 foreign and domestic debt from *Fenn's Compendium*. It appears that the entire debt was external before 1915. Yearbook presents total debt from 1880 to 1901 and then only foreign debt from 1901 to 1915, but the values for external and total debt in 1901 are the same. If we consider the data from *Fenn's,* the ratio of external to total was 88 percent in 1881 and 92 percent in 1891.
Government revenue: Not available.
Terms of trade: Obstfeld and Taylor (2003).
Real exchange rate: Obstfeld and Taylor (2003).
Exports: Mitchell (1992).
Imports: Mitchell (1992).
Nominal GDP: Bordo et al. (2001).
Yield spread between British consols: Obstfeld and Taylor (2003).
Growth of the money supply: Data generously made available by Alan M. Taylor, UC Davis.
Gold reserves: Obstfeld and Jones (2003).
Notes in circulation: Mitchell (1992).

France

Total outstanding government debt, external hard-currency debt, and domestic paper debt: Flandreau and Zúmer (2004).
Government revenue: Flandreau and Zúmer (2004).
Interest service on debt: Flandreau and Zúmer (2004).
Terms of trade: Obstfeld and Taylor (2003).
Real exchange rate: Obstfeld and Taylor (2003).
Exports: Flandreau and Zúmer (2004).
Imports: Barbieri (2000).
Nominal GDP: Bordo et al. (2001).
Yield spread between British consols: Obstfeld and Taylor (2003).
Growth of the money supply: Bordo et al. (2001).
Gold reserves: Flandreau and Zúmer (2004).
Notes in circulation: Flandreau and Zúmer (2004).

Germany

Total outstanding government debt, external hard-currency debt, and domestic paper debt: State debt is excluded; Flandreau and Zúmer (2004).
Interest service on debt: Flandreau and Zúmer (2004).
Government revenue: Flandreau and Zúmer (2004).
Terms of trade: Obstfeld and Taylor (2003).
Real exchange rate: Obstfeld and Taylor (2003).
Exports: Flandreau and Zúmer (2004).
Imports: Barbieri (2000).
Nominal GDP: Bordo et al. (2001).
Yield spread between British consols: Clemens and Williamson (2004).
Growth of the money supply: Data underlying Bordo et al. (2001).
Gold reserves: Flandreau and Zúmer (2004).
Notes in circulation: Flandreau and Zúmer (2004).

Greece

Total outstanding government debt, external hard-currency debt, and domestic paper debt: 1881, external and total debt from *Fenn's*. 1885–1913, Flandreau and Zúmer (2004).
Interest service on debt: Flandreau and Zúmer (2004).
Government revenue: Flandreau and Zúmer (2004).
Terms of trade: Obstfeld and Taylor (2003).
Real exchange rate: Prices from Flandreau and Zúmer (2004), exchange rates, Bordo and Jonung (1996).
Exports: Flandreau and Zúmer (2004).
Imports: Barbieri (2000).
Nominal GDP: Kostelenos (1995).
Yield spread between British consols: Obstfeld and Taylor (2003).
Growth of the money supply: Data underlying Bordo et al. (2001).
Gold reserves: Flandreau and Zúmer (2004).
Notes in circulation: Flandreau and Zúmer (2004).

India

Total outstanding government debt, external hard-currency debt, and domestic paper debt: Funded rupee debt and funded sterling debt from Reserve Bank of India *Banking and Monetary Statistics of India* (1954). No information about domestic gold debt. Money supply data from Goldsmith (1983).
Government revenue: Mitchell (1993a).
Terms of trade: Obstfeld and Taylor (2003).
Real exchange rate: Obstfeld and Taylor (2003).
Exports: Mitchell (1993a).
Imports: Mitchell (1993a).

Nominal GDP: Obstfeld and Taylor (2003).
Yield spread between British consols: Obstfeld and Taylor (2003).
Growth of the money supply: Data underlying Bordo et al. (2001).
Gold reserves: Not available.
Notes in circulation: Mitchell (1993a).
Population: Clemens and Williamson (2004).

Italy

Total outstanding government debt, external hard-currency debt, and domestic paper debt: Total and foreign debt from Zamagni (1998, 1999). Foreign debt includes only rendita interest paid abroad in foreign currency or gold. See Flandreau and Zúmer (2004) for a short discussion on this point.
Interest service on debt: Flandreau and Zúmer (2004).
Government revenue: Flandreau and Zúmer (2004).
Terms of trade: Obstfeld and Taylor (2003).
Real exchange rate: Obstfeld and Taylor (2003).
Exports: Flandreau and Zúmer (2004).
Imports: Barbieri (2000).
Nominal GDP: Bordo et al. (2001).
Yield spread between British consols: Obstfeld and Taylor (2003).
Growth of the money supply: Bordo et al. (2001)
Gold reserves: Flandreau and Zúmer (2004).
Notes in circulation: Flandreau and Zúmer (2004).

Japan

Total outstanding government debt, external hard-currency debt, and domestic paper debt: Internal and external debt from 1892–1913, *Statistical Yearbook of Japan,* no information was given about domestic gold debt. 1882 and 1887 foreign and total debt from Fenn's (no information about domestic gold debt). Total debt 1880–91 from Kikuchi (1904). 1897 foreign debt source is Furuya (1928), which includes government foreign bonds, domestic bonds sold abroad, domestic bonds shipped abroad, and corporation bonds. This series hence may contain some paper bond issues held abroad which would contaminate our measure of original sin. The amounts would not be large, we conjecture.
Government revenue: Mitchell (1993a).
Terms of trade: Obstfeld and Taylor (2003).
Real exchange rate: Obstfeld and Taylor (2003).
Exports: Mitchell (1993a).
Imports: Barbieri (2000).
Nominal GDP: Bordo et al. (2001).
Yield spread between British consols: Obstfeld and Taylor (2003).

Growth of the money supply: Data underlying Bordo et al. (2001).
Gold reserves: Jones and Obstfeld (2000).
Notes in circulation: Masayoshi (1899).

Mexico

Total outstanding government debt, external hard-currency debt, and domestic paper debt: External and internal debt from Bazant (1968), Ludlow & Marichal (1998) and Perez-Siller (1995). Only includes federal debt, no information about domestic gold or silver debt. Total debt and foreign debt 1881, 1883, 1885, 1891, 1892, 1895, 1897–1904, 1906–10, Ferguson and Schularick (2006).
Government revenue: Mitchell (1993b).
Terms of trade: Obstfeld and Taylor (2003).
Real exchange rate: Obstfeld and Taylor (2003).
Exports: Barbieri (2000).
Imports: Barbieri (2000).
Nominal GDP: Not available.
Yield spread between British consols: Obstfeld and Taylor (2003).
Growth of the money supply: Mitchell (1993b). Money supply includes deposits in commercial banks and currency and bank notes in circulation.
Gold reserves: Not available.
Notes in circulation: Mitchell (1993b).
Population: Clemens and Williamson (2004).

The Netherlands

Total outstanding government debt, external hard-currency debt, and domestic paper debt: Total consolidated debt sources are statistical yearbook and *Fenn's*. Except 1882–85, Flandreau and Zúmer (2004). Following Flandreau and Sussman (2005), Netherlands had no hard currency debt.
Interest service on debt: Flandreau and Zúmer (2004).
Government revenue: Flandreau and Zúmer (2004).
Terms of trade: Obstfeld and Taylor (2003).
Real exchange rate: Obstfeld and Taylor (2003).
Exports and Imports: Smits, Horlings, and van Zanden (1999).
Exports: Flandreau and Zúmer (2004).
Imports: Barbieri (2000).
Nominal GDP: Obstfeld and Taylor (2003).
Yield spread between British consols: Obstfeld and Taylor (2003).
Growth of the money supply: 1880–99 measured as the growth of M3. 1901–13, growth of money supply is the growth of M2. Data generously made available by Alan M. Taylor.

Gold reserves: Flandreau and Zúmer (2004).
Notes in circulation: Flandreau and Zúmer (2004).

New Zealand

Total outstanding government debt, external hard-currency debt, and domestic paper debt: Bordo, Meissner, and Redish (2005).
Government revenue: Mitchell (1993a).
Terms of trade: Obstfeld and Taylor (2003).
Real exchange rate: Obstfeld and Taylor (2003).
Imports: Mitchell (1993a).
Exports: Mitchell (1993a).
Nominal GDP: Bordo et al. (2001), Obstfeld and Taylor (2003).
Yield spread between British consols: Obstfeld and Taylor (2003).
Growth of the money supply: Data underlying Bordo et al. (2001).
Gold reserves: Not available.
Notes in circulation: Mitchell (1993a).

Norway

Total outstanding government debt, external hard-currency debt, and domestic paper debt: External and domestic debt from statistical yearbook. No information about whether the domestic debt was payable in specie. It is possible that the domestic debt actually had gold clauses. Still, the amount of domestic debt as a part of the total is very small.
Interest service on debt: Flandreau and Zúmer (2004).
Government revenue: Flandreau and Zúmer (2004).
Terms of trade: Obstfeld and Taylor (2003).
Real exchange rate: Obstfeld and Taylor (2003).
Exports: Flandreau and Zúmer (2004).
Imports: Mitchell (1992).
Nominal GDP: Bordo et al. (2001).
Yield spread between British consols: Obstfeld and Taylor (2003).
Growth of the money supply: Data underlying Bordo and Jonung (1996).
Gold reserves: Flandreau and Zúmer (2004).
Notes in circulation: Flandreau and Zúmer (2004).

Peru

Total outstanding government debt, external hard-currency debt, and domestic paper debt: Not available.
Government revenue: Mitchell (1993b).
Terms of trade: Clemens and Williamson (2004).
Real exchange rate: Not available.
Current account surplus: Not available.
Nominal GDP: Not available.

Yield spread between British consols: Clemens and Williamson (2004).
Growth of the money supply: Not available.
Gold reserves: Not available.
Notes in circulation: Not available.
Population: Clemens and Williamson (2004).

Portugal

Total outstanding government debt, external hard-currency debt, and domestic paper debt: Total debt, 1880–1913, Flandreau and Zúmer; percentage of debt serviced in gold, Flandreau and Zúmer (2004).
Interest service on debt: Flandreau and Zúmer (2004).
Government revenue: Flandreau and Zúmer (2004).
Terms of trade: Obstfeld and Taylor (2003).
Real exchange rate: Obstfeld and Taylor (2003).
Exports: Flandreau and Zúmer (2004).
Imports: Barbieri (2000).
Nominal GDP: Bordo et al. (2001).
Yield spread between British consols: Obstfeld and Taylor (2003).
Growth of the money supply: 1880–90. Growth of circulation in hands of public and commercial bank deposits. Data from Alan M. Taylor by private correspondence. 1891–1913, Bordo et al. (2001).
Gold reserves: Flandreau and Zúmer (2004).
Notes in circulation: Mitchell (1992).

Russia

Total outstanding government debt, external hard-currency debt, and domestic paper debt: 1880, 1887, 1891 total debt from *Fenn's*. 1880 hard currency debt from *Fenn's*. Foreign debt is reported as including domestic gold debt and internal debt. Total debt: 1881–84, 1885–86, 1888–90, 1893, 1894, Ferguson and Schularick (2004). 1885 total debt, Pasvolsky and Moulton (1924). 1895 to 1913, total debt. Percentage of debt serviced in gold, 1884–1913, Flandreau and Zúmer (2004).
Interest service on debt: Flandreau and Zúmer (2004).
Government revenue: Flandreau and Zúmer (2004).
Terms of trade: Clemens and Williamson (2004).
Real exchange rate: Obstfeld and Taylor (2003).
Current account surplus: Obstfeld and Taylor (2003).
Exports: Flandreau and Zúmer (2004).
Imports: Barbieri (2000).
Nominal GDP: Obstfeld and Taylor (2003).
Yield spread between British consols: Obstfeld and Taylor (2003).
Growth of the money supply: Kahan (1989).
Gold reserves: Flandreau and Zúmer (2004).
Notes in circulation: Flandreau and Zúmer (2004).

South Africa

Before union the data is constructed as an aggregate from available data from Cape of Good Hope, Natal, Orange Free State, and Transvaal.

Total outstanding government debt, external hard-currency debt, and domestic paper debt: Bordo, Meissner, Redish (2005).
Government revenue: Mitchell (1993a).
Terms of trade: Not available.
Exports: Global Financial Database.
Imports: Global Financial Database.
Nominal GDP: 1911–13, Mitchell (1993a).
Yield spread between British consols: Not available.
Growth of the money supply: Mitchell (1993a).
Gold reserves: Not available.
Notes in circulation: Not available.
Population: Schuman (1938).

Spain

Total outstanding government debt, external hard-currency debt, and domestic paper debt: External and internal debt from Acha (1976). No information about gold debt.
Interest service on debt: Flandreau and Zúmer (2004).
Government revenue: Flandreau and Zúmer (2004).
Terms of trade: Obstfeld and Taylor (2003).
Real exchange rate: Obstfeld and Taylor (2003).
Exports: Flandreau and Zúmer (2004).
Imports: Barbieri (2000).
Nominal GDP: Bordo et al. (2001).
Yield spread between British consols: Obstfeld and Taylor (2003).
Growth of the money supply: Data underlying Bordo et al. (2001).
Gold reserves: Flandreau and Zúmer (2004).
Notes in circulation: Flandreau and Zúmer (2004).

Sweden

Total outstanding government debt, external hard-currency debt, and domestic paper debt: Total debt (dette publique en obligations) and internal debt 1913 *Statistical Yearbook* of Sweden. Foreign debt 1880, 1887, 1891 from *Fenn's*. No information about domestic gold debts.
Government revenue: Flandreau and Zúmer (2004).
Terms of trade: Obstfeld and Taylor (2003).
Real exchange rate: Obstfeld and Taylor (2003).
Exports: Flandreau and Zúmer (2004).
Imports: Barbieri (2000).
Nominal GDP: Bordo et al. (2001).

Yield spread between British consols: Obstfeld and Taylor (2003).
Growth of the money supply: Bordo et al. (2001).
Gold reserves: Flandreau and Zúmer (2004).
Notes in circulation: Flandreau and Zúmer (2004).

Switzerland

Total outstanding government debt, external hard-currency debt, and domestic paper debt: 1880–1913, Flandreau and Zúmer (2004).
Interest service on debt: Flandreau and Zúmer (2004).
Government revenue: Flandreau and Zúmer (2004).
Terms of trade: Obstfeld and Taylor (2003).
Real exchange rate: Obstfeld and Taylor (2003).
Exports: Flandreau and Zúmer (2004).
Imports: Barbieri (2000).
Nominal GDP: Bordo et al. (2001).
Yield spread between British consols: Obstfeld and Taylor (2003).
Growth of the money supply: Bordo et al. (2001).
Gold reserves: Flandreau and Zúmer (2004).
Notes in circulation: Flandreau and Zúmer (2004).

Turkey

Total outstanding government debt, external hard-currency debt, and domestic paper debt: Not available.
Government revenue: 1884–1900, Du Velay (1903); for 1880, 1901–03, 1908–10 Shaw (1975).
Terms of trade: Obstfeld and Taylor (2003).
Real exchange rate: Not available.
Exports: Global Financial Database.
Imports: Barbieri (2000).
Nominal GDP: Not available.
Yield spread between British consols: Obstfeld and Taylor (2003).
Growth of the money supply: Not available.
Gold reserves: Not available.
Notes in circulation: Not available.
Population: Clemens and Williamson (2004).

Great Britain

Total outstanding government debt, external hard-currency debt, and domestic paper debt: 1880–1913 total debt, Flandreau and Zúmer (2004). Great Britain had no hard currency debt in this period, to the best of our knowledge.
Government revenue: Flandreau and Zúmer (2004).
Interest service on debt: Flandreau and Zúmer (2004).
Terms of trade: Obstfeld and Taylor (2003).

Real exchange rate: Obstfeld and Taylor (2003).
Exports: Flandreau and Zúmer (2004).
Imports: Barbieri (2000).
Nominal GDP: Bordo et al. (2001).
Growth of the money supply: Bordo et al. (2001).
Gold reserves: Flandreau and Zúmer (2004).
Notes in circulation: Flandreau and Zúmer (2004).

United States

Total outstanding government debt, external hard-currency debt, and domestic paper debt: Total debt, 1880–1913: Ferguson and Schularick (2006). All debt is payable in gold following Bordo, Meissner, and Redish (2005).
Government revenue: Mitchell (1993b).
Terms of trade: Obstfeld and Taylor (2003).
Real exchange rate: Obstfeld and Taylor (2003).
Exports: Barbieri (2000).
Imports: Barbieri (2000).
Nominal GDP: Bordo et al. (2001), Obstfeld and Taylor (2003).
Yield spread between British consols: Obstfeld and Taylor (2003).
Growth of the money supply: Bordo et al. (2001).
Gold reserves: Obstfeld and Jones (2003).
Notes in circulation: Mitchell (1993b).

Uruguay

Total outstanding government debt, external hard-currency debt, and domestic paper debt: Internal and external debt from *Statistical Yearbook,* no information about domestic gold debt.
Government revenue: Mitchell (1993b).
Terms of trade: Not available.
Real exchange rate: 1900–13, Obstfeld and Taylor (2003).
Exports: Barbieri (2000).
Imports: Barbieri (2000).
Nominal GDP: Clemens and Williamson (2004).
Yield spread between British consols: Obstfeld and Taylor (2003).
Growth of the money supply: 1901–13, Mitchell (1993b).
Gold reserves: Not available.
Notes in circulation: Mitchell (1993b).
Population: Clemens and Williamson (2004).

Table 4A.1 Crisis dates, 1880–1913

Year	Argentina	Australia	Austria	Belgium	Brazil	Canada	Chile	Denmark	Egypt	Finland	France	Germany	Greece	India	Italy	Japan	Mexico	Netherlands	New Zealand	Norway	Portugal	Russia	South Africa	Spain	Sweden	Switzerland	Turkey	U.K.	U.S.	Uruguay
1880							DC										DC										DC			
1881			BC																											
1882																								DC						
1883																														
1884																	BC												BC	
1885	CC							BC														DC								
1886													CC																	
1887							CC				CC																			
1888					BC, CC						BC												BC							
1889					BC																									
1890	BC, CC, DC																											BC	CC	
1891	BC				CC								BC						BC, CC									DC		
1892		BC													BC						DC									
1893						CC						CC			CC														BC, CC	
1894													DC						BC											
1895																														
1896					BC																									
1897					CC													BC												
1898					DC		BC, CC																							
1899					BC																									
1900					BC				CC	BC						CC														
1901												BC				BC														
1902																														
1903																							BC							
1904																CC														
1905																			CC											
1906																														
1907							BC	BC	BC		BC				BC	BC	BC								BC				BC	
1908	CC					CC		BC				CC			CC	CC														
1909																														
1910																														
1911																														
1912																														
1913																														BC

Note: CC represents currency crises; BC represents banking crises; DC represents debt crises.

Table 4A.2 Data availability for countries and years

Variable	Argentina	Australia	Austria	Belgium	Brazil	Canada	Chile	Denmark	Egypt	Finland	France	Germany	Greece	India	Italy	Japan	Mexico	Netherlands	New Zealand	Norway	Portugal	Russia	South Africa	Spain	Sweden	Switzerland	Turkey	U.K.	U.S.	Uruguay
Original sin	1880-1913	1880-1913	1880-1913	1880-1913	1880-1913	1880-1913	1880-1913	1880-1913	—	1881, 1891	1880-1913	1880-1913	1885-1913	1880-1913	1880-1913	1880-1913	1880, 1881, 1883, 85-86, 1890-1912	1880-1913	1880-1913	1880-1913	1880-1913	1880, 1884-1913	1880-1913	1880-1913	1880, 1887, 1881, 1913	1880-1913	—	1880-1913	1880-1913	—
Debt/Revenue	1880-1913	—	1880-1912	1880-1913	1880-1913	1880-1913	1880-1913	1880-1913	1880-1913	—	1880-1913	1880-1913	1881, 1882, 1884-1913	1880-1913	1880-1913	1880-1913	1880, 1881, 1883, 85-86, 89-1912	1880-1913	1880-1913	1881-1913	1880-1912	1880-1912	1910-1913	1880-1913	1880, 1887, 1891, 1813	1880-1913	—	1880-1913	1880-1913	1880, 1884-1913
Mismatch																1882, 1887														
Debt	1880-1913	—	1880-1913	1880-1913	1880-1913	1880-1913	1887-1895	1880-1913	—	1881, 1891	1880-1913	1880-1913	1881, 1885-1913	—	1880-1913	1892-1897, 1903-1913	—	1880-1913	—	1880-1913	1880-1913	1880, 1884-1913	—	1880-1913	1880-1913	1885-1913	1881-1913	1880-1913	1880-1913	1880-1913
Interest	1881-1913	1881-1913	1881-1913	1881-1913	1881-1913	1831-1913	1881-1913	1881-1913	1881-1913	1881-1913	1881-1913	1881-1913	1881-1913	1881-1913	1881-1913	1881-1913	1881-1913	—	1881-1913	1881-1913	1881-1913	1881-1913	—	1881-1913	1881-1913	1885-1913	—	1881-1913	1881-1913	1881-1913
Terms of trade	1885-1913	1880-1913	1880-1913	1880-1913	1880-1913	1880-1913	—	1880-1913	1886-1913	1880-1913	1880-1913	1880-1913	1880-1913	1880-1913	1880-1913	1885-1913	1886-1913	1880-1913	1880-1913	1880-1913	1880-1913	1885-1913	—	1880-1913	1880-1913	—	—	1880-1913	1880-1913	1900-1913
Real exchange rate	1884-1913	1880-1913	1880-1913	1880-1913	1880-1913	1880-1913	1881-1913	1881-1913	1886-1913	1880-1913	1881-1913	1880-1913	1880-1913	1880-1913	1880-1913	1880-1913	1880-1913	1880-1913	1880-1913	1880-1913	1880-1913	1880-1913	1881-1913	1880-1913	1880-1913	1880-1913	1880-1913	1880-1913	1880-1913	1900-1913
Trade balance	1880-1913	1880-1913	1880-1913	1880-1913	1880-1913	1880-1913	1880-1913	1880-1913	1880-1913	1911-1913	1880-1913	1880-1913	1880-1913	1880-1913	1880-1913	1881-1913	1880-1913	1880-1913	1880-1913	1880-1913	1880-1913	1881-1897	—	1880-1913	1880-1913	1893-1912	1880-1913	1880-1913	1880-1913	1880-1913
Bond spread	1880-1913	1880-1913	1881-1913	1881-1913	1881-1913	1885-1913	—	1880-1913	1886-1913	1880-1913	1880-1913	1881-1913	1880-1912	1881-1913	1880-1913	1881-1913	1880-1913	1880-1913	1880-1913	1881-1913	1880-1913	1880-1913	1881-1913	1880-1913	1880-1913	1880-1913	1880-1913	1881-1913	1880-1913	1880-1913
Gold standard	1880-1913	1880-1913	1880-1913	1880-1913	1880-1913	1880-1913	1880-1913	1880-1913	1880-1913	1880-1913	1880-1913	1880-1913	1881-1913	1880-1913	1880-1913	1885-1913	1880-1913	1880-1913	1880-1913	1880-1913	1880-1913	1880-1913	1881-1913	1880-1913	1880-1913	1880-1913	1880-1913	1880-1913	1880-1913	1885-1913
Growth of money supply	1885-1913	1881-1913	1881-1913	1881-1913	1881-1913	1881-1913	—	1886-1913	1902-1913	1880-1902, 1912-1913	1881-1913	1881-1913	1881-1913	1881-1913	1881-1913	1881-1913	1902-1911	1881-1913	1881-1913	1881-1913	1881-1911	1881-1913	—	1881-1913	1881-1913	1881-1913	—	1881-1913	1881-1913	1901-1913
Ratio of gold reserves to notes	1880-1913	1880-1913	1880-1913	1880-1913	1880-1913	1880-1913	1887-1895	1880-1913	—	1880-1913	1880-1913	1880-1913	1880-1913	1880-1913	1880-1913	1880-1897	1880-1913	1880-1913	—	1880-1913	1880-1913	1880-1913	1880-1913	1880-1913	1880-1913	1883-1913	1880-1913	—	—	—
Central bank indicator	1880-1913	1880-1913	1880-1913	1880-1913	1880-1913	1880-1913	1880-1913	1880-1913	1880-1913	1880-1913	1880-1913	1880-1913	1880-1913	1880-1913	1880-1913	1880-1913	1880-1913	1880-1913	1880-1913	1880-1913	1880-1913	1880-1913	1880-1913	1880-1913	1880-1913	1880-1913	1880-1913	1880-1913	1880-1913	1880-1913

Note: Long dash indicates no data are available for this variable and country.

References

Acha, Valentin Fernández. 1976. *La dueda pública*. Vol. 2 of *Datos básicos para la historia financiera de Espaana (1850–1975)*. Madrid: Instituto de Estudio Fiscales.
Adalet, Muge, and Barry Eichengreen. 2005. Current account reversals: Always a problem? NBER Working Paper no. 11634. Cambridge, MA: National Bureau of Economic Research.
Barbieri, Katherine. 2000. *The liberal illusion: Does trade promote peace?* Ann Arbor: University of Michigan Press.
Bazant, Jan. 1968. *Historia de la deuda exterior de México (1823–1946)* Nueva serie Colegio de Mexico. Centro de Estudios Históricos México: El Colegio de México.
Becker, Thorvald. 1913. *Les emprunts d'etat Finlandais*. Helsinki: Societe d'Imprimerie Sana.
Beim, David O., and Calomiris, C. W. 2001. *Emerging financial markets*. New York: McGraw-Hill.
Berg, Andrew, and Catherine Patillo. 1999. Are currency crises predictable? A test. *IMF Staff Papers* (June): 46–2.
Bordo, Michael D. 2003. Market discipline and financial crises policy: An historical perspective. *Research in Financial Services: Private and Public Policy* 15: 154–82.
Bordo, Michael D., Barry Eichengreen, Daniela Klingebiel, and Maria Soledad Martinez-Peria. 2001. Is the crisis problem growing more severe? *Economic Policy* 32:51–75.
Bordo, Michael D., and Lars Jonung. 1996. Monetary regimes, inflation, and monetary reform: An essay in honor of Axel Leijonhufvud. In *Inflation, institutions, and information: Essays in honor of Axel Leijonhufvud*, ed. D. Vaz and K. Velupillai, 157–244. London: Macmillan.
Bordo, Michael D., Christopher M. Meissner, and Angela Redish. 2005. How "original sin" was overcome: The evolution of external debt denominated in domestic currencies in the United States and the British Dominions 1800–2000. In *Other people's money*, ed. Barry Eichengreen and Ricardo Hausmann, 122–53. Chicago: University of Chicago Press.
Bordo, Michael D., and Anna Schwartz. 1996. The operation of the specie standard: Evidence for core and peripheral countries. In *Currency convertibility: The gold standard and beyond*, ed. Jorge de Macedo, B. Eichengreen, and J. Reis, 11–82. London: Routledge.
Caballero, Ricardo, Kevin Cowan, and Jonathan Kearns. 2004. Fear of sudden stops: Lessons from Australia and Chile. NBER Working Paper no. 10519. Cambridge, MA: National Bureau of Economic Research.
Calomiris, Charles. 1992. Greenback resumption and silver risk: The economics and politics of monetary regime change in the United States, 1862–1900. NBER Working Paper no. 4166. Cambridge, MA: National Bureau of Economic Research.
Céspedes, Luis Felipe, Roberto Chang, and Andrés Velasco. 2004. Balance sheets and exchange rate policy. *American Economic Review* 94 (4): 1183–1193.
Clemens, Michael, and Jeffrey G. Williamson. 2004. Wealth bias in the first global capital market boom 1870–1913. *The Economic Journal* 114 (04): 304–37.
Córtes Conde, R. 1995. La Dueda Externa Argentina 1880–1906. In *La Dueda pública en América Latina en perspectiva histórica*, ed. Reinhard Liehr. Frankfurt am Main, Germany: Vervuert.

Crouchley, Arthur Edwin. 1938. *The economic development of modern Egypt.* London: Longmans, Green and Co.
Dowd, Kevin. 1992. Free banking in Australia. In *The experience of free banking,* ed. Kevin Dowd, 48–78. Routledge: New York.
Du Velay, A. 1903. *Essai sur l'histoire financière de la Turquie depuis le règne du Sultan Mahmoud II jusqu'à nos jours.* Paris: A. Rousseau.
Edwards, Sebastian. 2003. Exchange rate regimes, capital flows and crisis prevention. In *Economic and financial crises in emerging markets,* ed. Martin Feldstein, 31–78. Chicago: University of Chicago Press.
Eichengreen, Barry. 1999. The Baring crisis in a Mexican mirror. *International Political Science Review* 20 (3): 249–70.
Eichengreen, Barry, and Ricardo Hausmann. 1999. Exchange rates and financial fragility proceedings, Federal Reserve Bank of Kansas City; *New challenges for monetary policy,* 329–68.
Eichengreen, Barry, Ricardo Hausmann, and Ugo Panizza. 2003. Currency mismatches, debt intolerance, and original sin: Why they are not the same and why it matters. NBER Working Paper no. 10036. Cambridge, MA: National Bureau of Economic Research.
———. 2005. The pain of original sin. In *Other people's money,* ed. Barry Eichengreen and Ricardo Hausmann. Chicago: University of Chicago Press.
Ferguson, Niall, and Mortiz Schularick. 2006. The empire effect: The determinants of country risk in the first age of globalization, 1880–1913. *The Journal of Economic History* 2 (66): 283–312.
Flandreau, Marc. 2003. Crises and punishment: Moral hazard and the pre-1914 international financial architecture. In *Money doctors: The experience of international financial advising, 1850–2000,* ed. Marc Flandreau. London: Routledge.
Flandreau, Marc, and John Komlos. 2002. Core of periphery? The credibility of the Austro-Hungarian currency, 1867–1913. *The Journal of European Economic History* 31 (2): 293.
Flandreau, Marc, and Clemens Jobst. 2005. The ties that divide: A network analysis of the international monetary system, 1890–1910. *The Journal of Economic History* 65 (4): 977–1007.
Flandreau, Marc, Jacques Le Cacheux, and Frederic Zúmer. 1998. Stability without a pact: Lessons from the European gold standard, 1880–1914. *Economic Policy* 13 (26): 115–62.
Flandreau, Marc, and Nathan Sussman. 2005. Old sins. In *Other people's money,* ed. Barry Eichengreen and Ricardo Hausmann, 154–89. Chicago: University of Chicago Press.
Flandreau, Marc, and F. Zúmer. 2004. *The making of global finance.* OECD: Paris. Data retrieved from http://www.eh.net/databases/finance/
Frankel, Jeff, and Andrew K. Rose. 1996. Currency crashes in emerging markets: An empirical treatment. *The Journal of International Economics* 40 (1–2): 209–24.
Furuya, S. Y. 1928. *Japan's foreign exchange and her balance of international payments.* NY: Columbia University Press.
Global Financial Database. N.d. Global financial data. Available at http://www.globalfinancialdata.com/
Goldsmith, Raymond W. 1983. *The financial development of India, 1860–1977.* New Haven, CT: Yale University Press.
Goldstein, Morris, and Philip Turner. 2004. *Controlling currency mismatches in emerging market economies.* Washington, DC: Institute of International Economics.

Jones, Matthew T., and Maurice Obstfeld. 2000. *Saving, investment, and gold data for 13 countries.* Available at http://www.nber.org/databases/jones-obstfeld/
———. N.d. Saving, investment, and gold: A reassessment of historical current account data. Available at http://www.nber.org/databases/jones-obstfeld/
Kahan, Arcadius. 1989. *Russian economic history: The nineteenth century.* Chicago: University of Chicago Press.
Kikuchi, Gunzo. 1904. *Das Staatsschuldenwesen seit der Restauration Japans.* Kaemmerer, CA: Halle.
Komlos, John. 1987. Financial innovation and the demand for money in Austria-Hungary, 1867–1913. *Journal of European Economic History* 3 (16): 587–605.
Kostelenos, George C. 1995. *Money and output in modern Greece: 1858–1938.* Athens: Centre for Planning and Economic Research.
Levy, M. B. 1995. The Brazilian public debt domestic and foreign 1824–1913. In *La deuda pública en América Latina en perspectiva histórica.* Vol. 58 of Bibliotheca Ibero-Americana, ed. Reinhard Liehr, 209–54. Frankfurt am Main, Germany: Vervuert.
Ludlow, Leonor, and Carlos Marichal (coordinadores). 1998. *Un siglo de deuda pública en México. Lecturas de historia económica mexicana.* México, DF: El Colegio de México.
Masayoshi Matsukata, M. 1899. *Report on the adoption of the gold standard in Japan.* Tokyo: Government Press.
Meissner, Christopher M. 2005. New world order: Explaining the international diffusion of the gold standard, 1870–1913. *Journal of International Economics* 66:385–406.
Mishkin, Frederic S. 2003. Financial policies and the prevention of financial crises in emerging market countries. In *Economic and financial crises in emerging markets,* ed. Martin Feldstein, 93–130. Chicago: University of Chicago Press.
Mitchell, B. R. 1992. *International historical statistics: Europe, 1750–1988.* 3rd ed. Basingstoke, England: Macmillan.
———. 1993a. *International historical statistics: Africa, Asia, Oceania, 1750–1988.* 2nd ed. Basingstoke, England: Macmillan.
———. 1993b. *International historical statistics: The Americas, 1750–1988.* 2nd ed. Basingstoke, England: Macmillan.
Molino, Evaristo. 1898. *Bosquejo de la hacienda pública de Chile, desde la independencia hasta la fecha.* Santiago de Chile: Imprenta nacional.
Nash, Robert Lucas. 1876. *Penn's compendium of the English and foreign funds.* Various issues. London: Effingham Wilson.
Obstfeld, Maurice, and Alan M. Taylor. 2003. Sovereign risk, credibility and the gold standard, 1870–1913 versus 1925–1931. *Economic Journal* 113 (487): 1–35.
Pasvolsky, Leo, and Harold Moulton. 1924. *Russian debts and Russian reconstruction: A study of the relation of Russia's foreign debts to her economic recovery.* New York: McGraw-Hill.
Pérez Siller, J. 1995. La deuda y consolidacion del poder en Mexico, 1867–1896: Bases para la modernidad porfirista. In *La deuda pública en América Latina en perspectiva histórica.* Vol. 58 of Bibliotheca Ibero-Americana, ed. Reinhard Liehr, 293–336. Frankfurt am Main, Germany: Vervuert.
Reinhart, Carmen, Kenneth Rogoff, and Miguel Savastano. 2003. Debt intolerance. *Brookings Papers on Economic Activity,* Issue no. 1:1–74.
Reserve Bank of India. 1954. *Banking and monetary statistics of India.* Bombay: Reserve Bank of India.
Schumann, Christian Gustav Waldemar. 1938. *Structural changes and business cycles in South Africa, 1806–1936.* London: P. S. King.

Shaw, Stanford. 1975. The Nineteenth Century Ottoman Tax Reforms and Revenue System. *International Journal of Middle East Studies* 6 (4): 421–59.
Smits, J., E. Horlings, and J. van Zanden. 1999. *The measurement of gross national product and its components: The Netherlands, 1800–1913.* Discussion paper. Utrecht: N. W. Posthumus Institute, Utrecht University.
Statistical Yearbook of Belgium (*Annuaire Statistique de la Belgique*). Various issues. Brussels, Belgium: Institut national de statistique, Ministère des affaires économiques.
Statistical Yearbook of Brazil (*Anuario Estatistico do Brasil*). Various issues. Rio de Janeiro, Brazil: Instituto Brasileiro de Geografica e Estatistica.
Statistical Yearbook of Chile (*Anuario Estadistico de Chile*). Various issues. Santiago, Chile: Instituto Nacional de Estadisticas.
Statistical Yearbook of Finland (*Annuaire Statistique pour la Finlande*). Various issues. Statistics Finland.
Statistical Yearbook of Holland (*Annuaire Statistique des Pays-Bas*). Various issues. Gravenhage, Holland: Centrale Commissie voor de Statistek.
Statistical Yearbook of Japan (*Résumé statistique du Japon*). Various issues. Tokyo: Bureau of Statistics.
Statistical Yearbook of Portugal (*Annuario estatistico do Reino de Portugal*). Various issues. Lisbon, Portugal: The National Statistical Institute of Portugal.
Statistical Yearbook of the Republic of Uruguay (*Anuario estadistica de la Republica Oriental del Uruguay*). Various issues. Montevideo, Uruguay: Direccion General de Estadistica.
Tattara, G. 2003. Paper money but a gold debt: Italy on the gold standard. *Explorations in Economic History* 40 (2): 122–42.
Vázquez-Presedo, Vicente. 1989. *Estadísticas históricas argentinas (comparadas).* Buenos Aires: Ediciones Macchi.
Zamagni, V. 1998. Il debito pubblico Italiano 1861–1946: Riconstruzione della serie storica. *Rivista di storia economica* 3 (19): 207–42.
———. 1999. Una rettifica. *Rivista di storia economica* 3 (15): 339–42.

5

The True Measure of Country Risk
A Primer on the Interrelations between Solvency and the Polity Structure of Emerging Markets, Argentina 1886–1892

Gerardo della Paolera and Martín Grandes

5.1 Introduction

This paper looks into the heterogeneous effects that the process of financial integration with the world capital market had on different government bodies in Argentina. It covers the period from 1886 until the run-up to the Baring Crisis in 1891.

Among the first to analytically recognize that the nature of emerging capital markets is far more complex than the arbitrage parity conditions in the conventional goods and services markets were Harberger (1980) and Eaton (1985). In this essay we add an extra dimension to their analysis and ask how credit constraints and potential defaults are to be analyzed by considering the behavior of different political entities within the same sovereign nation.

The asymmetric havoc wrought by the Baring collapse was reflected by a credit crunch for the provinces and the municipal entities, leading them to a default on their obligations by the end of 1891. By contrast, the Bank of England acted as a timely lender of last resort for the national government. Unlike other developed countries at the time, whose financial markets at different levels were well integrated into the world capital markets—meaning their borrowings were regarded as perfect substitutes—the Argentina experience suggests an opposite fate.

This contribution aims to demonstrate that the public sector borrowings at all three levels—national, provincial, and municipal—were not perceived as holding the same risk class—that is, they were seen as imperfect substitutes. Moreover, our approach suggests that an analysis of the public

---

Gerardo della Paolera is president and professor of economics at the American University of Paris. Martin Grandes is an assistant professor of economics and business administration at the American University of Paris.

debt dynamics should take into account the political structure of the country in question. It is always the case that, in spite of their different political jurisdictions, provincial and municipal debt was always recognized ex post facto as a federal liability. Hence, we will reconsider the true measure of country risk: political structure matters for the management and assessment of public debt. The paper intends to (a) first, set out a simple framework to address the reality of the different political entities; (b) then construct the time series data of the yield to maturity of the relevant bonds and financial instruments with the purpose of (c) computing the true measure of country risk, as defined by the weighted average of sovereign and subsovereign default risk premia.

The lessons drawn by this paper are very telling regarding the recent build-up of debt that drove the surprising collapse of the Argentine currency board and its financial system in early 2002. It also points out that to analyze the dynamics of monetary and fiscal policies by looking only at central government institutions is at best a partial equilibrium exercise (della Paolera and Taylor 2003). The intertemporal effects of the country's polity structure on economic outcomes should be taken into account to correctly assess the risk premium of an emerging market country and the real debt burden borne by its residents. Also, this exercise opens the question of what it means to exercise the role of lender of last resort in the international financial architecture (della Paolera 2001).

5.2 The Rationale to Recalculate the Country Risk Premium

In much of the recent literature on political economy—for instance, in Persson and Tabellini (2003)—the main issue is that economic policymaking generates conflicts in different dimensions and therefore, political economy outcomes are a function of the political institutions' structure. These authors highlight the different games played by the political actors within a political system to influence political economy outcomes, but very little is said about how the engineering of the decision-making process in a republic can affect economic outcomes, and, more importantly, the perception of state solvency.[1]

Surprisingly enough, when it comes to analyzing the conduct of fiscal policy, the question of how different political parties coalesce or not is more often studied when the so-called common-pool problem in fiscal policy is addressed, rather than the issue of the political structure, delegation of authority, and sovereign and subsovereign jurisdictions. The importance of taking into account the political structure for the conduct of public policy is recognized by Persson and Tabellini (2003, 38): "We are confident that fo-

---

1. One crucial exception to this is Elster (1995) on the impact of constitutions on economic performance and Drazen (2000, 134–37).

cusing on central rather than general governments does not bias our inferences. Nevertheless, we always include an indicator variable for federal political structures in our cross-country analysis. . . . These are likely to control all levels of government more easily in unitary than in federal states."

In this vein, we want to investigate the linkages between the political structure and the pricing and management of the public debt in a federal republic such as Argentina for the period 1886–92. This period is fertile in terms of access to the international capital markets, and is one that has both good data and institutional qualitative information available. In economic history, there are three or four candidates of newly settled federal countries that could be outstanding laboratories for analyzing the dynamics and moral hazard of public government debt under a federal constitutional design: the United States, Mexico, Brazil, Argentina.[2]

The importance of analyzing whether subsovereign becomes in fact a sovereign debt liability was clearly recognized in the case of Argentina some time ago by Marichal (1989, 162–63): "The long term consequences of Financial Dependency: While the debt arrange of 1893 provided substantial relief for the Argentine National Treasury, the drain of capital from Buenos Aires to Europe continued despite the large payments remitted from Argentina, the foreign debt of the national government did not decline. In fact, between 1891 and 1900 it rose from 204 million to 389 million gold pesos. This huge increase did not come from fresh loans as such, but rather from a series of conversions of previous debts. Specifically, the Argentine National Government assumed responsibility for all existing debts of the provincial governments and the municipalities."

Also, Shepherd's (1933, 59) paper on the default and adjustment of Argentine foreign debts states: "More than 15 years elapsed from the first defaults in Argentina, July 1, 1890, to the last settlement in December, 1906. . . . Holders of provincial and municipal bonds . . . lost all accrued interest and suffered reduction of principal in most instances. It is needless to speculate upon what the outcome of debt negotiations with individual Provinces would have been if the National Governments had not assumed responsibility for the provincial foreign debts."

As we can appreciate here, the theoretical aspects of country risk, moral hazard, and incomplete information have to take into account the political structures of nations. At some point, in times of financial turmoil the common-pool fiscal problem emerges, so the question is: what is the true counterfactual (or actual) country risk measure of the state under consideration? What is the true measure of the expected solvency of a sovereign state with a complex and fuzzy federal structure?

---

2. For Brazil, there is a discussion about the federal level by De Paiva Abreu (1999): "Brazil: 1824–1957: Born on Mau Pagador." However, the author makes no account of the consolidated debt.

To our knowledge, to analyze the process of capital arbitrage and convergence, previous estimations of interest rates in emerging countries or newly settled economies restricted their data analysis to liquid central government bonds. We claim that these estimates might only show an incomplete picture of that process. Furthermore, we may even have to reexamine the process of interest rate convergence of countries such as the United States, Mexico, Brazil, and Argentina once the ex ante and ex post economic effects of the subsovereign bodies (i.e., provinces and municipalities) are taken into account. Roberto Cortes Conde (1989) clearly addresses the problem of the fiscal linkages between the federal government of Argentina and the provinces, but his aim is not to analyze the dynamics of debt in a consolidated fashion.[3] Della Paolera (1988) and della Paolera and Taylor (2001) analyze the dynamics of fiscal and monetary policy coordination, though they emphasize the role of the central fiscal authorities. Finally, Fishlow (1989) looks into the public debt burden for an open economy, but again, like the previous authors, mostly looks at the convergence of interest rates of Argentina to the world economy by considering the standard real yield spread of a sovereign bond over the world risk-free interest rate. To be fair, the macroview is also present in more general studies, such as in Ferguson (2001, 142), who recognizes the problem in his seminal work: "Although, the American federal government never defaulted on its debt, the same cannot be said of the American States themselves. In the recession of 1837–43, there were defaults on around half of the outstanding state debts; 10 per cent of the total amount owed by the states were repudiated altogether."

Also, E. Cary Brown (1990, 232) states while analyzing the U.S. 1843 crisis: "Unsuccessful efforts were made to persuade the federal government to assume or support these debts, and many foreign lenders clearly failed to distinguish the two levels of government." Also, the same author mentions an important economic history episode which reveals the ex ante and ex post importance of the consequences of the political entity fiscal structure on the calculation of the real ex ante cost and real burden of the public debt: "European lenders were ready purchasers of many states' debts, but were understandably put off by the defaults and, after, repudiations. Secretary of the Treasury Bibb in his Annual Report for 1844 stated: "If aliens, not understanding the texture of the National Government, do not distinguish accurately between engagements entered into by the several States . . . have distrusted the credit of the National Government . . . such distrust is to be regretted."[4]

Another interesting case wherein a province or municipality defaulted and was not bailed out by the national government, and where the fact that

---

3. See, however, Cortes Conde (1987).
4. See E. Cary Brown (1990, 252). The United States definitely had a consolidating view of the debt after the Civil War. Our a priori hunch here is that unitarian political regimes are less prone to public debt recursive crises, but this is a topic for further research.

the subsovereign borrower defaulted did not affect, at all, the risk of other entities and the national government, is provided by the experience of Brazil in 1894–1904. This is the case of the state of Espiritu Santo, which defaulted on its 1894 bond issue in 1901 and resumed payments in 1904. The default risk of other entities was not affected by the actions of this state. In fact, Brazil was de facto on gold and capital was flowing to the country. The same state that defaulted got a new loan four years later at a good price.[5]

The Argentine experience is both quantitatively and theoretically compelling. As della Paolera (1988, 28) states: "Revised estimates confirmed the importance of the European capital transfers to the Argentine economy: in between 1884–90 the country absorbed 11 per cent of the new portfolio issues of the London market; North America (including Canada) with a population twenty times that of Argentina absorbed 30 per cent of the new issues." In this first draft, we attempt to construct the true measure of country risk for Argentina for the important 1886–92 period, and then to analyze the differences that are obtained from the standard view of Argentina's behavior and state of affairs in international capital markets. This exercise should be seen as a first modest attempt to open the question about differing political economic goals of different subsovereigns within the same country.

5.3 Analytical Framework

5.3.1 Public Debt and the True Measure of Country Risk

For the reasons sketched previously, Argentina's true country risk premia should not be viewed as strictly equal to the premium paid by the national government during the booming years of the first era of financial globalization (1880–91), when international liquidity was plentiful. Since different subnational entities (provincial and municipal) should have been perceived as holding (substantially) different risk classes compared to the national sovereign, the calculation of country risk premium could be misleading if one assumed it to be equal to such national sovereign risk. We argue that if Argentine bonds are perceived as better risks than their provincial and municipal counterparts, the market is implicitly recognizing that the different political bodies run an independent fiscal policy. However, the recurrent story of emerging capital markets is that when international capital markets dry up, the sovereign body, the nation, envelops and bails out the subsovereign bodies. Hence, the assessment of country risk should take into account this institutional feature.

Let us call RA, RP, and RM the national, provincial, and municipal yield, respectively, spread over a risk-free rate. We argue that the true cost of transferring financial resources to Argentina (RT), measured by the

---

5. We thank Aldo Musacchio for bringing this episode to our attention.

Table 5.1   Public borrowings, in thousands of gold pesos and percent of total loans

Year	National	θ_A	Provincial	θ_P	Municipal	θ_M	Total
1886	16,128	0.39	25,459	0.61	0	0.00	41,587
1887	33,744	0.72	10,912	0.23	1,892	0.04	46,548
1888	31,750	0.35	48,810	0.53	11,200	0.12	91,760
1889	13,067	0.42	1,620	0.05	16,146	0.52	30,833
1890	11,420	1.00	0	0.00	0	0.00	11,420
1891	2,506	1.00	0	0.00	0	0.00	2,506
Average		0.65		0.24		0.11	

yield spread over a comparable risk-free bond, the British Consol yield, for instance, would be more adequately defined by the weighted sum of RA, RP, and RM. The implicit weight is given by the share of each entity's borrowings in the total supply of loans at some time T (θ_A, θ_P, and θ_M):

$$RT = \theta_A RA + \theta_P RP + \theta_M RM$$

where $\theta_i = L_i / L_{TOT}$ with $i = A$, P, and M.

We calculate the θ_is using public borrowing figures, drawn from Shepherd (1933), over the period 1886–91. The debt incurred by the different political entities had a manifold purpose: (a) expansion of the railway network or other public works; (b) capitalization of provincial banks; (c) consolidation of other outstanding debt; and (d) the financing of mortgage loans, which ultimately encouraged land speculation. The θ_i are reported in table 5.1.

Marichal (1989) computes an average θ_i for the period 1880–90 and obtains $\theta_A = 0.5$, $\theta_P = 0.42$, and $\theta_M = 0.08$. As these estimates reflect more accurately the average debt stock share of each political entity in the total indebtedness over the whole decade (i.e., the 1880s),[6] we will use them in section 5.4 to compute the true measure of country risk, RT, notwithstanding our sample being constrained to 1886–92, as was argued earlier.

5.3.2 Supply of External Funds and Risk Premia

The uneven degree of financial integration of the different Argentine governmental bodies into the international capital market becomes apparent, not only through the assessment of country risk, but also through their counterpart: the external supply of loanable funds available for those entities. That is, when international liquidity crunched the response of interest rates or yield differentials (measured by subtracting the risky yield from a risk-free benchmark yield) to a variation in the external supply of loanable funds, it should have been felt as having an asymmetric impact on the different governmental entities.

---

6. Table 5.1 demonstrates that provincial and municipal entities were credit rationed in 1890 and 1891.

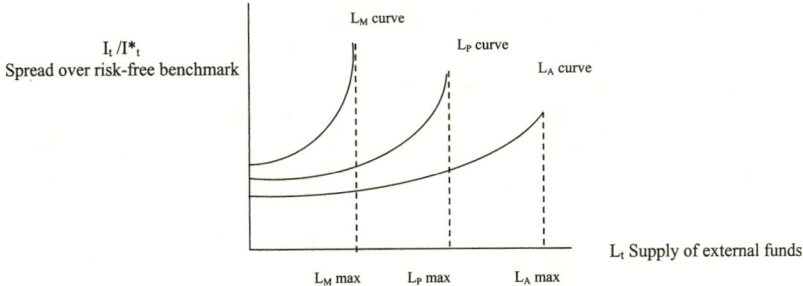

Fig. 5.1 Supply of external funds under the assumption of rationed credit markets

A first rationale of such asymmetric response may be found in the popular perception that the Bank of England would only bail out the national government in case of financial distress. A second plausible rationale could be the broad tax collection privileges and export-import levy monopoly of the national government over the subsovereign entities, and perhaps a stronger provincial than municipal fiscal stance. In other words, provinces and municipalities had less guarantees to offer to foreign creditors in case of financial distress. A third and last rationale of the asymmetric reaction in yield spreads of different government bodies to a contraction in the external supply of loanable funds lies in transfer risk. Transfer risk (or direct sovereign intervention risk) refers to the probability that a government with (foreign currency) debt servicing difficulties imposes foreign exchange payment restrictions (e.g., debt payment moratoria, strict capital controls) on otherwise solvent companies and/or subsovereign entities in its jurisdiction, forcing them to default on their own foreign-currency obligations. All this is equivalent to saying that the degree of credit rationing or the conditions under which new borrowings would have been undertaken by the national and subnational entities has to be perceived as plainly different.

Figure 5.1 illustrates the supply of external funds each borrower faced under the assumption of rationed credit markets—that is, the impossibility of borrowing unlimited financial resources at a constant interest rate. L_A, L_P, and L_M stand for the external supply of loans faced by the Argentine Republic and the provincial and municipal entities, respectively. Here it can be seen that a tightening of the credit constraint hits first at those low-quality, high-risk borrowers, that is, provinces and municipalities.[7]

---

7. When credit markets are not rationed, though, some municipal entities may be able to borrow cheaper than provinces. In a database containing the time series of default risk premia for a number of subsovereign Brazilian entities over 1895–1930, Musacchio (2005) demonstrates that for certain years—especially since 1900—the risk premium borne by the municipality of Rio de Janeiro was lower than the spreads paid over the British Consol yields by states such as Minas Gerais or Espirito Santo. This fact could be explained by the relatively higher export and import revenue of Rio de Janeiro.

In other words, the elasticities of their respective risk premia to the foreign credit supply that each borrower faced would have been different.

Figure 5.1 replicates previous work by Harberger (1980) and Eaton (1985) on the recognition of different perception of risk, but is extended to the case of various subsovereign entities. Harberger was a pioneer in explaining why the small country/open economy assumption that those countries face an infinitely elastic supply of funds was at best, a very weak assumption in understanding how financial and debt markets work in developing countries. Another important theoretical study was done by the pioneering works of Calvo (1988) and Calvo and Guidotti (1990) on the importance of expectations for interest price formation and the volatility of maturity. Here, as a first approximation, we deal with the true process of debt pricing in a federal republic that has foggy linkages with its different subsovereign entities.

5.3.3 Sovereign and Subsovereign Risk Premia in a Simple General Equilibrium Framework: The "Cascade" Effect

For a foreign-currency denominated bond (either in British pounds or gold), the premium over a risk-free asset (typical benchmarks at the time were the British Consols, denominated in British pounds) borne by an emerging market issuer can be defined as follows. First, let $R^{*A}_{t,k}$, $R^{*P}_{t,k}$, and $R^{*M}_{t,k}$ denote the annualized gross yields (i.e., one plus the interest rate) at time t on foreign-currency debt issued on the London market by the resident emerging sovereign A (or subsovereigns P and M, respectively), with k-period maturity; let $R^{*f}_{t,k}$ denote the gross yield on foreign-currency debt of the same maturity issued by the benchmark foreign debtor, typically a risk-free instrument issued by the British Treasury at the same market. Letting $i^A_{t,k} = \ln(R^{*A}_{t,k})$ and similarly with the other yields, we can write the following interest-rate equilibrium conditions:

(1) $$i^{A*}_{t,k} = i^{f*}_{t,k} + \mu_t$$

(2) $$i^{P*}_{t,k} = i^{f*}_{t,k} + \delta_t$$

(3) $$i^{M*}_{t,k} = i^{f*}_{t,k} + \varepsilon_t$$

where $\mu_t = \mu(i^{f*}_{t,k}; i^{A*}_{t,k}; L_A)$; δ_t and ε_t are the national, provincial, and municipal pure default or simply entity risk premia, respectively. In line with our assumptions, it should be clear that: $\delta_t = \mu_t + \phi_P$ and $\varepsilon_t = \mu_t + \phi_P + \phi_M$, being ϕ_P, ϕ_M the specific province and municipal premia over (and typically above) the national government default premium. Therefore, it is straightforward that $\phi_{Pt} = \phi_P(i^{A*}_{t,k}; i^{P*}_{t,k}; L_P)$; $\phi_{Mt} = \phi_M(i^{P*}_{t,k}; i^{M*}_{t,k}; L_M)$. The equilibrium of interest rates of the sovereign and different subsovereign bodies as shown in equations (1), (2), and (3) can be rewritten as follows:

(1') $\quad i_{t,k}^{A*} = i_{t,k}^{f*} + \mu_t$

(2') $\quad i_{t,k}^{P*} = i_{t,k}^{f*} + \mu_t + \phi_{Pt}$

(3') $\quad i_{t,k}^{M*} = i_{t,k}^{f*} + \mu_t + \phi_{Pt} + \phi_{Mt}$

The relevant spreads are obtained as:

(4) $\quad RA = i_{t,k}^{A*} - i_{t,k_t}^{f*} = \mu_t$

(5) $\quad RP = i_{t,k}^{P*} - i_{t,k}^{f*} = \mu_t + \phi_{Pt}$

(6) $\quad RM = i_{t,k}^{M*} - i_{t,k}^{f*} = \mu_t + \phi_{Pt} + \phi_{Mt}$

Equations (4) to (6) reveal a cascade effect in the determination of each risk premium. Furthermore, recalling that

(7) $\quad L_{TOT} = L_A + L_P + L_M,$

where all borrowings are expressed at present values, it turns out that the total country risk premium is

(8) $\quad RT = \theta_A \mu_t + \theta_P RP + \theta_M RM$, as laid out in section 5.3.1.

As a special case we might have that when $\theta_P = 0$ and $\theta_M = 0$ (as 1890–91 proves) $RT = \mu_t$. Certainly, this is not the case when international liquidity abounds and market sentiment improves, as in the earlier period. The exception would be the case of a federal country where subsovereign entities are fiscally independent, perceived as solvent as the federal state and there are no moral hazard problems. In this case, assuming that $\theta_P > 0$, $\theta_M > 0$, both ϕ_P, ϕ_M would be zero and again $RT = \mu_t$.

Based on this framework, we now aim to: (a) compute the true measure of country risk, RT_t, and (b) compare it to μ_t. Section 5.4 presents the data set and an estimate of RT.

5.4 Preliminary Evidence on the True Measure of Country Risk

5.4.1 Data Set

We work with bimonthly data from *The Economist* newspaper, covering the period January 1886–January 1892. More specifically, we collect current market (bid) price observations corresponding to foreign and colonial stocks, namely the Argentine Republic, provincial entities, and municipalities. Besides the sovereign bond prices, which are easy to identify and are traded on a liquid market, we should ideally include all twenty-three provincial and municipal loans as reported by Shepherd (1933, table 6). Unfortunately, this is not possible because (a) *The Economist* does not re-

Table 5.2   Loan features: Sovereign and sub-sovereign issuers

Agent	Entity	Denomination and issue date	Original amount placed (sterling)	Issue price	Coupon payments
Baring Bros.	Argentine Republic	5% loan, 1884	1.714.200	84[a,b]	semi-annual
Baring Bros.	Province of Buenos Aires	6% loan, 1882–1886	4.098.300	92 and 98	quarterly[a]
Morton, Rose & Co.	Province of Cordoba	6% loan, 1887–1888	1.190.400	91 and 92	semi-annual
Murrieta & Co.	Province of Entre Rios	6% loan, 1886	800.000	91[a,b]	semi-annual
Morton, Rose & Co.	Province of Santa Fe	6% loan, 1883–1884	1.434.426	90 and 86[a,b]	semi-annual
Heinemann & Co.	City of Rosario	6% loan, 1888	992.000	103	semi-annual

Source: The Economist, January 1886–January 1892.
[a] All loans contained an accumulative sinking fund provision of 1 percent over the principal.
[b] Admittedly there will be an unaccounted "coupon size and payout frequency" effect on the yield differential of Buenos Aires.

port bond market prices for all those loans,[8] (b) some reported bonds are quoted on an irregular basis (i.e., illiquidity) or (c) secondary market data is not available for a specific loan at all times. Thus, we try to find loans with the closest issue date, coupon payments, and maturity, when possible.

Table 5.2 summarizes the national, provincial, and municipal bonds we have selected, as well as their main features.

5.4.2 The True Measure of Country Risk: Some Preliminary Estimates

In a first step, we proceed to compute μ_t, RP, and RM so as to be able to compute the true measure of country risk, RT. To this end, we first calculate a current yield for each loan at a given date as the ratio coupon-to-bid price. This current yield is a rough proxy of the bond yield to maturity. Coupon bond (clean) prices should indeed reflect the relationship between the coupon rate and the yield to maturity: when the former is higher than the yield to maturity the price should be above par (i.e., higher than 100) and vice versa. As we are unable to retrieve the yield to maturity for each bond, we assume they are equal to the bond's current yield.

Most of these bonds had maturities of about thirty years. We recall that we are calculating a pure default premium, as all loans are floated and traded in the same jurisdiction (London) and are denominated in the same currency, that is, sterling. Then, μ_t, RP, RM are obtained by subtracting each current

---

8. We were unable to find the unquoted loan prices in other sources such as www.globalfin.com or The Corporation of Bond Holders, at least on a regular and high-frequency basis.

Table 5.3   θ per province

	Buenos Aires	Cordoba	Entre Rios	Santa Fe	Total
Sterling	9,154,686	3,785,600	5,276,400	6,619,526	24,836,212
Share	0.369	0.152	0.212	0.267	

Source: Shepherd (1933).

Notes: Based on those provinces for which data are available in *The Economist.* Adds up all loans contracted by a province in 1880–1890.

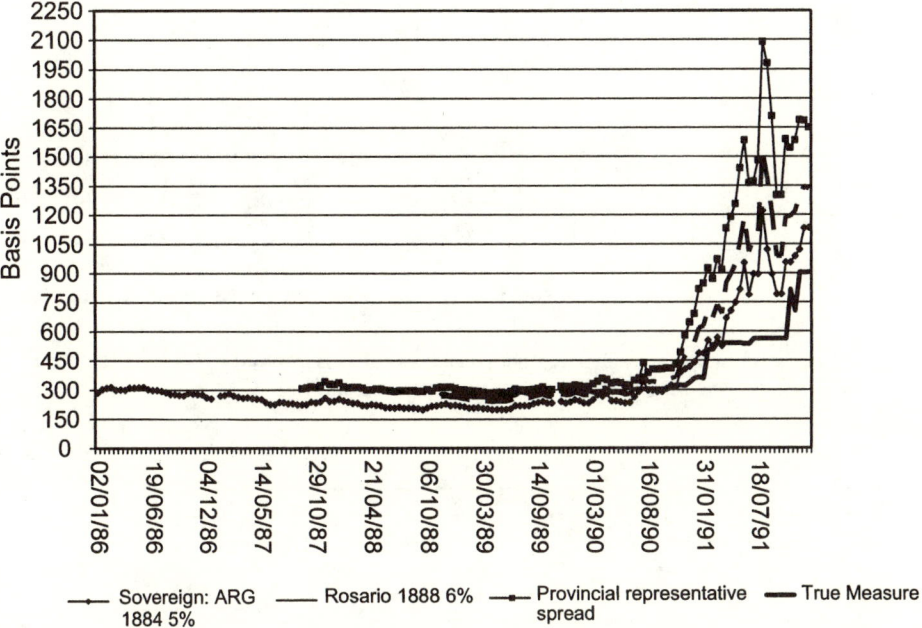

Fig. 5.2   Sovereign and sub-sovereign spreads over British Consol yields 1886–91: National, provincial, and municipal issuers

yield from the current yield of a risk-free bond, namely British Consols perpetuities of 3 percent or 3.5 percent, depending on the year. In the case of *RP*, we calculate a weighted average of the four provincial current yields corresponding to those loans reported in table 5.2 above. The loan weights are estimated using data from Shepherd (1933) and are shown in table 5.3.

Figures 5.2, 5.3, and 5.4 plot μ_t, *RP*, *RM*, and *RT*, respectively, over the relevant period and over two subsample periods, namely tranquil times (1886–89) and turmoil times (1890–92).[9]

---

9. *RT* starts from October 1888 due to the constraint imposed by our municipal loan, Rosario (1888) 6 percent, and the lack of alternative data prior to this year.

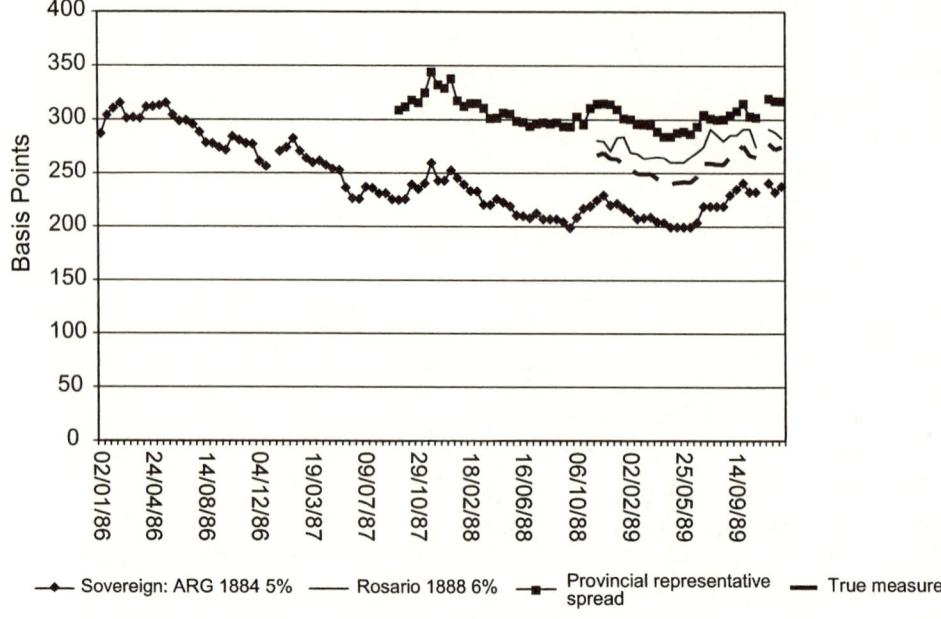

Fig. 5.3 Sovereign and sub-sovereign spreads over British Consol yields II 1886–89: National, provincial, and municipal issuers; tranquil times

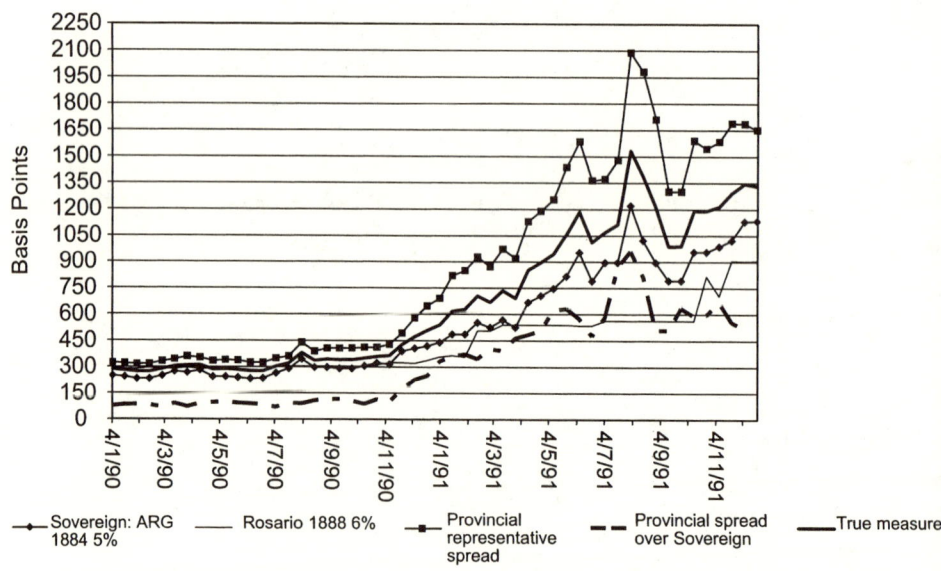

Fig. 5.4 Sovereign and sub-sovereign spreads over British Consol yields III 1890–91: National, provincial, and municipal issuers; financial turmoil

Figures 5.2, 5.3, and 5.4 illustrate several important facts:

1. Until November 1890 provincial and municipal (represented by Rosario) bonds were traded at an average spread of 100 to 120 basis points (bps) above the sovereign. In particular, we see that the true measure of country risk stood close to the sovereign bond spread in tranquil times (figures 5.2 and 5.3). Put differently, when liquidity was plentiful investors were attaching a slightly higher probability of default to subsovereign entities in comparison with the sovereign.

2. All yields start to rise from July–August 1890, when the first defaults are declared (Shepherd 1933), amid political upheaval and deep concerns about the financial health of the different entities (figure 5.4).

3. However, the decoupling between the sovereign and subsovereign entities' spreads over the British Consol yield only becomes apparent in November 1890 (bold dotted line in figure 5.4), when Baring's troubles are known. For instance, the provincial spread over the sovereign yield widens to 900 bps by June 1891 and never comes down to below 600 bps afterward.

4. Since November 1890 we observe how the yield differential between the true measure of country risk (RT) and the representative sovereign bond (Argentina 1884 [5 percent]) start to increase. Figure 5.5 presents evidence in this direction: RT trades at 200 to 300 bps over the typical sovereign risk premium in 1891 (bold solid line, right hand scale). This excess spread would be wider should one exclude the loan incurred by Rosario, our representative municipal bond, which may be regarded as a special bond that traded at tighter than even provincial spread levels.[10]

5.5 Historical and Political Economy Side: Politics and Debt

The downward bias of the true country risk during tranquil times was of about 100 to 200 basis points, a magnitude that represents one third of the absolute value of the spread. It is important to note that the band of divergence is maintained until the late 1890s, but afterward the divergence becomes clear even before the defaults of 1892. Hence, one might say that not only did Argentina start a period of financial autarky, but also the opportunity cost of its staging a comeback to the international capital markets was higher. This higher cost was not due to the performance of its own fed-

---

10. Indeed, one should caution against the use of the bond floated by Rosario in 1888 as a municipal benchmark issue. This loan may not be representative of other Argentine municipal bonds, given its specific features and low discount. On the other hand, as we said earlier, *The Economist* does not report bond market prices/yields for all other Argentine municipal loans entered into in 1886–92, or some reported bonds are quoted on an irregular basis (e.g., illiquidity), hence not allowing any expanded calculation of the municipal default risk premium. Notwithstanding this data availability constraint, our hunch is that other municipal bonds were at least riskier than national government bonds.

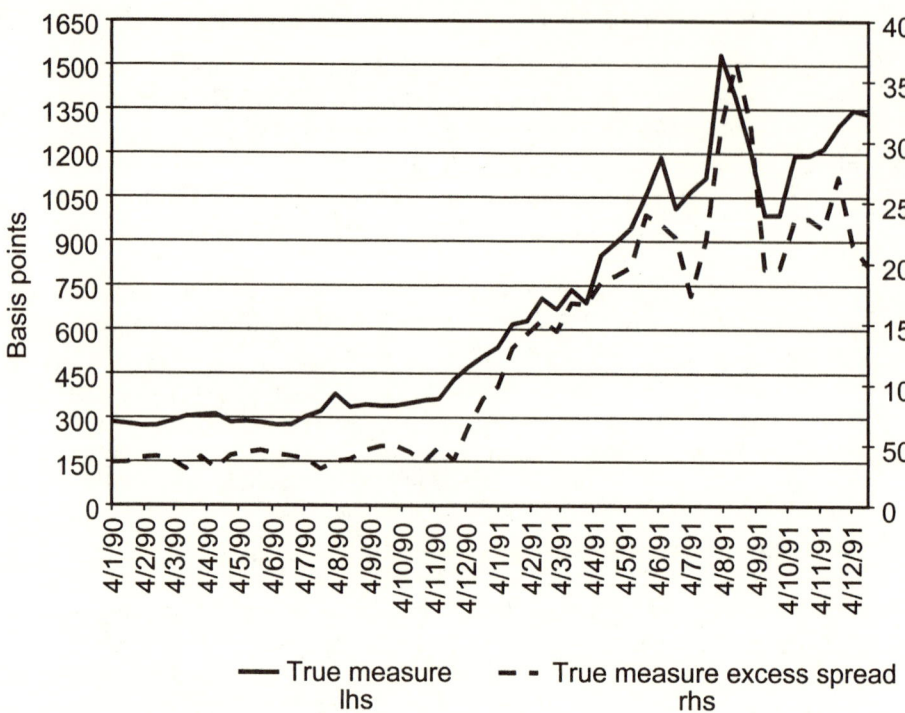

Fig. 5.5 Excess spread between "True Measure of Country Risk" and typical Sovereign Spread (ARG 84.5%): 1890–91 financial turmoil

eral bonds but to the attribution of solvency involved now in turbulent-time bonds that originally have had a different seniority.

It is apparent from this historical performance that institutions' subtleties matter more and more fully appear in harsher rather than in more tranquil times. It is a surprising but well-known asymmetric result from credit markets that the spread (and its volatility) between good and lemon assets flattens when markets are hugely liquid and goes nuts when conditions worsen. While the borrower might have the usual time-inconsistent and moral hazard macroeconomic feature in credit markets, here the creditor has a time-inconsistent institutional appraisal and enforceability of the different fixed-income instruments. The endgame outcome of whether Argentina had to bail out subsovereign bonds rests on the bargaining power of the international creditors and the cost-benefit perception of the borrowing nation.

What was the strategy followed by Argentina to manage the 1890–91 Baring crises to eventually return to the international capital markets?

First, we must say that the first political entity that recognized the service payments difficulties was the Argentine Republic in July 1890, stating that it might default on all foreign debt obligations (della Paolera and Taylor 2001, 72–73). This announcement produced a cascade effect on the foreign obligations of the provinces and municipalities, which by the end of 1891 defaulted both on their interest and amortization payments. The incumbent President Juarez Celman resigned in August 1890 and was replaced by his Vice-President Carlos Pellegrini, a well-seasoned cosmopolitan politician and financier.

The strategy of the Argentine central government was implemented in two steps: (a) Pellegrini stated first that Argentine bonds would and should never be in default, and quickly produced the famous Funding Loan agreement of 1891 with the Bank of England to avert the full default on the Argentine bonds; (b) he insisted to the Corporation of Foreign Bondholders that the situation of the provincial and municipal debt was a separate problem, and placed it in a different jurisdiction. Hence, the Bank of England acted as a lender of last resort in 1891 to the central Argentine government, bailing out both the Argentine Republic and Baring.

In the Romero agreement of 1893, the relief on service and amortization payments still referred to the Argentine republic debt, and the provincial and municipal debts were in limbo after having quoted in good times only 50 basis points above the best Argentine fixed income security! However, in 1898, Argentina, in a virtual state of autarky, recognized the provincial and municipal external obligations, which were definitely consolidated in the year 1905. That is, in spite of the clearly different conditions and collateral implied by different type of bonds, the ex post facto here as in the previous case of the Baring loan undertaken by the province of Buenos Aires in 1824, the federal government nationalized the whole debt obligations, which means that in an emerging country in which most of the debt incurred in order to finance expenditure is floated in hard currency in international markets, institutional moral hazard is king.

Therefore, the true measure of the opportunity cost of funds for Argentina and the real cost of the debt burden for the whole citizenry should take into account this feature. Again, to have concluded that in January 1890, because Argentina's federal bond yield was converging to the world yield and hence we were witnessing a more mature capital market, is at best a partial equilibrium statement. And this is a lesson that was not learned by economists for the contemporaneous economies. Ex ante sovereign property right constraints might not be constraints at all after certain events arise. So both the cost of capital in the buoyant period and the cost of being in autarky for some many years after the crash should internalize the true measure of country risk.

5.6 Concluding Remarks

In this paper we ask about the importance of the political structure of an emerging market economy in determining its degree of participation and strategies in the international debt markets. We think we have added another angle to the discussion by recognizing that debt strategies depend not only on political polarization, election probabilities, or standard forward-looking time inconsistencies; the economic effects of the political structure of emerging nations are an important consideration in analyzing their economic development.

And this political structure effect should be priced accordingly.

In this first exercise, we have calculated the true measure of country risk in light of the Argentine experience of 1886–1892. It was shown that the true measure decoupled from the typical sovereign risk spread by 200 to 350 basis points when liquidity crunches and political upheaval set up a tough scenario after July 1890. More importantly, the credit crunch had an effect on the strategic behavior of both borrowers and lenders in an ex post facto.

The lessons drawn here are very telling to the recent build-up of debt that drove the surprising collapse of the Argentine currency board and the financial system in early 2002, and the public debt disarray.[11] Moreover, it informs policymakers and investors about the correct way of assessing country risk in federal countries where subsovereign entities are fiscally dependent on the central government finances and where moral hazard is present.

For further research, the paper invites political economy researchers to analyze the actual costs and consequences of ex ante pitfalls in evaluating country risk when the polity of a country differs. Our first prognosis here is that when a federal republic cannot develop well-integrated capital markets, it probably means that the polity structure is clearly suboptimal and fails to effect economic development and progress for its citizens.

Finally, as an extension of the present study, an econometric model will be performed in order to test (a) the different elasticities of μ_t, RP, and RM (or each of the implicit bond yields) to a shock in the international liquidity constraint (e.g., a change in L^* faced by each entity or I_f^*) and (b) the endogenous responses of an entity spread to a change in other domestic entities spreads; that is, how fast and sensitive is the cascade effect.

References

Brown, E. Carey. 1990. Episodes in the public debt history of the United States. In *Public debt management: Theory and history,* ed. Rudiger Dornbusch and Mario Draghi, 227–54. Cambridge: Cambridge University Press.

---

11. Ongoing research is addressing the question of whether the lessons drawn from this paper could apply to recent default episodes in federal republics where subsovereign entities are essentially fiscally reliant on the central government's public finances. In particular, the case of Argentina 2001–2002 is being studied.

Calvo, Guillermo. 1988. Servicing the public debt: The role of expectations. *The American Economic Review* 78:647–61.
Calvo, Guillermo, and Pablo E. Guidotti. 1990. Indexation and maturity of government bonds. In *Public debt management: Theory and history,* ed. Rudiger Dornbusch and Mario Draghi, 52–82. Cambridge: Cambridge University Press.
Cortes Conde, Roberto. 1987. Nuevos aspectos en la crisis de 1890. Series Documentos de Trabajo Instituto Torcuato Di tella. Documento no. 145.
———. 1989. *Dinero, deuda y Crisis: Evolucion fiscal y monetaria en la Argentina, 1862–1890.* Buenos Aires: Editorial Sudamericana.
Della Paolera, Geraldo. 1988. How the Argentine economy performed during the gold standard period: A reexamination. PhD diss., University of Chicago.
———. 2001. Wrapping up: Britain as a lender (. . . of last resort) of Argentina 1820–1914. Paper presented at St. Antony's College, Oxford (May).
Della Paolera, Gerardo, and Alan M. Taylor. 2001. *Straining at the anchor: The Argentine currency board and the search for macroeconomic stability: 1880–1935.* Chicago: University of Chicago Press.
———. 2003. Gaucho banking redux. *Economia LACEA* 3 (2): 1–42.
De Paiva Abreu, Marcello. 1999. Brazil: 1824–1957: Bom ou Mau Pagador? Unpublished manuscript. Department of Economics, PUC-Rio. Texto para Discussao 403.
Drazen, Allan. 2000. *Political economy in macroeconomics.* Princeton: Princeton University Press.
Eaton, Jonathan. 1985. Sovereign debt: A primer. *World Bank Economic Review* 7: 137–72.
Elster, John. 1995. The impact of constitutions on economic performance. In *Proceedings of the 1994 World Bank Annual Conference on Development Economics* 209–39. Washington, DC: World Bank.
Ferguson, Nial. 2001. *The cash nexus: Money and power in the modern world, 1700–2000.* New York: Basic Books.
Fishlow, Albert. 1989. Conditionality and willingness to pay: Some parallels from the 1890s. In *The international debt crisis in historical perspective,* ed. B. Eichengreen and P. Lindert, 86–105. Cambridge, MA: MIT Press.
Harberger, Arnold. 1980. Vignettes on the world capital markets. *American Economic Review* 70 (2): 331–37.
Marichal, Carlos. 1989. *A century of debt crises in Latin America: From independence to the Great Depression, 1820–1930.* Princeton, NJ: Princeton University Press.
Musacchio, Aldo. 2005. *Brazil's stock and bond market database.* Cambridge, MA: Harvard Business School.
Persson, Torsten, and Guido Tabellini. 2003. *The economic effects of constitutions.* Cambridge, MA: The MIT Press.
U.S. Department of Commerce. 1933. Shepherd Report. *Default and adjustment of Argentine foreign debts, 1890–1906.* Washington: Government Printing Office.

6 Related Lending: Manifest Looting or Good Governance?
Lessons from the Economic History of Mexico

Noel Maurer and Stephen Haber

6.1 Introduction

Close ties between banks and their borrowers are common in many less-developed countries (LDCs). Indeed, in many LDCs these ties are so close that banks lend primarily to firms controlled by their own directors, or their directors' close friends and families. The standard view among policymakers is that these arrangements are pernicious: they allow insiders (bank directors) to expropriate outsiders (minority shareholders and depositors). The incentives to expropriate outsiders are likely to be particularly strong during a financial crisis, as the insiders seek to use the resources of the bank to rescue their other enterprises.[1] Related lending, according to this view, is therefore "a manifestation of looting" (La Porta, López-de-Silanes, and Zamarripa 2003, 231).

Noel Maurer is assistant professor in the Business, Government, and the International Economy department at the Harvard Business School. Stephen Haber is the A. A. and Jeanne Welch Milligan Professor in the department of political science, and the Peter and Helen Bing Senior Fellow of the Hoover Institution, Stanford University.

Earlier versions of this paper were presented at the National Bureau of Economic Research Corporate Finance Group, the National Bureau of Economic Research Inter-American Development Seminar, the World Bank, and the Stanford Center for International Development. The authors would like to thank Nicola Cetorelli, Robert Cull, Alex Galevotic, Simon Johnson, David Kaplan, Todd Keister, Randall Kroszner, Luc Laeven, Naomi Lamoreaux, Ross Levine, Ethan Ligon, César Martinelli, Aldo Musacchio, Roger Noll, Sangeeta Pratap, Armando Razo, James Robinson, Jordan Siegel, Tridib Sharma, Paul Sniderman, Kenneth Sokoloff, Michael Tomz, and Paul Wilson for their comments on earlier drafts. Financial support was provided by a grant from the U.S.-Latin American Relations Program of the William and Flora Hewlett Foundation to Stanford's Social Science History Institute.

1. See Akerlof and Romer 1993; La Porta, López-de-Silanes, Shleifer, and Vishny 1997, 1998; Rajan and Zingales 1998; Johnson, Boone, Breach, and Friedman 2000; Johnson, La Porta, López-de-Silanes, and Shleifer 2000; Laeven 2001; Bae, Kang, and Kim 2002; Mitton 2002; Habyarimana 2003; La Porta, López-de-Silanes, and Zamarripa 2003.

If related lending is so bad, then why did it characterize the banking systems of the United States, Germany, and Japan during their most rapid periods of growth?[2] Indeed, as Kroszner and Strahan have shown, related lending is *still* widespread in the United States, continental Europe, and Japan (Kroszner and Strahan 2001). These findings suggest, in turn, that there are conditions under which related lending is pernicious and conditions under which it is not.

What might those conditions be? One might posit either of two hypotheses. The first is that the impact of related lending varies with the quality of property rights. According to this view, related lending was (and is) positive in the United States, continental Europe, and Japan because the rule of law and efficiently specified property rights make looting difficult.[3] In developing countries, on the other hand, the lack of well-specified property rights, coupled with the lack of rule of law, allows directors to loot their banks with impunity. The second hypothesis is that the impact of related lending varies with the quality of corporate governance. This view stresses that what determines the growth outcomes of related lending is the presence (or absence) of institutions that lower the cost of monitoring bank directors.[4]

We argue that the weight of the evidence supports the second view: the outcome of related lending depends on the incentives and monitoring costs faced by bank directors, minority shareholders, and depositors. Our view is motivated by several curious features of what is perhaps the most intensively studied case of looting through related lending: Mexico from 1995 to 1998. During this period, bank directors made loans to the firms in which they held an interest that had lower levels of collateralization, lower interest rates, and higher default rates than arm's-length loans (La Porta, López-de-Silanes, and Zamarripa 2003). The first curious feature of this episode is that it took place in the context of an ongoing taxpayer-financed bailout of depositors, bank debtors, and stockholders.[5] The second odd feature of the 1995–1998 banking crisis is that the directors of Mexico's

---

2. See Aoki, Patrick, and Sheard 1994; Lamoreaux 1994; Calomiris 1995; Fohlin 1998.

3. For example, looting via default on existing debt will be more difficult in countries where bankruptcy law allows creditors to replace the management of bankrupt companies.

4. The term *corporate governance* is often used to capture two conceptually separate issues. It sometimes refers to the general enforcement of property rights. At other times, it refers to the institutions that allow shareholders and directors to monitor one another. We use the term in its second sense. Indeed, the institutions that allow shareholders and directors to monitor each other are important precisely because the agency problems between residual claimants (like depositors, shareholders, and directors) rise along with the cost of information and the difficulty of using the state to enforce property rights.

5. From 1991 to 1995, Mexico's banks were characterized by extremely high levels of loan default and negative real rates of return on assets. In early 1995 the Mexican government carried out a bailout designed to protect depositors. This bailout was originally intended as a one-time event, but it quickly became an open-ended mechanism that not only protected depositors but protected bank debtors and bank shareholders as well (Haber 2005).

banks had very little of their own capital at risk well before the crisis began. When Mexico privatized its banking system in 1991, the new owners borrowed much of the capital they used to purchase the banks *from the very same banks they were purchasing.* Many of the banks, therefore, effectively had capital-adequacy ratios close to zero well *before* they ran into trouble (Mackey 1999). In other words, neither depositors nor shareholders had any incentive to monitor the activities of the bank directors, and the directors had no incentives to monitor each other. In short, both property rights and corporate governance were poor in Mexico's 1995–1998 episode, which greatly limits its utility in adjudicating between the competing hypotheses.

We assess these two hypotheses by exploring the causes and consequences of related lending in a case in which there was widespread related lending, an externally generated financial shock that occasioned a government-organized rescue of the banks, weakly enforced property rights, and the unambiguous absence of the rule of law. This country did, however, have institutions that provided bank directors with incentives to monitor one another, and allowed depositors and minority shareholders to monitor bank directors. The country is Mexico during the thirty-five-year dictatorship of Porfirio Díaz (1876–1911). If the property rights view of related lending is correct, then one would expect that Mexican bankers should have looted their own banks or used them as mechanisms to transfer resources to firms under their control. At the very least, they should have allocated credit inefficiently, overinvesting in firms that they controlled. If the corporate governance view is correct, then one would expect that there would have been neither looting nor capital misallocation.

We find that bankers neither looted their own banks nor did they misallocate capital. Rather, we find that Mexican bankers primarily lent to their own firms because information was costly and contract rights were extremely difficult to enforce through the legal system.[6] Related lending provided an informal means to assess ex ante risk and enforce contracts ex post. We also find that even when the economy was hit with a large external shock, Mexico's bankers did not use related loans as a mechanism to loot their own banks. In addition, the loans they made to their own enterprises were no worse an allocation of credit than that which they could have obtained by making arm's-length loans to comparable enterprises. These results are consistent with the literature on the financial history of the developed nations, the literature about business groups in India, and recent

6. For a discussion of the importance of the legal system for financial development and economic growth see Levine 1998, 1999 and La Porta, López-de-Silanes, Shleifer, and Vishny 1998. For a discussion of the advantages that accrue to creditors from long-term relationships in the credit market see Greenbaum, Kanatas, and Venezia 1989; Sharpe 1990; Rajan 1992; Petersen and Rajan 1994, 1995.

work on the Asian crisis of 1997–98 (Friedman, Johnson, and Mitton 2003). The implication is that there is no necessary connection between related lending and looting, even in countries with weak property rights.

Related lending did not produce looting in Porfirian Mexico because various institutions aligned the interests of bank directors, shareholders, and depositors. The first were the institutions that allowed bank directors to monitor each other and enabled shareholders to police the directors. The second were the institutions that governed the banking sector. These institutions mandated high capital requirements, placed strong restrictions on note issue, and created limited liability. The third was the design of the banking rescue of 1908, the year in which Mexico was hit by a severe economic downturn originating from the Panic of 1907 in the United States. The Mexican government intervened as a lender of last resort, buying illiquid loans from the banks, but it carefully structured the terms of its intervention to ensure that the banks could not pass off their bad loans to taxpayers. The end result was a remarkably stable and efficient banking system, despite the ubiquitous use of related lending.

We do find that related lending gave rise to a more concentrated industrial structure in downstream industries. That outcome, however, was a result of Mexico's concentrated banking system. That is, bankers allocated credit to entrepreneurs on the basis of relational ties, but few entrepreneurs enjoyed such ties, because there were few banks. Nevertheless, it is not clear that the degree of concentration in Mexico was sufficiently high to create a significant degree of market power.

Our findings have implications beyond related lending. In recent years, a large literature has emerged on the effects of institutions on economic growth.[7] One of the findings of the literature is that there are numerous cases of dictatorial governments that are unable or unwilling to effectively specify or enforce property rights, but that nevertheless experience prolonged periods of rapid growth (Przeworski et al. 2000, 177). Our findings imply that economic actors may be able to compensate for weak legal institutions (at least for a time) by exploiting ties based on longstanding social and business relationships.

The rest of this paper is organized as follows. Section 6.2 provides a discussion of the data sets we develop. Section 6.3 provides a discussion of how related lending came to be the dominant business strategy of Mexico's bankers. Section 6.4 analyzes our data on the performance of the banking industry. Section 6.5 examines the impact of related lending on a downstream industry—cotton textiles. Section 6.6 concludes.

---

7. See North and Weingast 1989; Barro 1991, 1997; Engerman and Sokoloff 1997; Rajan and Zingales 1998; Przeworski et al. 2000; Bates 2001; Acemoglu, Johnson, and Robinson 2001, 2002; Keefer (forthcoming).

6.2 Sources and Methods

The analysis that we carry out on the causes and consequences of related lending in Mexico draw on three bodies of evidence that we have developed. The first body of evidence consists of bank financial reports. These reports were published in the Mexican financial press and allow us to estimate bank rates of return, share prices, dividend payments, and capital-asset ratios.

The second body of evidence focuses on bank lending strategies. For two of Mexico's largest banks, the Banco Nacional de México and the Banco Mercantil de Veracruz, we retrieved internal bank records that allowed us to estimate the extent of related lending over long time periods—1884–1911 and 1898–1906, respectively. These records were located in the Archivo Histórico Banamex and the Archivo de la Nación, both in Mexico City. For four other large banks, we were able to develop a data set for a cross-section of the loans they made in 1908. These records were also retrieved from the Archivo General de la Nación.[8] The two banks for which we have collected time series information (Banamex and the Banco Mercantil de Veracruz) accounted on average for nearly half of total bank assets. When we add the four banks for which we have cross-sectional data, our sample of banks covers two-thirds of all bank assets.

The third body of evidence focuses on a downstream industry that received related loans from the banks—cotton textiles. We note that the Mexican cotton textile industry is an ideal natural laboratory with which to study the impact of related lending on the real economy. In the first place, cotton textiles were Mexico's largest manufacturing industry. In the second place, the industry was finance-dependent, but at the same time it approximated the requirements of perfect competition to an unusual degree. Mexican law posed no direct barriers to entry into the industry. Nor were their indirect barriers to entry posed by patent protection, proprietary technology, control of raw materials, advertising, branding, or control of wholesale or retail distribution. The capital equipment was easily divisible and scale economies were exhausted at small-firm sizes, compared to such industries as steel, cement, paper, and chemicals. The industry was also characterized by a high degree of entry and exit. Finally, high tariffs protected the industry from foreign competition.

We study the effect of related lending on this industry by employing the Razo-Haber textile data set. We draw seven censuses from their data set:

---

8. We retrieved records of these loans by examining interbank loan sales to the state-owned Caja de Préstamos para Obras de Irrigación. See the *Sesiones Administrativas de la Caja de Préstamos,* Box 1, located in Galería 2 of the Archivo General de la Nación in Mexico City. Data for the total size of the loan portfolios of these banks were retrieved from their end-of-year balance sheets published in the *Economista Mexicano.*

1888, 1891, 1893, 1895, 1896, 1912, and 1913.[9] These censuses are enumerated at the mill level and contain information on inputs and outputs as well as information about location and ownership. We also draw state and national data on textile inputs and outputs from their data set for every year from 1891 to 1913. This state and national data allow us to make certain that the years for which we have mill-level censuses are not outliers. Table 6.1 presents data on the overall size and growth of this industry.

We then coded the data set in order to capture relationships between bankers and textile mill owners. Specifically, we code for bank board members who were also the sole proprietors of a textile mill, a partner in a firm that owned a textile mill, or who served on the board of directors of a joint stock corporation that owned a textile mill. We denote such mills as being "bank-related."[10]

Table 6.2 presents aggregate data on the relationships between mill owners and bankers. In 1888, 21 percent of textile mills were owned by bank directors or their close relatives. Eighty-eight percent of the bank-related mills were fully owned by directors, the remainder being organized as joint stock companies. By 1913, the proportion of bank-related mills had grown to 54 percent, and the proportion of such mills organized as joint-stock

9. This data set links mills and firms across manufacturing censuses and excise tax records over the period 1850–1932. For a discussion of the sources and methods used to build the panel, see Razo and Haber 1998. The census records employed in this study can be found in García Cubas (1893); *Mexico, Dirección General de Estadística 1894;* Mexico, Secretaría de Fomento (1890); Mexico, Secretaría de Hacienda (1896a); Mexico, Secretaría de Hacienda (1896b); Archivo General de la Nación, Ramo de Trabajo, box 5, file 4; Archivo General de la Nación, Ramo de Trabajo, box 31, file 2. We have recoded their data set to more effectively follow firms during the 1888–1913 period. We have also recalculated the real value of output by substituting the Gómez-Galvarriato and Musacchio price index for the INEGI cotton textile price index employed by Razo and Haber (1998). In addition, we have culled stamping and knitting mills from the data set and checked the data set against original manuscripts to verify observations with inordinately high or low values.

10. We note that our definition of bank connection is restrictive. Entrepreneurs who were connected to a bank in some way other than overlap between their membership on a bank board and ownership of a textile firm (for example, overlapping board memberships in a third, unobserved firm in a different industry, or marriage to a relative of a member of a bank board) are coded as "non-related" firms. We note that the assumption that overlap between mill ownership and a bank dictatorship is a good proxy for bank credit is consistent with three fundamental facts about Mexican banking. First, we know from case studies by historians that some banks were founded by textile entrepreneurs for the purpose of financing their existing manufacturing ventures (Gamboa Ojeda 1985; Gamboa Ojeda and Estrada 1986; Rodríguez López 1995). Second, in the case of Banamex (Mexico's largest bank), some of its board members were textile industrialists and the bank itself was a major stockholder in one of the country's largest textile companies. We know from the minutes of the bank's board meetings that it lent heavily to these enterprises (Maurer 2002, 98). Third, evidence from other large banks (reviewed below) makes it clear that they lent primarily to their own board members, members of their families, and their business associates. We also know that the directors of many of these banks also owned textile mills. The list of banks related to textile entrepreneurs or joint stock textile companies consists of Banamex, the Banco de Londres y Mexico, the Banco Oriental, the Banco de Nuevo León, the Banco de Durango, the Banco de Coahuila, the Banco Mercantil de Veracruz, the Banco de Guanajuato, the Banco de Estado de México, and the Banco de Zacatecas.

Table 6.1   The Mexican textile industry

	Number of mills	Output in 1900 pesos	Output in meters	Spindles	Workers	Price index
1878	73	n.a.	73,597,000	249,294	11,922	
1888	84	11,484,000	n.a.	249,591	15,083	94
1891	85	13,795,758	93,526,834	277,784	14,051	87
1893	113	19,925,011	122,550,335	370,570	21,963	96
1895	98	26,013,666	170,928,751	411,090	18,208	91
1896	100	25,338,269	206,411,839	430,868	19,771	93
1898	112	n.a.	n.a.	469,547	n.a.	93
1899	120	32,564,462	231,685,692	491,443	23,731	91
1900	122	35,458,578	261,397,092	588,474	27,767	100
1901	133	35,553,376	262,043,539	591,506	26,709	95
1902	124	27,938,569	235,955,965	595,728	24,964	103
1903	115	31,338,693	262,169,838	632,601	26,149	118
1904	115	34,645,972	280,709,989	635,940	27,456	123
1905	130	46,097,321	310,692,041	678,058	30,162	111
1906	130	44,894,422	349,711,687	688,217	31,673	114
1907	129	41,325,963	376,516,577	693,842	33,132	125
1908	132	35,303,315	368,370,354	732,876	35,816	121
1909	129	36,656,495	314,227,874	726,278	32,229	118
1910	121	39,118,584	315,322,022	702,874	31,963	129
1911	119	39,286,480	341,441,477	725,297	32,147	131
1912	126	46,848,154	319,668,409	762,149	32,209	136
1913	128	36,642,671	298,897,198	752,804	32,641	147

Sources: Haber 1989, table 8.1; Haber, Razo, Maurer 2003, tables 5.2 and 5.8. Original censuses for 1888, 1891, 1893, 1895, 1896, 1912, and 1913 can be found in: México, Secretaría de Fomento, 1890; México, Departmento de Fomento, 1893; México, Dirección General de de Estadística, 1894; México, Secretaría de Hacienda, 1896a; México, Secretaría de Hacienda, 1896b; México, Archivo General de la Nación, Ramo de Trabajo, Box 5, file 4; and Box 31, file 2.
Note: n.a. = not available.

Table 6.2   Mexico's textile industry, by bank relation, 1888–1913

	Number of mills related to banks	Percent of mills related to banks	Percent of output (by value) produced by bank related mills	Percent of output (by volume) produced by bank related mills	Percent of capacity (by spindlage) installed in bank related mills
1888	18	21		32	33
1891	17	20		32	
1893	33	30	48	51	51
1895	38	39	58	59	59
1896	40	40	58	60	62
1900	70	57	75		
1904	64	55	75		
1912	69	55	79	80	82
1913	69	54	77	78	80

Source: See table 6.1.

companies had risen to 27 percent. The percentage of installed capacity controlled by related mills increased from 33 percent in 1888 to 80 percent in 1913.[11]

6.3 Related Lending and the Mexican Banking System

In 1878, the Mexican banking system was so small as to be practically nonexistent. Only two chartered banks existed in the entire country. One was a branch of a British bank that operated in Mexico City and focused primarily on financing foreign trade. The other was a small American-founded operation chartered by the government of the border state of Chihuahua.[12]

Within a few years, however, Porfirio Díaz (Mexico's ruler from 1876 to 1911) enacted legislation that engendered the rapid expansion of the banking system from this extremely low base—by providing bankers with a series of segmented monopolies and duopolies. Only the two national banks—the Banco Nacional de México (henceforth Banamex) and the Banco de Londres y México (henceforth BLM)—were permitted to branch freely across state lines. Other banks were prohibited from branching outside their concession territories, which were generally contiguous with state lines. Federal law also erected extremely high barriers to entry. First, banks without a federal charter were prohibited from issuing notes, meaning that they could not effectively compete against chartered banks.[13] Second, the government levied a 2 percent tax on bank capital and a 5 percent tax on banknotes—but exempted the first bank in each state to receive a federal charter. Third, it established a minimum capital requirement of 250,000 dollars—five times the minimum capital needed to found a national bank in the United States. Finally, in case these barriers proved insufficient, the law gave the Finance Minister the right to approve all issues of new bank stock, which was one of the primary ways Mexican banks raised new resources during this period. The fact that the brother of the finance minister between 1893 and 1911 sat on the board of directors of the country's largest bank provided him with an obvious incentive to exercise his veto.[14]

---

11. Following Kane 1988, we measure installed capacity by spindles, which constitute the most important capital input for the production of cotton textile goods.

12. Until the growth of the chartered banking system in the decades after 1884, most financial intermediation took place in merchant houses, which issued bills of exchange and advanced credits to entrepreneurs in their social networks. These institutions did not, however, have any of the advantages of banks: they did not sell equity to outside investors, they did not have limited liability, they did not take deposits, and their bills of exchange had to be 100 percent backed by specie reserves. In short, they were different from modern banks in a fundamental sense: they made money by speculating with the funds of their proprietor, rather than with funds that belonged to people other than the proprietor. For an examination of how such a merchant house operated see Walker 1987.

13. See Maurer 2002, ch. 2; Haber, Razo, and Maurer 2003, ch. 4.

14. See Maurer 2002 and Haber, Razo, and Maurer 2003.

Table 6.3   The Mexican banking industry, 1896–1912

	Number of reporting banks[a]	Total bank assets (in U.S.$ millions)	Banamex market share (%)	BLM market share (%)	Herfindahl index[b]
1896	6	50	58	28	0.42
1897	10	54	n.a.	n.a.	n.a.
1899	13	78	51	26	0.34
1900	17	113	39	25	0.22
1901	20	107	38	22	0.20
1902	23	107	35	19	0.17
1903	25	130	37	17	0.18
1904	26	184	41	15	0.20
1905	26	205	39	18	0.20
1906	28	264	40	16	0.21
1907	28	301	44	14	0.23
1908	34	339	40	12	0.19
1909	35	283	37	12	0.17
1910	35	302	39	12	0.18
1911	35	385	39	12	0.18
1912	34	342	36	11	0.16

Source: Calculated from balance sheets published in El Economista Mexicano.
Note: Banamex indicates the Banco Nacional de México. BLM indicates the Banco de Londres y México.
[a]In 1911 there were 42 banks in operation, but only 35 reported data to the Secretary of the Treasury. The banks that did not report were small operations.
[b]Computed nationally, this assumes that banks with territorial concessions could operate in one another's concession territories. Thus, this is a lower bound estimate.

The short-term consequence of these high barriers to entry was a rapid expansion of the banking system. By 1897, when the law took its final form, the number of banks had risen to 10, with total assets of 50 million dollars. By 1911, there were 42 banks, controlling assets of 385 million dollars (see table 6.3). The ratio of commercial bank assets to GDP was 27 percent, roughly the same as its ratio in 2004 (33 percent).

The long-term consequence of high barriers to entry, however, was that Mexico remained relatively under-banked. In 1910, even if we include mortgage banks and private unchartered banks dedicated primarily to financing foreign trade, there were only 42 banks in the entire country with assets totaling US$414 million. Mexico possessed 364,286 inhabitants per bank, compared to 3,852 in the United States. The ratio of bank assets to GDP was only 27 percent, versus 65 percent in the United States.

The level of concentration in this banking system was extremely high. Banamex's share of total assets never fell below 36 percent. The Herfindahl concentration stabilized around 0.20, meaning that a system with 42 banks (35 of which provided data) was roughly as concentrated as one with five equally sized banks. In fact, measures of the total Mexican banking market greatly overstate the degree of competition. The lack of interstate competition (outside a few northern border states and the Distrito Federal) and limits on the number of banks in any given region meant that Banamex and the BLM were able to use their privileged position to operate like inefficient monopolists: they held excess liquidity to ration credit and drive up their rate of return (Maurer 2002, 70–92).

One might think that powerful politicians might have objected to this cozy arrangement, until you consider that they received a steady stream of rents from the banks. For example, Banamex's board of directors was populated by members of Díaz's coterie, including Pablo Macedo (the President of Congress and long-serving congressman from the Distrito Federal), Roberto Núñez (the under-secretary of the treasury), Sebastián Camacho (senator for the Distrito Federal), Pablo Escandón (congressman from Guanajuato, governor of Morelos, and Porfirio Díaz's chief of staff), and Julio Limantour (the brother of the finance minister). The chairman of the board of Banamex's largest competitor, the Banco de Londres y México, was none other than the secretary of war (and former mayor of Mexico City, former secretary of the interior, and former secretary of development), Manuel González Cosío. Joining him on the board was Rafael Dondé (senator from the state of Sonora). In addition, Julio Limantour was a major stockholder in the bank. The Banco Internacional Hipotecario, a mortgage bank, was similarly populated with political notables, including Julio Limantour, Porfirio Díaz Jr. (the dictator's son), and Emilio Pardo (federal deputy from the states of Hidalgo, México, and the Distrito Federal, senator from Tlaxcala, and ambassador to Belgium and the Netherlands). The board of the Banco Mexicano de Comercio e Industria also contained insiders. Its chairman was Pablo Macedo (see above). Joining Macedo on the board was Guillermo de Landa y Escandón (a senator from the state of Chihuahua and governor of the Federal District; Haber, Razo, and Maurer 2003).

These arrangements were paralleled at the state level. The only difference was that state governors, rather than cabinet ministers, sat on the banks' boards and received a steady stream of directors' fees, stock distributions, and dividends. In some cases, the governor himself received the bank concession. In point of fact, the banking system was deliberately conceived to distribute benefits to the state governors, and give them a stake in the maintenance of Porfirio Díaz's rule.[15]

The banks of the southern states of Chiapas and Oaxaca clearly illustrate the pattern. Emilio Rabasa served as governor of Chiapas in 1891–1894. Rafael Pimentel succeeded him in 1895–99. The Rabasa family owned a large stake in the Banco de Chiapas, and a member of the Pimentel family sat on the bank's board of directors. Another member of the Pimentel family, Emilio Pimentel, governed Oaxaca from 1902 to 1911, and

---

15. See Maurer 2002, 33–47, 93–114; Razo 2003; Haber, Razo, and Maurer 2003.

it should come as no surprise that the Pimentel family was represented on the board of the Banco de Oaxaca as well. The president of the Banco de Oaxaca, Luis Mier y Terán, had himself served as governor of the state between 1884 and 1887.

Northern state governors played as prominent a role in the banking system as their southern counterparts. In Durango, the founders of the Banco de Durango placed Governor Juan Manuel Flores on their board of directors (Rodríguez López 1995, 22). In San Luis Potosí, two members of the Díez Gutiérrez family governed the state between 1881 and 1898—both sat on the board of the Banco de San Luis Potosí. In the state of Sinaloa, Governor Mariano Martínez de Castro (governor from 1881 to 1884 and again in 1888–92) sat on the board of directors of the Banco Occidental. In the state of Zacatecas, Governor Génaro García Valdez (1900–04) served as president of the Banco de Zacatecas and sat on the board of the Banco Occidental in Sinaloa. In Chihuahua, Luis Terrazas and his relatives sat on the boards of all the state's major banks. In fact, Enrique Creel, Terrazas' son-in-law, received the concession for the Banco Minero de Chihuahua. Creel himself would later serve as governor of the state. In the central state of Mexico, the founders of the Banco del Estado de México reserved a board position for the former governor, José Zubieta, who governed from 1881 to 1889.[16]

In other cases, the connection to the state governor was less direct than a seat on the board, but strong nonetheless. In Puebla, for example, Governor Mucio Martínez received neither stock in the Banco Oriental nor a seat on the board. The Banco Oriental did, however, lend over 264,000 pesos to Martínez. This debt, along with an additional 400,000 pesos held by individual creditors, was never repaid. Instead, the major financiers of Puebla, among whom were the principal shareholders of the Banco Oriental, bailed Martínez out by forming a partnership with him and effectively assuming his liabilities (Gutiérrez Alvarez 2000, 125–26).

Financial markets could not substitute for banks in an environment characterized by high information costs. Mexico created a general incorporation law in 1889, but very few firms used the law to sell stock directly to the public. The reason was that stockholders had few ways to monitor the directors of public companies. Financial reporting requirements were not enforced. In fact, firms often went for years without publishing their financial statements, despite a law mandating that they do so. Moreover, investors had no way of determining whether the founders of a firm (who typically served as its directors) had divested themselves of their holdings in the firm. The result was that the public tended to invest only in enterprises controlled by individuals with established reputations for political

---

16. Board members from the *Boletín Financiero y Minero,* 2/28/1907, 6/18/1907, 6/10/1908, and 4/14/1908. Political careers from Camp (1991), appendix F.

connections and financial solvency: that is, enterprises that were already connected to banks (Maurer 2002).

In an environment characterized by extremely high information costs, bank directors had strong incentives to protect their reputations and monitor one another. There was neither deposit insurance nor guarantees that banks would redeem their notes for specie on demand. As Huybens, Luce, and Pratap have shown, depositors policed bank behavior by withdrawing funds from banks that pursued risky strategies (Huybens, Luce, and Pratap 2005). In addition, Mexico's banks typically had capital-adequacy ratios of 30–35 percent. In part, these capital ratios were driven by the legal requirement that note issues not exceed two (sometimes three) times a bank's cash on hand, or three times its paid-in capital (Maurer 2002, 43, 111). In equal part, however, these capital ratios were driven by risk aversion on the parts of both bankers and their creditors (depositors and noteholders). Banks usually did not, in fact, issue notes up to their legal maximum.

Bank directors owned substantial stakes in their banks. As of the 1884 Commercial Code, receiving a bank charter required the founding group (who became the directors) to subscribe to the first tranche of the bank's capital. Banks could later sell additional tranches of capital to outsiders. In addition, bank directors could (and often did) sell parts of their original stakes. These outside shareholders (who owned a majority of bank stock) then insisted on the appointment of independent directors (typically other bankers) who monitored the founding board members. This meant that directors had strong incentives to monitor each other (because their own capital and reputations were at risk) and that shareholders possessed a mechanism to monitor directors.[17] In fact, we have direct historical evidence that this mechanism was employed by outside shareholders. In March 1908, the outside shareholders of the Banco de Jalisco, displeased with the discovery of severe irregularities in the bank's books, replaced the entire board of directors save Vice President Eugenio Cuzin (Maurer 2002, 113).

Mexico's bankers started out by making arm's-length loans, but quickly shifted to related lending. Banamex, the largest bank in the country, received one of the first federal charters (in 1884). It began by making arm's-length loans. The problem was that it lacked good mechanisms to assess the quality of borrowers or the collateral they offered. It therefore responded by placing onerous requirements on borrowers, but these only worked to create adverse selection. The history of one of its largest manufacturing loans is perhaps instructive in this regard. In 1884, it opened a 200,000 peso credit line (roughly $200,000) to the Hercules textile factory for the purpose of purchasing a new plant and equipment. Banamex charged an in-

---

17. See Ludlow 1985, 299–346; Gamboa Ojeda 2003, 106, 111, 116, 129, 132; Ludlow 2003, 147–49, 152; Cerutti 2003, 196, 211–13; Romero y Barra 2003, 229; Rodriguez Lopez 2003, 271–2; Maurer 2002, 74–80, 94–95, 111–13.

terest rate of 8 percent and required that the loan be collateralized with 250,000 pesos worth of the factory's inventory, with the warehousing costs to be borne by the factory. Given that the factory had to finance the cost of the inventory, this implied an effective interest rate of 18 percent. Terms like these, of course, tend to attract low-quality borrowers—and this case was not an exception to that general rule. The Hercules mill was unable to make its payments. Eventually, Banamex sold a portion of the loan to a New York trading house (for only 65 percent of its face value) and recouped the rest by converting the loan into an equity interest in the mill.

This loan, as well as a series of others in which the collateral turned out to be fictitious or unrecoverable, caused Banamex's directors to shift strategy: after 1886 it lent primarily to its own directors, members of their families, or their close business associates. In fact, from 1886 to 1901 *all* of the private (nongovernment) loans made by Banamex went to its own directors. After 1901 Banamex extended credit to nonrelated borrowers, but only if they satisfied one of two criteria: the borrower had a loan guarantee from the federal government (as was the case with some railroad companies); or the borrower was either the Banco Oriental or one of that bank's directors. The reason given by Banamex board members for the latter exemption is instructive: most of the loans made by the Banco Oriental went to its own directors, all well-known textile magnates. Loans to them, and to their bank, were a means of investing in their manufacturing enterprises. Thus Banco Oriental loans were deemed low risk precisely because the bank practiced related lending.[18]

Related lending, in fact, appears to have been standard business practice. Data we have retrieved on the loan portfolio of the Banco Mercantil de Veracruz indicates that 86 percent of its loans to individuals from 1898 to 1906 went to the bank's own directors.[19] Banamex's largest competitor, BLM (which controlled, on average, 17 percent of total bank assets), also made sizable loans to its own board members to finance manufacturing start-ups (Maurer 2002, 103). A cross-section of loans we have drawn for 1908 for four other banks indicate similar lending strategies. Twenty-nine percent of the Banco de Nuevo León's loans went to a single firm, owned by one of its directors. Thirty-one percent of the Banco Mercantil de Monterrey's loans also went to a single firm owned by one of its directors. Fifty-one percent of the Banco de Durango's loans went to enterprises owned by the family members of one of its directors. An astounding 72 percent of the Banco de Coahuila's loans went to a single firm owned by family members

---

18. See Maurer 2002, 95–103, 108–10; Maurer and Sharma 2001, 953–56. The case of the Banco Oriental and its relationship to the Puebla textile industry is detailed in Gamboa Ojeda (1985) and Gamboa Ojeda and Estrada (1986).

19. The data for this estimate come from a random sample of 50 entries in the *Libro de Responsibilidades* of the Banco Mercantil de Veracruz, located in Galería 2 of the Archivo General de la Nación in Mexico City.

of a director.[20] Qualitative evidence from case studies by historians on the Banco de la Laguna, the Banco Occidental, and the Banco de Durango concur with our quantitative analysis.[21]

Mexico's bankers did not choose to lend to a particular company and then demand a seat on that company's board of directors. Rather, a group of textile mill owners, for example, would obtain a bank charter in conjunction with a powerful politician, sell shares in the bank to outside investors, issue bank notes, and then lend those notes to textile mills that he already owned (or, in some cases, found an entirely new mill). Of the 34 textile mills that switched from being nonrelated to being bank-related between 1888 and 1912, only one was a firm that was purchased by an existing banker. Thirty-three were owned by textile entrepreneurs who later became bankers. In short, bankers did not look at their banks as independent credit intermediaries in the textbook sense of the term. Instead, they looked at them as the investment arms of their widespread commercial and industrial interests.

6.4 Related Lending and the Performance of the Banking System

Did Mexican bankers use related loans to loot their own banks? One would imagine that they had strong incentives to do so. Mexico was hit by an external shock in 1908 that drove down the prices of its major export commodities by between 14 and 56 percent, depending on the product. Export prices declined 19 percent in the 1908–1909 fiscal year. They declined an additional 2 percent in 1909–10 (Cárdenas 2003, 240). The decline in prices caused mineral and agricultural producers to curtail production by between 20 and 64 percent (depending on the product), which in turn caused the demand for manufactured goods to fall by 9 to 20 percent (also depending on the product). The export crisis coincided with a severe drought in northwestern Mexico and the Gulf states, which caused the price of corn (Mexico's primary staple crop) to rise 128 percent between June 1908 and June 1909, and engendered a spike in agricultural imports (Cárdenas 2003, 242–43). The decline in Mexico's export, agricultural, and manufacturing sectors soon threatened the banking system. Deposits fell, interest rates on commercial paper rose from 8 percent to 10 percent, and net new lending dropped to zero. Indeed, total bank assets declined 17 percent from 1908 to 1909.[22]

---

20. We retrieved records of these loans by examining interbank loan sales to the state-owned Caja de Préstamos para Obras de Irrigación. See the *Sesiones Administrativas de la Caja de Préstamos,* Box 1, located in Galería 2 of the Archivo General de la Nación in Mexico City. Data for the total size of the loan portfolios of these banks were retrieved from their end-of-year balance sheets, published in the *Economista Mexicano.*
21. See Aguilar Aguilar 2003, 74; Rodriguez López 2003, 272, 278–79; Cerutti 2003, 169-70, 196, 204.
22. Bank balances and the interest rate on commercial paper from *Economista Mexicano.* Bond price data from Escalona Salazar (1998).

In response to the crisis, the government quickly organized a rescue. In September 1908 the federal government chartered the Caja de Préstamos para Obras de Irrigación y Fomento de la Agricultura. The Caja was financed by requiring Mexico's four largest banks to purchase 10 million pesos of its shares, 25 percent of which they were not permitted to sell. The Caja then issued 44.5 million pesos of government-guaranteed bonds in Europe, with an effective coupon rate of 5.1 percent. (The nominal yield on Mexican government bonds in 1908 was 4.3 percent.) The Caja used the funds from the bond and equity sales to purchase bank loans and bank-issued mortgage bonds in order to inject liquidity into the banking system (Maurer 2002, 66–68). The financial press greeted the plan with cries of relief. "Inasmuch as it is empowered to take over from the other chartered Banks the long-time loans to agricultural and industrial concerns which they are now carrying," wrote the *Mexican Herald* (Sept. 3, 1908), "its foundation will greatly ease the local business situation, and enable the other Banks to give more efficacious financial assistance to the commercial community and to the general public."[23]

By mid-1909, the Caja's outstanding purchases of bank loans totaled 23.8 million pesos. In addition, it had purchased an additional 8.9 million pesos of securities (mostly bonds issued by the clearinghouse used by the regional banks), and it had deposited 20.7 million pesos directly into the banking system (Maurer 2002, 67). The Caja de Préstamos was particularly vital in rescuing Mexico's second-largest bank, the Banco de Londres y México. In inflation-adjusted terms, the Banco de Londres y México's loans and discounts fell an astonishing 40 percent between the beginning of 1908 and the end of 1909 (Maurer 2002, 68). By June 1910, funds advanced from the Caja to BLM made up 21 percent of the Caja's asset portfolio.[24]

The Caja de Préstamo's statutes were carefully written to reduce the incentive for the banks to pass bad debts to the taxpayers. First, the Caja's charter required the banks to "unconditionally" guarantee the loans they sold to the Caja (*Economista Mexicana* 1908). Second, as a matter of policy, the Caja often agreed to rebate to the banks 1 percentage point of the interest it collected on the loans that the banks transferred to Caja.[25] Third, the banks were required to purchase 25 percent of the equity in the Caja, which they were not allowed to resell (*Economista Mexicana* 1908). Through these measures, the designers of the 1908 bank bailout hoped to be able to act as a lender of last resort and provide the banks with desperately-needed liquidity without creating moral hazard and a liability for the federal government.

23. See the *Mexican Herald* (9/3/1908).
24. Calculated from data in the *Sesiones Administrativas de la Caja de Préstamos,* Archivo General de la Nacion, Mexico City.
25. *Sesiones Administrativas de la Caja de Préstamos,* Box 1, various entries.

6.4.1 Did Directors Loot?

The most obvious sign of bankers extracting resources from their own banks would be an unstable banking system. The evidence indicates, however, that Mexico's banking system was remarkably stable. As shown in table 6.3, the number of reporting banks and total bank assets increased steadily. The only downturn in real bank assets occurred in 1909, as a result of the crisis of 1908, but the system's growth resumed in 1910.

One might argue that although the system was stable, directors were still able to extract resources from outside shareholders. That hypothesis, however, is not consistent with the fact that Mexican banks were extremely profitable. The real return on the book value of equity in 1901–12 was 12 percent. These returns were not driven by the profits earned by a few large banks: the unweighted average real return-on-equity for all banks was 10 percent per year.

Mexican banks returned high profits to shareholders by paying out regular dividends. In fact, over the 1901–10 decade, the banks paid out almost all of their profits in the form of dividends.[26] Steady dividends translated into high returns from banking stock. As table 6.4 shows, someone who purchased an index of banking stock weighted by market capitalization would have earned a real return of 9 percent per year. Our estimate of market returns is not driven by the high returns available from owning the stock of the largest banks: an investment strategy based on purchasing equally sized stakes in all the banks would have yielded a slightly higher real annual return of 10 percent. The returns available to investors in Mexican banking stock were, in fact, more than twice those available from investing in the Dow Jones Industrials (see table 6.4).

One might argue that the high returns investors earned in the banking sector were simply compensation for risk. If this were the case, then we would expect the value of banking stock to be highly discounted. We therefore estimated two measures of the discount on banking stock: market-to-book ratios and dividend yields. Table 6.5 shows the average (weighted and unweighted) market-to-book value ratio for Mexican banks in 1900–11. Bank stock traded at an average premium of 33 percent over its book value.[27]

---

26. In fact, banks paid dividends worth 106 percent of their profits over the 1901–10 period. We estimated this figure from balance sheets published in the *Economista Mexicano*. Profits were calculated as changes in real net worth (adjusted for issues of new stock) plus dividends in 1900 pesos. Real net worth was calculated by revaluing assets and liabilities in 1900 pesos and subtracting the value of new stock issues, if any.

27. Only the Banco de Michoacán in the years 1909 and 1910 was valued at less than its book value. The Banco de Michoacán was hard hit by the financial panic in 1909. Banamex agreed to accept responsibility for redeeming the Banco de Michoacán's banknotes if the Banco de Michoacán would agree to abandon its right to issue further notes. There were no losses to depositors or noteholders (Maurer 2002, 80).

Table 6.4   Real rates of return on Mexican banking, 1901–1912 (%)

	Real returns on book equity		Real returns from owning an index of bank stocks		Real returns from the Dow Jones index (peso terms)
	Weighted average[b]	Unweighted average	Weighted average[b]	Unweighted average	
1901	10	10	11	17	−7
1902	14	13	16	17	−7
1903	1	0	8	14	−24
1904	4	7	6	7	41
1905	40	29	33	29	37
1906	23	13	16	20	−5
1907	4	6	6	8	−41
1908	0	4	2	3	52
1909	14	9	12	−1	7
1910	4	3	9	10	−21
1911	20	14	−8	−4	9
1912[a]	11	10	−2	1	1
Average	12	10	9	10	4

Source: Stock prices and dividends reported in the *Economista Mexicano*. Dow Jones data from Haber, Razo, Maurer, table 5.12.
Note: All values converted to 1900 pesos using the Gómez-Musacchio (1998) index.
[a]First semester, annualized.
[b]Weighted by market capitalization.

Table 6.5   Market-to-book ratios for Mexican banks

	Weighted average[a]	Unweighted average
1901	1.52	1.20
1902	1.63	1.27
1903	1.69	1.25
1904	1.84	1.27
1905	1.95	1.35
1906	1.81	1.44
1907	1.76	1.41
1908	2.09	1.45
1909	2.14	1.33
1910	2.09	1.37
1911	1.90	1.33
Average	1.86	1.33

Source: Stock prices and dividends reported in the *Economista Mexicano*.
[a]Weighted by market capitalization.

Table 6.6   Banking stock yields (%)

	Average yield on bank shares[a]	Average yield on government bonds	Bank share premium
1901	9.4	5.0	4.4
1902	8.4	4.9	3.5
1903	8.3	4.9	3.4
1904	7.5	4.8	2.7
1905	8.1	4.3	3.8
1906	8.0	4.3	3.7
1907	7.1	4.4	2.7
1908	7.5	4.3	3.2
1909	6.8	4.3	2.5
1910	7.4	4.3	3.1
1911	7.7	4.5	3.2
1912	7.6	4.6	3.0

Source: Stock prices and dividends reported in the *Economista Mexicano.* Government bond yields from Escalona Salazar (1998, 93).

[a] Dividends divided by market price of common stock.

The data on banking yields is also inconsistent with the hypothesis that investors heavily discounted banking stock. As table 6.6 demonstrates, between 1901 and 1912 the difference between the yield on Mexican banking stock and Mexican government bonds dropped from 4.4 percentage points to 3.0 percentage points. In other words, the risks associated with owning banking stock appear to have declined over time.

Did the banks succeed in weathering the crisis through the expedient of passing off their bad related loans to the Caja de Préstamos—much the way that Mexican banks passed off their bad loans to the fund for the protection of bank savings (FOBAPROA) after the 1995–98 bailout? If that were the case, then we would expect the Caja de Préstamos to have lost money. The evidence, however, indicates that the opposite occurred—the Caja de Préstamos earned positive returns. In point of fact, the Caja de Préstamos may be the only government-organized banking rescue in world history to have made money. We calculate that the Caja generated a real return to all claimants on its assets (bondholders and shareholders) of 4.9 percent in 1909, 6.0 percent in 1910, and 5.7 percent in 1911.[28]

6.5 Did Related Lending Misallocate Capital?

One might argue that even if bankers did not loot enough to jeopardize the health of the banking system, they may have nonetheless used their related enterprises to transfer resources from bank depositors and outside

28. Calculated from the balance sheets of the Caja de Préstamos, published in *Economista Mexicano.*

Table 6.7 **Average annual growth in capacity across census periods (%)**

	Years between censuses	Bank-related mills	Nonrelated mills
1888–1893	5	5.5	4.0
1893–1895	2	11.0	8.4
1895–1896	1	7.6	4.1
1896–1912	16	2.4	0.4

Source: See table 6.1.

Note: Annualized rate of growth in capacity, measured in spindles, among firms listed in both censuses. Thus, the 1888–1993 cohort represents firms listed in both the 1888 and 1893 censuses.

shareholders to themselves. In order to test this hypothesis we turn to our panel of textile mills. If bankers were using their textile mills to channel resources from the banks to themselves, then we would not expect bank-related mills to grow. The mills would simply be mechanisms to extract the wealth of the bank.

When we look at the growth in the size of mills, however, we find precisely the opposite: not only did bank-related mills grow, they grew faster than their nonrelated competitors. In table 6.7 we calculate the growth rates of mills that existed across various census periods. In each intercensus period, we find that mills that were bank-related outgrew mills that were not.

One might argue, however, that bank directors used their banks in order to quickly build up their enterprises and then sell them for cash. The evidence, however, indicates that bankers who invested in textile mills viewed them as long-term investments. Of the 70 bank-related mills in 1900 (when the number of bank-related mills peaked) only seven had changed hands by 1913.[29]

6.5.1 Technical Efficiency

A somewhat weaker argument would suggest that bankers may have used their banks to support their own relatively inefficient firms. In this view, bank-related mills may have been productive enterprises (rather than zombie firms whose purpose was to extract bank resources), but would be less productive than their competitors. If this hypothesis holds, it implies that related lending misallocated capital.

We estimate a time series, cross-sectional regression on labor productivity. The results are in table 6.8.[30] We control for mill age, location, bank re-

---

29. An additional seven mills shut down over the period.
30. We measure output as the real value of production. Following Atack (1985) and Sokoloff (1984) on productivity in the United States, and Bernard and Jones (1996) on international productivity comparisons, we took the number of workers as the measure of the labor input. We adjusted, however, for changes in the legal length of the workday. We also estimated an OLS regression on labor productivity in which we controlled for mill size and capital intensity. That regression produced similar results. We therefore do not report them.

Table 6.8   Labor productivity regressions

	Spec 1	Spec 2
No. of observations	486	486
No. of mills	164	164
R^2	0.2706	0.2808
Constant	6.47***	6.45***
	(98.69)	(83.78)
1895	0.59***	0.62***
	(8.19)	(6.69)
1896	0.60***	0.64***
	(8.29)	(6.91)
1912	0.58***	0.53***
	(7.94)	(4.73)
1913	0.60***	0.57***
	(8.25)	(5.18)
Bank-Related		
1893		0.06
		(0.46)
1895		−0.13
		(−0.10)
1896		−0.05
		(−0.40)
1912		0.10
		(0.85)
1913		0.09
		(0.76)

Source: See table 6.1.

Notes: Functional form is OLS. Controls for mill age, location, and traded status did not materially affect the results. Dependent variable = (ln) output per worker (in 1900 pesos). *T*-statistics in parentheses.

***Significant at the 99 percent level.
**Significant at the 95 percent level.
*Significant at the 90 percent level.

lation, and whether it was publicly traded.[31] The results do not support the hypothesis that bank-related mills had lower labor productivity than their nonrelated competitors: none of the coefficients on bank-relation are significant.[32]

A skeptical reader might argue that our productivity measures treat each

---

31. We do not report the results on mill age, location, and traded status because none of the coefficients were large or significant, and because the addition of these variables had no material impact on our cross-sectional dummies or the interaction of the cross-sectional dummies with the dummy for bank relation.

32. The year dummies indicate rapid productivity growth from 1893 to 1895, and then flat productivity growth after 1895.

Table 6.9 Weighted labor productivity, by mill type

	Output per worker (1900 pesos)		
	Nonrelated	Bank-related	Difference (%)
1893	991	1,049	6
1895	1,243	1,266	2
1896	1,204	1,201	0
1912	1,371	1,403	2
1913	1,384	1,373	−1

Source: See table 6.1.

observation (one mill-year) equally. The regressions do not weight the results by firm sizes. Thus, it might be the case that small, particularly efficient, related mills drive the regression results. We therefore break the sample of mills into two sectors, nonrelated and bank-related, and calculate the labor productivity of each sector in the aggregate for individual census years. The results, reported in table 6.9, indicate that for the entire period under study, there were no significant differences in productivity between the bank-related mills, taken as a whole, and their nonrelated competitors.

6.5.2 Economic Efficiency

An even more skeptical reader might argue that the lack of difference in technical efficiency between bank-related and nonrelated mills is to be expected. The inefficient mills went out of business and hence dropped out of our data set. Such a reader would argue that the right criterion is economic efficiency, and that bank-related mills were less economically efficient than their nonrelated competitors. In order to test this hypothesis, we employ a Cox maximum-likelihood proportional hazards model to estimate the effect of bank relation on the probability of mill failure. Mills are defined as "failed" when they disappeared from the subsequent census, never to reappear. All coefficients (and standard errors) are transformed into hazard rates.

Our findings, presented in table 6.10, are not consistent with the hypothesis that bank-related mills were less economically efficient. In fact, we find exactly the opposite: bank-related mills were only 23 percent as likely to fail as their nonrelated competitors. This result is robust to the addition of conditioning variables for mill size, labor productivity, and age.

The Cox hazard model also suggests that being big was endogenous to being bank related. Bank-related firms lived longer and therefore grew larger. This is consistent with our finding—that bank-related mills grew much faster than their competitors (reported in table 6.7).

Table 6.10   Cox proportional hazard model

	Spec. 1	Spec. 2	Spec. 3	Spec. 4
No. of observations	467	431	275	271
Prob > χ^2	0	0	0.0001	0.0004
Bank-related dummy	0.23***	0.39**	0.32***	0.34**
	(–3.96)	(–2.53)	(–2.62)	(–2.45)
ln (installed spindlage)—Proxy for size		0.59***	0.63**	0.66*
		(–3.92)	(–2.06)	(–1.76)
ln (output per worker)—Real value			0.89	0.92
			(–0.49)	(–0.36)
Age of mill				0.98
				(–1.25)

Source: See table 6.1.

Notes: Dependent variable = 1 if survive, 0 if fail. *T*-statistics in parenthesis. When coefficients are transformed into hazard rates they represent the effect that the independent variable has on the mill failing. The smaller the coefficient, the greater the independent variable's impact. For example, a coefficient of 0.23 on the bank connection dummy means that a bank-connected mill has a 23 percent chance of failing in any given period compared to an independent mill. Output per worker data adjusted for changes in length of legal workday.
***Significant at the 99 percent level.
**Significant at the 95 percent level.
*Significant at the 90 percent level.

6.5.3 Relative Returns

A dedicated skeptic might argue that although there is no evidence that bank-related mills were less efficient than other mills, the textile sector as a whole might have been less profitable than other sectors of the economy. From the available evidence, however, this seems unlikely. An investor who purchased shares in a comprehensive sample of Mexican manufacturing stocks (excluding textiles) would have earned a real return of only 3.3 percent between 1902 and 1910 (Haber 1989, 120). A similar sample of mining stocks available on the Mexico City stock exchange would have *lost* money between 1902 and 1910, returning an average real return of –5.9 percent. (This calculation includes mining stocks that paid high dividends for a few years and then disappeared, as befits a bonanza industry like mining.)[33] Railroads did little better: all of the major trunk lines lost money during the first decade of the twentieth century at annual rates ranging between –0.3 percent and –2.2 percent (Maurer 2002, 105). In short, it seems difficult to argue that related lending caused overinvestment in cotton textiles, as compared to other industries for which we have data.

33. Calculated from stock prices and dividend coupons published in *Economista Mexicano*.

Table 6.11   Average textile mill size (in spindles), by mill type

	Nonrelated mills	Bank-related mills	Size ratio (bank related/nonrelated)
1888	2,549	4,611	181%
1893	2,320	5,467	236%
1895	2,759	6,711	243%
1896	2,862	6,417	224%
1912	2,303	8,725	379%
1913	2,234	8,680	389%

Source: See table 6.1.

6.5.4 Related Lending and Market Structure

If bank-related firms grew at a much faster rate than their nonrelated competitors, then it logically follows that there should have been big size differences between bank-related and nonrelated mills. Table 6.11 is unambiguous on this point: in 1888, bank-related mills were, on average, almost twice the size of unrelated mills; by 1913, they were nearly four times as large.

If bank-related mills were larger than nonrelated mills, then it logically follows that the market structure of the textile industry became more concentrated as the proportion of bank-related mills grew. In order to measure concentration, we aggregate mills into firms, and estimate four-firm concentration ratios and the Herfindahl index.

In order to determine how low concentration would have been in the absence of related lending, we specify three counterfactuals. The first compares Mexico to itself over time. Constant returns to scale and the absence of entry barriers characterized cotton textile manufacturing. We should expect that, in the absence of related lending, concentration should have fallen as the industry grew. The second compares Mexico to countries that had large textile industries but that did not have Mexico's banking system. We focus on the United States, Brazil, and India (Haber 1991, 1997, 2003). The third, following Sutton, compares the Mexican textile industry's actual market structure to a hypothetical fully-competitive industry, in which the market structure was a function solely of industry size and a stochastic growth process.[34]

The results of all three experiments, displayed in table 6.12, indicate that the Mexican cotton textile industry was too concentrated. First, concentration in Mexico actually increased over time, even though the industry

---

34. The method assumes that all firms in a market have an identical chance of gaining or losing market share over time. Even under perfect competition, therefore, firms will have unequal market shares in equilibrium, but the market share of the largest firms will solely be a function of the number of firms in the industry and a stochastic growth process (see Sutton 1998).

Table 6.12 Industrial concentration in cotton textiles: Mexico, Brazil, India, and the United States

	Four firm ratio (%)					Herfindahl index		
Circa	Mexico	Mexico expected	Brazil	India	United States	Mexico	Brazil	India
1888	18	19	37		8	0.022	0.058	
1891	20	19				0.020		
1893	29	15				0.038		
1895	33	17	35			0.042	0.059	
1896	30	16				0.041		
1900	30	14		19	7	0.038	0.028	0.018
1904	33	15	21			0.042		
1912	30	14		19	8	0.039		0.018
1913	31	14	14			0.041	0.014	

Sources: For Mexico, see table 6.1; for Brazil, Haber 1997; for India and the United States, Haber 2003.

was growing quickly (in the United States, brazil, and India, concentration fell or remained stable as the textile industry grew). Second, the Mexican cotton textile industry was much more concentrated than the U.S., Brazilian, or Indian cotton textile industry. Third, the Mexican cotton textile industry showed much higher four-firm ratios compared to the ratio that would be expected in a perfectly competitive market, given the number of firms in the industry.

We note that even though Mexico's textile industry was concentrated by world standards, the industry did not depart very far from perfect competition. The four-firm ratio never exceeded 38 percent, and the number of firms hovered around 110. It is hard to believe that this level of concentration was sufficient to allow even the largest firms to exercise market power. This interpretation is consistent with the historical evidence about firm behavior during this period.[35]

6.6 Conclusions and Implications

We argue, based on a study of a banking system characterized by widespread related lending, that there is no *necessary connection* between related lending and looting. We also argue that there is no *necessary connection* between related lending and a misallocation of capital. Mexican bankers during the Porfiriato did not choose to lend to firms that were systematically less productive than their competitors.

We also argue that related lending is not a consequence of inadequate regulation and supervision, but rather is a rational response to high levels

---

35. See Haber 1989, 94–95, and Gómez-Galvarriato 1999.

of default risk. High levels of default risk can exist for any number of reasons, but prominent among them are weak institutions to enforce contract rights and high costs of obtaining information about potential borrowers. Related lending mitigates these problems. First, bankers do not need recourse to the formal legal system to sanction related borrowers. Rather, they can do so through a wide variety of informal means. Second, bankers can obtain information about related borrowers at relatively low cost.

It logically follows that attempts to eliminate related lending through supervision and regulation will not produce the first-best outcome of arm's-length lending based on objective performance criteria. Rather, in the context of high default risk, the close regulation and supervision of banks so as to preclude related lending will produce very little lending of any type. The canonical case of this phenomenon also comes from Mexico, where regulators have been quite effective in curtailing related lending since a series of accounting and regulatory reforms in 1997. The response of Mexico's banks has been to drastically curtail private lending, shifting their assets into corporate and government securities, as well as loans to states and municipalities (Haber and Musacchio 2004).

Unfortunately, the institutional problems that give rise to high levels of default risk (weak property rights and high costs of information) cannot be reformed at the stroke of a pen. Enhancing the enforcement of contract rights requires, in the first place, that governments actually have the capacity to adjudicate and enforce those rights. This requires more than the power of coercion. It requires that the government has an efficient administrative apparatus that can adjudicate disputes at low cost to the contracting parties.[36] The *capacity* to enforce contracts is, however, only half the battle. As a large literature in economic history and political science has demonstrated, any government that has the power to effectively adjudicate contract rights also has the power to abrogate or selectively enforce them. Thus, the effective enforcement of contract rights also requires that there be self-enforcing political institutions that limit the authority and discretion of public officials.[37] To argue, therefore, that governments can

---

36. If the cost of adjudication to the parties is high, then economic agents will only make contracts whose rate of return exceeds the cost of contract enforcement. This will curtail the number of contracts into which agents enter, and thereby depress economic activity.

37. Constraints on public officials and government capacity are causally linked. If the power of public officials is not limited, economic agents will be subject to expropriation risk. They will therefore refrain from investments whose rate of return does not compensate them for expropriation risk. The result will be lower levels of investment, which, in turn, will reduce the pool of wealth and income that the government can tax. With fewer resources, the government will be less able to develop an effective administrative and coercive apparatus that can adjudicate property rights. This fundamental dilemma of governance was noted as long ago as the Middle Ages (Greif et al. 1994), but in recent years it has spawned a sizable political science literature. For representative works see: North and Weingast 1989; Shepsle 1991; Hoffman and Norberg 1994; McGuire and Olson 1996; Weingast 1997a, 1997b; North et al. 2000; Olson 2000; Bates 2001; Haber, Razo, and Maurer 2003.

enhance property rights enforcement at the stroke of a pen is to engage in a nirvana thesis.

Related lending need not, however, be economically inefficient. Three conditions appear to be necessary to prevent related lending from turning into organized looting. First, the banks must be well-capitalized. In our case, for example, the capital asset ratios were four times the levels recommended by Basel. Second, bank directors must own substantial equity shares in their own banks. This gives bank directors incentives to monitor one another. Third, outside shareholders must have their own money at risk, and depositors must not be fully insured. This gives depositors and outside shareholders incentives to monitor the activities of the directors.

We note that the results we obtained for the Mexican case are consistent with those of other cases—particularly, contemporary India.[38] They are also consistent with the results obtained in historical case studies of the nineteenth-century United States and continental Europe.[39] We would submit, therefore, that more research is needed into the causes and consequences of related lending before academics and public officials embrace any particular set of policy recommendations.

References

Acemoglu, Daron, Simon Johnson, and James Robinson. 2002. Reversal of fortune: Geography and institutions in the making of the modern world income distribution. *Quarterly Journal of Economics* 117:1231–94.

Aguilar Aguilar, Gustavo. 2003. El sistema bancario en Sinaloa (1889–1926): Su influencia en el crecimiento economico. In *La banca regional en Mexico,* ed. Mario Cerutti and Carlos Marichal, 47–100. District Federales, Mexico: Fondo de Cultura Económica.

Akerlof, George, and Paul Romer. 1993. Looting: The economic underworld of bankruptcy for profit. *Brookings Papers on Economic Activity,* Issue no. 2:1–73.

Aoki, Masahiko, Hugh Patrick, and Paul Sheard. 1994. The Japanese main banking system: An introductory overview. In *The Japanese main banking system,* ed. Masahiko Aoki and Hugh Patrick, 3–50. Oxford: Oxford University Press.

Atack, Jeremy. 1985. *Estimation of economies of scale in nineteenth century United States manufacturing.* New York: Garland.

Bae, Kee-Hong, Jun-Koo Kang, and Jin-Mo Kim. 2002. Tunneling or value added: Evidence from mergers by Korean business groups. *Journal of Finance* 57 (6): 2695–2740.

Barro, Robert. 1991. Economic growth in a cross section of countries. *Quarterly Journal of Economics* 106 (2): 407–43.

———. 1997. *Determinants of economic growth: A cross-country empirical study.* Cambridge, MA: MIT Press.

---

38. See Khanna and Fisman 2004; Khanna and Palepu 2000a, 2000b.
39. See Calomiris 1995; Lamoreaux 1994.

Bates, Robert H. 2001. *Prosperity and violence: The political economy of development.* New York: W. W. Norton.
Bernard, Andrew, and Charles Jones. 1996. Productivity across industries and countries: Time series theory and evidence. *Review of Economics and Statistics* 78 (1): 135–46.
Calomiris, Charles. 1995. The costs of rejecting universal banking: American finance in the German mirror, 1870–1914. In *Coordination and information: Historical perspectives on the organization of enterprise,* ed. Naomi Lamoreaux and Daniel Raff, 257–322. Chicago: University of Chicago Press.
Cárdenas, Enrique. 2003. *Cuando se originó el atraso económica de México: La economía mexicana en el largo siglo XIX, 1780–1920.* Madrid: Editorial Biblioteca Nueva.
Cerutti, Mario. 2003. Empresarido y banca en el norte de Mexico, 1879–1910: La fundacion del Banco Refaccionario de la Laguna. In *La banca regional en Mexico, 1870–1930,* ed. Mario Cerutti and Carlos Marichal, 168–215. Mexico, DF: Fondo de Cultura Económica.
Dirección General de Estadística. 1894. Auario estadístico de la Republica Mexicana 1893–94.
Economista Mexicano. 1908. End of year bank balance sheets. December 12.
Engerman, Stanley, and Kenneth Sokoloff. 1997. Factor endowments, institutions, and differential paths of growth among new world economies. In *How Latin America fell behind,* ed. Stephen Haber, 260–306. Palo Alto, CA: Stanford University Press.
Escalona Salazar, Ana Maria. 1998. La entrada de México al patrón oro y el aceso a los capitales extranjeros. BA thesis, México, DF: ITAM.
Fohlin, Caroline M. 1998. Relationship banking, liquidity, and investment in the German industrialization. *Journal of Finance* 53:1737–58.
Gamboa Ojeda, Leticia. 1985. *Los empresarios de ayer: El grupo dominante en la industria textil de Puebla, 1906–1929.* Puebla, Mexico: Universidad Autonoma de Puebla.
———. 2003. El Banco Oriental de Mexico y la formacion de un sistema de banca, 1900–1911. In *La banca regional en Mexico, 1870–1930,* ed. Mario Cerutti and Carlos Marichal, 101–33. Mexico, DF: Fondo de Cultura Económica.
Gamboa Ojeda, Leticia, and Rosalina Estrada. 1986. *Empresas and empresarios textiles de Puebla: Analisis de dos casos.* Puebla, Mexico: Universidad Autonoma de Puebla.
Gómez Galvarriato, Aurora. 1999. The impact of revolution: Business and labor in the Mexican textile industry, Orizaba, Veracruz, 1900–1930. PhD diss., Harvard University, Cambridge, MA.
Gómez Galvarriato, Aurora, and Aldo Musacchio. 1998. Un nuevo índice de precios para México, 1886–1930. Working paper no. 113. Mexico City: Centro de Investigacíon y Docencia Economicas.
Greenbaum, Stuart, George Kanatas, and Itzhak Venezia. 1989. Equilibrium loan pricing under the bank-client relationship. *Journal of Banking and Finance* 13: 221–35.
Grief, Avner, Paul Milgrom, and Barry R. Weingast. 1994. Coordination, commitment, and enforcement: The case of the merchant guild. *Journal of Political Economy* 102 (4): 745–46.
Gutiérrez Alvarez, Coralia. 2000. *Experiencias contrastadas: Industrialización y conflictos en los textiles del centro-oriente de México, 1884–1917.* México: El Colegio de México Centro de Estudios Históricos; Benemérita Universidad de Puebla Instituto de Ciencias Sociales y Humanidades.

Haber, Stephen. 1989. *Industry and underdevelopment: The industrialization of Mexico, 1890–1940.* Palo Alto, CA: Stanford University Press.

———. 1991. Industrial concentration and the capital markets: Mexico, Brazil, and the United States, 1840–1930. *Journal of Economic History* 51 (3): 559–80.

———. 1997. Financial markets and industrial development: A comparative study of governmental regulation, financial innovation, and industrial structure in Brazil and Mexico, 1840–1930. In *How Latin America fell behind: Essays on the economic histories of Brazil and Mexico, 1800–1930,* ed. Stephen Haber, 146–78. Palo Alto, CA: Stanford University Press.

———. 1998. The efficiency consequences of institutional change: Financial market regulation and industrial productivity growth in Brazil, 1866–1934. In *Latin America and the world economy since 1800,* ed. John H. Coatsworth and Alan M. Taylor, 275–322. Cambridge, MA: Harvard University Press.

———. 2003. Banks, financial markets, and industrial development: Lessons from the economic histories of Brazil and Mexico. In *Latin American macroeconomic reforms: The second stage,* ed. José Antonio González, Vittorio Corbo, Anne O. Krueger, and Aaron Tornell, 257–92. Chicago: University of Chicago Press.

———. 2005. Mexico's experiments with bank privatization and liberalization, 1991–2003. *Journal of Banking and Finance* 29:2325–53.

Haber, Stephen, and Aldo Musacchio. 2004. Foreign banks and the Mexican economy. Harvard Business School Working Paper no. 05-024.

Haber, Stephen, Armando Razo, and Noel Maurer. 2003. *The politics of property rights: Political instability, credible commitments, and economic growth in Mexico, 1876–1929.* New York: Cambridge University Press.

Habyarimana, James. 2003. The benefits of relationships: Evidence from Uganda's banking crisis. Harvard University. Unpublished paper.

Hoffman, Philip, and Katherine Norberg, eds. 1994. *Fiscal crises and the growth of representative institutions.* Palo Alto, CA: Stanford University Press.

Huybens, Elisabeth, Astrid Luce Jordan, and Sangeeta Pratap. 2005. Financial market discipline in early-twentieth-century Mexico. *The Journal of Economic History* 65 (3): 757–78.

Johnson, Simon, Peter Boone, Alasdair Breach, and Eric Friedman. 2000. Corporate governance in the Asian financial crisis. *Journal of Financial Economics* 58 (1–2): 141–86.

Johnson, Simon, Rafael La Porta, Florencio López-de-Silanes, and Andrei Shleifer. 2000. Tunnelling. Harvard Institute of Economic Research Paper no. 1887.

Kane, Nancy. 1988. *Textiles in transition: Technology, wages, and industry relocation in the U.S. textile industry.* Westport, Connecticut: Greenwood.

Keefer, Philip. Forthcoming. What does political economy tell us about economic development—and vice versa? *Annual Review of Political Science.*

Khanna, Tarun, and Raymond Fisman. 2004. Facilitating development: The role of business groups. *World Development* 32 (4): 609–28.

Khanna, Tarun, and Krishna Palepu. 2000a. Emerging market business groups, foreign investors, and corporate governance. In *Concentrated corporate ownership,* ed. Randall Morck, 265–94. Chicago: University of Chicago Press.

———. 2000b. Is group affiliation profitable in emerging markets: An analysis of diversified Indian business groups. *Journal of Finance* 55:867–91.

Kroszner, Randall, and Philip Strahan. 2001. Bankers on the boards: Monitoring, conflicts of interest, and lender liability. *Journal of Financial Economics* 62 (3): 415–52.

Laeven, Luc. 2001. Insider lending and bank ownership: The case of Russia. *Journal of Comparative Economics* 29 (2): 207–29.

Lamoreaux, Naomi. 1994. *Insider lending: Banks, personal connections, and eco-*

nomic development in industrial New England. Cambridge: Cambridge University Press.

La Porta, Rafael, Florencio López-de-Silanes, Andrei Shleifer, and Robert W. Vishny. 1997. Legal determinants of external finance. *Journal of Finance* 52: 1131–50.

———. 1998. Law and finance. *Journal of Political Economy* 106 (6): 1113–55.

La Porta, Rafael, Florencio López-de-Silanes, and Guillermo Zamarripa. 2003. Related lending. *Quarterly Journal of Economics* 118 (1): 231–68.

Levine, Ross. 1998. The legal environment, banks, and long run economic growth. *Journal of Money, Credit, and Banking* 30 (pt. 2): 596–620.

———. 1999. Law, finance, and economic growth. *Journal of Financial Intermediation* 81 (1-2): 36–67.

Ludlow, Leonor. 1985. La construccion de un banco: El Banco Nacional de Mexico, 1881–1884. In *Banca y poder en Mexico,* 1800–1929, ed. Leonor Ludlow and Carlos Marichal, 299–346. Mexico: Editorial Grijalbo.

———. 2003. El Banco Mercantil de Veracruz, 1898–1906. In *La banca regional en Mexico,* 1870–1930, ed. Mario Cerutti and Carlos Marichal, 134–67. Mexico, DF: Fondo de Cultura Económica.

Mackey, Michael. 1999. Report of Michael W. Mackey on the comprehensive evaluation of the operations and functions of the fund for the protection of bank savings "Faboproa" and the quality of supervision of the Fobaproa program, 1995–1998. Unpublished paper.

Maurer, Noel. 2002. *The power and the money: The Mexican financial system, 1876–1932.* Palo Alto, CA: Stanford University Press.

Maurer, Noel, and Andrei Gomberg. 2004. When the state is untrustworthy: Public finance and private banking in Porfirian Mexico. *Journal of Economic History* 64:1087–1107.

Maurer, Noel, and Tridib Sharma. 2001. Enforcing property rights through reputation: Mexico's early industrialization, 1878–1913. *The Journal of Economic History* 61 (4): 950–73.

Mitton, Todd. 2002. A cross-firm analysis of the impact of corporate governance on the East Asian financial crisis. *Journal of Financial Economics* 64 (2): 215–41.

Musacchio, Aldo. 2005. Can civil law countries get it right? Institutions and financial market development in southeastern Brazil, 1890–1940. PhD diss., Stanford University.

North, Douglass C., William Summerhill, and Barry R. Weingast. 2000. Order, disorder, and economic change: Latin America versus North America. In *Governing for prosperity,* ed. Bruce Bueno de Mesquita and Hilton L. Root, 17–58. New Haven, CT: Yale University Press.

North, Douglass, and Barry Weingast. 1989. Constitutions and commitment: The evolution of institutions governing public choice in seventeenth-century England. *The Journal of Economic History* 49 (4): 803–32.

Olson, Mancur. 2000. *Power and prosperity: Outgrowing communist and capitalist dictatorships.* New York: Basic Books.

Petersen, Mitchell, and Raghuram Rajan. 1994. The benefits of lending relationships: Evidence from small business data. *Journal of Finance* 49:3–37.

———. 1995. The effect of credit market competition on lending relationships. *Quarterly Journal of Economics* 110:407–44.

Przeworski, Adam, Michael Alvárez, José Antonio Cheibub, and Fernando Limongi. 2000. *Democracy and development: Political institutions and the material well-being of the world, 1950–1990.* New York: Cambridge University Press.

Rajan, Raghuram. 1992. Insiders and outsiders: The choice between informed and arms-length debt. *Journal of Finance* 47:1367–1400.

Rajan, Raghuram, and Luigi Zingales. 1998. Financial dependence and growth. *American Economic Review* 88 (3): 559–86.
Razo, Armando. 2003. Social networks and credible commitments in dictatorships: Political organization and economic growth in Porifiran Mexico, 1876–1991. PhD diss., Stanford University.
Razo, Armando, and Stephen Haber. 1998. The rate of growth of productivity in Mexico, 1850–1933: Evidence from the cotton textile industry. *Journal of Latin American Studies* 30 (3): 481–517.
Rodríguez López, Maria Guadalupe. 1995. La banca porfiriana en Durango. In *Durango (1840–1915): Banca, transportes, tierra e industria,* ed. Mario Cerutti, 7–34. Monterrey, Nuevo León: Impresora Monterrey.
———. 2003. Paz y bancos en Durango durante el Porfiriato. In *La banca regional en Mexico, 1870–1930,* ed. Mario Cerutti and Carlos Marichal, 254–90. Mexico, DF: Fondo de Cultura Económica.
Romero y Barra, Maria Eugenia. 2003. El Banco del Estado de Mexico 1897–1914. In *La banca regional en Mexico, 1870–1930,* ed. Mario Cerutti and Carlos Marichal, 216–51. Mexico, DF: Fondo de Cultura Económica.
Secretaría de Fomento. 1890. Boletín semestral de la República Mexicana. Mexico City.
Secretaría de Hacienda. 1896a. Memoria de la Secretaría de Hacienda. Mexico City.
———. 1896b. Estadística de la República Mexicana. Mexico City.
———. 1904. Boletín de estadística fiscal, 1903–04. Mexico City.
Sharpe, Steven. 1990. Asymmetric information, bank lending, and implicit contracts: A stylized model of customer relationships. *Journal of Finance* 45:1069–87.
Shepsie, Kenneth. 1991. Discretion, institutions, and the problem of government commitment. In *Social theory for a changing society,* ed. Pierre Boudieu and James Coleman, 245–63. Boulder, CO: Westview Press.
Sokoloff, Kenneth. 1984. Was the transition from the artisanal shop to the non-mechanized factory associated with gains in efficiency? Evidence from the U.S. manufacturing censuses of 1820 and 1850. *Explorations in Economic History* 21 (4): 351–82.
Sutton, John. 1998. *Technology and market structure.* Cambridge, MA: MIT Press.
Stulz, René. 2001. Does financial structure matter for economic growth? A corporate finance perspective. In *Financial structure and economic growth: A cross-country comparison of banks, markets, and development,* ed. Asli Demirgüç-Kunt and Ross Levine, 143–88. Cambridge, MA: MIT Press.
Walker, David W. 1987. *Business, kinship, and politics: The Martinez del Rio family in Mexico, 1824–1867.* Austin: University of Texas Press.
Weingast, Barry R. 1997a. The political foundations of limited government: Parliament and sovereign debt in 17th- and 18th-century England. In *The frontiers of the new institutional economics,* ed. John N. Drobak and John V. C. Nye, 213–46. San Diego, CA: Academic Press.
Weingast, Barry R. 1997b. The political foundations of democracy and the rule of law. *American Political Science Review* 91 (2): 245–63.

7

Sudden Stops and Currency Drops
A Historical Look

Luis A. V. Catão

7.1 Introduction

A prominent strand of international macroeconomics literature has recently devoted considerable attention to what has been dubbed "sudden stops"; that is, sharp reversals in aggregate foreign capital inflows. While there seems to be insufficient consensus on what triggers such reversals, two consequences have been amply documented—namely, exchange rate drops and downturns in economic activity, effectively constricting domestic consumption smoothing. This literature also notes, however, that not all countries respond similarly to sudden stops: whereas ensuing devaluations and output contractions are often dramatic among emerging markets, financially advanced countries tend to be far more impervious to those disruptive effects.[1]

These stylized facts about sudden stops have been based entirely on post-1970 evidence. Yet, periodical sharp reversals in international capital flows are not new phenomena. Leaving aside the period between the 1930s Depression and the breakdown of the Bretton-Woods system in 1971 (when stringent controls on cross-border capital flows prevailed around

---

Luis A. V. Catão is Senior Economist at the research department of the International Monetary Fund.

I thank my discussant, Lorenza Martínez, as well as Michael Bordo, Gian Maria Milesi-Ferretti, and participants of the 2004 NBER Inter-American Seminar in Economics for comments on an earlier draft. I am also grateful to George Kostelenos, Pedro Lains, Agustín Llona, Leandro Prados, Irving Stone, Bill Summerhill, Gail Triner, and Jeffrey Williamson for kindly sharing their data with me. The views expressed here are the author's alone and do not necessarily represent those of the IMF.

1. Calvo, Izquierdo, and Mejia (2004) note, for instance, that whereas 63 percent of sudden stop episodes have been associated with devaluations in emerging markets, the proportion drops to 17 percent among advanced economies.

the globe), a large body of the historical literature has highlighted the fact that the pace of international capital flows has been anything but smooth (Eldstein 1982; Stone 1999; DeLong 1999; Eichengreen 2003). In particular, past financial crises in emerging economies have been shown to be frequently associated with dramatic downturns in capital flows that often seemed hard to rationalize (Kindleberger 1978). Partly because of data limitations, however, cross-country evidence on historical patterns of sudden stops and their relationship to exchange rate developments has been unsystematic at best.

This paper aims to fill some of this gap. First, it describes the historical evidence on sudden stops (SS henceforth) using a new international data set on capital inflows spanning sixteen countries since the early days of financial globalization, around 1870—when asset market arbitrage was greatly spurred by the advent of the transatlantic telegraph in 1866—through the eve of World War I. Two key features that underpin the current relevance of this period are the high degree of world capital market integration and the widespread use of bond financing as the main instrument of sovereign borrowing—two clear similarities with its late twentieth-century/early twenty-first century counterpart.[2]

Four sets of questions are then asked about the nature of SSs, namely:

- Are SSs an exclusive feature of a class of countries, or do they hit capital-importing economies more generally, irrespective of their level of development and monetary regimes?
- How large are such SSs relative to the size of the recipient country's economy, and what is their average duration?
- Do SSs display some systematic cross-country pattern and time bunch, or is there evidence that they are typically triggered by idiosyncratic country shocks?
- Is there a systematic relationship between SSs and shifts in monetary policy and interest rates in major capital-exporting countries?

Against this background, the second contribution of the paper is to establish the links (if any) between SSs and currency crashes. A feature of the pre–World War I period, which makes it especially interesting for looking at this relationship, is the existence of an international monetary system that provided one key incentive for countries to peg their currencies to gold and thus forestall devaluations or depreciations. Bordo and Rockoff (1996) and Obstfeld and Taylor (2003) argue that membership of the "gold club" tended to shave off between 40 to 60 basis points in countries' spreads. This represented nonnegligible savings to sovereign borrowers, given the generally high ratios of countries' foreign-currency-denominated debts to GDP

---

2. See Obstfeld and Taylor (2004) for measures of international capital integration over the past century and a half.

at the time, and the much narrower dispersion of country spreads relative to today (Mauro, Sussman, and Yafeh 2002). In this late nineteenth/early twentieth-century setting, a currency drop following an SS would thus tend to be starkly revealing about other costs of keeping the peg. As discussed subsequently, these costs include the need of accumulating large gold reserves yielding low returns (relative to other domestic investment opportunities) as well as forgoing the role of the exchange rate as a shock absorber. Further, decisions to abandon the peg or not to join gold may also be revealing of the existence of institutional frictions that mitigated the political cost of currency crises in some countries relative to others.[3]

To shed light on this relationship between SSs and currency drops, a central ingredient of the analysis is consideration given to the various factors that drive exchange rate behavior. Based on a simple model of nominal exchange rate determination and using probit panel regressions, the paper looks at what distinguishes successful peggers to those that experienced currency crashes. As will be seen, this approach helps discern country-specific from common international factors driving the relationship between SSs and currency drops.

The remainder of the paper is structured as follows. Section 7.2 documents SS patterns across the sixteen countries comprising the study. Section 7.3 looks at the distinct exchange rate responses to capital account shocks in the context of a simple exchange rate model and probit regressions. Section 7.4 zooms in on country-specific monetary and fiscal stances as well as financial structures that may account for the different outcomes to common international shocks. Section 7.5 concludes with a summary of the main findings and a discussion of some salient implications.

7.2 Patterns of Sudden Stops

A first issue in the definition of an SS is whether capital inflows are measured in net or gross terms. The recent literature overwhelmingly uses the net concept—the capital or financial account balance—for which data is available at higher (usually quarterly) frequencies.[4] However, this choice is not inconsequential. For instance, straightforward balance of payments

---

3. For instance, if interest groups linked to export sectors have a higher leverage on domestic policymaking in some of these countries, this would tend to mitigate such political costs and foster the politics of a weaker currency, delaying or even thwarting efforts to join or rejoin gold. There is considerable controversy in the literature, however, on whether such export lobbies systematically succeeded in shaping currency policies in the various countries during the late nineteenth and early twentieth centuries. See, for instance, Fritsch (1988) on the case of Brazil. Using a broader cross-country sample, Meissner (2005) finds no significant econometric evidence that inflationist agricultural interests played a significant role in the timing of gold pegs.

4. See, e.g., Dornbush, Goldfajn, and Valdez (1995), Edwards (2004), and Calvo, Izquierdo and Mejia (2004). One study that considers both gross and net flow variables is Caballero, Cowan, and Kearns (2004).

(BOP) accounting indicates that an exogenous improvement in a country's net barter terms of trade automatically translates in a drop in net capital inflows, all else being constant. In an economic sense, this is very different from a situation in which the country faces a sudden drop in the supply of external financing, to which the current account has to improve (unless the country possesses sufficient international reserves to smoothe the capital account shock) through a devaluation or a contraction of income. In principle, the concept of sudden stops should refer to the latter and not to the former type of event.

In what follows, lack of data on *total* gross inflows for every country requires a somewhat eclectic approach. Specifically, I combine a measure of net capital inflows to countries for which the series is available, with information collected by Stone (1999) on *gross* portfolio calls on the London market. Since Britain was then by far the largest capital-exporting nation (in terms of both absolute annual flows and ratios to GNP) and the most important lending center for the overwhelming majority of emerging markets, one would expect such a portfolio call measure to closely trace fluctuations in gross flows to most countries. As shown below, information about SS patterns derived from these different sources yields a broadly consistent story.

Figure 7.1 plots net capital flows into capital importing countries for which data is available.[5] As expected from countries with very different commodity specializations and under distinct policy regimes, there is clearly some diversity in the time pattern of capital inflows. Yet, what is arguably much more striking about figure 7.1 is the apparent synchronicity of the downswings across most countries. Three main episodes stand out in particular: the downswing of 1874–80, that of the early 1890s, and the shorter downturn of 1906–08. Clearly, not all countries were equally affected and, in a couple of occasions, foreign capital flows moved in opposite directions in a subset of them (e.g., Norway and Russia in the early 1890s). But overall, such downswings hit the overwhelming majority of countries at about the same time and were often abrupt. This suggests that pre-WWI SSs did display some time bunching similar to that observed over the past decade and a half (Calvo, Izquierdo, and Mejia 2004).

As discussed further, it is also striking that SSs hit countries with widely disparate per capita income levels and distinct monetary regimes. They struck countries as poor as Brazil (with an estimated per capita GDP of US$811 in 1913 on constant 1990 purchasing power parity [PPP] basis) and as rich as the United States (with a per capital GDP of US$5,301 on the same PPP basis in 1913).[6] Some of them remained on

---

5. Net capital import data are not available for Greece and Portugal throughout the period, or for Argentina and Russia before the 1880s and Brazil after 1900. See appendix 2 for information on the respective data sources.

6. International data on per capita GDP on a constant PPP basis since 1870 is available in Maddison (2003).

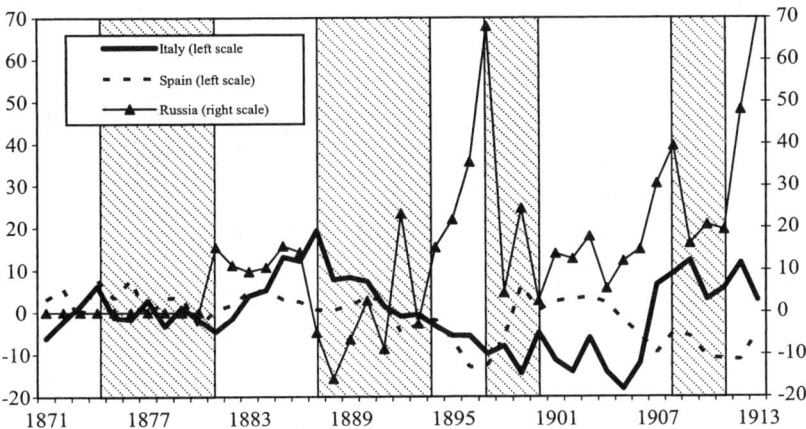

Fig. 7.1 Net foreign capital inflows (million pounds)
Source: See appendix B.

gold throughout, such as Scandinavia and North America since the late 1870s, whereas others experimented with distinct monetary regimes such as bimetallism, temporary gold-pegs, and plain inconvertible paper money; none of these regimes could prevent a capital importer from being hit by an SS.[7]

These inferences are broadly corroborated by available data on gross

---

7. It may well be that more flexible exchange rates helped insulate domestic output from the SS, as argued in Edwards (2004) based on post-1970 evidence. A comparison between output responses to SSs across the different exchange rate regimes in the prewar era is not discussed here, however, and constitutes an interesting topic for future research.

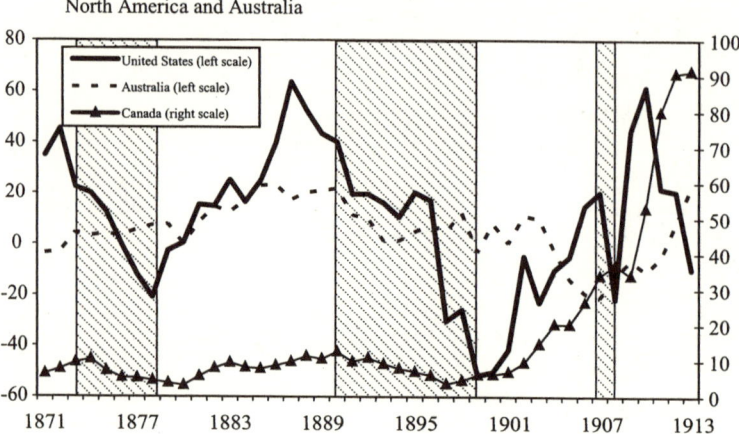

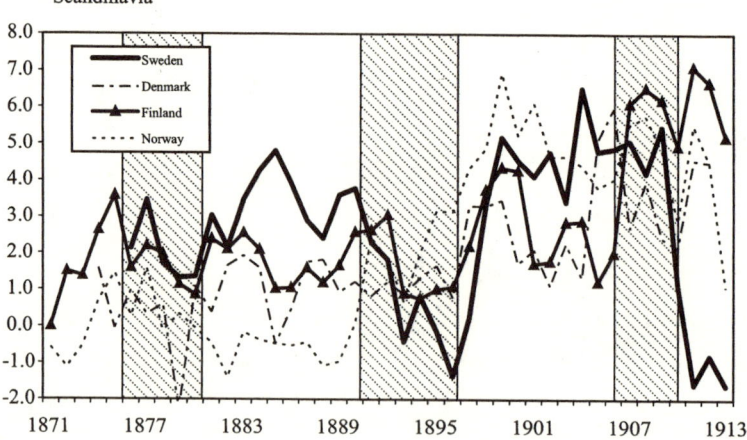

Fig. 7.1 (cont.)

flows based on portfolio calls on the London market. While the latter seem to account for a smaller share of total gross foreign investment in southern Europe and Russia—where French and German capital flows were prominent—bond flotations in London were by far the most important external financing instrument to capital-importing countries in Latin America and the Anglo-Saxon New World. Starting with Argentina, this gross inflow indicator portrays a very similar pattern as that of the net inflow data, both highlighting the major SS of 1889–1994, which was closely associated with a famed financial crisis that brought down the Baring's investment bank (see della Paolera and Taylor 2001 for a detailed account). Similarly, sharp downturns in gross portfolio inflows around the same period are also ob-

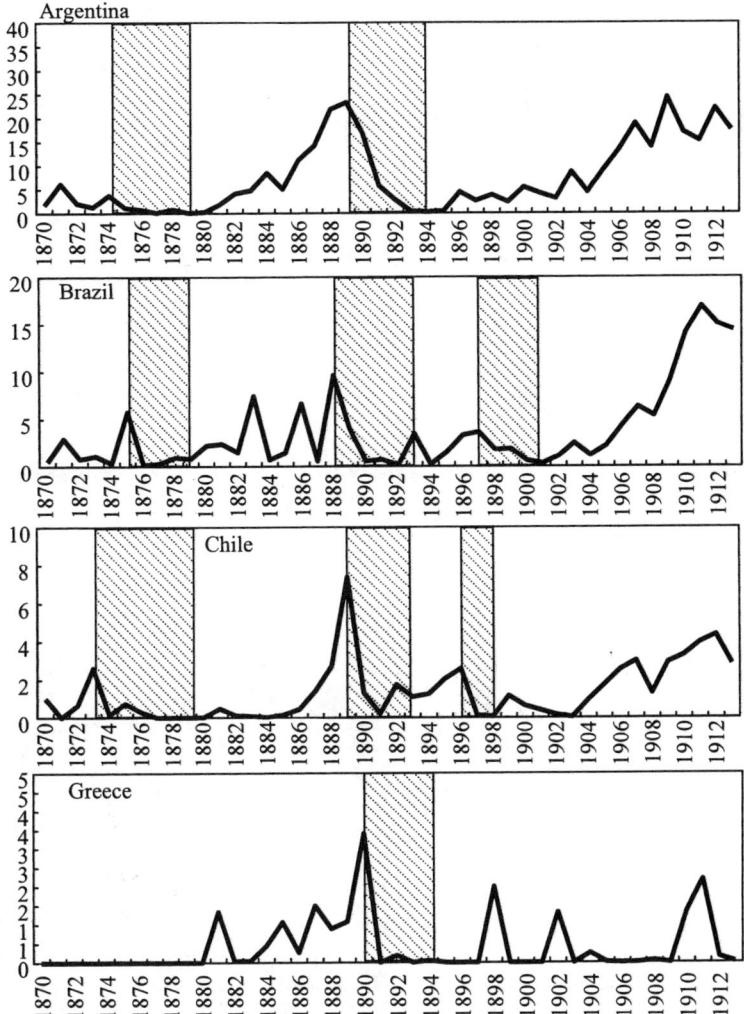

Fig. 7.2 Gross portfolio calls on London (million pounds)
Source: Stone (1999).

served for Brazil and Chile which, in addition, experienced another SS earlier in the 1870s and later in the 1890s—in the Brazilian case leading to a sovereign debt rescheduling in 1898 and in the Chilean case in an abandonment of the gold peg.[8] With regard to southern Europe, and bearing in

8. For further specifics, see Franco (1990) and Llona Rodriguez (2000).

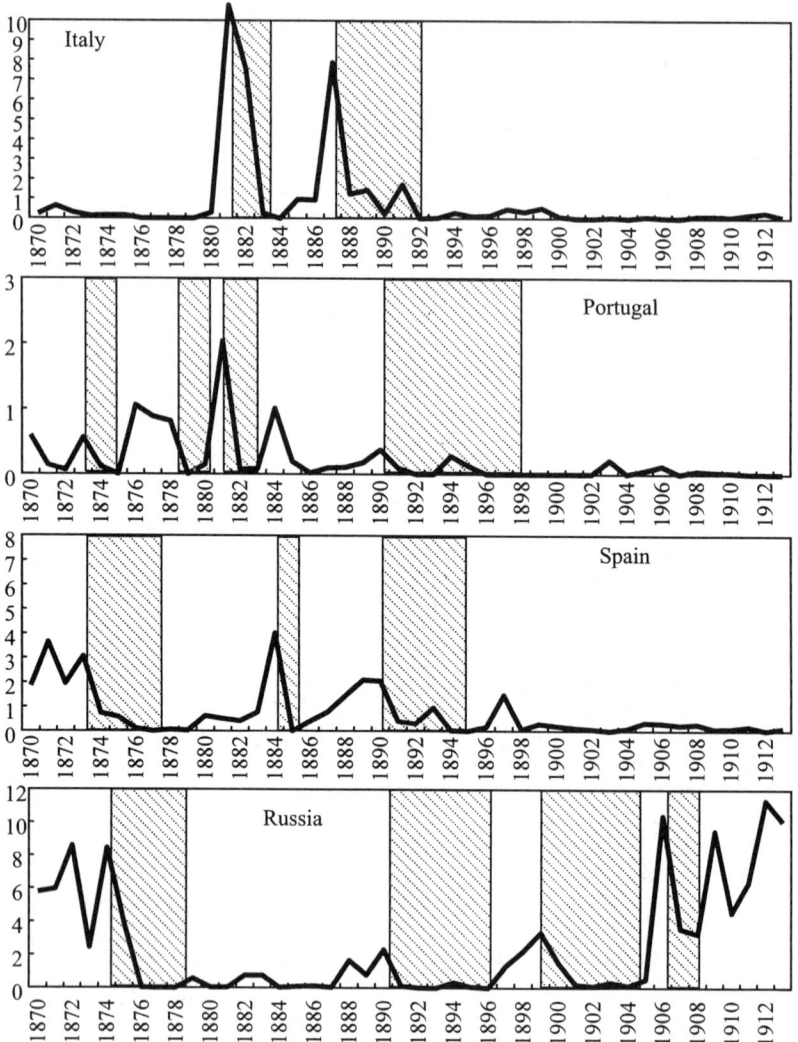

Fig. 7.2 (cont.)

mind the above-mentioned caveat about the limitations of gross flow data for these countries, figure 7.2 also fleshes out a similar timing of SSs in much of southern Europe.[9]

9. In the case of Russia, discrepancies in the timing of the SSs between the gross and the net capital inflow series plotted in figure 7.1 suggest that capital flows into Russia other than those associated with London floatations were important and may have dominated in the aggregate. Another possibility is that, since the net capital flow series was derived from the difference between the current account balance and changes in international reserves, it may reflect large inaccuracies in the measurement of these two variables. See appendix 2.

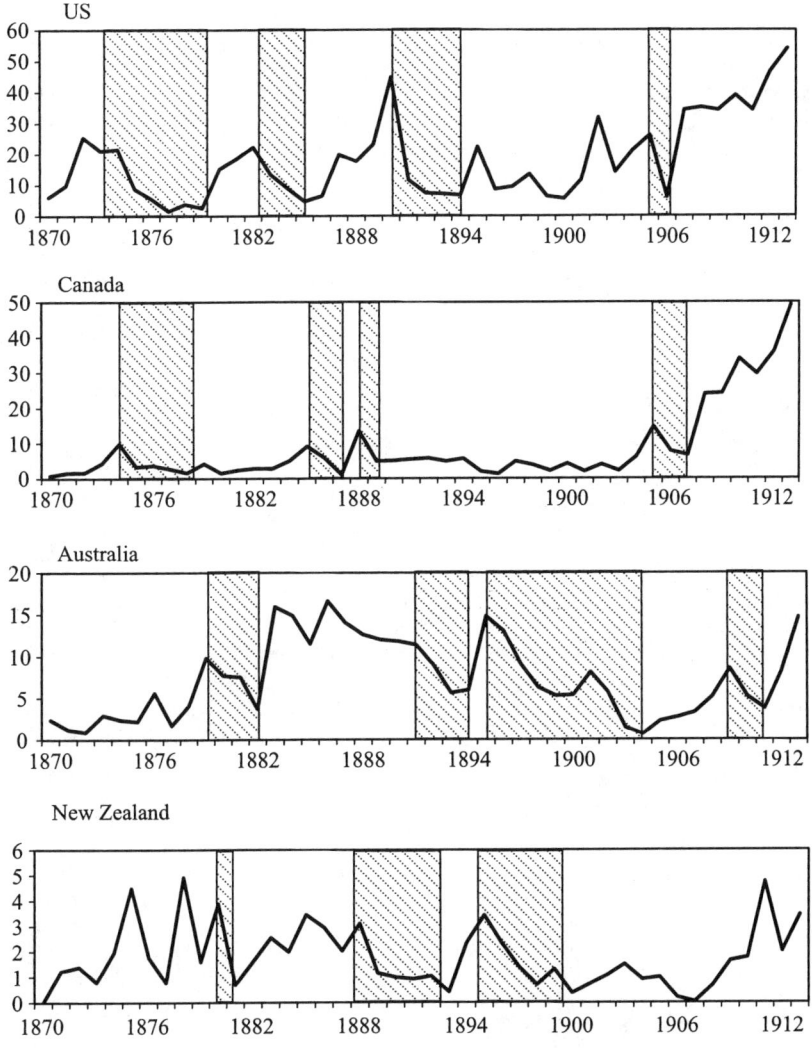

Fig. 7.2 (cont.)

Turning to the Anglo-Saxon capital importers, the gross capital inflows indicator further highlights the fact that these countries also experienced SSs, despite operating a more rules-based monetary regime, displaying greater fiscal discipline overall and remaining pegged to gold throughout.[10]

10. The United States formally adopted the gold standard in 1879 but policy actions and statements, as well as a gradual appreciation of the currency under way since the mid-1870s toward the antebellum parity, signaled to market participants that gold resumption was imminent.

Table 7.1   **The chronology of sudden stops and currency drops**

	Sudden stops		Currency drops
	NKF definition	GKF definition	
Argentina		1874–1879	1876–1878
	1889–1895	1889–1895	1885–1886
			1889–1891
Brazil	1876–1880	1875–1879	1876–1880
	1888–1894	1888–1894	1890–1898
Chile	1875–1881	1873–1880	1876–1880
			1885–1886
	1891–1893	1889–1893	1891–1894
	1897–1899	1896–1898	1898–1899
	1907–1908	1907–1908	1907–1908
Greece		1890–1897	1886–1887
		1911–1913	1891–1895
Italy	1874–1881	1881–1884	
	1887–1899	1887–1892	1892–1894
Portugal		1873–1875	
		1878–1880	
		1884–1886	
		1890–1893	1891–1898
			1907–1908
Spain	1876–1880	1873–1877	
		1884–1885	
	1890–1896	1889–1895	1892–1894
	1904–1907		1897–1901
Russia		1874–1878	1876–1878
	1885–1888	1890–1992	1891–1892
	1897–1900	1899–1901	
		1906–1908	
Australia	1890–1894	1886–1893	None
	1898–1899	1895–1899	None
	1903–1907		None
Canada	1875–1880	1874–1880	None
	1890–1897	1888–1896	None
Denmark	1875–1880		None
	1884–1886		None
	1906–1908		None
Finland	1875–1880		None
	1883–1885		None
	1892–1894		None
	1899–1901		None
New Zealand		1888–1893	None
		1895–1900	None
		1903–1907	None
Norway	1899–1902		None
Sweden	1890–1893		None
	1909–1913		None
United States	1872–1878	1872–1877	None
	1887–1994	1890–1894	None
	1907–1908	1905–1906	None
	1910–1913		None

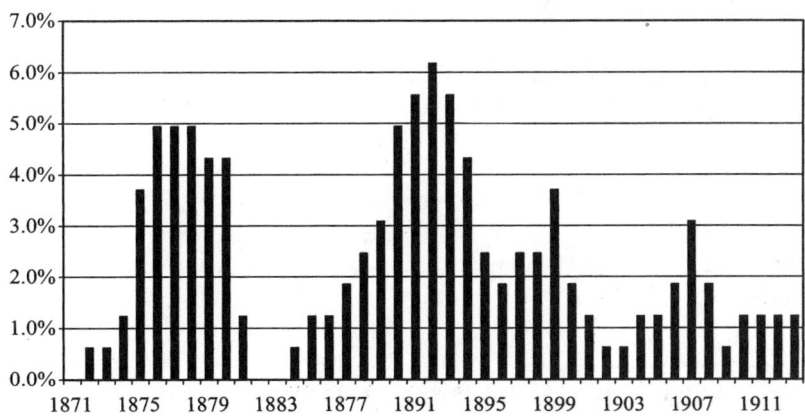

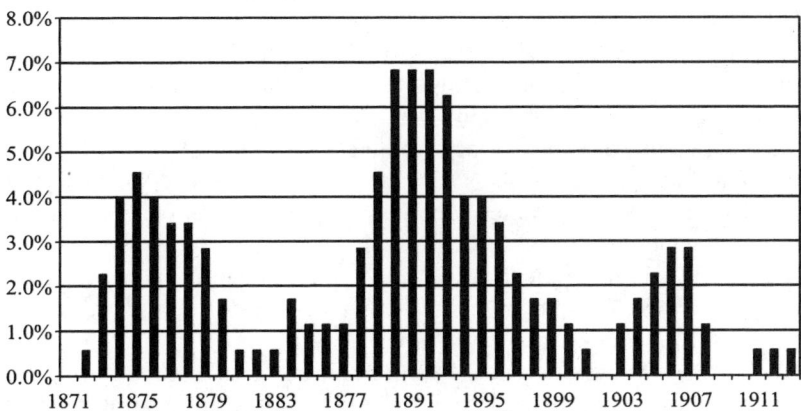

Fig. 7.3 Frequency distribution of sudden stops
Source: See appendix A.

Similar considerations apply to all four Scandinavian countries (Denmark, Finland, Norway, and Sweden).[11]

Further corroboration of the evidence that SSs usually bunch over time is provided in the more formal classification of these episodes, reported in

---

11. Fiscal discipline was especially remarkable among Scandinavian countries where public debt averaged between 15 to 20 percent of GDP during 1870–1913. On this front, Scandinavian countries were only superseded by the United States, for which the public debt to GDP ratio averaged 9 percent and fell to a low around 3 percent by the eve of World War I. This contrasts with much higher period averages for countries such as Argentina, Chile, Greece, Italy, Portugal, and Spain. The implications of these differences in fiscal performances are examined later.

table 7.1. Although figures 7.1 and 7.2 make reasonably clear what episodes should qualify as SSs, table 7.1 summarizes this information, using the following working definition: an SS is defined as a drop (from peak to trough) of no less than two standard deviations of the deviations of respective series from a linear trend, and/or any drop that exceeds 3 percent of GDP over a period shorter than four years. Timing the beginning of SS as the year where capital inflows (measured in million pounds) peak, then SS is then said to end in the year when capital flows start rising relative to trend without falling back to its lowest level (also relative to trend) within a four-year window. On this basis, it is clear that both the net and the gross flow data yield a broadly similar picture about the timing of SSs in most countries.

Using the same definition, figure 7.3 plots the incidence of SSs over time, normalized by total SS observations in the sample. Both the net and gross measures clearly indicate that SSs bunched around the mid-1870s, the early 1890s, in 1906–1907, and also, albeit to a lesser extent, in the late 1890s, according to the net flow measure. Such a pattern is consistent with that of the net capital outflow series from Britain, France, and Germany—the three main capital exporting countries of the late nineteenth century, which is plotted in the upper panel of figure 7.4. At the same time, the lower panel of the same figure also show that *all* SSs were, in turn, preceded with a one or two year lag by a hike in core central banks' discount rate. This has striking parallels with the more contemporary evidence on the adverse impact of advanced countries' monetary tightening on capital exports to emerging markets (Calvo, Leiderman, and Reinhart 1993; Fernandez-Arias 1996), indicating that exogenous monetary shocks were key drivers or "push factors" in capital flow reversals during the prewar period as well.

To further gauge the macroeconomic importance of SSs during the period, figure 7.5 plots the usual metric of scaling net capital flows by GDP.[12] As one would expect in an era of free capital mobility and extensive international borrowing, figure 7.5 shows that fluctuations in net foreign capital inflows (NFKIs) were sizeable. Absolute annual deviations from a balanced capital account indicate that the macroeconomic impact was largest in Argentina (where such deviations averaged 10 percent of GDP over the entire period), then followed by Canada (7.5 percent of GDP), Finland (6.25 percent of GDP), and Australia (5.5 percent). Pooling together all SS events in countries for which the respective NFKI series is available, the peak-to-trough median drop in inflows amounted to 5.1 percent of GDP. This is of a very similar magnitude as the trough-to-peak magnitude of current account reversals identified by Calvo, Izquierdo, and

---

12. It would be useful, as suggested by Calvo, Izquierdo, and Mejia (2004), to use tradable sector output as a scaling factor if such information were available.

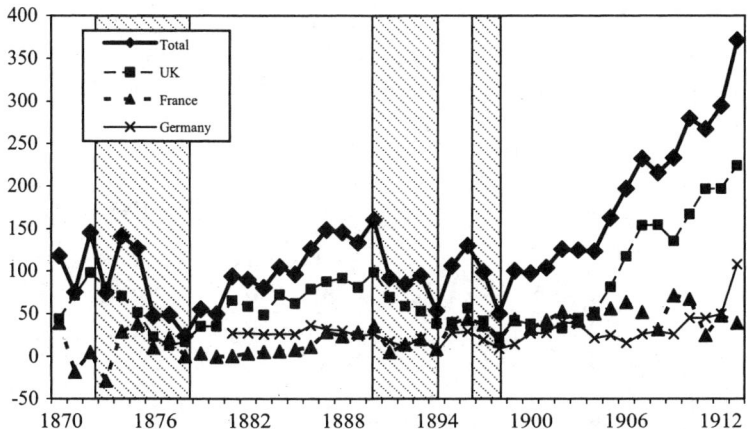

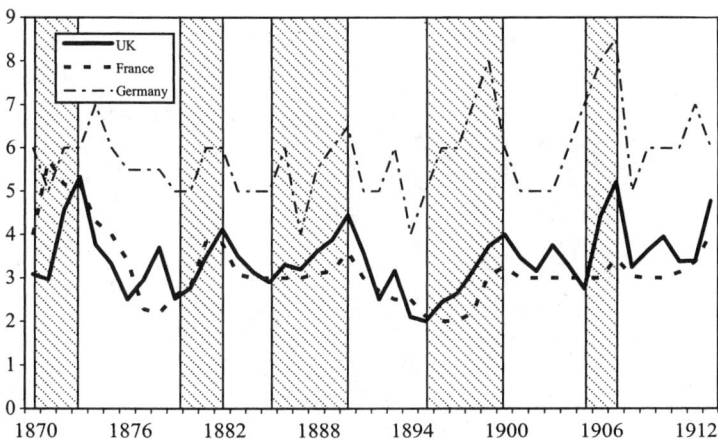

Fig. 7.4 Core countries: Net capital exports and interest rates (%)
Source: See appendix B.

Mejia 2004, appendix table 3) in the more recent vintage of SSs (4.9 percent). Further, as with its contemporary counterpart, pre-WWI SSs tended to be persistent: measured in terms of mean or median, and regardless of whether one uses the available gross or net capital inflow measures, the average duration of SSs is four years over the whole panel.

Also consistent with the prima facie evidence presented earlier, standard tests on mean differences in the magnitude of SSs (again measured from peak to trough) show no statistically significant difference between fixers

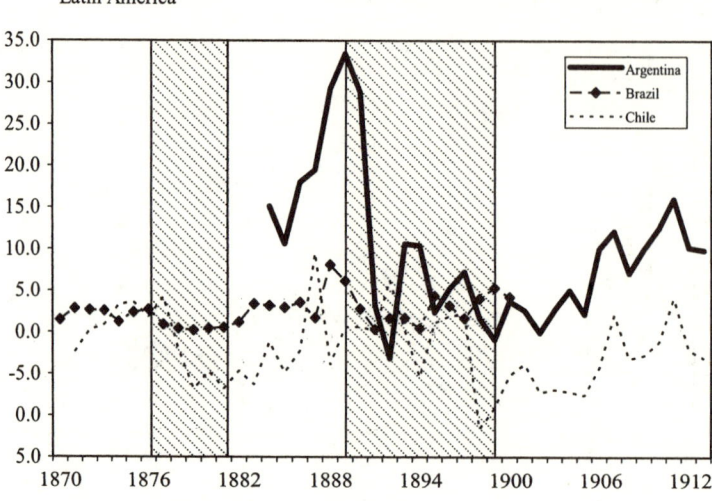

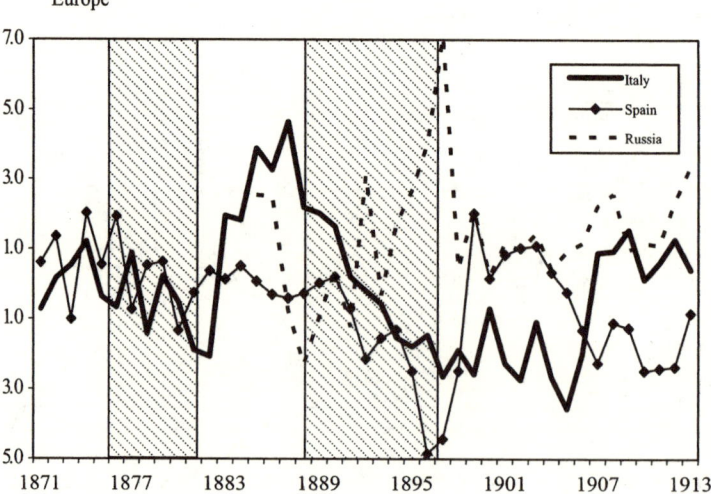

Fig. 7.5 Ratio of net capital inflows to GDP (%)
Source: See Appendix A.

and floaters.[13] No less interestingly, there is no statistically significant difference in the duration of SSs between the gold and nongold country groups: SSs are reasonably persistent in both cases, with mean durations

13. The mean for the floating (off-gold) group was 10.3 percent, whereas that for gold-peggers was 5.6, but this large mean difference results from one large outlier—Argentina in 1890–92. Dropping the latter, the mean for the off-gold group falls to 5.1 percent. Partly because of that outlier intragroup standard errors are large, at 12 and 3 percent. Not surpris-

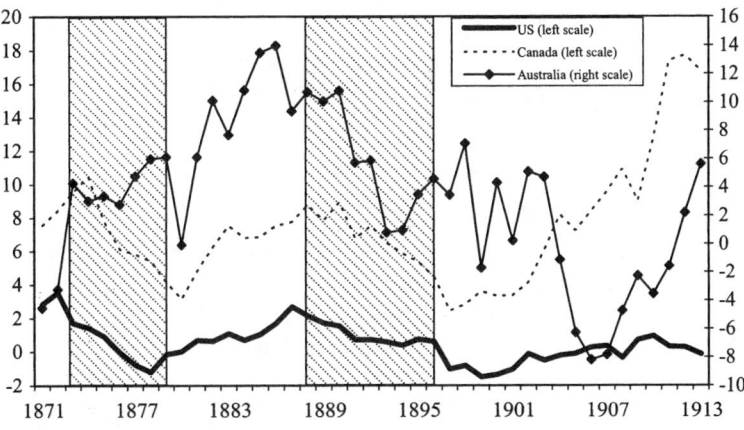

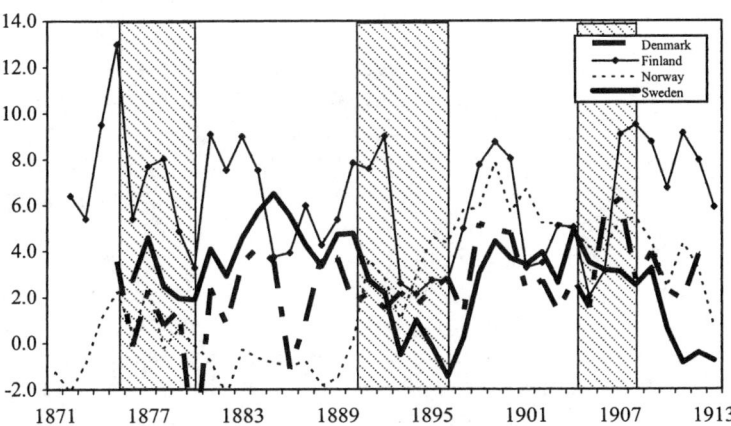

Fig. 7.5 (cont.)

of 3.7 and 4.2 years, respectively, and again with no statistically significant difference in means.[14] This evidence calls into question the view that fixing the exchange rate was a sine qua non condition for attracting and/or stabilizing capital inflows. The fact that SSs also struck other gold-pegged countries with histories of sensible macropolicies suggests that neither the mon-

---

ingly in light of such high variance, the respective z-statistic for differences in mean is 0.99, thus well below the 10 and 5 percent critical threshold levels of 1.64 and 1.96.

14. The respective z-statistic is 0.69. In computing this statistic, the duration of SSs in Greece, Portugal, and New Zealand (countries for which a NFKI series is unavoidable), as well as in Argentina and Russia prior to 1880, was measured using gross capital inflow series as reported in table 7.1.

etary regime nor the fiscal policy stance can insulate a country from a capital account shock, an evidence with striking parallels to that amassed by Calvo, Izquierdo, and Mejia (2004) who find that neither differences in monetary regimes nor country-specific fiscal behavior can explain the incidence of SSs in their sample of 32 countries over 1990–2001.

7.3 Capital Flows and Currency Crashes

Despite the relatively rapid international spread of the gold standard from the 1870s and the fact that all core industrial nations consistently pegged their currencies to gold until the eve of World War I, many capital-importing countries continued to operate distinct monetary regimes during the period. In several cases what one observes is either a repeated switch between a gold peg and a floating regime (for instance, in Argentina, Brazil, Chile, and Greece),[15] or countries that postponed gold standard membership until a later stage, once substantial gold reserves were accumulated, facilitating uninterrupted adherence to the peg, as in India, Japan, and Russia from 1897 (see Catão and Solomou 2005 for specifics). Within this wide spectrum of country-specific monetary arrangements, there were also those that never pegged to gold (China and Spain), one (Portugal) that adopted gold much earlier (1856) but also left earlier (1891), and countries such as Austria-Hungary and Italy, which were formally off-gold during much of the period but saw their national monetary authorities successfully shadowing the gold parity, which yielded relative exchange rate stability as a result.

This diversity is apparent in the behavior of the various spot exchange rates. While Anglo-Saxon and Scandinavian currencies were kept within the narrow gold points and thus were virtually flat, figure 7.6 shows how widely the price of the domestic currency relative to gold varied elsewhere.[16] Among Latin American economies, not only did exchange rates display long-term depreciating trends, but they also witnessed large discrete downward adjustments in the mid-to-late 1870s and between the late 1880s and early 1890s, which, in the case of Chile, was compounded a further downward adjustment in 1906–1908. Several European countries un-

---

15. Argentina stabilized its exchange rate and held on to a gold peg in 1870–75, 1883–84, and 1899–1913. Brazil was on gold for a few months between 1888 and 1889 and from 1906 to 1913. Chile was on a bimetallic standard through 1879 and on gold between 1895 and 1898. Greece was on gold in 1885 and then in 1910–13.

16. Since the British pound was then the main international currency that adhered to a preestablished gold content throughout, all the nominal indices are measured relative to the pound. To facilitate comparison, all series are rebased to 1900 = 100. Defining the exchange rate as the foreign price of domestic currency implies that a rise in the index corresponds to an appreciation of the respective national currency relative to the pound. The experience of countries that pegged their currencies to silver, such as Mexico, China, India and Japan, is not reviewed here but is examined in Catão and Solomou (2005).

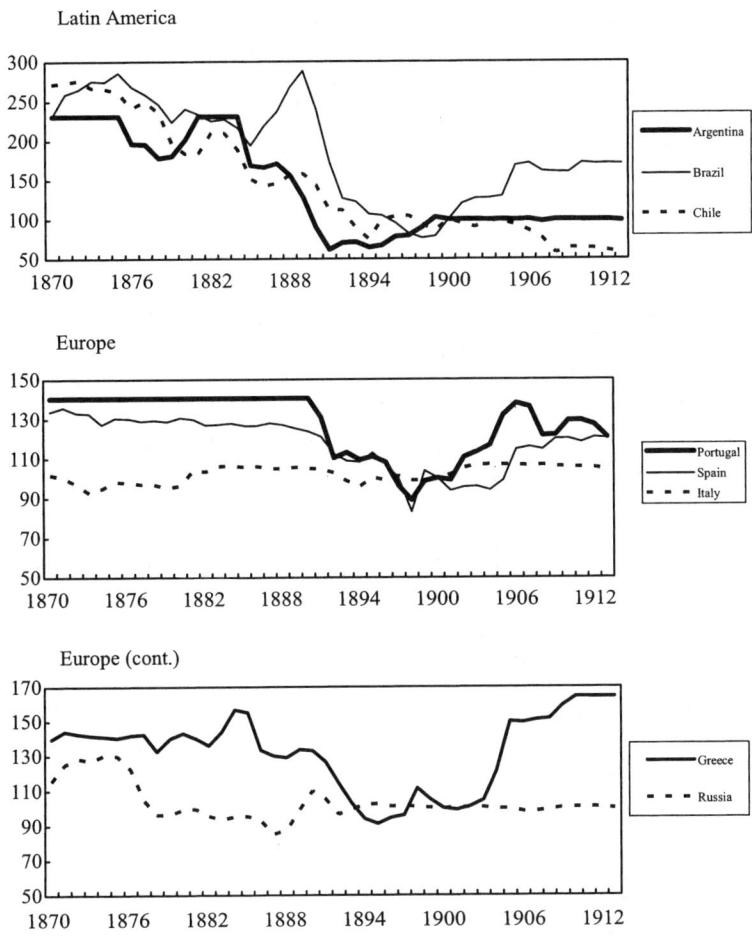

Fig. 7.6 Nominal exchange rates in currency crisis countries (pound sterling/domestic currency, 1900 = 100)

der paper money regimes also witnessed nontrivial fluctuations in the gold parity of their currencies. Although relatively mild in Italy, sizeable depreciations are observed in Russia in 1875–78, Greece in both 1884–86 and 1890–95, Spain in 1890–93 and 1895–98, and Portugal in 1891–94. Comparing the timing of these various exchange rate drops or currency crash episodes with the timing of SSs in each countries reported in table 7.1, it is clear that currency crashes were either concomitant with SSs or followed the latter with a one- or two-year lag.

Three main questions then arise. First, to what extent are SSs driving these exchange rates relative to other factors? Second, is the causality running from SS to exchange rates or from exchange rate risk (driven by, say, contagion, or by factors that may be common to several countries, such as primary commodity terms of trade) to SSs? Third, why did some large capital exporters who also faced SSs managed to stick to the peg when others did not?

To shed light on these questions, one needs to consider the role of other potential explanatory variables in explaining the exchange rate as well as the possibility of reverse causality running from exchange rate changes to SSs. A useful starting point is a model of exchange rate determination that nests the various possible relationships—for instance, along the lines of the monetary models of the 1970s and 1980s, which allow for short-run price rigidity (see Frankel [1979] and Frankel and Rose [1995] for a synthesis). Appendix 1 shows how these earlier models can be straightforwardly extended to allow for a time-varying country risk premium—which becomes a function of the supply of international liquidity—and for violations to long-run PPP; instead, the real equilibrium exchange is let to be driven by terms of trade trends, long-run productivity differentials between home and abroad, and the country's fiscal position—consistent with a wide class of open-economy macromodels (see, for example, Edwards 1989, and Obstfeld and Rogoff 1996 for surveys).

The formal derivation of the model laid out in appendix 1 yields the following reduced-form equation for expected parity deviations of the spot exchange rate:

$$(1) \quad E(e_t - \bar{e}_t) = \mu - (\Delta m_t - \rho \Delta y_t) + \alpha(tot - \overline{tot})_{t-1} + \varphi(\bar{y}_{pc} - \bar{y}^*_{pc})_{t-1} - \eta\left(\frac{g}{t} - \frac{\bar{g}}{\bar{t}}\right)_{t-1} + \frac{1}{\theta}(i_t - i^*_t) + \upsilon(\Delta b^* + \psi \Delta res)_t$$

where tot stands for the respective country's net barter terms of trade; m is domestic money supply, and y for domestic real output; y_{pc} and y^*_{pc} stand for domestic and foreign per capita GDP respectively, and i and i^* for the short-term domestic and foreign interest rates; g/t is the ratio of public expenditure to revenues;[17] Δb^* stands for changes in the supply of foreign capital flows and Δres for changes in the ratio of international reserves to paper currency in circulation. All variables are expressed in natural logarithms, with the bar subscript denoting the respective long-run or trend equilibrium levels.

Recalling that the exchange rate is defined here as the foreign price of the domestic currency, equation (1) states that the expectation of a currency drop will be higher as: (a) money supply grows relative to output; (b) terms of trade deteriorate relative to trend; (c) domestic productivity declines rel-

---

17. The ratio of fiscal expenditure (G) to revenues (T) is used instead of the more conventional of scaling $G-T$ by GDP for two reasons. One is that it is always a nonnegative number, which allows working with a log specification. Second, it circumvents the problem of the well-known deficiencies of GDP data for many of the sample countries during the period.

Table 7.2 Probit estimates of the determinants of currency crises

	(1)	(2)	(3)	(4)	(5)	(6)	(7)	(8)
$\Delta \ln(M2)_t$	3.37 (4.76)***	2.50 (5.10)***	2.56 (5.29)***	2.52 (5.83)***	4.29 (6.02)***	4.30 (6.32)***	5.28 (5.75)***	2.45 (7.27)***
$\Delta \ln(Yreal)_t$	−2.47 (−1.44)	−1.45 (−1.12)	−1.49 (−1.10)					
$TOTgap_{t-1}$	0.58 (0.13)	0.17 (0.31)						
$\ln(yreal/n)_{t-1} - \ln(yreal*/n*)_{t-1}$	−0.15 (−3.18)**	−0.11 (−4.12)***	−0.12 (−4.09)***	−0.12 (−4.28)***	−0.16 (−2.97)***	−0.15 (−2.83)***	−0.16 (−2.77)***	−0.10 (−3.65)***
$G/T\ gap_{t-1}$	1.34 (3.49)***	1.22 (4.03)***	1.22 (4.06)***	1.40 (4.19)***	1.74 (3.14)***	1.64 (3.93)***	1.88 (4.39)***	1.42 (5.13)***
$\Delta \ln(World\ K\ flows)_t$	−1.32	−1.00	−0.77	−1.05	−1.37	−1.3	−1.57	−1.02
$\Delta(res/M0)_t$	−6.11 (−6.11)***	−5.06 (−5.06)***	−5.05 (−5.05)***	−5.01 (−5.01)***	−4.35 (−4.35)***	−4.52 (−4.52)***	−4.45 (−4.45)***	−5.32 (−5.32)***
	−2.34 (−4.73)***	−1.34 (−4.25)***	1.13 (−4.97)***	−1.39 (−6.74)***	−1.94 (−5.24)***	−1.82 (−4.93)***	−2.17 (−5.16)***	−1.37 (−6.86)***
$(i - i^*)_{t-1}$	0.01 (1.55)							
i^*_{t-1}		0.24 (1.82)*	0.18 (1.71)*	0.26 (1.73)*	0.25 (1.49)	0.42 (1.59)	0.38 (1.69)*	0.25 (1.84)*
$\ln(Ext.Debt/X)_{t-1}$					−0.17 (−0.92)			
$\ln(Total\ Debt/Y)_{t-1}$						−0.08 (−0.42)		
$\ln(Ext.Debt/Total\ Debt)_{t-1}$							0.11 (0.27)	
$\ln(X/M)_{t-1}$								0.27 (0.81)
No. of observations	471	559	559	599	468	497	467	559
Pseudo R^2	0.49	0.47	0.46	0.46	0.49	0.49	0.48	0.46
Percent correctly classified ($p = 0.5$)	97.88	97.67	97.5	97.67	98.08	98.19	98.07	97.85
Percent correctly classified ($p = 0.2$)	96.60	96.60	96.42	96.06	96.37	97.78	96.36	96.06

Notes: Coefficients refer to marginal effects at mean. Robust z-statistics in parentheses.
***Significant at the 1 percent level.
**Significant at the 5 percent level.
*Significant at the 10 percent level.

ative to foreign countries' productivity; (d) the domestic interest rate drops relative to its foreign counterpart; (e) the foreign supply of capital flows shifts down without the offsetting of rising reserves relative to the currency in circulation. It is straightforward to see in equation (1) that once the terms $1/\theta(i_t - i_t^*)$ and $\psi \Delta res$ are shifted to the left-hand side, we have an index analogous to that of currency pressure popularized in the work of Eichengreen, Rose, and Wyplosz (1996).[18]

On the basis of that model, table 7.2 reports probit estimates of the determinants of a currency crash. In the absence of a commonly agreed-on criterion in the literature,[19] a currency crash is defined here as an exchange rate depreciation greater than at least one standard deviation of the annual percentage change of the nominal exchange rate (relative to sterling) over the entire 1870–1913 period, provided that this depreciation is not fully reversed within a three-year window. Thus defined, our sample comprises nineteen such events, which are listed in table 7.1.[20] As in Frankel and Rose (1996) and many others, the dependent variable is set to one in the first year of a crisis episode and zero otherwise; the observations pertaining to the period during which the crisis is ongoing (i.e., as the exchange continues to slide) are dropped, since they are part of the same crisis already counted once. Specifics on measurement and data sources are provided in appendix 2.

The first column of table 7.2 shows the estimates for the baseline model. Nearly all variables yield the sign predicted by theory and most of them are statistically significant at 1 percent. The exceptions are the terms of trade (TOT) gap (i.e., deviations of actual TOT from a log linear trend),[21] output growth ($\Delta \ln[Yreal]$), and the interest rate differential ($i - i^*$). While the coefficient on output growth yields the correct sign, the interest rate differential indicator (which enters the regression with a one-year lag to mitigate endogeneity) actually yields the opposite sign as that predicted by the model—not an uncommon result in many empirical estimates of the uncovered interest parity condition (cf. Frankel and Rose 1995). Overall, the

---

18. An advantage of the present formulation is that the weights of the interest rate differential and the reserve terms can be econometrically determined through the estimation of $1/\theta$ and ψ, rather than being imposed so as to equalize the respective unconditional variances as in Eichengreen, Rose, and Wyzplosz (1996).

19. See Frankel and Rose (1996), Kaminsky and Reinhart (1999), and Milesi-Ferretti and Razin (2000) for the different classification criteria employed in this literature. One feature of the pre-1914 period which helps minimize disagreements on crisis dates is the more stable price environment and the absence of policy devices such as crawling pegs, which make it harder to separate currency crashes from noncrisis related discrete exchange rate adjustments in response to high inflation bouts.

20. Due to lack of data on relevant covariates for Russia in the 1870s, the effective number of crisis events is reduced to eighteen in the probit estimation.

21. Throughout this paper, detrending is made on a linear or log-linear time trend given evidence of trend stationarity from augmented Dickey-Fuller tests. These are available from the author upon request.

coefficients show M2 growth to be a main determinant of currency crashes, with a 1 percentage point increase in the former increasing the likelihood of the latter by 3.4 percentage points. The other main drivers of currency risk are the ratio of government expenditure to revenues, measured relative to its log linear trend (G/T gap), and changes in the supply of foreign capital (World K flows), and net of changes in the reserve-to-currency ratio ("res/Mo"). The relative productivity differential is an additional significant predictor with the expected negative sign, though the estimated elasticity is a lot lower. Overall, the model fits the data reasonably well: a pseudo R-squared of about 0.5 is high relative to that found in similar studies and, more importantly, the model correctly predicts some 98 percent of events once a cutting-off point for refinancing a crash is of a predicted likelihood of greater than 50 percent. Employing a lower cut-off point of 20 percent reduces the prediction rate slightly, but even then the model correctly predicts 11 of the 18 crash events in the sample.

The two ensuing columns in table 7.2 fine tune the previous results by dropping the TOT (which had been statistically insignificant throughout), and replacing the interest rate differential variable by the foreign interest rate i^*, which is proxied by the Bank of England discount rate—the closest proxy to a short-run, risk-free rate during the period. Consistent with the prima facie evidence presented in section 7.2, higher foreign interest rates in the year prior to the currency crash had a positive and significant impact on the crash at 10 percent. This corroborates the finding that monetary tightening in the core is a significant driver of currency pressures in capital-importing countries. As also expected, given the evidence presented in section 7.2, the inclusion of i^* lowers the estimated coefficients on both the capital flow and reserve variables. This is consistent with the results of Eichengreen (1992) who, using Granger-causality tests in a vector auto-regressive (VAR) model of the U.K. economy, finds that changes in the Bank of England discount rate Granger-caused capital exports. To the extent that the two other core European central banks in France and Germany tended to follow the Bank of England lead around cyclical turning points—as illustrated in the bottom panel of figure 7.4 and also noted in Lindert (1969)—the effect of hikes in the U.K. discount rate on net capital importing countries was thereby reinforced.

Finally, columns (5) to (8) check the robustness of the foregoing regressions to the inclusion of three other potentially important variables. One is the ratio of external public debt to exports—a usual yardstick of country solvency in the sovereign debt literature. The respective estimate is statistically insignificant and has the opposite sign as that postulated by theory. A similar finding obtains for the ratio of total public debt to GDP (column [6]). The following column reports results for the inclusion of the ratio of external to total public debt—an indicator of the extent of currency mismatches in countries' balance sheets that is commonly associated with the concept of original sin, that is, a country's incapacity to issue debt denominated in its own currency. This idea, much popularized by Eichengreen and Hausman (1999) and further elaborated in many subsequent contributions, suggests that the greater the mismatch the higher the risk of sovereign defaults and currency crashes; so, one would expect the coefficient on this variable to be positively signed. Column (7) of table 7.2 shows that while the respective point estimate is indeed positive it is small and not statistically different from zero. So, there is no evidence that currency denomination of the country's debt is a significant determinant of currency risk. Finally, the last column of table 7.2 gauges whether trade imbalances (defined as the log of export to import values) add any significant additional explanatory power to the regressions and help predict crash events. The estimates show that this does not seem the case, likely reflecting the fact that such imbalances are already captured by the other covariates in the model.

In short, the preceding econometric results indicate that fluctuations in international capital flows are significant determinants of currency risk. Accordingly, it is not surprising that SSs tend to be associated with currency crashes. Further, since SSs are often preceded by interest rate hikes in core countries, it thus appears that financial developments exogenous to net capital-importing countries are at the root of currency crises. Yet, this econometric evidence also indicates that this is not the full story: since not all countries respond similarly to those external shocks, country-specific factors do matter—notably the growth of money supply, the cyclicality of fiscal balances, and variations in the international reserve coverage of the domestic money stock. Each of these factors is discussed next.

7.4 Domestic Financial Imperfections and Procyclical Behavior

Two broad generalizations seem to command wide consensus in the historical literature on the financial markets of countries that witnessed currency crashes before WWI.[22] One is that their financial markets were much shallower relative not only to the so-called European core (Britain, France, and Germany) but also relative to other emerging economies of the Anglo-Saxon world and Scandinavia. This can be unambiguously gauged by a broad range of financial development indicators such as the number of banks and bank capitalization per capita, or the ratios of broad money and domestic bank credit to GDP. In addition, banks in these economies were deemed to be poorly regulated, and information about borrowers' credit history usually hard to obtain. While these imperfections were in some

---

22. See, for instance, della Paolera and Taylor (2001) on Argentina; Goldsmith (1986), Haber (1997), and Trimer (2000) on Brazil; Llona Rodriguez (1990) on Chile; Fratianni and Spinelli (1997, children. 3) on Italy.

cases mitigated by stringent controls restricting entry (as in Brazil, for instance), such regulations appear to have greatly hindered efficiency—a point stressed in Cameron's classic comparative study on early banking (Cameron 1972). To these structural features, one added ingredient in those economies was the existence of multiple issuing banks and the lack of a national bank holding the monopoly of fiduciary money and soundly performing the role of a lender of last resort.[23]

Some salient implications follow. First, shallower domestic bond markets and limited access to bank credit by firms imply that borrowers were typically credit constrained; hence, any outward shift in the external supply of funds would tend to automatically translate into faster credit growth. Second, once information about creditworthiness is hard to obtain, lending becomes more responsive to current collateral values pledged against loans. Third, illiquid domestic markets would make it harder for banks to borrow from the local private sector or sell to others the illiquid (but otherwise solvent) items in their portfolios during monetary crunches, exacerbating the risk of fire sales and bank runs in the wake of SSs and business cycle downturns. Finally, the decentralization of note issuing rights combined with deficient regulations and governments that were dependent on banks to finance large deficits tended to exacerbate moral hazard and thus undermine the practice of backing of outstanding bank notes with safe levels of specie holdings. This was likely to heighten the depressing effects of money creation on the exchange rate.

Figure 7.7 shows that countries that experienced currency crashes were indeed the ones that embarked upon rapid monetary expansion, which far exceeded domestic income during cyclical upswings. Argentina is the most notable case, with the ratio of M2 to GDP rising from 28 to 65 percent of GDP between 1880–89, even though real GDP itself nearly tripled during the same period. The flip side of such a rapid monetary expansion was a sharp drop in the international reserve coverage of the domestic currency in the later stages of the boom, which left banks highly vulnerable to a run when capital flows dried up in the run-up to the Baring's crisis of 1890–91. Likewise in Brazil, where monetary expansion had been previously curbed by stringent regulations on bank entry, the sudden stop of 1890–91 was preceded by unprecedented monetary expansion resulting from the sudden lift of controls on bank issuance (the Encilhamento), leading to a twofold increase in the broad money to GDP ratio between 1889 and 1891.

Data for other countries is likewise suggestive of the significant role of

---

23. This seems to have been an important distinguishing feature of successful financial development in northern Europe. On the less well known but interesting experience of countries other than the European core and the United States, see the key role played by the Nationalbanken in Denmark, the Nederlandsche Bank in the Netherlands, and the Riksbank in Sweden which are discussed in Hansen (1991), Jonker (1997), and Jonung (1984), respectively.

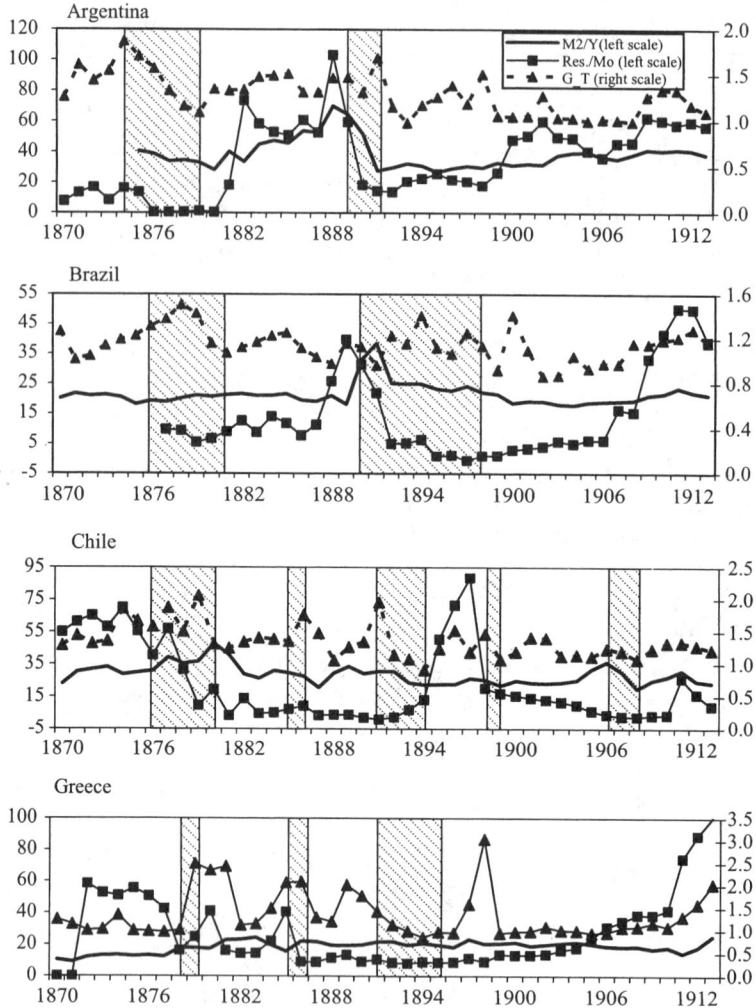

Fig. 7.7 Monetary and fiscal indicators in currency crisis countries (currency crashes in shaded areas)
Source: See appendix A.

monetary expansion in brewing currency crashes during SSs. In Chile, Portugal, and to a lesser degree Spain, the elasticity of broad money to income rose well above unity in the two to three years prior to the 1890–1892 crashes. This contrasts with the smoother behavior of money supply in other countries, which either managed to stick to the peg or that experienced a relatively mild depreciation, such as Italy and Russia in the early 1890s. Figure 7.8 corroborates the view that a high procyclicality of domestic bank credit, as proxied by the M2 multiplier, contributed to cur-

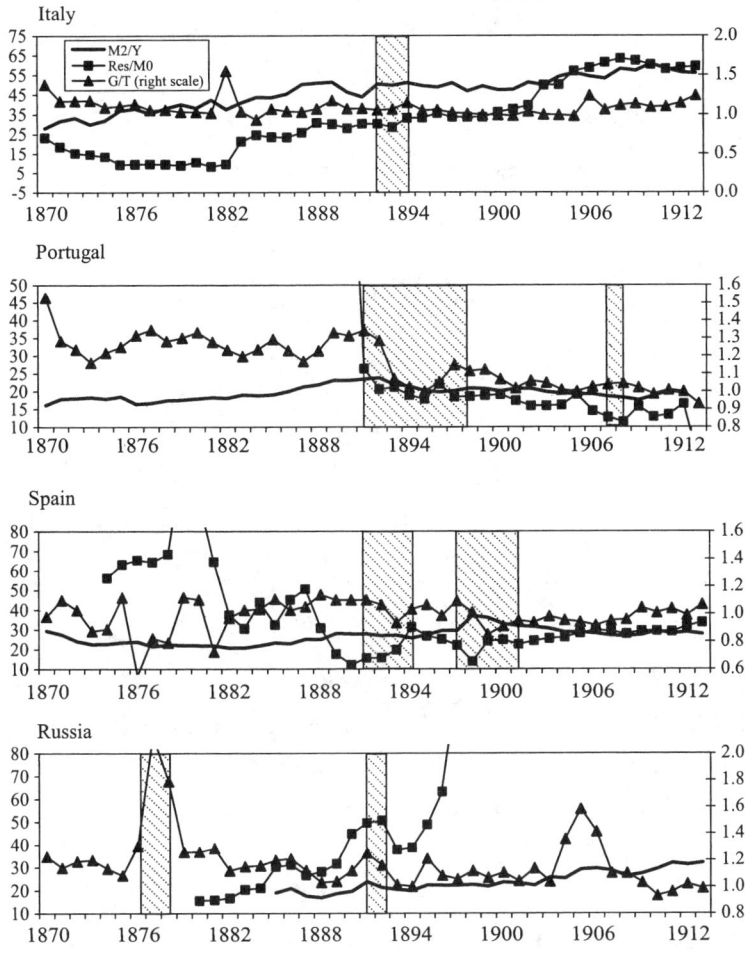

Fig. 7.7 (cont.)

rency crashes:[24] as with the ratio of broad money to GDP, the money multiplier is noticeably more cyclical in crisis countries than in noncrisis ones.

The other distinguishing feature of countries in which SSs were followed by currency crashes pertains to fiscal behavior. Gauged by either the ratio

---

24. The focus on M2 rather than on domestic bank credit is motivated by two considerations. One is that theoretical models of nominal exchange rate determination (including the one outlined in appendix 1) commonly postulate a direct link between monetary expansion and the exchange rate. The other is the lack of data on domestic bank credit for several countries. An alternative indicator considered was to derive aggregate bank credit by the difference between broad money and international reserves of the consolidated banking system, using available data on the two variables. This yields a very similar pattern as that of M2.

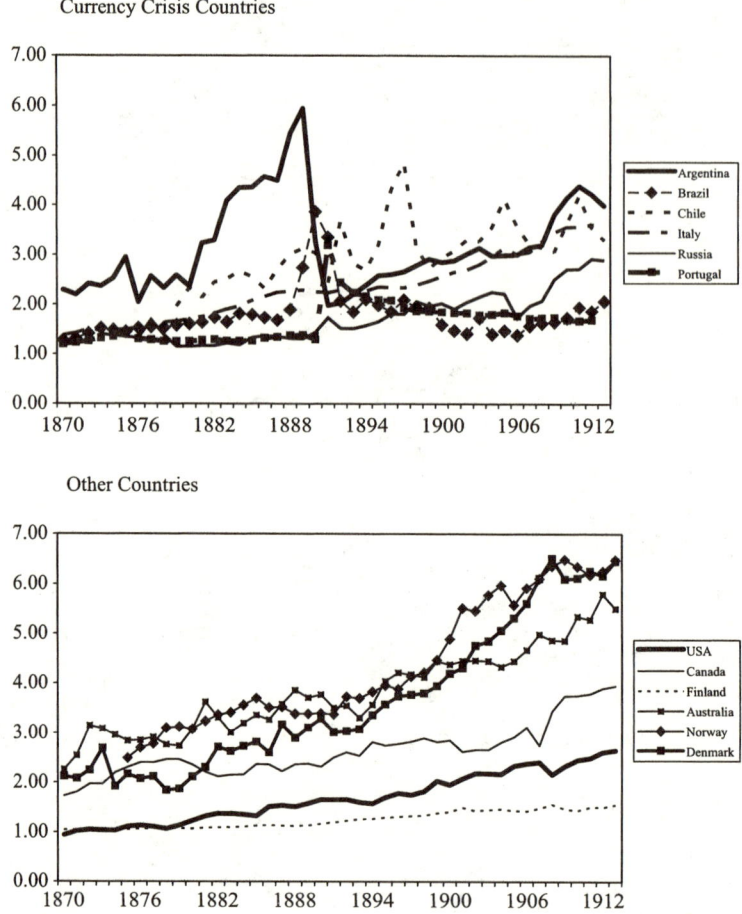

Fig. 7.8   The M2 multiplier
Source: See appendix B.

of public expenditure to revenues or the ratio of public debt to GDP averaged by country over the entire period, it appears that fiscal behavior was generally more relaxed in currency-crash countries. The upper panel of figure 7.9 shows that three of the countries that experienced the worst currency crashes in the pre-WWI era (Argentina, Chile, Greece) were precisely the ones with the highest average ratios of public expenditures to revenues, whereas countries that managed to stick to gold throughout tended to display lower ratios. Clearly there were exceptions, such as Brazil (which experienced large currency drops without strikingly high fiscal imbalances on average), and the association is certainly not one-to-one for all countries (Australia and New Zealand being two other obvious outliers).

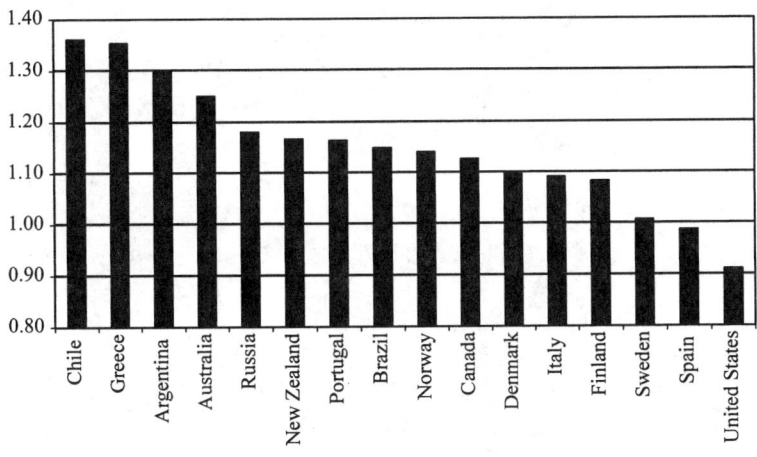

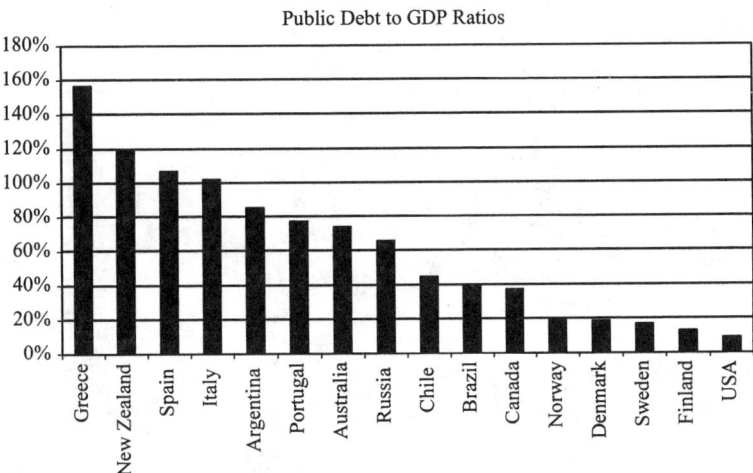

Fig. 7.9 Fiscal indicators: Country averages over 1870–1913
Source: See appendix B.

Overall, the ratio of expenditure to revenues in the currency-crash group was around 10 percent higher than that for the noncrash group. The lower panel of figure 7.9 further reinforces this point: not only did six of the eight noncrash countries lie at the bottom of the debt to GDP distribution over the entire period, but also the average ratio of debt to GDP was twice as high among crash countries (85 percent) than among noncrash ones (38 percent).

No less importantly, such period averages obscure the fact that fiscal behavior was more procyclical in currency-crash countries. While there are

Table 7.3 OLS regression measures of fiscal procyclicality

	Output gap$_t$ (1)	Output gap$_{t-1}$ (2)	Kinflow gap$_t$ (3)	Kinflow gap$_{t-1}$ (4)
Argentina	1.138	1.127	0.037	0.089
	(4.46)***	(4.33)***	(0.60)	(1.15)
Brazil	0.943	0.903	0.157	0.155
	(6.11)***	(5.28)***	(2.85)***	(2.69)***
Chile	1.938	1.807	0.323	0.248
	(3.55)***	(3.21)***	(4.02)***	(2.76)***
Greece	2.284	1.930	0.050	−0.029
	(5.17)***	(3.97)***	(0.39)	(−0.22)
Italy	−0.039	−0.118	0.057	0.073
	(−0.14)	(−0.41)	(1.67)*	(2.08)**
Portugal	1.097	1.090	0.030	0.047
	(9.49)***	(8.54)***	(0.82)	(1.26)
Spain	0.130	0.316	−0.018	−0.018
	(0.62)	(1.54)	(−0.71)	(−0.69)
Russia	0.369	1.023	−0.110	−0.110
	(0.98)	(3.06)***	(−1.96)**	(−1.89)*
Australia	1.249	1.299	−0.093	−0.060
	(6.68)***	(7.30)***	(−1.47)	(−0.91)
Canada	1.026	1.236	0.177	0.169
	(4.21)***	(5.30)**	(2.72)*	(2.51)**
Denmark	0.669	0.933	0.044	0.113
	(1.16)	(1.60)	(0.84)	(2.18)
Finland	0.235	0.227	0.054	0.039
	(0.27)	(0.27)	(0.59)***	(0.41)
New Zealand	1.571	1.687	0.052	−0.006
	(5.34)***	(6.60)***	(0.75)	(−0.09)
Norway	0.005	1.035	−0.241	−0.230
	(0.01)	(1.48)***	(−5.63)***	(−5.10)***
Sweden	−0.043	0.098	0.040	0.034
	(−0.18)	(0.39)	(1.64)*	(1.33)
United States	−0.644	−0.853	−0.027	−0.050
	(−1.80)*	(−2.54)**	(−0.62)	(−1.17)
Mean				
Crash countries	0.982	1.010	0.066	0.057
Noncrash countries	0.508	0.708	0.001	0.001

Note: Dependent variable: Real government expenditure cycle.
***Significant at the 1 percent level.
**Significant at the 5 percent level.
*Significant at the 10 percent level.

different metrics to gauge the degree of fiscal procyclicality across countries (see, e.g., Bayoumi and Eichengreen 1995; Gavin and Perrotti 1997), one measure that mitigates endogeneity issues is that of regressing the cyclical component of real government expenditure on the cyclical component of real GDP and/or foreign capital inflows. As discussed in Kaminsky, Reinhart, and Végh (2004), this is because tax revenues are themselves a direct function of the real GDP cycle—a relationship that is bound to be strong among emerging markets, where tax bases are highly procyclical. This is especially the case during the period under consideration, where import and consumption taxes account for over 80 to 90 percent of tax revenues in most countries comprising our sample (see Bordo and Cortes-Conde 2001 as well as Sokoloff and Zolt's paper in this volume).

The first column of table 7.3 reports the estimated coefficients of a regression of the cyclical component of real government expenditure (as before, measured as deviations from a log linear trend) on the cyclical components of real GDP (also defined as deviations from a log linear trend). While such a regression potentially suffers from well-known biases associated with the use of generated regressors (a downward bias) as well as the potential omission of other explanatory variables (a bias that can go either direction), it is still valuable for the task at hand, which is to highlight cross-country differences in fiscal reactions to the business cycle. The bivariate regression estimates in the first column of table 7.3 suggest that fiscal policy was highly procyclical in the countries that experienced the worst currency crashes during the period (Argentina, Brazil, Chile, Greece, and Portugal). While there is evidence that the fiscal stance was also procyclical in three other countries that stuck to gold throughout (Australia, Canada, and New Zealand), averages over crash and noncrash groups indicate that the former was about twice more procyclical than the latter (0.98 versus 0.51). A similar inference about the higher fiscal procyclicality of the first group of countries also follows when using the one-year lagged instead of current real GDP cycle, as reported in the second column of table 7.3.

In assessing the procyclicality of fiscal policies during this period of free capital mobility, it is also of interest to gauge the extent to which real government expenditure responded to the international cycle in capital flows. More procyclical policy stances should be also associated with a higher elasticity of spending to the supply of external finance. As before, I proxy the latter as the total net capital outflows from the three main capital exports of the late nineteenth century (Britain, France, and Germany), all denominated in sterling (or gold) and measured in terms of deviations from a log-linear trend. The results are reported in columns (3) and (4) in table 7.3. Regardless of whether one uses current or one-year lagged values of the explanatory variable, the group averages reported at the bottom of the table suggest that crash countries tended to display a more responsive fiscal behavior to the push of international capital flows. While the estimated coefficients are not as large nor as statistically significant as before, these regressions again suggest that currency crash countries tended to be more procyclical overall.

Such procyclicality tended to heighten currency risk by inducing looming fiscal imbalances during cyclical upswings. This can be seen in figure

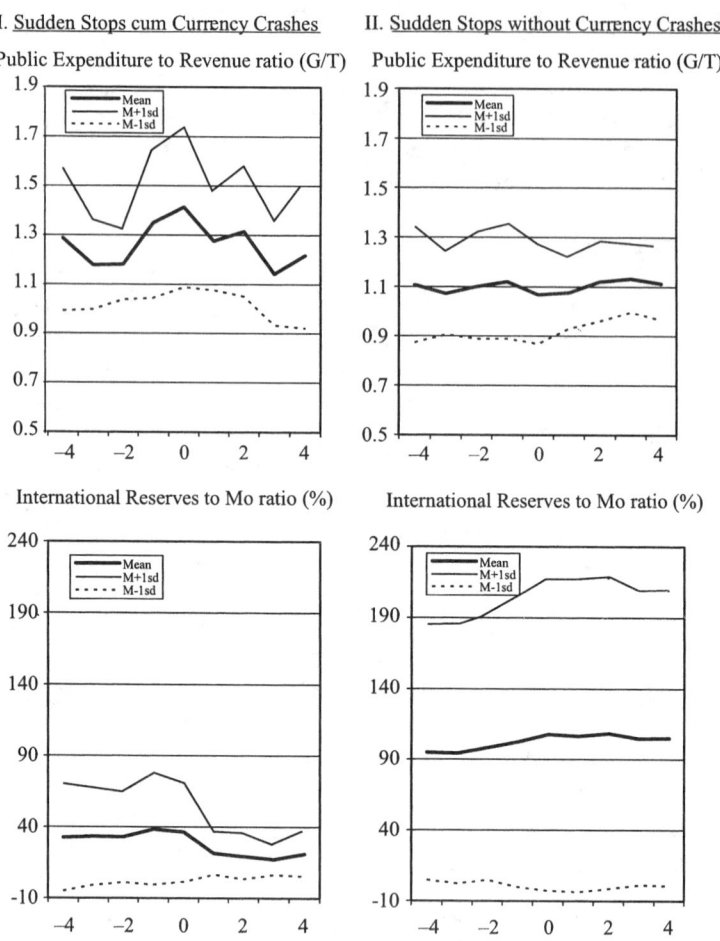

Fig. 7.10 Fiscal and reserve positions around sudden stops
Source: See appendix A.

7.10, which contrasts the fiscal behavior (again measured in terms of the ratio of public expenditure to revenues) between currency crash events and noncrash ones. Noting that $t = 0$ corresponds to the year immediately before the downturn in capital inflows, it is apparent that fiscal imbalances rose and were much larger, on average, in the subset of countries in which SSs were accompanied by currency crashes. Likewise, the during- and post-shock contrast is no less striking: while the fiscal stance appears to be notably contractionary and hence procyclical among crash countries, noncrash countries engaged in a mildly expansionary—and hence, countercyclical—fiscal behavior. By imparting a further impulse to absorption during cyclical upswings, fiscal procyclicality tends to exacerbate imbalances, which in turn will call for a real exchange rate depreciation and/or a sufficiently large drop in absorption. Given the more limited reserve coverage of the monetary base in those countries as well as the presence of nontrivial nominal rigidities even in that earlier period (as discussed in Catão and Solomou 2005), the nominal exchange rate would emerge as a natural candidate to shoulder the burden of the adjustment. Thus, one would thus expect this fiscal expenditure-to-revenue imbalance (G/T gap) to be a significant predictor of currency crashes, and this is precisely what the probit results of table 7.2 show to be the case.

Finally, there is the channel related to the coverage of paper money in circulation (Mo) with hard-currency reserves (mostly gold at the time). The bottom panel of figure 7.10 indicates that, on average, noncrash countries entered the capital inflow cycle with twice as high reserve coverage than their crash-prone counterparts. While the standard error bands are strikingly large for noncrash (reflecting the ratios of bank gold reserves to paper money above 200 percent in the large gold-producing economies of Australia and New Zealand), median comparisons that play down such outliers tell a similar story (25 percent versus 56 percent in the year just before the SS). So, the noncrash countries clearly counted on a much larger reserve cushion against the capital account outflow. In addition, the behavior of the reserve coverage ratio during SS events in the noncrash countries suggest that their respective monetary authorities appear to have played more closely by the so-called "rules of the game": absolute reserve losses were accompanied by a roughly concomitant drop in currency in circulation, so that the reserve coverage ratio of Mo remained about stable on average. By contrast, countries with initially lower reserve coverages, and that also missed the opportunity of the boom in capital inflows to prop up their coverage ratios, saw the latter drop by nearly one half (from 38 to 17 percent) between the year preceding the capital inflow peak ($t = -1$) and the second year after the SS ($t = 3$). To the extent that reserve accumulation is inversely related to fiscal and domestic credit expansion as in first-generation currency crisis models a la Krugman (1979), the procyclicality of the domestic fiscal and monetary stances shows up again as a key culprit.

7.5 Conclusion

As with the post-Bretton Woods era, international capital flows in the pre-World War I world were anything but smooth. This paper has shown that all net capital-importing countries for which the relevant annual data exist experienced sporadic but often large and abrupt reversals in foreign capital inflows. These sudden stops hit countries with widely disparate per capita GDPs, levels of financial development, and exchange rate regimes, as well as countries with low and high gold reserve coverages of their domestic currencies. This suggests that none of these factors can prevent a capital importer from being hit by a large capital account reversal—even though deeper financial markets, exchange rate flexibility, and high levels of precautionary reserves should help mitigate the associated side-effects on economic activity, as the recent literature on SSs indicates (Calvo, Izquierdo, and Mejia 2004; Edwards 2004).

The dataset assembled in this paper also allows us to highlight other striking parallels between SSs now and SSs then. One is the large magnitude of drops in net foreign capital inflows during these episodes, with a median of about 5 percent of GDP (measured peak-to-trough) on a various cross-country basis. The other is the relatively lengthy period it takes for capital inflows to fully recover (four years on average). A third similarity is the time bunching of such events. We have seen earlier that sudden stops bunched around the early to mid-1870s, the early 1890s, and 1906–1907. As is well known from the late nineteenth century and early twentieth century economic historiography, all these subperiods were characterized by financial crises and a higher incidence of sovereign defaults (Kindleberger 1978; Lindert and Morton 1989; Kelly 1998; Eichengreen 2003). While in principle these SSs could have been triggered by country-specific factors in capital importers (such as the U.S. railways bankruptcies of 1873 or Argentina's mortgage bond repayment crisis of early 1890), which then irradiated to other emerging markets, possibly via mechanisms highlighted in the international financial contagion literature (Eichengreen, Rose, and Wyzploz 1996), the evidence provided in this paper points to one common factor in all these events—preceding hikes in central bank discount rates in the core capital exporting countries, typically with a one- to two-year lag. Once again, this has striking parallels with the post-1970 evidence, in that changes in U.S. interest rates appear to be a main driver of capital flows to developing countries (Calvo, Leiderman and Reinhart 1993; Fernandez-Arias 1996) and of shifts in overall emerging market risk (Catão and Kapur 2006). This obviously does not imply that domestic or regional factors (including wars and other political conflicts) have been unimportant during the period in some countries, but simply that monetary tightening in the core of the world economy played a significant role, sometimes reinforcing those country-specific effects.

Against this background, a main question addressed in this chapter is why such SSs led to currency crashes in some countries but not in others. Consistent with the evidence just discussed, the probit regression results of section 7.3 indicate that SSs in capital exports from core countries to the rest of the world, together with lagged international interest rates, did raise the likelihood of currency crises generally, all else constant. But the same regressions also show that country-specific factors related to money growth, reserve coverage of domestic currency, and fiscal imbalances played a no less significant role. Countries where money growth was highly responsive to cyclical conditions and grew well in excess of aggregate income and international reserves during upswings were the ones in which the worst currency drops followed. Unsurprisingly, these are countries for which historical literature finds the strongest evidence of a prevalence of loose regulations on banks of issues, institutional obstacles to loan recovery, and high credit elasticity to cyclically sensitive collateral values. Conversely, economies with seemingly better-regulated banks and deeper financial markets typically had a smoother broad money multiplier and also managed to maintain a consistently higher backing of domestic bank liabilities or paper money with international (gold) reserves; they were the ones that managed to overcome the SS shock while sticking to their currency pegs. This evidence brings back to the fore Whale's (1937) and Ford's (1962) earlier views—grounded on a much slimmer data set and limited econometric apparatus—on the importance of the domestic financial imperfections in propagating capital account shocks and accounting for cross-country differences in macroeconomic adjustment during the classic gold standard era.

Similar considerations apply to the role of fiscal policy in affecting currency risk. Countries where fiscal deficits were higher on average and real government spending more procyclical typically witnessed a juxtaposition of SSs and currency drops. The channels through which fiscal imbalances affect the exchange rate are well known from currency crisis literature and, as discussed previously, the probit results are broadly consistent with the prediction of first-generation currency crisis models (Krugman 1979) about the role of fiscal deficits in currency crashes: countries where government expenditures typically grew significantly faster than the tax base during upswings experienced reserve losses and large real exchange rate appreciations that called for sharp correction when capital inflow suddenly dried up. As discussed in Catão and Solomou (2005), nonnegligible nominal rigidities, combined with limits to the necessary decline in absorption and a low elasticity of capital flows to domestic interest rates, implied that the nominal exchange rate would bear much of the burden of adjustment in these cases.

What implications or lessons can be drawn from this evidence? A first lesson is that history often repeats itself, and that the documented patterns of SSs over the past two decades have some striking similarities with those in the past. Thus, they can be regarded as stylized facts about SSs more broadly, and indicate that high capital mobility need not automatically translate into stabilizing cross-border financial flows and greater consumption smoothing. Then, as now, individual countries' capacity to reap benefits and minimize the risk of capital mobility to degenerate into disruptive currency crashes and competitive devaluations lie most critically on fiscal and monetary management and the resilience of countries' domestic banking systems. Those in which the monetary transmission mechanism and fiscal policies are more procyclical—be it because of the kind of voracity effects discussed in Tornell and Lane (1998) or other political imperfections (Végh and Talvi 2000) that discourage both public saving and reserve accumulation during good times—are more likely to face greater exchange rate instability and disruptive currency drops as a result.

Two other salient policy implications should also be briefly mentioned. Time bunching in SSs implies that country insurance type of contracts are likely to be more effective, if not only feasible, when drawn between net capital exporters and net capital importing countries, since the latter tend to be badly hit at about the same time, thus limiting the scope for risk sharing among them. Last but not least, to the extent that SSs take place in the wake of monetary tightening in core advanced countries, this suggests that a high international reserve coverage of domestic monetary liabilities when world interest rates start creeping up is an important ingredient in minimizing the risk of abrupt and often contractionary currency drops. This underscores the importance of precautionary reserve accumulation at the earlier upswing stage of the international investment cycle.

Appendix A

A Benchmark Model of Nominal Exchange Rate Determination

This appendix briefly outlines a benchmark model of nominal exchange rate determination that guides the empirical analysis of currency crashes provided in the main text. The model assumes that prices are sticky in the short run and that risk-adjusted uncovered interest parity (UIP) holds, so that the expected change in the log of spot exchange rate (Δe^e_{t+1}) responds to the nominal short-term interest rate differential between onshore (i_t) and offshore (i_t^*) asset markets, adjusted by a time-varying country risk premium (δ_t):

$$(2) \qquad \Delta e^e_{t+1} = i_t^* - i_t + \gamma \delta_t$$

where positive values for Δe_{t+1} denote an appreciation between t and $t + 1$, and $0 < \gamma \leq 1$.[25] Thus, when the country risk premium rises (or equivalently, foreign finance supply drops), and in the absence of arbitrage failures, a fixed exchange ($\Delta e_{t+1} = 0$) can only be expected if the short-run domestic interest rate rises relative to the foreign rate. Otherwise, the exchange rate would overshoot at time t, depreciating beyond its long-run

---

25. The risk premium is thus being broadly defined to include bank failure or any confiscation risk that affects the representative asset holding.

equilibrium (to be defined in the following); only in this case could the home country investor be compensated for the rise in country risk by an expected currency appreciation between t and $t + 1$. By the same asset market equilibrium condition, the only way that a rise in the foreign interest rate would be compatible with a fixed exchange rate under unchanged domestic interest rates is if the country risk premium drops: only in this case would equilibrium be maintained without entailing an expected exchange rate change.

In the long run, the exchange rate has to converge to a level that is consistent with good market equilibrium. As is standard in the literature, sticky prices imply that the adjustment process is expected to eliminate differences between actual and equilibrium exchange rate levels gradually:

$$(3) \qquad \Delta e^e_{t+1} = -\theta(e_t - \bar{e}_t) + E(\Delta \bar{e})_t.$$

where $\bar{e}$ is the log of the long-run equilibrium nominal exchange rate, and θ characterizes the speed of adjustment, $0 < \theta < 1$. This implied adjustment dynamics can be shown to be consistent with rational expectations under sticky prices (Frankel 1979).

Combining equations (2) and (3) yields:

$$(4) \qquad e_t = \bar{e}_t + \frac{1}{\theta}[(i_t - i^*_t) - E(\Delta \bar{e}_t)] - \frac{\gamma}{\theta}\delta_t.$$

Equation (4) postulates that at any given point in time the nominal exchange rate moves along its long-run equilibrium level, adjusted upward (downward) by any positive (negative) short-term interest rate differential between home and abroad, a decline (increase) in the country risk premium, and expected changes in the *equilibrium* nominal exchange rate.

The second pillar of the model hinges on what determines $\bar{e}$. In the long run, PPP may not necessarily hold, so that the equilibrium real exchange rate is possibly time varying:

$$(5) \qquad \bar{rer}_t = \bar{e}_t + \bar{p}^*_t - \bar{p}_t$$

where p and p^* are the domestic and foreign price indices, respectively. Using the foreign price as the numeraire and since long-run world price inflation under a gold standard should be negligible, it follows that

$$(6) \qquad \Delta \bar{rer}_t = \Delta \bar{e}_t + \Delta \bar{p}_t.$$

Given long-run price flexibility, the standard log-linear version of the Keynes-Hicks money market equilibrium condition allows us to map long-run domestic price inflation onto the behavior of money supply and output aggregates, assuming a log-linear trend in secular velocity:

$$(7) \qquad E(\pi)_t = \Delta \bar{m}_t - \phi \Delta \bar{y}_t + \vartheta,$$

where π is the inflation rate, y and m are the logs of the domestic real output and money stock, respectively; ϑ is the trend growth rate in money velocity and $\phi > 0$.

Substituting equations (5), (6), and (7) into equation (4) yields

(8) $\quad e_t - \bar{e}_t = \dfrac{1}{\theta}[i_t - i_t^* - \gamma\delta_t] + \dfrac{1}{\theta}E(\overline{\Delta rer_t}) - \dfrac{1}{\theta}(\Delta\overline{m}_t - \phi\Delta\overline{y}_t + \vartheta).$

Equalizing long-run to actual values in money and output as is commonly done in empirical applications (see Frankel and Rose 1995), and assuming that expected changes in the real exchange rate are directly proportional to preceding deviations of terms of trade, international productivity differentials, and fiscal positions from their respective long-run trends, this yields

(9) $\quad e_t - \bar{e}_t = \mu - \dfrac{1}{\theta}(\Delta m_t - \phi\Delta y_t) + \alpha(tot - \overline{tot})_{t-1} + \varphi(\bar{y}_{pc} - \bar{y}_{pc}^*)_{t-1}$

$\qquad - \eta\left(\dfrac{g}{t} - \dfrac{\bar{g}}{t}\right)_{t-1} + \dfrac{1}{\theta}(i_t - i_t^*) - \gamma\delta_t + \varepsilon_t,$

where $\mu = -\vartheta/\theta$.

The final step is to characterize what determines the country risk premium δ. As in Jeanne and Rose (2002), this is modeled as proportional to the external inflow of liquidity. As discussed in the main text, such an effect is bound to be directly related to the push of capital exports from the core advanced economies (Δb^*) net the degree to which domestic authorities or the banking system can offset changes in capital inflows with changes in the foreign exchange reserves to money ratio (Δres). This yields the benchmark equation that guides the empirical analysis in the main text:

(10) $\quad e_t - \bar{e}_t = \mu - \dfrac{1}{\theta}(\Delta m_t - \phi y_t) + \alpha(tot - \overline{tot})_{t-1} + \varphi(\bar{y}_{pc} - \bar{y}_{pc}^*)_{t-1}$

$\qquad - \eta\left(\dfrac{g}{t} - \dfrac{\bar{g}}{t}\right)_{t-1} + \dfrac{1}{\theta}(i_t - i_t^*) + \upsilon(\Delta b^* + \psi\Delta res)_t + \varepsilon_t$

Appendix B

Data Construction and Sources

Argentina

Net foreign capital inflow: Obtained by the difference of changes in specie reserves in domestic banks and the balance on the external current ac-

count provided in della Paolera, Gerardo and Alan Taylor (2003, data appendix).
Foreign trade and external terms of trade: see Catão and Solomou (2005, appendix 2).
Gold reserves: 1870–1882: bank specie reserves from della Paolera (1992); 1883–1913: della Paolera (1988, 173, col. 3).
Central government expenditures and revenues: Mitchell (2003).
Central government debt: della Paolera and Taylor (2003).
Money: Money in circulation (Mo) from della Paolera (1992). Broad money (M2) computed by splicing the Baiocco's 1870–83 series with that computed by Gerardo della Paolera, both of which reported in della Paolera and Taylor (2003).
Exchange rate: della Paolera and Taylor (2003).
Domestic interest rate: average annual yields on domestic mortgage bonds provided in della Paolera (1988).
Domestic price index: Catão and Solomou (2005).
GDP: della Paolera and Taylor (2003).
Population: Maddison (2003).

Brazil

Net foreign capital inflow: Franco (1988).
Foreign trade and external terms of trade: IBGE (1986).
Gold reserves: 1870–1900 from Franco (1988); extended through 1913 based on linear interpolation between 1900 and 1905 and using data from Paulo Neuhaus, Rio de Janeiro.
Central government expenditures and revenues: IBGE (1986).
Central government debt: Foreign debt from IBGE. Domestic debt obtained from Levy (1995), "The Brazilian Public Debt—Domestic and Foreign, 1824–1913," in *The Public Debt in Latin America in Historical Perspective,* ed. Richard Liehr, 209–54. Frankfurt: Vervuert.
Money: Mo and M2 both from IBGE (1986).
Exchange rate: IBGE (1986).
Domestic interest rate: kindly provided by Summerhill and Triner, based on primary data on domestic prices of 5 percent and 6 percent domestic perpetual bonds (polices).
Domestic price index: see Catão and Solomou (2005).
GDP: Contador and Haddad 91975); 1900–13 from C. Haddad (1978).
Population: Maddison (2003).

Chile

Net foreign capital inflow: derived by difference between changes in specie reserves in the banking system and the external current account balance estimated in Braun et al. (2000).
Foreign trade and external terms of trade: Braun et al.

Specie reserves: Llona Rodriguez (1990).
Central government expenditures and revenues: Braun et al.
Central government debt: Braun et al.
Money: 1870–78: Mo based on outstanding bank notes from Llona Rodriguez (1990, tables 73 and 75), then spliced with the currency-in-circulation series provided in Mitchell (1998). M2 adds total deposits to these series using Llona Rodriguez's estimates, provided in the same source.
Exchange rate: Braun et al.
Domestic interest rate: short-term average loan interest rate charges by domestic banks from Braun et al.
Domestic price index: see Catão and Solomou (2005).
GDP: Braun et al.
Population: Maddison (2003).

Greece

Net foreign capital inflow: not available.
Foreign trade and external terms of trade: Foreign trade data from Mitchell (2001). Terms of trade series kindly furnished by Jeffrey Williamson.
Specie reserves: Lazaretou (1993).
Central government expenditures and revenues: Mitchell (2001).
Central government debt: Lazaretou (1993).
Money: Lazaretou (1993).
Exchange rate: Catão and Solomou (2005).
Domestic price index: GDP deflator, as provided in Kostelenos et al. (forthcoming).
GDP: Kostelenos et al.
Population: Maddison (2003).

Italy

Net foreign capital inflow: Calculated as the difference between changes in specie reserves in the banking system and the current account balance reported in Tattara (2000).
Foreign trade and external terms of trade: Foreign trade data from Mitchell (2001), *International Historical Statistics: Europe,* London. Terms of trade series kindly furnished by Jeffrey Williamson.
Specie reserves: Fratianni and Spinelli (1984).
Central government expenditures and revenues: Mitchell (2001).
Central government debt: Zamagni (1998).
Money: Fratianni, Michele and Franco Spinelli.
Exchange rate: Catão and Solomou (2005).
Domestic price index: Maddison (1991).
GDP: ibid.
Population: Maddison (2003).

Portugal

Net foreign capital inflow: not available.
Foreign trade and external terms of trade: Lains (1995). The figures used are based on the author's revision of the respective official series.
Specie reserves: Mata and Valério (1994).
Central government expenditures and revenues: Mitchell (2001).
Central government debt: Mata and Valério.
Money: Fratianni, Michele and Franco Spinelli.
Exchange rate: Catão and Solomou (2005).
Domestic price index: see Catão and Solomou (2005).
GDP: das Neves (1994).
Population: ibid.

Russia

Net foreign capital inflow: calculated as the difference between changes in specie reserves in the banking system and the current account balance reported in Gregory (1982).
Foreign trade and external terms of trade: export and import values from Mitchell (2000). Terms of trade series kindly provided by Jeffrey Williamson.
Specie reserves: Flandreau and Zulmer (2004).
Central government expenditures and revenues: Mitchell (2001).
Central government debt: Flandreau and Zulmer (2004).
Money: Mo from Crisp (1976, 138–39). M2 adds Mo to bank deposits taken from Mitchell (2001).
Exchange rate: Catão and Solomou (2005).
Domestic price index: see Catão and Solomou (2005).
GDP: in the absence of a GDP series, the net national product estimate provided in Gregory (1982, table 3.1, 56–57), (variant 1) was used.

Spain

Net foreign capital inflow: unpublished estimates by Leandro Prados, kindly provided by the author.
Foreign trade and external terms of trade: Prados de la Escosura (1988).
Specie reserves: Carreras and Tafunell (1988), and Aceña and Reis (2000).
Central government expenditures and revenues: Mitchell (2001).
Central government debt: Carreras and Tafunell (1988).
Money: Aceña.
Exchange rate: ibid.
Domestic price index: the deflator for private consumption from Prados de la Escosura (2003).
GDP: Prados de la Escosura (2003, Table A.13.5, 681–82).
Population: ibid.

Australia

Net foreign capital inflow: calculated as the difference between changes in specie reserves in the banking system and the current account balance underlying Jones and Obstfeld (2001). The database is available at: http://www.nber.org/databases/jones-obstfeld. The Butlin series was chosen for the estimates reported in this paper, since the new current account estimates which completely exclude gold flows yield surprisingly high absolute levels of net capital inflows to GDP in the early 1890s. Both series yield, however, similar inferences on the timing and magnitude of *changes* in net capital inflows to GDP.
Foreign trade and external terms of trade: trade values from Mitchell (2002). Terms of trade from Bordo and Rockoff (1996).
Specie reserves: Obstfeld and Jones.
Central government expenditures and revenues: Mitchell.
Central government debt: Obstfeld and Taylor (2003).
Money: Mitchell.
Exchange rate: Obstfeld and Taylor (2003).
Domestic price index: ibid.
GDP: ibid.
Population: Maddison (2003).

Canada

Net foreign capital inflow: calculated as the difference between changes in specie reserves in the banking system and the current account balance from Urquart and Buckley (1965).
Foreign trade and external terms of trade: trade values from Mitchell (2002). Terms of trade from Urquart and Buckley.
Specie reserves: Obstfeld and Jones.
Central government expenditures and revenues: Mitchell.
Central government debt: Obstfeld and Taylor (2003).
Money: Mitchell (2001).
Exchange rate: Obstfeld and Taylor (2003).
Domestic price index: ibid.
GDP: ibid.
Population: Maddison (2003).

Denmark

Net foreign capital inflow: calculated as the difference between changes in specie reserves in the banking system and the current account balance underlying Jones and Obstfeld (2001). The database is available at: http://www.nber.org/databases/jones-obstfeld.
Foreign trade and external terms of trade: trade values from Mitchell (2002). Terms of trade from Andres Olgaard (1993).
Specie reserves: Obstfeld and Jones.

Central government expenditures and revenues: Mitchell.
Central government debt: Flandreau and Zulmer (2004).
Money: Mitchell.
Exchange rate: Obstfeld and Taylor (2003).
Domestic price index: ibid.
GDP: nominal GDP from Obstfeld and Taylor (2003). Real GDP from Maddison (2003).
Population: Maddison (2003).

Finland

Net foreign capital inflow: calculated as the difference between changes in specie reserves in the banking system and the current account balance underlying Jones and Maurice Obstfeld (2001). The database is available at: http://www.nber.org/databases/jones-obstfeld.
Foreign trade and external terms of trade: trade values from Mitchell (2001). Export and import prices, and terms of trade from Hjerppe (1989, 259–60).
Specie reserves: Obstfeld and Jones.
Central government expenditures and revenues: Mitchell.
Central government debt: Flandreau and Zulmer (2004).
Money: Mitchell.
Exchange rate: Obstfeld and Taylor (2003).
Domestic price index: ibid.
GDP: Hjerppe.
Population: Maddison (2003).

New Zealand

Net foreign capital inflow: not available.
Foreign trade and external terms of trade: Mitchell (2002). Terms of trade kindly provided by Jeffrey Williamson.
Specie reserves: reserves (coins and bullions) in trading banks from Bloomfield (1984, table IX.1, 386–87).
Central government expenditures and revenues: Mitchell.
Central government debt: Obstfeld and Taylor (2003).
Money: sum of currency in circulation from Mitchell and deposits in trading banks from Rankin (1992).
Exchange rate: Obstfeld and Taylor (2003).
Domestic price index: ibid.
GNP: Rankin.
Population: Maddison (2003).

Norway

Net foreign capital inflow: calculated as the difference between changes in specie reserves in the banking system and the current account balance

underlying Jones and Obstfeld (2001). The database is available at: http://www.nber.org/databases/jones-obstfeld.
Foreign trade and external terms of trade: trade values from Mitchell. Terms of trade from Edison and Klovland (1988).
Specie reserves: Obstfeld and Jones.
Central government expenditures and revenues: Mitchell.
Central government debt: Flandreau and Zulmer (2004).
Money: Mitchell.
Exchange rate: Obstfeld and Taylor (2003).
Domestic price index: Mitchell (2001).
GDP: nominal GDP from Obstfeld and Taylor. Real GDP from Maddison (2003).
Population: Maddison (2003).

Sweden

Net foreign capital inflow: calculated as the difference between changes in specie reserves in the banking system and the current account balance underlying Jones and Obstfeld (2001). The database is available at: http://www.nber.org/databases/jones-obstfeld.
Foreign trade and external terms of trade: trade values from Mitchell. Terms of trade and foreign trade prices from Fridlizius (1963).
Specie reserves: Obstfeld and Jones.
Central government expenditures and revenues: Mitchell.
Central government debt: Flandreau and Zulmer (2004).
Money: Mitchell.
Exchange rate: Obstfeld and Taylor (2003).
Domestic price index: Maddison (1995).
GDP: nominal GDP from Obstfeld and Taylor. Real GDP from Maddison (2003).
Population: Maddison (2003).

United States

Net foreign capital inflow: calculated as the difference between changes in specie reserves in the banking system and the current account balance underlying Jones and Obstfeld.
Foreign trade and external terms of trade: trade values from Mitchell. Terms of trade from Williamson (1964, table B4, 262).
Specie reserves: Obstfeld and Jones.
Central government expenditures and revenues: Mitchell.
Central government debt: Obstfeld and Taylor (2003).
Money: Mitchell.
Exchange rate: Officer (2001).
Domestic price index: Balke and Gordon (1989).
GDP: Jones and Obstfeld.
Population: Maddison (2003).

European Core Countries

Central bank discount rates: Bank of England's discount rate for Mitchell (1988); Bank of France's discount rate from Lévy-Leboyer and Bourguignon (1985); German discount rate from Homer and Sylla (1991).
Capital exports: U.K. data from Stone (1999); French data from Lévy-Leboyer and Bourguignon (1985); German data from Bloomfield (1968).

References

Aceña, Pedro M., and Reis Jaime. 2000. *Monetary standards in the periphery, paper, silver and gold, 1854–1933.* London: Palgrave Macmillan.
Balke, Nathan S., and Robert J. Gordon. 1989. The estimation of prewar gross national product: Methodology and new evidence. *Journal of Political Economy* 97:38–92.
Bayoumi, Tamim, and Barry Eichengreen. 1995. Restraining yourself: The implications of fiscal rules for economic stabilization. *Staff Papers* 42 (1): 32–48.
Blattman, Chris, Jason Hwang, and Jeffrey Williamson. 2003. Terms of trade and economic performance in the periphery 1870–1940. NBER Working Paper no. 9940. Cambridge, MA: National Bureau of Economic Research.
Bloomfield, Arthur. 1968. Patterns of fluctuation in international investment before 1914. Princeton Studies in International Finance no. 21, Princeton University, Department of Economics.
Bloomfield, G. I. 1984. *New Zealand: A handbook of historical statistics.* Boston: G. K. Hall.
Bordo, Michael, and Roberto Cortes-Conde. 2001. *Transferring wealth and power from the old to the new world: Monetary and fiscal institutions in the 17th through the 19th century.* New York: Cambridge University Press.
Bordo, Michael, Christopher Meissner, and Angela Redish. 2003. How original sin was overcome: The evolution of external debt denominated in domestic currency in the United States and British dominions. NBER Working Paper no. 9841. Cambridge, MA: National Bureau of Economic Research.
Bordo, Michael, and H. Rockoff. 1996. The gold standard as a "Good Housekeeping Seal of Approval." *Journal of Economic History* 56 (2): 384–428.
Braun, Juan, Matías Braun, Ignacio Briones, José Diaz, Rolf Luders, and Gert Wagner. 2000. Economía Chilena 1810–1995: Estadísticas Históricas. Catholic University of Chile, Instituto de Economía, Documento de Trabajo no. 187.
Caballero, Ricardo, Kevin Cowan, and Jonathan Kearns. 2004. Fear of sudden stops: Lessons from Australia and Chile. NBER Working Paper no. 10519. Cambridge, MA: National Bureau of Economic Research.
Calvo, Guillermo, Leonardo Leiderman, and Carmen Reinhart. 1993. Capital inflows and real exchange rate appreciation in Latin America: The role of external factors. *IMF Staff Papers* 40 (1): 108–51.
Calvo, Guillermo, Alejandro Izquierdo, and Luis Fernando Mejia. 2004. On the empirics of sudden stops: The relevance of balance sheet effects. NBER Working Paper no. 10520. Cambridge, MA: National Bureau of Economic Research.
Cameron, Rondo. 1972. *Banking and economic development: Some lessons from history.* New York: Oxford University Press.

Carreras, A., and X. Tafunell, eds. 1988. *Estadísticas Históricas de España. Siglos XIX y XX.* Madrid: Fundación Banco Exterior.
Catão, Luis A. V., and Sandeep Kapur. 2006. Volatility and the debt intolerance paradox. *IMF Staff Papers* 53 (2): 195–218.
Catão, Luis A. V., and Solomos Solomou. 2005. Effective exchange rates and the classical gold standard adjustment. *American Economic Review* 94:1259–75.
Contrador, Claudio, and Claudio Haddad. 1975. Produto Real, Moeda e Preços: A Experiência Brasileira no Periodo 1861–1970. *Revista Brasileira de Estatística* 36 (143): 407–40.
Crisp, Olga. 1976. *Studies in the Russian economy before 1914.* London: Macmillan.
das Neves, João Luís César. 1994. *The Portuguese economy: A picture in figures: XIX and XX centuries with long term series.* Lisbon: Catholic University.
della Paolera, Geraldo. 1988. How the Argentina economy performed during the international gold standard: A re-examination. PhD diss., University of Chicago.
———. 1992. The performance of the Argentine economy during the international gold standard, 1860–1930. Paper presented at the conference Long-Run Economic Growth in Argentina, Brazil and Mexico. London: Institute of Latin American Studies.
———. 2003. *A new economic history of Argentina.* Cambridge: Cambridge University Press.
della Paolera, G., and A. M. Taylor. 2001. *Straining at the anchor: The Argentine currency board and the search for macroeconomic stability, 1880–1935.* Chicago: National Bureau of Economic Research.
DeLong, B. 1999. Financial crises in the 1890s and the 1990s: Must history repeat? *Brookings Papers on Economic Activity* 2:253–94.
Dornbusch, Rudiger, Ilan Goldfajn, and Rodrigo Valdes. 1995. Currency crises and collapses. *Brookings Papers in Economic Activity* 2:221–42.
Edelstein, M. 1982. *Overseas investment in the age of high imperialism.* New York: Columbia University Press.
Edison, Hali J., and Jan Tore Klovland. 1988. A quantitative reassessment of the purchasing power parity hypothesis: Evidence from Norway and the United Kingdom. *Journal of Applied Economics* 2:309–33.
Edwards, Sebastian. 1989. *Real exchange rates, devaluation and adjustment: Exchange rate policy in developing countries.* Cambridge, MA: MIT Press.
———. 2004. Thirty years of current account imbalances, current account reversals, and sudden stops. *IMF Staff Papers* 51 (January).
Eichengreen, Barry. 1992. The gold standard since Alec Ford. In *Britain in the international economy 1870–1939,* ed. S. N. Broadberry and N. F. R. Crafts, 47–79. Cambridge: Cambridge University Press.
———. 2003. *Capital flows and crises.* Cambridge, MA: MIT Press.
Eichengreen, Barry, and Ricardo Haussman. 1999. Exchange rate regimes and financial fragility. NBER Working Paper no. 7418. Cambridge, MA: National Bureau of Economic Research.
Eichengreen, Barry, Andrew Rose, and Charles Wyzplosz. 1996. Contagious currency crises: First tests. *Scandinavian Journal of Economics* 98 (4): 463–85.
Fernandez-Arias, Eduardo. 1996. The new wave of private capital inflows: Push or pull? *Journal of Development Economics* 48:389–418.
Flandreau, Marc, and F. Zulmer. 2004. *The making of global finance 1880–1913.* Paris: OECD.
Ford, A. G. 1962. *The gold standard 1880–1914: Britain and Argentina.* Oxford: Clarendon.
Franco, Gustavo H. B. 1988. O Balanco de Pagamentos do Brasil: Novas Estimativas, 1870–1896. PUC Discussion Paper no. 201. Rio de Janeiro.

———. 1990. *A década republicana: Brasil e a economia internacional, 1888–1900.* Rio de Janeiro: IPEA.
Frankel, Jeffrey. 1997. On the mark: A theory of floating exchange rates based on real interest differentials. *The American Economic Review* 69 (4): 610–22.
Frankel, Jeffrey, and Andrew Rose. 1995. A survey of empirical research on nominal exchange rates. In *Handbook of international economics,* ed. Kenneth Rogoff and Gene Grossman, 1689–1729. Amsterdam: North Holland.
———. 1996. Currency crises in emerging markets: An empirical treatment. *Journal of International Economics* 41:351–66.
Fratianni, Michele, and Franco Spinelli. 1984. Italy in the gold standard period, 1861–1914. In *A retrospective of the classical gold standard 1821–1931,* ed. Michael D. Bordo and Anna J. Schwartz, 405–51. Chicago: University of Chicago Press.
———. 1997. *A monetary history of Italy.* Cambridge: Cambridge University Press.
Fridlizius, Gunnar. 1963. Sweden's exports 1850–1960. *Economy and History* 2: 38–96.
Fritsch, Winston. 1988. *External constraints on economic policy in Brazil, 1889–1930.* Pittsburgh, PA: University of Pittsburgh Press.
Gavin, Michael, and Roberto Perotti. 1997. Fiscal policy in Latin America. *NBER Macroeconomics Annual,* 11–61. Cambridge, MA: National Bureau of Economic Research.
Goldsmith, Raymond W. 1986. *Brasil 1850–1984: Desenvolvimento Financeiro sob um Século de Inflação.* São Paulo, Brazil: Harper & Row.
Gregory, Paul R. 1982. *Russian national income, 1885–1913.* Cambridge: Cambridge University Press.
Haber, Stephen. 1997. Financial markets and industrial development: A comparative study of governmental regulation, financial innovation, and industrial structure in Brazil and Mexico, 1840–1930. In *How Latin America fell behind: Essays in the economic histories of Brazil and Mexico,* ed. S. Haber, 146–78. Stanford, CA: Stanford University Press.
Haddad, Claudio. 1978. *O Crescimento do Produto Real Brasileiro.* Rio de Janeiro: Vargas Foundation.
Hansen, H. 1991. From growth to crisis: The Danish banking system from 1850 to the interwar years. *Scandinavian Economic History Review* 39 (3): 20–40.
Hjerppe, Riitta. 1989. *The Finnish economy, 1860–1985: Growth and structural change.* Helsinki: Bank of Finland.
Homer, Sidney, and Richard Sylla. 1991. *A history of interest rates.* Rutgers, NJ: Rutgers University Press.
IBGE. 1986. *Estatisticas Historicas do Brasil.* Rio de Janeiro: IBGE.
Jeanne, Olivier, and Andrew Rose. 2002. Noise trading and exchange rate regimes. *Quarterly Journal of Economics* 117 (2): 537–69.
Jones, Matthew T., and Maurice Obstfeld. 2001. Saving, investment, and gold: A reassessment of historical current account data. In *Money, capital mobility, and trade: Essays in honor of Robert A. Mundell,* ed. Guillermo A. Calvo, Maurice Obstfeld, and Rudiger Dornbusch, 303–64. Cambridge, MA: MIT Press.
Jonker, Joost. 1997. The alternative road to modernity: Banking and currency, 1814–1914. In *A financial history of the Netherlands,* ed. M. Hart, J. Jonker, and J. Van Zanden, 94–123. New York: Cambridge University Press.
Jonung, Lars. 1984. Swedish experience under the classical gold standard, 1873–1913. In *The classical gold standard in retrospective,* ed. M. D. Bordo and A. Schwartz, 361–99. Chicago: University of Chicago Press.
Kaminsky, Graciela, and Carmen Reinhart. 1999. The twin crises: The cause of banking and balance of payments problems. *American Economic Review* 89 (3): 473–500.

Kaminsky, Graciela, Carmen Reinhart, and Carlos Végh. 2004. When it rains it pours: Procyclical capital flows and macroeconomic policies. NBER Working Paper no. 10780. Cambridge, MA: National Bureau of Economic Research.

Kelly, Trish. 1998. Ability and willingness to pay in the age of the pax Britannica. *Explorations in Economic History* 35:31–58.

Kindleberger, Charles P. 1978. *Manias, panics, and crashes.* New York: Macmillan.

Kiyotaki, N., and J. Moore. 1997. Credit cycles. *Journal of Political Economy* 105 (2): 211–48.

Kostelenos, G., S. Petmezas, D. Vasileiou, E. Kounaris, and M. Sfakianakis. Forthcoming. *Gross domestic product 1830–1939, sources of economic history of modern Greece, quantitative data and statistical series 1830–1939.* Athens: Historical Archives of the National Bank of Greece.

Krugman, Paul. 1979. A model of balance of payments crisis. *Journal of Money, Credit and Banking* 11:311–25.

Lains, Pedro. 1995. *A Economia Portuguesa no Século XIX. Crescimento Económico e Comércio Externo.* Lisbon: Imprensa Nacional.

Lazaretou, Sophia. 1993. Monetary and fiscal policies in Greece: 1833–1914. *Journal of European Economic History* 22 (2): 285–311.

Levy, Maria Barbara. 1995. The Brazilian public debt—domestic and foreign, 1824–1913. In *The public debt in Latin America in historical perspective,* ed. Reinhard Liehr, 209–54. Frankfurt: Vervuert.

Lévy-Leboyer, M., and François Bourguignon. 1985. *L'Economie Français au XIXe Siécle.* Paris: Éditions Économica.

Lindert, Peter. 1969. Key currencies and gold, 1900–1913. Princeton Studies in International Finance no. 24. Princeton University, Department of Economics.

Lindert, Peter, and Peter Morton. 1989. How sovereign debt has worked. In *Developing country debt and economic performance,* ed. Jeffrey Sachs, 225–35. Chicago: National Bureau of Economic Research.

Llona Rodriguez, Agustin. 1990. Chilean monetary policy: 1860–1925. PhD diss., Boston University.

———. 2000. Chile during the gold standard: A successful paper money experience. In *Monetary standards in the periphery: Paper, silver and gold, 1854–1933,* ed. P. M. Acena and J. Reis, London: Macmillan.

Maddison, Angus. 1991. *Dynamic forces in capitalist development.* Oxford: Oxford University Press.

———. 2003. *The world economy: Historical statistics.* Paris: OECD.

Mata, Maria Eugénia, and Nuno Valério. 1994. *História Económica de Portugal.* Lisbon: Presenca.

Mauro, Paolo, Nathan Sussman, and Yishay Yafeh. 2002. Emerging market spreads: Then versus now. *Quarterly Journal of Economics* 117 (2): 695–733.

Meissner, Christopher. 2005. A new world order: Explaining the international diffusion of the gold standard, 1870–1913. *Journal of International Economics* 66:385–406.

Milesi-Ferretti, Gian Maria and Assaf Razin. 2000. Current account reversals and currency crises: Empirical regularities. In *Currency crises,* ed. P. Krugman, Chicago: University of Chicago Press.

Mitchell, Brian. 1988. *British historical statistics.* Cambridge: University of Cambridge Press.

———. 2001. *International historical statistics: Europe, 1750–1993.* London: Macmillan.

———. 2002. *International historical statistics: Asia and Oceania.* London: Macmillan.

———. 2003. *International historical statistics: The Americas, 1750–1993*. London: Palgrave Macmillan.
Obstfeld, Maurice, and Kenneth Rogoff. 1996. *Foundations of international macroeconomics*. Cambridge, MA: MIT Press.
Obstfeld, Maurice, and Taylor, Alan M. 2003. Sovereign risk, credibility and the gold standard: 1870–1913 versus 1925–31. *Economic Journal* 113 (487): 241–75.
———. 2004. *Global capital markets: Integration, crisis, and growth*. Cambridge:
Officer, Lawrence H. 2001. Exchange rate between the United States dollar and the British pound, 1791–2000: Source notes. Economic History Services. http://www.eh.net/hmit/exchangerates/poundsource.html
Olgaard, Andres. 1993. The Danish terms of trade in foreign trade, 1875–1963. In *The economic development of Denmark and Norway since 1870*, ed. Karl Gunnar Persson. Hants, England: E. Elgar.
Prados de la Escosura, Leandro. 1988. *De impirio a nación. Crecimiento y atraso económico en España (1780–1930)*. Madrid: Alianza.
———. 2003. El progreso economico de España, 1850–2000. Madrid: Fundacion BBVA.
Reis, Jaime. 2000. The gold standard in Portugal 1854–91. In *Monetary standards in the periphery: Paper, silver and gold, 1854–1933*, ed. P. M. Aceña and Jaime Reis, 69–111. London: Macmillan.
Stone, Irving. 1999. *The global export of capital from Great Britain, 1865–1914*. London: Macmillan.
Tattara, Giuseppe. 2000. Was Italy ever on gold? In *Monetary standards in the periphery: Paper, silver and gold, 1854–1933*, ed. P. M. Aceña and Jaime Reis, 18–68. London: Macmillan.
Tornell, Aaron, and Philip Lane. 1998. Are windfalls a curse?: A nonrepresentative agent model of the current account. *Journal of International Economics* 44 (1): 83–112.
Triner, Gail. 2000. *Banking and economic development: Brazil, 1889–1930*. New York: Palgrave.
Urquart, M. C., and Kenneth H. A. Buckley. 1965. *Historical statistics of Canada*. Cambridge: University of Cambridge Press.
Végh, Carlos, and Ernesto Talvi. 2000. Tax base variability and procyclical fiscal policy. NBER Working Paper no. 7499. Cambridge, MA: National Bureau of Economic Research.
Whale, P. B. 1937. The working of the prewar gold standard. *Economica* 18–32.
Williamson, Jeffrey G. 1964. *American growth and the balance of payments 1820–1913*. Chapel Hill: University of North Carolina Press.
Zamagni, Vera. 1998. Il Debito Pubblico Italiano 1861–1946: Riconstruzione della serie storica. *Rivista di Storia Economica* 14:207–42.

8   Establishing Credibility
The Role of Foreign Advisors in Chile's 1955–1958 Stabilization Program

Sebastian Edwards

8.1 Introduction

The adoption of stabilization programs is usually a painful process, both politically and economically. History is replete with instances where, even in the light of obvious and flagrant macroeconomics disequilibria, the implementation of stabilization programs is significantly delayed. Why do policymakers and/or politicians prefer to live with growing inflationary pressures and implement price and other forms of highly inefficient controls instead of tackling the roots of macroeconomic imbalances? Is the prolongation of inflation the consequence of mistaken views on the mechanics of fiscal deficits and money creation, or is it the unavoidable result of the political game? Why, after months of apparent political stalemate, are stabilization programs all of a sudden adopted that closely resemble others proposed earlier? These questions are at the heart of the political economy of stabilization and inflationary finance.[1] In recent years the analysis of these issues has attained new interest, as a number of authors have applied the tools of game theory to the study of macroeconomic policymaking. Although important theoretical progress has been achieved in

---

Sebastian Edwards is the Henry Ford II Professor of International Economics at UCLA's Anderson Graduate School of Management and a research associate at the National Bureau of Economic Research.

This is a revised version of a paper presented at the National Bureau of Economic Research's Inter-American Seminar on Economics, held at the Colegio de Mexico, December 2–4, 2004. I thank Roberto Alvarez for his comments and assistance.

1. Latin American debates on inflation and stabilization have traditionally emphasized political economy angles. It is only recently, however, that these issues have begun to be tackled using a formal economics framework. See, for example Edwards (1994).

Table 8.1 Inflation rate: Dec. 1946–Dec. 1958 (Consumer Price Index % change)

Year	Inflation rate
1946	30.1
1947	23.1
1948	16.8
1949	20.4
1950	16.7
1951	22.8
1952	12.0
1953	56.6
1954	71.0
1955	84.0
1956	37.8
1957	17.1
1958	32.5
1959	32.9
1960	5.4
1961	10.2
1962	26.7

Source: International Financial Statistics, IMF.

the explanation of some of these phenomena, the amount of empirical and historical work on the subject is still rather limited.[2]

The purpose of this paper is to investigate an important historical stabilization episode in Chile, a country with one of the longest histories of chronic inflation in the world. Starting in the late nineteenth century, Chile suffered recurrent and increasingly frequent inflationary outbursts. Of the many stabilization programs adopted to tackle this problem, the 1955–1958 package implemented with the advice of the U.S. consulting firm of Klein-Saks, is, undoubtedly, one of the most fascinating ones.[3] Its interest is based on a number of factors: first, at the time the program was put in place inflation had reached the extremely high annual level (for that time) of 85 percent (see table 8.1). Second, the policies adopted contradicted the newly dominant orthodoxy in Latin America that associated inflation to *structural* problems.[4] Third, the Klein-Saks program took place in a period of acute political confrontation. Fourth, the episode is interesting because after what was considered to be an initial success—inflation declined to 38 percent in 1956 and was further reduced to 17 percent in 1957—the program failed to achieve durable price stability (see figure 8.1). Finally, what makes this episode particularly noteworthy is that the program proposed

---

2. For a masterful presentation of recent advances in the political economy of macroeconomics policymaking, see Drazen (2000).
3. It is certainly a stabilization attempt that has attracted considerable attention from academic economists. See, for example, Hirschman (1963), Felix (1960), and Edwards (1986).
4. On the structuralist view of inflation see, for example, Sunkel (1958).

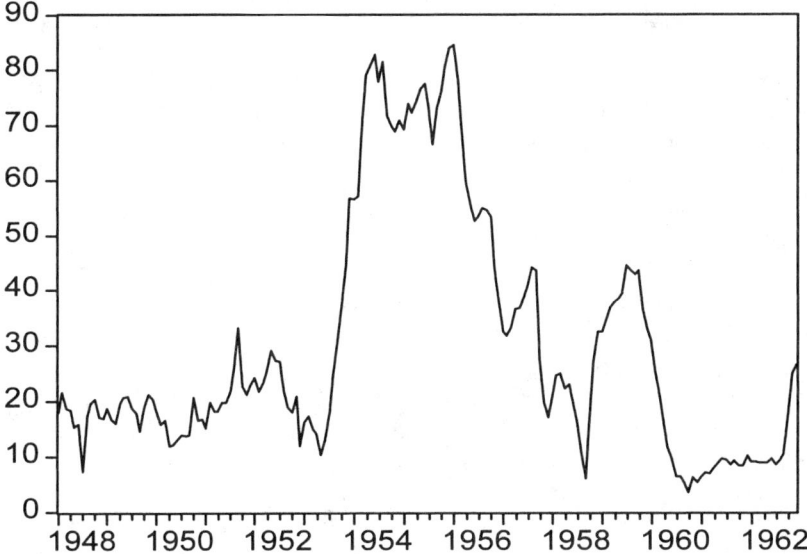

Fig. 8.1 Inflation rate

by the Klein-Saks Mission was very similar to anti-inflationary plans that had been previously elaborated by several government agencies, including the Ministry of Finance and the Central Bank, in the period 1954–55. However, while these earlier stabilization efforts were rejected by Congress, most (but not all) of the Mission's program was approved. This characteristic of the episode raises the issue of the role of foreign advisors in the design (and implementation) of economic policy.

In this paper I argue that the foreign advisors of the Klein-Saks Mission gave *initial* credibility to the stabilization program launched in 1955. These foreign advisors played the role of independent, nonpartisan technocratic arbiters. It was precisely because they were foreigners that they could rise above the political fray and suggest a specific program whose main components were rapidly approved by a highly divided Congress. The fact that the program was very similar to one proposed earlier by the government— and that was rejected by Congress—underscores the view that, while locals are suspect of being excessively partisan, foreigners are often (but not always) seen as independent policy brokers. But providing *initial credibility* was not enough to ensure success. In spite of supporting trade reform, foreign exchange rate reform, and the deindexation of wages, Congress failed to act decisively on the fiscal front. Consequently the fiscal imbalances that had plagued Chile for a long time were reduced, but not eliminated. In 1957 a sharp drop in the international price of copper—the country's main export—resulted in a major decline in fiscal revenue and in an increase in the fiscal deficit. The Mission recommended a series of belt-tightening measures, but politicians had had enough of orthodoxy. No adjustment was made, and inflationary expectations once again shifted for the worse. By October of 1958 the Mission had left the country, and an opportunity for achieving stability had been lost.

The rest of the paper is organized as follows: In section 8.2 I provide a broad historical background on the Ibañez del Campo presidency in Chile during 1952–58. In section 8.3 I present the analytical framework for interpreting the Klein-Saks episode. This framework is based on the modern theory of credibility, and makes use of concepts such as war of attrition and external enforcers. Section 8.4 focuses on Chile's inflationary experience. Here, I discuss in great detail economic conditions in the early 1950s and I focus on the mechanisms behind the country's increasing rate of inflation. I discuss President Ibañez del Campo's original populist program, and I deal with two failed stabilization programs implemented during the early 1950s. In section 8.5 I discuss in detail the program proposed by the Klein-Saks Mission, focusing on two of its main components: wage deindexation and the reform of the exchange rate system. In section 8.6 I focus on the role played by the Klein-Saks Mission in the stabilization effort launched in late 1955. In this part of the paper I concentrate on three interrelated issues: first, I analyze whether the diagnosis of inflation causes differed significantly from previous analyses. That is, I investigate whether from a *purely technical* perspective the Mission provided new approaches and insights. Second, I explore the extent to which the Mission's program was credible; more specifically, I investigate the presence of the external advisors provided a precommitment technology. And third, I use congressional records and correspondence files to analyze the political process—including the formation of alliances and coalitions—that led in early 1956 to the adoption of the so-called "stabilization package." In section 8.7 I use time series econometric techniques to analyze whether the Mission's stabilization program was credible to the public. Finally, in section 8.8 I present some concluding remarks.

8.2 Historical Background

In 1952 former army general Carlos Ibañez del Campo was elected president of Chile by a significant margin.[5] His campaign had been carried out on the basis of a "new beginning"—he was called by his supporters "the General of Hope" (*El General de la Esperanza*)—and as a reaction against the political establishment. He was supported by a loosely knit coalition of

---

5. Ibañez del Campo obtained 47 percent of the votes. The right-wing candidate Arturo Matte got 28 percent, while the radical Pedro Enrique Alfonso obtained 20 percent. The socialist candidate and future president, Salvador Allende, obtained less than 6 percent.

populists, nationalists, and socialists. The general himself, however, was not a member of any political party, and from the very beginning of his campaign stated his intentions of being highly independent from the parties. His program's rhetoric was decisively populist and had an antiestablishment content. The presence of socialists in the coalition was not window dressing; they participated in the first Ibañez del Campo cabinet with three ministers, including finance.[6] As time progressed, however, it became apparent that Ibañez del Campo's personalistic approach to government was increasingly incompatible with the socialist program. In October of 1953, less than a year after Ibañez del Campo had taken office, the socialist party abandoned the governing coalition.[7]

Carlos Ibañez del Campo inherited a country with serious macroeconomic disequilibria, stemming mostly from significant fiscal imbalances financed by the Central Bank. During the first two years of the Ibañez del Campo presidency no serious attempt at fighting inflation was made. Quite the contrary, influenced by a combination of populist views and an approach to monetary policy based on the "real bills doctrine," monetary policy became increasingly lax, generating a rapid acceleration of inflation. The propagation of price increases was greatly helped by the existence of a broad-based wage indexation system that mandated wage adjustments by the amount of accumulated past inflation.[8]

After a failed stabilization attempt, inflation surged in 1955 toward the 100 percent level. Politically, Ibañez del Campo became increasingly isolated as both the right (conservative and liberal), the centrist Radical Party, and the left stepped up their opposition tactics. Labor unrest was mounting and a generalized political dissatisfaction was apparent. It was at this juncture of Chile's political and economic history that the men of the Klein-Saks Mission arrived in Chile.[9] Their task was to tame inflation, attain stability, and help set the stage for a recovery program.

The emphasis in this paper is not on the actual policies and results of the Klein-Saks Mission, but rather on the political economy process that led to the hiring of these consultants and to the (at least partial) adoption of their policies. That is, I am interested in understanding what was the role of the external advisors, and, in particular, whether their advice helped the Ibañez del Campo administration solve its credibility and commitment

---

6. In Chile the socialist party had strong Marxist inclinations. It was not a social democratic party.

7. See, for example, Ampuero (1969), and Jobet (1971).

8. This process of backward-looking indexation was informally initiated in the late 1950s and legalized through Law 10,343 in mid-1952.

9. The Mission was hired in July 1955; the five-man team arrived in Santiago in September. Their first memorandum was delivered to the president in November. The Mission was led by Preston Carter, a man with ample practical experience both in the private and government sector. His colorful Spanish and straightforward manners rapidly established him as a trusted advisor. See Correa Prieto (1962).

problem. I also investigate whether the fact that the Mission was hired affected how different players perceived the costs of delaying the resolution of inflationary pressures.

8.3 The Basic Analytics of the Political Economy of Inflation and Stabilization

Since the early 1990s there has been renewed interest in analyzing the political economy dimensions of macroeconomics policymaking. Many of these theoretical developments have formally used game theory to describe the way in which different actors interplay in the policymaking process. The purpose of this section is to provide an analytical framework for the historical analysis that follows. I briefly review some of the most important features of the theoretical literature on inflation, placing particular emphasis on stabilization programs.

Generally speaking, political economy models of macroeconomic policymaking stress the distributional impact of both inflation and stabilization. The existence of distributional and political conflict fuels the inflationary process. There are many possible channels through which political conflict may result in higher inflation. Cukierman, Edwards, and Tabellini (1992), for instance, have suggested a model wherein politicians have different preferences and act strategically. This strategic interaction results in an inefficient tax system and in the inflationary finance of the fiscal deficit. In this type of model, a higher degree of political instability will result in higher seignorage and higher inflation; a greater degree of political polarization—measured as the difference in political parties' preferences—will also result in higher inflation.

Interestingly, this approach not only explains the origin of inflation but also provides insights about the timing of the stabilization. In this framework, stabilizing the price level means changing the political status quo. This, in turn, may generate new disputes among political groups about the share of the burden of the fiscal adjustment. These political disputes are likely to take the form of a war of attrition, during which all the conflicting groups wait for one of them to finally give up. The group that blinks first is forced to bear a disproportionate burden of the adjustment.[10] This war of attrition results in a delay of the stabilization. A particularly interesting feature of these models is that this delay takes place even in situations where there is general agreement among conflicting groups about the overall form of the adjustment policies needed to stop inflationary pressures. Of course, postponing stabilization will usually increase the size of the adjustment effort needed, and thus exacerbate the political conflict.[11]

---

10. For more details on this outcome, see Alesina and Drazen (1989), and Drazen (2000).
11. For an early study on the effects of a postponed adjustment, see Edwards and Montiel (1990). See also Drazen (2000).

Existing theoretical models based on the war of attrition concept have been quite general, and have not always specified the precise mechanism (or mechanisms) through which the conflict is finally resolved. What makes one of the players retreat? Why, at some point, does the perceived cost of waiting exceed the benefit? What is the role of political negotiations? Can a third party, or mediator, help bring the conflict to a faster end? Addressing these issues at a theoretical level is well beyond the scope of this paper. However, in discussing and interpreting the Klein-Saks episode, I consider some (possible) complications of the straightforward war of attrition model.

A somewhat different, although not contradictory, approach to inflation and stabilization is based on the role of institutions and credibility. After the rational expectations revolution, many authors emphasized the importance of expectations during stabilization episodes. A number of them, and most notably Sargent, concluded that in order to put an end to any inflationary process, a credible change of the monetary and fiscal regimes was needed.[12] To the event that stabilization is not credible—that is, the stabilization program is not expected to achieve the intended results—the costs of adjustment escalate and the probability of a successful stabilization becomes smaller.[13] This view led naturally to look for ways of modifying and influencing expectations during a stabilization program. The role of policy announcements has been analyzed as a possible means of affecting inflationary expectations. In this connection, however, it has been stressed that in order for these announcements to be credible—and thus to actually affect expectations—it is necessary for the government to be able to precommit itself to a given course of action. This, of course, turns out to be difficult to do, since societies many times lack the institutional setup required for government to credibly precommit itself.

Credibility-based models have also emphasized the role of *reputation* as a substitute for precommitment. According to this approach, the desire of governments to preserve their reputation—or even, possibly, to improve it—provides them with a constrained set of policy options.[14] Some authors have suggested that expectations can be coordinated and that credibility can be established if it is supported by an external institution, such as the League of Nations in the 1920s and the International Monetary Fund after 1950.[15] The reason is that by granting its seal of approval to a stabilization plan, an external institution enhances the confidence in the program. In principle, this seal of approval is independent of the financing that the external institutions can provide.[16] In fact, the presence of external in-

12. This was the message of Sargent (1983, 1986).
13. Along similar lines see Dornbusch (1991).
14. See Preston and Tabellini (1990, 2000).
15. See Sachs (1989), Edwards (1989), and Santaella (1993).
16. Accounts of the support given by external credits and loans to stabilizing countries are in the League of Nations (1946), Dornbusch and Fischer (1986), and Persson and Tabellini (2000). On the IMF as a provider of a "seal of approval" see Boughton (2001, 2003) and Vreeland (2003).

volvement can endow the stabilizing government with a commitment technology that gives an assurance that the announced program will indeed be fully carried out.

8.4 Inflation in the Early 1950s in Chile

In this section I provide some background information on the Chilean inflationary process before the arrival of the Klein-Saks Mission. I concentrate on the path that led to very rapid inflation in 1954–55 and I discuss the characteristics of the most important stabilization attempts undertaken during the years prior to the arrival of the Mission.

8.4.1 The End of the "Radical" Presidencies

During the years 1938 to 1952 the centrist Radical Party was the dominant political force in Chile. Throughout this period the country underwent a rapid industrialization process based on import substitution policies, and experienced a fairly rapid rate of growth.[17] Gabriel Gonzalez-Videla, the third Radical President, came into power in 1946 supported by a coalition of Radicals, Socialists, and Communists. The Communist Party, however, had a short stay in office: in 1948 the so-called "Law of Defense of Democracy," which outlawed the Communist Party, was enacted. For the rest of its period, Gonzalez-Videla governed with the support of the rightest liberal and conservative parties.

During the Gonzalez-Videla presidency, Chile experienced increasingly large macroeconomic imbalances that led to rapid inflation, low savings and investment, and recurrent external sector difficulties. Wages were under continuous pressure, monetary policy was dominated by supporters of the "real bills doctrine," which believed that money creation channeled toward industry was not inflationary, and public finances became extremely fragile. In spite of the fact that after the expulsion of the communists the Ministry of Finance was controlled by austere, conservative politicians, the rate of money creation was extremely high. For instance, between 1945 and 1951 the stock of high-powered money increased at a rate that exceeded 30 percent per year.[18]

These inflationary pressures resulted in two important macroeconomic developments that shaped many of the policies that were to be taken in the next ten years: first, in order to deal with external sector imbalances and to fight tendencies toward real exchange rate overvaluation, a system of multiple nominal exchange rates was developed. While during the first year of the Gonzalez-Videla administration there were three official exchange

---

17. See, for instance, Mamalakis (1976).
18. The two most important finance ministers were Jorge Alessandri (who in 1958 became President of the Republic) and Carlos Vial. As stated in Felix (1960), they did not always agree on the causes behind the country's rapidly increasing rate of inflation.

Table 8.2   Multiple exchange rates: 1947–1955 (Chilean pesos per U.S. dollar at end of year)

Year	Government	Preferential	Official	Banking	Special	Commercial
1947	19.37	25	31			
1948	19.37	25	31	43[c]		
1949	19.37	25	31	43		
1950	19.37	25[a]	31	43	50[d]	60[e]
1951	19.37		31	43	50	60
1952	19.37		31	43	50	60
1953			110[b]			
1954			200[f]			
1955			200			

Source: Pick's Currency Yearbook, several issues.
[a]Discontinued January 9th.
[b]Devaluation October 5th.
[c]Beginning February 4th.
[d]Beginning August 1st.
[e]Beginning January 10th.
[f]Devaluation November 10th.

rates, ranging from 37 to 31 pesos per U.S. dollar, by 1952 the number of official rates had increased to five, with their range going from 19.37 to 60 pesos per U.S. dollar (see table 8.2).[19] However, in spite of the adoption of this discriminatory exchange rate system and of the imposition of generalized controls and trade restrictions, the external sector was under continuous pressure during this period. Not surprisingly, the foreign exchange parallel (or black) market premium increased from a level of around 30 percent in 1946 to almost 400 percent toward the end of the Gonzalez-Videla administration (see figure 8.2). As a result of this situation, increasing amounts of resources left the country in the form of capital flight.[20]

The second important macroeconomic development of this period was the institutionalization of a wage rate indexation mechanism. As inflation increased, a 1941 law mandating the yearly adjustment of minimum wages for white collar workers became a more and more important piece of the existing economic legislation. Although this law did not specify all the details of this adjustment process—it did not say, for example, to what percentage wages should be adjusted relative to past inflation—actual man-

---

19. These rates were "official" in the sense of being sanctioned by the authorities. However, one of them only received the technical name of "official exchange rate." What made things more complicated was that there were also a number of "mixed" rates, corresponding to weighted averages of the six official rates.

20. See, for example, the United Nation's *Technical Assistance Report on Chile's inflation* (1951, 3). This report was written by a team of foreign experts led by Erik Lindahl from the University of Upsala.

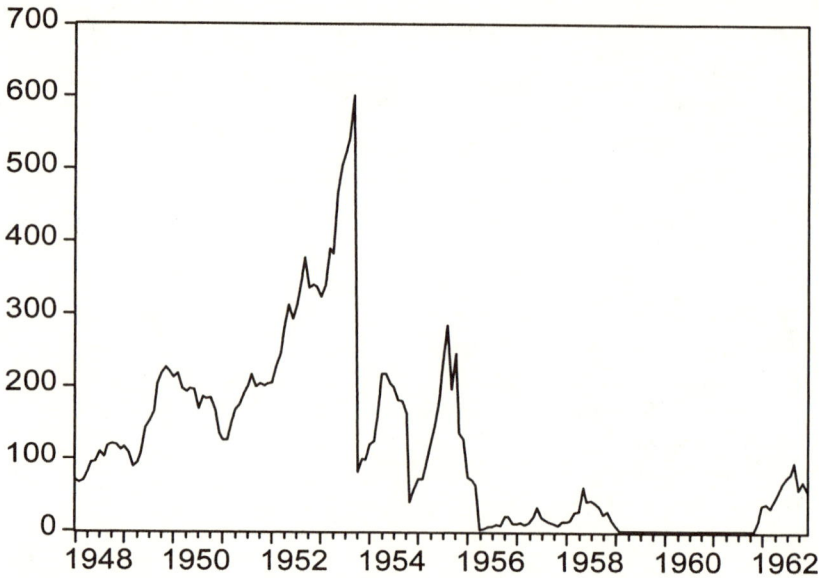

Fig. 8.2 Black market premium

dated wage increases became de facto fully linked to past inflation. Moreover, in some years (1949–50, for instance) the wage adjustment decreed by the government greatly exceeded accumulated inflation during the preceding year.[21] These autonomic wage adjustments fed back into prices, generating to a highly self-feeding process that was constantly validated by the Central Bank. The process became more entrenched in late 1952, when a law mandating an automatic backward-looking wage adjustment for public sector wages of 90 percent of past inflation was enacted. Initially this legislation applied only to public servants. By 1954, however, its reach had increased greatly; approximately half a million public and private sector workers' salaries were adjusted according to the mechanism determined by this law.

The combination of this indexation mechanism with the increasing importance of the parallel market for foreign exchange resulted in a highly inertial inflationary process, as well as important distortions in the external sector. The contribution of the indexation mechanism to inflation was understood early on by many (but not all) Chilean economists. In fact, in the period 1949–55 the elimination, or at least partial control, of this indexation procedure was at the center of policy discussion and was considered an essential component of most stabilization attempts. In 1949 the govern-

---

21. See Hirschman (1963). The Chilean indexation scheme of this period is described, in a comparative setting, in Sen Gupta (1958).

ment requested two foreign advisory reports on the causes of inflation and on possible ways to stop it. Although these two reports—by a United Nations team and by the staff of the International Monetary Fund—differed in many respects, they agreed that an elimination of the inflationary pressure would require dealing with wage adjustments.[22]

8.4.2 Ibañez del Campo's Populist Program

In 1952 Carlos Ibañez del Campo became the candidate of the disillusioned. The 72-year-old retired army general captured voters' frustration and disappointment with the traditional political parties. Not being himself a member of a political party, he was supported by a loose coalition of personal followers (*Ibañistas*), nationalists (Partido Agrario Laboristas [PAL]) and socialists. From early on the Agrario Laboristas became the backbone of the coalition, helping determine the main social, foreign, and economic policies.[23]

Although during the presidential campaign Ibañez del Campo was (deliberately) vague regarding the details of his economic program, his discourse had a clearly populist tone.[24] He promised to eliminate inflation, to increase the standard of living, to create a strong government-owned bank, and to put an end to corruption. The Partido Agrario Laborista (PAL), however, had a more clearly defined economic program that explicitly called for increased subsidized credit for productive purposes; higher public investment in transportation and other forms of infrastructure, modernization of agriculture, the encouragement of exports, and the creation of a heavy industry.[25]

After taking power in November, 1952, Ibañez del Campo named Juan B. Rosetti, a socialist, to the Ministry of Finance. In spite of the government's statements that defeating inflation was a high priority, during the period 1952–1955 the fiscal deficit and money creation reached record proportions.[26] Wage increases, higher transfers, and growing bank credit were rapidly feeding higher price increases. Between December of 1951 and December of 1954 the Central Bank's credit to the government increased by 43 percent (see figure 8.3 on monetary growth).

In 1953, Minister of Finance Felipe Herrera, a socialist who later became the president of the Interamerican Development Bank, put together

---

22. These two reports differed, however, in their emphasis. While the Fund considered the elimination of indexation as the *center* of a stabilization program, the UN proposal revolved around a price freeze and an obligatory savings scheme.
23. On the PAL, see Garay Vera (1990).
24. Interestingly enough, and contrary to other populist experiences in Latin America, in addition to courting the urban masses, Ibañez del Campo sought (and obtained) support among the rural voters.
25. On the PAL economic program, see Garay Vera (1990).
26. Ffrench-Davis (1973) points out that the rate of money expansion during this period had only been exceeded during the Socialist Republic of 1932.

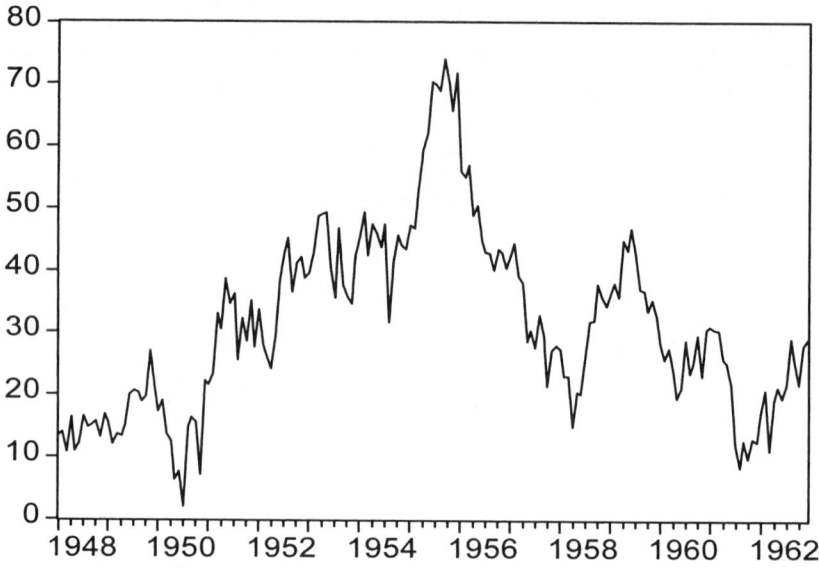

Fig. 8.3 M1 growth

a stabilization program based on a devaluation of the peso, credit controls, and higher income taxes. No effort, however, was made to put an end to the wage indexation scheme. Quite on the contrary, the devaluation—most commercial transactions became subject to a 110 pesos per dollar rate—was accompanied by a 15 percent increase in the so-called *Family-Allowance,* a per head bonus paid to each worker. Moreover, the program was not fully implemented; after an intense debate, Congress refused to increase taxes, with inflation continuing its rapid acceleration.

Instead of following up on the Herrera program and trying to work out a political solution to the impasse, President Ibañez del Campo decided to alter the course of economic policy. Herrera was replaced by an Ibañez del Campo supporter of clear populist inclinations, who immediately eliminated credit controls and increased government expenditures and wage adjustments.[27] Undoubtedly Ibañez del Campo's own personality affected the nature of the inflationary process. His sudden changes of heart, his political gyrations, and his stubborn independence from political and economic advisors more often than not added fuel to inflation.

A second stabilization attempt took place in mid-1954 under the leadership of Jorge Prat, a nationalist politician that had been a member of the conservative party until 1947. This program was even broader and more ambitious than that proposed by Felipe Herrera. Its main components included:

27. See Hirschman (1963) and Ffrench-Davis (1973) on this episode.

- government austerity through lower expenditures;
- a new devaluation;
- higher taxes;
- the reestablishment of credit controls;
- reforming the system of wage indexation by reducing the extent of the adjustment to 60 percent of accumulated past inflation;
- increasing the coverage of the minimum wage;
- imposing a forced profits reinvestment policy on corporations.

This program—which was known as the "Program of Economic Rectification" (*Programa de Rectificación Económica*)—received some initial political support by Congress, and some of its components, including the devaluation and a partial adjustment of taxes, were undertaken. Once again, however, the complete program was not approved by Congress, and once again taxes and wages were at the heart of the political impasse: the right, the radicals, and the left voted against tax increases and the wage deindexation rules. At that point, political bickering increased significantly, with the opposition parties stepping up their antigovernment campaign. In December, Congress stripped the government of executive privileges and put an end to a state of emergency imposed earlier that year. A succession of finance ministers went in and out of office in rapid succession.[28] The leftist opposition rapidly began to gather momentum, and major labor conflicts ensued. A number of major strikes took place, with political dissatisfaction becoming ever more apparent. The government was clearly on the defensive.

In January 1955, under the fifth minister of finance of the Ibañez del Campo administration, a 60 percent generalized wage adjustment was granted. In that month inflation reached an annual rate of almost 57 percent and the premium in the parallel market for foreign exchange surpassed the 70 percent mark, almost doubling from its level in November of 1954, when the Prat devaluation was engineered.

As the year 1955 began, the political situation became increasingly fragile, with a group of Ibañez del Campo supporters—including the so-called "grey wolves" (*lobos grises*)—discussing with some high military officers—the "Straight Line" (*Linea Recta*) group—the possibility of staging a coup that would have dissolved Congress, while retaining Ibañez del Campo as the head of state. The extent of the plot, and the vulnerability of the democratic system, became starkly clear when Senator Guillermo Izquierdo, the Chairman of the Partido Agrario Laborista, realized that he himself had been involved in discussions with the military Straight Line group.[29]

---

28. A drastic decline in the price of copper made things more complicated (Zahler 1978; see Ffrench-Davis 1973).

29. See Garay Vera (1990, 178).

8.5 The Klein-Saks Mission: Diagnosis and Policy Recommendations

In July of 1955 the government of Chile hired the Klein-Saks consulting firm to evaluate the economic conditions of the country and to provide a set of recommendations regarding anti-inflationary policy.[30] Two months later the five-man Mission arrived in Santiago for what was originally supposed to be a six-month visit. Things, however, were not so simple; the Mission worked continuously in Chile until September of 1958. By then, however, inflation had not been tamed. In October of 1958 the 12 months' rate of inflation was 16 percent, significantly higher than what the Mission had expected when it had arrived in Chile three years earlier.[31] But the worst was yet to come. By December 1958 inflation had climbed to 33 percent, and by mid-1959 it was almost 45 percent. By then the Klein-Saks Mission had been added to a long list of Chile's failed stabilization programs.

In this section I discuss the diagnosis made by the Mission, as well as its original policy recommendations. I also analyze the political discussion that surrounded the first year of the Mission's work. Although the main interest of this paper is on the *adoption and implementation* of the Mission's program, in subsection 8.5.2. I briefly deal with the final phases of the program, and I discuss the reasons behind its eventual failure.

8.5.1 Diagnosis

Approximately forty-five days after its arrival, on November 19, 1955, the Mission delivered its first policy memorandum to President Ibañez del Campo, stating its overall view on Chile's economic conditions and sketching some of its most important policy recommendations. The Mission's diagnosis of Chile's inflationary pressures revolved around four basic areas: (1) fiscal deficit, (2) monetary expansion, (3) exchange rate policy, and (4) wage rate policy.

The mission forcefully argued that the state of government finances and, in particular, the extremely high fiscal deficit was at the heart of the inflationary process. It was suggested that this problem was to be tackled by a combination of higher revenues, to be obtained via the combination of a tax reform that would include stiff penalties for tax evasion and payment delays, and reduced expenditures. Among the specific measures recommended to cut down public expenditures the Mission included the "suppression of foreign travel by public functionaries," the "elimination, if pos-

---

30. Government leaders debated intensively on who could provide the best advice. The candidates included Dr. Dagmar Schacht, of Nazi fame, and the French economist Pierre Mendes-France. A number of elements seem to have determined the selection of the Klein-Saks group, including the fact that this was a U.S. firm and that it had helped in implementing a successful (or so perceived) program in Peru in 1949.

31. According to the Mission's program, price stability would have been achieved by 1958-1959. See Ffrench-Davis (1973, 27).

sible, of subsidies to public railways, maritime freight, airlines, buses, and electricity," and the reduction (again if possible) "of the acquisition of arms and weapons."[32]

The Mission also pointed out that while fiscal laxity was the main cause of inflation, price increases themselves had helped to further weaken the efficiency of the tax system.[33]

> The entire tax system had become distorted, with the incidence of taxes being far different from the intentions of the legislators. All taxes fixed in numbers of peso and *all taxes paid with a time lag had a lesser incidence than had been intended*. . . As a consequence tax revenue had become insufficient to finance even a constant level of real expenditures. (Klein-Saks 1958, 3; emphasis added)

Of course, the statement in italics means that the Mission recognized what in time has come to be known as the Olivera-Tanzi effect: lagged tax collection in an inflationary environment can greatly erode tax revenues. Consequently, an important recommendation of the Mission was to replace specific taxes for ad valorem ones and to reduce the tax collection lag.

With respect to credit policy, the Mission argued that excessive money creation, mostly (but not exclusively) devoted to finance government expenditures, constituted an important element fueling inflation. Their monetary analysis was traditional and based strictly on the quantity theory of money. For instance, in evaluating Chile's capacity to conduct noninflationary monetary creation a Mission report stated.

> Considering that the Chilean economy is fully employed, that population grows at a 1.6% annual rate and that national income has rarely exceeded 3.5%, it is not justifiable to expend liquidity at a rate exceeding 5 to 6% per annum.[34]

And the letter went on to say:

> It is, thus, not surprising that with an increase in monetary means of almost 70% in 1955, price increases had reached almost 80%.

In terms of policy, the Mission suggested imposing quantitative credit limits to the banking system, and urged the Central Bank to make use of the control attributions that a new charter had provided in 1953. Additionally, it recommended that the Central Bank charge an interest rate close to the market rate for its own loans and other operations. Much of the Mission's early work on monetary policy consisted of persuading the public, and especially a prominent group of industrialists, that money cre-

---

32. Letter from the Mission to the President of the Republic, dated November 19, 1955.
33. Most letters and memoranda from the Mission to the government were in Spanish. This and other quotes correspond to my own translation.
34. Letter to the minister of finance, dated December 27, 1955.

ation devoted to increasing credit to industry was still inflationary. In fact, as was suggested earlier, at the time Chilean entrepreneurs were highly influenced by the real bills doctrine, and argued that it was crucial to distinguish between speculative and productive credit.

With respect to exchange policy, the Mission argued that under a situation of multiple exchange rates and severe overvaluation, as the one prevailing in Chile in late 1955, the rest of the anti-inflationary measures would be self-defeating. Without introducing rapid and substantial corrective measures in the foreign sector it was clear that the public would continue to speculate against the peso, introducing a dangerous instability into the financial and banking sectors.

In a letter to the minister of finance dated January 16, 1956, the Mission argued that it was urgent to implement in the *very short run* a reform of the exchange rate system:

> An anti-inflationary program that excludes a reform of the exchange rate system will, at best, generate a temporary and short run reduction of inflation. It would fail, however, to provide the country with a solid base for future economic growth and development.

In April of 1956, and after the IMF had granted its approval, a new exchange rate system consisting of a single *fluctuating exchange rate* for commercial transactions and a freely floating rate for capital movements was adopted. In fact, this dual floating exchange rate system was vintage Julius Klein. In 1949, Klein, one of the principal partners of the consulting firm, had advised the government of Peru recommending, among other things, the adoption of a dual-rate fluctuating system. This regime lasted in Peru from November 1949 to December 1954.[35]

Initially it was thought that the Central Bank would occasionally intervene in the foreign exchange market in order to smooth excessive fluctuations. In fact, with the aid of the IMF the government created a US$70 million stabilization fund for this purpose. Rather quickly, however, the government began to intervene in the market in a direct way, by de facto pegging the commercial rate. By 1957 the exchange rate became a serious area of disagreement between the government and the Mission. While the latter argued that new world and national conditions required a substantial depreciation of the peso, the government refused to do so, on the grounds that it would increase inflation.

The exchange system reform of 1956 was accompanied by a series of measures geared at organizing the control of international trade systems. The most important elements of the new foreign trade regime were the existence of a list of forbidden commodities that could not be imported into the country and the implementation of a system of previous import de-

---

35. The Peruvian program can be found in Klein (1949). See also Edwards (1983).

posits whereby, at the time of requiring an import license, importers had to make a deposit (in the Central Bank) equivalent to a percentage of the merchandise to be imported.

Although the Mission's reports recognized from the beginning that the anti-inflationary policy should be seen as a *package* with multiple interrelated components, they also stressed that limiting the extent of *wage indexation* was the most important short-run measure. This position was based on both economic and strategic considerations. First, the Mission recognized that the automatic wage adjustment mechanism introduced inertia into the system through both cost pushes and higher inflationary expectations. Thus, eliminating (or even limiting) indexation would provide an important blow to inflationary psychology and to cost increases. Second, according to the existing legislation, the annual wage adjustment was due at the end of January of 1956. When the Mission issued its first report in mid-November 1955, Congress was already devoted to the discussion of the nature of the upcoming wage bill. It was, thus, fundamentally important to handle this situation head on, without much delay. It was considered that tackling the wage adjustment issue could *not* wait until a consistent and comprehensive package was fully available.

The central role given by the Mission to limiting the extent of indexation is apparent in the following quote from a letter to the Minister of Finance dated December 17, 1955:

> [I]t is clear that unless the current system of automatic wage readjustments is eliminated (or at least modified), it will be impossible to have a successful implementation of the restrictive credit and budget policies.

In a grave and fateful mood the letter stated that:

> [t]he country is now a prisoner of a past that invented the current automatic [wage] adjustment system.

A large fraction of the Mission's efforts during the first few months in Santiago was devoted to convincing government officials, politicians, and civic leaders of the necessity of limiting wage adjustment for 1956 to no more than 50 percent of accumulated past inflation.[36] The specific proposal (Law 12,006) was presented to Congress in November of 1955 and was approved by the Lower House (the *Cámara de Diputados*) on December 22 by a comfortable margin.[37] The PAL, other *Ibañista* groups, and the right-wing parties (conservatives and liberals) voted for its approval, with the left and the radicals opposing it.

The Senate, however, was a different story; the government and its new allies did not have a clear majority in the higher chamber of congress. Jan-

---

36. Law 12,006 also established that during 1956, prices of basic goods and necessities—which were controlled by the government—would only increase by 40 percent.

37. The vote was 56 in favor and 48 against.

uary 3, 1956, was probably one of the most memorable days in Senate history. The debate was long and intense and after two votes a nineteen-nineteen draw persisted. It was only on the 6th of January that this piece of legislation, known as the "Stabilization Program" (*Programa de Estabilización*) was approved, when ailing Senator and former Presidential candidate Cruz-Coke was brought to the Senate floor to participate in the third vote.

From a political economy perspective, perhaps the most important aspect of this episode is that Law 12,006 and, more generally, the Klein-Saks stabilization package as a whole was supported by both conservative and liberal parties. These were the same parties that had so vehemently opposed Ibañez del Campo in the past. Not only that, but these were the same politicians that in November of 1954—during the Prat stabilization attempt—had refused to support legislation that would put an end to indexation. Why did they support this legislation in early 1956, and not in 1954? Was it only because inflation has crossed some threshold number that made it so costly as to make some political parties change their position?[38] Did the presence of the Klein-Saks Mission have anything to do with this change in the right's position? Some of these issues are addressed in sections 8.6 and 8.7 of this paper.

8.5.2 The End of the Affair: Unraveling and Departure

As soon as Law 12,006, which restricted wage indexation, was approved, the Mission turned its efforts to the fiscal deficit. In a letter addressed to the minister of finance dated January 16, 1956, the Mission said:

> We need to note that . . . the limits on wage indexation and the control of credit would lose their effectiveness unless they are immediately followed by . . . [the] *control of fiscal expenditure* . . . [and] . . . *tax measures*. (1956; emphasis in the original)

Among the expenditure-related measures the Mission recommended putting an end to were low income housing subsidies, canceling public construction projects, reducing the personnel in diplomatic missions, increasing the price of postage, and suspending military purchases. In terms of tax measures the Mission suggested levying taxes on the basis of current (as opposed to last year's) income, raising fuel taxes, enforcing the tax code, and sending tax evaders to prison.[39]

The fiscal accounts, however, did not evolve in the way the Mission had envisaged them. On the one hand, Congress was reluctant to enact a major tax reform; on the other, the Ibañez del Campo administration was unwill-

---

38. This is unlikely, since in November of 1954, when the Prat program was rejected, inflation was already 70 percent. It is difficult to think that some magic threshold is crossed when inflation moves from 70 to 80 percent.

39. Mission letter to the minister of finance, January 16, 1956.

Table 8.3   Fiscal deficit: 1952–1964

Year	Deficit fiscal (% GDP)
1952	4.3
1953	4.9
1954	4.0
1955	4.2
1956	2.2
1957	3.6
1958	3.2
1959	3.9
1960	5.3
1961	5.1
1962	6.2
1963	5.5
1964	4.9

Source: Ffrench-Davis (1973) and IMF.

ing to reduce expenditures in a significant way. Paradoxically, the IMF program of 1956—under which the country borrowed US$81.3 million—had a negative effect on fiscal austerity. The reasons for this were simple: at that time the IMF had not yet developed the concept of *conditionality,* and thus there were no formal (and legal) austerity conditions attached to the program. Once the IMF funds became available, the administration felt that a serious financial constraint had been lifted, and considered that there was no need to reduce expenditures drastically.[40] After declining in 1956, the fiscal deficit again increased in 1957; in 1958 it experienced a slight decline, but it was still being financed mostly by money creation (see table 8.3).

A drastic drop in the price of copper in late 1956 and 1957 greatly affected fiscal revenues, and contributed to the higher deficit in 1957 and 1958 (see figure 8.3 on the price of copper). The government reacted to the lower price of copper by increasing its indebtedness from abroad and, especially, by money creation. In a report to Congress' Joint Budget Committee, the Mission argued that the negative effects of a lower copper price had been amplified because the country lacked sufficient international reserves:

> The lack of a policy aimed at accumulating reserves . . . during periods when the price of copper was high, has implied that during the current year the monetary authorities have had to make a major effort to maintain the foreign exchange situation under control. . . . Thus, it has been impossible to provide fiscal or credit assistance . . . to depressed regional industries.[41]

---

40. See Remmer (1986) on the IMF programs in Latin America during the 1950s.
41. Report to the Congress' Joint Budget Committee, November 7, 1957.

As the fiscal imbalance increased, the stabilization program unraveled. In 1957 the wage rule was weakened, and a general wage increase equal to 80 percent of accumulated inflation was decreed. Moreover, credit controls were relaxed and the money supply started to expand at a more rapid pace. As a result of the decline in the price of copper the peso came under pressure. The authorities reacted negatively to the faster depreciation of the peso by increasing trade barriers. More specifically, during the second half of 1957, and against the Mission's recommendations, prior import deposits were increased very significantly.[42]

By early 1958 the Mission's program was rapidly losing political support and credibility. In May of that year the Mission issued a report of its work, including a set of recommendations for the future. Many of these had to do with fiscal policy, foreign exchange policy, and the creation of strong public institutions.[43] But perhaps the most important set of recommendations had to do with inflation. The Mission insisted that inflationary financing would not provide a path to prosperity. By October of that year the Mission's work came to an end; inflation was rapidly creeping up. By December of 1958 it was 33 percent, and by June of 1959 it had already reached the 50 percent mark.

8.6 The Politics of Credibility and the Klein-Saks Mission

In order to understand fully the sequence of events that led to the adoption of the 1955–56 stabilization program it is necessary to explain the role played by the Klein-Saks Mission. What was the actual contribution of these foreign advisors in the implementation of this specific program? How does their work fit, if at all, within the political discussions and debates of that time? In what follows I look at these questions from three different perspectives. I first analyze what was new in the Mission's recommendations. I then investigate the political reception of the Mission's proposals, and I finally deal with the issue of the Mission's work and credibility.

8.6.1 The Klein-Saks Mission as a Technocratic Team

The simplest explanation of the Mission's role is the purely technical one. According to this view, foreign consultants would provide policymakers with a type of expertise otherwise unavailable in the country. Once the technical diagnostic work is done, domestic politicians and policymakers

---

42. See Ffrench-Davis (1973).
43. Interestingly, the Mission made two recommendations that were considered to be extreme at the time, but that today are at the core of Chile's economic institutions: a (relatively) independent central bank, governed by a small technical board; and the reform of social security, where "the individual himself would make decisions regarding the disposition of a substantial part of his income" Klein-Saks (1958, 48).

will have a clearer view of the problems at hand and, with the help of the advisors, could proceed to design a specific stabilization program. This interpretation of foreign advisors as providing technical expertise not available in the country does not require that all participants in the debate agree on the causes of inflation and on the most desirable course of action. In fact, it is perfectly possible to think that this technical knowledge is more in line with a particular political view of the world than with others.[44]

Some authors have endorsed the view of the Klein-Saks Mission as technocrats providing expertise not available in Chile at that time. In fact, this was the way the Mission was presented by the government in 1955: repeatedly, administration spokesmen and (part of) the media referred to the Mission as a group of politically neutral foreign experts that, similar to medical doctors, were coming to the country to provide a diagnosis of the nature of the sickness and suggest a specific treatment. This is, for example, the view of Correa Prieto (1962), who argues that the display of technical knowledge made by the Mission's chief, Preston Carter, greatly contrasted with the low level of preparedness of the local technocrats.[45] While Ffrench-Davis (1973) has rejected the view that the Mission was politically neutral, he has argued that it did indeed provide a type of technical expertise unavailable at that time in Chile. According to him most Chilean economists were then of a leftist-structuralist persuasion and, consequently, a government that wanted to pursue an orthodox type of adjustment program could not elaborate such a program with local experts.

Although there is little doubt that the Mission was formed by experienced professionals that contributed a number of technical details in the design of policies, it is also true that their overall contribution to the diagnosis and formulation of policy was limited. As we have already seen, the failed Prat stabilization proposal (the "Program of Economic Rectification") of November of 1954 included a large number of the components of the Klein-Saks program, including limiting the extent of indexation, fiscal austerity, and higher taxes.

A lengthy report presented by the Central Bank to the Chamber of Deputies in July of 1955 clearly indicates that at that time at least part of the economics profession in Chile had understood the country's inflationary problems in a way that fully coincided with that later developed by the Mission. For example, the proposed Central Bank program called for fiscal restraint, for the elimination of legislation that allowed the Treasury to borrow from the Central Bank, for the adoption of a freely fluctuating exchange rate, and for the implementation of an imports deposit scheme to control foreign trade. With respect to wages, the report argued that controlled their rate of increase was an essential component of the stabilization

---

44. See Felix (1960).
45. See Correa Prieto (1963, 50); Wurth Rojas (1958).

program (Banco Central de Chile 1956). It is interesting, however, to note that the report was not as forceful regarding wage deindexation as it was with respect to the other components of adjustment policies. This may be explained by the fact that it was at that time an exceedingly sensitive political issue, which the Bank Board tried to avoid to the extent possible.

From the analysis of both the Prat 1954 program and the Central Bank 1955 document, it is clear that, at least in terms of diagnosis and broad policies, the Klein-Saks program did not add novel aspects. Hirschman (1963) has argued that the only new device suggested by the Mission was the system of advanced deposits on imports. This, however, is not completely correct. The Central Bank program specifically proposed "requiring [to importers] a deposit in domestic currency in the Central Bank" (Banco Central 1956, 77). What was new in the Mission's program was the suggestion of a *dual* floating rate system. The Central Bank program and other proposals that circulated at the time called for a unique floating rate. The absence of spectacular (and almost mythical) new policy propositions in the Mission program contrasts sharply with a UN report of 1950, which suggested a forced savings scheme as a sort of panacea that would quickly, and with little cost, help solve most (if not all) economic problems in Chile.[46]

The fact that the Mission had not suggested significant new perspectives or policy measures was a source of some irritation in Chile. Many felt that national pride was at stake, since foreigners were coming into the country, recommending measures already discussed many times in the past. As Hirschman has pointed out, many considered the Mission's program as a (convex) combination of the Herrera and Prat programs of 1953 and 1954. The resentful sentiments of a large number of Chileans toward the Mission are captured from the opening statement from then Senator (and eventually President of the Republic) Salvador Allende, during the debate of Law 12,006:

> [I] have stated that there are Chilean professionals with the required knowledge and ability to design, on the basis of an organic plan, the measures to be taken.[47]

8.6.2 War of Attrition, Umpires, and Mediators

A popular interpretation of the role of foreign advisors and foreign agencies is that of an umpire that helps the locals select one of many alternative proposals for action. Hirschman (1963), for example, offers this explanation with respect to the role of the Kemmerer 1925 Mission, which resulted in the foundation of Chile's Central Bank. According to him, when Kemmerer arrived, so many proposals for monetary reform had been discussed

---

46. See United Nations (1951).
47. See Congreso Nacional de Chile, Diario de Sesiones del Senado, January 3, 1955, 1137.

that the politicians and the public had become utterly confused. According to this view the role of the foreign advisors is just to pick one of many proposals and thus help solve an impasse. It is worth quoting Hirschman on this point:

> Examination of the many proposals that were put forward with ever-increasing frequency in the period 1913–25 makes it clear that the final Kemmerer bills did not contain any substantial innovations with respect to the crucial topics of restoration of the gold standard and the establishment of the Central Bank. The conclusion is therefore inescapable that the mission served principally as an *umpire*. (Hirschman 1967, 176–77; emphasis added)

Alternatively, one can think that foreign advisors provide new information to different groups on the costs and consequences of the crisis, thus convincing some of them that they should give up their extreme positions. According to this interpretation, by pointing out angles previously unseen by the different groups, the foreign advisors contribute to obtaining an earlier end to the war of attrition. Players that would have refused to give up in the absence of this new information decide to compromise earlier on. This interpretation is close to that provided by the Klein-Saks Mission itself in 1958. In a summary document published in May of that year, it said:

> [T]he only program with a chance of success was deemed to be a broad attack on many fronts, in which all factions would contribute, through a gradual retreat from their previous extreme positions. . . . In attention to aid in the implementation of such a program, the Mission has always seen its main contribution is acting as an objective advisor on the overall aspects of a balanced program. (Klein-Saks 1958, 6)

Although the interpretation of the role of the Klein-Saks Mission as an umpire and a mediator is quite appealing, it presents some problems.[48] First, and as has already been established, the Mission contributed very little in terms of new perspectives and provided little new information to what was already on the table in mid-1955. This casts serious doubt on the interpretation's being based on additional information provided in the context of a war of attrition.

A second problem is that war of attrition models assume that, although different groups struggle to obtain larger shares of national income and try to avoid playing a large fraction of the costs of stabilization, they basically agree on what should be done to eliminate inflation. In these models there is no ignorance or disagreement with respect to the way in which the world works. Inflation, and the inability to put together a timely stabilization pro-

---

48. In fact, in light of the previous discussion, if one were to replace the reference to Kemmerer for Klein-Saks and monetary reform for a stabilization program, the quote from Hirschman would appear quite plausible.

gram, is the unavoidable result of a distributive conflict; in these models there is no room for dissenting approaches to stabilizing. The only source of conflict is who pays a larger share of the costs of reducing inflation. This important assumption of the war of attrition models is flatly contradicted by the history of the Klein-Saks program.

The Congressional debate that preceded the approval of Law 12,006 shows that different groups and parties strongly disagreed on what was the most adequate course of action to defeat inflation. For example, when explaining his negative vote Senator Ampuero, the former secretary-general of the Socialist Party, argued that the proposed fluctuating exchange rate was contrary to the goal of solving inflation and staging a recovery. Another opposition senator, Socialist Senator Luis Quinteros stated:

> Honorable Senate, we should remember that even before any wage adjustment law was enacted, Chile already suffered from high inflation. . . . Consequently to argue that the law of wage adjustment is the main engine of inflation contradicts, in my view, Chile's economic and history experience. (Diario del Senado, January 3, 1956, 1181).

But it is perhaps the statement by radical deputy Muñoz-Horz that is the one that more vividly captures the opposing views on the mechanics of inflation:

> [T]he inflationary process has . . . increased in an exaggerated way profits of productive firms. This demonstrates that the automatic increase of wages is not precisely the engine of inflation. . . . From what has been said it follows that in order to end this serious inflationary process it is necessary, first and foremost, to fix and freeze prices and immediately to increase salaries, wages and pensions so that they achieve parity with prices." (Diario de la Cámara de Diputados, Dec. 22, 1955, 2549–50)

It is evident, then, that the views prevailing at the time regarding the causes of inflation, and the most appropriate course for the stabilization program, were significantly different. It is difficult, consequently, to agree with the view that the Klein-Saks Mission acted as a mediator that helped *all* factions decide how much to contribute toward the achievement of the stabilization of growth. Indeed, the Mission approach was considered to be completely erroneous by a large proportion of politicians, economists, and journalists.

8.6.3 Credibility and the Klein-Saks Mission

As was pointed out in section 8.2, modern theories of inflation and stabilization have emphasized the role of *credibility* in achieving a rapid and (relatively) costless adjustment process. To the extent that governments are able to affect expectations, and persuade the private sector that a change of regime will be engineered, the disinflation process will have a higher probability of success. The problem, however, is that governments tend to have difficulties in making credible promises. That is, there are usually few institutional arrangements that can assure the public that the government will not renege on its promises after the private sector has already made important decisions. A key issue in establishing credibility, then, is to design mechanisms that will allow the government to precommit itself.

An interesting line of analytical reasoning postulates that *reputational constraints* can sometimes act as good substitutes for precommitment technology.[49] Policymakers afraid to damage their reputation will tend to stick to their promises. This is an elegantly plausible idea, but the Ibañez del Campo government was particularly noncredible. The general had changed alliances, denounced former collaborators, and gyrated too rapidly to give any confidence to the public.

The Ibañez del Campo credibility problem is neatly evidenced in the speech given by Senator Luis Bossay, chairman of the opposition Radical Party, during the debate on Law 12,006 on the stabilization of prices and wages. After arguing that wage deindexation constituted only an isolated measure that did not go to the heart of the problem, he said:

> It is true that [Finance] Minister Herrera Palacios . . . referred to the adoption of complementary measures. . . . Do we have any assurance that after approving one measure, the rest of them will be implemented? . . . the cruel experience of three years shows that this hesitant, incoherent and contradicting government is unable of designing and maintaining, with perseverance, a financial and economic policy; we have no confidence that it is committed today of implementing a coherent plan that would put an end to the inflationary process." (Diario de Sesiones del Senado, January 3, 1956, 1152)

In fact, the Ibañez del Campo administration's announcements and promises had become noncredible for every political party in the opposition. Not only were the center and left skeptical regarding the government's ability to deliver on its promises, but the right wing, which the President was seeking as a new ally, was equally doubtful. Senator Moore, from the liberal party, described the government as following a "zig-zagging approach full of contradictions and incomplete attitudes."[50] On the other hand, Senator Marin, from the liberal party, questioned the government's ability to maintain an announced course of action.

The credibility problem had been compounded by the fact that after the abortion of the Prat stabilization program in November of 1954, there had been four different ministers of finance that had taken half-baked and often contradictory measures, while inflation continued its rampant pace.

In some way the Central Bank was the only public institutions that had some credibility. Its professional staff was well respected and, as we have

49. See, for example, Drazen (2000) and Persson and Tabellini (2000).
50. Diario Sesiones del Sanado, January 3, 1955, 1146.

seen, its proposed stabilization program of July 1955 was sophisticated and suggested a number of fundamental measures. The Bank, however, was handicapped by its lack of independence from the government. In spite of a reform to its charter in 1953, the Board was still dominated by representatives of the executive. This lack of independence was so evident that during his short tenure as minister of finance the populist Guillermo del Pedregal strongly maneuvered to oust the Central Bank Governor Arturo Maschke.[51]

When looked at from the perspective of a government with a total lack of credibility and virtually no reputational capital, resorting to external advisors begins to make sense. By taking this measure the government was signaling its intentions of altering its behavior. It is also possible that government officials expected that by hiring the Mission they were acquiring some reputational capital. Additionally, by doing this, a sense of continuity was introduced into the program. Even if Ibañez del Campo decided to replace the minister of finance, the mission technocrats were still around to carry on the battle.

A number of authors have recently argued that external agencies such as the World Bank and the International Monetary Fund can provide credibility to adjustment and stabilization programs (Edwards 1989; Drazen 2000). This can happen in two related ways: first, by violating agreements with these agencies the country in question will incur costs that will usually come in the form of losses of resources obtained through specific programs. These costs, of course, will make policy changes less probable than otherwise. Second, through the monitoring of the country's economic performance, the external agencies provide information to other (external) actors, including foreign governments and private creditors. In a way, through the provision of information, these external institutions make the country's reputation more transparent and easy to control, thus making this constraint more binding.

Although the Klein-Saks Mission did not have funds of its own to provide to the Chilean government, its connections with the international financial community and the U.S. government made its role rather effective. In fact, after putting together the most important element of the stabilization program, the mission helped the government obtain US$70 million in fresh resources. Additionally, the mission's work during late 1955 and early 1956 paved the path for Chile's standby agreement with the IMF in April of 1956. This, however, leaves open the question of why the

---

51. For a fascinating insider's view of economic policymaking during this period, see Maschke's memoirs (Maschke 1990). I had the opportunity to interview Mr. Maschke in 1991, when I first got interested in studying this period of Chile's economic history. I must say that I had the most wonderful and interesting time talking with him at his Providencia apartment. That same year I also interviewed Dr. Anibal Pinto, one of Chile's most influential academic economists during the time of the Klein-Saks Mission, and Mr. Arturo Fontaine Aldunate, who had been the Under Secretary of Finance during Jorge Prat's tenure as minister. These interviews were extremely useful in helping me understand better the politics and economics of the second Ibañez administration.

Chilean government decided to hire private advisors rather than going directly to the IMF. There are two explanations for this decision. First, at this time the IMF had relatively little experience in setting up programs with the developing countries. For instance, during 1953–1955 a total of only *five* standby agreements had been signed, with most of them being with European nations. Additionally, the fact that the Klein mission to Peru in 1949–1954 had been well received by the international community made the Washington consultants natural candidates for this job. Second, hiring a private advisory group that would take residency in Santiago and that would provide a daily monitoring of the economic situation helped the government to gain *political* credibility with the domestic right, whose support it required to approve key elements of the program.

The mounting political tension of 1955 greatly influenced the right's decision to change its strategy and to support the Ibañez del Campo administration's anti-inflation program. It became apparent at that time that the increasing economic chaos had generated serious antidemocratic sentiments among sectors of the military. The "Straight Line" (*Linea Recta*) movement was acting opening, and a number of nationalistic elements were calling on Ibañez del Campo to close Congress and to establish itself as an autocratic ruler who would return order and put an end to inflation. This possibility represented great political danger for the rightist politicians, who clearly remembered the setbacks suffered during the first Ibañez del Campo authoritarian rule in 1924. Moreover, at this point the conservative-liberal coalition had great expectations that their candidate could win the upcoming Presidential election in 1958.[52] In a way, then, the right was caught between two undesirable alternatives: to continue opposing Ibañez del Campo at all costs and, thus, risking a coup that would seriously jeopardize their chance of getting the presidency; or to support an untrustworthy administration that was well known for its gyrations and changes in policies.

The fact that the right weighed the political consequences of not supporting the stabilization program is apparent from liberal Senator Moore's speech on January 3, 1955.[53] He candidly stated:

> The liberal Party does not favor a coup d'etat; it does not expect . . . to resolve this issue by force and by spilling blood. . . . We desire that Mr. Ibañez serves his full term. (1147)

And he went on to say:

> We do not favor a coup. . . . Should we, then, blindly oppose the government from Congress? No. That would damage even more the reputation of the political parties; it would offer a motive to finish them and to close Congress. (1148)

---

52. Jorge Alessandri, the right-wing candidate, in fact won that election.
53. The quotes that follow come from the Diario de Sesiones del Senado, January 3, 1955.

And, he referred to the dilemma faced by his party in the following way:

> We will continue to defend legality, and we are demonstrating this by providing Mr. Ibañez with a legal tool. We place a delicate tool in clumsy hands. (1148)

However, it was one thing to weigh the costs of not supporting the government and see the economic situation further deteriorate, and a different thing to provide Ibañez del Campo with a blank check. In order to support the government, the right required certain guarantees that the overall package would include policies particularly important for this group. Among these policies, perhaps the most controversial one referred to the reform of the exchange rate system, including the adoption of a freely fluctuating rate. The key importance attached by the right to the exchange rate policy is manifest in a number of instances in the Congressional debate of that time. For example, conservative Senator Prieto stated:

> [T]here is no possibility of expanding production if the [foreign exchange law] retains . . . fixed and discriminatory rates. (Diario de Sesiones del Senado, January 3, 1955, 1167)

In this regard, then, the Klein-Saks Mission, with its historical record of supporting fluctuating rates and its good relation with the International Monetary Fund, provided an important element in persuading the Right to support the government. The Klein-Saks Mission provided, to the extent possible, an assurance that the policies were going to be consistent with what had been (implicitly) agreed upon. In other words, by having hired the Klein-Saks Mission the government not only sought to obtain domestic and international *economic* credibility, but it was also trying to credibly precommit to a key *political* group that there would be no sudden changes in the future course of action. But, how credible was the Mission's program? Did the Mission's work in fact, affect expectations? And if it did, was this a short-term break in expectations, or was it relatively long-lasting?[54] This, and related issues, are tackled in detail in section 8.7 of this paper.

8.7 Policy Credibility and Structural Breaks: An Empirical Investigation

In his highly influential work on inflation and stabilization, Sargent (1983, 1986) has argued that a credible anti-inflationary program results in a rapid change in the monetary and inflationary regimes. If the public believes that the policy will work—that is, that the policy is *credible*—it will incorporate its changed expectations into its decision-making process, including decisions on pricing, speculation, wage bargaining, capital flows, and so on. These changes in expectations, in turn, will be translated into a

---

54. Of course, we know that it was not *that* long lasting. After all, the Mission did fail, and by December 1958 inflation was already 33 percent.

change in the behavior of endogenous variables, such as interest rates, exchange rates, and inflation. This, for instance, was what happened during Raymond Poincare's stabilization program in France in the 1920s. It is also what happened with the founding of the Federal Reserve System in the United States in late 1914.[55]

From an econometric point of view, credible changes in regime will be reflected in break-points in the time series of the key endogenous variables. For example, as argued in Edwards (1993, 1998), a credible stabilization program would be reflected in a decline in the degree of *inertia* in the rate of inflation. In this section I use data on the black market exchange rate premium, as well as on inflation, to analyze the extent to which the policies of the Klein-Saks Mission were indeed credible.[56] Generally speaking, a credible stabilization program should be reflected in a very rapid—that is, instantaneous—break in the time series properties of financial variables, such as interest rates and (market determined) exchange rates. A credible stabilization program would also be reflected, although more slowly, on structural breaks in the time series behavior of inflation. In particular, if the stabilization program is indeed credible, the rate of persistence (or inertia) would rapidly decline, as would the expected long-term rate of inflation.

8.7.1 The Credibility of the Klein-Saks Mission and the Exchange Rate

In figure 8.4 I present the evolution of the official exchange rate, as well as the parallel (i.e., free) market exchange rate for the period January 1953–December 1956. As may be seen, the month the mission arrived in Chile, in September 1955, the parallel market rate (PER) experienced a drastic decline of 23 percent—it went from 770 pesos per dollar, in August, to 595 pesos per dollar in September. This is quite impressive considering that at that point the Mission had very little to show for its work. In the next two months, however, the public became increasingly skeptical, with the parallel rate climbing back to high levels—although not as high as the maximum attained in August of 1955. In January of 1956, once Law 12,006 was approved, the parallel rate fell by 24 percent, and the premium declined by almost 70 percent. During 1956 the parallel market rate was rather stable, and after the adoption of the new exchange rate regime in April the premium virtually disappeared (see figure 8.4), suggesting that the private sector perceived the Klein-Saks effort as a serious attempt at changing the na-

---

55. See Mankiw, Miron, and Weil (1987) for an analysis of the change in interest rate behavior after the founding of the Fed, a policy that the authors (rightly) consider to represent a major change in regime in U.S. monetary policy. In Edwards (1998) I used short-term interest rate data to analyze whether changes in Chile's capital controls policy were credible and effective.

56. Since there are no data on market-determined interest rates, I have not attempted to analyze structural breaks in interest rate behavior.

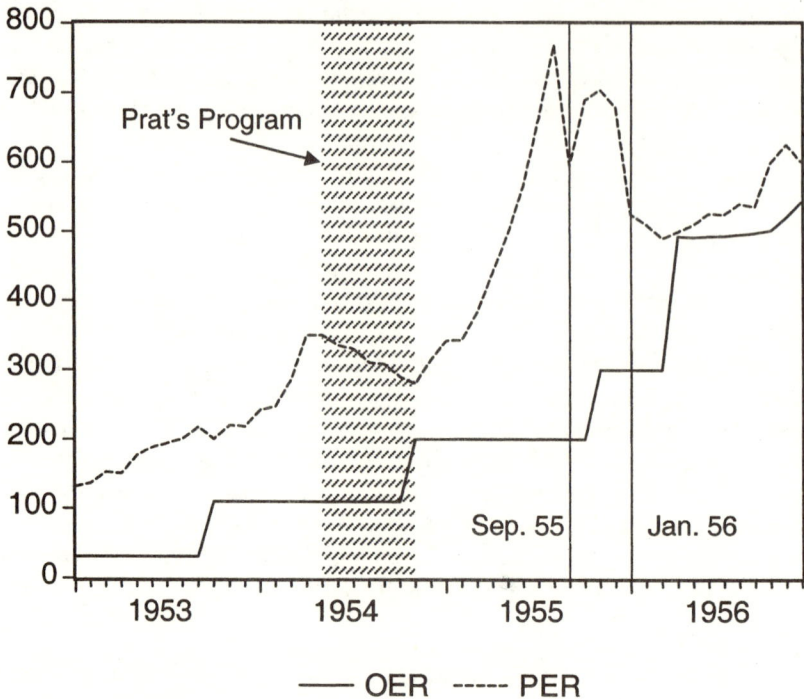

Fig. 8.4 Parallel and official exchange rate

ture of the inflationary process. Interestingly enough, as can be seen from the figure, the only other period with a significant decline in the free market rate corresponds to Prat's tenure as minister of finance. However, as soon as it became apparent that his program was not going to be approved by Congress, the free market rate rapidly climbed to higher levels (see shaded area in figure 8.4). This figure, then, suggests that there was a short-lived break in expectations that took place at the arrival of the Mission.

In order to formally analyze the extent to which the Mission affected expectations, I estimated a series of equations for the parallel market exchange rate premium, and I analyzed whether the equation had exhibited a structural break around the time the Mission began its work. The basic equation has the following form:

(1) $$premium_t = \alpha_0 + \alpha_1(\log \overline{OER_t} - \log OER_t) + \alpha_2 \frac{\Delta M_{t-1}}{M} + \alpha_3 \, premium_{t-1} + \varepsilon_t,$$

where *premium* is the parallel market premium; OER_t is the official exchange rate; $\overline{OER_t}$ is the equilibrium nominal exchange rate, which would prevail in the absence of rationing; $\Delta M_{t-1}/M$ is the excess supply of money M1; and ε is an error term assumed to have the standard properties. As long as there are exchange restrictions, the intercept will be significantly positive. Generally speaking, we would expect α_1 to be positive, indicating that the larger the gap between the equilibrium and the actual official nominal exchange rate, the larger will be the premium. Notice that this means that, to the extent that the equilibrium nominal exchange rate is unchanged, a nominal devaluation of the official rate (that is, an increase in log OER_t) will result in a decline in the parallel market premium. The α_2 coefficient is expected to be positive, indicating that a larger excess supply for money will result in a larger premium. Coefficient α_3 is expected to be positive and smaller than one. This coefficient measures the degree of inertia of the foreign exchange premium; the closer this coefficient to one, the higher is the degree of inertia.

A credible stabilization plan is expected to be reflected in a structural beak in equation (1), governing the foreign exchange premium. More specifically, when a credible stabilization plan is implemented, it is expected that the values of both α_0 and α_1 will decline. Indeed, under extreme credibility that eliminates inflationary pressures and exchange restrictions, it would be expected that α_0 and α_1 would very rapidly converge to zero. Notice that in this case the equilibrium (steady state) value of the premium would be equal to zero.

In order to analyze whether the adoption of the Klein-Saks program indeed affected expectations, I followed the following strategy. First, I use equation stability tests to analyze whether there is a breakpoint in equations of the type of (1) around the time of the program's adoption. Second, I add a number of dummy variables to the estimation of equations of the type of (1), as a way of analyzing this issue in greater detail. I am particularly interested in investigating whether α_0 and α_1 experienced a significant decline at the time of the program. In this analysis I have used the Hodrick-Prescott stochastic trend component of (the log of) the official exchange rate as a proxy for OER_t.[57] All the results discussed in this section were obtained using monthly data. See the appendix for exact variables' definitions and sources.

In table 8.4 I present regression results for equation (1). The first column uses a 1948–58 sample, while in column (2) the sample covers the 1948–62 period. The results are quite similar across these two base equations; all the coefficients have the expected signs and are significant at conventional levels. These estimates suggest that during this period the parallel market premium had a very high degree of inertia. Indeed, the estimated coefficient

---

57. I also assumed that for the period under study the equilibrium nominal rate was a constant. In this case, instead of the nominal exchange rate gap, the estimated equation will only have the log of the official rate. In terms of the credibility analysis, the results obtained when this alternative specification was used were similar to those discussed here, and have not been reported due to space considerations.

Table 8.4   Credibility and exchange rate premium: Regression analysis

	(1)	(2)	(3)
Constant	0.283	0.139	0.208
	(3.896)***	(3.028)***	(3.913)***
Nominal exchange rate disequilibrium	1.771	1.494	1.657
	(7.355)***	(7.477)***	(8.167)***
M1 excess of supply	0.020	0.016	0.018
	(1.905)*	(2.109)**	(2.329)**
Lagged premium	0.779	0.847	0.827
	(21.772)***	(32.252)***	(29.473)***
D552 · lagged premium			−0.721
			(−2.113)**
D561 · lagged premium			−0.721
			(−1.993)**
D562 · lagged premium			−1.107
			(−0.425)
D571 · lagged premium			1.865
			(0.408)
D572 · lagged premium			−0.409
			(−0.225)
D581 · lagged premium			−0.277
			(−0.294)
D582 · lagged premium			−0.414
			(−0.191)
D552			1.162
			(1.531)
D561			0.163
			(0.620)
D562			0.133
			(0.390)
D571			−0.426
			(−0.730)
D572			−0.175
			(−0.527)
D581			−0.183
			(−0.619)
D582			−0.165
			(−0.221)
Adjusted R^2	0.88	0.90	0.91
Durbin-Watson	1.67	1.80	1.73
Akaike info criterion	10.41	10.18	10.21
Schwarz criterion	10.50	10.25	10.53
F-statistic	313.28	535.78	100.34
Prob(F-statistic)	0.00	0.00	0.00
Sample	48-3: 58-12	48-3: 62-12	48-3: 62-12
No. of observations	130	178	178

Note: T-statistics in parentheses.
***Significant at the 1 percent level.
**Significant at the 5 percent level.
*Significant at the 10 percent level.

for the lagged premium is 0.78 and 0.85. In the discussion that follows, I focus on the results obtained when the 1948–62 sample is used.[58] As pointed out earlier, an important question for the credibility analysis is whether there was a change of regime at the time of the Mission's program. An F-test for equation stability suggests that equation (1) indeed experienced a structural break during the September 1955 and the September 1958 period: the value of the test is 15.8, indicating that the null hypothesis of no structural breaks is rejected at conventional levels.[59]

As a way of understanding further the reaction of expectations and of the foreign exchange market to the Mission's program, I included dummy variables for the period 1955–58 in the estimation of equation (1). In total, seven dummies were included: the first one (D552) takes a value of one for the September–December 1955 period, and zero otherwise. The other dummies—D561, D562, D571, D572, D581, and D582—take a value of one for the respective six-month period, and a value of zero otherwise (that is, D561 has ones for January–June 1956). The results, which are in column (3) of table 8.4, indicate that the effects of the Mission's program on expectations and the foreign exchange market were quite complex. As soon as the Mission arrived—and even before it started working—there was a sharp decline in the degree of persistence of the premium: the coefficient of (D552 × $premium_{t-1}$) is –0.721 and significant at the 5 percent level. This suggests that by the end of 1955 the parallel market premium had completely lost persistence—indeed, a χ^2 test indicates that the null hypothesis of equality of coefficients cannot be rejected at conventional levels. The results also indicate that the coefficient of (D561 × $premium_{t-1}$) is significantly negative, with a point estimate of –0.721; moreover, the null hypothesis that the degree of inertia in the first half of 1956 is zero cannot be rejected. These results, indeed, suggest that the hiring of the Mission did alter expectations, and changed the structural behavior of the parallel market premium.

This decline (or disappearance) in the degree of persistence was short-lived, however. As may be seen from table 8.4, starting in the second half of 1956, the coefficients of the dummy variables interacted with the lagged premium are not significantly different from zero, and the degree of persistence in the parallel market for foreign exchange goes back to what it had been before the Mission's arrival in Chile. As may be seen, the intercept dummies are not significantly different from zero.

8.7.2 Credibility and Inflationary Inertia

An important question is whether inflationary inertia declined in Chile in the period surrounding the Klein-Saks stabilization program. In order to do this I estimated a number of equations of the following type:

---

58. This is appropriate, since in 1960–1961 a new and bold stabilization program based on the pegging of the exchange rate and the elimination of all capital account restrictions was put into place. For details see, for example, Ffrench-Davis (1973).

59. This is a Chow F-test. The null hypothesis is that there are no structural breaks.

(2) $$Inf_t = \beta_0 + \beta_1 \frac{\Delta M_{t-1}}{M} + \beta_2 DevPar_{t-1} + \beta_3 DevOff_{t-1} + \beta_4 Inf_{t-1}$$
$$+ \beta_5(Dummy \times Inf_{t-1}) + \sum \sigma_j S_j + \psi_t$$

Inf is inflation, measured as the percentage change in the (CPI) relative to the same month in the prior year; $\Delta M_{t-1}/M$ is the rate of growth of M1, also measured relative to the previous year; *DevPar* is the rate of change in the parallel (i.e., free) exchange rate; *DevOff* is the rate of change of the official exchange rate; *Dummy* is a dummy variable that takes the value of one during the stabilization program; S_j are seasonal dummies; and ψ_t is an AR(12) error term.[60] To the extent that the stabilization program has indeed resulted in a decline in the degree of inertia, the estimated coefficient for β_5 would be significantly negative. As in the analysis of the exchange rate market, in the estimation I considered several alternative dummy variable that cover different time spans.

In table 8.5 I present the results obtained from the estimation of several versions of equation (2). Since the rate of devaluation in the parallel (i.e., free) market is endogenous, I used instrumental variables in the estimation; the standard errors were estimated using the Newey-West procedure.[61] The estimates in column (1) assume that there are no structural breaks during the period under study. In column (2) I have used one dummy variable (*DKS*) for the complete Klein-Saks period; it takes the value of one for September 1955–September 1958, and zero otherwise. In column (2) I have distinguished seven subperiods; as in table 8.4, the dummies D552, D561, D562, D571, D572, D581, and D582 refer to six successive six-month periods.[62] As may be seen, during the period under study inflation experienced a very significant degree of inertia. For instance, the estimate of the lagged dependent variable in column (1) is 0.896. The coefficients of money creation and exchange rate changes are positive, as expected, and with the exception of the coefficient of $\Delta M_{t-1}/M$ they are significant at conventional levels. Column (2) suggests that the degree of the Klein Saks program there was a very small, statistically significant, decline in inertia: the estimated coefficient of $(DKS \times Inf_{t-1})$ is equal to –0.044 and has a *t*-statistic of –2.36. The results in column (3) look at this issue in greater detail, by replacing *DKS* with the array of dummies D551–D582. As may be seen, these results give a rather more textured and complex story: according to these esti-

---

60. Since the monthly rate of inflation is defined as a year-over-year variable, equation (2) has to be estimated under the assumption of an AR(12) error.

61. The following instruments were used: the interaction between the dummy variable DKS and logged of inflation and lags of inflation rate, M1 growth, free exchange rate growth, and official exchange rate growth.

62. A preliminary analysis indicates that the intercept did not change during the period under study. Consequently, no dummies for the intercept were included in the regressions reported in table 8.5.

Table 8.5   Credibility and Inflation Inertia: Regression Analysis (IV)

	(1)	(2)	(3)
Constant	0.096	−0.583	−0.067
	(0.123)	(−0.702)	(−0.071)
Lagged inflation	0.896	0.938	0.940
	(26.801)***	(31.188)***	(26.370)***
Lagged M1 growth	0.028	0.037	0.020
	(0.689)	(0.922)	(0.555)
Lagged free exchange rate growth	0.045	0.043	0.035
	(4.330)***	(4.098)***	(2.884)***
Lagged official exchange rate growth	0.021	0.013	0.014
	(3.018)	(1.601)	(1.386)
DKS · lagged inflation		−0.044	
		(−2.358)**	
D552 · lagged inflation			0.007
			(0.237)
D561 · lagged inflation			−0.052
			(−1.738)*
D562 · lagged inflation			−0.036
			(−1.217)
D571 · lagged inflation			−0.017
			(−0.658)
D572 · lagged inflation			−0.088
			(−1.082)
D581 · lagged inflation			0.002
			(0.039)
D582 · lagged inflation			0.042
			(0.355)
AR(12)	−0.400	−0.423	−0.413
	(−4.479)***	(−4.999)***	(−4.113)***
Adjusted R^2	0.97	0.98	0.97
Durbin-Watson	1.44	1.56	1.56
F-statistic	1,158.96	1,023.07	496.10
Prob(F-statistic)	0.00	0.00	0.00
Sample	50:2–62:12	50:2–62:12	50:2–62:12
No. of observations	155	155	155

Note: T-statistics in parentheses.
***Significant at the 1 percent level.
**Significant at the 5 percent level.
*Significant at the 10 percent level.

mates the decline in inflationary inertia was small and very short lived, and took place during the first half of 1956. This is immediately after Law 12,006, which reduced the extent of wage indexation that was approved by Congress. If the program had been credible, one would have expected that during the next few months, inertia would have fallen further. According to the results in column (3), the opposite actually happened: beginning in

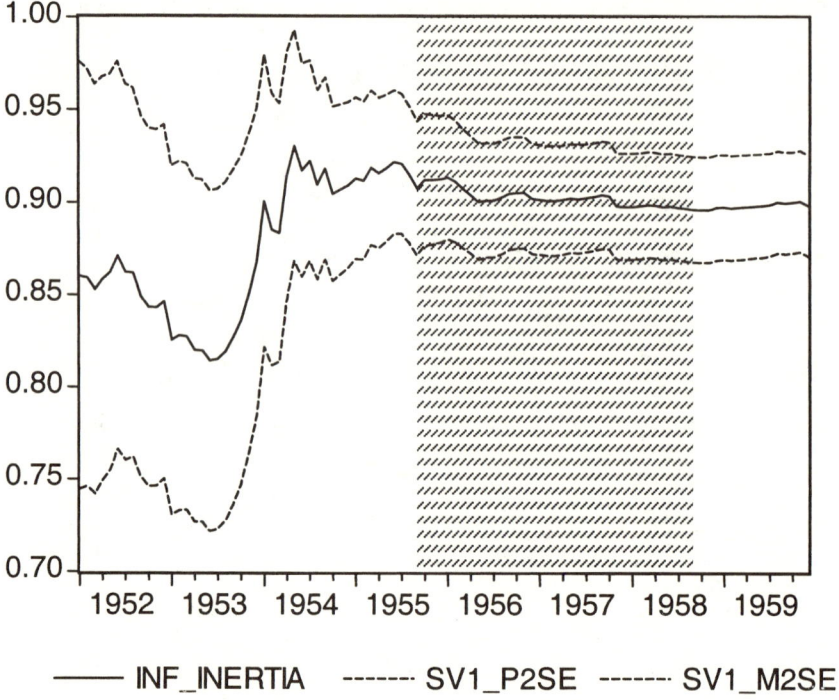

Fig. 8.5 Inflationary inertia coefficient: Kalman filter estimation

the second half of 1956 the degree of inflationary inertia was back to the level it had had prior to the program.

As a final step in this analysis I used a Kalman-Filter approach to estimate a time-varying coefficient version of equation (2). In the estimation I assumed that the coefficient of Inf_{t-1} was the only time-varying coefficient. As before, I assumed that the error term was characterized by an AR(12) process. The result obtained for the inertia coefficient is displayed in figure 8.5. This figure shows very clearly that in the months preceding the arrival of the Klein-Saks Mission the degree of inflationary inertia in Chile was increasing rapidly. Indeed, the coefficient of Inf_{t-1} climbed from 0.81 in mid-1953 to 0.92 by mid-1955. This figure also confirms the findings in table 8.5: immediately after the Klein-Saks Mission began its work there was a very small reduction in inertia. This, however, did not gather force, nor was it very significant. By late 1958, the degree of inertia continued to be substantial; indeed much higher than in mid-1953.

8.8 Concluding Remarks

In this paper I have analyzed Chile's experience with anti-inflationary policies in the mid-1950s. In 1955–1958 Chile implemented a stabilization package with the advice of the U.S. consulting firm of Klein-Saks. The Klein-Saks program took place in a period of acute political confrontation. After what was considered to be an initial success—inflation declined to 38 percent in 1956, and was further reduced to 17 percent in 1957—the program failed to achieve durable price stability. I have argued that the foreign advisors of the Klein-Saks Mission gave *initial* credibility to the stabilization program launched in 1955. The Mission's foreign advisors played the role of independent, nonpartisan, technocratic arbiters. It was precisely because they were foreigners that they could rise above the political fray and suggest a specific program, whose main components were rapidly approved by a highly divided Congress. The fact that the program was very similar to one proposed earlier by the government—and that was rejected by Congress—underscores the view that, while locals are suspect of being excessively partisan, foreigners are often (but not always) seen as independent policy brokers. But providing *initial* credibility was not enough to ensure success. In spite of supporting trade reform, foreign exchange rate reform, and the deindexation of wages, Congress failed to act decisively on the fiscal front. Consequently, the fiscal imbalances that had plagued Chile for a long time were reduced, but not eliminated. In 1957 a sharp drop in the international price of copper—the country's main export—resulted in a major decline in fiscal revenue and in an increase in the fiscal deficit. The Mission recommended a series of belt-tightening measures, but politicians had had enough of orthodoxy. No adjustment was made, and inflationary expectations once again shifted for the worse. In section 8.7 I presented empirical results on the evolution of inflation, exchange rates, and interest rates that support my historical analysis.

Appendix

Monthly Data

Variable	Definition	Source
Inflation	Rate of growth of Consumer Price Index	International Financial Statistics, IMF, various issues.
Official exchange rate	Chilean pesos per U.S. dollar	Monthly bulletin, Central Bank of Chile, various issues.
Market exchange rate	Chilean pesos per U.S. dollar	Pick's Currency Yearbook, Pick Publishing Corporation, New York, various issues.
Money supply	Monetary base: M1	Mamalakis (1983).

References

Alesina, A., and A. Drazen. 1989. Why are stabilizations delayed? *American Economic Review* 81 (5): 1170–88.
Ampuero, R. 1969. *La Izquierda en Punto Muerto.* Santiago: Editorial Orbe.
Banco Central de Chile. 1955. *Memoria annual.* Santiago: Banco Central de Chile.
Boughton, James. 2001. *Silent revolution: The International Monetary Fund 1979–1989.* Washington, DC: The International Monetary Fund.
Boughton, J. 2003. Who's in charge? Ownership and conditionality in IMF-supported programs. IMF Working Paper no. WP/03/191. Washington, DC: International Monetary Fund, September.
Correa Prieto, L. 1962. *El Presidente Ibáñez: La Política y los Políticos.* Santiago: Editorial Orbe.
———. 1963. *Nuestra economía y sus flaquezas: análisis no comprometido.* Santiago, Chile: Editorial Orbe.
Cukierman, A., S. Edwards, and G. Tabellini. 1992. Seigniorage and Political Instability. *American Economic Review* 82 (3): 537–55.
Diario de Sesiones del Senado. Congreso Nacional, Santiago de Chile (various issues).
Dornbusch, R. 1991. Credibility and stabilization. *Quarterly Journal of Economics* 106 (3): 837–50.
Dornbusch, R., and S. Fischer. 1986. Stopping hyperinflations past and present. *Weltwirtschaftliches-Archiv* 122 (1): 1–47.
Drazen, A. 2000. *The political economy in macroeconomics.* Princeton, NJ: Princeton University Press.
Edwards, S. 1983. Floating exchange rates in less developed countries: A monetary analysis of the Peruvian experience, 1950–1954. *Journal of Money, Credit and Banking,* 15 (1): 73–81.
———. 1986. Monetarism in Chile, 1973–1983: Some economic puzzles. *Economic Development and Cultural Change* 34 (3): 535–59.
———. 1989. *Real exchange rates, devaluation, and adjustment: Exchange rate policy in developing countries.* Cambridge, MA and London: MIT Press.
———. 1994. The political economy of inflation and stabilization in developing countries. *Economic Development and Cultural Change* 42 (2): 235–66.
———. 1998. Capital flows, real exchange rates, and capital controls: Some Latin American experiences. NBER Working Paper no. 6800. Cambridge, MA: National Bureau of Economic Research.
Edwards, S. and P. Montiel. 1990. Devaluation crisis and the macroeconomic consequences of postponed adjustment in developing countries. *IMF Staff Papers* 36 (4): 857–903.
Felix, D. 1960. Structural imbalances, social conflict, and inflation: An appraisal of Chile's recent anti-inflationary effort. *Economic Development and Cultural Change* 8 (2): 113–47.
Ffrench-Davis, R. 19873. *Políticas Económicas en Chile: 1952–1970.* Santiago: Centro de Estudios de Planificación Nacional, Ediciones Nueva Universidad.
Garay Vera, C. 1990. *El Partido Agrario Laborista, 1945–1958.* Santiago: Editorial Andrés Bello.
Hirschman, A. 1963. *Journeys towards progress: Studies of economic policy-making in Latin America.* New York: W. W. Norton.
Jobet, J. C. 1971. *El Partido Socialista de Chile.* Santiago: Eds. Prensa Latinoamericana.
Klein, J. 1949. Reforma monetaria en el Perú. *El Trimestre Económico* 16:600–19.

Klein-Saks Mission. 1958. *The Chilean stabilization program and the work of the Klein and Saks economic and financial Mission to Chile.* Santiago. (This volume contains copies of most of the correspondence sent by the Mission to the Chilean authorities; unpublished manuscript.)

League of Nations. 1946. *The course and control of inflation.* Geneva: League of Nations.

Mamalakis, M. 1976. *The growth and structure of the Chilean economy, from independence to Allende.* Yale Economic Growth Center. New Haven, CT: Yale University Press.

———. 1983. *Historical statistics of Chile: Money, prices, and credit services.* Westport, CT: Greenwood.

Mankiw, G. N., Miron, J. A., and D. N. Weil. 1987. The adjustment of expectations to a change in regime: A study of the founding of the Federal Reserve. *American Economic Review* 77:358–74.

Maschke, Arturo. 1990. *Cuatro presidentes de la república desde el Banco Central de Chile, 1940–1960.* Santiago, Chile: Editorial Andres Bello.

Persson, T., and G. Tabellini. 1990. *Macroeconomic policy, credibility and politics.* New York and Melbourne: Harwood Academic.

———. 2000. *Political economics: Explaining economic policy.* Cambridge, MA: MIT Press.

Remmer, K. 1986. The politics of economic stabilization: IMF standby programs in Latin America, 1954–1984. *Comparative Politics* 19 (October): 1–24.

Sachs, J. 1989. Conditionality, debt relief, and the developing country debt crisis. In *Developing country debt and economic performance,* ed. J. Sachs, 255–95. National Bureau of Economic Research Progress Report. Chicago: University of Chicago Press.

Santaella, J. A. 1993. Stabilization programs and external enforcement: Experience from the 1920s. *IMF Staff Papers* 40 (3): 584–621.

Sargent, T. 1983. The end of four big inflations. In *Inflation,* ed. R. E. Hall, 124–79. Chicago: University of Chicago Press.

———. 1986. Stopping moderate inflation. In *Inflation, Debt and Indexation,* ed. R. Dornbusch and M. Simonsen, 54–95. Cambridge, MA: MIT Press.

Sen Gupta, A. K. 1958. Survey of wage price links in a prolonged inflation. Appendix II in Bernstein, E. M., Wage-price links in a prolonged inflation. *IMF Staff Papers* 6:3 (November): 323–68.

Sunkel, O. 1958. Inflation in Chile: An unorthodox approach. *International Economic Papers* 10:107–31.

United Nations. 1951. *Technical Assistance Reports on Chile's Inflation.* New York: United Nations.

Vreeland, J. R. 2003. Why do governments and the IMF enter into agreements? Statistically selected cases. *International Political Science Review* 24 (3): 321–43.

Würth Rojas, E. 1958. *Ibáñez: Caudillo Enigmático.* Santiago: Editorial del Pacífico.

Zahler, Roberto. 1978. La inflacíon Chilena. In *Chile, trienta y cinco años de disconitnuidad económica, 1940–1975,* ed. Roberto Zahler et al., 17–72. Santiago, Chile: Instituto Chileno de Estudios Humanísticos.

III
Protectionism and Economic Performance

9   Some Economic Effects of Closing the Economy
The Mexican Experience in the Mid-Twentieth Century

Gerardo Esquivel and Graciela Márquez

9.1 Introduction

As a result of the recent wave of trade liberalization that has spread around the world, there have recently been numerous attempts to study the implications of opening up an economy. As a consequence, we now have studies on the relationship between openness and growth, openness and productivity, openness and relative wages, openness and regional distribution of economic activity, and so on. Some of these studies have been used to test implications of basic trade theory models (Stolper-Samuelson theorem, the Rybczynski theorem, industrial concentration models, etc.), while others have tested more recently developed implications of geography and trade models (agglomeration effects, regional dispersion effects, etc.).[1]

An outcome of this growing branch of the economic literature is that we now have an important body of empirical evidence regarding these effects. Unfortunately, in many aspects of this literature we have contradictory empirical evidence. For example, on the one hand, there are results showing a positive effect of trade on growth (Sachs and Warner 1995). However, there are also other studies that have a more skeptical view about the robustness of such a relationship (i.e., Rodrik and Rodriguez 2000). Some-

---

Gerardo Esquivel is a professor of economics at El Colegio de Mexico. Graciela Márquez is a professor of history at El Colegio de Mexico.

We thank comments from participants at the NBER Inter-American Seminar on Economics, held in Mexico City, December 2–4, 2004. We also thank the excellent assistance of Pedro José Martinez, Jose Manuel del Muro, and Rosario Castro. We gratefully acknowledge financial support from Conacyt (grant G32774D).

1. A far-from-exhaustive list includes papers by Edwards (1998), Goldberg and Pavcnik (2004), Greenaway, Morgan, and Wright (2002), Hanson (1998b), and Fujita and Hu (2001).

thing similar occurs with the implications of the Stolper-Samuelson theorem.[2]

In this paper we take a different approach to study some of the economic implications of the commercial policy. Instead of focusing on a situation of opening up an economy, we focus on the opposite situation, namely, the closing of an economy. For that purpose, we focus on an economy that was recently opened and that has been the subject of many of the empirical studies mentioned previously: Mexico.

Mexico is an economy that substantially reduced its tariff and nontariff barriers, starting in the mid-eighties (Tornell and Esquivel 1997). Later on, in the early 1990s, Mexico joined NAFTA and effectively became a very open economy. However, despite the fact that we know that the Mexican economy was relatively closed in the early 1980s, it is not quite clear how long the Mexican economy had been closed. In this paper we argue that, even though the Mexican industry has been protected for a long period, which in some cases goes back to the late nineteenth century, the structure of protection that existed in the Mexican economy in the second half of the twentieth century comes from an important modification in the commercial policy that took place around 1947.

We then use this result to analyze two economic implications of closing an economy. First, we study the impact of closing the economy on the relative wages and employment levels of skilled and unskilled workers in the Mexican industry between 1945 and 1965. Second, we study the regional dispersion of economic activity that took place in Mexico between 1945 and 1965. For that matter, we apply recently developed methodologies to analyze the opening up of an economy in order to analyze the inverse situation: that is, the closing of an economy. In principle, we should expect that the effects of closing an economy should be exactly the opposite of opening up an economy.

The objective of this paper is twofold: on the one hand, we show how the Mexican economy got closed in the mid-twentieth century. In order to do that, we revisit the empirical evidence on tariff and nontariff protection in the first half of the century and we also document the structural change in the protection scheme for the Mexican industry that took place after 1947. On the other hand, we evaluate two economic implications of closing an economy. This evaluation may be seen as an additional test of whether the economy was indeed closed in those years, but could also be seen as an evaluation of some implications of standard international trade theory models.

Besides this introduction, the structure of this chapter is as follows: section 9.2 describes Mexico's commercial policy in the past century, with an

---

2. See Esquivel and Rodriguez-Lopez (2003) and the references cited therein (see also Davis 2005).

emphasis on the change of the instrument being used by the Mexican authorities. Section 9.3 evaluates the implication of the protectionist policy on the wage and employment of skilled and unskilled workers. Section 9.4 evaluates the implications of the protectionist policy in the dispersion of regional economic activity in Mexico after the implementation of quantitative restrictions on foreign goods. Finally, in section 9.5 we present our conclusions.

9.2 Protectionism in Mexico: A Brief Historical Review

Recent scholarship on commercial policy has demonstrated that protectionism in Latin America had its origins in the nineteenth century.[3] On the one hand, fiscal and administrative goals fueled high tariffs and imparted an inertial component to tariff levels. On the other, deliberate efforts to promote manufacturing also drove tariff rates upward across the region.

In the case of Mexico, its commercial policy featured a strong fiscal component until the mid-1880s, when the Porfirian regime (1876–1911) used tariff rate changes to create a structure of protection conducive to import substitution, where finished goods generally held higher tariff rates than machinery and inputs. To protect the economy, the Mexican government established specific rates for a range of goods. However, these tariffs lost their protective power over time due to the continuous increases in import prices (in terms of silver pesos) between 1892 and 1902, as shown in figure 9.1.[4]

Besides tariff protection, Mexican manufacturers also benefited from the devaluation of the domestic currency (the silver peso). As a result of the continuous depreciation of the local currency in international markets, the exchange rate became an additional source of protection for domestic producers. Even though rising prices in pesos eroded protection conferred by specific tariffs during the 1890s, the exchange rate protection sheltered domestic industry from foreign competition. Once Mexico joined the gold standard in 1905, the exchange rate protection came to an end, and thus domestic producers had to increasingly rely on import duties as a source of protection. Indeed, between 1905 and 1911, textile, iron and steel, cement, and beer producers succeeded in negotiating protective tariffs for their manufactures in accordance with the industrial promotion goals of the Porfirian regime.

3. See Coatsworth and Williamson (2004) and Haber (2006).
4. We are aware that the measure of protection used in figure 9.1, the ratio of total tariff revenues to total value of imports, could be misleading, since extremely high tariffs may discourage imports. Yet, we lack any other measure of protection suitable for long-run comparisons. Nonetheless, there is evidence that this ratio approximates reasonably well the direction of protection and correlates well with more precise measures of protection. According to Bueno (1972), the rank correlation between nominal and effective protection for 1960 was 0.87 (see also Mexico, Nacional Financiera 1971, 141–42).

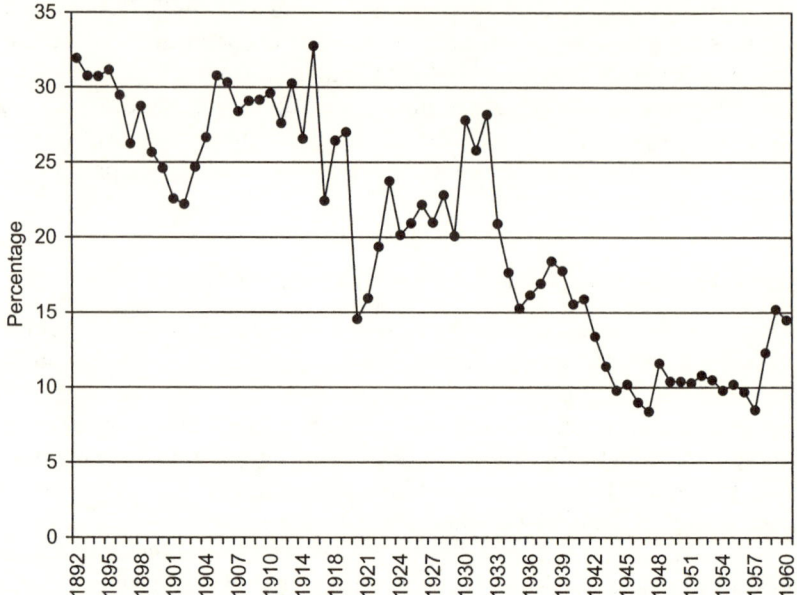

Fig. 9.1 Total duties as a percentage of total imports, 1892–1960

The Mexican Revolution, which started in 1910, brought about modifications in the design of Mexico's commercial policy. The new policy consisted of a simultaneous increase in protection levels for various sectors, therefore breaking the emphasis on industrial protection that was characteristic of the late Porfiriato. Indeed, fiscal deficits forced the federal government to decree tariff increases to all types of goods in the same percentage. Beginning in 1915, the government decreed tariff reductions aimed at curbing inflationary pressures, affecting consumption goods, particularly foodstuffs and coarse cotton textiles. Thus, in 1920 the average nominal tariff rate was significantly lower than in the Porfirian era (see figure 9.1).

During the 1920s, negotiation among sectors was the driving force behind tariff rate changes. Most tariff modifications emerged as recommendations of the Tariff Commission, where representatives from industrialists, labor unions, merchants, and government officials deliberated over a wide range of demands for protection. In general, tariff levels increased for manufactured final goods. However, other sectors such as agricultural and intermediate products also benefited from tariff protection, thanks to pressures exerted by agricultural and industrial interests.

9.1.1 Tariff Policy, 1929–1946

In November 1929, the Executive decreed a new Trade Ordinance, the first since 1891. A substantial part of the Ordinance was the tariff schedule, listing 2,771 categories and their corresponding specific duties. The Tariff Commission played an important role in drafting the new schedule. Over the years, the number of modifications had become a major obstacle to importers who needed to know an ever-changing classification and its rates.

The Tariff Commission not only compiled the long series of tariff rate modifications and updated classifications to avoid undertaxation of high-value products that fall into generic categories, but it also increased tariff rates. Most of the increases responded to the incorporation of consular fees and other surcharges formerly assessed on import duties.[5] As shown in figure 9.1, the average tariff rose to 28 percent in 1930, elevating this indicator above the averages reached in the 1920s and reaching a similar level to the one achieved at the end of the Porfirian era in 1910.[6]

Although the cascading structure of the late Porfirian regime had been blurred by generalized rate increases on intermediate goods that were approved during the 1920s, the structure of protection revealed that tariffs still served as a device to promote manufacturing activities.[7] In terms of the structure of the tariff, clothing and textiles bore the heaviest duties, ranging from 40 to 100 percent. Duties on agricultural products and foodstuffs competing with domestic production also increased to levels above 40 percent, showing an intention to cater to the demands of strong political supporters of the political regime that emerged after the Revolution of 1910. A third group, consisting of iron and steel products, alcoholic beverages, and other manufactures exhibited import duties above 25 percent. At the bottom end were duties on raw materials, machinery, and equipment.[8]

Currency devaluations in the 1930s and the early 1940s (1930–33, 1938–39, and 1941) eroded the protective power of specific tariffs because of the inverse relationship of specific rates and import prices in pesos. During the 1930s, relatively few tariff rate changes were specifically addressed to satisfy the demands for protection in import-competing industrial branches. In contrast, major tariff revisions occurred as a response to balance-of-payments problems and due to the need to curtail imports. This was the case in 1937 when the Executive decreed increases for 633 categories. Further

---

5. See U.S. Tariff Commission (1942).
6. Cárdenas (1987) argues that there exists a bias in the implicit tariff after 1929 because a higher level of nominal protection simply reflected the inclusion of consular fees and other surcharges (see Cárdenas 1987, 104).
7. For a more detailed discussion on the changes in the structure of the tariffs between 1905 and 1930 see Márquez (2001).
8. The general description of the structure of protection is drawn from Oficina de Estudios Especiales del Comité de Aforos y Subsidios al Comercio Exterior, 1946, 241–42. Other estimates of ad valorem rates by group of products or individual categories confirm the structure of protection just described: clothing (68.91 percent), textiles (59.39 percent), foodstuffs (31.57 percent), iron and steel products (33.94 percent), coarse unbleached cloth (76.4 percent), and fine unbleached cloth (84.5 percent). For group estimates of nominal protection see Márquez (2001); for cloth categories see Gómez-Galvarriato, in this volume.

increases in specific tariffs for 233 categories took place during the following year.

Figure 9.1 shows that in 1938, the average nominal rate of protection reached its highest level since 1934. Later, a revision in 1940 changed classifications but left rates practically unaltered (U.S. Tariff Commission 1942, 181). The few tariff rate changes that took place in Mexico between 1940 and 1947 coincided with the unavailability of imports associated with trade disturbances provoked by WWII. Furthermore, in an inflationary context, a passive commercial policy meant the erosion of existing tariff rates (average nominal protection in 1940 reached 15.55 percent, and declined to 8.40 percent in 1947). It is worth noting that a declining nominal protection did not hinder manufacturing growth: in fact, the Mexican economy grew at an annual average rate of 7.3 percent, whereas the manufacturing sector achieved an average growth rate above 10 percent in the period 1940–45.[9]

The flexibility in the design and management of commercial policy in the 1930s allowed the government to accommodate tariff rate changes to fiscal needs, balance-of-payment problems, or demands for protection. A yearly authorization from Congress allowed the Executive to decree tariff rate changes as it deemed necessary. Thus, the design of commercial policy responded to the behavior of revenues and the commercial deficit as well as to recommendations from the Tariff Commission. In the late 1930s and early 1940s, two forces from institutional changes limited the ability of the government to modify tariff policy. First, a Constitutional reform of August 1938 ruled that tariff legislation was an exclusive attribution of the Federal Congress. Therefore, the Executive no longer had the power to introduce changes in tariff rates in a discretional manner. The need of congressional approval limited the ability of the Executive to introduce tariff rate changes according to different economic policy goals.

Second, the commercial agreement between Mexico and the United States, in effect since 1943, also contributed to further reduce the flexibility of commercial policy. Among the provisions of the agreement was the obligation to maintain the level of duties for 120 tariff categories. A November 1943 decree increased tariff rates of nearly 600 categories, but it was later revoked before it went into effect. According to Sanford Mosk (1954, 70), Mexican officials ruled out duty increases after the U.S. government claimed that "tariff increases violated the spirit, if not the letter, of the Mexican-American trade agreement." A year later, Mexican authorities approved tariff increases again, but it only affected a small fraction of the categories projected in 1943. Protective and fiscal concerns continued driving duty increases in the following three years.

---

9. On the role of tariff protection and other policy instruments on the growth record in the period 1940–46 see King (1970, 22–32).

Table 9.1   Average ad valorem tariffs by sector (%)

Sector	1935–1939	1939–1944
Animal products	23	18
Vegetable products	40	28
Mineral products	20	14
Textiles and yarns	50	29
Textile manufactures	70	52
Chemicals	12	8
Sundry manufactures	32	23
Machinery and apparatus	5	3
Automobiles and its components	14	10

Source: Oficina de Estudios Especiales (1944), p. 252.

Because of the nature of the revisions in the late 1930s and early 1940s, the structure of the tariff changed little in terms of the stimulus that tariff protection provided to manufacturers. Finished products remained as the most heavily protected sector, whereas raw materials and machinery tariffs were significantly lower than the rest of the sectors. In table 9.1, the decline in nominal protection is apparent (measured as equivalent ad valorem rates) between 1935 and 1944, but it is also noticeable that the structure of protection remained practically unaltered.

9.1.2   From 1947 Onward: A New Form of Protectionism

By the end of WWII, Mexico promoted an inward-looking development strategy in which protectionist policies played a central role. Unlike early twentieth-century protectionism, the new instruments of commercial policy were mainly ad valorem rates and quantitative controls, both introduced in 1947. Whereas ad valorem rates isolated tariff protection from the eroding effect of inflation on specific rates, quantitative controls elevated protection beyond the level provided by tariffs. Thus, inward-looking policies adopted during the postwar era erected a new form of protectionism by redefining tariff protection and introducing quantitative controls.

In an attempt to avoid the erosion of the protective power of tariffs, the Mexican authorities shifted from specific to ad valorem tariffs in November 1947. The government set a list of official prices for the computation of ad valorem rates, but importers were required to use invoice prices in case these were higher. By setting ad valorem rates and official prices, policymakers controlled the level of nominal tariff protection conferred on domestic producers, thus eliminating the major disadvantage of specific rates. In addition, the government recovered a certain degree of flexibility by introducing the list of official prices, since increases in these prices require no more than an Executive decree, whereas tariff increases entailed cumbersome procedures including congressional authorization.

Between 1947 and 1960, changes in tariff rates and official prices affected individual categories, yet none of these modifications aimed at a particular group of imports (King 1970, 75). Similarly, when commercial policy was used to ameliorate balance-of-payments problems, the government implemented undifferentiated tariff increases. This was the case in 1954, when a decree elevated all tariff rates by 25 percent as a complementary measure to the devaluation of the peso. After this episode, ad valorem tariff rates changes occurred rarely, indicating that tariff policy was no longer the instrument for the promotion of industrial growth. In its place, nontariff devices occupied a central role in the industrialization strategy of the mid-twentieth century.

Rules for quantitative restrictions on imports were first announced in 1944, but they were actually applied until 1947. Import licenses were first used as a device to reduce imports in the face of balance of payments problems after the WWII. In an early stage, licenses applied only to luxury goods; in 1947 controlled imports represented 18 percent of total imports. But the number of categories subject to licenses soared in the following years. Table 9.2 shows the proportion of controlled imports in total from 1956 to 1964. In 1956, 27 percent of total imports were subject to licenses, whereas in 1964 the proportion grew to 65 percent. By groups, all imports in the beverages and tobacco industries required licenses in 1963, whereas manufactured goods and arms and munitions were the only groups in which controlled imports were less than 50 percent of the total (see table 9.2).

How did the license system work? The list of controlled imports depended on public and private initiatives. The government took an active

Table 9.2 Participation of controlled imports in total

Sector	1956	1957	1958	1959	1960	1961	1962	1963	1964	Average 1956–65
Total	27.7	35.1	42.5	43.2	37.8	53.6	52.5	63.3	65.4	46.8
Food	18.8	4.4	66.7	25.6	28.2	46.7	65.8	83.6	64.1	44.9
Drink and tobacco	45.2	47.6	34.2	20.0	33.1	23.2	99.9	100.0	99.9	55.9
Raw materials	23.4	27.5	39.6	36.1	36.6	41.1	71.1	68.3	62.9	45.2
Fuels and lubricants	40.0	40.0	39.5	95.5	91.8	87.6	92.0	86.2	83.6	73.0
Chemical products	76.2	71.3	57.1	83.2	73.7	93.5	67.0	72.7	76.6	74.6
Fats and oils	37.3	39.3	43.9	42.7	41.3	67.8	44.8	45.1	55.9	46.5
Manufactures, classified by	47.5	54.4	50.0	57.3	54.5	66.7	68.3	63.7	60.4	58.1
Machinery and equipment	25.3	36.1	39.5	42.3	33.4	50.1	48.6	66.7	71.0	45.9
Manufactured goods	8.5	12.8	16.8	17.6	15.7	21.5	28.3	27.4	30.4	19.9
Arms and munitions	44.0	45.1	36.9	51.3	52.8	79.0	18.4	56.4	36.1	46.7

Source: León Figueroa, 1966.

role in determining the list of imports subject to control in 1947 and 1954, both corresponding to episodes of balance-of-payments adjustments. Private interests channeled their demands for protection through applications filed in the Ministry of Industry and Trade. Applicants provided information on costs, prices, production, and distribution capacity. A committee consisting of representatives from industrial and importers' organizations, as well as officials from the Ministry of Industry and Trade, first reviewed applications and then submitted a recommendation to the ministry. In the early 1960s, more than thirty different committees reviewed the 3,000 applications filed, on average, each week. According to King (1970, 79), the committees had almost no influence on the decisions taken in the period 1955–58, when recommendations were rarely taken into account. Still, the participation of the private sector in the decision-making process offered manufacturers an opportunity to "learn something about the market for a number of products still imported."

Licenses for products on the list of controlled imports required another application, whose approval took between four to six weeks. Importers had to document why the product in question was needed. According to Gerardo Bueno (1971, 182), the Ministry of Industry and Trade approved only one third of the applications. An excessive administrative burden on industrialists and contraband were two side effects of licenses. In addition, lack of coordination between the Finance Ministry and the Ministry of Industry and Trade ensured that the license system as a device to face balance-of-payments problems was rarely implemented.[10]

Had the new type of protectionism any role in explaining patterns of growth for individual industries? Up tot his point we have only referred to average nominal protection. A better indicator of protection, known as the effective rate of protection, discounts the protection conferred on inputs from the tariff on the final product. It is also possible to compute the implicit rate of protection, by directly comparing price differentials between domestic products and potential competing imports. Unfortunately, these two measures of protection require detailed information that is not available for the years before 1960. Using some estimates of effective and implicit rates of protection for 1960, it is possible to infer some of the growth pattern shaped by protectionist policies after 1947.

Table 9.3 compares nominal and effective rates of tariff protection for ten economic sectors.[11] The effective rate of protection rose above nominal protection in industrial sectors, contrasting with the case of primary sectors (agriculture, mining, and energy), where nominal rates were higher than the effective rates of protection. This is typical of a policy that aims at

10. For a critical assessment of the license system see Bueno (1972, 151).
11. Note that industry classification in table 9.3 is different from that in table 9.2. Such discrepancy is due to the aggregation problems when using either trade data or production data. This problem persists throughout the paper. Unfortunately, this is an issue beyond this paper.

Table 9.3   Nominal and effective rates of protection, 1960 (%)

Sector	Nominal tariff	Effective Tariff protection	Effective Implicit protection
Agricultural production	6.7	1.7	3.7
Mining	4.6	1.8	13.0
Fuels and oils	3.0	1.2	9.7
Food products	55.9	108.3	47.7
Clothing, textiles, and shoes	55.2	83.1	26.5
Wood and paper	33.8	50.9	24.2
Chemical products	17.8	21.1	24.5
Nonmetallic mineral products	29.5	46.8	0.7
Basic metallic products	19.3	30.0	46.6
Machinery and miscellaneous	31.6	51.5	45.2

Source: King (1970, tables 6.1 and 6.3, 129–131).

promoting the development of manufactures. In particular, the gap between nominal and effective protection widened in consumer goods industries like food products, clothing, textiles, and shoes. As a response to tariff protection, the process of import substitution in these branches advanced swiftly and was almost complete by the late 1950s. However, a pattern of protection that was extended over time caused serious difficulties for long-term growth. Domestic producers did not achieve international competitive standards and their growth depended on the behavior of internal demand.[12] A study of Mexican industry conducted by the Finance Ministry and the Bank of Mexico concluded that consumer goods industries not only ranked among the less-dynamic areas, but also that they depended heavily on tariff protection. This study singled out food, beverages, tobacco shoes, clothing, and textiles as areas of slow growth during the 1950–65 period.[13]

In addition to tariffs, domestic producers enjoyed price margins derived from quantitative controls. Yet, a differentiated pattern in the use of this advantage was closely related to the levels of tariff protection. Table 9.3 shows that effective tariff rates were higher than those found in price differentials (effective implicit rates) in six sectors, which indicates that domestic producers in these areas did not fully exploit the margins provided by tariffs. Therefore, licensing and other quantitative controls became a redundant source of protection for sectors for which tariffs already provided a sufficient price margin over competing imports. Extreme cases of the redundancy of licenses were food products, clothing, textiles, and shoes,

---

12. Cárdenas argues that by the early 1950s, domestic firms supplied 95 percent of domestic demand in textiles, food products, beverages, tobacco products, shoes, soap, rubber, alcohol, and glass industries (see Cárdenas 2003, 257).

13. See México, Secretaria de Hacienda y Crédito Público (1966, 8–9).

where the effective rates differed more than fifty percentage points. Costs reductions, the smuggling trade, price control policies, and a potential shift in the application of licenses might explain the behavior of price setting in the presence of excessive tariff protection. In sectors where domestic protection was required to fully exploit tariff protection and the licensing system, the effective rate of protection implicit in price differentials was higher than the effective rate of protection.

A closer look at the manufacturing sector demonstrates the effects of tariff levels and licenses. Table 9.4 shows that in fourteen manufacturing areas the effective rate was higher than the implicit tariff rate. This group consisted mostly of traditional industries where tariff protection dated as far back as the Porfirian era. Industrialists secured nominal tariff protection for their finished products and tariff reductions for their inputs over decades of lobbying and negotiations with the government. Beverages, textiles, shoes and clothing, soap, and metal manufactures are some examples

Table 9.4 Effective tariff and implicit rates of protection, 1960 (%)

Sector	Tariff rate	Implicit rate
Beverages	141.2	41.4
Leather	104.4	13.4
Tobacco	89.5	52.5
Soft textiles	83.1	35.5
Shoes and clothing	73.5	6.9
Soap and detergents	67.7	1.0
Pulp and paper	65.1	31.0
Metal manufactures	64.4	19.8
Other textiles	50.6	38.2
Printing	49.6	9.3
Other food products	48.6	44.9
Nonmetallic products	36.9	–0.2
Synthetic fibers	32.9	26.9
Wood and cork	32.8	26.8
Meat and dairy products	77.4	102.1
Motor vehicles	57.1	83.1
Other manufactures	45.6	50.3
Electrical machinery	44.2	49.4
Basic metals	43.4	48.6
Other chemicals	34.5	59.3
Rubber	31.3	49.1
Basic chemicals	22.7	41.4
Perfumes and cosmetics	20.8	25.6
Fertilizers and insecticides	8.2	11.1
Pharmaceutical products	6.5	11.2
Nonelectrical machinery	6.0	34.3
Transport equipment	4.6	29.8

Source: King (1970, 132).

of manufacturing areas for which import substitution relied primarily on tariff protection.

Another thirteen branches representing intermediate goods, consumer durables machinery, and transport equipment required quantitative controls in addition to tariff protection to close the gap between domestic and world prices. These sectors maintained lower tariffs for various reasons: users requested tariff reduction to control costs, and production of this type of product took off when policy instruments privileged the use of quantitative controls. In the chemical industry, the average proportion of controlled imports in the period 1956–64 was above any other industry (see table 9.1).

In sum, tariffs and quantitative controls, the two main components of the pattern of protectionism in the postwar era, produced a differentiated effect in the manufacturing sector. For traditional industries, quantitative controls became redundant in the presence of excessive levels of tariff protection, whereas the promotion of import substitution in branches producing intermediate and durable consumer goods depended heavily on an extensive system of import licenses. More importantly, however, is that starting in 1947 the combination of tariff and nontariff instruments gave rise to a generalized system of protection for domestic producers in Mexico, and with that, the Mexican economy became, de facto, a much more closed economy than it used to be. In the next two sections, we evaluate two likely implications of this commercial policy.

9.3 Effects of Closing the Economy on Skilled Labor Employment and Wages

By the mid-twentieth century, Mexico was clearly an unskilled, labor-abundant country: for example, in 1940, 54 percent of the population older than fifteen years was still illiterate, and even in 1950, only 5.4 percent of the population older than fifteen years had attained some postprimary education. Therefore, closing the economy, according to the standard international trade theory, should have had specific implications on the intensity of use of different types of labor, as well as on skilled-unskilled relative wages. The reasoning is as follows: when an economy is open to international trade, relative wages are only a function of technological parameters and relative prices, and they do not depend on supply and demand parameters. However, when the economy gets closed, supply and demand factors start affecting relative wages. Now, because the economy is closed, and it cannot longer specialize in the production of goods that intensively use its abundant factors, domestic production will shift from unskilled labor toward skilled labor-intensive sectors. This, in turn, will increase demand for skilled labor and reduce demand for unskilled workers, thus producing an increase in the relative wage of skilled workers.

For a given labor supply, this result would induce domestic producers to reduce the use intensity of the factor that has become relatively more expensive, that is, skilled labor, and to increase the demand for the factor that has become relatively less expensive, unskilled labor. As a result of these effects, the mix and the use intensity of labor factors in each sector should change and we should observe the following results: higher relative wages for skilled workers, an increase in the use intensity of unskilled workers across the economy, and an increase in the production and employment of skilled labor-intensive sectors. Of course, the composition of the labor supply is usually changing over time, and therefore we should take that into account when evaluating labor market effects of trade policies.

9.3.1 Methodology

In order to test whether this implication of standard international trade theory actually occurred when the Mexican economy closed, we will use a methodology that has been widely applied in studies of the labor market effects of recent trade liberalization policies.[14] The methodology provides a simple decomposition of changes in the skilled-labor employment and skilled-labor wage bill shares into two different components: *between*-industry and *within*-industry terms. The decomposition is the following:

$$(1) \quad \Delta\left(\frac{L^S}{L^U + L^S}\right) = \sum_j s_j \Delta\left(\frac{L^S}{L^U + L^S}\right)_j + \sum_j \left(\frac{L^S}{L^U + L^S}\right)_j \Delta s_j$$

where subindex j refers to industry j,

$$L^S = \text{skilled labor}$$

$$L^U = \text{unskilled labor}$$

$$\text{and } s_j = \frac{(L^U + L^S)_j}{L^U + L^S},$$

so that s_j is the employment share of industry j.

Equation (1) decomposes the total change in the skilled-labor employment share of the economy (the left-hand side term) on two components: the first right-hand side term denotes the *within-industry* effect, which is the change in the skilled-labor employment share at the industry level for a given industry employment share (s_j), whereas the second right-hand side term is the *between-industry* effect, which captures the change in the industry employment shares for given skilled-labor employment shares at the industry level. An analogous procedure is used to decompose changes in the wage bill for skilled labor.

---

14. See, for example, Berman, Bound, and Machin (1998), Cañonero and Werner (2002), and Gonzaga, Menezes-Filho, and Terra (2002) and Meza (2003).

9.3.2 Data and Results

To implement equation (1) for the Mexican case during the period when the economy was closed, we compiled statistical information from the Mexican Industrial Census of 1935, 1945, 1955, and 1965.[15] We have data on the number of blue collar and white collar workers at the industry level as well as data on the wage bill of each type of labor for a subset of 64 industries. These industries represent close to 70 percent of total output and total employment in every census year. We have not made use of information from all industries due to comparability problems and because information about certain industries could not be found at all.

As it is standard in the literature, we will associate blue collar (production) workers with unskilled workers and white collar (nonproduction) workers with skilled workers. Of course, we acknowledge that such a simple classification is far from ideal, but we have no other information available at the individual level that could help us to overcome this problem (i.e., we do not have data on type of employment or on educational level).[16]

The results of our decomposition are shown in table 9.5. Before commenting on this table, it is worth discussing the role of a changing labor supply, which could also be affecting our results. If the labor supply of skilled people was growing relative to that of unskilled workers (as surely it was during the period when the economy was closed) and if commercial policy had played no role at all in the labor market, then this situation would be reflected through a reduction in the relative wages of skilled workers and through an expansion of the industries which use the skilled labor factor more intensively. That is, it would generate a positive between-industry effect. In addition to that, the reduction in skilled-labor relative wages would induce a generalized increase in the use of skilled labor in the economy, and therefore would generate an increase in the employment of this type of labor in all industries, i.e., a positive within-industry effect. However, it should be noted that these results should necessarily be accompanied by a reduction in the relative wage of skilled labor.

On the contrary, if labor supply were unchanged, and all the effects on the labor markets were only the result of commercial policy, we should expect to observe an increase in the relative wages of skilled workers and an increase in the relative price of skill-intensive sectors. This, in turn, should be reflected into a positive between-industry effect and a negative within-

---

15. We did not use information from the first Mexican Industrial Census of 1930 due to data comparability problems.

16. Results in Krueger (1997) and Slaughter (2000) suggest that using either education or production status information produce similar results for the case of the United States. However, note that in some cases classification decisions could be relevant (see Gonzaga, Menezes-Filho, and Terra 2002).

Table 9.5 Changes in employment and wage bill shares for skilled labor in Mexico's industry

Period	Total	Within	Between
Decomposition of changes in skilled labor			
1935–45	0.044	0.024	0.020
1945–55	0.060	0.036	0.023
1955–65	–0.027	–0.023	–0.004
1935–55	0.104	0.066	0.038
1945–65	0.032	0.012	0.021
1935–65	0.076	0.038	0.038
Decomposition of changes in skilled labor wage bill			
1935–45	0.015	0.001	0.015
1945–55	0.124	0.079	0.045
1955–65	0.036	0.018	0.018
1935–55	0.140	0.093	0.047
1945–65	0.160	0.096	0.064
1935–65	0.175	0.089	0.086

industry effect. The last result would follow from the natural reaction of industries to the increase in the relative wages of skilled workers.

Table 9.5 shows the results of our decomposition for both the employment and the wage bill share of skilled labor in Mexico for different subperiods between 1935 and 1965. There are several interesting results: first, the share of skilled labor employment increased in the Mexican industry between 1935 and 1955. However, between 1955 and 1965, the share of skilled labor employment decreased. Note that in all cases both effects go in the same direction, thus reinforcing each other. In fact, between 1935 and 1965 the share of skilled labor in Mexico increased by 7.6 percentage points, with half of this increase explained by between-industry adjustments and the other half by within-industry changes.

In terms of the wage bill for skilled labor, the bottom panel of table 9.2 shows that it increased substantially and continuously since 1935. Indeed, between 1935 and 1965 the wage bill share of skilled labor increased by more than 17 percentage points, with most of the increase taking place after 1945. Note that, as with the employment effects, almost half of the increase in the wage bill came as a result of between-industry movements and the other half from within-industry adjustments.

More importantly, however, is the fact that the increase in the wage bill for skilled workers in all subperiods, with the exception of the 1935–1945 period, was greater than the increase in the share of skilled labor employment. This means that not only were there more skilled workers being employed in the Mexican industry, but also that the remuneration they were receiving was growing relative to that of unskilled workers.

The pattern of employment, wage bill, and relative wages for skilled labor in Mexico between 1945 and 1965 is not compatible with a pure labor supply story. Instead, it is perfectly compatible with a labor supply story combined with the effects of a commercial policy that protected domestic industries and therefore shifted resources from the production of unskilled labor-intensive sectors toward skilled labor-intensive production.[17] Moreover, the reduction in the share of skilled-labor employment that took place between 1955 and 1965 is also compatible with the substantial rise in the wage premium for skilled labor that occurred between 1945 and 1965. In that sense, we may conclude that the behavior of employment, wage bill, and relative wages for skilled labor in Mexico after 1945 is compatible with the implications of standard trade policy models when an economy gets closed. In that regard, these results provide a strong and unequivocal support in favor of the labor market implications of standard trade theory models. This conclusion stands in sharp contrast to the ambiguous results that have been typically obtained in studies analyzing the opening of an economy. This suggests that studying cases of closing an economy in more detail could help to shed light on debates about the labor market implications of commercial policy.

9.4 Effects of Closing the Economy on the Regional Dispersion of Economic Activity in Mexico

There are several recent papers that relate trade to geographic aspects. One line of study analyzes whether trade policy affects the regional dispersion of economic activity. For example, there is a line of research that combines elements from trade, agglomeration economies, and geography. A far-from-exhaustive list of papers along these lines includes Krugman and Hanson (1996), Krugman and Livas-Elizondo (1996) and Krugman and Venables (1996). These papers argue that as a result of greater economic integration, there may be a shift in the relevant market for domestic producers, who may want to reallocate their economic activities in order to attend the enlarged market, not only the domestic market. If this occurs and there are agglomeration economies, this may prompt a circular cumulative process of increases in demand and economic activity in a completely different region from the one that predominated before the economic integration. Not surprisingly, most of these papers were somehow inspired by NAFTA and their likely implications for the Mexican economy. Indeed,

---

17. This result seems, at first sight, incompatible with empirical evidence presented in Hanson and Harrison (1999), wherein they argue that the structure of protection in Mexico was designed to protect unskilled labor-intensive sectors. However, they are not necessarily incompatible for at least two reasons: first, because they focused on the structure of production in the 1980s, which was obviously different from that in the 1940s or 1950s, and second, because what they actually showed is that the reduction in trade barriers in Mexico in the 1980s was more dramatic in low-skill industries—not that they were the only sectors being protected.

Krugman and Livas Elizondo (1995) even suggested that the inward-looking policy followed in Mexico could have produced a pattern of industrial concentration in and around Mexico City.

Hanson (1996b) has emphasized the role of regional production networks to attempt to identify the pattern of production in a country that moves from an import-substitution strategy to a more open regime. His model has location economies arising from the provision of specialized inputs and congestion costs created by agglomeration. The model emphasizes the fact that for a developing country, trade openness involves moving from a vertically integrated industry towards a more specialized pattern of production, probably through subcontracting with developed-country firms. He concluded that NAFTA would not only shift relatively unskilled jobs to Mexico, but also that there would be a substantial reallocation of jobs within Mexico, since these would move from Mexico City to the U.S. border region.

In one of the few empirical applications of this line of research, Hanson (2001) studied whether integration between Mexico and the United States has contributed to the expansion of economic activity at the border. The intuition is that if transport costs are the main nontrade policy barrier to trade, the elimination of all trade policy barriers should provide a geographical advantage to the border cities. His results tend to support the hypothesis that integration produces an expansion of economic activity at the border. He finds that an increase in exports from Mexican cities to the United States increases labor demand in the neighboring U.S. city.

In sum, this line of analysis suggests that, as a result of greater trade openness, port and border cities will tend to attract higher levels of economic activity. In the remaining parts of this section, we discuss the possibility that closing the economy could have affected the dispersion of economic activity in Mexico in the opposite way—that is, provoking a greater concentration in the main domestic markets and reducing the dispersion of economic activity.

9.4.1 Methodology

We will compute two different measures of regional dispersion of economic activity. On the one hand, we will compute Krugman's index of regional specialization. On the other, we will compute Hoover's coefficient of localization.[18]

Krugman's index of regional specialization (SI) is defined as follows:

$$SI_{jk} = \sum_{i=1}^{n} \left| \frac{E_{ij}}{E_j} - \frac{E_{jk}}{E_k} \right|$$

where

---

18. Both indexes have been used, amongst others, by Kim (1995).

E_{ij} is the level of employment in industry $i = 1, \ldots, n$ and region j, and E_j is the total industrial employment for region j and similarly for region k.

On the other hand, Hoover's coefficient of localization is based on the location quotient, which is defined as

$$L_{ij} = \frac{E_{ij}}{E_{imex}} \bigg/ \frac{E_j}{E_{mex}}$$

where E_{ij} and E_j are defined as before, E_{imex} is total employment in industry i in Mexico, and E_{mex} is total industry employment in Mexico. Note that if the location quotient is greater (smaller) than one, region j has a higher (smaller) share of employment in industry i relative to its share of total industry employment.

With the location quotient estimates we then proceed to construct the *localization curve* for each industry. This curve is built in a similar fashion to a Lorenz curve. That is, first we rank the regions by their L_{ij} estimates for a given i in descending order, then we plot the cumulative percentage of total industry employment over the regions in the *x*-axis and the cumulative percentage of employment in industry i over the regions in the *y*-axis. Of course, both cumulative series add up to 100 percent. Note that if employment in industry i is distributed in the same pattern as total employment, then location quotients for each region would be all equal to one and the localization curve would be a 45-degree line. However, if that were not the case, then the localization curve would be always above the 45-degree line. Therefore, we may compute the *coefficient of localization* as the area between the 45-degree line and the localization curve divided by the entire upper triangular area. Note that the coefficient of localization is analogous to the Gini coefficient.

9.4.2 Results

Table 9.6 shows the results of calculating the specialization index for seven Mexican regions for specific years between 1940 and 1965. Data come from the industrial census of the corresponding years. A map of Mexico and the definition of Mexican regions are included in the appendix.

Results in table 9.6 show several interesting aspects of regional development in Mexico. For example, it shows that the industrial composition (as defined by industry employment characteristics) in the capital region of Mexico is indeed relatively different from that of the rest of the country. This can be inferred from the fact that the value of the index for all region pairs that include the capital region are almost always above unity, with the largest differences being those between the capital and the southern and

Table 9.6 Mexico's regions: Specialization Index (Krugman), 1940–1965

	Capital	Center	Center-North	Gulf	North	Pacific	South
1940							
Capital	0.0						
Center	1.295	0.0					
Center-North	1.201	0.870	0.0				
Gulf	1.298	1.265	1.474	0.0			
North	1.018	1.092	0.755	1.321	0.0		
Pacific	1.060	0.843	0.842	0.957	0.919	0.0	
South	1.436	0.897	0.621	1.289	0.852	0.877	0.0
1945							
Capital	0.0						
Center	1.267	0.0					
Center-North	1.042	0.944	0.0				
Gulf	1.293	1.274	1.349	0.0			
North	1.008	1.078	0.822	1.217	0.0		
Pacific	0.991	0.862	0.987	1.054	1.029	0.0	
South	1.273	1.025	0.449	1.334	0.960	1.028	0.0
1955							
Capital	0.0						
Center	1.542	0.0					
Center-North	1.387	1.220	0.0				
Gulf	1.620	1.280	1.181	0.0			
North	1.321	1.356	0.887	1.185	0.0		
Pacific	1.269	1.153	0.854	0.949	0.945	0.0	
South	1.336	1.219	0.875	0.999	1.029	0.739	0.0
1965							
Capital	0.0						
Center	1.251	0.0					
Center-North	1.096	0.952	0.0				
Gulf	1.406	1.241	1.217	0.0			
North	1.028	1.125	0.805	1.204	0.0		
Pacific	0.991	0.991	0.674	0.995	0.826	0.0	
South	1.257	0.932	0.839	1.167	0.976	0.706	0.0

Gulf regions. On the opposite side, the most similar region to the capital throughout this period was the northern region of Mexico. Table 9.6 also shows that the most similar regions in Mexico during this period were the South and the center-North before 1955 and the South and the Pacific after 1955.

Interestingly, table 9.6 does not show any specific trend in terms of regional specialization throughout the period. In fact, the only significant pattern is a generalized increase in all coefficients related to the capital and center regions between 1945 and 1955. Such increases, however, were reverted in the next decade. In most cases (13 out of 21 region pairs), the index of specialization in 1965 was indeed lower than in 1945. These results suggest that regional specialization in Mexico was not substantially affected by the change in commercial policy implemented since 1947 or, in any case, the effects were short-lived, and they did not have permanent effects on regional specialization in Mexico.

Table 9.7 shows the results of computing the Hoover's coefficient of localization for Mexican industries for selected years between 1940 and 1965. We have grouped industries according to their pattern of geographic concentration between 1945 and 1965. A few industries showed an erratic pattern in their index and therefore they are not included in this table. Table 9.7 is divided into three panels. The top panel includes industries that show a relatively stable pattern throughout the period, while the panel in the middle includes industries that show a declining trend in the value of their index. Finally, the bottom panel includes those industries that present an upward trend in the value of their index. The first interesting result to notice is the relatively large value of the localization index for Mexican industry. For example, in 1945 the unweighted average value of the index was 0.652, while in 1965 it had diminished to 0.596. These values stand in sharp contrast with analogous measures for the U.S. industry reported in Kim (1995), where the unweighted average of the localization index was 0.327 and 0.284 in 1947a and 1967, respectively.

The top panel of table 9.7 shows that the geographical dispersion of twelve Mexican industries remained practically stable between 1945 and 1965. Most of these industries already had relatively high values of their coefficient of localization (with only one exception, all industries had an initial index above 0.67, and their index average in 1940 was 0.846), which means that they were already very highly concentrated within relatively few states in Mexico. This is mainly the case of industries associated to a certain type of raw material that can only be found in specific states (this is the case of the hackled sisal, coke, coal mining, and oil and gas industries). However, there are other highly concentrated industries that seem to be associated with the existence of a certain knowledge or skill, or even by a certain inertia in their degree of localization. This seems to be the case of the pharmaceutical and perfumes and cosmetics industries.

Table 9.7 also shows that relatively more industries present a declining trend in their index of localization than otherwise. The average index of these industries decreased from 0.767 in 1940 to 0.482 in 1965. Interestingly, the industries that present this pattern come from the whole range of the initial distribution of the localization index. For example, in this case we have industries that were completely concentrated in 1940, like tanks and metallic structures and metal furniture, but also industries like pastries and bakeries, which were already very dispersed by 1940. All of these industries present an important reduction in their localization index, which

Table 9.7   **Hoover's coefficient of localization for Mexican industries**

Industry	1940	1945	1955	1965
Coal mining	1.000	1.000	1.000	1.000
Coke and other mineral coal products	1.000	1.000	1.000	0.974
Hackled sisal	0.961	0.986	0.985	0.942
Inks of all kinds	0.861	0.974	0.983	0.932
Pharmaceutical products of all kinds	0.933	0.939	0.915	0.947
Gin and packing cotton plants	0.920	0.920	0.968	0.887
Perfumes and cosmetics	0.935	0.907	0.931	0.963
Coffee	0.861	0.831	0.886	0.813
Oil and gas	0.760	0.797	0.666	0.790
Paints and varnishes	0.799	0.779	0.846	0.823
Wood conservation and preparation	0.670	0.733	0.698	n.a.
Cotton textiles and manufactures thereof	0.451	0.398	0.483	0.464
Average	0.846	0.855	0.863	0.867
Tanks and metallic structures	1.00	1.000	0.442	0.600
Paper manufactures of all kinds	0.916	0.972	0.921	0.724
Metal furniture	1.000	0.971	0.894	0.790
Rubber manufactures of all kinds	0.960	0.955	0.942	0.837
Iron and steel	0.824	0.889	0.554	0.589
Hats and caps	0.908	0.873	0.379	0.482
Basic chemicals	0.907	0.839	0.883	0.430
Baking powder, hops and maize products	0.870	0.829	0.426	0.356
Cardboard manufactures of all kinds	0.817	0.814	0.779	0.686
Clothing	0.772	0.759	0.728	0.425
Cardboard, and cardboard in sheets	0.866	0.747	0.381	0.637
Glass	0.840	0.746	0.705	0.590
Agave beverages excepting pulque	0.757	0.662	0.646	0.635
Nonelectrical machinery and equipment	0.564	0.658	0.431	0.302
Woolen textiles	0.678	0.652	0.473	0.568
Workers Uniforms	0.769	0.645	0.582	n.a.
Metallurgical plants and metallic mining	0.641	0.605	0.312	n.a.
Cement	0.725	0.560	0.327	0.243
Coffee mills and roasting shops	0.634	0.559	0.548	0.315
Repairing shops for nonelectrical machinery and equipment	0.591	0.311	0.358	0.364
Pastries and alimentary pastes of flour	0.652	0.306	0.332	0.310
Metallurgical plants and metallic mining	0.377	0.287	0.331	0.148
Bakeries	0.568	0.239	0.089	0.098
Average	0.767	0.690	0.542	0.482
Metallic beds	0.772	0.837	0.863	n.a.
Sugar	0.609	0.668	0.748	0.680
Wire manufactures, wire fences, and wire sheets	0.861	0.662	0.960	0.883
Beer	0.623	0.495	0.574	0.586
Metallic mining	0.499	0.467	0.679	0.674
Sawmills	0.430	0.440	0.579	0.583
Wheat mills	0.476	0.326	0.392	0.385
Soap of all kinds	0.477	0.321	0.469	0.754
Ice	0.411	0.217	0.396	0.414
Nixtamal (maize) mills	0.136	0.165	0.278	0.373
Average	0.529	0.4597	0.5938	0.5925

Note: n.a. = not available.

means that they tended to become more dispersed throughout the country between 1945 and 1965.

The bottom panel of table 9.7 shows that there are ten industries with an increase in their index of localization after 1945. This group includes some industries where the increase was only observed between 1945 and 1955, but most cases show an increase between 1945 and 1965. All in all, increases in the index of localization were moderate: the unweighted index for these industries increased only from 0.46 to 0.59 between 1945 and 1965. The most noticeable case is the soap industry, which increased from 0.32 in 1945 to 0.75 in 1965. This case is interesting because it is one of those industries that had a relatively large tariff protection, and therefore we could think that it is probably the only industry that seems to fit the predicted pattern of regional concentration after being protected. However, not even this case may fit the prediction of the geography and trade literature, for at least two reasons: first, this industry had benefited from tariff protection well before the 1940s (therefore, it is not clear why it should become more concentrated now), and second, the implicit protection level for this industry was nil (1 percent; see table 9.4).

Figures 9.2 and 9.3 illustrate the patterns of regional dispersion of economic activity that took place in two Mexican industries after 1945. These are the cases of the soap industry, which is the only one that somehow fits the predictions of models of geography and trade, and the cement industry, which is one of the industries that was widely dispersed throughout the country, despite the fact that it was also a heavily protected industry. As mentioned before, most industries behaved in a similar fashion to the cement industry, and therefore their patterns of dispersion of regional activity closely resemble the one shown in figure 9.3.

In conclusion, the empirical evidence based on the specialization and localization indexes does not provide strong support for the implications of the geography and trade literature for the case of a closing economy. The evidence from the specialization index shows that if there was any effect, it was short-lived. On the other hand, the evidence from the localization index shows that there was no pattern of further regional concentration for most industries. Furthermore, the only industry that seems to have become more concentrated (the soap industry) does not necessarily fit the case of a recently protected industry.

Of course, there are some caveats to this conclusion. It could be the case that some industries tended to concentrate around a few domestic markets and that they may still show a tendency toward decentralization. This may be the case in those industries producing final goods and that could have increased their presence in some states associated to large cities (which could be the case of the states of Nuevo Leon and Jalisco, where the important cities of Monterrey and Guadalajara are located). However, we consider that the bulk of the empirical evidence is against the idea that

1940

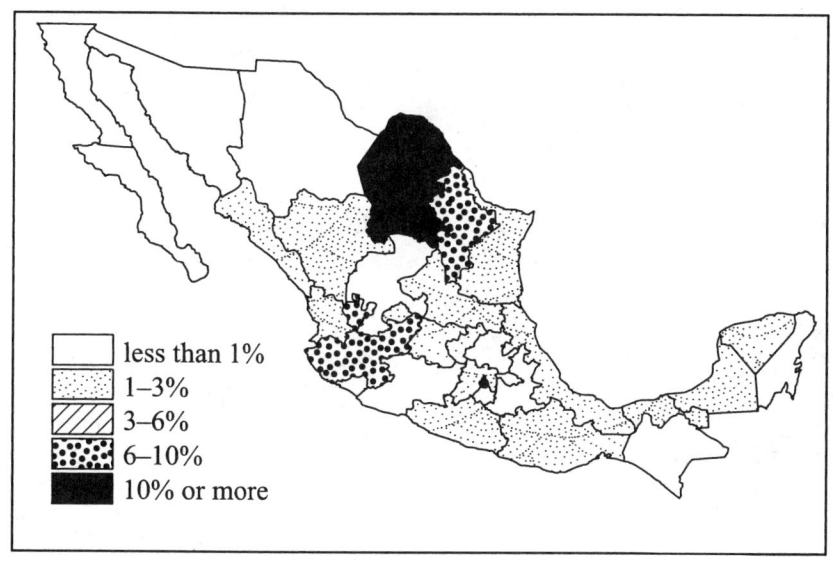

1965

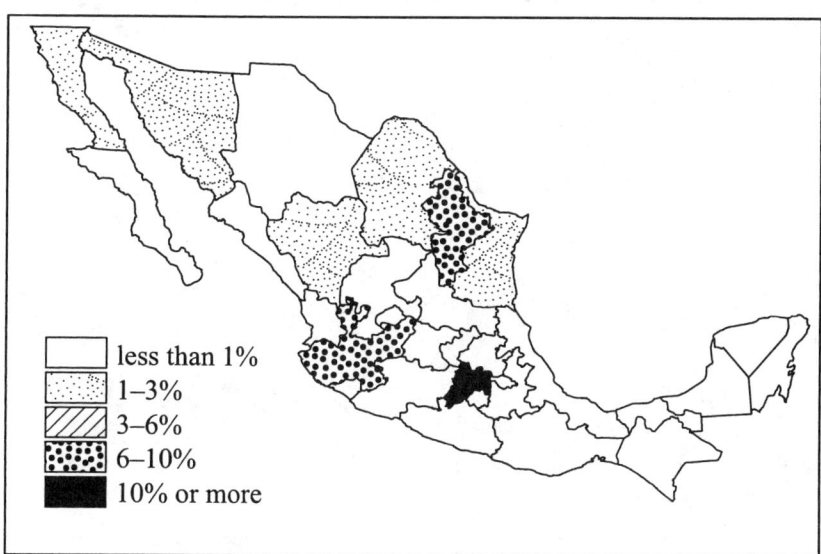

Fig. 9.2 Soap industry: Regional dispersion of industry employment, 1940–1965

1940

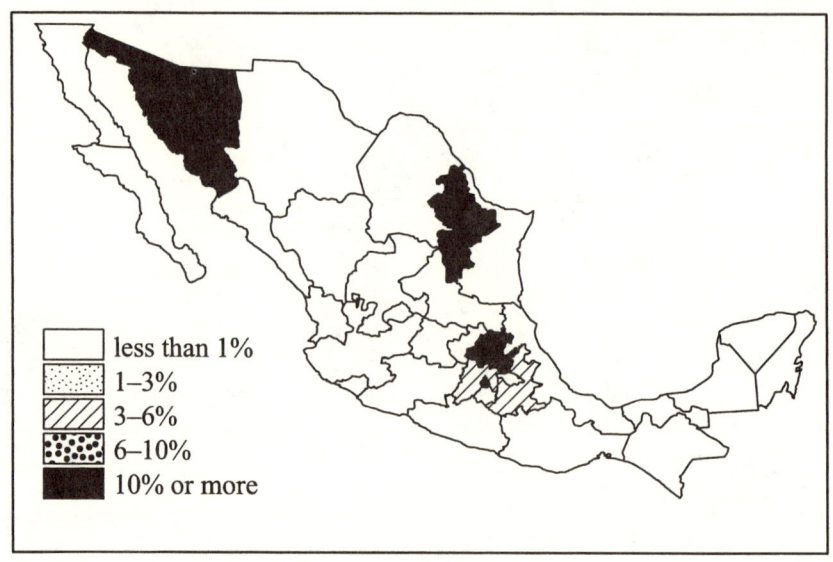

1965

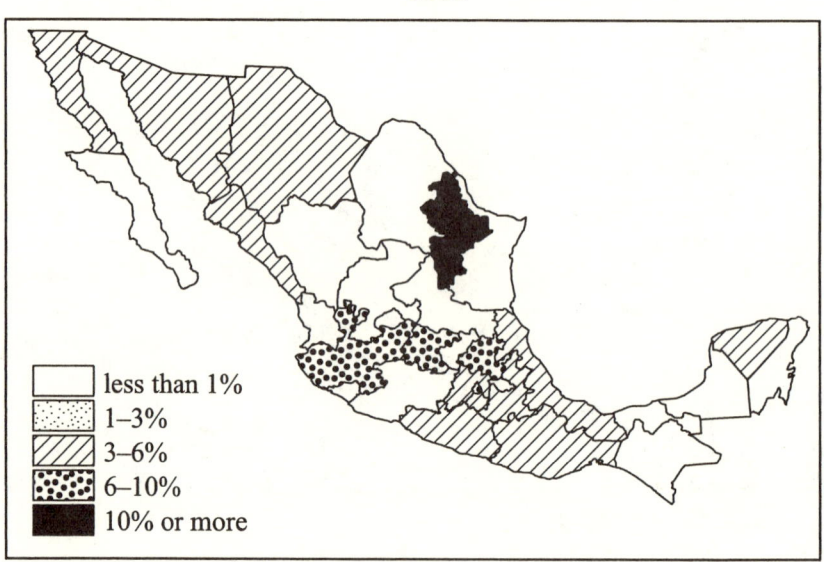

Fig. 9.3 Cement industry: Regional dispersion of industry employment, 1940–1965

closing the economy led to a higher regional concentration of economic activity in the Mexican economy.

9.5 Conclusions

In this paper we have argued that the Mexican economy started to become a closed economy in 1947. In that year, commercial policy in Mexico shifted from a traditional, industry-specific protectionist scheme based on tariffs toward a generalized protectionist policy based on nontariff instruments (quotas and import licenses). This scheme of protection is the one that prevailed until the mid-eighties, when the economy began to open up to trade with the rest of the world.

We have evaluated two economic implications of closing the economy that were derived from standard international trade models or from more recent trade and geography literature. Our results show that the behavior of employment, wage bill, and relative wages for skilled labor in Mexico after 1945 strongly support the labor market implications of standard trade theory models, and are in line with predictions based on the Stolper-Samuelson theorem. As mentioned before, this conclusion differs from the ambiguous results that have typically been obtained in studies analyzing the opening up of an economy and that have led some authors to declare the Stolper-Samuelson theorem dead (Davis 2005). This result suggests that studying cases of closing an economy in more detail could help to shed light on debates about the labor market implications of commercial policy.

On the other hand, the empirical evidence on the dispersion of regional economic activity in Mexico after 1945 does not provide strong support for the implications of the geography and trade literature for the case of a closing economy. The evidence from the specialization index shows that if there was any effect, it was short lived. On the other hand, the evidence from the localization index shows that there was no pattern of further regional concentration for most industries.

In general, we believe that moving away from the typical case of studying a liberalized economy in order to evaluate the implications of trade theory models, toward the study of the reverse implications for an economy that is being closed, can help us shed light on the validity of some implications of standard trade models, this could be an interesting line of analysis to pursue in the future.

Appendix

State	No.	Region	State	No.	Region
Baja California	2	North	Distrito Federal	9	Capital
Chihuahua	6	North	México	15	Capital
Coahuila de Zaragoza	7	North			
Nuevo León	19	North	Hidalgo	13	Center
Sonora	26	North	Morelos	17	Center
Tamaulipas	28	North	Puebla	21	Center
			Tlaxcala	29	Center
Baja California Sur	3	Pacific			
Colima	8	Pacific	Campeche	4	Gulf
Jalisco	14	Pacific	Quintana Roo	23	Gulf
Nayarit	18	Pacific	Tabasco	27	Gulf
Sinaloa	25	Pacific	Veracruz	30	Gulf
			Yucatán	31	Gulf
Aguascalientes	1	Center-North			
Durango	10	Center-North	Chiapas	5	South
Guanajuato	11	Center-North	Guerrero	12	South
Querétaro	22	Center-North	Michoacán	16	South
San Luis Potosi	24	Center-North	Oaxaca	20	South
Zacatecas	32	Center-North			

References

Berman, E., J. Bound, and S. Machin. 1998. Implications of skill-based technological change: International evidence. *Quarterly Journal of Economics* 113:1245–80.
Bueno, Gerardo. 1971. Implications of skill-biased technological change: International evidence. In *The structure of protection in developing countries,* ed. Bela Balassa, 169–202. Baltimore, MD: Johns Hopkins University Press.
Bueno, Gerardo. 1972. La estructura de la protección efectiva en México en 1960. *Demografía y Economía* 6 (2): 137–205.
Cañonero, Gustavo, and Alejandro Werner. 2002. Salarios Relativos y Liberaización del Comercio en México. *El Trimestre Económico* 69 (273): 123–42.
Cárdenas, Enrique. 1987. *La industrialización mexicana durante la gran depresión.* México, DF: El Colegio de México.
Cárdenas, Enrique. 2003. El proceso de industrializacíon acelerada en México (1929–1982). In *Industrializacion y Estado en América,* ed. E. Cárdenas, J. A. Ocampo, and R. Thorp, 240–76. Mexico DF: Fondo de Cultura Económica.
Coatsworth, John H., and Jeffrey Williamson. 2004. The roots of Latin American protectionism: Looking before the Great Depression. In *Integrating the Americas: FTAA and beyond,* ed. Antoni Estevadeordal, Dani Rodrik, Alan Taylor, and Andrés Velasco, 37–73. Cambridge, MA: Harvard University Press.
Davis, Don. 2005. Stolper-Samuelson is dead and other crimes of both theory and data. Forthcoming. In *Globalization and poverty,* ed. Ann Harrison. Chicago: University of Chicago Press.
Edwards, Sebastian. 1998. Openness, productivity and growth: What do we really know? *Economic Journal* 108 (March): 383–98.
Esquivel, Gerardo, and Miguel Messmacher. 2002. Economic integration and subnational development. Unpublished paper. New York: World Bank, June.
Esquivel, Gerardo, and Jose Antonio Rodríguez-López. 2003. Technology, trade, and wage inequality in Mexico before and after NAFTA. *Journal of Development Economics* 72 (December): 543–65.
Fujita, Masahisa, and Dapend Hu. 2001. Regional disparity in China 1985–1994: The effects of globalization and economic liberalization. *Annals of Regional Science* 35:3–37.
Goldberg, Pinelopi, and Nina Pavcnik. 2004. Trade, inequality, and poverty: What do we know? Evidence from recent trade liberalization episodes in developing countries. *Brookings Trade Forum,* 223–69.
Gonzaga, G., N. Menezes-Filho, and C. Terra. 2002. Trade liberalization and evolution of skill earnings differentials in Brazil. Working paper no. 463, Pontificia Universidade Católica do Rio de Janeiro (September).
Greenaway, D., W. Morgan, and P. Wright. 2002. Trade liberalization and growth in developing countries. *Journal of Development Economics* 67:229–44.
Haber, Stephen. 2006. It wasn't all Prebisch's fault: The political economy of Latin American industrialization. In *The Cambridge economic history of Latin America,* ed. Victor Bulmer-Thomas, John Coatsworth, and Roberto Cortes Conde, 537–84. Cambridge: Cambridge University Press.
Hanson, Gordon. 1996a. Integration and the location of activities: Economic integration, intraindustry trade and frontier regions. *European Economic Review* 40:941–49.
———. 1996b. Localization economies, vertical organization, and trade. *American Economic Review* 86 (5): 1266–77.

———. 1998a. North American economic integration and industry location. *Oxford Review of Economic Policy* 14 (1998): 30–44.
———. 1998b. Regional adjustment to trade liberalization. *Regional Science and Urban Economics* 28:419–44.
———. 2001. U.S.-Mexico integration and regional economies: Evidence from border-city pairs. *Journal of Urban Economics* 50:259–87.
Hanson, Gordon, and Ann Harrison. 1999. Trade liberalization and wage inequality in Mexico. *Industrial and Labor Relations Review* 52 (2): 271–88.
Kim, Sukkoo. 1995. Expansion of markets and the geographic distribution of economic activities: The trends in U.S. regional manufacturing structure, 1860–1987. *Quarterly Journal of Economics* 110 (4): 881–908.
King, Timothy. 1970. *Mexico: Industrialization and trade policies since 1940*. New York: Oxford University Press.
Krueger, Alan B. 1997. Labor market shifts and the price puzzle revisited. NBER Working Paper no. 5924. Cambridge, MA: National Bureau of Economic Research, February.
Krugman, Paul, and Gordon Hanson. 1993. Mexico-U.S. free trade and the location of production. In *The Mexico free trade agreement*, ed. Peter M. Garber, 163–86. Cambridge, MA: MIT Press.
Krugman, Paul, and Raúl Livas-Elizondo. 1996. Trade policy and the third world metropolis. *Journal of Development Economics* 49:137–50.
Krugman, Paul, and Anthony Venables. 1996. Integration, specialization, and adjustment. *European Economic Review* 40:959–67.
León Figueroa, Julio. 1966. *El control directo a las importaciones en México*. BA thesis, Universidad Nacional Autónoma de México.
Marquez, Graciela. 2001. Protección y Cambio Institucional: La política arancelaria del Porfiriato a la Gran Depresión. Documento de Trabajo no. 2001-V. Central Estudios Económicos, El Colegio de México.
México, Nacional Financiera. 1971. *La politica industrial en el Desarrollo economico de América Latina*. México, D.F.: Nafinsa.
México, Oficina de Estudios Especiales del Comité de Aforos y Subsidios al Comercio Exterior. 1946. Problemas del comercio exterior. In *Memoria del Segundo Congreso Mexicano de Ciencias Sociales*. Sociedad Mexicana de Geografía y Estadística, México: Artes Gráficas del Estado.
México, Secretaría de Hacienda y Crédito Público. n.d. *Evolución de la industria manufacturera en México 1950–1965*, 2 vols. México: Centro Nacional de Productividad.
México, Secretaría de Hacienda y Crédito Público. 1966. *El desarrollo industrial de México*. México: Centro Nacional de Productividad.
Meza, Liliana. 2003. Apertura Comercial y Cambio Tecnológico. Efectos en el Mercado Laboral Mexicano. *El Trimestre Económico* 279 (Julio-Septiembre): 457–506.
Mosk, Sandford A. 1954. *Industrial revolution in Mexico*. Berkeley: University of California Press.
Rodrik, Dani, and Francisco Rodríguez. 2000. Trade policy and economic growth: A skeptic's guide to the cross-national evidence. In *NBER macroeconomics annual 2000*, ed. Ben Bernanke and Kenneth S. Rogf, 261–325. Cambridge, MA: MIT Press.
Sachs, Jeffrey, and Andrew Warner. 1995. Economic reform and the process of global integration. *Brookings Papers on Economic Activity*, Issue no. 1:1–118.
Slaughter, Matthew J. 2000. What are the results of product-price studies and what can we learn from their differences? In *The impact of international trade on wages*,

ed. Robert C. Feenstra, 129–70. National Bureau of Economic Research Conference Volume. Chicago: University of Chicago Press.

Tornell, Aaron, and Gerardo Esquivel. 1997. The political economy of Mexico's entry into NAFTA. In *Regionalism versus multilateral trade agreements,* ed. T. Ito and A. Krueger, 25–55. Chicago: University of Chicago Press.

U.S. Tariff Commission. 1942. *The foreign trade of Latin America: A report on the trade of Latin America with special reference to trade with the United States.* Washington, DC: Government Printing Office.

10
The Political Economy of Protectionism
The Mexican Textile Industry, 1900–1950

Aurora Gómez-Galvarriato

10.1 Introduction

After several years of closing up their economies from international trade as a means of fostering internal industrial development, several Latin American nations realized that their industrial sectors, which had prospered under protection, were not capable of surviving international competition. Once it became clear that it was too costly or even impossible for a country to continue pursuing protectionist policies, it also appeared that the sacrifices they had undertaken to acquire industrial development had been in vain.

The backwardness of Latin American industry has generally been blamed on protectionist policies, which, for their part, have been generally considered the result of ideology. In particular, this backwardness is said to be a result of the development of the dependentist and structuralist schools of economic thought sponsored by the Economic Commission for Latin America (ECLA) from the 1940s to the 1970s. This explanation has often been complemented by the development of economic models describing how a government can be captured by interest groups to generate such

---

Aurora Gómez-Galvarriato is a professor in the Economics department of the Centro de Investigación y Docencia Económicas (CIDE) and the Peggy Rockefeller Visiting Scholar (2006–7) at Harvard University.

I am indebted to John Coatsworth, Alan Dye, Stephen Haber, David Lederman, Aldo Musacchio, Kenneth Sokoloff, John Womack, Jeffrey Williamson and several other scholars' comments and advice given this paper when presented in the Inter-American Seminar on Economics 2004; New Perspectives on Economic History December 2–4, 2004; the Economic History Workshop, Columbia University/Barnard University, April 3, 2002; the Von Gremp Workshop in Economic and Entrepreneurial History, University of California, Los Angeles, October 30, 2001; the Economic History Workshop, Social Science History Institute, Stanford University, November 5, 2001; and the Workshop in Economic History, Department of Economics, Harvard University, April 3, 1998. All errors are of course my own.

policies. However, very few historical studies have been undertaken to find out how protectionist policies and industrial backwardness came about.

From Coatsworth and Williamson (2002) we know that Latin American tariffs were far higher than anywhere else in the century before the Great Depression. Yet they experienced a huge surge during this period, as they did in the rest of the world. However, while most countries decreased tariffs earlier on, Latin America persisted in its protectionism for several decades after World War II. What were the forces driving this process?

This paper addresses this question from a microperspective, by studying the evolution of international competitiveness and protection levels in Mexican textile manufactures, which is a paradigmatic example of an overprotected industry unable to compete internationally. By 1990 most mills in the traditional Mexican textile regions of Puebla, Tlaxcala, and Veracruz were on the verge of bankruptcy, if they had not already closed. A visit to several of them evidenced the use of outdated technology, which in some cases dated back to the nineteenth century.

What happened to the Mexican textile industry? What were the causes of its demise? Was it always as noncompetitive internationally as it appeared by the mid-1980s? If not, how did it evolve to become so? Why?

Because data on the textile industry at the national level are not rich and accurate enough to provide answers to many of these questions, I am going to study the case of a particular firm, the Compañía Industrial Veracruzana S.A. (CIVSA). This firm owned one of the biggest and most modern mills operating in Mexico during Porfirian times (1880–1910). Although operating until the present time with great struggle, it is but a shadow of what it used to be. Through this study CIVSA's archival material will be complemented with information available on a national basis, in order to set it in a more general context.

The plan of the paper is the following: First, a brief overview of the textile industry of the period is provided to give an idea of how representative CIVSA was. Then, CIVSA's prices, costs, and productivity levels will be contrasted with those of the United States and Great Britain, to make an assessment of CIVSA's international stature. Information to carry out this comparison was available for 1911, providing an accurate picture of CIVSA's situation at the end of the Porfiriato. An analysis of the reasons behind CIVSA's relative production cost level is carried out to get a full picture of CIVSA's competitive situation from an international perspective around 1911. Then, the evolution of CIVSA's labor productivity from 1900 to 1930 will be explored. This will give an idea of how the institutional changes that came about with the Revolution affected this variable. A study of the evolution of tariff protection for the textile industry will be undertaken in order to understand how levels of protection changed and interacted with productivity and the level of competitiveness.

10.2 CIVSA and the Mexican Textile Industry: A General Background

The Compañía Industrial Veracruzana S. A. was founded in 1896. Its textile mill, Santa Rosa, started working in 1898 (by that time there were around 120 cotton textile mills operating in Mexico). The first textile mills were established in Mexico in the 1830s and slowly developed through the nineteenth century, having to face Mexico's difficult political and economic conditions. Between 1890 and 1910 the textile industry experienced an era of rapid modernization and expansion as a result of political stability, greater economic growth, and the modernization in communications and transportation that the arrival of railroads and the telegraph in the previous decade had brought about. During this period, several textile corporations like CIVSA were founded. They built new mills and modernized old ones, enlarged the scale of production, introduced hydroelectric power to run the mills, and introduced state-of-the-art technologies of production.

This process also meant a concentration of the industry, since due to a slow development of the financial sector only a few companies could undertake the investment required to carry out such transformation.[1] Eight textile conglomerates founded by the turn of the century owned only 12 percent of the mills but 41 percent of the spindles, 45 percent of the looms, and 60 percent of the printing machines of the entire industry. These companies employed 38 percent of the labor force in the industry and paid 40 percent of the taxes. CIDOSA (13.5 percent) and CIVSA (6.3 percent) alone accounted for 20 percent of the total sales in the industry and employed 18 percent of the labor force. In 1912, CIVSA's Santa Rosa mill was the second largest mill operating in Mexico (after only the Compañía Industrial de Orizaba S.A., Río Blanco mill), working with 40,184 spindles, 1,685 looms, and 1,560 workers, compared to a national average of 6,299 spindles, 229 looms and 254 workers per mill. The average mill in the United States in 1910 operated with 20,714 spindles, 502 looms and 286 workers. By 1912 only 23 percent of the textile mills were corporations (*sociedades anónimas*) and only six of them traded stock in the stock market. CIVSA was one of them. As this makes clear, CIVSA was representative only of the fraction of the textile sector that had modernized their mills during the period (roughly 12 percent of the mills, but which made 40 percent of the cotton textile production). The Santa Rosa mill is still operating today, but it has recently been declared bankrupt.

10.3 CIVSA's International Competitiveness

How competitive were CIVSA's selling prices, compared with English and American prices for similar products? Because yarn was produced us-

---

1. See Stephen Haber (1997).

ing standard measures throughout the world, it is usually easier to compare its costs and prices than those for cloth, produced in a myriad of different brands and of varying qualities. Yet because CIVSA did not sell yarn, no information on yarn costs and sale prices exists in its archives. Thus, it was necessary to find information on types of cloth made in foreign countries similar to those produced by CIVSA. Table 10.1 shows a list of American and English fabrics, which by weight and type were similar to those CIVSA manufactured. Because CIVSA's cloth was generally narrower than American and English cloth, all prices were transformed into pesos per square meter. Data on production costs provided by CIVSA's records did not include general expenses, depreciation, and a return on capital. Thus these items were estimated and added to the original cost figures, assuming returns on capital of 5 percent, 8 percent, or 10 percent (see table 10.1).

As table 10.2 shows, CIVSA's prices were 64 percent higher than American prices and 28 percent higher than English prices on average. However, once the tariff is added to foreign prices, CIVSA's prices were only 1 percent higher than American prices and 14 percent below British prices, on average. If transportation costs for foreign cloth were added, CIVSA's relative prices would have been even lower. Foreign competition, tariffs included, seems to have been an important benchmark for defining CIVSA's prices, which were basically the same as those of its domestic competitors (e.g., CIDOSA). This was true because there was not much domestic competition in the Mexican market for higher-quality cloth.

Table 10.2 also shows that CIVSA required much lower tariffs than those established to compete with American competitors and practically none to compete with the British for most of the types of cloth in the sample. Assuming a return on capital of 8 percent, in 1911 several of the types of cloth shown in table 10.1 could have competed with English imports, but practically none with American imports. However, much lower tariffs than those established would have sufficed to enable CIVSA to compete with foreign imports (on average only 41 percent of the tariff was necessary for CIVSA to compete with American cloth and no tariff to compete with English weaves). Because Mexico imported fabrics mostly from England, cloth prices from this country were more relevant for the Mexican industry (see table 10.3).[2] Thus a great part of the tariff served merely to provide CIVSA with higher profit margins. It would be revealing to make a similar comparison for some year in the 1920s, but the relevant information is not available.

Although the Mexican cotton textile industry enjoyed high protection

---

2. It is difficult to understand why Mexican textile imports came mostly from England, given that American goods of similar qualities had lower prices. I believe this situation resulted from the commercial networks England had already established in these type of products, which must have taken some time for Americans business to build.

Table 10.1   Prices and production costs of cloth: CIVSA, England, and the United States, 1911 (current pesos)

American brand	m²/kg	Price (pesos/m²)		CIVSA's brand	m²/kg	Production cost (pesos/m²)	Cost (pesos/m²)			Price (pesos/m²)
		U.S.	England				5%	8%	10%	
Denim	3.97	0.32	0.40	Dril necoxtla blanco	3.92	0.34	0.39	0.40	0.41	0.55
Canton flannel	4.58	0.24	0.33	Franela velours	4.17	0.21	0.26	0.27	0.28	0.43
Brown drills	5.22	0.20	0.27	Dril kaki	4.95	0.32	0.37	0.39	0.39	0.52
				Dril palmita blanco	5.59	0.20	0.25	0.27	0.27	0.31
Shirting	7.30	0.20	0.24	Toile sublime	7.25	0.19	0.24	0.25	0.26	0.33
Table damask	7.08	0.31	0.27	Bramante 7/4	7.63	0.17	0.22	0.23	0.24	0.34
Madras	8.23	0.18	0.23	Santa rosa 1	8.26	0.14	0.19	0.20	0.21	0.24
				Flor de lys 1	8.26	0.13	0.18	0.19	0.20	0.21
				Tela francesa 1	8.26	0.16	0.21	0.22	0.23	0.28
Calico print	10.89	0.14	0.23	Nansu mulhouse	10.10	0.17	0.22	0.23	0.24	0.30
Printed percale	11.74	0.15	0.17	Percal un color	11.90	0.13	0.18	0.19	0.20	0.21
Printed lawn	15.47	0.12	0.16	Cotelina fantasia	15.63	0.12	0.17	0.18	0.19	0.21

Source of English and U.S. data: House of Representatives, Cotton Manufactures, Report of the Tariff Board (Washington, 1912), I, 443–444.

Source of Mexican data: Archive of the Compañia Industrial Veracruzana S.A.

Notes: In order to calculate the additional cost represented by general expenses, depreciation, and return on capital, the following data were used: general expenses for 1911 were $350,000, depreciation according to calculations explained in chapter 7 (Gómez-Galvarriato, 1999) was $217,254.08, equity and reserves were $6,765,678.63, and meters of cloth produced in that year were 17,744,142. Prices for English and American goods are prices in the home country.

Table 10.2 Tariffs, comparative prices, and production costs of cloth: CIVSA, England, and the United States, 1911

CIVSA brand	Fraction	Specific tariff (pesos/mt2)	Tariff required[a] U.S.	Tariff required[a] U.K.	Mex. price – U.S. price + tariff	Mex. price – U.K. price + tariff	Mex. price/ U.S. price	Mex. price/ U.K. price	Mex. price/ Cost (8%)
Dril necoxtla blanco	334b	$0.14	$0.08	$0.00	1.20	1.01	1.73	1.36	1.37
Franela velours	335	$0.11	$0.04	–$0.05	1.23	0.98	1.79	1.31	1.56
Dril kaki	336	$0.17	$0.18	$0.11	1.41	1.18	2.61	1.92	1.36
Dril palmita blanco	333a	$0.10	$0.07	–$0.01	1.02	0.83	1.53	1.13	1.16
Toile sublime	334a	$0.11	$0.04	$0.01	1.06	0.95	1.63	1.38	1.34
Bramante 7/4	333a	$0.10	–$0.08	–$0.04	0.83	0.90	1.10	1.23	1.47
Santa Rosa 1	333a	$0.10	$0.02	–$0.03	0.84	0.71	1.31	1.01	1.18
Flor de lys 1	333a	$0.10	$0.01	–$0.05	0.76	0.64	1.18	0.92	1.14
Tela francesa 1	334a	$0.11	$0.04	–$0.01	0.98	0.83	1.57	1.22	1.30
Nansu mulhouse	335a	$0.14	$0.09	–$0.01	1.08	0.81	2.17	1.29	1.33
Percal un color	335	$0.11	$0.04	$0.02	0.80	0.75	1.38	1.23	1.08
Cotelina fantasia	335	$0.11	$0.06	$0.02	0.92	0.79	1.73	1.33	1.18
Average		$0.12	$0.05	$0.00	1.01	0.86	1.64	1.28	1.29

Sources: See table 10.1 and table 10.4.

[a]Tariff required by CIVSA to compete with those foreign products in the Mexican market. It is overestimated because the prices for English and American prices are those effective in the home country and transportation costs would have to be added to them.

Table 10.3 Cloth imported by Mexico from the United States and the United Kingdom as a percentage of total cloth imports

	U.S. (% imports)		England (% imports)	
Year	Quantity	Value	Quantity	Value
1903	11.00	11.87	77.28	71.63
1904	17.51	18.28	70.85	66.25
1905	16.93	16.62	66.82	61.70
1906	13.20	14.91	70.79	64.73
1907	10.91	13.66	70.64	63.53
1908	8.03	8.52	72.30	67.83

Sources: México, SHCP, Boletín de Estadística Fiscal, various years.
Notes: Tariff schedule paragraphs considered were 458–61 from 1903 to 1905 and 333–36 from 1906–08.

levels during the Porfiriato (see tables 10.4 and 10.5), they were not higher than those of the United States. A comparison of Mexican and American tariff levels indicates that levels of protection for cloth in Mexico were actually lower than in the United States in 1911. In that year the American ad valorem equivalent duty for coarse unbleached cloth, similar to those table 10.4 describes (paragraphs 315–17 of the U.S. tariff schedule), rose from 20.68 percent to 52.22 percent, depending on the particular kind of cloth. The simple average of all duties for unbleached cloth in paragraphs 315–17 was 34.9 percent. American tariffs for fine unbleached cloth comparable to that described in table 10.5 (paragraphs 318–19 of the U.S. tariff schedule) ranged from 36.45 percent to 48.05 percent; its simple average was 41.8.[3] In Mexico the comparable ad valorem equivalent tariffs for 1911 were 20.1 percent and 26 percent, respectively. American tariffs for 1911 were even higher than the average Mexican duties for 1900–1910 of 33.3 percent and 40.5 percent, respectively. Because raw cotton was tariff-free in the United States, effective protection rates[4] were even higher in that

---

3. The American tariff schedule was far more specific than the Mexican one, providing for several duties, depending on square yards per pound, threads per square inch, and value per square yard, whereas the Mexican tariff schedule provided for a single duty (House of Representatives, *Cotton Manufactures*, I, 69). The Mexican duty only divided unbleached and white cloth between that with fewer than 30 threads per 5 square millimeters and that with more than 30 threads in that area; that is, with fewer or more than 152.28 threads per square inch.

4. The effective rate of protection (EPR) is the percentage excess of the domestic price of the value-added unit over its world market price. The effective rates of protection are calculated using the following formula: ERP = $(W_i - V_i)/V_i$, where W_i is the percentage excess of domestic value added and V_i is the world market value added. The numerator can be calculated either as a difference between domestic and world market value added, or as the difference between the tariff on the product and the tariff on the material input weighted by the latter's share in the product price on the world market. Thus it is calculated as: ERP = $(T_t - A_{ct}T_c)/(V_t)$, where T_t is the nominal tariff for cloth, T_c is the nominal tariff for cotton, A_{ft} is the coefficient of cotton as a share of the value of cloth under free trade, and V_t is the world market value added for the textile industry. See Bela Balassa and Associates (1971, 5–6, 315–18). I am grateful to Graciela Márquez for her explanations of this subject.

Table 10.4 Tariffs for coarse unbleached and white cloth

Year	Pesos/m² or KL	Specific tariff ($)	Nominal tariff (%)	Raw cotton nominal tariff (%)	ERP (%) (1)	ERP (%) (2)
1901	0.22	0.09	41.5	19.6	72.2	78.8
1902	0.24	0.09	38.2	16.7	67.8	73.5
1903	0.32	0.09	28.5	13.6	49.3	53.9
1904	0.25	0.09	36.1	13.8	66.3	71.0
1905	0.27	0.10	36.3	18.6	61.4	67.7
1906	0.32	0.10	30.0	16.4	49.5	55.1
1907	0.23	0.10	41.6	15.1	77.5	82.7
1908	0.36	0.10	27.2	15.7	44.0	49.4
1909	0.31	0.10	30.7	13.0	55.0	59.5
1910	0.40	0.09	22.4	10.6	38.9	42.5
1911	0.45	0.09	20.1	12.5	31.4	35.7
1912	0.35	0.09	26.0	15.1	41.9	47.1
1913	0.49	0.05	10.3	13.2	8.3	12.8
1914	0.58	0.05	8.7	7.9	10.7	13.4
1915	1.54	0.05	3.2	2.9	4.0	5.0
1916		0.08		12.4		
1917a		0.08		8.0		
1917b		0.04		0.0		
1918	0.37	0.05	13.1	1.6	27.9	28.4
1919	0.52	0.05	9.4	1.4	19.9	20.4
1920	0.71	0.05	6.9	1.3	14.2	14.6
1927	2.63	5.05	186.3	10.7	411.1	414.8
1928	2.63	5.10	177.9	10.4	392.4	396.0
1929	2.59	5.10	183.5	48.0	362.5	378.8
1930	2.75	2.15	76.4	27.2	142.8	152.0
1931	3.34	2.15	73.2	38.5	122.5	135.7
1932	2.77	2.15	76.7	39.2	1229.9	143.2
1933	3.21	2.15	72.2	52.4	104.5	122.3
1934	4.39	2.15	48.8	24.9	82.6	91.1
1935	3.86	2.15	58.0	23.6	105.1	113.1
1936	4.05	2.15	52.7	21.4	95.5	102.8
1937	4.35	2.15	50.7	20.4	91.9	98.9
1938	4.91	2.15	51.5	20.3	94.0	101.0
1939a	4.72	2.15	5.19	26.0	88.4	97.2
1939b	4.19	2.21	62.5	26.0	112.5	121.3
1940	6.31	2.21	36.0	16.7	63.0	68.7
1941	5.96	2.21	50.5	20.6	91.4	98.4
1942	6.79	2.21	40.7	12.8	78.0	82.3
1943	6.43	2.21	41.1	10.2	81.8	85.3
1944	6.16	2.21	41.2	13.2	78.7	83.2
1945	12.84	2.21	33.1	4.7	69.8	71.4
1946	8.76	2.21	27.3	15.4	44.5	49.7

Year							Year					
1921	0.36	0.08	20.9	29.2	14.2	24.2	1947	9.73	2.21	22.7	9.6	40.7	44.0
1922	0.40	0.10	23.5	25.9	24.0	32.8	1948	18.97	13.96	73.6	32.7	130.1	141.2
1923	0.46	0.11	24.1	14.9	37.9	43.0	1949			forbidden	10.0		
1924	3.17	0.96	28.3	32.0	28.0	38.9	1950			forbidden	16.7		
1925	3.11	0.96	30.1	8.2	59.0	61.8	1951	58.01	23.42	40.4	12.3	77.8	82.0
1926	2.87	0.96	32.5	11.1	61.4	65.2	1952	56.36	23.42	41.6	13.0	79.6	84.1
							1953	62.44	22.41	35.9	20.6	58.2	65.2
							1954	57.92	23.42	40.4	15.4	74.4	79.6
							1955	57.38	23.42	40.8	13.1	77.9	82.3
1901–1910			33.3	15.3	58.2	63.4	1927–1933			129.0	32.4	237.9	249.0
1911–1920			12.2	6.9	19.8	22.2	1934–1947			46.3	17.7	81.2	87.2
1921–1926			26.6	20.2	37.4	44.3	1948–1955			45.4	16.7	83.0	89.1

Sources: Data for the value added and raw cotton coefficient are taken from the U.S. Manufacturing Census of 1905. The U.S. industry was chosen as a proxy of the world's industry for lack of other data. In order to transform nominal into ad-valorem tariffs, information on prices were necessary. This was obtained for the period 1900–23 from the United States, Foreign Commerce and Navigation of the United States (Washington, D.C.), various years. Cloth prices were obtained by dividing the total value of U.S. exports to Mexico by its total quantity. It was transformed from square yards to square meters. (1 m² = 1.196 yd²). For the rest of the period both prices and tariffs were in terms of pesos per kilo. The sources are: Estados Unidos Mexicanos, Departamento de la Estadística Nacional, Anuario Estadístico. Comercio Exterior y Navegación, Estados Unidos Mexicanos, Secretaría de la Economía Nacional, Estadística del Comercio Exterior, and Estados unidos Mexicanos, Anuario Estadístico del Comercio Exterior de los Estados Unidos Mexicanos. I am indebted to Edward Beatty for his help in the calculation of these figures and for providing me very valuable information.

Notes: The value added in the industry was 44 percent. It was calculated by subtracting the cost of materials, fuels, and purchased electric energy from the value of products. It is reported as a percentage of the value of the final product. The ERP was calculated as indicated in footnote 5. Two coefficients for raw cotton were used for the ERP calculation. The first coefficient for raw cotton, .50, was that which prevailed in the U.S. industry in 1905; the second, .35, was the 1900–10 average of cotton expenses as a percentage of net sales at CIVSA. The first was used for ERP(1) and the second for ERP(2). 1917a goes from January to July 18, 1917. 1917b goes from July 19 to December 14, 1917. Given that the number of tariff schedules increases with time, they were weighted after 1924 according to the share of kilos imported of each kind in three periods: 1924–29, 1931–39, and 1939–55. 1939 appears twice because the first was calculated using both shares.

Table 10.5   Tariffs for fine white and unbleached cloth

Year	Pesos/m² or KL	Specific tariff ($)	Nominal tariff (%)	Raw cotton nominal tariff (%)	ERP (%) (1)	ERP (%) (2)	Year	Pesos/m² or KL	Specific tariff ($)	Nominal tariff (%)	Raw cotton nominal tariff (%)	ERP (%) (1)	ERP (%) (2)
1901	0.22	0.11	50.7	19.6	93.1	99.8	1927	3.46	7.33	215.0	10.7	476.5	480.1
1902	0.24	0.11	46.7	16.7	87.0	92.7	1928	3.64	8.38	228.4	10.4	507.3	510.8
1903	0.32	0.11	34.8	13.6	63.7	68.3	1929	3.52	8.38	241.5	48.0	494.2	510.6
1904	0.25	0.11	44.1	13.8	84.5	89.2	1930	4.09	3.42	84.5	27.2	161.1	170.3
1905	0.27	0.12	43.8	18.6	78.4	84.7	1931	4.02	3.42	86.9	38.5	153.6	166.8
1906	0.32	0.12	36.2	16.4	63.6	69.2	1932	4.19	3.42	83.1	39.2	144.3	157.6
1907	0.23	0.12	50.2	15.1	97.1	102.2	1933	5.15	3.42	70.3	52.4	100.1	118.0
1908	0.36	0.12	32.8	15.7	56.8	62.1	1934	6.57	3.42	53.3	24.9	92.9	101.4
1909	0.31	0.12	37.1	13.0	69.4	73.9	1935	6.11	3.42	55.6	23.6	99.6	107.6
1910	0.40	0.12	29.0	10.6	53.9	57.5	1936	5.64	3.42	59.8	21.4	111.6	118.9
1911	0.45	0.12	26.0	12.5	44.9	49.2	1937	5.90	3.42	59.6	20.4	112.2	119.1
1912	0.35	0.12	33.7	15.1	59.4	64.5	1938	7.48	3.42	46.7	20.3	83.0	90.0
1913	0.49	0.07	13.4	13.2	15.3	19.8	1939a	8.61	3.42	40.0	26.0	61.3	70.1
1914	0.58	0.07	11.3	7.9	16.6	19.3	1939b	9.66	3.68	40.5	26.0	62.6	71.4
1915	1.54	0.07	4.2	2.9	6.3	7.3	1940	11.68	3.68	36.2	16.7	63.4	69.1
1916				12.4			1941	10.42	3.68	36.2	20.6	58.9	65.9
1917a		0.11		8.0			1942	14.65	3.68	25.3	12.8	42.9	47.3
1917b		0.11		0.0			1943	16.79	3.68	22.7	10.2	40.1	43.5
1918	0.37	0.10	25.6	1.6	56.4	56.9	1944	19.98	3.68	20.7	13.2	32.0	36.5
1919	0.52	0.10	18.5	1.4	40.5	41.0	1945	20.28	3.68	18.1	4.7	35.8	37.5
1920	0.71	0.10	13.5	1.3	29.3	29.7	1946	23.98	3.68	17.9	15.4	23.2	28.5
1921	0.36	0.11	31.3	29.2	37.9	47.9	1947	31.87	3.68	12.1	9.6	16.5	19.8
1922	0.40	0.14	33.4	25.9	46.5	55.3	1948	18.97	13.96	73.6	32.7	130.1	141.2
1923	0.46	1.52	30.6	14.9	52.6	57.7	1949	24.30	forbidden	forbidden	10.0		
1924	3.90	1.52	38.9	32.0	52.1	63.0	1950	30.78	forbidden	forbidden	16.7		
1925	4.06	1.52	37.5	8.2	75.8	78.6	1951	58.01	23.42	40.4	12.3	77.8	82.0
1926	3.71	1.52	40.8	11.1	80.2	84.0	1952	56.36	23.42	41.6	13.0	79.6	84.1
							1953	62.44	22.41	35.9	20.6	58.2	65.2
							1954	57.92	23.42	40.4	15.4	74.4	79.6
							1955	57.38	23.42	40.8	13.1	77.9	82.3
1901–1910			40.5	15.3	74.8	80.0	1927–1933			156.5	32.4	291.0	302.0
1911–1920			18.3	6.9	33.6	36.0	1934–1947			38.4	17.7	62.4	68.4
1921–1926			35.4	20.2	57.5	64.4	1948–1955			45.4	16.7	83.0	89.1

Sources: See sources for table 10.4.
Notes: See notes for table 10.4.

10.4 Explaining CIVSA's Higher Costs during the Porfiriato

Part of the difference in prices between Mexico and the United States resulted from the cost of raw cotton, which on average was 20 percent more expensive at CIVSA than in the United States during the Porfiriato. CIVSA purchased its raw cotton from either New Orleans or the Laguna region in Mexico, depending on its price and availability. Generally, Mexican cotton reached CIVSA at almost the same price as the New Orleans cotton, with a variation of only a few cents.[5]

Since cotton represented between 57 percent (shirting) and 79 percent (brown drills) of the cost of cloth in the United States, if the U.S. industry had paid the extra 20 percent cotton cost in Mexico it would have faced an additional cost of between 11 and 15 percent in these fabrics. Considering machinery costs were approximately 20 percent more in Mexico due to transportation costs, we can assume that erecting a mill in Mexico would cost 20 percent more than in the United States.[6] If this was true, and because depreciation and return on capital (of 8 percent) were 12 percent of the cost of cloth per yard in the United States,[7] the extra cost of the mill would represent an additional 2.4 percent over the American cost of cloth production. Together, the extra cost of cotton and of mill establishment would have accounted, at the most, for an extra cost of 17.4 percent. Yet CIVSA's costs of producing these fabrics (assuming an 8 percent return on capital) were on average 28 percent above U.S. prices for such fabrics. An important part of the difference was the result of labor productivity, partly determined by technology.

In the category of spinning, the low wages in Mexico relative to those in the United States and the United Kingdom allowed CIVSA to enjoy lower costs of labor per pound of yarn spun than in American or English mills.[8]

---

5. This is an upper-bound estimate, because the average value of the cotton used in the American mill reported by the Tariff Board in 1911 was 15.568 cents per pound, instead of 13 cents as indicated by the historical statistics of the United States and used in table 10.4. Because the price of cotton at CIVSA in 1911 was 16.203 cents per pound, the Tariff Board figure would make the price difference only 4.1 percent instead of 25 percent (as table 10.4 indicates). See House of Representatives (1912, 410). Prices compared were spot prices of "Upland Middling" at New York, from U.S. Department of Commerce (1975, 208). Prices for CIVSA come from company documents, including inventories, purchase invoices, and the cost of cotton reported in its books for *Movimientos Generales*. CIVSA bought American Strict Middling and Good Middling cotton, Mexican cotton of similar qualities to the American cotton it purchased, and Egyptian cotton.

6. This corresponds to the average cost of importing machinery from England to Mexico in the 1900s. See Aurora Gómez-Galvarriato, *The Impact of Revolution*, 156.

7. Ibid., 467.

8. This disagrees with Gregory Clark's conclusions that once the efficiency of the local labor is taken into account, "real labor costs turn out to be as high as those in Britain in most

Table 10.6 Pounds per spindle and cost of labor per pound: CIVSA, the United States, and the United Kingdom

Yarn	CIVSA (ring spindles)		U.S. (ring spindles)		U.K. (mule spindles)	
	Pounds per spindle (11 hrs)	Cost of labor per pound ($)	Pounds per spindle (10 hrs)	Cost of labor per pound ($)	Pounds per spindle (10 hrs)	Cost of labor per pound ($)
Warp 29	0.1951	0.0080	0.2440	0.0151	0.1940	0.0126
Warp 36	0.1339	0.0106	0.1730	0.0212	0.1440	0.0170
Weft 30	0.1673	0.0088	0.2590	0.0142	0.1810	0.0135
Weft 36	0.1121	0.0098	0.2060	0.0178	0.1370	0.0168
	CIVSA vs U.S. mill (%)		CIVSA vs U.K. mill (%)			
	Pounds per spindle	Cost of labor per pound	Pounds per spindle	Cost of labor per pound		
Warp 29	80	53	101	64		
Warp 36	77	50	93	62		
Weft 30	65	62	92	65		
Weft 36	54	55	82	58		

Sources: CV, Payrolls 1911 (Week 6) and U.S. House of Representatives, Cotton Manufactures (Washington, 1912), I, 410–12.

Notes: Costs presented here are the costs per pound of yarn as spun, excluding spooling or other processes beyond spinning. Because pounds of yarn at CIVSA were not reported per spindle but per worker, pounds per spindle were calculated using the reported average number of spindles per warp spinning frame (380.27) and per weft spinning frame (428.74) at CIVSA in 1911, considering that one spinner tended one spinning frame. Data from England and the United States was taken from the most efficient mill in each country on which the Tariff Board had information. Since there was no information for warp yarn number 29 in England and the United States the figure for warp number 28 was used.

Yet CIVSA produced a considerably lower quantity of yarn per spindle than its American counterpart (see table 10.6). Although CIVSA used ring spindles instead of mule spindles, its pounds per spindle were similar to those produced by the mule-spinning English mill.[9] CIVSA was obviously not taking advantage of using ring spindles. However, while the American mill sold 85.05 pounds of yarn spun from 100 pounds of cotton used, and the English mill 89.21, CIVSA reported production of 90 pounds of yarn per 100 pounds of cotton. If this is true, it might have been that CIVSA was

---

countries [including Mexico] except for the very low-wage competitors of Asia." In weaving, however, findings for CIVSA are in accordance with Clark's argument. It is clear, however, that the weaving technologies used were not equal throughout the world (Clark 1987, 51).

9. Output per spindle in Lancashire was considerably higher for ring spindles than for mule spindles, particularly for lower counts of yarn. For example, in 1907, 100 ring spindles produced 167.6 pounds of yarn number 28 weekly, but 100 mule spindles produced only 111.6 pounds (Leunig 1996, 174).

saving on cotton, which was relatively more expensive than in the United States and in England.[10]

A comparison of the number of employees necessary to operate a 40,000-spindle spinning mill in the United States and Japan with the workers employed in CIVSA's spinning department (40,184 spindles) explains how CIVSA paid lower labor costs than U.S. mills in yarn manufacturing. While CIVSA employed almost twice the number of workers U.S. mills did (183 percent), labor costs were only 70 percent of those in the United States (see table 10.7). However, the Japanese industry, paying even lower wages, but not competing with Mexican mills, had lower labor costs than CIVSA (94 percent), in spite of employing more than twice the workers CIVSA did (240 percent).

In weaving, however, lower wages at CIVSA were not enough to counterbalance the extra labor it employed relative to the U.S. industry. As table 10.8 shows, CIVSA (with 1,380 looms) employed almost seven times (676 percent) the number of workers U.S. mills employed to tend a 1,000 loom weaving mill, and paid more than twice the wages (219 percent). Because wages per worker were higher in Mexico than in Japan, CIVSA paid more than twice the total wages Japanese mills did (261 percent), although it employed almost the same number of workers (98 percent). While American weaving mills required only 53 weavers to tend 1,000 looms, Japanese mills required 700 weavers, and CIVSA 613 weavers (to tend 1,380 looms). Thus, although American weavers earned $1.59, weavers at CIVSA $0.45, and Japanese weavers $0.19 per day, their daily cost to the mills was $84.27, $274.08, and $129.50, respectively. Labor costs at CIVSA's weaving department were far higher than in the United States, higher even than in Japan.

The crucial difference between the American mill compared here and the Japanese and Mexican mills is that the U.S. firms used Northrop automatic looms.[11] When tending power looms "the most time-consuming tasks of the weaver were, first, to keep looms supplied with weft shuttles and, second, to piece together broken threads. Both these operations required that the machine be stopped.[12] The Northrop system replaced the weft automatically without stopping the loom, allowing for an increase in the number of looms tended.[13] Additionally, Northrop looms stopped instantly

---

10. According to the U.S. Tariff Board, the cotton value at the American mill was so similar to that used by the English mill that the same price was used to make comparisons. U.S. House of Representatives, (410). However, according to Gregory Clark, in 1910 "once the costs of getting the cotton from the port to the mills are included, the major New England textile towns had an advantage of about $0.0015 per pound over Lancashire mills using American cotton." Clark, "Why Isn't the Whole World Developed?" (1987, 144).

11. Whereas in 1911 less than 1 percent of the looms working in England were automatic, more than 30 percent of the American looms were automatic. In other words, 200,000 out of 665,049 looms working in 1910 (House of Representatives, 1912, 11, 169).

12. See Lazonick, *Competitive Advantage,* 163.

13. Anna P. Benson (1983, 27); George Draper & Sons (1896, 174).

Table 10.7 Employees necessary to operate a mill with 40,000 spindles in the United States, Japan, and CIVSA (40,184 spindles), 1911

Occupation (English)	Occupation (Spanish)	U.S. (southern mill)			Japan			CIVSA		
		No. of workers	Approx. total daily earnings (10 hrs)	Approx. daily earnings per worker (10 hrs)	No. of workers	Approx. total daily earnings (11 hrs)	Approx. daily earnings per worker (11 hrs)	No. of workers	Approx. total daily earnings (11 hrs)	Approx. daily earnings per worker (11 hrs)
Card room										
Overseer		1	3.50	3.50	1	0.45	0.45	5	6.08	1.22
Second hand		1	1.75	1.75						
Assistants					4	1.20	0.30			
Grinders		2	3.00	1.50	4	1.20	0.30			
Strippers	Abridora	4	4.60	1.15	4	1.20	0.30	6	1.58	0.26
Card minders	Carderos	4	5.00	1.25	6	1.80	0.30	15	4.00	0.27
Section hands		1	1.25	1.25						
Scutchers	Batientes							9	2.86	0.32
Mixing (cotton selectors)	Mezcla				20	2.50	0.13	3	0.76	0.25
Can boys	Cajonero				4	1.02	0.26	5	1.26	0.25
Lap carriers					4	1.10	0.28			
Draw-frame tenders	Estirador	10	7.00	0.70	48	8.40	0.18	20	7.31	0.37
Slubber tenders	Pabilador	12	14.70	1.23	15	1.48	0.10	10	4.56	0.46
Intermediate tenders	Intermedio	14	27.60	1.97	34	5.44	0.16	15	4.79	0.32
Fine-frame tenders	Fino y Super fino	24	57.76	2.41	49	7.35	0.15	29	22.88	0.79
Oilers	Aceitador	2	2.00	1.00	2	0.30	0.15	1	0.37	0.37
Sweepers		2	1.80	0.90	7	1.05	0.15			
General spare hands	Ayudantes	4	a		a			12	1.65	0.14
	Cepillador							4	1.33	0.33

		Mexican			Japanese			U.S.		
		N	Total	Avg.	N	Total	Avg.	N	Total	Avg.
Ring spinning room										
Overseer	Cabo	1	3.50	3.50	2	1.00	0.50	1	1.13	1.13
Second hand	Cabos	1	1.75	1.75	3	1.05	0.35	4	3.48	0.87
Section hands		4	6.00	1.50						
Spinners	Troxiles	50	37.50	0.75	300	55.80	0.19	118	68.14	0.58
Roving carriers		4	3.60	0.90	3	0.68	0.23	2	0.95	0.48
Oilers		4	4.00	1.00	2	0.45	0.23	6	1.78	0.30
Sweepers	Barrendero	3	2.40	0.80	[a]			19	3.17	0.17
Doffers	Mudadores	30	21.00	0.70	[b]			1	0.81	0.81
Band boy	Bandero									
Scrubber		2	1.80	0.90						
Torzal								2	0.38	0.19
Cuendero								3	0.75	0.25
Maq. Cuendera								1	0.78	0.78
Not defined								37	6.13	0.17
Yarn preparation room										
Overseer					1	0.50	0.50			
Assistants					2	0.70	0.35			
Reelers	Rodillero				260	41.50	0.16	2	1.93	0.96
Balers					4	1.30	0.33			
Bunding press hands					15	2.10	0.14			
Total		180	211.51	1.18	794	139.57	0.18	330	148.87	0.45

Sources: House of Representatives, Cotton Manufactures, Report of the Tariff Board on Schedule I of the Tariff Law (Washington, 1912), 524, and CV, Payrolls, 1911 (Week 6). Data from the Report of the Tariff Board were compiled from figures obtained from typical Japanese mills for seven months in 1911, similar U.S. mills were chosen by the Tariff Board to make the comparison.

Table 10.8 Employees necessary to operate a mill with 1,000 looms: The United States, Japan, and CIVSA (1,380 looms), 1911

Occupation (English)	Occupation (Spanish)	U.S. (southern mill)			Japan			CIVSA		
		No. of workers	Approx. total daily earnings (10 hrs)	Approx. daily earnings per worker (10 hrs)	No. of workers	Approx. total daily earnings (11 hrs)	Approx. daily earnings per worker (11 hrs)	No. of workers	Approx. total daily earnings (11 hrs)	Approx. daily earnings per worker (11 hrs)
Yarn preparation room										
Overseer	Cabo				1	0.30	0.30	1	2.26	2.26
Assistants					2	0.46	0.23			
Spoolers	Cañoneros	15	15.50	1.03	60	7.80	0.13	57	18.52	0.32
Warpers	Urdidor	10	11.97	1.20	20	3.20	0.16	20	10.62	0.53
Weft builder	Tramero							7	3.17	0.45
Slasher room										
Overseer		a			1	0.50	0.50			
Slasher tenders	Engomadores	6	7.50	1.25	b			13	9.75	0.75
Drawing-on hands	Repasador	b			50	5.00	0.10	21	10.60	0.50
Warp dressing	Peine							2	0.89	0.45
Folders (doublers)	Doblador							4	2.97	0.74
	Devanado							3	1.08	0.36
Weave room										
Overseer	Pagador	1	5.00	5.00	1	0.60	0.60	1	2.49	2.49
Second hand	Receptor de Mantas	2	5.50	2.75	10	3.50	0.35	1	1.58	1.58
	Receptor de Mantas (Ayudantes)							3	3.32	1.11
	Apuntador							2	3.47	1.73

Weighter	Pesador							4	3.15	0.79
Stamper	Revisador							4	2.63	0.66
Loom fixers	Correiteros	16	25.60	1.60	[b]			16	23.84	1.49
Loom fixer helpers	Ayudantes Correiteros							5	4.82	0.96
Weavers	Tejedor[c]	53	84.27	1.59	700	129.50	0.19	613	274.08	0.45
Filling carriers	Carretero	3	3.42	1.14	5	0.70	0.14	15	3.57	0.24
Extra day hands	Aviaduras	4	4.01	1.00	[b]			1	0.38	0.38
Smash hands		1	1.58	1.58	[b]					
Oilers	Aceitador	3	4.06	1.35	[b]			9	3.88	0.43
Sweepers (loom cleaners)	Barrenderos	8	10.50	1.31	[b]			6	2.33	0.39
	Limpia							1	0.32	0.32
Quill man		1	1.33	1.33						
Cloth carrier	Cargador de Telas							3	1.19	0.40
General spare hands	Ayudantes							18	3.78	0.21
Waste handlers	Desperdicio							2	0.64	0.32
Total		123	180.24	1.47	850	151.56	0.18	832	395.31	0.48

Sources: See table 5, House of Representatives, Cotton Manufactures, *Report of the Tariff Board on Schedule I of the Tariff Law* (Washington, 1912), 526.

[a]The slasher room was supervised by the weaving-room overseer.
[b]Note obtained.
[c]Northrop looms used in the United States.
[d]Oiling done by weavers.

when a thread was broken, reducing imperfections in the cloth that appeared whenever a weaver failed to repair a broken warp yarn immediately.[14]

While American weavers were tending an average of 18.87 automatic looms each, CIVSA's were only tending 2.25 power looms,[15] and Japanese weavers 1.43. At CIVSA, as in the English mills, weavers seldom tended more than four plain power mills, while in the United States a weaver generally tended twenty automatic looms.[16]

In the United States, however, weavers working with plain power looms rarely tended fewer than six, more often eight, and even twelve, if equipped with warp-stop motions, which made work much easier.[17] A U.S. weaver tended so many looms because he (or she) tended strictly to the skilled work of weaving, and all the other work was performed by other, less skilled workers;[18] this way of operating was called the "American System."[19] Although there were many unskilled workers helping weavers at CIVSA and the Japanese textile mill, they represented only 26 percent and 18 percent, respectively, of the total labor force in the weaving department, compared to 57 percent in the American mill. A significant part of the difference between the number of looms tended in the United States and CIVSA may also have been due to the fact that CIVSA's weavers were not relieved of unskilled chores to the same extent that American weavers were. Although it is difficult to know which other tasks CIVSA's weavers performed besides strictly weaving, it is clear that cleaning the looms was part of their weekly duties, since quarrels with employers on this issue often arose at the mill. Some of the difference in labor productivity levels could also have resulted from the fact that CIVSA produced a broader range of fabrics than American mills, which usually specialized in certain types. CIVSA payrolls indicate that the same weaver could produce as many as four kinds of different fabrics in a single week, which implied much additional work in resetting the loom for the different types of weave.

Overall, one can conclude that in 1911 CIVSA was less productive than the best English or American textile mills. While lower wages for spinning helped CIVSA offset its greater labor and machine requirements per pound of yarn, this was not the case in weaving, particularly when compared with the American industry. This, together with its greater cotton and machinery costs, made it produce at higher costs than those of the

---

14. See George Draper & Sons, 163–73.
15. On week six of 1911, 15 percent tended one loom, 60 percent two looms, 3 percent three looms, and 22 percent four looms. (CV), Payrolls, 1911 (Week 6).
16. See House of Representatives (1912, 11).
17. Ibid.
18. Such as bringing the weft from the storeroom, sweeping, oiling, cleaning, examining the roll of cloth, repairing imperfections, trimming the edges, picking off threads, and carrying cloth to cloth room (House of Representatives, 1912, 480).
19. Ibid.

American and British industries. Yet CIVSA's production costs, even considering rates of return of 8 percent or 10 percent, were fairly similar to the sales prices of English cloth of similar kinds. CIVSA would have thus required much lower duties than it had to be able to compete internationally.

The comparison between CIVSA and American and Japanese spinning and weaving mills indicates that by 1911 CIVSA and the Japanese mills had an important labor productivity gap with the United States. While labor productivity was greater in CIVSA's spinning department than in the Japanese spinning mills, it was about the same in the case of weaving. U.S. weaving mills appear to have been enjoying by then a huge advantage vis-à-vis the rest of the world by their early employment of Northrop automatic looms, helped by a better organization of labor within the mills. Whereas Japanese low wages allowed its mills to produce at competitive costs in spite of their low productivity of labor, this was not the case for CIVSA, particularly in weaving.

As we will see in the following section, the development of future events in Mexico would pose serious problems for CIVSA's ability to compete internationally, by creating greater disadvantages in two aspects of the problem: real wages and the ability to introduce new technology and devise changes in the ways labor is organized at the shop floor.

10.5 The Industry's Secular Decline in International Competitiveness

During the Mexican Revolution (1910–20) a major transformation in the relative power of workers and employers took place in the Orizaba textile mills, which would become an important factor to explain changes in productivity and competitiveness from then on. From a laissez-faire regime, where employers dealt with an unorganized labor force, which prevailed until 1905, a totally different situation emerged. The labor movement grew stronger as a consequence of weaker governments and the need for those groups seeking to establish themselves as governments to co-opt the labor movement, whose support had become necessary to reestablish peace (Gómez-Galvarriato 2002). Textile workers, and particularly those in the Orizaba valley, acquired particular strategic relevance for the revolutionary armies, given that they were the largest organized group along the corridor that goes from the port of Veracruz to Mexico City (where most textile mills were located and on which the railroad line Orizaba lies). This corridor was the main commercial route that linked the capital to foreign nations, and the port of Veracruz collected the major share of import and export duties, a substantial share of Mexico's fiscal revenues. This gave textile workers an important leverage in obtaining substantial improvements in their living conditions and to substantially improve their relative power vis-à-vis their employers.

By 1925 CIVSA workers were organized in powerful unions and workers' confederations, with an important role in the way work was done on the shop floor. Labor was now hired through collective contracts negotiated between unions and employers, and it was now unions, rather than employers, who made the major hiring and firing decisions among blue collar workers. The government, previously totally supportive of employers, was by then divided between the interests of employers and workers, and in many crucial turning points it gave decisive support to labor at the expense of company owners (see Gómez-Galvarriato 2002).

Although the levels of international competitiveness and comparative productivity attained in 1911 by CIVSA were modest, as time passed they deteriorated. A similar situation probably prevailed across the Mexican textile industry as a whole. Thus, at least until the late 1980s, when the Mexican economy opened up to international trade, the Porfiriato would become the period when the industry had reached its peak in terms of international competitiveness.[20]

Productivity levels at Santa Rosa, measured as machine per worker and production per worker, remained virtually unchanged from 1900 to 1950. Looms per worker remained constant throughout the period, while meters per worker produced weekly diminished by a small amount from the first decade of the century to the 1920s and a little more during the Revolutionary decade; the same was true for spinning. However, because working hours diminished and production per worker did not, productivity per hour worked increased (see tables 10.9 and 10.10).[21] Whereas real wages increased substantially after 1917, productivity did not; therefore, real wages per meter of output rose notably after that date (see figure 10.1). This result explains, in part, the deterioration in profitability rates that the firm experienced after that date (see table 10.11).

After 1930 the number of looms tended per weaver gradually increased, reaching almost four. This implied an improvement in productivity rates in terms of meters per worker, although with a concomitant small reduction in meters per loom. Yet this represents a minor increase in productivity when compared to what was attainable by introducing automatic looms.

In the spinning department there was no parallel productivity improvement after 1930. On the contrary, data shows a reduction in productivity after 1940. Further research must be undertaken to understand its causes.

Given the radical change experienced on the shop floor from control by

---

20. From 1984 to 1988 a substantial reduction of the tariff fractions subject to import permits was carried out. Whereas in June 1985 88.4 percent of yarn and cloth imports were subject to import permits, these were reduced to 3.4 percent in December 1985 and to 1.9 percent in May 1988. Average ad valorem tariffs went down from 42.5 percent in December 1985 to 13.8 percent in December 1987 (Carlos Márquez Padilla, 1994, 110–11).

21. This would be in accordance with factual evidence introduced by Karl Marx that, when the workday was shortened from twelve to eleven hours, output per workday actually increased "entirely as a result of steadier application to the work and a more economical use of time on the part of the workers." Karl Marx, in Lazonick, *Competitive Advantage on the Shop Floor* (63).

Table 10.9   **Weavers' productivity, 1900–30**

Year	Meters per worker		Meters per loom (weekly)	Looms per worker	Real wage per meter ($)	Real wage per week ($)	Meters per loom per hour
	Weekly	Hourly					
1900	533.3	7.4	231.9	2.30	0.008	3.66	3.09
1901	676.8	9.4	294.3	2.30	0.008	3.99	3.34
1902	683.4	9.5	298.4	2.29	0.008	4.37	4.40
1903	540.5	7.5	229.0	2.36	0.008	3.55	3.22
1904	527.4	7.3	211.0	2.50	0.008	3.48	3.70
1905	723.1	10.0	292.7	2.47	0.008	4.81	3.28
1906	623.4	8.7	238.9	2.61	0.009	3.83	2.74
1907	663.9	9.2	257.3	2.58	0.009	4.44	3.51
1908	634.5	8.8	275.9	2.30	0.010	5.68	3.85
1909	712.6	9.9	300.7	2.37	0.009	5.43	3.93
1910	561.5	8.2	257.6	2.18	0.009	4.78	4.41
1911	418.4	6.3	181.1	2.31	0.009	3.71	3.82
1912	694.3	11.0	276.6	2.51	0.010	7.91	5.01
1913	615.6	9.8	218.3	2.82	0.011	7.62	4.30
1914	774.6	12.3	289.0	2.68	0.008	6.72	5.03
1915	598.2	10.5	229.2	2.61	0.004	3.35	4.43
1916	703.2	12.4	236.0	2.98	0.008	6.46	4.85
1917	572.9	11.3	220.3	2.60	0.013	10.61	4.33
1918	542.3	10.7	203.9	2.66	0.012	8.19	4.58
1919	421.8	8.3	160.4	2.63	0.012	7.25	4.18
1920	535.1	10.5	209.0	2.56	0.011	8.52	4.74
1921	627.7	12.3	266.0	2.36	0.012	10.19	4.84
1922	558.3	11.0	229.8	2.43	0.017	13.23	4.25
1923	548.2	10.8	227.5	2.41	0.018	13.56	3.69
1924	542.6	10.7	220.6	2.46	0.015	11.52	5.04
1925	592.7	11.7	248.0	2.39	0.014	12.70	4.96
1926	628.5	12.4	265.2	2.37	0.013	12.68	5.18
1927	572.0	11.3	239.3	2.39	0.018	15.33	4.86
1928	631.0	12.4	251.4	2.51	0.018	15.49	4.52
1929	617.2	12.1	250.9	2.46	0.018	16.09	4.74
1931	824.1	16.6	240.0	3.43	0.016	13.48	4.85
1932	537.0	16.8	157.9	3.40	0.017	9.38	4.94
1933	929.9	19.4	275.5	3.38	0.015	13.74	5.74
1934	928.4	19.3	269.8	3.44	0.014	13.02	5.62
1935	842.5	17.0	248.4	3.39	0.016	13.54	5.02
1936	681.6	15.6	201.0	3.39	0.018	12.18	4.59
1937	559.2	12.2	165.0	3.40	0.020	11.01	3.59
1938	624.8	14.2	183.8	3.40	0.019	11.85	4.18
1939	680.1	14.2	200.5	3.39	0.023	15.85	4.18
1940	527.5	13.9	155.1	3.40	0.024	12.65	4.08
1941	761.5	14.6	216.0	3.53	0.022	16.88	4.15
1942	760.7	15.8	195.0	3.90	0.020	14.95	4.06
1943	773.1	16.1	196.5	3.93	0.019	14.60	4.09
1944	787.0	16.4	200.9	3.92	0.016	12.47	4.19
1945	595.5	15.3	151.4	3.93	0.018	10.49	3.88
1946	794.1	16.5	201.9	3.93	0.018	13.93	4.21
1947	732.9	15.3	199.9	3.66	0.019	13.61	4.16

(continued)

Table 10.9 (continued)

Year	Meters per worker Weekly	Meters per worker Hourly	Meters per loom (weekly)	Looms per worker	Real wage per meter ($)	Real wage per week ($)	Meters per loom per hour
1948	745.6	15.5	209.5	3.56	0.017	12.33	4.37
1949	776.9	16.2	213.8	3.63	0.019	15.15	4.45
1950	788.8	16.4	207.6	3.67	0.018	14.19	4.32
1900–10	625.5	8.7	262.5	2.39	0.009	4.36	3.59
1911–20	587.6	10.3	222.4	2.64	0.010	7.03	4.53
1921–29	590.9	11.6	244.3	2.42	0.016	13.42	4.68
1931–40	713.5	15.9	209.7	3.40	0.018	12.67	4.68
1941–50	751.6	15.8	199.3	3.77	0.018	13.86	4.19

Sources: Meters per loom and wage per meter was obtained from a sample of thirty weavers from CV, Payrolls, June and November 1900–30 and looms per workers were taken from CV, Payrolls Week 6, 1900–30. From 1900 to 1929 wages deflated with Index I AB, Aurora Gómez-Galvarriato, *The Impact of Revolution,* 700, 703, with Index I AB. From 1929 to 1942 wages were deflated with Federico Bach and Margarita Reyna (1943, 1–63). From 1943 to 1950 the price index came from NAFINSA (1963, 109).

managers to a situation where the union had great influence, it might seem surprising that productivity levels did not fall as a result of the Revolution. The fact that they did not means that the Santa Rosa union was effective at guaranteeing workers' discipline and effort. Moreover, workers were able to produce more per hour as the shift was reduced, despite the fact that they were performing their tasks with basically the same machinery they had worked with during the Porfiriato. The intensity of labor was higher during the shorter working day, perhaps because workers were not as tired. Since they were paid per piece, they tried to produce as much as their strength allowed. In addition, once the shift was reduced, companies became more strict about arrival and departure times.[22]

However, this was not all that was required to keep the industry's international competitiveness at the levels it had maintained during the Porfiriato, let alone improve them. The reduction in investment rates at CIVSA described in figure 10.2 were partly a consequence of the decline in profit rates. A regression of Santa Rosa's fixed assets growth on the average of the previous three years' profit rates yields the following relationship.[23]

---

22. Once the eight-hour shift was established punctually became very important for the company, since it considered that the shift should consist of eight effective hours. Thus the gates were closed strictly on time. On June 12, 1917, for example, Rio Blanco shut out between sixty and seventy workers who had arrived late. At first, this factory policy elicited complaints, but then workers apparently became used to it Archive of the Compañía Industrial de Orizaba S.A. (CD) correspondence, letter from Río Blanco office to the governor of Veracruz, Cordoba, June 13, 1917.

23. Where $GROWTH_t$ is investment in fixed assets in Santa Rosa as a percentage of total assets in the year t, and $PROFITRATE_t$ is CIVSA's return on assets in the year t. Two other versions of regression were run, one using the average of profitrates for two years instead of three and another using the logarithms of the variables. Both closely resembled the one shown.

Table 10.10 Spinners' productivity, 1900–30 (1900 pesos)

	Spinners (Warp No. 29)			Spinners (Weft No. 30)		
Year	Real wage per kilo	Kilos per worker (weekly)	Kilos per worker (hourly)	Real wage per kilo	Kilos per worker (weekly)	Kilos per worker (hourly)
1900	0.029	244.2	3.14	0.038	277.2	3.61
1901	0.029	220.9	3.02	0.037	222.0	3.12
1902	0.027	241.0	3.35	0.035	262.0	3.68
1903	0.027	234.3	3.12	0.035	232.0	3.03
1904	0.026	181.5	2.78	0.034	238.8	2.75
1905	0.026	256.3	3.05	0.034	239.7	2.91
1906	0.012	231.8	3.22	0.034	221.0	2.44
1907	0.036	225.3	3.13	0.038	227.9	2.49
1908	0.035	213.4	2.96	0.034	231.3	3.47
1909	0.030	229.4	3.19	0.034	225.1	3.75
1910	0.026	281.9	4.70	0.031	201.8	3.36
1911	0.027	232.3	4.22	0.029	219.4	3.99
1912	0.028	253.8	4.23	0.032	211.1	4.00
1913	0.028	212.9	3.88	0.032	205.3	3.95
1914	0.021	208.1	3.50	0.024	218.3	3.89
1915	0.011	190.7	3.68	0.012	214.8	3.48
1916	0.021	183.0	3.90	0.33	211.6	4.49
1917	0.037	176.3	3.67	0.040	212.5	4.22
1918	0.032	178.5	4.46	0.035	215.2	4.70
1919	0.034	160.3	4.21	0.035	216.9	5.07
1920	0.029	176.5	4.17	0.032	236.3	4.73
1921	0.036	190.3	4.24	0.037	206.3	4.35
1922	0.045	198.0	5.54	0.044	205.0	4.73
1923	0.044	204.9	3.90	0.046	210.1	3.93
1924	0.043	185.1	4.73	0.046	204.5	5.20
1925	0.037	208.2	4.14	0.044	220.4	4.71
1926	0.038	242.6	4.74	0.043	224.9	5.00
1927	0.048	219.9	3.98	0.049	257.8	5.61
1928	0.053	224.7	4.41	0.056	268.8	5.14
1929	0.051	268.2	5.09	0.054	260.6	5.40
1931	0.052	256.8	5.18	0.047	346.0	6.99
1932	0.059	190.5	4.65	0.057	296.2	5.99
1933	0.047	278.4	5.65	0.056	245.4	5.95
1934	0.046	275.5	5.74	0.045	281.4	6.94
1935	0.052	197.0	4.40	0.057	293.8	5.40
1936	0.049	109.6	2.76	0.062	319.1	2.43
1937	0.047	126.3	2.77	0.052	333.0	4.54
1938	0.054	131.7	3.20	0.050	298.4	3.77
1939	0.058	132.0	2.75	0.074	239.8	3.92
1940	0.076	139.3	3.53	0.061	191.5	4.19
1941	0.058	92.8	3.17	0.060	120.0	5.94
1942	0.055	103.9	3.66	0.065	105.7	4.34
1943	0.050	110.7	4.03	0.057	212.3	6.58
1944	0.048	119.0	4.24	0.049	201.9	3.38

(*continued*)

Table 10.10 (continued)

	Spinners (Warp No. 29)			Spinners (Weft No. 30)		
Year	Real wage per kilo	Kilos per worker (weekly)	Kilos per worker (hourly)	Real wage per kilo	Kilos per worker (weekly)	Kilos per worker (hourly)
1945	0.045	99.8	4.27	0.055	154.9	4.00
1946	0.051	107.0	4.46	0.056	198.8	4.55
1947	0.053	91.9	2.83	0.057	188.1	4.20
1948	0.049	146.5	4.89	0.055	190.1	4.91
1949	0.052	107.7	3.88	0.057	165.6	4.38
1950	0.052	119.6	3.93	0.055	138.5	4.90
1900–10	0.028	232.7	3.24	0.035	234.4	3.15
1911–20	0.027	197.2	3.99	0.030	216.2	4.25
1921–29	0.044	215.8	4.53	0.047	228.7	4.90
1931–40	0.054	183.7	4.06	0.056	284.5	5.01
1941–50	0.051	109.9	3.93	0.057	167.6	4.72

Source: A sample was taken from CV, Payrolls, June and November 1900–30. Wages were deflated.

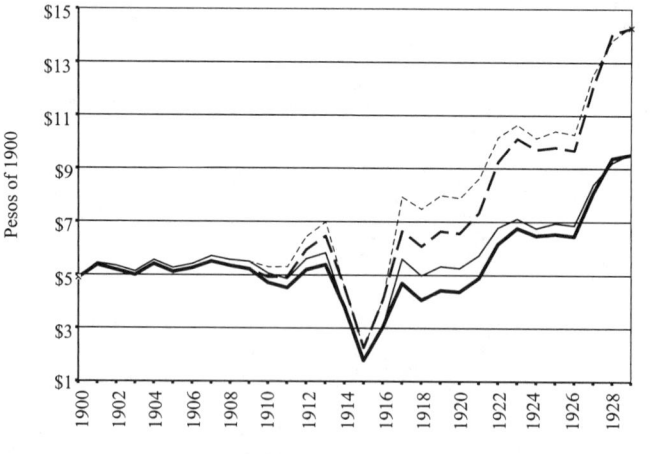

— Real Wages (I)   ▬ Real Wages (II)   --- Real Wages (I) Hourly   – – Real Wages (II) Hourly

Fig. 10.1 Average weekly and hourly real wages (pesos of 1900)
Source: CV, Payrolls 1900–30.

$$\text{GROWTH}_t = \underset{(-0.29)}{-0.005} + \underset{(2.02)}{0.62}(\text{PROFITRATE}_{t-1} + \text{PROFITRATE}_{t-2} + \text{PROFITRATE}_{t-3})/3$$

$$R^2 = 0.14,\ \text{adjusted}\ R^2 = 0.10,\ N = 28$$

with *t*-statistics in parentheses. Past profits are used as a proxy of expected future profits, of which investment in fixed assets should be a function. Re-

Table 10.11 CIVSA's return on assets and equity, 1899–1929

Year	Price index[c]	Return on assets[a] (%)	Return on equity[a] (%)	Return on assets[b] (%)	Return on equity[b] (%)
1899	92.50	−1.42	−1.63	−1.49	−1.76
1900	100.00	5.67	6.94	5.74	6.94
1901	104.72	4.35	5.29	4.32	5.05
1902	114.89	12.18	14.54	11.39	12.65
1903	115.29	11.73	13.79	11.02	11.96
1904	116.57	12.42	14.46	11.56	12.40
1905	117.94	12.41	14.39	11.41	12.20
1906	117.79	7.75	8.95	7.11	7.60
1907	122.35	8.17	9.47	7.32	7.74
1908	123.97	4.86	5.70	4.31	4.60
1909	132.24	6.34	7.48	5.33	5.66
1910	146.45	5.91	7.14	4.65	4.88
1900–10		7.53	8.88	6.89	7.49
1911	146.05	3.83	4.67	3.02	3.20
1912	148.68	9.28	11.14	7.24	7.50
1913	150.70	6.10	7.19	4.73	4.77
1914	171.90	−0.39	−0.44	−0.27	−0.26
1915	196.09	−2.63	−2.86	−1.63	−1.46
1916	223.68	6.72	7.19	3.68	3.21
1917	255.14	13.61	15.77	7.42	6.18
1918	305.88	8.04	9.21	4.07	3.01
1919	293.42	11.58	12.71	6.14	4.33
1920	319.01	11.01	12.68	5.77	3.97
1911–20		6.72	7.73	4.02	3.45
1921	285.68	14.81	17.49	8.41	6.12
1922	228.96	11.4	13.23	7.42	5.78
1923	200.26	8.96	10.06	6.32	5.02
1924	207.44	1.76	1.89	1.19	0.91
1925	241.69	6.61	6.94	4.04	2.87
1926	238.46	−3.20	−3.33	−1.97	−1.40
1927	210.63	7.23	7.53	4.82	3.57
1928	197.86	2.95	3.13	2.08	1.58
1929	201.44	2.47	2.59	1.71	1.29
1921–29		5.89	6.61	3.78	2.86

Sources: CV, Balances Generales y Estados de Resultados 1898–1910.
[a]Calculated using nominal equity and assets.
[b]Calculated correcting equity and fixed assets for inflation.
[c]Price Index II, AB, Gold. Aurora Gómez-Galvarriato, *The Impact of Revolution,* table A4.15 in Appendix to chapter 4.
[d]Net of depreciation.

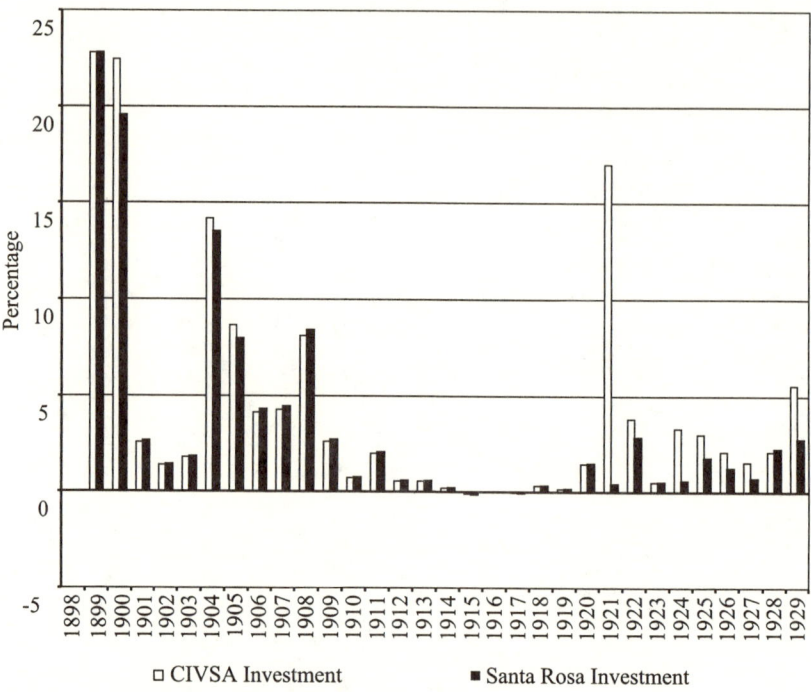

Fig. 10.2 Investments in real estate, machinery, and equipment at CIVSA (as percentage of total fixed assets)
Source: CIVSA and Santa Rosa General Balances 1900–1929.

sults of this regression show a clear association between investment and profits for CIVSA, indicating that the decline in profit rates after the Porfiriato accounts for a significant part of the drop in investment rates after 1912.[24] Yet, there were other forces behind the reduction of investment rates; namely, labor regulation restrictions on the adoption of new technology and the tariff policy adopted in the late 1920s.

New technology adopted by the textile industry worldwide was not introduced into Mexican mills. One of the most notable improvements in textile production was the introduction of automatic looms.[25] Other important technological changes that became widespread in the 1920s were the following: (1) double-length looms, which increased weavers' productivity; (2) the one-process picker (*batiente de un solo proceso*), which reduced balebreaking, lapping, and picking to only one step; (3) high-speed warping

---

24. A similar regression was run by Susan Wolcott and Gregory Clark for the Indian textile industry (using panel data of several mills from 1907–38), yielding very similar results. Susan Wolcott and Gregory Clark (1999, 407).
25. México, Secretaría de la Economía Nacional (Juan Chávez Orozco) (1933, 66).

(*altos estirajes*), which reduced the number of times yarn was passed through the fly frames (*veloces*); and (4) the use of artificial silk (rayon) to mix with cotton.[26]

Automatic looms were not introduced by CIVSA in the 1900s because they demanded higher investment—their price was two-and-a-half times that of an ordinary power loom. Moreover, at their early stage of development, they required more technical assistance than power looms. Because specialized technical assistance was relatively expensive in Mexico, this meant a significant additional cost.[27] However, because this technology was new and not so widespread at the time, it was not so crucial for the Mexican textile industry to adopt it then as later, when, after being tested and improved, it became standard throughout the world. In the 1920s, certain Mexican textile companies tried to acquire automatic looms, but faced the opposition of unions against this labor-saving machinery.[28]

In the early 1920s, CIVSA attempted to install 100 Northrop automatic looms. However, its union did not permit them and the company was forced to sell them at a discount to several other companies in small sets. Atoyac Textil, one of the mills of the Rivero Quijano family, bought some of them. However, this company was also unable to put them into operation because of problems like those at Santa Rosa. Moreover, according to one of Atoyac Textil's owners, Jesús Rivero Quijano, it was necessary to have at least a hundred automatic looms running for a company to reap the benefits of this new technology; even if they had been adopted at Atoyac there would not have been enough to show what automation could accomplish (Quijano, 278).

In 1923, Atoyac Textil decided to give another chance to automatic looms, buying twenty-four Stafford looms. However, "in order to introduce them it was necessary that the president of Stafford Looms travel to Mexico to have an interview with General Calles and President Obregón, to deal later with Luis N. Morones about the installation and operation of these machines (Quijano, 278). The government accepted the installation of these automatic looms on condition that they were considered an "exhibition." Once they were mounted, however, unions blocked their operation. The worker who ran the looms was stabbed to death. His successor soon started receiving death threats and promptly

---

26. See Segunda Ponencia de la Companñía Industrial de Orizaba S.A. in *Primera Convención Mexicana de Empresarios Textiles (Rama del Algodón)*, April 9–12, 1945, 176–180; and Jesús Rivero Quijano (1990, 239–48, 257–62, and 279–80).

27. A full discussion of these issues can be found in Aurora Gómez-Galvarriato, *The Impact of Revolution*, 152–56.

28. Graham Clark suggests in his study of the Mexican textile industry of 1909 that opposition from workers to automatic looms was already present then. However, CIVSA managers never referred to labor discontent as a reason for not adopting automatic looms. Moreover, they were able to put some automatic looms in operation in the early 1900s without any problems with workers. (Graham Clark 1909, 22).

resigned. No one else dared to tend the looms, and they were abandoned until some technicians transformed them into ordinary power looms (Rivero, 278).

In the late 1920s, a legal restriction on the adoption of new technologies such as automatic looms, one-process pickers, and high-speed warping was imposed. The wage-list that was designed as a result of the Convention of Workers and Industrialists of 1925–27 fixed the maximum number of machines per worker and established specific wages-per-piece. Under these conditions, industrialists had no incentive to introduce better machinery because it would not enable them to reduce labor costs, since wages-per-piece and the workers-per-machine had to remain invariable.[29]

In spite of the important technological changes that the textile industry had undergone since 1912, no new technical studies were made to define the 1925–27 industrywide labor contract. The same technical principles adopted to build the 1912 Tariff (based on the Blackburn wage-list of 1905) were used for the new wage-list.[30] In spinning, the concept of one worker per machine prevailed, forcing Mexican mills to adopt larger spinning machines than was recommended by their builders, or to join two spinning machines, with several technical problems.[31]

As in England, by lowering piece-rates on larger and faster spinning frames, wage-lists encouraged capitalists to try to maximize spindles per workers.[32] In contrast, in weaving, by setting piece-rates irrespective of the number of speed looms tended, wage schedules encouraged employers to try to minimize the number of looms per weaver. This was so because "for a given intensity of labor, the lower the number of looms per weaver, the faster each loom could be run, the higher the output per loom, and the lower total unit factor costs."[33]

In carding, the 1925–27 wage-list, like the one created in 1912, established that one worker should operate eight carding machines. However, by introducing simple modifications to machinery and organization, it became possible for one worker to tend forty carding machines with no additional effort. The wage-list created no incentive for Mexican mills to introduce these changes since, if they were allowed to implement them, mills would have to pay five times more to the card tender that remained working and give severance pay to the four who would have to be dismissed. These costs, together with the investment required to modernize the card-

---

29. México, Secretaría de la Economía Nacional (Juan Chávez Orozo, 67).
30. Ibid., 418.
31. Ibid.
32. In England between 1896 and 1914 spinning frames were enlarged in order to maximize effort and at the same time comply with the wage-lists. See Lazonick, *Competitive Advantage* (163).
33. Ibid., 163–64.

ing machines, were greater than the benefits the mills would obtain through cost reductions (Naciones Unidas 1951, 14).

The decision to establish fixed wage schedules per piece and limits on machines per worker was not made unknowingly. In 1926, the Saco-Lowell Shops, fearing that the agreements of the convention would affect demand for their machinery in Mexico, sent a letter to the president of the convention, explaining how detrimental the new regulations were to the adoption of new technology. The letter described the advantages of automatic looms as well as that of machinery specifically designed for the processing of scrap cotton. It explained why these innovations would not be adopted with the new wage-list and regulations proposed by the convention.[34] However, the majority of votes in the convention were in favor of the rigid wage schedule. Workers regarded modern machines as a threat to employment, industrialists as a threat to the survival of their decrepit mills, while government perceived the threat of social discontent. It was easier to raise tariffs and let the industry survive as it was. The overrepresentation of smaller, more old-fashioned mills at the convention may also have contributed to this result.[35]

CIVSA documents show the effects of the convention regulations on the company's investment decisions. In 1927, for example, double-length looms, not considered in the convention's wage-list, were installed in Santa Rosa.[36] However, a year later, the CIVSA board of directors decided to remove them because the wages demanded by the Santa Rosa union for their operators made production too costly.

In May 1929, CIVSA's main engineer presented a cost-benefit analysis, explaining the advisability of installing new high-speed-warping machines, which would generate substantial savings. CIVSA's board of directors decided to postpone their purchase until they were able to get a fair wage rate for operating these new machines. Together with CIDOSA, CIVSA started negotiations with the Ministry of Industry on this matter; at least until the end of 1930, however, they proved fruitless.[37]

Although the effects of rigid regulations on technological innovation must have been worse in those states, such as Veracruz, where the labor movement was strongest, contemporary studies on the textile industry indicate that they prevailed throughout the entire country.[38] Aggregate data

---

34. Saco Lowell Shops to Presidencia de la Convención, August 7, 1926, Archivo General de la Nacíon, (AGN), Departamento del Trabajo (DT), 979/3.
35. According to the Convention's rules every mill had a vote regardless of its size. This gave a majority vote to smaller, usually more outdated, mills. México, Secretaría de la Economía Nacional, (Moisés T. de la Peña), (1934, 48).
36. CV, AC, July 12, 1927.
37. CV, Actas del Consejo del Administracíon (Board Meetings Minutes [AC]), May 14, 1929.
38. See México, Secretaria de la Economía Nacional, (Juan Chávez Orozco), (1933, 67), and México, Secretaría de la Economía Nacional (Moisés T. de la Peña), (1934, 187–91).

for Mexico's textile industry show little investment.[39] Although some new factories were built in the 1920s, most of them were small establishments devoted to the production of knitwear (*bonetería*), mainly of artificial silk. This is why, although the number of factories increased by 22 percent from 1921 to 1930, the number of active spindles and looms increased only by 9 percent and 8 percent, respectively (see table 10.12). Machinery per worker (measured in loom equivalents), which increased during the last decade of the Porfiriato by 18 percent, increased by only 7 percent during the twenties. During the Revolution, loom equivalents per worker grew on a per-shift basis because of the reduction in the length of the workday. And labor productivity increased between 1926 and 1930, not only when measured by loom equivalents per shift, but also when measured in sales and production per worker. However, this was the result of (a) the implementation of the Convention's wages per piece, which increased labor intensity, and (b) the reduction of employment and hours worked per mill as a consequence of the Depression. According to contemporary observers, "This increase was by no means the result of an improvement in machinery in the mills."[40]

Increased protection levels were necessary to keep Mexican mills running. As tables 10.4 and 10.5 show, there was a substantial increase in ad valorem tariffs after 1927, which came together with the conclusion of the Workers' and Industrialists' Convention. Before that year, governments that came out of the Revolution had been actually less protectionist than the Porfirian government. After 1916, Carranza's government began to pursue a liberalization tariff policy that drastically diminished tariffs on basic commodities, such as cloth. The rationale behind this policy was twofold. On the one hand, during 1917 Mexico suffered a severe shortage of products, which generated a significant increase in prices. Reducing tariffs was therefore an emergency strategy designed by the government to cope with the enormous scarcity of goods and the rising prices the country was facing (Cosío Villegas, 99). However, there was also a theoretical reason behind the liberalization policy. At the First National Congress of Industrialists held in Mexico City in September 1917, Alberto J. Pani, Minister of Industry and Commerce, made it clear in his inaugural address that

---

39. National data on the cotton textile industry was obtained from the following sources: For 1900–11: México, SHCP, *Boletín de Estadística Fiscal,* several issues, México, *The Mexican Year Book 1908* (523–31). For 1912: AGN, DT 5/4/4 "Manifestaciónes presentadas por los fabricantes de hilados y tejidos de algodón durante enero a junio de 1912." For 1913: AGN, DT, 31/2/4, "Estadística semestral de las fcas, de hilados y tejidos de algodón de la Reública Mexicana correspondiente al semestre de 1913." For 1914–20: Stephen Haber, (1989, 124); and México, Secretaría de la Economía Nacional, (Moisés T. de la Peña), 14, 126. For 1921–24: México, Poder Ejecutivo Federal, Departamento de Estadística Nacional, *Aspectos Económicos de un Quinquenio: 1921–1925,* 8–29; *Boletín de Estadística,* January 1924, 52–55; *Estadística Nacional,* September 30, 1925, 5–17. For 1925–30: México, SHCP, Departmento de Impuestos Especiales, Sección de Hilados y Tejidos, "Estadísticas del Ramo de Hilados y Tejidos de Algodón y de Lana," typewritten reports.

40. See México, Secretaría de la Economía Nacional (Juan Chávez Orozco), (1933, 63).

Table 10.12 The Mexican textile industry, 1900–1934

Year	Active mills	Spindles	Looms	Workers	Workers (adj)	Cotton Cons.	Sales (nominal; $)	Sales (in 1900 pesos)	Loom equity per worker	Loom equity per shift	Cotton per worker	Sales per worker ($)
1900	134	557,391	17,202	26,764	26,764	28,990	35,459	35,459	0.87	0.87	1,083	1,325
1901	133	602,223	18,885	27,663	27,663	30,262	33,877	35,553	0.92	0.92	1,094	1,285
1902	124	575,304	17,974	25,316	25,316	27,628	28,780	27,939	0.96	0.96	1,091	1,104
1903	115	630,201	20,124	26,249	26,249	27,512	36,907	31,339	1.03	1.03	1,048	1,194
1904	119	632,018	20,326	27,033	27,033	28,841	42,511	34,646	1.01	1.01	1,067	1,282
1905	127	666,659	21,932	29,483	29,483	31,230	51,214	46,097	0.99	0.99	1,059	1,564
1906	130	683,739	22,776	31,673	31,673	35,826	51,171	44,894	0.96	0.96	1,131	1,417
1907	129	693,842	23,507	33,132	33,132	36,654	51,686	41,326	0.94	0.94	1,106	1,247
1908	132	732,876	24,997	35,816	35,816	36,040	54,934	45,303	0.92	0.92	1,006	1,265
1909	129	726,278	25,327	32,229	32,229	35,435	43,370	36,656	1.03	1.03	1,099	1,137
1910	123	702,874	25,017	31,963	31,963	34,736	50,651	39,119	1.02	1.02	1,087	1,224
1911	119	725,297	24,436	32,147	32,147	34,568	51,348	39,286	1.01	1.01	1,075	1,222
1912	127	762,149	26,801	32,128	26,773	32,366	52,847	38,804	1.10	1.31	1,007	1,208
1913	118	752,804	26,791	32,641	27,201	32,821			1.07	1.29	1,006	
1914	90											
1915	84											
1916	93											
1917	92	573,072	20,489	22,187	14,791		64,130	29,974	1.21	1.81		1,351
1918	104	689,173	25,017	27,680	18,453		48,567	19,574	1.18	1.77		707
1919	110	749,237	27,020	33,185	22,123		69,778	25,169	1.06	1.59		758
1920	120	753,837	27,301	37,936	25,291	31,694	120,492	36,890	0.94	1.41	835	972
1921	121	770,945	28,409	38,227	25,485	35,924	93,942	28,329	0.97	1.45	940	741

(continued)

Table 10.12   (continued)

Year	Active mills	Spindles	Looms	Workers	Workers (adj)	Cotton Cons.	Sales (nominal; $)	Sales (in 1900 pesos)	Loom equity per worker	Loom equity per shift	Cotton per worker	Sales per worker ($)
1922	119	803,230	29,521	39,677	26,451	34,654	85,023	26,766	0.97	1.45	873	675
1923	110	802,363	29,668	39,629	26,419	32,344	97,490	35,376	0.97	1.46	816	893
1924	116	812,165	29,888	37,732	25,155	30,517	96,435	34,429	1.03	1.54	809	912
1925	130	831,524	30,800	43,199	28,799	40,997	108,396	38,038	0.92	1.39	949	881
1926	138	842,793	31,296	44,250	29,500	41,523	95,438	34,111	0.92	1.38	938	771
1927	144	826,702	30,614	41,226	27,484	39,356	91,069	32,520	0.96	1.44	955	789
1928	132	823,862		38,889	25,926	37,031	96,293	36,491			952	938
1929	144	831,486	30,090	38,804	25,869	39,417	97,162	37,233	1.01	1.52	1,016	960
1930	143	842,265	30,625	39,424	26,283	40,582	91,145	37,811	1.01	1.52	1,029	959
1931	146	840,876	30,596	36,989	24,659	34,627	74,244	34,816	1.08	1.62	936	941
1932	141	831,847	29,825	34,095	22,730	34,311	75,977	38,861	1.14	1.71	1,006	1,140
1933	147	855,256	30,878	35,422	23,614	20,614	47,622	22,332	1.14	1.71	582	630
1934	159	863,746	31,602	39,281	26,187	22,842	64,514	29,451	1.05	1.57	582	750
1900–10	−8.2%	26.1%	45.4%	19.4%	19.8%	42.8%	10.3%	0.97	0.97	1,079	1,277	1,036
1911–20	0.8%	3.9%	11.7%	18.0%	−21.3%	−8.3%	134.7%	−6.1%	1.08	1.46	981	812
1921–26	15.0%	11.8%	14.6%	16.6%	16.6%	31.0%	−20.8%	−7.5%	0.96	1.44	888	888
1927–34	10.8%	4.5%	3.2%	−4.7%	−4.7%	−42.0%	−29.2%	−9.4%	1.06	1.58	882	

Source: See footnote 39.

Notes: Loom equivalents have been calculated following Gregory Clark (1987, 19–49). The length of the workday was considered to be twelve hours from 1900 to 1911, ten hours from 1912 to 1916, nine hours in 1917, and eight hours from 1917 to 1930. This is shorter than in reality because workday regulations were not strictly followed in all mills. Prices have been deflated using the Textile (gold) Index.

"free national and international competition" was one of the main principles behind the revolutionary industrial policy (Pani, 46).

Once Obregón came to power the free-trade spirit waned, and duties were gradually increased. However, although specific tariffs for cloth were higher between 1921 and 1926 than during the Porfiriato, ad valorem tariffs were not, since prices had also increased. Moreover, the effective rate of protection for cloth fell, because between the two periods, ad valorem tariffs for raw cotton rose more than those for cloth.[41]

In the Workers' and Industrialists' Convention of 1925–27, the three major actors in the political economy of the textile industry—businessmen, labor, and the government—chose an institutional arrangement that offered no incentives for technological transformation and therefore required high tariffs. Moreover, the depression that affected the textile industry from 1926 onward also created incentives for increased protection throughout the world. This explains the substantial increases in the tariff on cloth from 1927 to 1933, which made them several times higher than those that prevailed during both the Porfiriato and the early 1920s. This enabled most mills to survive, jobs to continue, and social order to endure. However, the lack of technological innovation in an industry sheltered by high rates of protection condemned Mexico's textile industry to become increasingly more outdated and unable to compete in world markets.

From 1933 to 1947, ad valorem tariffs decreased as a result of the increase in cloth prices. However the depreciation of the peso from 2.6 pesos per dollar in 1931 (when Mexico left the gold standard) to 5.5 in 1940 provided the industry with a further margin of protection. World War II generated an exceptional situation, as the Mexican textile industry was even capable of exporting vast quantities of cloth. When the war ended the situation reversed, and the industry demanded a new increase in tariffs. This came about at the end of 1947, when the new tariff schedule was changed to include both an ad valorem and a specific duty. Yet, since an official price list was established, and this list did not change for several years, ad valorem tariffs gradually decreased from 1947 to 1955 as a result of price increases. However, the peso continued depreciating, going from 4.8 pesos per dollar in 1947 to 8.6 in 1940, and then to 12.50 in 1954, providing further protection. Moreover, after 1947 the import of specific items in the tariff schedule were forbidden for some years (see tables 10.4 and 10.5).

The 1925–27 convention agreements may be understandable under the circumstances of worldwide depression in the textile industry. Nevertheless, the precepts adopted there were ratified over and over again. In spite of the efforts made by industrialists in 1932 and 1935 to introduce a more

---

41. Increased foreign competition must be part of the reason why CIVSA's markup (price/costs) decreased from 96 percent from 1904–1908 to 45 percent from 1923–27.

flexible wage schedule, the Textile Workers' and Industrialists' Convention of 1937–1939 kept it unchanged.[42]

After World War II, when the old equipment was worn out and needed to be replaced, industrialists made another attempt to change the restrictions imposed on the implementation of new technology. In 1945 CIVSA's president explained at the annual shareholders' meeting that it was urgent for Santa Rosa, as well as for Mexican textile industry as a whole, to fully modernize its equipment in order to be able to produce intensely in "conditions of efficient competition." "It is a matter of life and death for the national industry," he argued, "but full modernization generates problems of personnel, wage-lists, etc., that need to be solved uniformly and evenly."[43] According to him, CIVSA and other companies were only waiting for a favorable agreement by the Convention of Workers and Industrialists of the Textile Industry to be held in that year, to carry out the project.[44] However, despite their efforts, they had no success.[45] Only new plants established after the war were exempt from restrictions imposed by the industrywide labor contract, and some modern mills were established (IBRD, 69; CV, AAG, February 28, 1928). Old mills had to replace their worn-out equipment with used equipment. In 1956, for example, a considerable share of the machinery imported was used (29.07 percent of the looms, 38.28 percent of the spinning frames, and 52.98 percent of the carding machines).[46]

In 1950, CIVSA's president explained that after several months of negotiations, restrictions on the modernization of the industry had not been lifted.[47] That same year, a National Union of Industrialists for Textile Modernization (*Unión Nacional de Industriales para la Modernización Textil*), to which CIVSA belonged, was created to fight for the liberalization

---

42. Segunda Ponencia de la Compañia Industrial de Orizaba S.A. In *Primera Convención Mexicana de Empresarios Textiles (Rama del Algodón)*, April 9–12, 1945, 175.

43. CV, Actas de la Asamblea General (Minutes of the General Shareholders Meeting; AAG), February 26, 1927.

44. Ibid.

45. An agreement was reached at the Convention of Workers and Industrialists of the Textile Industry held in May 1946, by which a special commission would undertake a study of the necessary conditions for the modernization of the industry. However this commission did not reach any conclusions and was dissolved. An Arbitration Organism contemplated in the agreement of May 1946 was left in charge of the study but the labor sector members were opposed to participate in the project and it was also dissolved. The Minister of Industry and Labor asked the parties interested in the modernization of the industry to carry out private meetings in order to propose solutions to the problem. As a result of these meetings an agreement was reached on July 7, 1950, that generated "the General Regulation for the Modernization of the Textile Industry," to be included in the collective contract (*Contrato Obligatorio*). It was approved by two-thirds of the labor force in the industry, but according to those firms that had already started modernizing their machinery it only froze the modernization process. The General Regulations for the Modernization of the Textile Industry was effective as of January 25, 1951 (*Diario Oficial*, October 23, 1950, February 6, 1951).

46. See Javier Barajas Manzano, Aspectos de la Industria Textil de Algodón en México (Mexico City, 1959), 51.

47. CV, AAG, March 20, 1950.

of the legal restrictions on the use of new technology. However, a minority of industrialists, who were in favor of continuing to work with outdated machinery, together with the unions were able to prevent any modification of the labor laws and wage-lists.[48]

Early in 1951, employers and workers finally agreed on the general rules to be followed in the modernization of equipment, rationalization of working methods and wage scales, and specialization within the industry. Yet this agreement was only "a preliminary outline of principles to be followed by other agreements to implement specific programs." According to the International Bank of Reconstruction and Development, although the agreement was an important initial step, it was "not expected to have significant consequences for the time being" (IBRD, 69).

From 1951 onward the "General Rules for the Modernization of the Textile Industry" were included as an addendum to the wage-list.[49] These rules allowed more flexibility in the operation of modern machinery,[50] and set rules for the dismissal of excess workers. However, the minority of firms that had already begun a modernization process, of which CIVSA and CIDOSA were part, were opposed to them, considering that the specific criteria the new regulations established in terms of wages, severance fees, and workloads imposed severe restrictions for the modernization of the industry.[51] The members of the National Union for the Modernization of the Textile Industry considered it inadequate that those rules were voted for by the whole industry rather than by only those mills that had begun modernizing their machinery since 1946. They argued that the interests of firms operating with old machinery "that only seek for their indefinite subsistence"[52] was opposed to modernization. Since outdated firms had the majority of votes in the Workers and Industrialists Congress, no set of regulations that would effectively promote modernization could come out from a process that included the whole industry on a basis of one vote per mill. Moreover, outdated firms had allied with labor in their hostility to modernization. Workers, traditionally reticent of modernization, were particularly opposed to it, since most of them worked in antiquated mills.[53] Although these new laws permitted the creation of some modern mills and

---

48. CV, AAG, March 21, 1951.
49. *Diario Oficial,* February 6, 1951.
50. Modern machinery was defined as that which reduced labor with respect to the machinery considered by the Workers and Industrialist Convention of 1937–1939. *Diario Oficial,* February 6, 1951, 9.
51. *Diario Oficial,* October 23, 1950.
52. *Diario Oficial,* October 23, 1950. Letter from several firms that were members of the Unión de Industriales para la Modernización Textil to the president of the Comisión Mixta Obrero-Patronal de Contrato Colectivo del Trabajo de la Industria Textil del Algodón y sus Mixturas.
53. Ibid. Letter from several firms members of the "Unión Nacional de Industriales para la Modernización Textil" to the president of the Convención Mixta Obrero-Patronal, del Contrato Colectivo de Trabajo de la Industria Textil del Algodón y sus Mixturas, 5.

Table 10.13   Reduction in the labor required to produce the same quantity of coarse cloth in the United States, 1910–1936

Yarn preparation (Preparación de Hilados)	49.6%
Spinning (Tróciles)	26.9%
Spooling and drawing (Cañoneros y Repaso)	36.3%
Weaving (Telares)	52.8%
Cloth reception (Recepción de Manta)	14.2%

Source: Segunda Ponencia de la Compañía Industrial de Orizaba S.A. in Primera Convención Mexicana de Empresarios Textiles (Rama del Algodón), April 9–12, 1945, 196.

the modernization of certain departments of old mills, the restrictions it imposed on the process, together with high rates of protection, generated few investments for the modernization of the industry.

The result was that the textile industry became increasingly more outdated. Whereas in Mexico there had been no major changes in the industry's methods of production since 1912, in the United States the introduction of new technologies between 1910 and 1936 had already generated a significant reduction in labor requirements (see table 10.13).

At the 1945 Textile Convention CIDOSA presented a detailed comparative analysis of productivity levels in the Mexican, American, and English industries.[54] Its results showed the disastrous state of the Mexican industry (see table 10.14). According to CIDOSA, the structure of the collective labor contract for the industry was one of the main reasons. In addition to the rigid wage-list, it forced the industry to keep the same number of workers hired; any worker who left the mill for any reason had to be replaced. Moreover, because it established a promotion system based on seniority, it prevented firms from choosing and promoting personnel on the basis of aptitude and effort.[55] England's productivity levels had also lagged behind those of the United States as a result of a fixed collective labor contract that determined the wages to be paid per unit of production and type of work, the number of workers per machine, and their duties. Nevertheless, in England modernization was gradually phased in, allowing the industry to implement certain technological changes (i.e., installing the warp-stop motion system in plain looms).[56]

A United Nations study on the productivity of the Latin American tex-

---

54. Data for the Mexican industry were calculated by CIDOSA; data for the United States and England CIDOSA were obtained from a formal report by the English Textile Commission on a visit to the United States in March–April 1944.

55. See Segunda Ponencia de la Compañía Industrial de Orizaba S.A., 195.

56. Ibid., 188 and 197. "In 1892, at the peak of prosperity in the weaving industry, a Uniform List covering all the weaving districts was adopted on terms very favorable to wages. In late 1932 the Uniform List was modified to accommodate the 'more-looms' system; but in 1935 it was altered again, this time to discourage the practice of giving weavers more than four powerlooms to tend. To ensure that all employers would adhere to the 1935 list, it was given the force of law by Act of Parliament" (Lazonick, *Competitive Advantage,* 56).

Table 10.14   Productivity comparisons, c. 1945

	U.S.	England	Mexico	Mexico vs. U.S. (%)	Mexico vs. England
Spinning					
Warp No. 9[a]					
Kilograms per worker per hour	10.45	7.22	2.61	25	36
Total labor	226	327	904	400	276
Warp No. 31, Filling No. 43[b]					
Kilograms per worker per hour	4.45	2.32	1.13	25	49
Total labor	101	195	399	395	205
Weaving					
Coarse unbleached cloth[c]					
Meters per worker per hour	32.4	12.8	9.8	30	77
Total labor	890	2,252	2,941	330	131
Medium quality unbleached cloth[d]					
Meters per worker per hour	44.5	14	9.4	21	67
Total labor	337	1,072	1,599	474	149

Source: Segunda Ponencia de la Compañía Industrial de Orizaba S.A. in Primera Convención Mexicana de Empresarios Textiles (Rama del Algodón), April 9–12, 1945, 175–90. Data for spinning and weaving are the sum of the different parts of both processes, including yarn preparation and cloth preparation and reception.
[a]Spinning mills that manufactured 13,605 kilos of No. 9 warp yarn in 48 hours.
[b]Spinning mills that manufactured 13,605 kilos of warp yarn No. 31, plus 8,154 kilos of No. 43 weft (filling) yarn in 48 hours.
[c]Weaving mills that produced 1,385,316 meters of coarse unbleached cloth in 48 hours.
[d]Weaving mills that produced 720,540 meters of medium quality, unbleached cloth in 48 hours.

tile industry, published in 1951, indicated that as many as 85 percent of the spindles and 95 percent of the looms working in Mexico were out of date; that is, built during the first quarter of the century or earlier (Naciones Unidas, 87). Likewise, a Mexican public financial study (Nafinsa) reported that in 1957, 34.4 percent of the spindles, 46 percent of the carding machines, and 33 percent of the looms operating that year had been built before 1910. Technological backwardness was worst in states such as Veracruz, where labor regulations were more strictly implemented because of their stronger labor movements,[57] and where the mills were older. In this state, 67 percent of the spindles, 72 percent of the carding machines, and 73 percent of the looms working in 1957 had been manufactured before 1910 (Barajas, 1959, 67–74, 97–99). The industry gradually moved away

---

57. Legal wages and regulations were only important where the labor movement was strong enough to enforce them. In 1959 Javier Barajas Manzano explained that wages established by the wage-schedule (*contrato colectivo de trabajo*) could not be taken as the wages workers were actually paid. "It is well known," he explained, "that this document is not complied with by most mills, especially by those established at the beginning of the century, but that wages are set through bilateral agreements between workers and employers" (Barajas, 28).

from those states where the labor movement was strongest, wages highest, and labor regulations most effective. In 1923, 20.8 percent of spindles and 22.37 percent of looms in Mexico were in Veracruz, but by 1950 these figures had declined to 14.81 percent and 17.81 percent, respectively.[58] In the end, the strength of Veracruz' labor movement was the cause of its own demise.[59]

According to the United Nations study, the number of man-hours-per-kilogram of production was 269 percent higher in the Mexican cotton textile industry than in a standard modern industry. Modernization of equipment could increase productivity by 260 percent in spinning and 281 percent in weaving. Yet this would have caused the displacement of more than 15,000 workers and would have required an investment of over one hundred million 1950 dollars (Naciones Unidas 1951, 87). In contrast, according to the Nafinsa study, the modernization of the industry was feasible, since its calculations indicated that in 1958 it would have required 103,394,800 pesos, which represented only 0.67 percent of the annual aggregate investment made in Mexico in 1957. If the process had taken place over ten years, it would have generated an annual displacement of 896.53 workers, who could have been relocated to other sectors (Barajas 1959, 149).

The consistent opposition of textile trade unions to the introduction of labor-saving methods and machinery was mirrored by the wage-list imposed by the labor law (*contrato-ley*), which rigidly limited the possibilities of modernizing and rationalizing the industry (IBRD, 69; Naciones Unidas, 87). Yet it is difficult to assess whether the unions' policy of keeping the wage-schedule unchanged responded to the wishes of their rank and file. Lack of investment in the textile industry generated a decline in the real wages of cotton textile workers that was greater than the reduction experienced by workers in other manufacturing sectors. Whereas between 1939 and 1954 real wages in the Mexican manufacturing industry as a whole declined by 11 percent, wages in the cotton textile industry fell by 38 percent (Barajas, 31). Moreover, wages paid by old mills were far lower than those established by law for modern ones. The 1955 wage-list (*contrato ley*) established, for example, a daily wage of $12.70 for a card tender working in an old mill, but $26.02 for one working in a plant with modern equipment (Barajas, 33).

---

58. Ibid., 44.

59. This result is similar to that of Przeworski's model of accumulation and legitimation, when the economic militancy of organized wage earners (r in the model) is high. Capitalists stop investing and wages cannot be maintained at the high level. However, the situation of the Mexican textile industry is more complex. Given that r is different in different regions, this lowers the level of r, which in the long run reduces wages in a region with a relative higher r, also shortening the length of time within which wages will decrease. An increase in tariffs does the opposite, allowing for a greater increase in r without lowering wages, and extending the time before this takes place. I am currently working to expand Przeworski's model in this direction. See Przeworski 1985, 148–59, 179–96.

The government's protectionist policy placed incentives to maintain the status quo indefinitely. "Since the high protective tariff has made it possible to operate profitably in spite of technical inefficiency, management and labor have become complacent about the prevailing state of affairs in the industry" (International Bank of Reconstruction and Development, 69). However, modernization of the industry could not be postponed forever, and as time went by and the industry became more outdated, the problem became increasingly difficult to solve.

Mexico was not alone in this difficult quandary. In Brazil and in Ecuador the textile industries in 1951 were in a similar or worse situation, facing restrictions on the adoption of new technology caused by a rigid organization of labor comparable to that in Mexico.[60] Because nothing like the Mexican Revolution had happened in these countries, we should be careful about the extent to which we attribute the growth of labor organization in Mexico and its consequences for industrial development to the Revolution.

10.6 Conclusions

As we have seen, CIVSA's international competitiveness and productivity levels during the Porfiriato, although modest, did not improve for most of the rest of the century, until the late 1980s, when the Mexican economy was opened up to world markets and most textile mills went bankrupt. In 1911, CIVSA's costs and technology were not so different from those prevalent in England, or the United States, although closer to the former than to the latter. This conclusion can be generalized to the Mexican cotton textile industry as a whole. As time went by, the gap between Mexican costs and productivity levels and those that prevailed in cloth-exporting countries increased.

Why did this happen? Whom should we blame? The deterioration of relative productivity and competitiveness that the Mexican industry suffered does not appear to have been caused by the action of either the unions, industrialists, or government alone.

What took place was a complex interaction in which unions, industrialists, and government found themselves better off in the short run by maintaining—unchanged—the technology employed by the industry. Unem-

---

60. It is interesting to note that in São Paulo, these restrictions were less important than in Rio de Janeiro. The United Nations report indicated that the excess of personnel in Brazil's old mills was not due to the incapacity of managers to recognize it, but by the perpetuation of a traditional organization of labor dating from the end of the nineteenth century or the beginning of the twentieth century, when most of the mills were founded. Because the textile industry developed later in São Paulo in Rio de Janeiro, restrictions on the organization of labor were less important. In Chile and Peru, where the textile industry developed after the 1930s, there was less excess labor and fewer institutional restrictions on reducing it (Naciones Unidas 1951, 1–17, 20, 55, 74, 112).

ployment, widespread bankruptcies, and social unrest were the alternatives. Yet every time the decision to change the textile labor contract and to start modernization was postponed, the problem for the future worsened. If, at a given moment, the status quo was maintained for fear of unemployment and of mills' bankruptcies, as the gap between the technology used by the Mexican industry and that in the industry's leaders elsewhere in the world widened, the danger of widespread unemployment and bankruptcies in the industry only increased. In the late 1980s, when the decision to modernize the industry and open up the economy was finally taken, the industry was hard hit.[61]

Thus the agreements reached in 1925–27, explainable on the verge of the Great Depression, were maintained without any changes until at least 1951, and with few modifications until 1972.[62] For those workers employed at textile mills, this was perhaps not a bad choice, as long as they trained their children to be something other than textile workers. Although industrialists faced important constraints on modernizing equipment, they could reap large enough profits from the mills to keep them operating without making any major investment in them; they could also diversify their interests into other sectors. The government could maintain a relatively peaceful and long-lasting regime for several decades without much trouble. Yet the country as a whole was not able to grow at the rates that a buoyant, exporting industry could have allowed, and for decades most Mexicans were forced to dress in expensive, poor-quality cloth.

The analysis of productivity levels in Mexican textile mills indicates that the relative power of workers to control the relation between effort and pay is a crucial factor in determining the technology employed and therefore lev-

---

61. Whereas manufacturing production increased by an annual rate of 4.60 percent between 1986 and 1990, textile industry production rose only by 0.97 percent. This hides the even worse performance of the weaving and spinning sector of the industry, which did worse than other subsectors in the textile industry. Its production in terms of real pesos declined by 13 percent from 1980 to 1991, and its employment by 8 percent. In 1998, only a third of textile mills in Mexico were considered capable of producing at the level of quality, volume, and prices required by the U.S. market. Sandra Martinez (1994, appendix, table 12). Gary Gerreffi and Jennifer Bair, "En Búsqueda del Desarrolo Integrado en México," in *Trabajo,* 1 (2) December 1998, 160; Márquez (1994, 98–100).

62. December 31, 1972, was the due date to implement a new operating system based on workloads (*Diario Oficial,* September 15, 1980, 15, chapter 6, article 45. The wage-list of 1966 was the first to allow that plain loom weavers tended more than four looms, on the condition that the union agreed to it and that the weaver was paid 45 percent of the wages set for the normal load on the extra quantities produced with the additional machinery (*Diaro Oficial,* December 24, 1966, chapter 6, article 45b, 7 and paragraph 190, 55). In the National Convention of the Textile Industry, held in October 1987, industrialists continued to complain about the wage-lists (*Contrato-Ley*), claiming that there was always a lag between the technology they contemplated and the state of the art technology necessary to compete internationally, and that it was erroneous to set a general contract for all the industry when it was very heterogeneous (Martínez 1994, 117–26). By 1994 the industrywide collective contract (*Contrato-Ley*) of the textile industry had recently been suppressed (Márquez 1994, 123).

els of competitiveness and productivity, as Lazonick has pointed out.[63] In accordance with the Wolcott and Clark findings for the case of India, it is clear that in Mexico the poor performance of the textile industry, particularly after the Revolution, was a problem of "the low labor input per mill worker" (Wolcott and Clark, 421). Yet it is also evident that this did not result from a "low taste for effort on the job," or from managerial incompetence, but from a more complex situation, caused in part by the power exercised by workers in the labor market to block manpower reductions for fear of unemployment. However, it was also determined by the power exerted by the owners of smaller mills, who were either unwilling or unable to make new investments and were fearful of going bankrupt. The power of these two actors, however, would probably have not been enough to shape the evolution of the industry without the support of a government that valued social and political stability above economic development, and therefore pursued the tariff and labor policies that maintenance of the status quo required.

This study suggests that structures of social power are important variables in explaining the various development paths taken by countries (or regions). The institutions that govern the social relations of production are not, however, determined solely by unions, employers, or the government, but by the interaction between them, in arrangements that are greatly influenced by path dependency, and therefore difficult to change.

This study also indicates that the protectionist policy for the Mexican textile industry carried out from the late 1920s on was not the result of an import substituting strategy. Protection was not meant to foster the creation of a nonexistent domestic industry. Rather, it was put into place to allow the subsistence of an industry that was forced by labor regulations to exist in technological and organizational terms as a frozen picture of the 1900s. Moreover, high levels of protection were not the result of a *dependentist* ideology, but the consequence of a self-perpetuating situation in which all deciding actors were better off in the short run by promoting such a policy.

References

Archive of the Compañía Industrial Veracruzana S.A. N.d. *Balances Generales y Estados de Resultados* (yearly balance sheets and profit-and-loss statements), 1898–1910. N.p.

---

63. This conclusion supports the views of William Lazonick on the importance of the institutions of social power and workers' power on the relationship between effort and pay. However, it challenges his idea that British entrepreneurs could have taken skills off the shop floor simply by investing in management and following a different managerial strategy. Lazonick, *Competitive Advantage on the Shop Floor*.

Archive of the Compañía Industrial Veracruzana S.A. N.d. *Libros de Precios y Costos* (prices and costs records), January–December 1911. N.p.
Archivo General de la Nación. 1984. Las Primeras Tarifas (Salarios) Mínimas en la Industria Textil (1912). *Boletín del Archivo General de la Nación,* Tercera Serie, 7 (3–4): 5–83.
Arnold, A. J. 1999. Profitability and capital accumulation in British industry during the transwar period, 1913–1924. *Economic History Review* 52 (1): 45–68.
Bach, Federico, and Margarita Reyna. 1943. El Nuevo Indice de Precios al Mayoreo en la Ciudad de México de la Secretaria de la Economía Nacional. *El Trimestre Económico* 10 (1): 1–63.
Balassa, Bela, and Associates. 1971. *The structure of protection in developing countries.* Baltimore: Johns Hopkins University Press.
Barajas Manzano, Javier. 1959. *Aspectos de la Industria Textil de Algodón en México.* México: Instituto Mexicano de Investigaciones Económicas.
Beatty, Edward. 1996. The political basis of industrialization in Mexico before 1911. PhD diss., Stanford University.
———. 2002. Commercial policy in Porforian Mexico: The structure of protection. In *The Mexican economy 1870–1930,* ed. Jeffrey Bortz and Stephen Haber, 205–52. Stanford, CA: Stanford University Press.
Benson, Anna P. 1983. *Textile machines.* Lowell, MA: Shire Publications.
Bureau of the Census, U.S. Department of Commerce. 1975. *Historical statistics of the United States, colonial times to 1970.* Washington, DC: U.S. Government Printing Office.
Clark, Graham. 1909. U.S. Bureau of Foreign and Domestic Commerce, Special Agents Series no. 31. *Cotton Goods in Latin America,* Part I. Washington, DC: Government Printing Office.
Clark, Gregory. 1987. Why isn't the whole world developed? Lessons from the cotton mills. *Journal of Economic History* 47 (1): 141–73.
Coatsworth, John H., and Jeffrey G. Williamson. 2002. The roots of Latin American protectionism: Looking before the great depression. NBER Working Paper no. 8999. Cambridge, MA: National Bureau of Economic Research, June.
Cosío Villegas, Daniel. 1965. *Historia Moderna de México: El Porfiriato. La Vida Económica.* México: Hermes.
———. 1931. *La Cuestión Arancelaria en México.* III. *Historia de la Política Aduanal.* Mexico City: Ediciones de Centro mexicano de estudios económicos.
De la Cueva, Mario. 1938. *Derecho Mexicano del Trabajo.* México: Porrúa.
Draper Corporation. 1896. *Facts and figures for textile manufacturers, concerning the proper methods of equipping and running mills.* Hopedale, MA: Cook & Sons.
García Díaz, Bernardo. 1981. *Un Pueblo Fabril del Porfiriato: Santa Rosa, Veracruz.* México: CONAFE y FCE.
Gerreffi, Gary, and Jennifer Blair. 1998. En Búsqueda del Desarrollo Integrado en México. *Trabajo* 1 (2): 155–68.
Gómez-Galvarriato, Aurora. 1999. The impact of revolution: Business and labor in the Mexican textile industry, Orizaba, Veracruz, 1900–1930. PhD diss., Harvard University, December 1999.
———. 2002. Measuring the impact of institutional change in capital-labor relations in the Mexican textile industry, 1900–1930. In *The Mexican Economy, 1870–1930: Essays on the Economic History of Institutions, Revolution and Growth,* ed. Jeffrey Borat and Stephen Haber, 289–323. Stanford, CA: Stanford University Press.
Gómez-Galvarriato, Aurora, and Aldo Musacchio. 2000. Un Nuevo Indice de Precios para México, 1886–1929. *El Trimestre Económico* 67 (January–March): 47–91.

Haber, Stephen. 1989. *Industry and underdevelopment: The industrialization of Mexico 1890–1940.* Stanford, CA: Stanford University Press.
———. 1997. Financial markets and industrial development: A comparative study of governmental regulation, financial innovation, and industrial structure in Brazil and Mexico 1840–1930. In *How Latin America fell behind,* ed. Stephen Haber, 146–78. Stanford, CA: Stanford University Press.
International Bank for Reconstruction and Development. 1953. *The economic development of Mexico.* Baltimore: Johns Hopkins University Press.
Knight, Alan. 1990. *The Mexican revolution,* vol. 1. Lincoln, NE: University of Nebraska Press.
Lazonick, William. 1990. *Competitive advantage on the shop floor.* Cambridge, MA: Harvard University Press.
Luenig, Timothy. 1996. The myth of the corporate economy. PhD diss., Oxford University.
Márquez Padilla, Carlos. 1994. La Competitividad de la Industria Textil. In *La Industria Mexicana en el Mercado Mundial: Elementos para una Política Industrial,* ed. Fernando Clavijo and José I. Casar, 95–157.
Martínez Aguilar, Sandra Elena. 1994. Implicaciones del Libre Comercio sobre la Industria Textil Mexican: 1986–1991. BA thesis, UNAM.
México. 1891. Ordenanza general de aduanas marítimas y fronterizas de los estados unidos mexicanos: Con su tarifa de importacíon, notas explicativas y vocabulario anexo. Aprobada por decreto de 12 de junio de 1891 y vigente desde 1o de noviembre de 1891. México: Macedo y Castillo.
———. trans. J. Mastella Clark. 1882. *Mexico's Tariffs and Custom House Laws.* Mexico City: Printing Office of The Two Republics.
———. Dirección General de Estadística. 1894. *Anuario Estadístico de 1893.* Mexico City.
———. Dirección General de Estadística. 1938–1960. *Anuario Estadístico del Comercio Exterior de los Estados Unidos Mexicanos.* México City.
———. Estadística, Dirección general de Estadística. 1930. *Primer censo industrial de 1930* (microform v. 1–36).
———. Estados Unidos Mexicanos. Departamento de la Estadística Nacional. 1924–1928. *Anuario Estadístico: Comercio Exterior y Navegación.* Mexico City.
———. Secretaría de la Economía Nacional. 1929–1933. *Estadística del Comercio Exterior.* México City.
———. Secretaría de la Economía Nacional. Departamento de Industrias (Juan Chávez Orozco). 1933. Monografía Económico-Industrial de la Fabricación de Hilados y Tejidos de Algodón (mimeograph).
———. Secretaría de la Economía Nacional (Moisés T. de la Peña). 1934. *La Industria Textil en México. El Problema Obrero y los Problemas Económicos.* Mexico: Talleres Gráficos de la Nación.
———. Secretaría de Hacienda y Crédito Público, Comisión de Aranceles (Ing. Fernando Pruneda R.). 1941. La Industria Textil del Algodón en México. Mexico City: mimeograph.
———. Secretaría de Hacienda y Crédito Público. Departamento de Impuestos Especiales, Estadística del Ramo de Hilados y Tejidos de Algodón y de Lana Correspondiente a los Semestres de Mayo de 1925 a Octubre de 1929 (mimeograph).
———. Secretaría del Trabajo y Previsión Social (Miguel A. Quintana). 1942. Los Problemas de la Industria Textil del Algodón (mimeograph).
México, Poder Ejecutivo Federal, Departamento de Estadística National. *Aspectos Económicos de un Quinquenio: 1921–1925.* Mexico City: Imprenta Mundial.
Nacional Financiera (NAFINSA). 1963. *50 años de Revolución en Cifras.* México.

Naciones Unidas, Departamento de Asuntos Económicos. 1951. *Productividad de la Mano de Obra en la Industria Textil Algodonera de Cinco Países Latinoamericanos.* New York: United Nations.
Padilla, Carlos Márquez. 1994. La Competitividad de la Industria Textil. In *La Industria Mexicana en el Mercado Mundial,* ed. Fernando Clavijo and José I. Casar, 110–11. Mexico:
Pani, Alberto. 1918. Alocución de bienvenida a los delegados por el Sr. Ingeniero D. Alberto Pani, Secretario de Industria y Comercio. In *Reseña y Memorias del Primer Congreso Nacional de Industriales,* Secretaría de Industria, Comercio, y Trabajo, 45–49. Mexico City: Secretaría de Industria, Comercio y Trabajo.
Primera Convención Mexicana de Empresarios Textiles (Rama del Algodón). 1945. *Memoria General.* Mexico City: National Advertising Service.
Przeworski, Adam. 1985. *Capitalism and social democracy.* Cambridge: Cambridge University Press.
Ramírez, Elia B. 1985. *Estadística Bancaria.* México: INAH.
Remolina Roqueñi, Felipe. 1974. *El Artículo 123.* Mexico City: Ediciones del V Congreso Iberoamericano del Derecho del Trabajo y de Seguridad Social.
Rivero Quijano, Jesús. 1900. *La Revolución Industrial y la Industria Textil en México.* Vol. 2. Mexico City: J. Porrúa.
Seguna Ponencia de la Compañía Industrial de Orizaba S. A. 1945. *Primera Convencíon Mexicana de Empresarios Textiles (Rama de Algodón) April 9–12, 1945.* Memoria General. Mexico City: National Advertising Service.
Seminario de Historia Moderna de México, n.d. *Estadísticas económicas del Porfiriato. Fuerza de Trabajo y Actividad Económica por Sectores.* México: El Colegio de México.
Seminario de Historia Moderna de México. 1965. *Estadísticas económicas del Porfiriato: Comercio exterior.* Mexico: El Colegio de México.
United States Department of Commerce. 1975. *Historical statistics of the United States.* Washington, DC: Government Printing Office.
United States Special Consular Reports. 1896. *Money and prices in foreign countries.* Washington, DC: Government Printing Office.
United States Tariff Board. 1912. Cotton manufactures. Report by the President of the United States on Schedule 1 of the tariff law. 2 vols. Washington, DC: Government Printing Office.
Vicenti Renate. 1993. *Elsevier's textile dictionary.* Amsterdam: Elsevier.
Warren, George F., and Frank A. Pearson. 1933. *Prices.* New York: Wiley.
Wolcott, Susan, and Gregory Clark. 1999. Why nations fail: Managerial decisions and performance in Indian cotton textiles, 1890–1938. *Journal of Economic History* 59–2 (June): 397–423.

Contributors

Michael D. Bordo
Department of Economics
Rutgers University
75 Hamilton Street
New Brunswick, NJ 08901

Luis A. V. Catão
Research Department
International Monetary Fund
700 19th Street, NW
Washington, DC 20431

Sebastian Edwards
Anderson Graduate School of
   Management
University of California, Los Angeles
110 Westwood Plaza, Suite C508, Box
   951481
Los Angeles, CA 90095-1481

Leandro Prados de la Escosura
Departamento de Historia Económica
   e Instituciones
Universidad Carlos III de Madrid
Campus de Getafe
C/ Madrid, 126 28903 Getafe
   (Madrid), Spain

Gerardo Esquivel
Centro de Estudios Económicos
El Colegio de México
Camino al Ajusco 20
Pedregal de Santa Teresa, Mexico, D.F.
   10740

Aurora Gómez-Galvarriato
División de Economía
CIDE
Carretera México
Toluca 3655 Col. Lomas de Santa Fe
01210 Mexico, D.F.

Martin Grandes
Graduate School of Government
The American University of Paris
6, rue du Colonel Combes
75007 Paris France

Stephen Haber
Bldg 200, Room 19
Stanford University
Social Science History Institute, MC
   2024
Stanford, CA 94305

Pedro Lains
Instituto de Ciências Sociais
Universidade de Lisboa
Av. Aníbal Bettencourt, 9
Lisbon 1600-189 Portugal

Graciela Márquez
Centro de Estudios Históricos
El Colegio de México
Camino al Ajusco No. 20
10740 Mexico, D.F.

Noel Maurer
Harvard Business School
Soldiers Field
Boston, MA 02163

Christopher M. Meissner
Faculty of Economics
University of Cambridge
Sidgwick Avenue
Cambridge CB3 9DD England

Gerardo della Paolera
President and Professor of Economics
The American University of Paris
6, rue du Colonel Combes
75007 Paris France

Kenneth L. Sokoloff
Department of Economics
University of California, Los Angeles
Los Angeles, CA 90095-1477

Eric M. Zolt
University of California, Los Angeles
School of Law
Box 951476
Los Angeles, CA 90095-1476

Author Index

Abramovitz, Moses, 61
Acemoglu, Daron, 16, 84n2, 216n7
Adelet, Muge, 155
Adelman, Jeremy, 95n22, 96n23
Aguilar Aguilar, Gustavo, 226n21
Ahmad, S., 18n7
Alesina, Alberto, 84n4, 295n10
Ampuero, R., 295n7
Aoki, Masahiko, 214n2
Astorga, Pablo, 15, 15n1, 16, 19n13, 24, 25, 45
Atack, Jeremy, 231n30

Bakija, Jon M., 86n11, 117n42
Baptista, A., 20, 22n17
Baqir, Reza, 84n4
Barajas Manzano, Javier, 399n57, 400
Bardini, C., 18n8
Barro, Robert, 216n7
Bates, Robert H., 216n7, 237n37
Batista, D. C., 59n2
Bayoumi, Tamim, 270
Bazant, Jan, 72n18
Becker, Thorvald, 173n37
Benson, Anna P., 375n13
Berg, Andrew, 148
Bergés, A. R., 15n1, 19n13, 24, 25, 45
Berman, E., 345n14
Bernard, Andrew, 231n30
Best, Michael H., 85n9
Bhagwati, J. N., 18n10
Bird, Richard M., 86n10, 117n41

Blair, Jennifer, 402n61
Bordo, Michael D., 7, 148, 149, 149n13, 151n15, 152, 171n33, 244
Bortz, Jeffrey L., 59n2
Boughton, James, 297n16
Bound, J., 345n14
Bourguignon, F., 17, 17n6, 33, 44
Braithwaite, S. N., 19
Brewer, John, 87n12, 98n26
Broadberry, S. N., 18n8
Brown, E. Cary, 198, 198n4
Brownlee, W. Elliot, 117n44, 118n45, 119n46, 119n48
Brunori, David, 120n49
Bruton, Henry J., 77
Bueno, Gerardo, 335n4, 341, 341n10
Bullock, Charles, 100n27
Bulmer-Thomas, Victor, 2n3, 4n8, 67, 122n53, 125n59
Burger, A., 18n8
Burgess, Robin, 85n5, 124n57
Burkholder, Mark A., 99n27

Caballero, Ricardo, 156n18, 171n34, 245n4
Calomiris, Charles, 156n17, 214n2
Calvo, Guillermo, 202, 243n1, 245n4, 254, 254n12, 274
Cameron, Rondo, 265
Campa, José M., 60n4
Cañonero, Gustavo, 345n14
Cárdenas, Enrique, 59n2, 62n7, 65, 65n13, 66, 72nn18–19, 226, 337n6, 342n12

409

Cardso, E., 17n4
Catão, Luis A. V., 8–9, 258, 258n16, 274, 275
Cerutti, Mario, 224n17, 226n21
Céspedes, Luis Felipe, 141n1
Chang, Roberto, 141n1
Chaudhary, Latika, 84n4
Chávez Orozco, Juan, 382n40, 388n25, 390n29, 391n38
Clark, Graham, 389n28
Clark, Gregory, 373n8, 374n8, 388n24, 403
Clemens, M. A., 59n1
Coatsworth, J. H., 15, 16, 20, 22n17, 29, 60n3, 61, 62, 63, 335n3, 364
Coatsworth, John, 2n2, 15
Correa Prieto, L., 295, 311n45
Cortés Conde, Roberto, 60n3, 198, 198n3
Cowan, Kevin, 156n18, 171n34, 245n4
Cross, Harry E., 64
Cubberly, Ellwood P., 93n19
Cuikerman, A., 295

De Ferranti, David, 86n10, 116n40
De Gregorio, J., 17n4
Della Paolera, Gerardo, 7–8, 196, 198, 199, 248, 264n22
DeLong, B., 24
De Paiva Abreu, Marcello, 197n2
Devereux, J., 18n8
Díaz, J., 20, 22n17
Dormois, J. P., 18n8
Dornbusch, Rudiger, 245n4, 297n13, 297n16
Dowd, Kevin, 155
Drazen, Allan, 196n1, 292n2, 295n10, 296n11, 315n49
Dunn, Richard S., 88n14

Easterly, William, 84n4
Eaton, Jonathan, 195, 202
Ebrill, Liam P., 125n61
Edwards, Sebastian, 9–10, 17n4, 160, 245n4, 247n7, 260, 274, 291, 292n3, 295, 295n11, 297n15, 306n35, 319, 319n55, 333n1
Eichengreen, Barry J., 60n4, 85n6, 139, 141n2, 142, 144, 145, 146, 146n7, 151n16, 155, 165, 171n33, 173n36, 262, 262n18, 263, 264, 270, 274
Einhorn, Robin, 120n51
Elliott, J. H., 98n26
Elster, John, 196n1

Ely, Richard T., 120n50
Engerman, Stanley L., 16, 62, 84n2, 88n13, 90n17, 90n18, 93n19, 109n38, 116n40, 216n7
Escalona Salazar, Ana Maria, 226n22
Esquivel, Gerardo, 10, 334, 334n2
Estrada, Rosalinda, 218n10

Fajnzylber, P., 25n18
Felix, D., 292n3, 298n18, 311n44
Fernandez-Arias, Eduardo, 274
Ffrench-Davis, R., 67, 301n26, 302n27, 303n28, 304n31, 310n42, 311, 323n58
Fischer, S., 297n16
Fishlow, A., 17n4
Fitzgerald, Valpy, 15, 15n1, 16, 19n13, 24, 25, 45
Flandreau, Marc, 143, 143nn3–4, 145, 147, 151n15, 163n29, 169n32, 173
Fohlin, Caroline M., 214n2
Ford, A. G., 275
Fraile, P., 20, 22n17
Franco, Gustavo H. B., 249n8
Frank, A. G., 16
Frankel, Jeff, 143n3, 148, 165, 260, 262, 262n19
Fratianni, Michele, 264n22
Fremdling, R. R., 18n8
Fujita, Masahisa, 333n1

Galenson, David W., 90n16
Galor, O., 32
Gamboa Ojeda, Leticia, 218n10, 224n17, 225n18
Garay Vera, C., 301n23, 301n25, 303n29
Garman, Christopher da C. B., 130n67
Gavin, Michael, 270
Gereffi, Gary, 402n61
Gerschenkron, Alexander, 61
Gipson, Lawrence, 98n26
Goldberg, Pinelopi, 333n1
Goldfajn, Ilan, 245n4
Goldsmith, Raymond W., 264n22
Goldstein, Morris, 140, 142, 146, 146n6, 147n8
Gómez-Galvarriato, Aurora, 10–11, 236n35, 389n27
Gonzaga, G., 345n14, 346n15
Goode, Richard, 85n7
Grandes, Martin, 7–8
Gratz, Wilfrid L. M., 85n6
Greenaway, D., 333n1

Greenbaum, Stuart, 215n6
Greene, Jack P., 90n16
Guidotti, Pablo E., 202
Gutiérrez Alvarez, Coralia, 223n16

Haber, Stephen, 8, 15, 59n2, 60n3, 61n5, 63, 64, 65, 125n59, 214n5, 218n9, 220nn13–14, 222, 234, 235, 236n35, 237, 237n37, 264n22, 335n3
Haggard, Stephan, 130n67
Halperin Donghi, Tulio, 122n53
Hansen, B., 18n10
Hansen, H., 265n23
Hanson, Gordon, 333n1, 348, 348n17, 349
Harberger, Arnold, 195, 202
Harrison, Ann, 348n17
Hausmann, Ricardo, 139, 141n2, 142, 144, 145, 146, 146n7, 165, 171n33, 173n36, 264
Hirschman, Albert O., 84n4, 292n3, 300n21, 302n27, 312, 313
Hoffman, Philip, 237n37
Hofman, André, 25, 25n18, 60n3, 63nn9–10, 67
Holden, Robert, 96n24
Hu, Dapend, 333n1
Huybens, Elizabeth, 224

Isenman, P., 18n10
Izquierdo, Alejandro, 243n1, 245n4, 254, 254n12, 274

Jaramillo Uribe, J., 20
Jobet, J. C., 295
Jobst, Clemens, 151n15
Johnson, Lyman L., 99n27
Johnson, Simon, 16, 216n7
Jones, Charles, 231n30
Jonker, Joost, 265n23
Jonung, Lars, 265n23

Kalmanovitz, S., 20
Kaminsky, Graciela, 262n19, 270–71
Kanatas, George, 215n6
Kane, Nancy, 220
Kapur, Sandeep, 274
Kearns, Jonathan, 156n18, 171n34, 245n4
Keefer, Philip, 216n7
Keen, Michael, 125n61
Keesing, Donald B., 72n19, 76
Kelly, Trish, 274
Keyder, C., 18n8

Kim, Sukkoo, 349n18, 352
Kindleberger, Charles P., 244, 274
King, Timothy, 338n9, 340, 341
Klein, J., 306n35
Komlos, John, 173
Kravis, I. B., 18n10
Krozner, Randall, 214
Krueger, Alan B., 346n15
Krugman, Paul, 275, 348, 349

Lains, Pedro, 5–6, 59n2, 62n6, 62n8, 65n14, 68n17
Lamoreaux, Naomi, 214n2
Lane, Philip, 276
La Porta, Rafael, 213, 214, 215n6
Lazonick, William, 375n12, 382n21, 390n29, 398n56, 403n63
Le Cacheux, Jacques, 169n32
Lederman, D., 25n18
Leff, N. H., 20
Leiderman, Leonardo, 274
Levine, Ross, 215n6
Levy, M. B., 153
Lindert, P. H., 17n6, 263, 274
Lipsey, R. E., 18n10
Livas-Elizondo, Raúl, 348, 349
Llona Rodriguez, Agustin, 249n8, 264n22
Lockhart, James, 89n15
López-de-Silanes, Florencio, 213, 214, 215n6
Luce Jordan, Astrid, 224
Lüders, R., 20, 22n17
Ludlow, Leonor, 224n17

Machin, S., 345n14
Mackey, Michael, 215
Maddison, A., 16, 17n5, 18n9, 19, 28, 68n16, 246n6
Madison, Angus, 4n9
Mamalakis, M., 298n17
Mankiw, G. N., 319
Marichal, Carlos, 2n4, 197, 200
Mariscal, Elisa V., 93n19, 109n38, 116n40
Márquez, Graciela, 337nn7–8
Márquez Padilla, Carlos, 382n20, 402n62
Martinez Aguilar, Sandra Elena, 402n62
Maschke, Arturo, 316n51
Matthew, W. M., 115n39
Maurer, Noel, 8, 62n7, 218n10, 220nn13–14, 222, 222n15, 224, 224n17, 225n18, 227, 228n27, 237n37
Mauro, Paolo, 245

McBride, George McCutchen, 96n24
Meisel, A., 20
Meissner, Christopher D., 7, 171n33
Mejia, Luis Fernando, 243n1, 245n4, 254n12, 255, 274
Menezes-Filho, N., 345n14, 346n15
Meza, Liliana, 345n14
Milesi-Ferretti, Gian Maria, 262n19
Miron, J. A., 319
Mishkin, Frederic, 140
Mitchell, B. R., 71
Montiel, P., 296n11
Morgan, W., 333n1
Morrisson, C., 17, 17n6, 33, 44
Morton, Peter, 274
Mosk, Sandford A., 338
Mulder, Nanno, 67
Muñoz, O., 67
Musacchio, Aldo, 199, 201n7, 237
Musgrave, Peggy B., 85n7
Musgrave, Richard A., 85n7

Navarette, Alfred, Jr., 64, 65
Newland, C., 22, 22n17
Norberg, Katherine, 237n37
North, Douglass C., 15, 16, 83n1, 216n7, 237n37
Nuxoll, D. A., 18n10

O'Brien, P. K., 18n8
Obstfeld, Maurice, 148n11, 244, 244n2, 260
Olson, Mancur, 237n37

Palma, J. G., 67
Panizza, Ugo, 141n2, 142, 144, 145, 146, 146n7, 165, 171n33, 173n36
Patillo, Catherine, 148
Patrick, Hugh, 214n2
Pavcnik, Nina, 333n1
Perkins, Edwin, J., 98n26, 100n29
Perotti, Robert, 270
Perry, David B., 117n43, 122n52
Perry, J. Harvey, 100n30, 106n36
Persson, Torsten, 196, 297n14, 297n16, 315n49
Petersen, Mitchell, 215n6
Phillips, Charles E., 94n20
Poulson, B., 22, 22n17
Prados de la Escosura, Leandro, 5, 16, 18n8, 19, 26
Prasada Rao, D. S., 19n11
Pratap, Sangeeta, 224

Prebisch, R., 16
Przeworski, Adam, 216n7, 400n59

Quijano, Jesús Rivero, 389, 389n26, 390
Quiroz, A. W., 20

Rajan, Raghuram, 215n6, 216n7
Razaghian, Rose, 102n33
Razin, Assaf, 262n19
Razo, Armando, 63, 63n10, 64, 218n9, 220nn13–14, 222, 222n15, 237n37
Redish, Angela, 171n33
Reese, Thomas J., 85n9
Reinhart, Carmen, 140, 142, 147, 262n19, 271, 274
Remmer, K., 309
Robinson, James A., 16, 216n7
Rockoff, H., 244
Rodriguez, Francisco, 333
Rodriguez López, Maria Guadalupe, 218n10, 224n17, 226n21, 334n2
Rodrik, Dani, 333
Rogoff, Kenneth, 140, 142, 147, 260
Romero y Barra, Maria Eugenia, 224n17
Rose, Andrew K., 143n3, 148, 165, 260, 262, 262nn18–19

Sachs, Jeffrey, 60n4, 297n15, 333
Sala i Martín, X., 44
Salazar-Carrillo, J., 19n11
Salvucci, L. K., 20, 22n17
Salvucci, R. J., 20, 22n17
Sandos, James A., 64
Santaella, J. A., 297n16
Santamaría, A., 20, 22n17
Sargent, T., 297n12, 318
Savastano, Miguel, 140, 142, 147
Schwartz, Anna, 151n15
Schwartz, Stuart B., 89n15
Seligman, Edwin R., 120n50
Sen Gupta, A. K., 300
Sharma, Tridib, 225n18
Sharpe, Steven, 215n6
Sheard, Paul, 214n2
Shepsie, Kenneth, 237n37
Shleifer, Andrei, 215n6
Shome, Parthasarthi, 117n41
Silva, Alvaro Ferreira da, 62n6, 62n8, 65n14
Singer, H. W., 16
Slaughter, Matthew J., 346n15
Slemrod, Joel, 86n11, 117n42
Sokoloff, Kenneth L., 6–7, 16, 62, 84n2,

88n13, 90n17, 92n18, 93n19, 109n38, 116n40, 216n7, 231n30
Solberg, Carl E., 95n22, 96n23
Solomou, Solomos, 258, 258n16, 275
Spinelli, Franco, 264n22
Stein, Barbara, 16, 16nn2–3
Stein, Stanley, 16, 16nn2–3
Stern, Nicholas, 85n5, 124n57
Steuerle, C. Eugene, 117n42, 120n49
Stone, Irving, 244, 246
Stotsky, Janet, 117n41, 127n62
Strahan, Philip, 214
Summerhill, W. R., 16
Sunkel, O., 292n4
Sussman, Nathan, 145, 173, 245
Sutton, John, 235n34

Tabellini, Guido, 196, 295, 297n14, 297n16, 315n49
Tait, Alan A., 85n6
Talvi, Ernesto, 276
Tannenbaum, Frank, 96n24
Tanzi, Vito, 85n5, 85n8, 117n41, 124n58, 127n63
Tattara, G., 173
Taylor, Alan M., 17n4, 60n3, 148n11, 196, 198, 244, 244n2, 248, 264n22
Tenenbaum, Barbara, 99n27
Terra, C., 345n14, 346n15
Theil, H., 33, 33n22, 39
Thorpe, Rosemary, 67, 122n53
Tirado de Alonso, I., 19n11
Tornell, Aaron, 276, 334
Treff, Karin, 117n43, 122n52
Triner, Gail, 264n22
Turner, Philip, 140, 142, 146, 146n6, 147n8

Urrutia, M., 20

Valdez, Rodrigo, 245n4
Végh, Carlos, 271, 276
Velasco, Andrés, 141n1
Venables, Anthony, 348
Venezia, Itshak, 215n6
Vishny, Robert W., 215n6
Von Humbolt, A., 2n1
Vreeland, J. R., 297n16

Wagner, G., 20, 22n17
Ward, M., 18n8
Warner, Andrew, 333
Weil, D. N., 319
Weingast, B. R., 16, 216n7, 237n37
Weisman, Steven R., 117n42, 117n44, 118n45
Werner, Alejandro, 345n14
Whale, P. B., 275
Wiesner, Eduardo, 128n66, 129n66
Williamson, J. G., 17n6, 18n8, 59n1, 335n3, 364
Wills, Eliza, 130n67
Wolcott, Susan, 388n24, 403
WoldeMariam, Asegedech, 117n41, 127n62
Wright, P., 333n1
Würth Rojas, E., 311n45
Wyplosz, Charles, 262, 262n18

Yafeh, Yishay, 245

Zahler, Roberto, 303n28
Zamarripa, Guillermo, 213, 214
Zanden, Luiten van, 18n8
Zee, Howell, 85n8, 124n58, 127n63
Zingales, Luigi, 216n7
Zolt, Eric M., 6–7
Zúmer, F., 143, 143nn3–4, 147, 163n29, 169n32

Subject Index

Alcabala, 99, 99n27
Argentina, 1; accumulation of external debt and, 3; analytical framework for measuring country risk of, 199–203; country risk of, 199–200; domestic manufacturing, 3; export sector of, 2; financial crises and, 151–53; governmental strategy of, for country risk, 207–9; land policy in, 96–97; preliminary evidence on measure of country risk of, 203–7; public debt in (1886–92), 197; sources of revenue to state/provincial governments in (1870), 112
Australia, financial crises in, 154–56

Backwardness, Latin American economies and, 1–2
Banamex. *See* Banco Nacional de México (Banamex)
Banco de Londres y México (BLM), 220, 225; directors of, 222–24; related banking and, 225
Banco Internacional Hipotecario, 222
Banco Nacional de México (Banamex): boards of directors of, 220; directors of, 222–24; related banking and, 225
Banking crises, 140–42; determinants of, 167; robustness of findings, 169–74; statistical findings for, 165–69. *See also* Financial crises
Baring crises, 151, 152–53, 194

BLM. *See* Banco de Londres y México (BLM)
Bourguignon's L, 33n22
Brazil: accumulation of external debt and, 3; direct taxes in, 112–15; domestic manufacturing, 3; financial crises in, 153–54; growth rates of, 20; property tax in, 111–12; sources of revenue to state/provincial governments in (1870–1910), 113; sources of tax revenue for, 99; taxes in province of Minas Geraes, 112–14

Caja de Préstamos (Mexico), 227
Canada, 1; breakdown of types of national government revenue for, 103; distribution of tax revenues across levels of government in, 104; land policy in, 96–98; local government taxation in, 106; patterns of national government taxation in, 100–102; property taxes in, 109; provincial governments in, 106–9; schooling institutions of, 93–95; sources of revenue for municipal governments of, 106; sources of tax revenue for central governments in, 126; sources of tax revenue in, 108, 108t; tax systems in nineteenth-century, 98–116; tax systems of, 87; twentieth-century tax systems in, 117, 121–22

415

Subject Index

Chile: domestic manufacturing, 3; Gonzalez-Videla presidency and, 298–99; growth rates of, 20; historical background to stabilization program in, 294–96; Ibañez del Campo presidency and, 301–3; inflation in, 292–93; inflation in early 1950s in, 298–303; property taxes in, 109; sources of municipal government tax revenues in, 109; stabilization program in, 292–93. *See also* Klein-Saks Mission

CIVSA (Compañía Industrial Veracruzana S.A.), 364; explaining higher costs of, during the Porfiriato, 373–81; explaining secular decline in international competitiveness of, 381–401; general background of, 365; international competitiveness of, 365–73. *See also* Mexican textile industry

Closing of economies: effects of, on regional dispersion of economic activity, 334–57; effects of, on skilled labor employment and wages, 344–48; introduction to, 333–35. *See also* Protectionism, historical review of, in Mexico

Colombia: domestic manufacturing, 3; growth rates of, 20; property taxes in, 109; sources of municipal government tax revenues in, 110; sources of revenue to state/provincial governments in (1870), 112

Colonial taxation policies: of Great Britain, 98, 99–100; of Portugal, 99; of Spain, 99

Common school movement, 93

Compañía Industrial Veracruzana S.A. *See* CIVSA (Compañía Industrial Veracruzana S.A.)

Country risk, 199–200; analytical framework for measuring, 199–203; introduction to, 195–96; preliminary evidence on measure of, 203–7; rationale to recalculate premium for, 196–99

Cuba, growth rates of, 20

Currency crashes: domestic financial imperfections and, 264–65; fiscal behavior and, 267–73; rapid monetary expansion and, 265–67; sudden stops and, 258–64. *See also* Currency crises

Currency crises, 140–42; determinants of, 164; robustness of findings, 169–74; statistical findings for, 163–65. *See also* Currency crashes; Financial crises

Currency mismatches, 146–47

Debt crises, 140–42; determinants of, 159; robustness of findings, 169–74; statistical findings for, 158–63

Debt intolerance, 140, 147–48

Dependencia school, Latin America and, 16

Díaz, Porfirio, regime of: banking system and, 220–26; land reform during, 96–97

Direct contributions, 110

Dominion Lands Act (1872), 96

Europe, national government tax revenue per capita in (1870), 115

Exchange rates, in Chile, 319–23

External debt, Latin American economies and, 2–3

Financial crises, 7; in Argentina, 151–53; in Australia, 154–56; in Brazil, 153–54; data for, 148; from 1880–1913, 149–51; historical evidence for, 151–57; literature on predicting, 148; in U.S., 154–57

Fiscal behavior, currency crashes and, 267–73

Franchise, differences in, 90–92

Gonzalez-Videla, Gabriel, 298–99

Great Britain, colonial taxation policies of, 98, 99–100

Great Depression, 3

Green Revolution, 64

Growth rates, across Latin America, 20–26

Herrera, Felipe, 301–2

Homestead Act (1862), 95–96

Ibañez del Campo, Carflo, 301–3

Income taxes, 102; in Latin America, 128

Inequality: differences in, across Americas, 88–98; Latin American economies and, 1–2; long-run intercountry, for Latin America, 32–44, 47–52t; tax systems and, 86–87

Inflation: analysis of political economy of, 296–98; in Chile, 292–93; in 1950s Chile, 298–303

Inflation inertia, in Chile, 319

Institutions, economic growth and, 83–84

Klein-Saks Mission, 293–94; credibility and, 314–18; credibility and exchange

Subject Index 417

rate premium and, 319–23; credibility and inflationary inertia and, 323–24; departure of, 310; diagnosis of, 304–5; foreign advisors of, 293; policy recommendations of, 305–8; as technocratic team, 310–12; as umpires and mediators, 312–14; unraveling of, 308–10. *See also* Chile; Stabilization programs

Labor productivity, in Latin America, 24–25
Land policy, differences in, U.S. vs. Latin America, 95–98
Latin America: assessing success/failure of, 26–29; breakdown of types of national government revenue for, 103; colonial conditions and, 15–16; comparisons with United States and, 16; degree of centralization in, 128–30; distribution of tax revenues across levels of government in, 104; GDP sources for, 45–52; growth rates across, 20–26; hypotheses for failure of, 15–16; importance of indirect taxation in, 125–26; introduction to long-run relative decline of, 15–17; local government taxation in, 102; local/municipal tax revenues in, 108–9; long-run intercountry inequality in, 32–44, 47–52t; national government tax revenue per capita in (1870), 115; patterns of national government taxation in, 100–102; PPP and, 18–20; progressive taxes in, 124; property taxes in, 110–11; real income trends, 17–32; relative position of, in early nineteenth-century, 29–31; schooling institutions of, 93–95; sources of tax revenue for central governments in, 126; tax burdens in, 124; tax structures of, 86; tax systems in nineteenth-century, 98–116; twentieth-century tax systems in, 122–30; use of income taxes in, 128. *See also specific countries*
Latin American economies: average GDP growth rate (1950–60) for, 3–4; backwardness of, 1–2; external debt and, 2–3; features of, 1–2; Great Depression and, 3; susceptibility to external shocks and, 3
Liabilities dollarization, 7
Literacy rates, in Americas, 94t
Local/municipal governments: differences in taxation by, across Americas, 102; Latin American, sources of tax revenues for, 109; sources of revenue for Canadian, 106t; sources of revenue for U.S., 105t. *See also* State/provincial governments

Mean Logarithmic Deviation (MLD), 33–44, 33n22
Mexican banking system: boards of governors and, 222–24; looting by directors and, 228–30; performance of, and related lending, 226–30; related lending and, 220–26. *See also* Related lending
Mexican textile industry: introduction to, 363–64; Mexican banks and, 218–21. *See also* CIVSA (Compañía Industrial Veracruzana S.A.)
Mexico: domestic manufacturing, 3; effects of closing the economy on regional dispersion of economic activity in, 334–57; effects of closing the economy on skilled labor employment and wages in, 344–48; end of liberalism in, 63; growth rates of, 20; growth trends of, 68–72; historical explanations for economic backwardness of, 61–66; historical review of protectionism in, 335–44; impact of civil war on economy of, 63–64; impact of 1910 Revolution on agriculture in, 64–65; industrial growth in 1930s in, 65; inequality and, 2n1; introduction to similarities/differences to Portugal, 59–61; land policy in, 96–98; structural change in, 72–78; tariff policy, 336–39
Minas Geraes, province of, taxes in, 112–14
Municipal governments. *See* Local/municipal governments

Original sin, 139; role of, 142–46

Peru: domestic manufacturing, 3; growth rates of, 20
Portugal: colonial taxation policies of, 99; end of liberalism in, 63; growth trends of, 68–72; historical explanations for economic backwardness of, 61–67; interwar period of, 65–67; introduction to similarities/differences to Mexico, 59–61; structural change in, 72–78
PPP. *See* Purchasing power parity (PPP)
Prat, Jorge, 302
Progressive taxes, in Latin America, 124

Property taxes, 102–6; in Brazil, 111–12; in Canada, 108, 109; in Chile, 109; in Colombia, 109; in Latin America, 110–11; in U.S., 102–6, 105t, 108, 109
Protectionism, historical review of, in Mexico, 335–44
Provincial governments, Canadian, taxation and, 106–9
Purchasing power parity (PPP): Latin America and, 18–20

Real income trends, for Latin America, 17–32
Regional dispersion, of economic activity, in Mexico, 334–57
Regional integration, 4
Related lending: evidence for studying, 217; introduction to, 213–17; methods for studying, 217–19; Mexican banking system of, 220–26; misallocation of capital and, 230–36; performance of Mexican banking system and, 226–30. *See also* Mexican banking system
"Reversal of fortune" theory, 16
Rosetti, Jaun B., 301

Schooling institutions, differences in, U.S. vs. Latin America, 93–95
Spain, colonial taxation policies of, 99
SS. *See* Sudden stops (SS)
Stabilization programs: adoption of, 291–92 (*see also* Chile); analysis of political economy of, 296–98; credibility and, 293–94. *See also* Klein-Saks Mission
State/provincial governments: sources of revenue to, in Argentina (1870), 112; sources of revenue to, in Brazil (1870–91), 113; sources of revenue to, in Colombia (1870), 112; U.S., taxation and, 106–9. *See also* Local/municipal governments
Sudden stops (SS): currency crises and, 258–64; introduction to, 243–45; patterns of, 245–58; procyclical fiscal behavior and, 269–73; rapid monetary expansion and, 265–69; shallow financial markets and, 264–65

Suffrage institutions, differences in, U.S. vs. Latin America, 90–92

Tariff policy, in Mexico, 336–39
Tax instruments, relative use of, by central governments, 127–28
Tax policies, colonial: of Britain, 99–100; of Portugal, 99; of Spain, 99
Tax systems, 84–85; of Canada, 87; inequality and, 86–87; of Latin America, 86; in nineteenth-century Latin America, 98–116; twentieth century, in Canada, 117, 121–22; twentieth century, in Latin America, 122–30; twentieth century, in U.S., 117–21; of U.S., 87; variation of, 85
Textile industry. *See* Mexican textile industry
Trade liberalization, 333

United States, 1; breakdown of national government revenue for, 103; distribution of tax revenues across levels of government in, 104; financial crises in, 154–57; land policy in, 95–98; local government taxation in, 102–5; local/state taxes as shares of income by region in (1860 and 1880), 111; national government tax revenue per capita in (1870), 115; patterns of national government taxation in, 100–102; property taxes in, 109; schooling institutions of, 93–95; sources of tax revenue for central governments in, 126; sources of tax revenue for state governments of, 105; sources of tax revenue in, 108, 108t; state governments in, 106–9; tax systems in the nineteenth-century, 98–116; tax systems of, 87; twentieth-century tax systems in, 117–21

Value-added Tax (VAT), 124, 125, 125n61
Venezuela, growth rates of, 20
Voting participation, differences in, U.S. vs. Latin America, 90–92